Masses in Latin America

Masses
in
Latin
America

EDITED BY IRVING LOUIS HOROWITZ

NEW YORK

OXFORD UNIVERSITY PRESS

1970

FOR DANIELLE

ACKNOWLEDGMENTS

All of the articles in this volume, with the exception of the essay by Bryan Roberts, first appeared in *Studies in Comparative International Development*. To the authors of these essays goes my sincere appreciation both for their initial contribution and for their willingness to see them reproduced in bound volume form. I would also like to express my appreciation to Richard N. Adams from whose large-scale research in Guatemala the study by Mr. Roberts has been taken.

Contents

III   Masses and Politicalization

I

Masses
and
Mobilization

1

IRVING LOUIS HOROWITZ

Masses
in Latin America

The thesis that I wish to present is simple, yet elusive: to understand the processes that go under the rubric of social development it is necessary to study masses as well as elites, nameless peasants and urban dwellers no less than military manipulators and political celebrities. That such a thesis should require explication at this late date in social history represents a tribute to the tenacity of investigators who continue to project their own intellectual preferences and social upbringing onto the course of events in remote and faraway places. Those who study development, in contrast to those who participate in it, naturally tend to celebrate "achievers" and denigrate "ascribers." Perhaps for this reason no book or collection of papers on the subject of the masses of Latin America presently exists. This observation is not primarily intended as criticism of the manner in which academic disciplines have viewed Latin America, but, more to the point, as a commentary on the nature of Latin American societies.

From the time that Spain and Portugal extended their dynastic empires to Latin America until the present day, when the region is dominated by foreign powers, Latin America's economic and political life has been analyzed primarily as the product of its middle and higher elites. Social science literature cautiously

3

but insistently leaves the impression that Latin America is impervious to mass protest, habits, culture, or influence. Indeed, even the Mexican and Cuban revolutions have been analyzed by charting the actions and influences of their leaders. At best, meager credit is extended to the impact of modernizing intellectuals or disenchanted middle-class professionals.

Of course, every revolution and every major social change has a leadership that is well known. But what is often overlooked is that leaders are sensitized by masses of people to whom they owe the habits and concepts they acquire, the skills they exhibit and the purposes they serve, and the very political terms in which they speak. Leaders merely formalize, act out, or articulate what is generated by large and various populations; they must be placed back in that midst so that we do not distort the political values which define Latin America.

Ideologists and intellectuals alike ought not to forget that, while elites may do the "developing," masses still do the "dying." Nothing is more ludicrous than the traditional assumption that Latin peoples either do not or will not fight. The effete properties of the traditional ruling classes have bred a myth of pacifism, with the cowardice of their betrayal. But the pages of Latin American history are filled with tales of mass heroism. From the long marches of Simon Bolivar, through the Chaco Wars—in which ignorant Paraguayan Guaranis defended their homeland with a fanaticism and bravery that have become legendary—to the illiterate revolutionary Pancho Villa, through the romantic adventures of the Cuban Revolution led by Guevara and Fidel Castro, the masses of Latin America have exhibited a bravery and a consciousness that have made their national existence possible.[1] The *Guerrillero* was no invention of Ché Guevara or Mao Tse-tung—but has remained a constant factor in the civil wars through which Latin Americans reached nationhood.

To recount the deeds of heroism performed by the disenfranchised peasants and urban ghetto dwellers in Latin America is not required, since it has already been done well by chroniclers and historians of the era. Yet most developmentalists seem blinded to social change in anything but entrepreneurial terms and do not so much as give a nod to the role of the masses, even when they are discussing the military liberation of the hemisphere. Such populist *caudillos* as Antonio Vicente Mendes Maciel in Brazil, Tupac Amaru in Peru, Maclovio Herrera in Mexico, Facundo Quiroga in Argentina must be accorded a role in the developmental process at least equal to that of the *comerciantes* and *cientificos* who followed in their wake. This is a matter of causal priorities no less than elemental historical justice.

THE MEANING OF MASS

One definition of "mass" includes everyone functioning in a political order except the top elites. In this sense it is a negative concept, describing people who exert little appreciable control over their own economic or political lives at either local or national levels. A variant of this definition considers the mass to be those that do not, for one reason or another, occupy any significant rung on a decision-making ladder in politics or industry. In short, all those excluded from the major formal processes of national decision-making comprise the mass.

A somewhat different definition of mass sees it as determining the cultural apparatus through mass influence. When those in power believe their purposes are determined and defined by the mass, then the term signifies an appeal to the "lowest common denominator." This definition, which has much in common with elitist manipulation of sentiments, and which strangely enough became the chief ideological tool of post-World War Two "neo-Marxism," is closer to the Platonic rejection of democracy as a form of worthwhile government than it is a precise rendering of the term mass.

The difficulty with a negative definition is that in Latin America, at least, the mass may include the entire population: people of high culture, the highly educated, those informally involved with powerful people, some with economic but little political power (such as a large foreign-born immigrant population) and others with "status" but no significant capacity to influence those who formulate public policy. All of these, as well as others infinitely less advantaged, would have to be categorized "mass," leaving the "elite" stratum a narrow and thin one indeed. We ought then to attempt to formulate a positive definition of "mass," one that is more descriptive and selective.

The most generic concept of mass, employed by many social scientists throughout Latin America, includes those who exist either randomly and externally in relation to the main participants in the social system, or else exist as total dependents excluded from political, economic, or educational institutions. Within the social framework of modern Latin America, this concept would include those social sectors which neither participate economically nor are politically mobilized. Even in advanced nations like Mexico and Brazil, such a definition would categorize from 40 to 60 per cent of the population as mass instead of ascribing to them some kind of defined class role within the system.

If this definition is rigorously applied, it turns out that for Latin America, at least, the mass tends to be identified with the unorganized rural peasant sector, while more functional class roles are ascribed to members of the urban working and middle class. Often, those who define the stratification network along a mass-class axis describe Latin America as a dual economy, with a feudal sector and a capitalist sector. Mass is said to be diffused through the feudal sector, while class identities develop with much greater clarity in the urban-capitalist sector. The work of Jacques Lambert makes this distinction most forcefully. However, distinctions are also possible within the rural sector. For example, some rural proletarians work for their wages; rural sharecroppers may arrange with their landholders for the marketing and distribution of profits of the produce; and some peasants simply work the land of the holders and owners in exchange for privileges of living on the land. A feudal-capitalist separation makes only the crudest of distinctions. For instance, the deeper the situation is examined, the clearer it becomes that rural landlords really function almost exclusively as participants in the urban "marketplace." Clearly, within such a framework, classes as well as masses exist in the rural sector.

A further refinement in the concept of mass might be called a Marxian distinction, in which masses are identified not simply by their economic position in the social hierarchy, but by their attitude toward that position. Masses in the Marxist sense are those people in the society who comprise the working classes— the factory proletariat and the peasantry—as well as marginal intellectuals, who perceive their purpose not primarily as the achievement of their particular class needs but as the elevation of an entire mass of "oppressed" persons. This concept equates "mass" to forces in the old society (old in the sense of pre-socialist, rather than pre-modern) who are responsive to the need to promulgate a new society. The difficulty with a Marxian framework is that the notion of mass leads to a debate about who presently rules versus who is fit to rule. It further assumes that the masses have an historical mission and a pre-tested political direction. For the Marxists, in sharp contradiction to the modernizers, elites are those who resist the tendencies toward change for their own special class interests, instead of divinely ordained, innovative types.

Once the concept of mass became identified with a Marxian pattern of history, it *was,* and of course *is,* inevitable that the same concept would be turned against the mass by spokesmen for the elites. Many of the *cientificos* and *caudillos* maintain that the mass constitutes those people who by nature are unfit to rule. This attitude is even more prevalent in Latin America than in North America. The synopsis of the caudillo sentiment given by Chester Lloyd Jones pinpoints it with remarkable accuracy. Particularly noteworthy is that, unlike the previously mentioned definitions, this definition provides little parallel with the elite and egalitarian traditions of both Western Europe and North America. Delivered by a synthetic yet sympathetic Guatemalan dictator, the statement is a far cry from the caretaker elitism of an Edmund Burke or a Lord Bryce.

However defensible in theory, universal suffrage works badly or not at all in Guatemala, since the Indian seldom wishes to vote and the elections are practically never free. When they are free the political factions struggle to record the Indian vote in their favor. When they are not free those in power vote the Indians as a part of political routine. In any case Indian voting means the blind voting of masses of electors who have no conception of the issues espoused by the candidates. Manhood suffrage in Guatemala has not stimulated the Indian population to interest in politics, it does not result in division of opinion on policies, it has not fostered democracy. It has made the Indian vote only a counterweight which the *ladino* politicians feel they must control.[2]

One can see that from an elitist standpoint, ethnic stratification is at least as important as class stratification in defining mass and elite. Thus any full-fledged definition of elites must take cognizance of the many faceted nature of the mass, no less than its constantly shifting relationship to elites.

In defining the mass the following criteria can be applied: the mass are those people excluded from decision-making in politics, excluded from ownership or managerial participation in business and industry, non-participants in educational institutions, and, finally, those people consistently locked out of the power process. This definition makes it possible to have low status characteristics without being part of a mass. A person of color may be designated as one of low status in many Latin American countries, yet may perform elite functions within his racial group, or even within some of the society's major elite groups, such as the military.

Yet, a question certainly remains unresolved in even this open-ended definition, namely, whether mass and class are properly matters of consciousness and value rather than of social position and interest. While I choose to think that the definition in terms of interest is more appropriate, to some degree "class" refers to those groups of people who behave consciously to achieve their own ends. In this sense the very existence of well-defined values denotes the transformation of a mass acting by itself into a class acting for itself. It is to be hoped that this definition of mass provides a better explanation for the role of political action and awareness in creating group identity and is not merely a definition appended to certain static positions in a hierarchy.

The role of a mass in social development does not necessarily represent a perfunctory performance of duties by a large number of unthinking and unresponsive people, but specifically implies the creation of a climate in which newly emerging elites articulate mass sentiments.

Ultimately, then, the concept of mass is useful to identify a constantly diminishing reservoir of underprivileged manpower —those previously disenfranchised who constitute a potential "class" as they demand wider participation in the processes of social change, wider involvement in all those aspects of the national economy and culture which they see as touching upon their lives, and recognition as a group with rights and obligations. Whether this is realized through peaceful bargaining or violent struggle becomes a question of tactics rather than a matter of definition. But what is a matter of fact and not conjecture is the transformation of undifferentiated masses into individual laborers through the process of division of labor. We shall now consider more specifically the morphology of masses in Latin America.

TYPES OF MASS AND PATTERNS OF
LATIN AMERICAN INDUSTRIALIZATION

With respect to the requisites for economic development, we have seen, in a general way at least, that one has to begin to take seriously mass labor as well as deviant elites. In relation to Latin America, this would make necessary an analysis of the large majority of disenfranchised people who more closely approximate an underclass than they do membership in any established classes. Victor Alba has made this clear in his own vigorous rundown of the data on land ownership and occupancy.

> Statistics on Latin America's land-tenancy structure are out of date and frequently not worthy of credence. Nevertheless, it is safe to say that, in Latin America, only 5 per cent of the arable land surface is under cultivation, as opposed to the world figure of 7 per cent and the United States figure of 18 per cent. In Peru, 76 per cent of the cultivated land is owned by 1.6 per cent of the people; in Colombia, 1 per cent of the people own a quarter of the cultivable land; in Argentina, where current myth denies the need for agrarian reform, 5.1 per

9

cent of the people own 74.5 per cent of the land; in Bolivia, before the revolution of 1952, 91.1 per cent of the land was the property of 6.3 per cent of the inhabitants; in Chile, 2.2 per cent of the landholders own 73.2 per cent of the land; in Brazil, 50.9 per cent of the land belongs to 1.6 per cent of the people (yet Brazil has had no fewer than 200 agrarian-reform plans, 58 of them within the past twelve years; a good way of making sure none of them would be approved). Although in Chile and Colombia, for example, there have been plans for land reform, they have made such a cruel mockery of the aspirations of the landless peasants that Eduardo Frei's first step upon assuming office in Chile was to present an agrarian-reform plan "totally opposite to the earlier one passed during the administration of Jorge Alessandri." Frei's plan was approved by Congress in 1966.[3]

While the great majority of this underclass is still in the rural regions, migration has also placed many of its members in an urban context, where distinctions between masses and elites are made in terms of money, rather than land, but are no less absolute. It is important to realize that, when we speak of masses in Latin America, we include in the typology roughly eight different groupings or clusters: tribal Indians, modern Indians, peasants, small plantation laborers, large plantation laborers, small town types, metropolitan underclass, and the more familiar urban proletariat.[4] Only by such distinctions can an oversimplified identification of masses with rural peasants be avoided.

What makes the analysis so difficult and yet so necessary is that as industrialization increases it becomes more efficient, better able to fuse smaller properties into large centralized commercial properties. However, this consolidation and condensation takes place without a corresponding nonviolent transformation of mass into a popular class; despite modernization, the size of the industrial proletariat remains relatively low. Claudio Véliz has ably summed up the situation in Latin America, where industrialization occurs without the formation of a large-scale proletariat, as it did in Europe:

Latin America has industrialized rapidly, but this has not been the result of the exertions of an industrial bourgeoisie; nor has it produced an industrial proletariat. In the 1870's, Britain was the first industrial power on earth and was producing her first million tons of steel. To achieve this, over 370,000 workers were employed. In Latin America today, Argentina, Brazil and Mexico are well over the million-ton mark (Brazil is moving close to four million tons per year) and a rough estimate shows that only seven or eight thousand workers are needed to produce each million tons of steel. Peru is the first fishing nation on earth, but the total labor force engaged in the fisheries and processing plants does not exceed thirty thousand men. Such examples abound and they all point to a fairly obvious development: industrial technology has changed; it is now more capital than labor intensive. The industrial labor force in Latin America is not the modern equivalent of the traditional proletariat. Working with an advanced industrial technology, it is smaller, better trained and better paid. It is in fact an aristocracy of labor with incomes which all too often rise above those of vast numbers of white collar workers in the tertiary sector.[5]

As Véliz further points out, the transformation of a peasant class into an industrial proletarian class has not occurred to any appreciable degree. Urbanization takes place at a much faster pace than industrialization in many of the leading countries of the hemisphere; this huge influx of people is absorbed into a service sector of the economy, which, though well organized and politically active, remains economically marginal. In this way, Latin America becomes "modernized" without being industrialized.

The coming of industry resulted in a sharp decrease of self-employed artisans and craftsmen and a spectacular rise in the number of people in service occupations, but this increase was only the continuation of a process that had been going on for well over a century. These professionals, white collar employees, bureaucrats and domestic and service workers are not the Latin American equivalent of, say, the rising English middle class of 1832; for the most part they are directly or indirectly associated with, or dependent upon, either the central government or the traditional social structure. Few are involved in industry, and their political activities have been directed principally toward securing greater participation in the existing social organization rather than in seeking to demolish it and replace it with another.[6]

Not only is an integregated proletariat absent as a result of the special features of Latin American industrialization, but Latin America also lacks an innovative bourgeoisie. The oft-praised "demonstration effect," in which advanced nations show the face of the future to less developed nations, works to the disadvantage of Latin America precisely because expertise can be brought in from the outside. Technological innovation can be purchased at a much lower cost than the creation of an internal scientific core would demand—particularly if technology is geared toward consumer goods for a limited portion of society. This, coupled with the fact that profits and earnings on foreign investments are more certain than those on domestic investments, makes Latin America subject to foreign manipulation as well as making its middle class even less able to adjust to the new demands of economic planning. Thus, the entrepreneurial class serves even less as a source of development in Latin America than in any other part of the Third World, and the concept is certainly far less applicable than in the traditional Western European and North American economies.

The Colonial Factor of the Mass

Class interests rather than status values are the key factor in the structure of Latin American societies. The emphasis on issues of social status and inherited privilege derived from the colonial tradition has tended to obscure the sharp class polarizations within Latin American societies. Class in Latin America functions much more akin to class in European society than to that in North American society. Patterns of mobility oftentimes involve upward movement within a social class rather than a change from one social class to another. The element that is different from European societies is the link between mass and ethnicity.

Stavenhagen has pointed out that any study of inter-ethnic relations must consider both the class character and colonial character of mass life. In each case what may seem to be movement from feudal colonialism to capitalist class relations is in Latin American societies better described as a liquidation and replacement of medieval cultural forms by sharp dichotomies of upper class and working mass.

> We cannot over-emphasize that the class character and colonial character of inter-ethnic relations are two intimately related aspects of the same phenomenon. They are separated here only for the purpose of our analysis. Class relationships have developed parallel to and simultaneous with colonial relations and tend to displace them more and more. But the colonial character of inter-ethnic relations impresses particular characteristics upon class relations, tending to stop their development. In this context, class relations mean mutual interactions between persons holding opposed economic positions, independent of ethnic considerations. These relations develop together with the region's economic development. As agricultural production increases, as the market for industrial products expands, as monetary economy develops, and as the labor market expands, colonial relations lose their importance and give way to the predominance of class relations. The latter's development also depends, to a great degree, upon structural factors of national economy and is not the result of decision-making at the regional or local level. At any rate, this development tends to impress upon the class relations between Indians and Ladinos a characteristic mark while the "feudal" or "semi-feudal" aspects, so frequently indicated in the literature, tend to disappear.[7]

In terms of an international stratification system the masses are those portions of the underdeveloped society that are exploited by the very national classes—the bourgeoisie and the proletariat alike—that are in turn subject to the severe pressures from an international cosmopolitan "center." The pecking order enriches the national "class" sectors at the expense of the internal "mass" sectors, while it weakens the nationalist's resolve to seek revolutionary methods for pressing economic and social demands on the nation.

In an international context, the Latin American mass functions as a "safety valve" for the national classes; just as, internally, urbanization acts as a safety valve that prevents any undue buildup of pressure within the mass. How well this system works depends on one's criteria of efficacy. Yet, the fact remains that there have been few revolutions in Latin America—with the possible exception of the Cuban Revolution of 1956–1959— that have challenged, much less threatened, this pecking order of classes.

The volatile, or at least unstable, nature of economic and political processes in Latin America derive largely from their failure to move the entire society from a mass base into a class base. The result is a steady polarization of haves from have-nots, urbanized workers from rural peasants, and all of the other familiar dualisms which characterize the area.

Latin America is an area which has a diverse array of political parties without a corresponding level of mass participation in politics. One can more easily speak of *party pluralities* combined with *political monism* than of genuine democratization. Indeed, in recent years the tendency—witness events in Brazil and Argentina—has been to diminish mass participation still further by institutionalization of a norm of illegitimacy—by the emergence of single party, military-led systems. Alba has documented the atrophied character of Latin American politics.

> The general level of Latin American electoral participation is at about 20 per cent of the citizenry; that is, one out of every five inhabitants is registered to vote; the level falls still lower if those who are registered but fail to vote are subtracted. In the 1964 Mexican elections, 21.5 per cent of the population participated. In Brazil in 1967, 17.3 per cent participated. In the United States, average participation in presidential elections is about 55 per cent. In Great Britain, almost 70 per cent of the registered voters vote. Venezuela heads the list of Latin American countries; in the 1963 elections, 39 per cent voted.[8]

MASS MOBILIZATION AND POLITICAL PARTICIPATION

As a political issue the relationship between mass and elites can be defined in terms of participation and mobilization. To be a member of the mass is very nearly identical to being outside the framework of social participation. Robert E. Scott indicates that, at least for Mexico, there is a direct correlation between social class and political socialization: "The 10 or so per cent who share participant political cultured norms are found primarily in the upper and in the stable middle middle class. Of these, no more than 1 or 2 could be characterized as viewing politics from the perspective of the more nearly democratic 'civic culture' of Almond and Verba." [9] Scott accounts for this lag in mass politicalization by psychological factors such as the authoritarian values inculcated by the Church, and the traditionalist aspects of Mexico City. Whatever the bases of this lag in politicalization, its consequences are clear enough: the crystallization of the power structure and its tendency to become a bureaucratic elite, without any corresponding "great leap forward" in the economic structure. This process tends to confirm Latin Americans' stereotyped visions of politics. The politics of reform has become well-nigh impossible in the rural regions; it is difficult even in urban areas because the interest parties have never succeeded, and the ideological parties have never been required to meet the pragmatic test of success—which in Latin America would mean the integration of the rural and urban mass. This kind of elite politics implies the total control of social processes characteristic of backward nations rather than of modernizing nations. In this sense the study of mass in Latin America is the study of democratic and counter-democratic tendencies within the area. Furthermore, the struggle between the ideologies of socialism and capitalism is a rhetorical reflection of democratic and elitist trends in Latin America, rather than a serious choice between economic systems. As Daniel Goldrich pointed out: "Extreme depoliticalization will result from severe sanctions being levied against lower class people relatively inexperienced in politics. The effect can 'help' a government by reducing demands and therefore stress, but there is also a loss in the capacity to mobilize support." He goes on to show how

. . . a high level of politicalization may not be established despite an important demand-making experience. One such experience may not establish the psychological basis for continuing demand-making. Furthermore, the general case regarding the Latin American urban lower class is one where

15

alternative solutions to serious problems are not defined, and this retards politicalization. Consequently, meeting an important demand concerning housing and urban services, for example, does not necessarily trigger a chain of additional demands which would overwhelm governmental capacity in transitional societies.[10]

By the same token, we might begin to take more seriously the degree to which the struggle for democracy and development in the area is defined by the extent of mass participation and mobilization. As Kling points out: "In the light of the evidence, political violence cannot be regarded as aberrant behavior in Latin America. It is recurring, chronic, and rule-conforming. . . ."[11] But as Kling also shrewdly indicates, the culture of political violence may yet lead to participation in political life *per se*. The cult of violence, if positively channeled, may very well widen the base of democratic participation. This deserves a great deal more attention than it has received, if we are to arrive at a basis for mass democracy in the hemisphere. Toward this end the elaboration of Kling's position is well worth repeating; especially since it has clear implications for Black liberation struggles in North America no less than Latin American politics.

The sequel to elections in a culture of political nonviolence may include limited changes in public policies, but is not likely to be marked by a radical rearrangement of the political system or drastic changes in a wide variety of public policies. In contrast, the range of possible outcomes accompanying a revolution, in a culture of political violence, is extremely broad: the greater the degree of compatibility between violence and the prevailing norms of a political system, the greater the range of policy outputs that may accompany the employment of violence in such a culture; since millennial aspirations need not be invoked to justify violence, a revolution, like an election in other cultures, may merely rotate personnel. Also like an election, it may serve as a prelude to the introduction of relatively limited changes in public policies. But unlike an election, a revolution may shift personnel, eliminate certain social classes, radically modify the capabilities of various interests to exert influence and power, and transform the system for absorbing and resolving public conflicts. The spectrum of changes engendered by elections in

16

a culture of political nonviolence forms a rather small arc. A much larger arc, however, is required to accommodate the range of changes generated by revolution in a culture of political violence. Revolutionary means are compatible with highly diverse ends.[12]

MASS EDUCATION AND MIS-EDUCATION

The question of education is also clearly linked to that of mobilization, since political participation demands some preparation. But the point is, that unless those who become educated acquire a class role, they drift toward a mass identity. Not unnaturally, they may eventually seek to convert a mass following to the cause of mutual assistance in defining new class roles and attempt to acquire as much sympathy and prestige for these as possible. Thus, education in Latin America is linked not only to social mobility, but to forms of technical change that may thwart and frustrate social change.

Pressures for participation are not relieved by a quantitative approach to education, by apportioning an amount of education for each child in a given area, so that he may pursue a more advantaged situation. These pressures are relieved by establishing class identities for those educated, identities which do not divorce them from the popular sectors. In part this problem arises from the special circumstances of intellectuals in Latin America. As Philip G. Altbach has observed:

> The student population in many of the developing nations is numerically small, and is often very much cut off from the rest of its peer group by vastly differing experiences, "Western" ideas, and educational opportunities. This alienation from the peer group, as well as from the mainstream of the traditional society in many cases, often makes the student community self-reliant and at the same time unsure of its roots. In addition, students often have to develop their own traditions, since established patterns of "modern" educational, political, and social behavior in many new states have not as yet evolved.[13]

The relatively minuscule size of the well-educated population and its alienation from the peer group leads this vital peripheral element within the Latin American traditional elites to identify with the mass.

What further emphasizes the educational elite's support of the masses is their widespread mis-education. The structure of university life continues to emphasize established elite systems by routing students through certain preferred disciplines such as law. These often have little consequence for social and economic development, and an educated entrant into an old elite group may find himself at odds or absorbed by traditional type of elites and thus more removed from the masses than he intended or desired. Myron Glazer points out, in his study of Chilean university students, that education creates problems not simply by training and forming new elites. More pointedly, conventional forms of education lead, first, to the mis-education of established elites and, second, to the non-education of the masses of population:

> Qualitative professional training is in itself not sufficient for solving the manpower shortages from which Chile is suffering. As is the case with many Latin American countries, the greatest problems exist in building new professional groups and motivating members of the traditional professions to work with low income groups in urban and rural areas, where professional services are desperately needed, but are virtually non-existent. In such situations a special kind of professional identification is demanded. Professionals are needed who are not only technically competent, but also aware of their country's problems and motivated to assist in their solution.[14]

And precisely such a technically proficient and nationally dedicated educated sector is absent; first, because of indifference to mass educational needs, and, second, because of class prejudice in favor of self-serving traditional professions and against basic scientific and social forms of training.

The issues of mass education have recently been well summarized in a study of Peruvian stratification, with conclusions of profound implication for the hemisphere. "Education has to bear an especially heavy burden of ambition which it creates or aggravates only to then frustrate due to either its nonfunctional or

18

poor quality. It is for this reason that the primary source of revolutionary ferment is in the universities rather than the factories. Rebel leaders are those who suffer the widest gap between their aspirations and achievements, rather than those at the most deprived level of existence or in 'classic' proletarian situations." [15] Thus, if sound mass education has a "liberalizing effect" by drawing closer together aspirations and achievements, the mis-education that prevails throughout Latin America has a "polarizing effect" by widening the gap between aspirations and achievements. The elite structure of higher learning thwarts the reform potentials of each Latin American nation. The revolutionary potential of education remains negligible.

Those who view education as the panacea for the ills of the masses of Latin America little realize that education entails socialization into life-styles and expectations based upon the achievements of other members of a given occupation or profession. Thus, to instill an abstract achievement orientation, even were there agreement about what it is and how it could be exercised, would require an overhaul of the character of the traditional classes. Even were it possible, such an overhaul would provide high risks for elites and few guarantees of success for society as a whole.

MASS MAN: REFORMIST OR REVOLUTIONARY?

Often enough the distinction between mass and elites is drawn as a contrast between revolutionary fervor from below and innovative imagination from above. This formulation is dangerously simplistic, for it presents the human dimensions of development in terms of a mysterious Archimedean lever, and exploitation or stagnation as a consequence of its nonfunctioning. Available sociological information indicates that the liberal potential of the mass is its most decisive and abiding characteristic.[16] In fact, impulses toward liberal democracy are usually attributes of masses seeking integration rather than of the new elites—the so-called middle sectors—seeking innovation. Some quarters have called for community control of power. But in Latin America, where community power is dependent upon and accountable to national power, such a demand can only be a halfway house to political mobilization. The question is never power itself, but the size and scope of power that is to be exercised. Established elites, for their part, tend to polarize around either reactionary or revolutionary activities. We have seen this in relation to the field of education. Elites are by no means uniformly conservative. As has been noted, sectors of the traditional elites may be particularly committed to radical approaches to social change—especially in the educational arena. The conversion of a disorganized mass to organized class participants, and not the impulses of the middle sector, or even of elite policy toward that new middle sector, is the central issue. Democracy and development, and how they intersect, must finally be brought into the open and resolved in terms of the maturation of the mass.

The Latin American mass is central to any reform program because it contains the bulk of people. The Latin American class system is a center of both reaction and revolution because class polarization and class differentiation are relatively complete and static, and because the class variable among the economically "viable" sectors is not mitigated by other factors.

Industrialization, bureaucratization, and modernization placed very great strains on this traditional style of non-politics. They created a need for symbolic representation of stratified, developed, and highly ambitious class forces, all of which crystallized in the urban sector. The multiparty system in effect arose in response to the impossibility of continuing further the *antipolitique* of violence. It did not take a national decision or an intellectual commitment to make the political order democratic, but instead the exhaustion of the rural classes, and an indication of the preeminence of the urban sector. The landed aristocracy is still in a position to command the loyalties of the tradition-bound peasant masses. Instead of having politics as a symbolic recognition of different class interests, the landed interests, through their feudal paternalism, compel the development of politics by other means, that is, by force of arms. This brings the situation to a full circle. The urban-rural dichotomy in Latin America is one in which the old aristocratic ruling classes have at their disposal a mass base of relatively loyal peasants, while the new middle classes have at their disposal the urban working classes who feel they have a vested interest in the ongoing social system. The dichotomization between urban and rural regions begins to develop an autonomous character, and instead of the classical Marxist or European pattern of a struggle between classes, a struggle between class and mass takes place, with the landed aristocracy becoming increasingly marginal in the political struggle.[17]

Lest this polarity seem to be drawn too sharply, we must remember the relatively successful "extremist" movements such as Peronism in Argentina and Vargas's New State in Brazil, which maintained enthusiastic working-class support while making precious little effort during their periods of power either to incorporate the rural masses into the New State or to break the system of landholding characterized as epifeudal. In contrast, the most thoroughgoing revolutions in the hemisphere—in Mexico and in Cuba—although separated by nearly fifty years, both started with a mass peasant base, and owe their security as well as success to the continued loyalty of that base. As noted earlier, given the narrow stratum embraced by the proletariat, the mechanical absorption of European socialism by Latin America merely transferred power from traditional elites to modern elites without effecting fundamental changes in the social structure. For this reason, proletarian ideologies quickly took on a fascist rather than a socialist cast; and the masses' frustrations with revolutionary slogans hardened into a mistrust of politics as such.

Mass behavior is traditionally based on obedience to the masters and to the elites of the area.[18] In turn, the elites have created an extensive system of paternalism to deal with mass. The consequences of this system are clearly drawn by Roger Bastide.

Paternalism prevented tensions and softened the relations between races. But, at the same time, it strengthened the domination of one coloured group over another; and it institutionalized the subordination of the Negroes, who could only benefit from the protection of the whites, or from a certain familiarity in the whites' treatment of them, on condition that they "knew their place" and proved their deference, gratitude and respect. It was therefore an instrument of political and economic control, which, by avoiding the competitive relations which are possible in an individualistic society like ours, by preventing a struggle, and by rendering useless any wish for collective mobility on the part of the Negroes, assured supremacy and security to the white class. Under these conditions, one can understand why prejudices are at a minimum in a paternalist society, or, at least, why they remain latent rather than finding external expression. The reason is that they are unnecessary. Their functions of controlling and damming up are fulfilled by paternalism.[19]

However, in a system under which the old and rigid system breaks down, victims usually seek a liberating revenge along with a new participatory style, often because few options are available. In Latin America, the obedience-paternalism axis was gradually displaced by a resistance-revolution axis. Every form of electoral chicanery arranged to block peasant participation elicited new peasant unions and peasant communes. Every attempt to keep the cities of Latin America under the control of the wealthy sectors created mass squatter movements, called by various names in different cities of the hemisphere, but uniformly representing a demand for mass participation in the process of urbanization and industrialization. For every bishop sent to a rural area to calm troubled waters, there are the many priests who identify their religious calling with mass demands. Every appeal to the mass to proceed by small and orderly steps and docile adjustment to lack of changes in their condition is responded to by militant energy bent on effective organization and immediate recognition.

STRATEGIES FOR THE MASS VS. STRATEGIES OF THE MASS

Three essential strategies of change are now current: the United States strategy of developing a multiclass national politics, the Soviet model of developing a politics of an industrial class, and a Chinese model of politics based on mass peasant movements. What is involved is nothing short of a choice between reform and revolution on one side and between two strategies of making revolution on the other. While it may well be, indeed is even likely, that Latin America will continue to create its own political mixtures, it is worth at least listing the choices as they are estimated by major world powers.

If the United States model is to succeed in Latin America, the elite-mass dichotomy must be eliminated, and a pluralistic politics of competitive, numerous, but autonomous groups must emerge. This has been thwarted until now by the remarkable ineptitude and even corruption of the middle sectors in moving toward an advanced industrial system with related occupational groupings.

The success of the Soviet model depends on radicalization of the industrial class in the cities and their cooperation with the peasant mass in the countryside. But more especially, it depends on control of the urban centers. According to this orthodox Soviet viewpoint, the group that controls the cities controls the nation. The aspirations of the working class, however, more closely approximate those of the middle sectors than of the peasant masses in most instances, and union-led bargaining rather than revolution is favored. The third model, the Chinese strategy, is the reverse.

In the Maoist approach, the peasant mass surrounds the urban centers and overwhelms all the minority classes. According to this doctrine, he who controls the countryside controls the nation, at least in the initial phase of revolution. The supreme difficulty with applying this strategy to Latin America is that population is heavily concentrated in the coastal regions—and that peasants continue to rely upon migration rather than revolution to secure mass goals. The failure of any nation to follow in the footsteps of Castro's Cuba is clearly the result of more than American imperialist vigilance and supervision of the area. What will take place after the "safety-valve" of migration is either exhausted or completed is still problematic. But at that point the mass-class dichotomy will also be problematic.

Masses desire what individuals desire: socio-economic *satisfaction,* not political *mobilization.* The organization of mass movements and the enlargement of trade unions results from basic human desires for occupational security, adequate housing, decent schooling, old-age pension programs, etc. A basic test for the primacy of socio-economic factors is satisfied by the fact that in nearly every nation of Latin America, levels of parliamentary and/or participatory democracy correspond precisely to critical points at which basic needs are finally met.[20] Mass discontent shows a remarkable decline of interest in political experimentation exactly to the degree that established elites are able to cope with demands for social and economic security. This is as true for the Rightist regime of Juan Carlos Ongania in Argentina as it is for the Leftist regime of Fidel Castro in Cuba.

Contemporary emphasis on the role of political mobilization and political violence among the Latin American masses should be tempered by a realization that this politicalization is a direct consequence of the chronic inability of most nations in the hemisphere to solve basic economic demands for increased wealth. In effect, those nations of the hemisphere that exhibit extreme unevenness of economic growth also have severe inflationary spirals that wipe out personal savings and commercial investments (Argentina, Brazil, Peru). They are also the places where the cycle of political mobilization is most evident and where regimes have been installed by illegitimate processes.

The tragedy of the moment in Latin America is precisely the fact that, while the masses remain enveloped in an economic struggle for survival, the elites, having solved such basic problems for themselves, have transformed this struggle into a political contest for power rather than meeting the political needs of immobilized masses. This is why the Latin American masses speak in a relatively inchoate and muted language of class interests, while Latin American elites speak in a relatively polished language of national values. The ruling *politicos* and *pensadores* tend to interpret their own class interests as universal values, and, more than that, to establish their values as fit objects of moral emulation for the total society. For this reason every elite counter-revolution in Latin America, every assault on democratic participation, comes in the language of national redemption and moral rejuvenation.

Through the reality of counter-revolution the "values" of an elite stratum are presented as the national ideology. Any threat to the elite structures of Latin America is identified as a threat to law, order, and stability. To have values is to assume the mantle of national pride and perform the role of national redeemer. The masses are in the anomalous position of far outnumbering the elites and thus being much more likely custodians of national goals, yet in rhetoric and in ideology they are far less able to develop broad formulas that can convince the whole society to act on their claims and demands.

Social science must always study Latin America so as to consider the interaction of masses and elites—which expresses itself on one hand through masses who share universalistic interests for social betterment (but with an accompanying ideology of particularistic claims), while on the other hand, through elites who have particularistic interests of social privilege (but with an accompanying ideology of universalistic claims). Underneath the interactional framework is an historical truth: the claims of masses represent the realities of where Latin America is and must go in order to achieve social justice, while the claims of the elites represent the illusions of where Latin America has been and must go in order to maintain social privilege.

Doubtless, every "revolt of the masses," to use Ortega y Gasset's felicitous phrase, brings in its wake nearly as many problems as it solves. And in the sense that mass society is complex society, the problems themselves become tougher to resolve. Nonetheless, social tensions can scarcely be ameliorated by the replacing of new, more sophisticated forms of managerial inequities for older, and hence less efficient, forms of inequities.

The rapid spread of a "natural history of revolution" doctrine, of the idea that in the morphology of social change one revolutionary outcome approximates the outcomes of previous upheavals, has had a disastrous effect on mass movements in Latin America and on their gain of the support of alienated sectors of the elite. For social change cannot be measured by the extent to which the rhetoric of revolution is matched by actual performance, but rather by the extent to which the realities of revolutions promote genuine social development and human betterment. We can still measure the present moment only by what is obtained in the past, not by what is expected of the future. In this sense, the removal of injustices one by one, the progressive emancipation of people from ignorance and the growing participation of the mass in the political process is a "right" just as thoroughly coveted by Latin Americans in the twentieth century as it was by North Americans in the eighteenth century.

The exercise of that right occurs in more complex circumstances in this age of instantaneous transportation and communication than it did in the earlier period, when years, let alone days and hours, would have meant little in terms of the outcome of international struggles for national liberation. In short, the "disadvantages" of coming last in the developmental race have had far more profound effects in influencing political life in the area than the advantages of economic improvements have had.

Factors which in past centuries counted for very little now loom central, particularly the role of foreign commerce and business in Latin America. Rich countries install labor-saving machinery and thus create increasingly difficult problems for nations burdened by unabsorbed mass labor. Wealthy nations increase dissatisfaction among the Latin American masses by accentuating the gap between wealth and poverty through the direct or indirect advertising of commodities. Just as raw labor is displaced by technological advances, raw materials are displaced by engineering advances. Finally, advanced nations have less need to pay proper attention to the masses of Latin America, for they now have long-range, high-powered weapons which minimize the possibility that any of these nations might "get out of line." Concomitantly, such weapons facilitate biopolarization of the world with restitution of devices for carving up the world between the have-nations, rather than readjustments leading to equity and relative parity between all nations.

But just as rigorously, these factors have produced a reaction in Latin America. The relative political "softness" of military "hardware" has become plainer after Vietnam. And the same technology which locks out masses from social and economic participation and integration creates the bases for forms of struggle, such as sabotage and guerrilla insurgency, previously thought incongruent with the modern world. Finally, although international control mechanisms make the tasks of social change difficult, inhibiting as they do the growth of a powerful national bourgeoisie, they make possible forms of class and ethnic struggle and clearly encourage mass liberation and the liberalization of the mass.

NOTES

[1] See the essays by Augusto Céspedes, Juan O'Leary, and Rómulo Gallegos in *The Green Continent*, ed. by Germán Arciniegas, New York, Alfred A. Knopf, 1954, pp. 480–507.

[2] Chester Lloyd Jones, "If I Were Dictator," *Guatemala: Past and Present*, Minneapolis, University of Minnesota Press, 1940, pp. 343–50, 350–56. Reprinted in *Dictatorship in Spanish America*, ed. by Hugh M. Hamill, Jr., New York, Alfred A. Knopf, 1965.

[3] Victor Alba, *Nationalists Without Nations: The Oligarchy Versus the People in Latin America*, New York, Frederick A. Praeger, 1968.

[4] Charles Wagley and Marvin Harris, "A Typology of Latin American Subcultures," *Contemporary Cultures and Societies of Latin America*, eds. Dwight B. Heath and Richard N. Adams, New York, Random House, 1965.

[5] Claudio Véliz, "Centralism and Nationalism in Latin America," *Foreign Affairs*, Vol. 47, No. 1 (Oct. 1968), pp. 68–83.

[6] Ibid.

[7] Rodolfo Stavenhagen, "Classes, Colonialism, and Acculturation," *Studies in Comparative International Development*, Vol. I, No. 6 (1965), p. 76.

[8] Victor Alba, *Nationalists Without Nations: The Oligarchy Versus the People in Latin America*, New York, Frederick A. Praeger, 1968, pp. 116–17.

[9] See Robert E. Scott, "Mexico: The Established Revolution," in *Political Culture and Political Development*, eds. Lucien W. Pye and Sidney Verba, Princeton, Princeton University Press, 1965, pp. 330–95. Quoted here from *The Urban Explosion in Latin America*, ed. Glenn H. Beyer, Ithaca, Cornell University Press, p. 250.

[10] Daniel Goldrich, Raymond B. Pratt, and C. R. Schuller, "The Political Integration of Lower-Class Urban Settlements in Chile and Peru," *Studies in International Comparative Development*, Vol. III, No. 1 (1967–1968), pp. 20–21.

[11] Merle Kling, "Political Violence in Latin America," *Latin American Radicalism*, eds. Irving Louis Horowitz, Josue de Castro, John Gerassi, New York, Random House, 1969, p. 196.

[12] Ibid., pp. 204–5.

[13] Philip G. Altbach, "Students and Politics," *Comparative Education Review*, Vol. 10, No. 2 (June 1966), p. 175.

[14] Myron Glazer, "The Professional and Political Attitudes of Chilean University Students," *Comparative Education Review*, Vol. 10, No. 2 (June 1966), p. 293.

[15] David Chaplin, "Peruvian Stratification and Mobility—Revolutionary and Developmental Potential," in *Structural Social Inequality: A Reader in Comparative Social Stratification*, ed. Celia S. Heller, New York, The Macmillan Company, 1969, p. 436.

[16] See, for example, Gino Germani, "El autoritorismo y las clases populares," in *Politica y Sociedad en una Epoca de Transicion,* Buenos Aires, Editorial Paidos, 1962, pp. 127–46; and Albert O. Hirschman, *Journeys Toward Progress: Studies of Economic Policy-Making in Latin America,* New York, The Twentieth Century Fund, 1963; especially pp. 251–297.

[17] See Irving L. Horowitz, "The City as a Crucible for Political Action," *The Urban Explosion in Latin America,* ed. Glenn H. Beyer, Ithaca, Cornell University Press, 1967, pp. 241–43.

[18] See Martin Luis Guzman, *The Eagle and the Serpent,* New York, Alfred A. Knopf, 1930.

[19] Roger Bastide, "The Development of Race Relations in Brazil," *Industrialisation and Race Relations,* ed. Guy Hunter, London-New York, Oxford University Press, 1965, pp. 9–29.

[20] Phillips Cutright and James A. Wiley, "Modernization and Political Representation: 1927–1966," *Studies in Comparative International Development,* Vol. V (pub. pending).

2

CELSO FURTADO

Development and Stagnation in Latin America: A Structuralist Approach [*]

INTRODUCTION

Latin American economists have been increasingly applying themselves over the last few years to two problems of fundamental importance to the region. The first concerns the tendency toward a persistent rise in the price level, chiefly noticed in countries which are developing, or trying to develop, under conditions in which there is a decline in the import coefficient. The second concerns a tendency toward a slowing down in the rate of growth of per capita income. This is particularly evident in those countries which have attained greater diversification in their economic structures.[1]

The present study attempts to illuminate certain peculiarities in the socio-economic structures which have served as a framework for the process of growth of the Latin American countries during the last decades. The assumptions about the structures, which serve as a social framework for economic analysis, are drawn from historical evidence about the national economies, although they do not always refer to specific examples. The study is partially based on a typology of the regional economies.

The interdependence between growth and the tendency toward the increase in price level arises as a simple by-product of the analysis, which aims to determine the origin of the forces working to reduce the rate of growth. There is some evidence that these forces are related to peculiarities of the socio-economic structures. This indicates that it may be possible to use the structuralist approach, preponderant in contemporary Latin American economic thought, to construct an overall theoretical explanation of the characteristics of the growth process, the persistent upward pressures on the price level, and the recent tendency to stagnation.

The study of the development of the Latin American economy generally begins with the integration of the national economies into the world markets. This integration occurred, in almost all cases, in the second half of the last century. The characteristics of Latin American social and political realities are generally ignored, thus the study is limited to an analysis of the pertinent economic factors, especially those related to foreign trade and public finance. Nevertheless, even though the economic variables could be defined in terms of concepts derived from general principles of economics, the behavior of these variables is conditioned by institutional parameters, the knowledge of which requires a specific study of the social reality underlying them. In the Latin American case this social reality shows peculariarities which require careful attention.

The prevailing social organization in Latin America, resulting from the Iberian colonization, presents two otustanding characteristics: (1) the existence of an urban sector through which power is exerted, which in the colonial phase had its centers of ultimate decision in the respective European metropolis; and (2) the existence of a special class of men connected to the central power by bonds of personal loyalty, to whom the factors of production—land and native labor where it existed— were granted by that central power.

The backbone of the colonization process was represented by a chain of urban centers, of various sizes and significance, which constituted the basic structure of political power and administrative organization. Together with this rigid administrative structure, responsible for guarding the interests of the metropolis, a highly decentralized economic system arose under the direction of men who had semi-feudal prerogatives. In those regions where metropolitan control was less strict, commercial activities, mainly based on contraband, developed more freely, opening the way to the formation of an urban social group with considerable economic influence. A similar phenomenon also took place where a highly lucrative activity could be practiced outside the landowners' control, as in the case of alluvial gold mining in Brazil. It is important to note that such activities were always attached to the urban centers and they were directed by men whose loyalty to the metropolitan power was not very strict. In this way, a ruling class was formed, made up of two groups with interests which were distinct but not necessarily in conflict. On one hand there was a group of landowners vested with considerable power over the population in their domain, and on the other hand, there were those elements whose wealth was derived from commerce and other activities, principally urban in character. The continual confrontation of "conservatives" and "liberals" through the first century of political independence, brings about, to some extent, this present dichotomy of attitudes in the ruling class.

As an instrument for domination over a society where some forms of semi-feudal decentralization prevailed, the State emerged in colonial times as a strong bureaucracy which came to constitute one of the essential elements in the urban social structure. As an intermediary responsible for the distribution of "prebends" adjudicated by the metropolitan power, and later as the creator itself of such prebends, the political-bureaucratic structure exterted a strong influence within the society, and for this reason its control was ardently fought for by the factions of the ruling class. In time, the expansion of the bureaucratic structure itself became a completely new social stratum, which, because of its infiltration into the state apparatus, mainly through the military, came to be an essential constituent element of the power system.

The rapid integration of Latin American economies into the expanding currents of international trade, which took place in the latter part of the nineteenth century, is due in large part to this "liberal" segment in the ruling class of the region. There can

31

be no doubt that the prime mover of this process of economic expansion lay in the dynamism created by the advanced capitalistic economies at that time. It was, in reality, a displacement of the European economic frontier. However, the rapid Latin American response can only be explained if the dichotomy within the ruling class of the region is taken into account. The liberal group, formed mainly by urban elements, was amenable to external influences. While the landowner segment managed to expand its power by a process of expanding the area under crop cultivation—taking new land and tithing the population settling in their land—the urban bourgeoisie depended essentially on foreign commercial relations in order to survive. To the urban bourgeoisie fell the double function of discovering new lines of commerce and of exercising their influence in the interior by financial and other means, toward production of what seemed suitable for marketing. Occasionally it was a question of introducing new crops or assuming financial risks in the initial phase of a venture, and this could only be undertaken by men with direct knowledge of the possibilities offered by the foreign markets. These urban elements were indeed the Schumpeterians of the development, "the forward marchers" of Latin America.

Under the influence of the liberal groups, into which many of the most dynamic people of the agrarian faction had become incorporated, the State played a very important part in the transition of the semi-isolated society, with feudal characteristics, to increasing integration with the rapidly expanding European economy. A typical example of such action by the State was the financing by the Brazilian Government of the European immigration which made it possible to develop coffee production during the last quarter of the last century. In sum, the phase of development through rapid expansion of exports can be explained, from the Latin American side, by taking into account the converging effect of the following factors: (a) the existence of a pre-capitalist economy, from which land and labor could be drawn; (b) the existence of a segment of the ruling class oriented toward opening up new lines of exports in order to increase their wealth and protect and augment their social prestige; and (c) the existence of a political organization sufficiently articulate to serve as an instrument of the more progressive factions of the ruling class in their attempt to eliminate the obstacles, imposed by the semi-feudal social structure, to the process of integration into a growing but unstable international economy.

CHARACTERISTICS OF THE PRE-CAPITALIST ECONOMY

The socio-economic system in Latin America during the late nineteenth century presented some particular features which have to be considered if we intend to understand the subsequent phases of growth. The territorial occupation, as we have already observed, was obtained through the organization of a network of urban centers, which were a projection of the metropolitan power. These cities formed a system for the defense of the territory against frequent enemy action from outside and from within. From them came men who had authorization to seek precious metals and other forms of wealth, which were believed to exist in the new lands, and to use the native labor so needed in certain areas. However, where the objective was to start an agriculture capable of producing surpluses, the large agrarian productive units of various types assumed great importance from the beginning—as economic and social centers—to the disadvantage of the cities. Because there was no overhead capital, the agrarian productive unit had to contain in itself a full system for production and marketing, attaching itself directly to some principal urban center. The sizes of such agrarian units had, therefore, to be extensive; thus the adjudication of lands had been limited to people of considerable means.

The beginning of the Latin American agricultural economy was a large capitalist enterprise for creating surpluses to be exported, in the case of some tropical products, or to be sent to the mining centers and the cities. With the decline of the initial dynamic economic surge arising from mining in certain areas, the markets which previously absorbed surpluses from agriculture also naturally declined. In the case of exported staples, there occasionally appeared competitive productive areas which were better situated geographically or which had access to protected markets. Thus, the sugar economy of northeast Brazil suffered in the 17th century from strong competition by producers in the

English and French Antilles, which were closer to Europe and protected in their large metropolitan markets. In other cases, obstacles arose to the export of products to the traditional markets as the result of wars that engaged the metropolis. Hence, various circumstances contributed to reduce the relative importance of the surplus sold outside the agrarian unit, which was losing its capitalist character and increasingly becoming a system of social organization with semi-feudal characteristics. The heavily capitalized plantation, on which slave or semi-slave labor was employed in organized groups, tended to be replaced by mixed systems, in which it was up to each worker to produce his own food. Where these transformations were complete, the agrarian unit disintegrated and ceased to exist as an organized system of agricultural production. Instead, it gave way to a multiplicity of family units, the *fazenda* remaining as a superstructure to levy the land rent and to manage commercial and financial activities.

To understand certain features of Latin American socioeconomic organization, it is necessary to take into account that, even though colonization took place under conditions of unlimited supply of land, all lands which could be utilized for the production of an economic surplus were automatically transformed into private property under the control of a small minority. The abundance of land assured a means of subsistence to the population, whose crops were not limited on this account. However, all who worked the land had to pay a tribute to a member of the landowner class. When the possibility of marketing surplus was short, the payment of such tribute assumed other forms, such as help with domestic work, guarding property, opening new lands, building roads, etc.

The pre-capitalist agricultural economy, which prevailed in Latin America, assumed diverse forms, extending from that of the semi-closed Indian community with collective ownership of land to that of the large fazendas in which the private ownership of land was the basis of a system of social organization which enabled those who controlled the land to appropriate more than half the produce from those who worked it. From the economic point of view, the fazenda was not organized on the basis of capitalist rationality, namely, maximization of profit. If we ignore the semi-closed Indian communities, which were simply vestiges of cultural systems existing before European colonization, it appears that the common characteristic of the regional pre-capitalist economy is the control of the basic factor of production —land—by a small minority welded to the centers of political power. In theory, the supply of land could be considered unlimited, and starting at a certain distance from the urban centers, land also could be considered as a free good. Nevertheless, the people who labored the land where it was free domain, in a family unit, by definition were unable to create a surplus that could be sold, because they did not benefit from external economies. However, the peasant's subsistence depended on his ability to sell part of his own production, however small, so as to make it possible to acquire in the market such things as salt, fuel, and other essentials. This explains why the peasant preferred to settle in lands benefiting from external economies, even though he was compelled to divide his production with a member of the proprietary class.

In the economic system outlined, from the landlord's point of view, or from the point of view of the landlord class, the land was always in unlimited supply, and its degree of utilization depended on the availability of labor. Since the surplus created by one family generally permitted another family to be maintained, whenever the availability of labor was increased it was easy to open new lands, prepare pastures, plant new crops, build free roads, etc. This explains why the *fazendeiro* of the pre-capitalist economy was always referring to the shortage of labor. In effect, each new family incorporated into the system meant an increase of the global surplus which benefited the land proprietor. Since it fell to each family to provide for its own subsistence, the admission of new families into the fazenda did not result in an increase in administration costs. Even if the new peasant produced a surplus much smaller than the preexisting average, his incorporation into the fazenda was an advantage to the landowner. In this way, the structure of a pre-capitalist economy under conditions of unlimited supply of land—the property of a small minority—caused a permanent shortage of labor, without contributing to the increase of the wage rate above the subsistence level. The problem can be looked at from another angle: the control of the land by a small minority, under pre-capitalist conditions, enabled this minority to levy a tax on everyone who worked the lands which benefited by external economies. It should be stressed that such an economic organization engendered a pattern of income distribution in which a substantial part of this income (more than 50 per cent) was concentrated in the hands of a minority that comprised barely 5 per cent of the population.

There were cases in Latin America, resulting from the rupture in the political system provoked by outside factors, in which the landowning class was suddenly eliminated. A good example is the liquidation of the Jesuit Missions, in the nineteenth century by the insurrectionary liberation forces which owned large areas of land, particularly in Paraguay. Because of this political cataclysm, the lands which had been the property of the Order were transferred to the control of those who worked them; thus rent as an instrument for the collection of an economic surplus disappeared. Indeed, land became a free good. The elimination of land rent under such conditions strengthens the position of middlemen able to buy that part of the production which the farmer does not consume directly. The surplus tends, in this manner, to change from the hands of the old landowner class to the control of the middlemen. However, the peasant gains a capacity to bargain which can bring about important modifications in the organization of the productive system, and in the pattern of income distribution. Where previously his relationship to the landowner left him with no alternative but to turn over a substantial part of his produce, he could now choose to reduce the marketable part of his agricultural production, thereby producing more for his own use, or providing time to pursue crafts not related to agriculture, or to improve his home, etc. To protect himself from the manipulation of prices by middlemen, he was able to diversify production for his own use, thus becoming highly independent of the market. To the economy as a whole, the result has to be a relative decline of commercial activity and a regression in the pattern of the social division of labor. However, this will not prevent the living standard in rural areas from rising, owing to substantial modifications in the pattern of the income distribution. In fact, one may readily observe that, in certain rural areas of Latin America where marketed production is relatively small, the regions of old colonization in Paraguay being a good example, the standard of living of the population is relatively high.

Let us consider now a similar situation—that is, the elimination of the landowner class resulting from a political cataclysm, but in a subsequent phase, long after the period of population growth. The evolution of Haiti illustrates, to a certain degree, such a case. The population pressure, resulting in an increasing shortage of arable lands, will compel the peasants to seek new lines of production, which would allow for a more economic utilization of the soil. Without this effort of specialization, the living standards would have to drop to levels which could stop the population growth. The only alternative to a Malthusian equilibrium of this type—the possibility of endogenous technological innovations having been excluded a priori—is the integration into a market economy of bigger dimension, which will open to the middlemen the possibility of recovering or increasing its influence. Under such conditions, the middlemen will tend to assume a similar role, in the economic and social system, to that previously performed by the landowner class.

THE EXPORT GROWTH PHASE

Up to the middle of the last century, the Latin American economies were chiefly made up of pre-capitalist systems with the general characteristics outlined above. The abundance of land allowed for a high rate of population growth. But there is no indication that labor productivity rose in a sustained way in any particular area of the region. The technological revolution brought about in shipping, the demonstration effect, that is, the successful example of English manufactures which were modifying patterns of consumption in certain segments of the population, the new possibilities for commodity production created in the European markets in the more advanced phase of capitalist development, as well as the challenging example of the rapid development of the United States, these and other factors caused a "progressive" attitude to appear, especially in those regions where the urban classes found greater social expression. In some countries this progressive attitude brought government to assume the initiative in the promotion of important overhead invest- ments, financing them with foreign loans or even undertaking all the costs incurred by the immigration of large masses of Europeans into the region. This inflow of European population, for many reasons, including difficulties in obtaining ownership of land, helped to bring about a more rapid urbanization process.

As we have already indicated, the rapid integration of the Latin American economies into world markets was due to a favorable convergence of exogenous and endogenous factors. In the case of the mining industry, the exogenous factors doubtless predominated. In other instances, the exogenous elements, such as the import of finance capital, the introduction of new tech- niques or the creation of external economies through the con- struction of seaports, railways, and public utilities arose at a later phase. These changes occurred, however, as a response to the growth of exports, and their fundamental characteristic was that they were obtained by the introduction of new forms of production organization, which came to co-exist, in each country, with the pre-capitalist economy. In the case of countries which exported minerals, the dualism in the economic system was par- ticularly obvious, since generally the new exporting sector was geographically isolated. In countries exporting agricultural prod- ucts, the dualism was less visible, but nevertheless equally real, at least in the initial phase. In Brazil, the production of coffee, cocoa, rubber, and most export products, with the sole exception of sugar, was organized on lands previously not in use, requiring important movements of population.

It is necessary to consider the features of the pre-capitalist economy to understand why the new export economy had to be organized at the border of the traditional economic structure. The *latifundia,* as we observed, had progressively become a basic institution of the social and political structure and decreasingly performed functions of a primarily economic nature. To them fell the function of absorbing the increase in rural population, main- taining order, and carrying out minor overhead investments re- quired for the opening of new lands. Within the social and political structure represented by the *fazenda,* the isolated peasant and his family increasingly came to represent the basic unit of production.

Under such circumstances of familial solidarity, the landowner class neglected tasks directly related to the productive process in order to become involved with other social and political activities. The entrepreneurial attitude which made the rapid development of lines of export possible originated within the merchant groups which operated out of the urban centers. Here arose the individuals who discovered new economic horizons, whether in relation to testing the capacity of absorption of foreign markets, or inducing farm producers to cultivate a product which had favorable prospects in such markets. Once the discovery was made, it was only natural that the imitators would multiply, thus starting a period of speculation in favorably situated lands which brought high yields. The movement of population, attracted by higher wages and by the delusions of easy wealth that the fortunes of a few had turned into legend, occurred spontaneously. The rapid shift of the coffee frontier, in the north of the Brazilian State of Paraná, is a recent example of this process of creating a new agricultural frontier under the dynamic stimulus of expanding foreign demand.

The agricultural exporting sector, organized along capitalist lines, tended to concentrate in certain areas, according to the products in which they specialized, which facilitated the construction of the infrastructure required for its expansion and its linkage to foreign markets. The amount of labor absorbed—assuming a foreign demand fully elastic at a given le, .l of prices —was determined by the availability of lands of suitable location and quality, the physical productivity of labor and the real wage rate, which was necessarily higher than the pay which the peasant formerly obtained in traditional agriculture.

In fixing a wage rate higher than the pay earned by the peasant in pre-capitalist agriculture, the export sector was assured of an unlimited labor supply. In effect, the old agricultural sector functioned as a labor reservoir; until this reservoir was exhausted, the export sector enjoyed a flexible labor supply at a wage rate defined by the living standard which prevailed in the semi-feudal fazendas. On the contrary, in the particular case of those areas in which the standard of living, within the scope of the pre-capitalist economy, was relatively high—as occurred where the lands were of good quality and the peasant did not have to pay rent on the soil—the development of an agricultural export sector faced serious obstacles. Paraguay illustrates this last case.

The coffee expansion in Brazil is a typical example of the combination of a great abundance of good and well-located lands, with a very flexible labor supply at a relatively low wage rate. The limit to expansion of production was the saturation of the import markets. Even without the dramatic features of the expansion of the huge Brazilian coffee economy, the Latin American experience in the classical phase of export growth generally followed the same basic lines. Land always appears as an abundant factor and the labor supply showed a high elasticity at a relatively low wage level. The equilibrium between supply and demand was obtained through a sequence of crises of overproduction, which in part explains the tendency toward deterioration of the terms of trade observed over a long period of time.

The rapid development of Latin American agricultural exports in the phase considered here, can be better understood if the process of capital formation within this agricultural sector is examined. If investment is defined in a restricted sense, as being capital formation brought about by savings generated in the previous time period, it can be said that the development of the new agriculture required relatively little investment. Investment of this type financed the building of feed roads, the purchase of hand tools used by the peasants and the limited advances required by the new labor that was being used in the tasks connected with the expansion of the productive capacity. The income earned by the last group of workers was provided by crops obtained from the same land that was being incorporated into the new export agriculture. The case of perennial crops lends itself better to the analysis of this process. In this case, capital formation is equivalent to land rent and such imputed rent would not exist if the agriculture were not expanding. Thus, the expansion itself of agriculture creates the means that feed the investment process. It explains why within a period of five or six years, in the decade of the 1950's, the production of coffee doubled in Brazil without imposing any major strain on the resources of the economy or any important diversion of investment from other sectors. This broader concept of investment, including how labor is utilized in agriculture, will be detailed below.

Let us try to illustrate in a quantitative way the relations referred to previously, with regard to the process of capital formation, taking as an example the Brazilian economy in the golden phase of the expansion of coffee, cocoa or other crops of the perennial type. In such cases, it can be shown that about 90 per cent of the investment in reproducible capital is made up of embodied labor, which is paid with agricultural production obtained from the same land during the gestation period of the perennial crop. Let us designate by $\triangle k$ this part of total investment. The remaining 10 per cent of the investment, which must be covered by savings generated during the previous productive period, will be denoted by the addition of $\triangle K$ to the capital stock K. If the output-capital ratio $(P/k + K)$ equals 0.4, then it follows that the ration P/K is ten times greater, or 4.

Let us see in more detail the process of producing k, which we know to represent labor embodied in the improvement of land for new crops, approximating the value of the rent of the land during this period. It is as if the peasant spent part of his time, say half of his working hours, planting the perennial crop, and the other half taking care of annual crops for himself, although this does not mean that such crops are exclusively destined for his own consumption. To render the analysis more simply, it is appropriate to consider the planting of new crops as an independent productive sector, i.e., a sector oriented to the creation of productive capacity. However, one has to take into account that this creation of productive capacity in the export sector occurs simultaneously with the expansion of agricultural production destined in the domestic market to cover the additional labor costs required to expand the export sector. We will assume, finally, that the worker employed in the production of k, required the same amount of K and earns the same wage rate as workers directly employed in the export sector.

The definitions and structural relations that we have presented enable us to divide agriculture into three sectors, each with

41

a specific production function. The first sector (P_1) is composed of the pre-capitalistic agriculture; the second (P_2) corresponds to those activities directly producing for the external markets, and the third sector (P_3) is made up of the activities responsible for expanding the productive capacity of P_2, i.e., for the production of k. It may be taken for granted that the productivity of labor is substantially greater in P_2 and P_3 than in P_1, as is also the wage rate. However, even if the wage rate were less in P_1, due to the lower productivity of the pre-capitalist economy, the share of the total produce required to pay the peasant is less in P_2 and P_3. In effect, in the export sector the income of the worker will seldom absorb 50 per cent of his output and at times less than a third, whereas in the pre-capitalist sector the peasant's income is generally equal to or greater than half of his output. In this way, if we consider agriculture as a whole, during the growth period of the exports, we realize that the rise of labor productivity and the increase in the average wage rate occur concomitantly with the reduction of the share of labor in the aggregate income generated in agriculture, namely, with a greater concentration of income in the hands of the landowner-capitalist class. If we consider this class by itself, we see that the capitalist group is increasing its share at the expense of the feudal group.

The expansion of the productive capacity of P_2 presupposes a previous increase of activity in P_3, which behaves like an industry specialized in the production of capital goods, therefore subject to a mechanism of acceleration each time the demand expands for the goods produced with such capital goods. In this manner, if the demand for coffee, cocoa, or any similar product increases, sector P_3 which is concerned with the creation of new capacity of production in the export sector tends to absorb new labor from the pre-capitalist sector. The absorption of this labor requires a certain mobilization of savings generated during the previous period ($\triangle K$) which, as we have indicated, is assumed to be equal, per worker, to that required to employ a person in P_2. Since it is assumed that the productivity of labor is of the same magnitude in P_2 and P_3, the relation P/K is also identical in the two sectors, with the difference that in sector P_2, K requires the complement of a sizable amount of k, while in P_3 the inputs are restricted to labor (L) and K. The three production functions can be expressed as follows:

Output	P_1	P_2	P_3
Inputs			
L	$\overline{l}_1$	l_2	$\overline{l}_3$
K	O	b_{K_2}	b_{K_3}
k	O	b_{k_2}	O

b_{ij} = amount of capital stock i needed per unit of output of sector j.
l_j = amount of labor needed per unit of output of sector j.

The share of P_3 in total agricultural output is bound to increase whenever the export growth rate is increasing. On the other hand, whenever the relative importance of P_3 in total agricultural production increases, the rate of investment in the agricultural sector as a whole will rise, at the same time that the output-capital ratio increases. The combined action of these two factors will speed up the process of growth. Let us call $\triangle K$ the total investment, where $\triangle k = 0.9 \triangle K$ and $\triangle K = 0.1 \triangle K$, according to the definitions previously given. Since the labor productivity is the same in P_2 and P_3, as is also true of the relation L/K in these two sectors, it follows that the output-capital ratio [P/K] in P_3 is ten times greater than in P_2. Since P_2 and P_3 must be considered together as two subsectors that interact, it can be deduced that the output-capital ratio in the capitalist agriculture as a whole will tend to be higher, the higher is the agricultural rate of growth. On the other hand, whenever we equate investment and savings ex-post, it can be shown that the increase in the share of P_3 in the total production implies an increase of the rate of savings, for with the relative growth of P_3 the production of k necessarily increases with the same intensity. Since k cannot be consumed or exported, but necessarily incorporated into productive capacity, it can be inferred that its relative growth means, *ceteris paribus*, an increase of the ex-post rate of savings.

43

If it is true that a relative growth of P_3 brings about an increase of the savings rate, it can be inferred that the latter is a function of the changes in the pattern of the allocation of resources. Thus, not only the level of demand, but also the composition of this demand, constitutes a basic factor in the determination of the rate of savings, hence of the pace of growth. When changes in the pattern of the aggregate demand cause people to transfer from P_1 to P_3, not only a rise of the labor productivity occurs, but also an increase in the rate of savings, which permits an acceleration of growth with minor inflationary pressures. Such conditions apply only when the annual increase of P_2 is growing in absolute terms, which means a stable or increasing rate of expansion of exports; they are incompatible with exports which may be growing but at a declining rate. However, if exports are expanding, even though at a declining proportional rate of growth, the production of P_3 will be able to keep increasing for some time. This means that a certain amount of labor, even though decreasing, is being transferred from P_1 to P_2, which causes an increase of the average productivity and of the average wage rate, but not a rise of the growth rate of total output. If the rate of growth of P_2 continues to decline, a point will be reached at which the sector P_3 will start to shrink. If this last tendency persists, a second point will be reached at which the absorption of new people in P_2 will be less than the unemployment created in P_3, which indicates that P_1 will get back some of its previous work force. At the first point, when P_3 starts to decline, the savings ratio begins to shrink; at the second point, which marks the beginning of the return of labor to P_1, the average labor productivity starts to decline. This fall of productivity will have secondary consequences in the urban zones, where the relative prices of the agricultural products will tend to increase.

We made reference to the fact that the new agriculture, which develops in response to an expanding external demand, benefits from an unlimited supply of labor, at a relatively low level of wages determined by the standard of living that prevails in the pre-capitalist sector. It can happen, however, that this last sector may be relatively small from the point of view of the labor force employed in it and that, in spite of this, the abundance of good and well-located land gives rise to a rapid expansion of an export agriculture. This was the case of Argentina, whose integration into the international markets was extraordinarily rapid. Under such conditions, it is expected that the pre-capitalist agriculture will be absorbed in a relatively short time, and that all the labor be incorporated into a new agriculture organized on a capitalist basis.

Once the pre-capitalist sector is absorbed, the labor market is unified. Thus, the wage rate will no longer be a function of the standard of living prevailing in a semi-feudal society but will instead increase with productivity, as occurs in any capitalist economy in which there is a limited labor supply. As soon as the wage rate attains a certain level, a significant influx of foreign labor occurs. The migratory stream will make possible a greater development of the export sector and, for some time, it will inhibit the tendency of the wage rate to increase. However, it will also introduce into the country new habits of consumption and, in the case of European immigration, new social attitudes that are conducive to more advanced forms of labor organization.

With respect to those countries in which the pre-capitalist sector has disappeared as a reservoir of labor and in which the wage rate has become dependent on forces operating in a basically unified labor market, the basic transition to a capitalist structure has been accomplished. The economies of these countries, of which Argentina and Uruguay constitute the only two examples in Latin America, cannot be strictly considered as underdeveloped, inasmuch as the concept of underdevelopment is related to the idea of structural dualism. With this dualism basically eliminated, the labor market already cannot be qualitatively differentiated from the markets for other factors of production. Under such conditions, it is expected that the wages paid in agriculture approximate those paid in industry and services, progressively bridging the gap between the living conditions prevailing in the urban and rural zones. The disparity between the living standards of these two groups is the principal feature of typically underdeveloped countries.

National economies which had developed lines of export of mineral products also show certain peculiarities which merit attention. The process of integration into the international markets creates, in this case, a sharp dualism in the productive

45

structure, since the export sector presents a high coefficient of capital and a high level of labor productivity but absorbs no more than a small fraction of the labor force. The sharp disparity of sectoral productivity levels allows the ratio of exports to GIP to rise to 25 or 30 per cent, even though the sector producing for export employs less than 5 per cent of the active population. In such cases, the fiscal capacity of the government increases substantially, and one of the multiple secondary consequences of this fact is the intensification of the urbanization process. The absorption of labor in the mining export sector and the growth of the urban population create a necessity for greater agricultural surpluses. But this impulse is not sufficient to cause transformations in the agrarian structure. If an export agriculture opens the way for the penetration of capitalist enterprise in agriculture, it is because its specialization makes possible a high rate of profit, even without the introduction of greater technical advances. In the case of a simple expansion of the domestic market, the possibility of this specialization does not exist, hence the capitalist enterprise must be supported from the beginning by significant technical advance, in order to compete with the surpluses coming from the traditional agriculture. However, in view of the favorable conditions of the external sector, the chance is that the demand for additional food will be totally or chiefly met by imports. In this manner, a high coefficient of exports could be reached in several Latin American countries—Bolivia in the pre-revolutionary period was an extreme example—without the agricultural sector showing significant modification. On the contrary, the steady demand for the small surpluses coming from traditional agriculture tend to cause a relative increase of the rent paid on the lands, allowing the landlord class to augment its share in aggregate income and to consolidate its position in the power system.

THE INDUSTRIALIZATION PHASE

During the last quarter of the nineteenth century and the first decades of this century, favorable conditions occurred for the development of diverse lines of Latin American exports, which benefited, though unequally, almost all countries of the region. In respect to the area as a whole, at the end of the 1920's exports already represented approximately a quarter of the gross product. Even if we take into account that one-third of the income generated by exports remained outside the region, it should be recognized that the Latin American economies had attained an exceptionally high degree of integration into the system of international division of labor. However, it is highly significant that, notwithstanding this high integration in the system of international division of labor—about 40 per cent of economic activity was related to the external sector, whether through exports or imports—the pre-capitalist sector maintained a relatively great importance in almost all the countries of the area. Since labor was a factor of unlimited supply in the productive sectors outside the pre-capitalist economy, development assumed basically the form of relative growth of those sectors which benefited from the elastic labor supply without causing greater modifications in the production functions of those sectors. Thus, production per unit of the input mix was growing for the economy as a whole, but remained stable within each productive sector, which is to say: the economic system was modifying its structure without the need to absorb technological innovations. Evidently, where mechanical equipment was needed it had to be imported and innovations had to be absorbed as a simple routine process and not as a result of any economic, endogenously generated force. In agriculture, this automatic penetration of new techniques was extremely limited simply because the process of capital formation required little capital equipment.

The 1929 world crisis, and the protracted depression that followed, put an end to the process of progressive integration into a system of international division of labor in almost all of Latin America. A reversal of previous trends then set in by which the majority of the national economies of the region had to reduce, in one form or another, their coefficient of integration in world markets. This closing process of the national economies assumed two forms. The first simply consisted in the return of part of the labor force engaged in activities related to the external sector to the pre-capitalist economy: agriculture or crafts. The second form consisted of industrialization. The two forms occurred in varying degrees everywhere, but the success of industrialization was very uneven, which is easily explained when we consider that this industrialization was based on domestic markets, the dimensions of which were very unequal. In a few countries the impulse given to the national economy by industrialization allowed those countries to attain, albeit in short periods, relatively high growth rates, equal to or greater than those attained in the golden age of growing exports. The problem is to identify the nature of this industrialization process. Is it a sure way to reach and maintain a high rate of growth in the region?

Latin American industrialization is known as a process of import substitution. In reality, it is a process of change in the productive structure, permitting a reduction in the share of imports in aggregate supply without reversion of labor to the pre-capitalist economy. The import of certain goods is reduced or eliminated and those goods substituted in the domestic markets by the local produce. At the same time, the import of items which are hard to substitute is enlarged. Since per capita income is increasing while the coefficient of imports is reduced, the composition of aggregate demand tends to change, requiring greater alteration in the structure of aggregate supply than that foreseen at the beginning of the substitution process. The period of time required for aggregate supply to adapt to the modifications in the pattern of the demand, a period that can be greatly prolonged by institutional obstacles, is a primary force responsible for the creation of inflationary pressures, particularly when the capacity to import shows little or no flexibility in the short run.

Let us consider the case of a country in which, in 1929, exports represented around one-fifth of the gross product and in which the imports contributed around 60 per cent of the aggregate supply of manufactured goods. Due to the lowering of the export prices and to the shrinkage of the quantum exported during the depression, the capacity to import is reduced by, say, 50 per cent. Exports consist of agricultural products and concern a large number of producers. This induces the government to expand credit to finance the stockpiling of agricultural surpluses, as well as to modify the exchange rate in favor of the exporters. The two measures allow the level of money income of the export sector to be kept stable. The structure of aggregate demand will adjust itself to a substantially lower level of imports. To absorb part of the pressure exerted on the balance of payments, the government will raise tariffs on manufactured goods which already had begun to be domestically produced.

The shrinkage of imports, the devaluation of the exchange rate, the expansion of credit for the financing of stocks and the raising of tariffs tend to determine a series of changes in the cost structure. The action of these factors, together with the struggle of various social groups in defense of their income, are bound to cause modifications in relative prices and in income distribution, so as to make the pattern of aggregate demand and the structure of aggregate supply compatible. The final result is, however, a rise in the general level of prices of final goods, embodying a relative increase in the prices of imported goods. One may expect, as a by-product of these changes, an improvement in the competitive position of the manufactured goods of domestic production, as well as a rise in the relative prices of such goods. Since the wage rate in the industrial sector is supposed to be kept stable, it is to be expected that the profit rate in this sector will increase. Taking into account the unlimited supply of labor, it is natural that, under such conditions, the industrialists should try to work two and three shifts per day, which will be accompanied by somewhat reduced complementary investments. The output-capital ratio will tend consequently to grow sharply. Let us assume that this ratio is equal to 1 : 1 in the initial situation, an investment of one million dollars in reproducible capital being thus expected to yield a flow of income (value added) of one million dollars per annum. Through a 10 per cent increase in investment (mainly to cover additional needs of working capital), the introduction of two daily shifts will raise the income flow to two million dollars, the output-capital ratio increasing to 1.82. The same phenomenon can be examined from the point of view of the profit rate. Let us assume that the capital stock per worker, in the initial situation, is 2,500 dollars and that the annual wage rate is 600 dollars. If the output-capital ratio is equal to 1, then the 2,500 dollars of capital is bound to yield a flow of income (wage plus gross profit) of 2,500 dollars. Since the wage rate is 600 dollars, it follows that the gross profit equals 1,900 dollars, which amounts to a 76 per cent gross rate of return. In the second situation, where there is a 10 per cent increase in investment, capital increases to 2,750 dollars, but gross profit reaches 3,800 dollars, corresponding to a rate return of 138 per cent. These figures are of course very rough and are limited to clarifying the tendency toward a rapid increase in the profit rate.

Observing the behavior of the economic system as a whole from the point at which external demand shrinks, we realize that the sector responsible for the expansion of productive capacity in agriculture (P_3) rapidly shrinks. This causes a decline in the output-capital ratio and a fall of the profit rate in the capitalist agricultural sector ($P_2 + P_3$) although the reduction of the level of activity in P_2 is avoided through the financing of surpluses by the government. Concomitantly, other forces start to operate which produce a rise in the output-capital ratio and in the profit rate of the industrial sector. It is to be expected, therefore, that part of the entrepreneurial capacity, and of the financial resources which were being absorbed by the export sector in its phase of growth, should be diverted to the growing manufacturing sector. This change in the destination of investment causes a series of secondary consequences, due to specific differences in the process of capital formation in the manufacturing as compared to the agricultural export sector.

In analyzing the phase of expansion of exports, we indicated that the share of K in the amount of capital required to increase the export capacity was rather small ($K = 0.1\overline{K}$). Taking into account the quantity of K necessary to produce k, which complements K in P_2, we should ascribe to the above referred to coefficient a larger value, however, not greater than 0.2. Therefore, it can be assumed that the ratio P/K is equal to or greater than 2, if we consider P_2 and P_3 together. In other words, for each increase of 100 dollars in the productive capacity of the capitalist agriculture, a maximum investment of 50 dollars is required in terms of K, which we know to consist of imported equipment. Let us consider now, for the purpose of comparison, the process of capital formation in the manufacturing sector, which we will call P_4. Due to the structure of relative prices, the productivity of labor, as well as of capital, are substantially greater in P_4 than in export agriculture. Let us assume that the labor productivity is 2.5 times greater and that the output-capital ratios are also 2.5 times greater.[2] Assume the wage rate to be only 50 per cent higher, which can be explained by the fact that this rate continues to be strongly influenced by the living standard of the large segment of the population remaining in the pre-capitalist sector. In the export sector, for the sake of simplicity, let the average annual production per worker be 1,000 dollars and the annual wage rate 400 dollars. The corresponding values for the industrial sector would, therefore, be 2,500 and 600 dollars. Since the average output-capital ratio $(P/\overline{K})$ in industry is equal to one and in export agriculture is equal to 0.4, it follows that the total capital $(\overline{K})$ per worker would be the same in the two sectors, namely, 2,500 dollars. The gross profit rate would be, therefore, 24 per cent in agriculture (600/2,500) and 76 per cent in industry (1,900/2,500). It should be stressed, however, that of the investment in the agricultural sector, only a fraction not greater than 20 per cent must be covered, directly or indirectly, by savings generated in the previous period, while in the industrial sector the total investment consists of $\triangle K$. Therefore, the ratio P/K is 2 in export agriculture and 1 in industry. In other words, given a certain rate of savings (defined as that part of the income generated in the previous time period which was not consumed) the growth rate attainable in industry corresponds to half of that which is possible in the export sector. The pattern of aggregate demand, of course, sets another constraint to the relative growth rates of the two sectors. This pattern constitutes, therefore, a basic factor determining the economy-wide output-capital ratio, if we measure capital only in terms of K. On the other hand, when the pattern of aggregate demand changes, and, as a result of such a change, the share of industrial investment grows, the gross profit rate will tend to rise, permitting a higher savings rate. In effect, as the P/K ratio tends to diminish from 2 to 1, as a result of the change in the destination of investment, it will be necessary to increase the rate of savings in order to maintain the same rate of growth. In view of the substantial rise in the profit rate to which reference has already been made, it is quite possible for the required increase in the savings rate to take place.

From the point of view of the balance of payments, the above-mentioned differences in the two processes of capital formation have a particular significance. With respect to the export sector, we already observed that K is composed almost wholly of imported equipment. In the industrial sector, the import content (including indirect imports) would not be less than 75 per cent of total investment. This being true, the coefficient of imports per unit of additional investment would rise from 0.5 to 0.75. In other words, to create an additional flow of income of 100 dollars, it would be necessary to import 50 dollars worth of equipment, in the first case, and 75 dollars worth in the second; this is equivalent to saying that in order to maintain the growth rate it would be necessary to increase by 50 per cent the import of capital equipment. Moreover, the rise of the profit rate and consequent concentration of income are bound to give an additional impetus to the demand for durable consumer goods, which are entirely imported. However, it can be assumed that, during the first phase in the process of substitutive industrialization, this tendency may very well be cancelled by the price-effect, due to the sharp increase in the relative price of such goods. If we classify imports into three groups—equipment and intermediate products, durable consumer goods, and nondurable consumer goods—we can expect that the effect on demand due to devaluation is likely to be smallest with regard to the first group and largest with regard to the third. Due to the rise in the profit rate, industrialists will try to import equipment and intermediate goods, in spite of the rise in their prices; on the other hand, the concentration of income caused by the shift in the allocation of investments enables the high income classes to face the price rise of imported durable goods. Thus, it is natural that the reduction of imports tends to center upon the group of nondurable manufactured consumer goods. It is this phenomenon that creates favorable conditions for the process of import substitution.

Industrialization under conditions referred to above requires an effort aimed at adapting the economic system to a progressive reduction of the import share in aggregate supply. It is clear that, once the possibilities of substitution of nondurable goods have been exhausted, particularly with regard to the final phase of the manufacturing process of such goods, all attempts at maintaining the investment rate will necessarily cause growing pressure on the balance of payments, pushing upward the relative prices of durable consumer goods and equipment still more sharply than in the previous phase. Since the rise in the price of machinery tends to affect the investment rate adversely, the economy can only maintain its growth rate if a phase of substitution of the durable consumer goods and equipment begins. Let us call P_5 this new productive sector, the basic characteristic of which is a high coefficient of capital. Thus, if for each worker occupied in P_4 the capital is of the order of 2,500 dollars, in the new sector P_5 at least 10,000 dollars per worker will be necessary. Strictly speaking, one cannot assert that *all* industries producing durable consumer goods and equipment present a high capital coefficient, and that the contrary necessarily holds true for industries producing nondurable consumer goods. But this is the general tendency, since textile and food processing count for more than half of the industrial output of that sector. This, together with the fact that the markets of durable consumer goods and equipment are of relatively smaller size than that of nondurable goods, explains the late development of such industries.

Assuming that the profit rate tends to become uniform in every industry (otherwise it would not be possible to explain why industries with a notorious inferiority with respect to the rate of return on investment could attract any new capital) and taking into account that approximately the same wage rate prevails in all branches of the industry, we can infer that the output-capital ratio is likely to be as low as the coefficient of capital per worker is high. In accordance with the assumption previously made, in P_4 the quantity of capital per worker is 2,500 dollars, the wage rate 600 dollars, and the gross profit rate 76 per cent, given an output-capital ratio of 1. If we maintain in P_5 the same wage and gross profit rates, the capital-labor ratio being 10,000, the output-capital ratio cannot exceed 0.82.

This second phase of substitutive industrialization presents another very relevant aspect. The capital goods industries, since they face greater obstacles arising from the limited size of the market and inadequate means for financing sales, encounter conditions favorable to development only when the relative prices in this sector attain extremely high levels. In reality, the relative price of equipment starts to increase when the substitutive process is begun, but it is only when this increase reaches a certain point that the production of equipment becomes economically viable. It is even possible that the rise of the relative price of equipment starts only 'when the substitutive process of nondurable manufactured consumer goods is quite advanced; or that it begins moderately and is accentuated in the final phase, as a result of the discontinuation of a tariff policy aimed at subsidizing the imports of equipment which held during the initial phase of industrialization. The abrupt rise of the relative price of equipment, which characterizes the second phase of the substitutive industrialization, has serious repercussions on the process of capital formation, both in industrial and agricultural sectors. Since the real wage rate is determined by nonmarket factors and can be assumed to be stable, it can be expected that the decline in the output-capital ratio caused by the rise of the relative price of equipment is likely to bring about a reduction in the profit rate. In this manner, one may exclude the possibility that the savings rate may increase to compensate for the decline in the productivity of K.

The increase in the share of sector P_5 (domestic production of durable consumer goods and equipment) in the aggregate investment has other repercussions which deserve to be considered. Due to the high coefficient of capital per unit of employment in P_5, the amount of labor being transferred from the precapitalist sector to the other productive activities will decline with the increase of the share of this sector in aggregate investment. If four times as much capital is required to employ a person in P_5 as in P_4, then with the increasing orientation of new investment to that sector, the tendency toward the concentration of income will become more pronounced, even though the profit rate is kept stable. If one assumes that the wage rate and the amount of investment are unaltered, then gross profit must increase more rapidly than the income of the working class, since less labor is being absorbed into the industrial sector $(P_4 + P_5)$ per unit of investment. The sluggish growth of the workers' purchasing power is bound to depress the demand for agricultural products. This will reduce the transfer of labor from P_1 to P_2 and P_3, since it may be assumed that the urban population enjoying a higher rate of wage is also likely to create demand for the capitalist branch of the agricultural sector. This is an additional factor fostering the tendency towards a decline in the output-capital ratio (P/K) of the economy as a whole. In sum, aggregate demand is changing its pattern in such a way that the allocation of productive resources is bound to bring an increasing share of investment to those sectors in which the productivity of K is relatively low (durable consumer goods), reducing the share of those sectors in which the productivity is relatively high (capitalist agriculture).

Thus, a circular causation process arises by which the changes in the pattern of the aggregate demand determine changes in the structure of supply which, as they are realized cause: (a) an increase in the capital-labor ratio of the economy as a whole (K/L); (b) a decline in the transfer of labor from the sectors of low to those of higher labor productivity, and (c) an increase in the capital-output ratio of the economy as a whole (K/P). The rise in the coefficient of capital per unit of labor, under conditions of a stable wage rate, works toward fostering the concentration of income; on the other hand, the investment being oriented towards industries for which the optimum size of the market is relatively greater, sets in motion factors that depress the output-capital ratio. In short, the process of income concentration acts in two directions. It tends to increase the coefficient of capital, unleashing a cumulative process, since a higher amount of capital per unit of employment means a more unequal distribution of income, if the wage rate remains stable. On the other hand, it tends to reduce the growth rate for two reasons. First, it produces a decline in the output-capital ratio through the concentration of investment in the durable consumer goods industries, for which the obstacles raised by the inadequate size of the market are greater. Secondly, it induces a relative reduction of investment in agriculture, where capital formation is largely derived from the absorption of labor from the pre-capitalist sector.

The special case of an economy which, in the phase of export growth, has absorbed the entire pre-capitalist sector and presents a practically unified labor market, should be considered separately. In connection with this special case, let us assume that to face the depression the government embarks upon a political course like that previously described, maintaining the level of the export sector's money income by financing the agricultural surplus and by depreciation of the exchange rate.

As in the previous case, the supply of imported manufactured goods will decline in real terms while the level of aggregate money income is maintained, which causes the relative prices of those manufactured goods to rise, stimulating their domestic production. Industrialization, however, will have to take place through the absorption of labor previously employed in the export sector, since the pre-capitalist sector no longer exists. In spite of the policy aimed at defending the income level of the export sector, it is natural that the wage rate as well as the profit rate will decline in real terms since the country's terms of trade are deteriorating. Under such circumstances, industrialists have no difficulty in attracting labor, since the profit rate in industrial activities increases as a result of the rise in the relative price of manufactured goods. The stepping up of industrial investment has two effects upon the agricultural export sector. It induces a rise in the wage rate, to the extent that it attracts labor into the urban zones, squeezing the agricultural labor force. On the other hand, it aggravates the tendency, caused by the deterioration of the terms of trade, towards the rise in the relative price of other agricultural inputs. Hence it diverts a substantial part of the import capacity to the industrial sector. The availability of foreign currency to meet the needs of the agricultural sector is reduced and this makes the latter acquire domestically manufactured goods at relatively higher prices. In this manner, a convergence of factors operates in the direction of reducing the profit rate of the agricultural export sector and, indirectly, of making industrial investment more attractive, so that the substitutive process is likely to advance with extrordinary rapidity.

Under such conditions, it is possible that under-utilization of the export capacity takes place, with negative effects on the productivity of the economy as a whole. In reaching the advanced phase of import substitution, characterized by the domestic production of equipment, new problems might arise. Since the capital coefficient in the agricultural sector is higher than was the case in economies with a pre-capitalist sector, the increase of the relative prices of equipment will also contribute to the reduction of the profit rate in the export sector. Indeed, it can be taken for granted that the closing of any national economy with a high level of per capita income, through integration into the system of international division of labor which [and that, in this manner] has absorbed its pre-capitalist sector, is bound to produce a reduction in the productivity of the new industrial sectors. This reduction in productivity will be particularly large when the relative advantage that favored the integration into the world market results from an extensive utilization of a highly favorable endowment of natural resources. The structural modifications required by substitutive industrialization may signify, in this case, a decrease of productivity that can only be offset by an upward shift in the production functions caused by technological progress.

Comparing the two cases, one of substitutive industrialization with an unlimited supply of labor at a wage level determined by the living standards prevailing in the pre-capitalist sector (Brazil), and one of substitutive industrialization with a limited supply of labor (Argentina), we can draw the following conclusion. In the first, industrialization can advance without effect on the agricultural wage rate and without significantly affecting the rate of profit of the export sector. Thus, there exists no incompatibility between the advance of substitutive industrialization and an occasional recuperation of the export sector at a time of favorable conditions in the external markets. This was evident in Brazil during the 1950's, when a great expansion of coffee production took place at the same time that the substitutive industrialization had reached a high rate of growth. In the second case, substitutive industrialization may seriously affect the rate of profit in the export sector, making its recuperation difficult at a time when favorable conditions in export markets appear. To avoid such negative effects, industrialization would have to be followed by an investment effort in the agricultural sector aimed at raising the technological level of this sector so as to free labor. This investment effort cannot take place spontaneously if agriculture is facing a decline in the profit rate as a consequence of the external crisis and of indirect effects from the effort of import substitution.

Let us return now to the general case in which the process of substitutive industrialization, having attained its most advanced phase, starts producing a relative increase in the price of equipment and a greater concentration of income. The relative rise of the price of equipment has inverse effects from those of capital-saving, technological innovations. It requires a greater amount of investment per unit of product, i.e., it raises the ratio of capital to other inputs in the production function. Thus, in the same way that a capital-saving technological change, under conditions of stable wages, tends to raise the profit rate, the contrary happens when the relative price of equipment increases. Evidently, such a tendency can be offset by a rise of the general price level to allow for a compensatory redistribution of income. However, as it is assumed that the real wage rate is constant, the decline of the output-capital ratio indicates a contraction of the profit rate, with negative effects on savings, therefore unleashing a tendency toward the reduction of the growth rate. In spite of this, the factors working simultaneously in the direction of a greater concentration of income could check the above-mentioned tendency to a decline in the rate of savings.

The process of income concentration in routing investment toward industries with a high coefficient of capital has effects quite similar to those of the introduction of technological labor-saving devices. Since the wage rate is stable, the reduction of the input of labor per unit of output necessarily causes a rise in the profit rate or a decline in the relative price of the product. However, if the wage rate is determined basically by other factors, the reduction in the relative price of a specific product means only that the increase in the profit rate will take place in the economic system as a whole and this will benefit more than a given industry. In any case a concentration of income occurs, which will raise the savings rate, making it possible to neutralize the tendency previously indicated. Thus, everything takes place as if the economic system were absorbing technological innovations causing a reduction in the productivity of capital and increasing that of labor. This being true, in order to increase the output, it is necessary to add increasing inputs of capital and decreasing inputs of labor. It may be inferred, therefore, that for each stable growth rate of total output there is a corresponding declining rate of absorption of labor outside the pre-capitalist sector and an increasing savings rate, assuming the relative prices unaltered.

It is most likely that the two tendencies will appear differently weighted in each concrete case. Where the actual and potential sizes of the domestic market are relatively large, as in the case of Brazil, it is quite conceivable that capital goods industries surmount the difficulties of the preliminary phase and come to benefit from some economies of scale, preventing the tendency toward a substantial increase in the relative price of equipment. Perhaps the basic difference between the substitutive processes in Chile and in Brazil lies here. In the Chilean case, substitutive industrialization, in reaching that phase in which the market size entails increasing inefficiency of investment, produced a reduction of the savings rate and a decline in the rate of growth. In the Brazilian case, the larger dimension of the market, together with a larger relative importance of the pre-capitalist sector, created conditions, such that on the one hand, a greater efficiency of the capital goods industry could be obtained, and on the other hand, the process of income concentration advanced sufficiently to produce in full its negative economic and social consequences. Brazil's success with the substitution process is the counterpart of the fact that it was in this country that development benefited a smaller number of people and begot the sharpest social tensions. These tensions, reaching a critical point, had to adversely affect the growth process. Therefore, substitutive industrialization, by different processes in Brazil and in Chile, engendered a series of obstacles which produced its exhaustion as a dynamic factor of economic development.

In all of the previous analysis, the fact was explicitly ignored that the structural matrix could be modified through the injection of a new technology. It was intended to show that the changes in the pattern of the aggregate demand, initially provoked by dynamic external factors, and in the following phase generated by a policy aimed at defending the level of the money income of the export sector, are sufficient to explain the modifications in the structure of supply which permitted the average productivity of labor to increase. Changes in the production functions which actually occurred find their explanation in factors exogenous to strictly economic decisions, as for example in the fact that imported machines were bearers of technological innovations. It would be appropriate, however, to ask if the introduction of technological innovations, in modifying the input-output relations, did not act toward cancelling the effect of the factors working to concentrate income. Taking into account that technological innovations find their principal vehicle of penetration in machinery, it follows that those sectors in better positions to obtain the benefits of these innovations are those which use greater amounts of equipment. Thus, the smallest probability of being positively affected pertains to agriculture, and the greatest to the industries of durable consumer goods and equipment. Let us assume that technological innovation is neutral, i.e., that it increases the productivity of capital and labor simultaneously. With stable wages, the increase of productivity of capital as well as of labor acts toward the reduction of the share of wages in aggregate income. However, it may be objected that the introduction of more advanced techniques, having the greatest impact on the manufacturing sector, comes to cause a decline in the relative prices of industrial products, somewhat benefiting the peasants of the pre-capitalist sector, whose pay is traditionally fixed as a constant fraction of their produce. The consequent improvement in their standards of living might produce an upward shift of all rural and urban wage scales. But taking into account the small weight of manufactured goods in the expenditure of peasants in the pre-capitalist sector, the advantage which they realize will be much smaller than that which accrues to groups with a relatively higher consumption of manufactured goods. In this manner, independently of the fact that they may bring about increases in average productivity, the technological innovations are likely to aggravate the above-mentioned tendencies toward income concentration.

In short, everything takes place as if the existence of a sizable pre-capitalist sector of feudal character, together with an industrial sector that absorbs a technology requiring a rapid increase in the coefficient of capital, gave rise to a pattern of income distribution which tends to affect the allocation of productive resources in a way to reduce their economic efficiency and to concentrate income still more, in a process of circular causation. More generally, the decline in economic efficiency is likely to provoke economic stagnation. In particular cases, increasing concentration of income, and its sequel of under employed population flowing into the urban zones, create social tensions which, by themselves, are capable of rendering the process of growth nonviable.

FINAL NOTE

Without presenting general conclusions from the above analysis, we can say that development as a spontaneous process—caused by the motivation of certain social groups dedicated to maximizing their material benefits and their influence over the other groups making up a national community—took place in Latin America from the beginning of the second half of the last century without requiring or producing fundamental changes in the social structure. This process, however, even if it could last for some time in certain areas, presents evident signs of having run its course in the area as a whole.

By its particular characteristics, Latin American development, as much in its phase of export growth as in its period of industrialization, constitutes a historic process quite different from the classical model of capitalist development, in which technological innovations play a fundamental role. Without a differentiation between certain basic types of capitalist economy, all attempts toward a theoretical generalization aimed at interpreting the actual problems of the Latin American economies based on historical evidence drawn from the advanced capitalist economies will yield scant intellectual fruit. Nothing warrants a view of the present stage of the Latin American economies as a phase of transition toward the type of capitalistic structures which we recognize today in Western Europe or the United States. There is sufficient empirical evidence that substitutive industrialization has been aggravating the dualism of the labor market and amplifying the gap between the modern sector and the pre-capitalist economy, without opening prospects for a reduction in the importance of the latter as a main source of employment for a rapidly increasing labor force. In the urban sector the aggravation of the same dualism is manifested by the rapid growth of underemployment.

In the theoretical models currently in vogue as the basis for the making of development policies it is implicitly assumed that the economic system is integrated by a combination of structural relations. Its relative stability results from the existence of an institutional framework and from the fact that men and social groups, in their efforts to maximize their income, rely on their own experience, preferring roads already known. This makes it statistically possible to predict their behavior. It is assumed, on the other hand, that inherent in the social behavior of individuals and groups of individuals is the propensity toward an increase of their share in the aggregate income, whether it be by reducing the share of the others or by producing an increase of aggregate income by means of the introduction of technological innovations in the productive process. It is also implicit in this type of theoretical model that if an adequate level of employment is maintained, compatibility, or even a necessary causal relation, exists between the most statistically probable behavior of social groups and maximization of social welfare, insofar as the latter concept may be defined in terms of macro-economic variables. A set of political signals that register the most significant structural tensions assure that the above-mentioned compatibility be maintained through the opportune introduction of corrections in the institutional framework. Contrary to this model, the institutional framework that prevails in Latin America produces patterns of income distribution responsible for behavior incompatible with the most rational utilization of the available resources, that is, with the maximization of total output within any specific time horizon. There exists an inconsistency between the interests of those groups which control the process of capital formation and the interests of the community as a whole, insofar as it is assumed that the latter aims at maximizing the possibilities of social welfare. As these economic groups also occupy all the strategic positions in the power system, it is not surprising that political signals become inadequate to register the structural tensions, and that the instruments for political decision are not fit to promote the timely removal of the obstacles to development. The core of the problem is not in the behavior of the agents that make decisions in the economic field, which may be guided by strict criteria of rationality, either from the means they utilize or their legitimate objectives; rather, the core of the problem resides in the structural relations that determine the field within which the relevant decisions are made. It is in this sense that to the problem of Latin American stagnation we can attribute a structural character.[3] This being so, we have to ask if a policy capable of stopping the long term tendency toward stagnation will not have to assume a form of conscious and deliberate action with the objective of creating structural relations and inducing behavior patterns capable of begetting social processes of which economic development is a necessary component.

NOTES

* A mathematical formulation of the basic ideas expressed in the present study is being developed by Andrea Maneschi, of the Economic Growth Center, whose co-operation has been of great value to the author while working on this paper.

[1] The cumulative annual rate of growth in per capita income of Latin America as a whole since 1950 was as follows: 1950–1955, 2.2; 1955–1960, 1.4; 1960–1963, 0.4. See ECLA, *Estudio Económico de América Latina,* 1963, Vol. I, pg. 3.

[2] Considering P_2 and P_3 together, the output-capital ratio has to be higher than 0.4. However, the relative share of P_3 can only be defined if an assumption about the rate of growth of the export agriculture (P_2) is previously introduced. Nevertheless, the ratio P/K is always stable, once we have assumed the same labor productivity and the same amount of K per worker in both subsectors of capitalist agriculture.

[3] The structural approach to the problems of development, which is being increasingly adapted to problems in Latin America, initially appeared in connection with theoretical studies trying to identify the primary causes of the inflationary disequilibrium (which results, as a rule, from the structural rigidities of supply inherent in underdeveloped economies) distinguishing them from the mechanisms of propagation of these disequilibria. Current attempts to control inflation by focusing only on the propagating mechanisms (inspired by the monetarist theory) constitute a classic example of sterile efforts toward modifying the behavior of economic agents without previous alteration in the structural parameters which condition that behavior. As the criteria of rationality implicit in the monetarist policies are established at a macro level, since it is impossible to adequately foresee or control their repercussions at the micro level it may happen that economic agents be required, by these policies, to follow an irrational behavior from the point of view of their legitimate economic objectives. The achievement of the objectives of an economic policy (defined in terms of maximization of social welfare) cannot be obtained by inducing the economic agents to abandon their own criteria of rationality, because these are indispensable in a system of decentralized economic decisions. The compatibility between the rational at the macro and micro levels will only be achieved through modifications in the structural rela-

tions themselves that condition the sense and direction of behavior of the economic agents, particularly of those which make strategic decisions. Concerning the structuralist theory of inflation, consult, as basic works: Juan Noyola Vasquez, "El desarrollo económico y la inflación en México y en otros países latinoamericanos," *Investigación Económica* (México), Cuarto trimestre 1956; and Osvaldo Sunkel, "La inflación Chilena: Un Enfoque Heterodoxo," *El Trimestre Económico* (Mexico), Vol. XXV, No. 4, 1958.

3

ALAIN TOURAINE AND DANIEL PÉCAUT

Working-Class Consciousness and Economic Development in Latin America

The sociology of development has been defined as the study of emerging aspects of industrialization in nonindustrial societies. Its objective is to analyze the origin and specificity of these aspects. But such a definition raises more problems than it solves. It may even result in two paradoxes.

The first paradox arises when a parallel is attempted between the terms "preindustrial" and "industrial." How can we refer to industrial civilization when we are dealing with the level of experience of a "traditional" world? This problem is a vicious circle well known to both sociologists and economists. Sociologists have trouble understanding why a "traditional" world begins to change. In the face of a non-monetary economy, economists cannot conceive how industrialization, which presupposes the existence of a monetary system, can yet serve as a device for bringing about such a system. The "demonstration effect" that is, the example of previously industrialized nations, is expected to break the vicious circle. The problem refers not so much to the existence of change as to the conditions under which planning for change can occur.

This paradox draws our attention to a second one, in which the sociologist and the economist exchange points of view. To

65

break the circle, the sociologist accepts the process of economic development as a fact. Economic development represents not only the movement, but also its significance. Growth is cumulatively defined by the levels of industrialization thus far attained by industrial societies. Once *the unity* of the movement is accepted, one needs only to study the different ways of adapting to it, defining social movements and individual orientation in terms of aspects of the whole process without the need to pinpoint their specific meaning. This is a reductionistic choice.

The economist breaks the circle by invoking the sociological conditions of industrialization, the phenomena being cultural, psychological, and so on. This exchange of positions is not accidental. It expresses both the need for and the difficulty of considering change not merely as a happening, nor as the simple trajectory from a point of departure to one of arrival.

A sociology of development ought to include not merely the study of conditions or consequences, but analysis of the process from which the efforts at social change arise as a function of the tensions and contradictions of the original situation.

Studies of development have usually focused upon elites, since European experience taught that the popular masses had no participation in the political system. It was assumed that the passivity and impotence of masses could be snapped only by elite stimulus. In developing countries the distinction between leaders and those led is not always so sharp. Industrialization is often brought about by nationalist or revolutionary groups. Economic or political leaders are often also the leaders of popular movements. The political system is indirectly open, and the masses have a greater opportunity for participation in a more or less spontaneous way. In this sense they ought to be viewed as actors in development. Economic processes are not as autonomous as they were in the first countries which became industrialized, particularly Great Britain. The influence of the masses upon the form and definition of change in developing countries ought to be emphasized.

The objective of our research is to show that among Latin American workers there may be indirect or direct relationships to development which help define its meaning. In changing societies, even the processes of adaptation involve a certain consciousness and definition of development by their members.

Such an approach based on *consciencia* seems venturesome in the case of Latin America. The working masses of most Latin American countries passively adapt themselves to changes; it would be hard to classify social legislation and the development of political rights as working-class achievements, since they are imposed by the political elites in order to maintain their control over the masses. The large popular movements, such as Peronism and Getulism, were highly ambiguous, and the role of the masses in them was that of objects rather than agents. Yet it is possible to find working-class orientations which prove that workers are not merely subjected to change, but that they contribute to it.

In order to justify this, we shall first consider the problems and conditions for legitimacy involved in other methods of analysis.

The assumptions underlying most analyses of change postulate the "traditional" social system as the point of departure and the "modern" social system as the point of arrival. The transition is defined as the gradual and functional adaptation to the "modern" system at the point of arrival. The resulting normative and psychosociological changes are analyzed within this framework, and as a function of the change in values judged necessary to attain the industrialized state. Change appears through a series of functional requirements referring to "modern" values.

Such an analysis is found in Hoselitz, who speaks of the transition from "ascription" and "particularism" to "achievement" and "universalism." [1] We also find it in Smelser, who points to the dual processes of structural differentiation and integration.[2] Such analyses leave many questions unanswered.

1. They do not explain the origin of change. Within the framework of the terms given, only the type of adaptation can be described. We are faced with the difficulty mentioned earlier: We are forced to accept the fact of economic growth without being able to explain it sociologically.

2. Insofar as the social system aimed at is postulated in advance, the whole transitional period can only be presented in negative terms, as a vacuum. "Anomie" and "lack of adaptation" result from the disintegration of the original system and the lack of adjustment between structural differentiation and reintegration.[2] Far from being defined as specific forms of orientation, they are presented as mere manifestations of the difficulties of development. Smelser considers social movements one among many disturbances reflecting change asynchrony.[3] Heintz studies individual, collective, and institutional forms of anomie and analyzes various policies as "patching policies." [4]

3. Even if we accept the method upon which those analyses are based, it is hard to infer the functional requisites of social change. The concept of "obstacles" to development is ambiguous. Hirschman has shown that theories built on the concept of obstacles can be empirically refuted.[5] Neither ascetic morals nor small families are necessary to bring about industrialization. Abegglen's [6] and Brochier's [7] studies on the Japanese factory show that neither impersonality nor rationalization are indispensable.

4. These analyses run the risk of being solely descriptive. They allow for easier typologies by means of categories constructed in accordance with the "traditional-modern" model, rather than offering explanatory hypotheses.

5. Even that descriptive value can be questioned, especially when one is dealing with societies which are precisely defined in terms of both past and future. Melvin Tumin and Arnold Feldman show, in their study on social stratification in Puerto Rico, the problems involved in a perspective [8] based on a doctrine of the social system. They find various systems of stratification based on a plurality of values. If the Parsonian categories are to be directly applied, it should be possible to define a system of values to which the other values are subordinated, but this condition is not met. We might challenge the authors' interpretation of that "plurality of values" which they view as a leveling factor of change. But while that interpretation is insufficient, the authors show, elsewhere, the impossibility of reducing the process of change to adaptation to a new system of homogeneous values.

An analysis based merely upon the traditional-modern dichotomy can only consider the breakdown of a traditional system and the formation of a modern system. These two parts of the description are disconnected. The question arises as to how people who belong to the old system come to build a modern one using methods which may exhibit characteristics of either system and which are often far from rational, either in themselves or with respect to the goal sought. The creation of a new goal by means of contradictions is replaced with the image of a senseless process. We are presented with the idea of a society heading bumpily toward a new equilibrium. From a Parsonian approach it seems useless to find out how the actors themselves contribute to the orientation of the change.

We must prove the legitimacy of a different kind of research. The conditions under which we are dealing, not only with adaptative behavior, but also with goal-oriented behavior,[9] can be analyzed at three levels: those of the psychological, the structuring of experience in subsystems, and normative orientations.

For a goal to exist, an individual must be able to glance beyond his present horizon, that is, live in the present as a function of a certain idea about the future. We do not find this, for example, in the semi-jobless Algerians studied by P. Bourdieu.[10] Submerged in a situation which they are unable to render meaningful, they define their future in utopian terms bearing no relation to actual possibilities. The idea of a future requires that the individual be capable of perceiving alternatives from his present perspective.

The individual must not only participate in organizations, but must also be conscious and critical of the prevailing decision-making systems. This has two aspects, participation as opposed to withdrawal, and involvement as opposed to passivity. Only when both occur, only when the individual participates in an environment which he simultaneously appraises in the name of his own principles, can there be a structuring of action.

For a goal to exist, the individual must wield those principles not only in defense of his personal interests, but also with reference to social issues. These issues can assume forms more or less complex. They can be expressed through the simple consciousness of change in society, or they can be expressed in a call to a comprehensive principle of action—class conflict, the national constitution, or the like. There must be a link, if only minimal, between the individual's private orientations and those of the society.

These three conditions will not always be found together. The Latin American worker might be directly aware of change in the society and of collective mobility without participating in organizations or questioning them. The worker might even make appeals in the name of that comprehensive change without having any future goal himself. Nonetheless, it is still legitimate to speak of goals, degraded and heteronomous as their form may appear. The individual who is aware of the movement of society but not able to imagine or build his own future is incapable of autonomously interpreting the meaning of that movement.

We have established certain conditions for the legitimacy of a sociology of change. We must still find out whether such conditions are present in Latin America—that is, we must empirically justify our analysis.

Were the urban workers we propose to study only defined as marginal masses always belonging to the "dangerous" revolutionary classes,[11] it would be senseless to undertake a study of their orientations. This would lead only to a study of the pathology of change. But many studies show that workers are often attracted by some goal for the future, that they are capable of defining and organizing critical appraisals within the framework of the subsystems (enterprises, cities, etc.) which they enter, and that they implicitly or explicitly formulate general orientations. For example, even though G. Briones and José Mejía Valera show that a certain number of workers have been "caught" by the city rather than having come to it voluntarily, most studies refer to migration for economic reasons.[12] A survey by J. Matos Mar indicates that many in the Lima settlements came in order to afford their children the opportunity of a good education.[13] These are rational motivations.

It would be insufficient to study those processes of penetration into the urban world merely as phenomena of individual adaptation. The massive character of urban migrations involves a profound transformation of the society itself. The consequences have often been described with reference to São Paulo or Buenos Aires. Apparently the study in terms of adaptation is particularly applicable to the stable urban workers, flooded by the new masses and forced to take into account the presence of a group lacking in trade union tradition. For the latter, problems of individual adaptation relate to the feeling of collective mobility. We may assume that there will be a direct relationship between individual and social change.

At the level of the relationship between individuals and social subsystems, we are not dealing with mere processes of adaptation, that is, of internalization or rejection of the norms, but with processes of goal-structuring. A study of trade-union leaders in Chile shows that their behavior is not a mere reaction to the normative systems of the enterprise, but that it is directly related to the general problems of economic development.[14]

Latin American workers have access to power, which differentiates them from European workers at the start of industrialization. This access may take indirect or symbolic forms, but it is essential for understanding the formation of working-class attitudes in Latin America. European industrialization took place when workers were still excluded from any form of political participation. Latin American workers have been rapidly admitted to various forms of participation. This has allowed for greater possibilities of influence.

This increased political participation as related to industrialization has manifested itself in the popular national movements analyzed by Germani.[15] It has assumed concrete form in the early development of social legislation. This allows increasing influence of the new urban masses and decreasing intervention by the state in economic life. Finally, it has included anticipatory socialization into the cultural and consumption models of industrialized societies.

Yet that anticipatory socialization is not expressed in terms

71

of a rational vision of development. It is the product of a complex relationship between the forces of social change. In Brazil, for example, the size and importance of the urban masses has not led to any corresponding influence by them on the rest of society. Weffort showed that those masses were used as an instrument in the struggle between the divided elites.[16] When considering the early participation of the masses in the political system, we should therefore keep in mind that this participation was the result of a "democratization by authoritarian means" rather than the expression of working-class achievements.[17]

This influence of the new urban masses is also profoundly ambiguous. It is exercised neither in the direction of social integration nor in the form of mere disintegration. It never appears as a direct will for social and economic change. It can often constitute an obstacle to development, especially where participation is highly institutionalized, as is the case in the more advanced countries in the Southern portion of the Continent.

The action of these popular forces comprises, by means of their access to power, the possibility of appealing to societal values. Yet that appeal is necessarily formulated in an indirect way, in terms of the links with the past. We find ambiguity present at the three stages through which expectations become efforts toward social change—in behavior related to mobility, in attitudes toward particular environments, and in general sociopolitical orientations.

The migrant is both a marginal stranger in urban society and the creator of a new facet of urban dwelling. Living in a new yet miserable district, integrated to industry but an unskilled laborer, insecure and ill-informed concerning the labor market, he tries to become integrated into the urban-industrial society while at the same time exercising a certain influence. On the one hand, he is a passive and manipulated citizen, on the other, a decisive element in the formation of new social movements.

The former traditional role has often been described, while the latter remains neglected. The migrant's marginality, his heteronomy, and his desire for integration have received more attention than his initiative, social struggles, and orientations. We wish to show that those analyses are complementary, and that the latter aspects are more significant in the study of development.

The actor does not merely act in response to a situation. He contributes to its definition as a function of his own ends. This not only implies an element of "rejection" with respect to that situation, but also the reexamination of the meanings contained in given notions of development. Without this, orientations would be nothing but empty forms lacking integration into a history and a dialectic of social relations. For this reason our foremost task is to relate the situation to orientations. The basic issue is the national "situation" within the framework of society as a decisions system. In order to have a normative orientation, there must be a link with the global system of decisions. Aside from their particular interests, which would merely imply the maximization of advantages within the existing value system, the actors must be motivated by a specific orientation toward the society as a whole. They must define their particular interests with reference to the general interest, thereby establishing a relationship with the national system of decisions.

The national situation of Latin American countries is characterized by dependence on foreign societies. This is manifest in the limited autonomy of the national decisions systems. Studies by F. H. Cardoso [18] and by C. Furtado [19] have shown the various aspects of this limitation. These countries, while recognizing the legitimacy of and the need for development, are defined by relative underdevelopment. They possess more or less mobilizing types of social control, according to the relationships between the "traditional" and "industrializing" classes, and the popular classes' access to power.

We may start from the hypothesis that in most Latin American countries the systems of action will lead to a complex set of orientations. Dependence will exhibit a corresponding orientation in terms of critical national appraisal. Underdevelopment will be coupled with a demand for development. A given type of social control will correlate with a class orientation. Linkages to class, nation, and development will be found in different "mixes."

Applied to workers, this hypothesis means that an analysis made only in terms of class would be highly insufficient. Such an analysis would limit the field of study by assuming that workers are confronted with an adversary which they define in terms of class, within a society subject to class conflict. This would mean forgetting that the system of political power is far from being unified, that the interests of industrialists and oligarches within it are often opposed, and that in many cases the workers are merely an element within the elites' conflict. A mere class dialectic leads to a closed issue, whereas this situation is flexible. If we think of massive migrations and industrial models of participation, it is clear that we are dealing with a dynamic process in which the simple class dialectic becomes modified. An exclusive class-oriented study would mean that the social actors define each other in homogeneous terms. Nothing justifies this assumption.

Tumin and Feldman's study of social classes in Puerto Rico shows that the actors have recourse to different terms: higher categories refer to economic distinctions, and lower ones follow traditional distinctions.[20] We are unable to agree when they interpret this phenomenon as proof of the acceptance of the new stratification brought about by industrialization. Yet we must recognize the heterogeneity of the references to which the various categories resort. This means that they are not placed within a framework of strictly class relationships.

The essence of our suggested analysis is to study how the relations between the categories—between class, nation, and development—modify their content. The majority of Latin American popular movements show the need for such analysis. An example is R. Patch's study of the Bolivian Revolution, where he shows the fusion, even within a peasant movement, of national, class, and developmental objectives.[21]

There are some working-class sectors which are defined solely in class terms. This was the case, in early twentieth-century São Paulo, for working-class groups of European origin who were faithful to the anarchic trade-union traditions which they had brought from Europe. It is still possible to find such groups among the skilled workers of certain sectors. Yet even in this case, we may doubt the validity of interpreting their orientation strictly in class terms, since their behavior takes place within a complex framework in which neither the adversary nor the recent popular masses are easily categorized in those terms.

It is necessary to indicate how the patterns into which orientations are grouped can be analyzed. Let us relate these orientations to the independent variables which have characterized national situations: phases of development, types of social control, and degrees of dependence.

Elsewhere we have shown how orientations become articulated as a function of the different phases of development.[22] In the first phase, preindustrial society is still hardly disturbed. In the last, the society is almost industrialized, yet still linked to the past by certain economic or institutional aspects. The intermediate phase represents the trajectory between those two points in time. These phases are not only related to stages of economic growth, but also imply the progressive constitution of a system of action in which the social control of economic growth is at stake.

Starting from the notion that the themes of nation, class, and progress are always found in popular social movements, we have suggested a simple hypothesis by which these three principles are diversely combined according to the phase of development being considered. Any given group defines its field of action in terms of the way it defines itself, its adversary, and what is at stake. We have suggested that, in its first phase, the popular movement is based upon a class—especially a peasant—struggle. It opposes foreign domination and is oriented toward the initiation of development. In the second phase, marked by a massive mobilization of the population, the action is in the name of the newcomers, of the emerging masses. It opposes a class system conceived primarily as a system of obstacles, privileges, and ascriptions, and tends toward the integration of the nation. In the third phase, the movement is formed in the name of the nation, that is, of the people conceived as the mass of active citizens. It opposes the irrationality and inertia of institutions and private interests, and it subscribes to a class ideology. No movement of social importance can be organized without combining these three orientations in some way.

These hypotheses hold only if all other factors remain constant. If we take into account the types of social control, it will be useful to make a few distinctions in terms of their mobilizing qualities. They are mobilizing when the industrializing elites supersede the traditional elites, and the masses have an access to power. This distinction allows us to contrast countries such as Mexico and Chile, where the power elites directly assumed the mobilizing role, with countries such as Colombia, Argentina, and Brazil, where they did not. It might seem that, where a mobilizing social control exists, orientations will be more strongly articulated. Let us consider the example of the Bolivian Revolution, and of the first years in power of the M.N.R. (National Revolutionary Movement). During this period there was an attempt to transform society as a whole. This national orientation was based upon class action and upon a developmental goal manifested among the peasants and even among the miners.

The degree of independence may be considered, at least provisionally, the same in almost all Latin American countries.

We will now describe in greater detail the way in which the structure of the various orientations, and the relationships according to which the latter combine, may be analyzed. We must interpret these first hypotheses according to a second set of hypotheses. We shall start with the traditional working-class groups of São Paulo.

If these working-class groups are defined mainly in class terms, with no reference to either national or developmental issues, they cannot be considered as an expression of a high level of mobilization. In order to have a high level of mobilization, the individuals must take into account all the significant elements in a situation, not so much in terms of a social issue as in defense of a particular category. The workers of São Paulo have a conception of a class society that oscillates between the defense of their interests as skilled workers—to the detriment of any solidarity with newcomers—and solidarity with the unskilled masses. Reference is no longer to class alone. It includes the other poles: nation and development. Even when these workers are really expressing themselves in homogeneous class terms, we assume an underlying categorical defense.

When we speak of orientations in terms of class, nation, or

development, we are really referring to a double movement. Orientation in terms of class no longer means the mere definition of a class-relations issue at the societal level; it also results in the defense of the particular interests of a given class. There is a movement of defense and simultaneously a movement to redefine the society as a whole. That is the meaning of class action among European workers during the nineteenth century. The same dualism is found in the case of national consciousness or of developmental consciousness. In the former case, the struggle for a system of autonomus decision, the rationality of which is willed by the actor, coexists with a struggle for integration, that is, the defense of a particular category. In the case of developmental consciousness, reference to development may assume the form of a societal principle, but it can also simply appear as a reference to consumption and the higher standard of living of a given category. There is always a connection between the struggle at a categorical and at a global level.

Aside from the defense of a category, which assumes a complex group consciousness, a vague consciousness of identity with other individuals may be formulated, implying a feeling of identity of interests. Thus an orientation in terms of class may not go beyond the simple consciousness of being part of a mass. An orientation in terms of development may not go beyond a poorly structured perception of change. An orientation in terms of the nation may not go beyond a feeling of national identity. Orientations may originate at this level without crystallizing into a consciousness of personal interest, much less into an awareness of global problems. This still implies a certain consciousness of society as a whole, even though only invoking a situation which is explained by it. Tumin and Feldman call this "consciousness of stratification in terms of plentiful qualities." [23] It is found in individuals who do not possess a clear knowledge of an economic hierarchy and of contradicting interests, and who, in the way they classify the various elements of the society, refer to moral qualities which are plentiful by definition. Tumin and Feldman seem to consider this level of consciousness as functionally equivalent to that in which the feeling of a socioeconomic hierarchy receives priority, but we believe that it represents only the first degree of a certain consciousness of society.

Every orientation can present three degrees of elaboration (see Table I). If the defense of a category and a global defense are compatible, they supersede and exclude the third form, which we call "situational" defense.

TABLE I

	Situational Struggle	Categorical Struggle	Global Struggle
Class	Consciousness of a mass	Defense of working-class interests	Reference to conflicts
Development	Consciousness of change	Desire for consumption	Reference to growth
Nation	Consciousness of a people	Desire for integration	Reference to the rationality of political power

It is not enough to speak of class consciousness or of national consciousness in general terms. In the case of national consciousness, for example, it is important to distinguish struggle for integration from struggle for autonomous political power. Rather than assume that every orientation is continuous in character, we should distinguish different forms.

There may be simple cases, in which the orientation appears simultaneously as a categorical defense and as a global goal, or even only as a categorical defense. The former case expresses a high level of mobilization; the latter indicates a certain reference to development, but without its being more than a means to attain advantages. Yet there can also be more complex situations, in which orientations exhibit unevenly structured forms.

Table I permits the formulation of hypotheses concerning the meaning of those differences. Particularly, it makes possible the distinction between orientations representing a principle of action and those which are mere ideology. If within one of those configurations only one orientation adopts a global form, it can be assumed that it expresses an ideological mobilization, the meaning and scope of which depends on the actual behavior of the actors within their working or urban environment. Hypotheses about the meaning of normative orientations must refer to attitudes and behavior within the subsystems—city and enterprise—as well as to the goals for mobility which define the individual's possibilities of being included in those subsystems and of acting through them.

When entrance into the urban world occurs within a framework of collective mobility, it is insufficient to consider the processes of individual adaptation alone. The individual is quite able to adapt rapidly to the norms of urban life, as well as to the norms of industrial labor. Even those who seem ill-adapted, such as the inhabitants of the Santiago settlements, do not seem willing to move or return to their original environments.[24] It is a risk to interpret the phenomenon of lack of adaptation without referring to the actors' orientations. Workers who do not adapt to the rules of modern work may be those who were too well adapted to their pre-industrial society. If they have difficulty accepting the norms of business enterprise, it is because they accept too easily the system of stratification of proto-industrial societies, in which factory work is devaluated.[25] This is a clear indication of the need to restate problems of adaptation within the study of individual goals of mobility and of orientations of action.

Elsewhere we have shown the significance of such a study, making a distinction between different types of goals of mobility and starting from the idea that the goal for the future is what allows a smooth adaptation.[26] Here we shall adopt the simplest classification. At the most elementary level, we find workers *in a situation of displacement*—that is, they have not made a decision to leave, but have "followed the movement." Then, workers who have made a *decision to leave*. And finally, those who have come to the city as a result of a *goal of mobility*, that is, they place a high value on this movement and are conscious of its part within a society also undergoing change.

This classification is less clear than might first appear. Our objective is not to understand the reasons for adaptation, but the determinants for action and the capacity to participate in the elaboration of new social norms and values. While it is true that those who have the least ambitions of mobility are likely to be the most marginal in the city and in industry, they can, by virtue of

79

their mere presence, be more instrumental than others in sub-
verting the social order. This is because those having high ambitions of mobility are more easily integrated, and for that very
reason less disrupting.

We must circumscribe the definition of goals of mobility in
a manner more in keeping with our purposes. It is necessary to
take into account both the individual's personal status and the
collective situation of which he is a part. Many European working-class militants of the nineteenth century were semi-independ-
ent workers with a rather high professional status, placed at the
heart of a crisis of economic transition. The case of the Lyon silk
weavers is one of the most famous. They were professionally
independent workers, confronted with commercial capitalism
and menaced by the development of the manufacturing industry.

Given a situation of crisis, the higher an individual's personal position, the greater his propensity to act. We can thus
define goals of mobility which are linked not only to modes of
adaptation, but to possibilities of action as well. We must consider both the individual's status in his community of origin and
the status of the community itself. Two cases may be distinguished. Either we have a community in a situation of crisis, that
is, menaced by the eruption of new methods of work or new types
of social relations, or we have an underprivileged community,
whose members tend to abandon it in an almost "natural" movement which leads them to the poles of development. By correlat-
ing personal situation and collective situation, we can arrive at
the following hypotheses, in which mobility is no longer a mode
of adaptation to a new environment but a mode of action toward
it (see Table II).

TABLE II

	Underprivileged collective situation	Collective situation of crisis
High personal situation	Adaptation	Protest
Low personal situation	Marginality	Rejection

The goal of mobility is not only the expression of individual
psychological traits, but the result of a relationship between two

situations. Thus structured, it is more than a simple vision of a more or less uncertain future. The goal of mobility introduces possibilities of participation in the new environment and new sociopolitical orientations.

It is true that the gap between goals of mobility and concrete sociopolitical orientations is not bridged so directly. There intervenes between those two variables the action of the particular social environments in which the migrant is involved: the industrial enterprise and the city. Nonetheless, we must also consider the relationship between type of mobility and nature of the political system. If the latter is not mobilizing, the degree of structuring of the migrant's social expectations may be lower than if the opposite were the case. Yet it might be asked whether the combination of a new goal of mobility and a mobilizing political system would not run the risk of establishing an immediate—and therefore utopian—link between personal expectations and national policy. The newcomer would be directly sensitive to the solicitations of those in power—such as the popular masses during the Perón period—but he would also be highly dependent with respect to that power. The nature of mobility leads to a dialectic of autonomous or heteronomous action, which becomes clearer if we consider behavior in the industrial enterprise or the city.

The incorporation into work and urban life transforms personal orientations into collective action. Orientations seem to lead to a renewal of the significant elements of the national situation. But that renewal depends on the way in which the process of structuring is carried on through the partial subsystems.

Here the analysis must define which elements of those subsystems are going to contribute the most to that process of structuring. It must particularly determine which—urban or working experience—is going to exercise the greatest influence. Many authors have insisted that urban experience exercises a far greater influence in the crystallization of attitudes than labor experience does.[27] This phenomenon would account for the inde-

81

pendence of urbanization with respect to industrialization. Urbanization has occurred far more rapidly than industrialization. The index of growth of secondary-branch jobs represents only a small part of the total index of growth of the active population, especially if we take into account only those individuals working in enterprises with a staff of ten or more. This means that the industrial worker represents only a small minority of the population within which the immigrants have preferentially moved toward dependent, tertiary-branch jobs.

Urban metropolises constitute privileged areas, in which the rent average is far higher than that of rural areas.[28] This dualism between urban affluence and rural poverty means that in certain cases the worker will define himself in terms of belonging to a privileged area rather than in terms of his underprivileged class position. Urban experience introduces a sudden break. Past experience as an agricultural laborer is completely severed from the new experience as an urban worker. But the difference lies in the urban-rural opposition rather than in that of the two types of activities.

Urban privilege manifests itself in the eyes of the new worker in terms of culture, consumption, and a certain kind of "participation," to the point that an economic difference between rural and urban ways of life—whatever its importance —becomes a "cultural" difference to the newcomer. If this hypothesis is true, there will be important consequences in terms of attitudes. The city brings about a rather unstructured form of participation. The "urban culture," very advanced with respect to industrialization, risks encouraging the actual dependence of those new workers. Political "participation," insofar as the workers are not conscious of their common interests defined in terms of their work situation, might lead to forms of manipulation by the political leaders. Urban models of consumption may further emphasize dependence, limiting social struggles to ill-articulated protests aimed at defending or improving the standard of living. By making the urban experience a privilege, the worker runs the risk of manifesting merely "negative" forms of action, disposed toward protest rather than toward struggle in the name of structured interests.

This brings us to three important hypotheses. Urban experience may prevail over work experience, so that what might seem lack of adaptation to the work situation is really a strong reference to the urban experience. The latter will determine a break in the individual's attitudes, makig it difficult for him to remain conscious of his past. Finally, urban experience will manifest itself in terms of certain forms of dependence.

We will circumscribe this problem by defining the main dependent variables and their relationship to the actors' orientations. In order to have a structuring of action and subsequently a strong orientation toward class consciousness, national consciousness, and developmental consciousness, the individual must effectively participate in organizations. He must not only take a stand in terms of that participation, he must question the values of those organizations. Were this not the case, he would merely be reacting against modes of functioning, not exercising real action.

This relationship between reaction and action can be formulated in another way. The new worker arrives in the city, where he finds district organizations, political organizations, and a state bureaucracy. He becomes incorporated into an enterprise, in which he encounters hierarchies, rules, and so on. Three types of behavior may result. In the first place, the individual may simply withdraw. He establishes a balance of satisfaction or dissatisfaction without really participating, that is, without relating to the norms of industrial work or of the city. Such would be the case for certain workers in Lota, who dream of becoming established on their own.[29] At an intermediate level, there is participation with acceptance of work norms. We shall call this adaptation, but without forgetting that this adaptation may be accompanied by dissatisfaction at another level. For example, workers of agriculural origin studied in France manifested both conformism and dissatisfaction. Finally, at a third level, there is questioning—reference to work norms and urban norms, together with a discussion of those norms. This type of behavior will be found among workers who, for example, participate in urban norms yet criticize the functioning of the bureaucracy. If adaptation and dissatisfaction with respect to the subsystem conceived as an organization are combined, they may lead to the formulation of protest.

In order to move from protest to action, it is necessary to refer to a more general perspective, to principles of action autonomously defined by the workers. If the conditions for the structuring of action are to be established, the possibility of autonomous formulation must exist.

We do not find this among the São Paulo workers when they question their present condition. They conceive of the trade union merely as a useful instrument to provide them with medical care and the like, not as an instrument for collective action in terms of its own values. Even when they effectively discuss entrepreneurial norms, they are highly heteronomous, depending on the employer's benevolence or state protection rather than union action.

This dialectic of questioning and autonomy is essential to the understanding of working-class attitudes in Latin America. In a large number of surveys, worker questioning and heteronomy were found to coexist in relationships with the state. The survey by Silva-Michelena and Frank Bonilla in Venezuela shows that individuals may simultaneously criticize the mode of functioning of the state, question the political parties or the bureaucracy, and still expect improvement of their condition to come from within.[30]

The study by Landsberger, Barrera, and Toro in Chile shows how Chilean union leaders may question the employers' management and denounce their lack of interest in the workers, yet expect from those same employers—much more so than from trade-union action—an improvement in the workers' condition. This points up the ambiguity of an analysis solely concerned with questioning attitudes. This notion in itself may lead just as much to an elementary mode of action as to a highly complex mode of action. When speaking of the gradual "radicalization" of Brazilian union leaders,[31] it must be kept in mind that the ambiguity remains. We therefore propose to study simultaneously the level of questioning and the degree of autonomy exhibited. The correlation of these two dimensions allows us to define four types of unequally structured attitudes (see Table III).

Table III

		+ Questioning −	
	+	Critical action	Pressure
Autonomy			
	−	Rejection	Withdrawal

These attitudes are closely related to normative orientations. The greater the number of critical attitudes observed, the greater the possibility of finding complex orientations. The combination of autonomy and questioning allows understanding of how the individual, far from becoming integrated or participating in multiple environments, refers to global principles in the name of which he questions those environments. Here we find in terms of formal conditions of action that which at the level of orientations is preferably expressed in terms of content. As in the case of goals of mobility, those formal conditions cannot be separated either from the individual's personal situation or from the nature of his environments.

Autonomy is linked to the individual's situation in the city or in the enterprise. A study on working-class attitudes in France, together with other studies in various countries, has shown that skilled workers are usually capable of organizing autonomously within the enterprise. Unskilled workers commonly react in terms of elementary reasoning; they correlate the professional responsibilities of their work, the salary received, and the possibilities of receiving that salary in another job.[32] Generally, skilled workers do not define themselves only in terms of belonging to an enterprise, but according to a more complex system of references. Thus they can formulate their criticisms not only from within the enterprise but in contradistinction to its goals.

The level of questioning depends on the relationships between the worker and the decisions system of the enterprise, or between the citizen and the municipal policy. Questioning and autonomy cannot therefore be made synonymous. The skilled worker may be less prone to question the decisions system of the enterprise than the unskilled worker insofar as his status may determine a greater identification with his work and a stronger acceptance of its norms. Yet the skilled worker may also feel strongly incited toward argument, insofar as he is more directly menaced by a system of organization which constantly tends to limit his autonomy. The former may also be more sensitive to the distinction between manual and nonmanual workers.

The same argument is valid for the questioning that may arise in the city. The citizen with high socioeconomic status is more likely to be autonomous and may adopt questioning behavior like that of the citizen belonging to a "marginal population." The latter may inhabit a new district, but he may feel menaced by a rise in the rent, suddenly straining his budget, or by the interruption of an urbanization project. He may be led to question these changes, owing to his marginal condition, but being less autonomous, he may also react by withdrawal.

The notions presented here are of the same nature as those used to define types of mobility. In both cases, the point is to correlate the factors of integration into the social system with those of questioning of that social system (in the name of personal expectations resorting to global principles against particular environments).

We must still define with greater precision the influence of the city and of the enterprise upon the formation of autonomous action. The influence of the city has been presented in different and seemingly contradictory ways. A study by M. Lowy and S. Chucid alludes to a certain radicalization of the trade-union leaders of Brazilian metallurgy.[33] F. Bourricaud, on the other hand, shows how the city tends to create profoundly heteronomous and manipulable masses.[34] Yet if we accept the interdependence of the dimensions of questioning and autonomy, these descriptions need not be contradictory. Let us specify the possible hypotheses.

1. The city is the point of convergence of two subcultures. The "traditional" subculture is characterized by adherence to primary relationships within the neighborhood, especially when the latter is constituted by individuals from the same place of origin. Its features include certain attitudes toward the family, women, and so on, which are usually described as "traditional," even though this term seems highly inadequate to designate a changing environment. The "urban" subculture is defined by relative partici-

pation and consumption. It is characterized by mass media, a direct relationship with political leaders, and so on.

Heteronomy is stronger when there is both a maintenance of "traditional" culture and awareness of the "urban" culture. Autonomy at the level of urban action correlates with the abandonment of "traditional" references. An example of heteronomy is offered by the voting pattern of dwellers in the Lima settlements, who remained attached to certain forms of "traditional" culture even while orienting themselves toward the urban culture. In 1962, the people of the settlements voted for General Manuel Odría, even though they had demonstrated an ideological affinity for Haya de la Torre.[35] Odría did not have the support of a structured party such as APRA; but through personal contacts and the clienteles which he had established, he was able to attract the votes of these urban masses.

2. The city introduces a new relationship with political power. On the one hand, the masses enter a relationship with political leaders; on the other, they encounter power in the form of the State and its various administrations. While this encounter with bureaucracy may frequently arouse a strong argumentative spirit among the new citizens, the direct or indirect contacts with local and national political leaders emphasize their heteronomy.

This heteronomy may be manifested in a differential vote according to whether the elections are presidential or local. This was the case in São Paulo.[36] In the presidential elections, the individuals were influenced by mass media and the candidate's charismatic power. They voted en masse for the "populist" candidate (Jânio Quadros). But in the local elections, they were more sensitive to the direct propaganda of the candidates and their representatives, and voted differently.

3. The city modifies individual hopes due to the prestige of urban symbols: consumption, education, and so on. Yet even here there is a possibility of heteronomy if the individual does not really internalize the new norms or relate them to the objective possibilities offered him. He may have hopes for his children's education that are entirely unrelated to his means. Like the semijobless Algerians studied by P. Bourdieu, he wants his sons to become doctors or lawyers. Clearly, there is a new link

87

here between urban norms and political heteronomy. This link represents the transition from disproportionate expectations and means to a relationship of dependence.

4. The more central the capital, the greater the likelihood of heteronomy. The research on Chilean union leaders shows that those from Santiago are most distrustful of political parties. This rejection of political action generally, and not only of certain political parties, is the expression of a strong heteronomy.[37]

5. Urban experience may contribute in defining working-class orientations. Yet by itself it is not likely to elicit more than simple forms. Isolation in the city may doubtless develop a certain consciousness of social barriers; but the result is more likely to be hierarchical order than class conflict. Access to the world of consumption may stimulate an impulse to development; but above all it elicits a vague consciousness of change. Similarly, mass media may promote a consciousness of national participation, but in a confused form. Urban experience is essential, yet by itself it encourages heteronomous styles of action. This experience should be more important for individuals with marginal jobs than for those who have attained a certain autonomy through the work experience.

Under certain conditions, the city may exercise a very different influence, favoring the development of autonomous movements. It may even manifest the crisis of the political system. For example, when the standard of living of the urban masses is corroded by inflation, what used to be a source of heteronomy may generate autonomy. The more the urban masses are oriented toward consumption, the more they will defend their power of acquisition and denounce the crisis of the State. What was no more than questioning may become organized action. This situation is more likely to occur when the laboring masses have already achieved a certain autonomy through work. This presupposes a relatively high level of overall development, as well as actual work experience leading to a certain autonomy.

We must therefore go back to the work experience and to the conditions under which it may serve as the point of departure for reforming action. We have already indicated the influence of training. The type of enterprise and its relationship with the political system must also be considered. Only in this way will it be possible to analyze under what conditions the individual's personal situation may serve as the basis for critical debate within the enterprise, and under what conditions this questioning will lead to autonomous political action.

The enterprise as an organization can influence action. Action could hardly arise within an archaic enterprise, where relationships between management and workers are still paternalistic. In such a situation, we would expect to find attitudes of withdrawal or adaptation, but very limited questioning. Consider the workers in a traditional enterprise studied by Juarez Brandão Lopes. They are so far from being capable of concerted reform that they passively adhere to the strikes organized by the union. They are neither aware of the strike's objectives nor would they dare break the picket lines.[38] Within a rationalized enterprise, strongly questioning attitudes are more readily found.

The economic status of the enterprise, in terms of which salaries will vary, is even more important to take into account. Nonetheless, it is impossible to assume a direct relationship between the status of the enterprise and styles of behavior. Working in a privileged enterprise increases the possibility of autonomous behavior insofar as the individual has a greater negotiating power and can have higher hopes for success. Yet he is also more tempted to accept the normative system of the enterprise. The behavior of the workers in such enterprises may shift within a framework of profound ambiguity. While they are capable of autonomy, they are at the same time the best adapted. They are capable of rational debate, which they can use not only as a form of defense of their own interests, but also as an instrument of political action. They fluctuate between economic rationality and the desire to guarantee, by negotiation, the privileges to which they are entitled. The opposite is true in the case of an underprivileged enterprise. There is frequently stronger questioning, but less autonomy.

Autonomy depends mainly on the relationship between the enterprise and the state. It is at this level that the possibilities of critical action are most relevantly judged. At least four cases may be distinguished. According to F. H. Cardoso's analysis, the enterprise is frequently itself heteronomous, with the employers seeking not so much innovation as protection from the state.[39]

In this case, questioning is likely to reach the political level, but it is weakly articulated within the enterprise, and its politicalization may be more ideological than active. Second, there are large enterprises which are economically dynamic, but which may function as isolated territories within the economic life of the nation. Working-class struggles in these will be confined within the bounds of the enterprise. A third case is an enterprise which is both weak and independent of the state. It may be traditionalistic or paternalistic; either would be unfavorable for the development of working-class action. The last case covers those dynamic enterprises which are strongly linked to the state, either because they are public or because their production has symbolic or economic value for the nation as a whole. This situation induces the state to a policy of active intervention. Oil or steel enterprises frequently fit this pattern. Here the gap between questioning and political action is readily bridged.

To conclude this analysis, we should consider the nature of the political system itself. Within an archaic political system, the worker in a privileged enterprise tends to negotiate directly with the employer rather than to struggle at the political level. We find an illustration of this, at the level of union politics, in UTECE's program in Colombia. It aims at constituting an overall economic policy by means of negotiation with the union and without the intervention of the state. In a mobilizing political system, working-class action is more likely to manifest itself at the political level. It may assume a merely ideological form, as in Mexico, where the government controls or inspires most collective conventions.[40]

We have followed the same path to analyze urban experience and labor experience. While it is true that questioning must be combined with autonomy in order to open the way for working-class action, this movement always implies a dialectic of three terms: personal status, type of subsystem, and relationship with the political system.

We thus return to the point that a goal of mobility can, in different environments, give birth not only to a process of integration, but also to different forms of action. We can sum up our analysis by distinguishing four possible types of behavior. At the lowest level, we find *withdrawal,* characterized by a rejection of the industrial world and by the desire to become independently established. Then there is *utilitarian* behavior, in which the individual aims at maximizing his own profit. Utilitarianism may coexist with questioning behavior, but it is mainly expressed through heteronomy. Unions appear as simple means for individual protection. Then we find *collective* behavior, in which the individual identifies with a professional or urban group. Autonomy is at least possible. Finally, we have *political* behavior, in which the labor and environmental situations are immediately experienced as the manifestation of a political situation. The union stops being only an instrument for the protection of the working class and becomes the means for political action.

Such behavior sums up the complex relationships established between goals of mobility and the environments encountered. We shall consider only two very different cases. In one, immigrants arrive in the city and industry with a high goal of mobility and obtain high-ranking or stable jobs in dynamic enterprises. They are likely to adopt political behavior insofar as their situation encourages autonomy. Yet they remain at the level of collective behavior—that is, according to Y. Delamotte's expression, within a kind of "conflicting participation." They do not even question the principles of the political and economic organization. In contrast, consider immigrants arriving in the city with a low goal of mobility, and having low-ranking or unstable jobs in traditional enterprises. These may adopt withdrawal behavior, but they may also attain the level of political behavior if they achieve mobility through a strong access to power by the masses, and a wide participation in urban politics.

There is no simple relationship between goals of mobility and forms of action. Just as at the level of the formation of working-class movements the problem is that of the relationships between the working-class aristocracy and the urban populace, at the level of the formation of behavior the problem resides in the link between more or less autonomous forms of politicalization and more or less dependent forms of mobilization.

This study would be incomplete if it did not comment on the actual content of orientations toward action. Our purpose is to examine how orientations may become combined in terms of class, development, and nationalism. This level of analysis allows us to approximate real social movements, those beyond simple individual attitudes. It also allows us to measure the influence of different types of leaders, observe the maintenance of authoritarian or "traditionalistic" attitudes within movements of social reform, and obtain confirmation of the degree of autonomy or heteronomy exhibited.

Our aim is to show the usefulness of a perspective that has too seldom been explored. This is not to minimize the importance of studies on the evolution of values and norms, on the transition from traditionalism to modernism, or on the social integration of urban immigrants. We simply wish to emphasize the importance of the movement by virtue of which Latin America is being transformed—the process by which the new social forces set in motion by economic revolution enter the stage and become the actors of their own history.

It is not enough to define the conditions and the consequences of development. It is necessary to grasp them directly, in terms of action.

NOTES

[1] B. F. Hoselitz, *Sociological Aspects of Economic Growth*, Glencoe, Ill., The Free Press, 1960.

[2] N. J. Smelser, "Mechanisms of Change and Adjustment to Change," in *Industrialization and Society*, eds. B. Hoselitz and W. Moore, The Hague, Mouton, 1963.

[3] N. J. Smelser, op. cit.

[4] P. Heintz, "El Problema de la Indecisión Social en el Desarrollo Económico," *Anales de la Facultad Latinoamericana de Ciencias Sociales*, 1 (1964), 95–116.

[5] A. O. Hirschman, "Obstacles to Development: A Classification and a Quasi-Vanishing Act," *Economic Development and Cultural Change*, 13 (1965), 385–93.

[6] J. C. Abegglen, *The Japanese Factory; Aspects of Its Social Organization*, Glencoe, Ill., The Free Press, 1958.

[7] H. Brochier, *Le Miracle Économique Japonais*, Paris, Calmann-Levy, 1965.

[8] M. M. Tumin and A. Feldman, *Social Class and Social Change in Puerto Rico*, Princeton, Princeton University Press, 1961.

[9] Alain Touraine, *Sociologie de l'Action*, Paris, Éditions du Seuil, 1965.

[10] J. Bourdieu, *Travail et Travailleurs en Algérie*, Paris and The Hague, Mouton, 1963, Vol. II.

[11] L. Chevalier, *Classes Laborieuses et Classes Dangereuses à Paris Pendant la Première Moitié du XIXe Siècle*, Paris, Plon, 1958.

[12] G. Briones and J. Mejía-Valera, *El Obrero Industrial; Aspectos Sociales del Desarrollo Económico en el Perú*, Lima, Instituto de Investigaciones Sociológicas, Universidad Nacional Mayor de San Marcos de Lima, 1964.

[13] J. Matos Mar, "Les 'Barriadas' de Lima: Un Exemple d'Intégration à la Vie Urbaine," *l'Urbanisation en Amérique Latine*, Paris, UNESCO, 1962.

[14] H. A. Landsberger, M. Barrera, and A. Toro, "The Chilean Labor Union Leader: A Preliminary Report on His Background and Attitudes," *Industrial and Labor Review* 17 (3), 399–420.

[15] Gino Germani, *Política y Sociedad en una Época de Transición (De la Sociedad Tradicional a la Sociedad de Masas)*, Buenos Aires, Paidós, 1965.

[16] Francisco C. Weffort, "State and Mass in Brazil," *Studies in Comparative International Development*, II, 12 (1966).

[17] Alain Touraine, "Industrialisation et Conscience Ouvrière a São Paulo," *Sociologie du Travail*, III, 4 (1961), 77–95.

[18] Fernando Henrique Cardoso, *Empresário Industrial e Desenvolvimento Econômico*, São Paulo, Difusão Européia do Livro, 1964.

[19] Celso Furtado, *The Economic Growth of Brazil: A Survey from Colonial to Modern Time*, Berkeley and Los Angeles, University of California Press, 1963.

[20] M. M. Tumin and A. Feldman, op. cit.

[21] R. W. Patch, "Peasantry and National Revolution: Bolivia," in *Expectant Peoples: Nationalism and Development*, ed. Kalman Silvert, New York, Random House, 1963.

[22] Alain Touraine, "Social Mobility, Class Relations, and Nationalism in Latin America," *Studies in Comparative International Development*, I, 3 (1965).

[23] M. M. Tumin and A. Feldman, op. cit.

[24] CEPAL, *Proyecto de Investigación Conjunta sobre Política Social y Poblaciones de Erradicación; El Caso de la Población José Maria Caro*, 1964 (mimeograph).

[25] W. E. Moore and A. S. Feldman, *Labor Commitment and Social Change in Developing Areas*, New York, Social Science Research Council, 1960.

[26] A. Touraine and O. Ragazzi, *Ouvriers d'Origine Agricole*, Paris, Éditions du Seuil, 1961.

[27] F. Bonilla, "The Urban Worker," in *Continuity and Change in Latin America*, ed. John J. Johnson, Stanford, Stanford University Press, 1964.

[28] J. Lambert, *Le Brésil*, Paris, Fondation Nationale des Sciences Politiques, A. Collin, 1953.

[29] T. Di Tella, L. Brams, J. D. Reynaud, and A. Touraine, *Huachipato el Lota*, Paris, Editions du C.N.R.S. (in press).

[30] J. A. Silva-Michelena, F. Bonilla, and J. Cotler, "La Investigación Sociológica y la Formulación de Políticas," *América Latina*, VIII, 2 (1965), 3–47.

[31] G. A. Dillon Soares, "Desenvolvimento Econômico e Radicalismo Político," *América Latina*, V (1962), 65–83.

[32] Alain Touraine, *La Conscience Ouvrière*, Paris, Éditions du Seuil, 1966.

[33] M. Lowy and S. Chucid, *Opiniões e Atitudes de Líderes Sindicais Metalúrgicos*, São Paulo, 1960 (unpublished).

[34] François Bourricaud, "La Place de Lima dans la Vie Politique Péruvienne," *Le Problème des Capitales en Amérique Latine*, Paris, Éditions du C.N.R.S., 1965.

[35] François Bourricaud, op. cit.

[36] A. Simão, "O Voto Operário em São Paulo," *Anais do Primeiro Congresso Brasileiro de Sociologia*, 1954, 201–14.

[37] H. A. Landsberger, M. Barrera, and A. Toro, op. cit.

[38] Juarez Brandao Lopes, "O Ajustamento do Trabalhador a Industria: Mobilidade Social e Motivação," *Mobilidade e Trabalho*, São Paulo, 1960.

[39] Fernando Henrique Cardoso, op. cit.

[40] F. Meyers, *Parti, Gouvernement et Mouvements Ouvriers au Mexique, Deux Études de Cas*, Geneva, Conférence de Recherches sur les Relations Professionnelles et le Développement Économique, International Institute for Labor Studies, 1964 (mimeograph).

4

SOLON L. BARRACLOUGH

Agricultural Policy
and Strategies of Land Reform

Agricultural production in Latin America as a whole has actually fallen by about 10 per cent per capita from estimated pre-World War II levels; it has just barely kept pace with population growth during the last two decades. Individual country data show Mexico to be the only notable exception to this general picture of relative stagnation. Malnutrition is widespread among large sectors of the Latin American population, both rural and urban. On the average the availability of calories and proteins is from one-sixth to one-third less in these countries than in those of Europe or North America. While the physical volume of Latin American agricultural exports is estimated to have increased by about 16 per cent since the pre-World War II period, the volume of agricultural imports, mostly foodstuffs, has gone up by over 80 per cent. This has had serious repercussions on the balance of payments of most Latin American countries.[1]

Admittedly these FAO estimates are subject to wide margins of error, but the general trends are unmistakable. One would have to be blind indeed to deny the existence of a Latin American agricultural problem.

Meanwhile, agrarian reform has become one of the principal public issues in Latin America since the war. Few topics arouse more passionate debate among politicians, laymen, or economists. This is especially true since the Cuban revolution and the continent's subsequent involvement in the Cold War.

95

Not surprisingly, there has been a tendency in Latin America to treat the agricultural production problem and the agrarian reform problem as being one and the same thing. A recent public-opinion poll in Chile found that 80 per cent of the population of greater Santiago believed agrarian reform to be necessary for the country; three-fourths of those favoring reform gave as their reasons the unsatisfactory levels of food production and the widespread prevalence of extensively used good lands.[2]

But International Bank missions, foreign "experts," and economic planners usually play down the urgency of agrarian reform. They put their emphasis on the necessity for greater agricultural investments, improved agricultural prices, accelerated rural-urban migration, and cheaper farm inputs in order to raise agricultural productivity and stem agrarian unrest. Some economists recognize an agrarian problem apart from the productivity problem. At best they regard it as a political matter outside their competence and responsibilities; more commonly they view it as an extraneous nuisance that may upset their projections and recommendations. Others, few in numbers but with no more analytical acumen than some of their contrary-minded colleagues, identify the agrarian problem as completely with the problem of modernizing agriculture as does Chilean public opinion. They seem to imply that reform by itself will automatically increase productivity.

Unfortunately, agricultural policy recommendations based only upon the conceptual paradigms and boundaries of the accepted academic disciplines are not likely to fit realities in Latin America, or elsewhere. This paper argues that it is useful to distinguish sharply between the "agrarian problem" and the "agricultural development problem" in analysis; but an understanding of the relationships between the two is of crucial importance in planning policy. To make recommendations based upon an analysis of either problem alone is an exercise in frustration and futility.

The data and ideas discussed below were largely drawn from recent studies of land tenure and agricultural development in seven Latin American countries. These studies have been carried out under the auspices of the Interamerican Committee of Agricultural Development.[3] To a lesser extent they are taken from research now under way in Chile by the Agrarian Reform Training and Research Institute (ICIRA).

To avoid falling into the more obvious errors of overgeneralization about Latin America as a whole, the discussion will be limited for the most part to the seven countries studied by ICAD. The experiences from these countries will be treated as case studies illustrative of various aspects of the Latin American situation.

AGRICULTURAL POLICY IN LATIN AMERICA

If anyone is naïve enough to think that most Latin American countries have national agricultural-development strategies made up of consistent policies and programs supporting national goals, he should immediately abandon this myth. The truth is that there are a multitude of policies affecting agriculture, often highly contradictory. Many were inherited directly from the Spanish and Portuguese mercantile systems.

Agricultural policy, like any other public policy, is an output of the political system. It is the product of political inputs.[4] To understand policy one must know something about the political structure and political processes.

An exhaustive analysis of agricultural policy in Latin America is beyond the scope of this paper. It was not attempted in any of the ICAD studies. Our purpose in briefly mentioning policies is to show how they are related to land-tenure institutions and the agrarian structure. Policy constitutes the principal direct linkage between the agrarian reform problem and the agricultural development problem in the countries studied.

The Clienteles of Agricultural Policies

If the goal of agricultural policies in Latin America has not been national development, what was it? This can best be understood by looking at the interest groups (clienteles) that are benefited. This is not so different from farm policy anywhere except in the matter of degree. But this difference of degree is all-important for agricultural development. It is directly related to the social organization and the political structure in Latin America in general and in rural areas in particular.

The broad groups or clienteles most directly concerned with agricultural policy may be defined by their common economic interests and social position.[5] The groups that are most successful in articulating their interests and influencing policy, however, are generally represented in the political process by pressure groups (associative groups) and by national political parties.

The principal interest-group affecting Latin American agricultural policy is composed of the large landholders and the commercial, banking, and bureaucratic groups whose social and economic interests closely coincide with those of these large farm producers. Within this broad interest group is a traditional *latifundista* sector and a more modern commercial sector whose interests sometimes diverge from those of the latifundistas.

A second group directly interested in farm policy is made up of the low-income small producers and landless workers. The workers' and smallholders' interests coincide on general redistributive measures but often conflict on specific means.

The third group that frequently has convergent agricultural policy interests includes urban consumers, agricultural raw-material users, manufacturers, and employers of rural migrants. There are other less well-defined clienteles such as middle-class medium-sized commercial farm producers, whose interests often coincide with those of the large producers, depending on the particular circumstances.

The large farm producers and the principal urban groups affected by agricultural policy are generally represented by well organized associations or pressure groups. The present national agricultural societies (e.g. the Sociedad Nacional de Agricultura in Chile and the Sociedad Rural in Argentina) and their predecessors have been highly influential since colonial times. The employers' trade associations, importers' and exporters' associations, bankers' clubs, and some urban-based labor unions also have a long history of articulating the interests of their members.

Many of the Latin American political parties are essentially institutions for aggregating the interests of these broad economic and social clienteles.[6]

Of course, there are many divergences of interest on particular policies within each group. The general policy strategy each would support, however, is sharply distinguished vis-à-vis those strategies that clearly benefit the others.

The development planners make up a relatively new pressure group occasionally affecting policy, at least marginally. They do not usually represent any clientele at all in the sense we have used the term. That these technocrats have not been more influential is easily explained by this absence of a firm political base.[7] What is remarkable is that the planners have been as successful as they have been in influencing policies, or at least the terminology and the rationale of policies.

As policy is as much a matter of rule application and adjudication as it is of legislation one must look at the net results. "Obedience without compliance" has been a characteristic of Latin American public administration since the first viceroys began receiving instructions from the king of Spain. Chile had laws on the books for over 20 years authorizing the expropriation of abandoned farms before the Agrarian Reform Law of 1963, but no land was expropriated. Carlos V had similar experiences with his decrees requiring more humane treatment of the Indians. In Latin America as elsewhere, policy is more clearly revealed by the functional public budget than by the legal codes.

Agricultural Policy and Administrative Institutions

One of the clearest connections between agricultural policy and clientele is seen in the history of the agricultural administrative agencies in some of the ICAD study countries. The present national Ministries of Agriculture were created in Brazil, Chile, and various other countries at the end of the nineteenth century.[8] Their primary purpose was to take over with public financial support certain regulatory functions such as animal disease control and crop quality and production control for export. These functions had previously been carried out by the landowners' associations. The agricultural ministries have worked since their inception almost exclusively with the traditional large owners and they have recruited much of their personnel from the land-owning families. They have not usually intervened in any very active way in promoting change or modernization.

Recent detailed field studies in Chile show that the Ministry of Agriculture personnel still work almost entirely with traditional medium- and large-sized producers. Although soil conservation and extension have been added to the ministries' activities, these services operate at minimal levels.

During the 1930's traditional Latin American agriculture was in serious trouble. The more aggressive large commercial producers influenced government policy toward stimulating commercial production, especially for export. The traditional Ministries of Agriculture proved entirely unsuited for promotional work of the kind required. As a result a whole series of new agricultural, developmental, and financing institutions blossomed forth. In this period the Banco Agrícola in Peru, the Banco del Estado and the Corporacion de la Reforma Agraria (Chilean Development Corporation, or CORFO) in Chile were created to provide public funds and assistance for commercial large farmers. In Brazil nearly a dozen commodity-oriented institutes were formed to finance production, provide technical information, market the crops, support prices, pay subsidies, control production, and perform other services for the larger producers. The Brazilian Alcohol and Sugar Institute, for example, had among its functions the fixing of export quotas; one of the principal objectives of these quotas was to control sugar production in São Paulo, where it could be produced more economically, in order to protect the profits of traditional high-cost producers in Pernambuco. The Chilean wine producers entrusted the Government with the control of new plantings in order to prevent "overproduction" for the domestic market.

These new organizations were publicly financed but generally were controlled by *Consejos* (boards of directors) composed in part by representatives of the Government and in part by representatives of the private interests of the clientele concerned. All important policy decisions of the Consejos were subject to veto by the private representatives. This made effective Government control of agricultural policy a practical impossibility.[9]

In recent years, and especially since the Alliance for Progress, political pressures to have some agricultural policies to benefit the small farmers and farm laborers have come both from progressive groups in Latin America and from the United States. If further proof is needed of the orientation toward the large-farmer clientele of the traditional ministries and agricultural development institutions, it is given by the need to create entirely new administrative institutions to reach this low-income clientele at all. The traditional technical assistance and lending institutions have now been supplemented by a new set of "agrarian reform" oriented organizations such as CORA and INDAP in Chile, ONRA in Peru, IERAC in Ecuador, SUPRA in Brazil, and INCORA in Colombia.[10] Operating with severe legal and budgetary restrictions and usually under Consejos in which the large landowners and other private interests still have a powerful voice, these reform institutes have been entrusted with policy application in benefit of the *campesinos*.[11]

Beneficiaries of Some Agricultural Policies

A quick review of a few of the major areas of agricultural policy only confirms the conclusion that policy primarily serves a very limited clientele, usually the large landowners and some urban groups. Those policies benefiting the agricultural workers and small producers are few and typically ineffective.

1) *Credit* offers the most obvious example of clientele-oriented agricultural policies. All of the ICAD study countries have various official agencies and institutions responsible for providing agricultural credit. Substantial amounts of credit are also made available to agriculture through the commercial banks, often with explicit or implicit state guarantees. Interest charges are usually subsidized and in inflationary periods they are often negative. Repayment terms are liberal and debt moratoriums an accepted emergency practice. For example, the large cattle producers' debts in Brazil were taken over by the Government in

1954–55, apparently following the philosophy that losses if not profits should be socialized.

Lending procedures for large borrowers are speedy and convenient. There is little or no control of how the credit is ultimately used once it is extended. Much of it ultimately finances urban residences and other non-agricultural investments.

The case of Chile may be taken as fairly typical. In 1960 agriculture received 36 per cent of all institutional credit granted by commercial banks and the Government. Of this, only 7 per cent went to family-sized and small producers (who accounted for over 40 per cent of the value of agricultural production). The remainder went to the large landowners.[12] The smallholders, on the other hand, had virtually no access to official or commercial bank credit. The campesino small producer was outside the formal credit market both for economic reasons (lack of security, small volume of business, etc.) and because of his social position. If he got credit at all it is from the moneylender, storekeeper, or large landowner.[13]

Various recent Government credit programs such as that of the Agricultural Development Institute in Chile (INDAP) and of INCORA in Colombia have been undertaken to reach this low-income clientele. Up until now, however, the total amounts involved in credit programs for low-income farmers have been relatively small (about 2 per cent of all state-financed agricultural credit in Chile in 1964). In Peru over 70 per cent of the credit from the State Agricultural Bank in 1963 was for the production of cotton and rice, both almost entirely large-farm crops in that country. Similar situations were found in other countries studied.

2) *Public investments* in irrigation, land reclamation, and the opening of new lands for colonization tend to benefit the same large-owner clientele. Private and public investments in irrigation projects in coastal Peru have left close to 90 per cent of the irrigated land in multifamily-sized farm units. Of six publicly financed irrigation projects recently constructed in Chile only one was primarily for small farmers; most of the newly irrigated lands are in holdings of over 200 hectares each. Wollman estimates that the repayment terms for these irriga-

tion investments are so favorable with the inflation that the Government will recover less than 6 per cent of its original costs.[14]

Investments in roads opening up new lands show the same trends. How this occurs is seen by the Peruvian example. During the last 50 years land titles have been granted private owners for about 5 million hectares in the eastern Peruvian frontier region which was being opened to settlement. Of this area 97 per cent was granted to only 1,205 owners of holdings greater than 100 hectares each. The average large grant was of 3,900 hectares per grantee. The figures for Brazil and other countries are not very different.

In recent years, public investment in the colonization of frontier areas has been advanced as a policy to benefit the small farmers and landless workers. Colonization policy is supported by both the larger landowners in settled areas and those who have speculatively obtained titles to low-value virgin lands. The former see it as a way to divert pressures for agrarian reform. The latter are aware of the importance for them of opening up the frontier areas; roads and an additional labor supply are a necessity if their own lands are to acquire real market value.

Those Government-directed and financed colonization projects, however, have not had much impact on low-income rural groups. In Guatemala, in the eight years from 1954 to 1962, only about 6,000 families were colonized on family-sized units, although 25,000 new units had been planned. The rate of settlement was less than 7 per cent of the rate of net demographic increase of the rural population. Many of the parcels were given to urban middle-class colonists rather than to campesinos. In Chile the Caja de Colonización was created in 1929 to subdivide large estates, and also to settle smallholders on new lands; this institution created some 4,000 small and medium holdings between 1929 and 1962.

In other countries official colonization has been proceeding at a similarly slow pace (See Table I). Nowhere has it approached the rate of new family formation in rural areas through population increase net of migration.

TABLE I   Colonization Activities in Selected ICAD Study Countries.

Country	Period	Units colonized	Land area (hectares)	Units per year	Area per year (hectares)
Argentina [a]	1940–56	5,731[b]	2,195,394	337	129,141
Chile	1929–63	4,708[c]	1,388,024[d]	134	39,664
Guatemala	1955–62	5,265[e]	95,260	619	11,207

Notes:

[a] Between 1961 and June 1963, 454 lots were colonized with an area of 35,281 hectares.
[b] Number of allotments.
[c] Number of parcels and lots. In addition there were 1,049 very small holdings ("micro parcelas" and "huertos").
[d] Includes the "micro parcelas."
[e] In addition, 4,524 "micro parcelas" with 11,660 hectares, and 12,081 "comuneros" with 52,402 hectares were adjudicated.

Source: ICAD reports.

3) *Land tenure and labor policy* has primarily supported the largeholders, at least until very recently. The Latin American national constitutions almost without exception contain provisions making land expropriation practically impossible. Compensation has to be at full market value and in cash; the court procedures for obtaining an expropriation decree are generally complex and weighted in the landowners' favor. Argentina requires that each expropriation be approved by Congress.

Recently, with the demands for agrarian reform, some of these constitutional clauses have been modified. How difficult it is to do this can be seen by the fact that although the Frei Government in Chile, which has a large parliamentary majority, has been pushing for three years for a new article on property rights to permit deferred payment of expropriated land, this amendment received preliminary approval late in 1967; hence it is still not officially enforceable even now.

Historically, in Latin America, the power of the state was used to assure landlords as plentiful, cheap, and docile a work force as possible. When legalized slavery and forced labor were abolished during the nineteenth century, a series of tenure institutions such as *peonaje, inquilinaje,* and various forms of share-

104

cropping took their place. These tenure arrangements tie the worker to the large farms by ceding him the use of a small parcel of land for his house and garden while limiting his alternative opportunities to obtain land or find other employment. Written contracts are seldom used for such tenure agreements. Public authority has been (and still is in many areas) at the disposal of the landowners to expel workers who do not accept all of the conditions required. Police power is also commonly used to control migration in rural areas. In Guatemala the Indian population living in smallholder communities was required legally to work on the large plantations in periods of labor shortage whether they wanted to or not. Rural labor organizations were, of course, strictly proscribed. The same situation still prevails in most rural areas today.

From earliest colonial times there were a few voices raised in defense of the Indians. Royal edicts were issued to protect Indian lands and prevent too flagrant exploitation. These, however, had little influence in practice.

There has recently been a proliferation of policies fostered by urban-based populist governments ostensibly designed to benefit low-income campesinos. The Arévalo Government abolished compulsory labor in Guatemala in 1945 while the Arbenz Government in 1952 commenced an agrarian reform that had conceded land to over 100,000 campesinos before it was overthrown in 1954 (with U.S. support) and the land returned to its former owners. The López Government in Colombia enacted Law 200 in 1936 which enabled tenants and squatters to claim title to their lands if they had occupied them for ten years.

All the ICAD study countries had laws in 1963 which proscribed tenancy contract abuses and established minimum wages and working conditions. In theory, farm workers often participate in social security programs along with urban groups. Under certain conditions they have the legal right to organize unions.

The evidence demonstrates that these laws have not been effective. Minimum wages are unenforced and practically unenforceable in rural labor-surplus areas with a public administration that is closely allied with the large landowners. In Brazil minimum wage laws were being observed in only one out of eight states according to one survey. In most rural areas of Chile, Peru, and Ecuador the situation was similar. Usually such legislation was adopted with tacit agreement that it would not be vigorously enforced.

The effects of such legislation may even be negative for the campesino groups they are supposed to benefit. For example, in Colombia, the owners' expulsion of many campesinos from the large properties immediately followed adoption of Law 200 giving them permanent rights to land if they had worked more than ten years on the farm.

In Argentina there have been special laws and regulations controlling farm wages and tenant contracts since the early 1940's. In spite of the protection they have given commercial tenants, these regulations generally failed to aid those whose tenure or farm employment was most precarious. This omission was in part deliberate, due to exclusions and deficiencies in the legislation, and in part administrative, as it proved impossible to enforce many provisions of the laws. A special appeals tribunal was created to facilitate consideration of tenant and worker claims, but its powers were progressively diminished until now few of the controls are actually enforced. Argentine farm laborers' "regulated" real wages declined by an estimated 30 per cent from the mid-1950's to 1960.

The enforcement of controls in rural areas depends largely on the willingness of the landowner groups to permit the application of laws that are against their own interests. This is because the clientele most damaged by strict enforcement of the laws has its greatest political and economic influence at the local level in rural areas.

4) *Tax policy* has also tended to favor the clientele of traditional large landowners. In all of the countries studied, taxation penalized the more productive farmers while those with large, idle estates escaped virtually tax-free. The bulk of tax revenue from agriculture is derived from taxes on sales, turnover, and exports or from taxes on wage payments. Meanwhile, the tax-take from land and capital, from net incomes or inheritances, is everywhere small.

In Argentina, for example, the ICAD study concluded that

only about one-third of the total tax revenue collected from the agricultural sector was derived from income taxes or capital taxes which, in theory at least, do not depress the level of farm output. In Peru land taxes are almost nonexistent. Land taxes and income taxes are easily evaded by large property owners. In Chile, it was estimated that on the average land-assessments for tax purposes were between one-tenth and one-fifth of actual commercial market prices for land when the present government took office in 1964. (New assessments in Chile are now changing this situation, however.)

Economic planners have often recommended a stiff tax on land, based on its market value or on its potential productive capacity, both as a revenue measure and as a means to force more intensive production on good idle land. For such policies to be effective the tax would have to be enforced strictly and impartially. Experience does not indicate that either the passage or enforcement of such tax laws is easily attainable. Tax policy suffers from the same political weaknesses as contract regulation. In rural areas dominated by latifundia the power to tax or to enforce tax laws normally depends on the same groups who benefit from the large landholdings. It is naïve to expect that these groups are voluntarily going to tax themselves out of their privileged positions.

Nor can public support for tax reforms be easily mobilized in urban areas. A tenure reform redistributing land to campesinos can generate strong support among the beneficiary groups. On the other hand tax reform, while invariably producing intense opposition, seldom finds strong support since the beneficiaries are diffused throughout society and receive their benefits only indirectly.

5) *Educational policy* as it affects the agricultural population can also be analyzed in terms of clienteles.[15] Throughout Latin America educational levels and opportunities are far lower in rural regions than in urban regions. Rural illiteracy rates of as high as 50 per cent are encountered in many parts of rural Chile, which along with Argentina boasts the best rural school-systems of the study countries. In many of the Indian areas of Guatemala and Peru 80 to 95 per cent of the adult population are unable to

read or write. The ICAD studies found several large *haciendas* in Ecuador and Guatemala on which there were no elementary schools nor were there any schools nearby, although legally every large property owner is supposed to aid in providing schooling for the residents of his estate.

This lack of adequate rural elementary schooling, however, does not mean that the large landowners' families do not have access to educational facilities. Instead, it reflects the fact that the substantial landowners are essentially an urban-oriented class. Many live in the nearby provincial towns or in state and national capitals. Those living on their farms often send their children to boarding schools in the cities or have means of transport to take them to the towns. There is simply a different school system to serve this clientele. This is largely a result of the agrarian class structure; it also serves to perpetuate it.

The secondary and university educational systems reflect the same policy orientation. Very few campesinos ever enter secondary school. There are occasional agricultural vocational schools to be found in the ICAD study countries but these are designed primarily to train technicians and administrators for the large estates. In any case, their total enrollment is minuscule compared either with the school-age population or the potential job opportunities for technicians in agriculture.[16]

Agricultural college curricula emphasize preparing professionals for the traditional government agricultural services and for managing large farms. The students are mostly from large landowning families or from the urban middle classes. First importance is placed upon courses dealing with commercial crops grown on the large farms. One Peruvian *agrónomo* told the author that he graduated from the agricultural university without having been taught anything concerning corn or potatoes or having been told that these were Peru's two leading crops —the management of cotton, rice, and sugar grown on the large plantations was the principal focus of the technical courses.

Extension services, technical-assistance programs, and agricultural research typically serve only the larger landowners. The social distance between educated technicians and illiterate campesinos is so great that the former naturally prefer to work with the better-educated large landowners. Even when specifically assigned to work only with low income groups, they gravitate toward helping the few more educated local leaders, often causing resentment among the majority of smaller owners.[17] More basic, however, is the fact that these technical assistance programs were created to serve the large owner clientele. It is only in the new agrarian-reform agencies that there is any incentive or possibility for contacts with lower income groups.

Most of what little agricultural research that has been carried out in Latin America has been directed to improvement of high-value export crops. The subsistence crops grown by the mass of peasantry are of little commercial interest. There are few pressures to improve varieties and management methods that can be readily adopted by small farmers.

6) *Price and marketing policies* most clearly reveal the conflicts of interest between the large landowner clientele and strictly urban groups. The Ministries of Agriculture and the large agricultural producers' organizations are dedicated to guaranteeing remunerative farm prices, securing subsidies for farm inputs, and promoting exports. The Ministries of Economy, however, supported by manufacturers associations, trade unions, and strong political parties, are charged with keeping food prices down and in protecting domestic industries from foreign competition. As Latin America has been urbanizing rapidly, the political weight of the urban clientele is increasing.

Outsiders are prone to regard the complicated labyrinth of price controls, production limitations, import and export subsidies, prohibitive tariffs, state-protected monopolies, exchange-rate manipulations, and special tax exemptions as a recent development imposed by misguided disciples of state intervention in the economy. Actually, the mercantilist systems of Spain and Portugal have much more to do with the present structure than is generally realized. The outlines of present networks of regulations, licenses, official monopolies or concessions, quotas, and red tape were already largely formed in the eighteenth century.[18]

Trying to control or to support agricultural prices without adequate rationing or production limitations leads to predictable complications. These are abundant in Latin America. Brazil's coffee stocks are now about three times annual exports and consumption and are equal to the total annual coffee harvest in the whole world. "Meatless days" are observed in Argentina, Chile, Colombia, and Uruguay in attempts to equate beef consumption with demand. In Brazil the price of the front quarter of the cow was controlled as a concession to the anti-inflationary efforts of the Minister of Economy while the hindquarter was sold free of price restrictions as a concession to the minister of agriculture.

After having observed how official prices are set, the wonder for an economist is that the system functions at all. Perhaps the best explanation is that price controls simply are not very effective for most products—there are too many ways to evade them through quality erosion, black markets, and smuggling. Where price fixing is even partially effective it is accompanied by production control (as with Chilean wine), by surpluses (Brazilian coffee), or by informal rationing through the distribution system that generally benefits more well-to-do groups (meat and milk).

Several countries have had policies of subsidizing certain agricultural inputs, such as fertilizers.[19] The domestic prices of Chilean nitrate and Peruvian guano have been heavily subsidized. In part this has been to aid these fertilizer industries that were losing their foreign markets because of the competition of cheaper sources of nitrogen; in part it has been to aid the large users of these inputs. Peruvian guano, for example, has been sold in recent years to domestic users at less than 50 per cent of its export price. Almost all of the guano used domestically is purchased by large coastal landowners, primarily producing sugar, cotton, and rice.

In the study countries it is accepted practice for governments to grant liberal tax-exemptions, foreign-exchange convertibility guarantees, liberal credit facilities, import privileges, and regional concessions or monopolies to foreign investors to install large-scale modern agricultural industries such as packing houses, milk plants, or poultry plants. The alleged purpose is to attract foreign investment and increase production. Often these investments are made in the name of a so-called "cooperative" to take advantage of special cooperative laws, although the "coop"

110

may be formed by no more than half a dozen large producers. The effects for small farmers and national processors is often disastrous, however, as it is impossible for them to compete successfully with the officially favored enterprises.

Imports of agricultural products, especially under U.S. Public Law 480, have been the most effective means of preventing rapid price rises of foodstuffs for urban consumers. During the last ten years, for example, Chilean imports of U.S. surplus wheat and milk have amounted to about 9 per cent of Chilean domestic wheat production and 7 per cent of milk production; in 1964 milk imports were estimated to be as much as 15 per cent of production. Imports of P.L. 480 wheat by Colombia and Brazil have also been relatively great. There is an inexorable political and economic logic involved here. Practically no Latin American government could withstand the consequences of a sharp increase in the relative prices of basic foods consumed by the urban population. When one considers that 50 per cent or more of the low-income groups' budget goes for food and that these groups make up a majority of the population, it is easy to see why.

If one examines the relative prices of agricultural products during the last 15 years, however, there are no clear downward or upward trends discernible in the ICAD study countries. Actually it is difficult for public policy in these countries to change very much the relationship of agricultural prices as a whole in relation to the general price level. A Michigan State University study in Colombia concludes that even wheat production has not been adversely affected by P.L. 480 imports.[20] The greatest effect on agriculture has not been to depress production directly, but to postpone the day when government policies will have to deal more effectively with the agricultural crisis.

Price policies have been primarily the result of interest articulation by the large-landowner groups, importers, exporters, credit agencies, processors, manufacturers (who demand high-tariff protection), and urban consumers. The low-income agricultural groups have had little or nothing to do with them one way or another. Actually their interests are neither clear nor united. The small producers often consume a large portion of their own production, sometimes more than 50 per cent. They also sell in local markets that may be little affected by national price policies. To the extent that they buy foodstuffs such as flour or sugar from national markets, they are affected by price levels more as consumers than as producers. Wage workers in agriculture are directly concerned with food prices only as consumers. The majority have very low incomes. Most of their annual cash expenditures are for food. On the other hand, they commonly receive part of their pay in kind and are consequently partly insulated from changes in relative prices.

Government marketing policies have been directed almost entirely at aiding the large producers. Publicly financed marketing organizations were initially organized to satisfy large-owner demands to support prices. The public construction of grain silos in Brazil (with U.S. aid) was advanced as an aid to efficient marketing. Only the big growers benefited. The proclivity of municipal government agencies to protect local marketing monopolies of agricultural products puts the small producers who cannot ship in bulk at a severe disadvantage. Recent attempts in Chile to provide government credit to small producers through special loans for marketing have proved frustrating. Most of the small producers affected were either sharecroppers or were in debt to large buyers or landowners who promptly got control of the small-marketing loans, using them to substitute for credit they customarily extended.

Foreign exchange and tariff policies have probably been more often beneficial to industrial interests than to agricultural producers. Even here, however, generalizations are difficult, especially for countries with large agricultural exports.

It can be seen that the policy picture is an extremely complicated one. Many programs counteract each other. The net effect of the complex of policies affecting agriculture in Latin America is not easily evaluated. The balance would certainly vary from country to country and from year to year.

If any group has been systematically discriminated against, it is the small-farm producers and landless workers. The reasons why these groups have so little voice in the political process are rooted in the structure of political power. This in turn is closely connected with land tenure.

THE AGRARIAN PROBLEM [21]

When one's values are threatened he senses a problem. Personal problems, however, only become public issues when the values believed to be endangered are held by politically influential groups. The "Negro problem" in the United States and the "agrarian problem" in Latin America are both issues of this type.

Many of the traditionally held values of the property-owning and governing classes in Latin America are being challenged. Pressures are mounting to reform the agrarian structure that concentrates power, status, and wealth in rural areas in the hands of a relatively small group of traditional landowners, tradesmen, and officials. As this structure is largely based upon land-tenure institutions, the agrarian problem and the land-tenure problem are nearly synonymous. In Spanish there is no distinction between the terms for land-tenure reform and agrarian reform—both are referred to as *reforma agraria.*

Our review of agricultural policies in the seven ICAD study countries has shown that they have usually benefiited the large landowners and various urban groups, and have seldom favored the low-income campesinos. Recruitment into political positions has generally been from large landlords' families and upper and middle urban classes. The campesinos have been unable to organize pressure groups or to influence policy at the national political level. Communications between campesino groups and governments have been practically nonexistent. There have been no political inputs from the campesinos. The vast majority of the rural population, and the most numerous group in the total population of Latin America, has little or no representation in the present political structures.

The political system, however, is only a part of the social system. The determinants of agricultural policy are to be found in the social structures of these Latin American countries, especially in their rural social structures.[22] The roots of the agrarian problem lie in the traditional social systems whose values are threatened by a changing world.

113

The Traditional Agrarian Structure

In the traditional rural economy, land is the main source of wealth. Income from land, however, cannot be realized without labor. Rights to land have therefore been accompanied by laws and customs (land-tenure institutions) that assure the land-owners a continuing and compliant labor supply.[23]

These land-tenure institutions were a product of the Spanish and Portuguese colonial systems. Once established, however, these same institutions served to perpetuate the traditional social structure. Ownership or control of land in traditional agrarian societies carries with it political power; the large landowners have the ability to make others do their will, if necessary by force.[24]

1) *Origins:* The general lines of the agrarian structure were laid down in the colonial period. The Indians and their lands were rapidly distributed among the more influential Spanish and Portuguese officers and civilians, wherever the possibilities for commercial farming or mining made it profitable to do so. A few relatively small grants of land (*caballerías* and *peonías*) were made to lesser officers and common soldiers in the hopes of encouraging intensive farming to feed the new settlements. Indian communities on poorer lands or in remote areas were left legally as wards of the Crown. Most of the territory, however, was distributed in vast geographically defined areas variously known as *encomiendas, mercedes* or *donatarias*—fictitious, but legally binding grants ostensibly made by the Indians to the Spaniards and Portuguese colonists.

The encomenderos in Spanish America and the donatarios in Brazil were given the right to use the Indians for profit. They were also made responsible for their religious welfare. These repartitions of Indians and land eventually became converted into real property in land. They formed the basis for the large estates (plantations, haciendas, *fazendas, estancias*, etc.) that have dominated the organization of Latin American agriculture ever since.

2) *Land-Tenure Institutions:* Latin American agriculture for

the most part is still organized in large estates worked by several families under the supervision of a single administration, and in communities of smallholdings where each family performs both entrepreneurial and labor functions. These two types of rural social organization co-exist in most of rural Latin America. They are frequently referred to as latifundia and minifundia. The number of family-sized commercial farms and small commercial estates has increased, but far less rapidly than colonial visionaries and liberal optimists had foreseen when they encouraged the handing out of peonías to disbanded soldiers and later when after independence from Spain and Portugal they abolished primogeniture and slavery.

In the seven countries studied by ICAD the owners of estates on the average hold over three-fourths of the agricultural land. Estates employing more than twelve workers include 82 per cent of all farmland in Peru, for example. Smallholdings (too small to provide work for more than one family) make up from 62 per cent (Brazil) to more than 96 per cent (Ecuador, Guatemala, and Peru) of the number of farm units although they have very little of the land. This situation is summarized by the data on the distribution of farms by size from all seven countries (Table II).

The agricultural population can be considered as being made up of four social groups—estate owners who may be entrepreneurs or merely *rentiers*, an intermediary group of estate administrators and supervisors, the landless workers on the estates, and the smallholders.[25] The estate owners comprise the upper strata or agrarian aristocracy; with their families and estate administrators they make up from 4 to 16 per cent of the farm population in the countries studied. The peasants who work the land as smallholders or landless laborers comprise the rest (Table III).

A few of the smallholders with family-sized or slightly larger parcels are in effect small commercial farmers employing some outside labor.[26] This is especially true of such immigrant groups as the Japanese colonists near São Paulo, Italians near Mendoza in Argentina, and Germans in southern Chile. This caveat aside, the countryside is divided into two broad social and economic classes: the peasants who work the land with their hands, and

TABLE II Relative Number and Area of Farm Units by Size Groups in ICAD Study Countries. (Percentage of country total in each size-class) *

Country	Small holdings Sub-family [a]	Family [b]	Estates Multi-family (medium) [c]	Multi-family (large) [d]	Total
Argentina					
Number of farm units	43.2	48.7	7.3	0.8	100.0
Area in farms	3.4	44.7	15.0	36.9	100.0
Brazil					
Number of farm units	22.5	39.1	33.7	4.7	100.0
Area in farms	0.5	6.0	34.0	59.5	100.0
Chile					
Number of farm units	36.9	40.0	16.2	6.9	100.0
Area in farms	0.2	7.1	11.4	81.3	100.0
Colombia					
Number of farm units	64.0	30.2	4.5	1.3	100.0
Area in farms	4.9	2.3	23.3	49.5	100.0
Ecuador					
Number of farm units	89.9	8.0	1.7	0.4	100.0
Area in farms	16.6	19.0	19.3	45.1	100.0
Guatemala					
Number of farm units	88.4	9.5	2.0	0.1	100.0
Area in farms	14.3	13.4	31.5	40.8	100.0
Peru					
Number of farm units	88.0	8.5	2.4	1.1	100.0
Area in farms	7.4	4.5	5.7	82.4	100.0

Notes: * Area in farms measured by hectares.

[a] *Sub-family:* Farms too small to provide employment for a single family (two workers) with the typical incomes, markets, and levels of technology and capital now prevailing in each region.

[b] *Family:* Farms large enough to provide employment for 2 to 3.9 people, on the assumption that most of the farm work is being carried out by the members of the farm family.

[c] *Multi-family (medium):* Farms large enough to provide employment for 4 to 12 people.

[d] *Multi-family (large):* Farms large enough to provide employment for over 12 people.

Source: ICAD studies.

the estate owners and administrators who do not. Composed originally of Indians and Negro slaves, with their numbers augmented later by miscegenation with the conquerors and the

TABLE III Distribution of Farm Families According to Socio-Economic Status, ICAD Study Countries.

	Argentina (1960)	Brazil (1950)	Chile (1950)	Colombia (1960)	Ecuador (1960)	Guatemala (1950)	Peru (1960)
Thousands of families in agriculture	768.6	5,404.2	344.9	1,368.8	440.0	417.4	1,124.5
Status (%) of families in agriculture [27]							
Operators of large-sized estates	0.4	1.8	3.0	1.1	.3	.3	.9
Operators of medium-sized estates	4.8	12.8	6.5	3.9	2.1	1.5	2.1
Administrators of large and medium-sized estates	1.3	2.1	2.1	1.5	2.0	2.2	1.0
Operators of family-sized smallholdings	32.6	14.9	17.7	23.3	9.5	7.8	7.6
Operators of sub-family-sized smallholdings	25.9	8.6	23.1	47.0	53.6	63.6	61.7
Landless farm workers (with and without rights to cultivate subsistence plots)	35.0	59.8	47.6	23.2	32.5	24.6	26.7
Total	100.0	100.0	100.0	100.0	100.0	100.0	100.0

[27] See Table II for definitions of farm size groups.

Source: ICAD studies.

absorption of the least fortunate among immigrants and disbanded soldiers, the peasantry has never enjoyed status or political power.

About half of the agricultural population depends upon the estates directly for employment. The landless laborers frequently receive small subsistence-sized parcels to cultivate as a partial wage, while many of the smallholders work part-time on the estates. Hence the dividing line between these two peasant groups is not sharp.

Slavery and forced labor were legally abolished during the nineteenth century. The estate owners now control their labor force largely by means of their monopoly of the land. Where there is no alternative employment and no other possibility to obtain sufficient land of his own for subsistence, the peasant is forced to work on the estate on the owner's terms. The workers provide labor to the estate owner at a low wage in return for the use of land and pasture. These tenure arrangements are institutionalized in a variety of sharecropping and quasi-feudal share-labor and tribute-paying agreements such as *huasipungaje* (Ecuador), *colonaje* (Peru and Guatemala), and *inquilinaje* (Chile).[28]

3) *Rural Social and Political Organization:* On the estates the social hierarchy is rigid, consisting of the land-owning class, an intermediary group of managers, accountants, straw bosses, and specialized workers, and at the bottom those who actually till the soil. In the Latin American traditional scheme of values these class differences take on an almost caste-like aspect. The peasantry remains in large measure socially "Indian" in Ecuador, Peru, and Guatemala. Elsewhere distinctive dress, manners, and skin-shading usually set the campesinos apart from the estate owners and administrators.

Control on the estates is autocratic, imposed from above. Discipline is maintained chiefly by the menace of eviction and by partial acceptance by the workers of the *patronal* scale of values. Corporal punishment is still occasionally found in traditional Andean haciendas. Throughout the Andean region, Brazil, and even parts of Chile it is commonplace to find that peasants living on the estates are prohibited from receiving non-resident visitors or visiting outside without authorization of the management.

118

In spite of great regional diversity in the types of estate, they exhibit similar organizational and social characteristics. There are only minor variations in the labor organizations of an Ecuadorian highland hacienda, a Brazilian cotton plantation, a Chilean *fundo*, a Brazilian mixed-farming fazenda, an Argentine cattle estancia, a Guatemalan coffee *finca*, a Peruvian sugar plantation, or a Central American banana plantation. All are characterized by a small managerial group and a relatively large number of dependent workers and tenants.

Estate owners not only rule in their properties but also hold considerable power in the wider society. Most of the largest landowners are closely linked by family and social contacts with the urban commercial and managerial classes; they are often partially or fully absentee, maintaining residences and business and political interests in the provincial or national capital and occasionally abroad. Their children attend schools in the cities and their social life centers there, making them in many ways an urban class. They constitute the principal nexus between the campesino and the national political system.

Local social, political, educational, and even religious institutions may depend upon the estate owners for continued existence. Priests who incur the large farmers' displeasure by advocating land reform and better farm wages are frequently transferred or sent abroad, and some are even jailed. Numerous Brazilian, Peruvian, and Guatemalan labor-union organizers have been jailed or simply disappeared in recent years for similar offenses.

The state's police power is generally at the estate owners' disposal. It may be supplemented by private strong-arm forces such as the *capangas* in Brazil's northeast. When Indians in 1962 pastured animals on lands of which they disputed the legal title with a large Peruvian hacienda, the Lima owner promptly had a company of soldiers sent up who only required lodging, food, and women of the resident administrator before chasing off the "invaders" at gun point the next morning.

In contrast to the estates, the smallholding communities are characterized by relatively minor social differences among their members. These communities are generally bound together by kinship ties and a strong group solidarity against either outside pressures or the disruptive effects for the community of any single member acquiring a too disproportionate share of land or income.[29]

While the estate owners have direct contact with national institutions, the smallholders generally depend upon a small town-dwelling elite of merchants, government officials, ecclesiastics, and landowners in their relationships with the broader society. These are not usually interested in jeopardizing their positions of influence by promoting closer direct contacts between the peasants and the outside world.

In one Chilean smallholding community, for example, the government sent in agricultural agents to give supervised credit and organize a smallholders' cooperative. Local merchants and political bosses, who in some cases were also the larger landowners in the community, quickly took advantage of the credit and got control of the so-called cooperative. Most of the smallholders received no substantial benefits at all and remain suspicious of the program.[30]

4) *Economic incentives:* To a surprising extent small-scale peasant farming prevails not only in the smallholding communities but also on the large estates. This is a result of the widespread practice of allotment to permanent workers of parcels of land and pasture rights for subsistence production, and of the prevalence of sharecropping in the production of some commercial crops, such as cotton in Brazil. Wolf observes that in many peasant economies "the concept of the operating unit begins to dissolve into a series of individual tasks, and corresponding claims on income." [31] This is clearly what happens in the more traditional subsistence-oriented communities and estates.

Many of the large commercial estates, however, also include a complex of individual operating units and enterprises, some small and some large.[32] Profit maximization for the managers of these multifamily units is a singularly complicated calculation, especially if the owner has other non-farm business interests for which his farm serves as a security for credit and as a political base.

The salient characteristic of both the smallholder communities and the estates is that the peasants' production surpluses above subsistence and capital replacement tend to be expropriated by other groups. In the smallholder communities, tradesmen, moneylenders, and local officials are generally able to take peasant surpluses. In the estates it is primarily the owners and managers who do so. In either case, economic incentives to produce are modified.

Anthropologists and sociologists usually take it for granted that production incentives are determined by the social system.[33] Many economists, on the other hand, assume that producers everywhere strive rationally to maximize their profits. "Economic man," however, is a concept relevant for explaining rural Latin American economic behavior only within the context of local social systems and the agrarian structure.[34]

When the Chilean Government provided improved wheat seeds and fertilizer to peasants in one Chilean smallholder community very favorable terms, the producers reacted by reducing the area planted. The wheat required for subsistence could now be produced on less acreage.[35] It would be a mistake to generalize from a few experiences of this kind. But we cannot assume that peasants act according to *our* concepts of what a rational economic man would do regardless of the local social system in which they are operating.

Limited resources cannot explain the extensive use of land or the technical backwardness on most large estates. One finds only a partial explanation in the high costs of many technical improvements and their relative unsuitability for Latin American conditions. The principal reasons, however, must be sought in the land-tenure structure.

Powerful, often absentee, landowners with an abundant supply of low-cost dependent tenants and laborers have few incentives to change their methods. To do so would require them to become agricultural entrepreneurs and full-time farm managers instead of traditional landlords. The economic risks and sacrifices required would usually outweigh the return that they foresee from such an effort. Most important, many would have to work very much harder, change their way of life, and give up their elite position at the apex of the traditional social pyramid. Also it should be recalled that large-estate owners already enjoy relatively large incomes by local standards; in economic terms, the marginal utility of additional income is relatively low. Why should traditional large landowners make the great effort to become commercial farmers? Why should they sacrifice a way of life through which they now enjoy prestige, power, and relative wealth solely for happening to own land? [36]

This is not to say that there are not many commercially-oriented agricultural entrepreneurs in Latin America. Obviously there are. The point is that what constitutes rational economic behavior is strongly influenced by the social structure—by land-tenure institutions.

Pressures on the Traditional Agrarian Structure

Symptoms of the agrarian problem are to be seen in numerous overt conflict situations between peasant groups and estate owners. Indian communities have invaded dozens of Peruvian haciendas during the past decade; a peasant strike forced the government to begin expropriating and distributing to the peasants the large estates in the Peruvian valley of La Convención.

The federation of rural unions with the independent peasant unions and the *Ligas Camponesas* in northeastern Brazil were able to call a strike in 1962 in which some 200,000 peasants participated, demanding better wages and working conditions. The present Brazilian military government has suppressed peasant union activity and many peasant leaders have been jailed, exiled, or murdered, but the conditions creating agrarian unrest continue unabated.

Rural Colombia has been torn by violence since 1946; although this has not assumed a primarily peasant versus estate-owner orientation, it has its roots in that country's traditional agrarian structure. In Guatemala, return of estate lands to former owners after the Arbenz Government had handed it out to some 100,000 peasants did no more to alleviate Central American agrarian problems than did the massacre of some 10,000 to 20,000 peasants by El Salvador's army in the 1930's.[37] The ICAD study has found several large Ecuadorian estates in

122

disintegration, with the peasants taking control of the land. The number of labor conflicts on Chilean estates has been growing at an exponential rate during the last few years.

1) *Causes of Disequilibrium:* Widespread consciousness of an agrarian problem and the rapid increase in conflict situations are more symptoms of the agrarian issue than its causes. Somehow one must explain why the seigneurial system that has survived in Latin America for nearly four centuries is only now being seriously threatened.

The English historian George Macaulay Trevelyan observed that "Politics is the outcome, not the cause of social change." Our hypothesis is that the principal "causes" of the agrarian problem are to be found in the population explosion, the rapid spread of modern technology, urbanization, and changing value patterns. All of these factors are largely exogenous to the local rural social systems affected. More than anything else they are the result of the relatively rapid economic and social development Latin America has experienced during the last half-century.

In the first place, Latin American population continues to increase at one of the most rapid rates ever recorded anywhere. The present rate of demographic increase implies a more than doubling of the region's population within the next quarter-century: the UN estimates that the 1965 Latin American population of 230 million may reach 700 million by the year 2,000.

Moreover, although rural population is growing much more slowly than urban because of migration to the cities, it is still increasing at an average of about 1.5 per cent annually. In rural areas such as central Guatemala, birth rates are close to the biological maximum, and death rates are rapidly decreasing due to the control of epidemics, while urban employment opportunities are minimal. The number of people in the smallholding community of San Juan de Ostuncalco in upland Guatemala, for instance, doubled between 1930 and 1960 although only marginal new areas could be brought into cultivation. The population explosion puts a double strain on the agrarian sector—that of accommodating more farmers and at the same time that of producing more per worker in order to feed the expanding cities.

123

Technological change and urbanization are accelerating: On the one hand, improved transport facilitates migration to city slum areas; in spite of relatively slow industrial growth the region is becoming increasingly urbanized (Table IV). It is easy to explain why urban interests, concerns, and values should increasingly predominate in national political debates.

TABLE IV   Estimated Urban and Rural Population Trends in ICAD Study Countries. 1950–1970.

Country	Thousands of people			Per cent	
	Urban	Rural	Total	Urban	Rural
Argentina					
1950	11,199.1	5,893.9	17,093.0	65.6	34.4
1960	15,001.9	5,664.1	20,666.0	72.6	27.4
1970	18,200.8	6,260.2	24,461.0	74.4	25.6
Brazil					
1950	18,783.0	33,161.0	51,944.0	36.2	63.8
1960	31,991.0	38,976.0	70,967.0	45.1	54.9
1970	51,000.0	44,300.0	95,300.0	53.5	46.5
Chile					
1950	3,389.7	2,364.2	5,753.9	58.9	41.1
1960	5,028.0	2,346.0	7,374.0	68.2	31.8
1970	6,925.0	2,467.0	9,392.0	73.7	26.3
Colombia ᵃ					
1950	3,160.7	8,107.5	11,268.2	28.0	72.0
1960	5,353.0	8,961.0	14,314.0	37.4	62.6
1970	8,394.0	9,897.0	18,291.0	45.9	54.1
Ecuador					
1950	944.0	2,289.0	3,203.0	28.5	71.5
1960	1,422.0	2,787.0	4,209.0	33.8	66.2
1970	2,235.0	3,395.0	5,630.0	39.7	60.3
Guatemala					
1950	701.0	2,101.0	2,802.0	25.1	74.9
1960	963.0	2,579.0	3,542.0	27.2	72.8
1970	1,353.0	3,172.0	4,525.0	29.9	70.1
Perú					
1950	3,058.6	4,773.4	7,832.0	39.0	61.0
1960	4,607.0	5,542.0	10,149.0	45.4	54.6
1970	7,229.0	6,433.0	13,662.0	52.9	47.1

Note:

ᵃ Meta, Chocó, *Comisarías e Intendencias* are not included.

Source: ICAD studies.

On the other hand, technological progress in the rural areas is extremely uneven. The ICAD study of nine municipalities in Brazil found only about 4 per cent of the farms using fertilizers; there were only 464 tractors and 3,000 vehicles for draft animals on 26,000 farms, the rest being worked entirely by hand.

Estate owners often tend to introduce labor-saving machinery rather than more labor-intensive farming methods. Mechanization reduces their dependence on a potentially unruly work-force and has greater prestige value. Modernizing and rationalizing one large commercial plantation in coastal Ecuador resulted in discharging one-half of the 600 resident workers although the value of output was increased by several times. The net effect is to increase peasant insecurity and unemployment.

Another effect of changing technology is to force a redefinition of the traditional relations between peasants and management. This is true even when the technology is labor intensive instead of labor saving. A tractor driver, even if he is a bare foot Indian, has a different status than he had when he drove a yoke of oxen.

Thirdly, values are changing. With improved communication, increasing literacy and growing urbanization, traditional Latin American values are being replaced by the more cosmopolitan and equalitarian values dominant in most of the industrialized world. While on some traditional Andean haciendas, peons still kneel to kiss the corner of the "patron's" poncho to show respect, in provincial towns, such anachronisms are not taken seriously any more.

With transistor radios, newspapers, and sometimes even television reaching remote rural hamlets and helping to stimulate aspirations, the peasant is questioning the unalterability of the established order. Politicians seeking populist support promise land for the landless, while intellectuals preach social justice, national integration, and economic development.[38]

One can see many parallels between contemporary rural Latin America and late nineteenth-century eastern Europe. What is surprising is not that rural unrest exists in Latin America but that it has been so long in coming.

2) *Whose problem?* For the estate owner the agrarian

problem consists principally of maintaining his wealth, social position, and political power in a changing world. Traditionally-minded landowners would prefer to do this with the least possible alteration of land-tenure institutions. They vigorously oppose attempts to organize agricultural labor or to substitute cash wages for quasi-feudal obligations.

Commercially-oriented producers, however, would generally support doing away with these cumbersome labor arrangements, substituting a "free" labor market, provided that their real power over the peasantry was not seriously undermined. Thus, in Ecuador, many of the more progressive hacendados are happy to have the government award *huasipungueros*—which are small, less than subsistence-sized plots of land—with the understanding that they will still have to depend upon the estates for employment; it is cheaper for good commercial estate owners than the old system. In Chile "liberal" large landowners often support for the same reasons the idea of creating workers' villages with garden plots (*villorrios*) outside the estate limits.

Practically everywhere estate-owners see the immediate cause of the agrarian problem as subversive agitation, unfavorable price relationships, and inadequate credit. They foresee economic and social disaster if the land is turned over to ignorant uncultured peasants.

The peasants see the problem rather differently. Their immediate aspirations are usually limited to greater security, better economic conditions, and more opportunities for their children.[39] Smallholders and tenants generally aspire to obtain title to the land they work, to have a little more, and if they are Indians they may dream of recovering some of the lands wrested from their forefathers. Workers on the estates, on the other hand, are more likely to be concerned with possible eviction, declining real wages, the personal treatment given to them by the management, and the little favors that can be increased or withheld by the "good" or "bad" patron, such as the right to pasture more animals or to obtain a loan when needed.

A recent study in central Chile of the aspirations of the *inquilinos* on the large estates revealed that most of them would like to be smallholders; however, the immediate problems of their everyday relations with the estate owner and administrator and of providing a living for their families were of much more pressing importance.[40] Temporary workers are often even more preoccupied with their economic conditions as laborers and they may see the smallholders' and permanent laborers' ambitions for land as a threat to their own job security. The peasants usually have no doubt, however, that they could cultivate the land better than the present estate owners. They are the ones who do the actual work now, and most of them believe they know the soils and requirements for careful husbandry from lifelong practice and experience.

If one reviews the history of agrarian-reform policies in Latin America, one is struck by the fact that they are usually inspired less by the estate-owners' foresightedness or peasant pressure than by urban politicians and intellectuals. This can in part be explained by chronic shortages and rising food prices and by the problems created by a swelling stream of migrants from rural areas.

Other factors may be of greater importance. One of these is the property-owners' fear that peasant unrest may trigger a Mexican, Bolivian, or Cuban style revolution if something is not done soon—much of the halfhearted support for agrarian reform by the Alliance for Progress may be explained on this basis. A second reason is the sympathy that organized labor has for reform and the hope of labor leaders that a victory over the estate owners will weaken the position of employers everywhere. In the third place, politicians seeking populist support can appeal to most urban groups for agrarian reform without fear of losing votes, while the example of Cárdenas in Mexico and Luis Muñoz Marín in Puerto Rico leads them to hope that it might be possible to create a solid peasant-based political machine to carry their party to sustained national power.

The most influential single group pressing for agrarian reform, however, is to be found among the Latin American intellectuals. Moved by a moral commitment to social justice and national development, by an antipathy to the traditional elite common among intellectuals everywhere, and by a strong desire to hold power and direct the national destiny, this group can be counted upon to maintain continuous pressure for building a new agrarian structure, although there is little consensus among them about what that new structure should be. Most would agree with Arnold Toynbee when he wrote "In Latin America agrarian reform is the necessary starting point for political, economic and social change alike." [41]

THE AGRICULTURAL DEVELOPMENT PROBLEM [42]

It should now be amply clear that the agrarian problem is primarily political and social. There is, however, the economic problem of how to increase Latin American agricultural productivities and incomes. This economic problem and the agrarian structure are interrelated, but not always in the ways that the politicians and many economists imagine.

Agricultural development implies increasing productivities of the resources used. It means greater specialization and trade. The relative importance of foodstuffs in consumption will necessarily decrease. Development will be accompanied by greater urbanization and a continued lowering of the proportion of the total work force engaged in agriculture. Besides all these things it means increasing incomes. While it is a tautology to say that the agricultural development problem is basically one of improving farm families' incomes, this is a good starting point for analysis.

Incomes of the vast majority of the Latin American peasant families, both smallholders and landless workers, range from an equivalent of less than US$ 200 to about US$ 600 per year, including the estimated value of home consumption. Per-capita annual peasant incomes in all of the ICAD study countries, except Argentina (where they are higher), average from an equivalent of less than $40 to a little over $180. Incomes tend to be lowest in the Andean region and in northeast Brazil, but considering the difficulties of accurate measurement, regional differences are frequently rather academic.

The estate owners and other larger producers, of course, have considerably greater incomes than the peasants, often several hundred times so. A rough estimate of the breakdown of agricultural income in Chile by socioeconomic group is made in Table V.

TABLE V   Distributions of Agricultural Income in Chile, 1960 (one escudo [Eo] = approximately one US$).

	Farm Families		Income		Average Family Income (Eo)
	Number (thousands)	Proportion (%)	Total (millions Eo)	Proportion (%)	
Workers and Small-scale Owners	243.9[a]	70.7	155.2[b]	33.4	636
Family-scale Producers [c]	61.1	17.7	59.0	12.7	966
Supervisory Personnel	7.3	2.1	8.6	1.8	1,178
Medium-scale Producers [d]	22.3	6.5	71.4	15.4	3,202
Large-scale Producers [e]	10.3	3.0	170.8	36.7	16,582
	344.9	100.0	465.0	100.0	1,348

Notes:

[a] Includes families of producers with sub-family scale units and share-croppers.

[b] Includes salaries, payment in kind, social security contributions, and incomes on sub-family units from shares and from the land ceded as part payment for labor to *inquilinos*.

[c] Includes for the most part producers with from 5–20 hectares in irrigated zones, and greater area in the middle and extreme south. Some such units have incomes close to those of sub-family producers.

[d] Includes the operators of farm units large enough to provide employment for 4 to 12 people (using typical present farming methods and technology in the region).

[e] Includes the operators of farm units large enough to provide employment for over 12 people.

Source: ICAD, *Tenencia de la Tierra y Desarrollo Socio-Económico del Sector Agrícola: Chile*, Washington, 1966.

Obstacles to Increasing Farm Incomes

In addition to the institutional structure that limits opportunities and incentives to produce, there are a great many economic reasons why the majority of farm families find it just about impossible to increase their real incomes. Peasant producers have such inadequate resources of land and capital that it is very difficult for them to increase their production using existing methods. Technology is often primitive. Services necessary for modern agriculture such as good transportation, research stations, education, technical assistance, and credit are inadequate. Markets are poorly organized and farm product prices are low in relation to the costs of many purchased inputs. Finally, peasants have few or no alternative job opportunities.

Any one of these obstacles to agricultural development might be a crucial limiting factor at any particular time and place. All are interrelated; if one is overcome, peasant economic progress is likely to be stopped short by one of the others. It is necessary to overcome all of them in order to assure continuous and dynamic agricultural progress.

1) *Limited resources* of land and capital present an obstacle for the majority of peasant families to increase their incomes significantly. Let us first consider the question of land.

As was noted earlier, census statistics show that from nearly two-thirds to nine-tenths of the agricultural population lives on small subfamily-sized farms (minifundia) or are landless workers (Table III). The minifundia by definition are too small to provide full employment for the family labor force using customary techniques. The laborers often cultivate small family plots as well as working on the estates' larger operations. In effect, many of the landless laborers are also small peasant producers or *minifundistas*. Adjusting the data to take account of this fact, the proportion of small producers with subfamily-sized parcels in Brazil (where sharecropping is particularly prevalent) and Chile approaches that in the other study countries where the census shows more minifundia.[43]

The operators and their immediate families of subfamily-sized farm units of various tenures apparently make up over half the Latin American rural population. These minifundistas could increase their incomes by working more land. So could you and I, or any large landowner for that matter. But these small producers now have insufficient land to use the labor supply available in their own families, and have few other job opportunities; it can be held that the lack of sufficient land now holds back their production.

There is no doubt that most campesinos who now cultivate small plots believe this to be the case.[44] The peasants are usually convinced that they would be better off enlarging their parcels than working as laborers on the estates, even with better pay. They see the lack of land as a limiting factor for their enterprise.

It is common knowledge in traditional rural areas that land sold as small plots brings a far higher price than land of similar quality and location sold as part of a large estate. One can suppose that this in part reflects the peasants' possibilities of using the land more intensively.[45]

The shortage of land for many peasants was brought home to us when visting an Indian community of over 100 families in the central Andes. The Indians were cultivating potatoes intensively on about 50 eroded hectares. In all directions around the village lay the uncultivated lands of the hacienda, many of them with better soil. The Indians, however, were unable to buy or rent more land. Many worked on the hacienda without wages several days per year in payment for permission to pasture a few animals in the mountains and for the privilege of using the hacienda's roads to reach neighboring town markets.

Looking at Latin America as a whole, however, it is not possible to maintain that the unavailability of potentially productive agricultural land is a serious limiting factor for immediate agricultural development. Much of the arable land now in large estates is left in natural vegetation while there are vast areas of jungle still not incorporated into agricultural production (Tables VI, VII, and VIII). René Dumont once shocked a Chilean audience by saying that a rational distribution of the world farm population in relation to the available land resources that are not now being used intensively would put 25 Asiatics working beside every native campesino. While this may be an exaggeration, anyone familiar with farming in Japan, Southeast Asia, or the Near East can appreciate the tremendous potential for Latin American agricultural expansion.

What is true for the region as a whole is not necessarily so for more limited areas. In the Andean highlands, for example, there is serious overpopulation in relation to available resources. Typical family plots have less than one or two hectares each. The same holds for parts of northeast Brazil and many other areas. It is necessary to take this fact into account when considering the possibilities of making more land available for small producers. In many regions there is a sharp resource limit that would permit at most a doubling in the amount of productive land available per family even if all the land were used as intensively as possible under present economic conditions.

Several studies indicate that the marginal productivity of land in the minifundia communities is relatively high while the marginal returns to additional labor tend to be greatest on the

TABLE VI   Density of Agricultural Population in ICAD Study Countries—1960.

Country	Population per 100 agricultural hectares in farms [a]	Population per 100 cultivated hectares in farms
Argentina	2.1	10.4
Brazil	13.6[b]	43.3[b]
Chile	9.7	79.4
Colombia	29.9	154.3
Ecuador	50.5	108.5
Guatemala	68.7	157.9
Peru	29.3	176.3

Notes:

[a] "Other uses" and "wasteland" are not included. See Table VII.
[b] 1950.

Source: ICAD studies.

large units.[46] Budget analyses of individual cases are particularly revealing about the possibilities of profitable expansion in production if more land and capital could be made available to small producers.

In the ICAD studies, subfamily-sized holdings consistently showed much higher average returns per hectare than the large estates (Table IX). This is true whether comparisons are made on the basis of total land area or only of cultivated land; the same differences were evident where it was possible to take account of

Table VII Land Use by Size Groups in ICAD Study Countries.

Country	Cultivated land [a] Thousands hectares	%	Natural pastures Thousands hectares	%	Forest and brush Thousands hectares	%	Other uses incl. sterile land Thousands hectares	%	Total land in farms Thousands hectares	%
Argentina										
Sub-family	2,232	38.0	2,748	46.8	560	9.5	333	5.7	5,873	100.0
Family	17,420	22.4	47,289	60.9	10,245	13.2	2,700	3.5	77,654	100.0
Multi-family (medium)	8,154	31.1	13,686	52.2	2,641	10.1	1,749	6.6	26,230	100.0
Multi-family (large)	5,934	9.2	45,366	70.8	8,187	12.8	4,606	7.2	64,093	100.0
Total	33,740	19.4	109,089	62.7	21,633	12.5	9,388	5.4	173,850	100.0
Brazil										
Sub-family	1,001	82.2	93	7.6	56	4.6	68	5.6	1,218	100.0
Family	8,287	59.8	2,409	17.4	2,240	16.2	921	6.6	13,857	100.0
Multi-family (medium)	28,705	36.4	29,929	37.9	14,504	18.4	5,790	7.3	78,928	100.0
Multi-family (large)	30,386	22.0	60,229	43.6	39,199	28.4	8,394	6.0	138,208	100.0
Total	68,379	29.4	92,660	40.0	55,999	24.1	15,173	6.5	232,211	100.0
Chile										
Sub-family	40	51.3	23	29.5	4	5.1	11	14.1	78	100.0
Family	306	15.6	862	43.8	594	30.2	204	10.4	1,966	100.0
Multi-family (medium)	535	17.0	1,432	45.5	855	27.1	328	10.4	3,150	100.0
Multi-family (large)	1,751	7.8	8,014	35.6	7,219	32.0	5,534	24.6	22,518	100.0
Total	2,632	9.5	10,331	37.3	8,672	31.3	6,077	21.9	27,712	100.0
Colombia										
Sub-family	941	69.4	247	18.2	67	4.9	101	7.5	1,356	100.0
Family	2,237	36.6	2,279	37.3	1,266	20.7	330	5.4	6,112	100.0
Multi-family (medium)	1,028	16.1	3,095	48.6	1,967	30.9	278	4.4	6,368	100.0
Multi-family (large)	849	6.3	9,001	66.5	3,099	22.9	587	4.3	13,536	100.0
Total	5,055	18.5	14,622a	53.4	6,399	23.4	1,296	4.7	27,372	100.0

133

TABLE VII (continued) Land Use by Size Groups in ICAD Study Countries.

Country	Cultivated land [a] Thousands hectares	%	Natural pastures Thousands hectares	%	Forest and brush Thousands hectares	%	Other uses incl. sterile land Thousands hectares	%	Total land in farms Thousands hectares	%
Ecuador										
Sub-family	740	74.1	106	10.6	55	5.5	98	9.8	999	100.0
Family	516	45.3	129	11.3	221	19.4	273	24.0	1,139	100.0
Multi-family (medium)	395	34.2	209	18.1	245	21.2	307	26.5	1,156	100.0
Multi-family (large)	430	15.9	811	30.0	615	22.7	850	31.4	2,706	100.0
Total	2,081	34.7	1,255	20.9	1,136	18.9	1,528	25.5	6,000	100.0
Guatemala										
Sub-family	444	83.3	20	3.8	37	6.9	32	6.0	533	100.0
Family	240	48.0	89	17.8	127	25.4	44	8.8	500	100.0
Multi-family (medium)	424	36.3	266	22.7	389	33.3	90	7.7	1,169	100.0
Multi-family (large)	367	24.2	208	13.7	780	51.3	164	10.8	1,519	100.0
Total	1,475	39.6	583	15.7	1,333	35.8	330	8.9	3,721	100.0
Peru										
Sub-family	935	68.2	197	14.4	195	14.2	44	3.2	1,371	100.0
Family	382	45.7	270	32.3	79	9.5	104	12.5	835	100.0
Multi-family (medium)	292	27.4	426	39.8	174	16.3	177	16.5	1,069	100.0
Multi-family (large)	937	6.1	9,595	62.6	1,837	12.0	2,961	19.3	15,330	100.0
Total	2,546	13.7	10,488	56.4	2,285	12.3	3,286	17.6	18,605	100.0

Note:

[a] Includes improved pastures.
See Table II for definitions of size classes.
Sources: ICAD Studies.

134

soil quality and location in the comparisons. Both the aggregate country data and individual case studies indicate that average labor returns are only from one-fifth to one-tenth as much on the

TABLE VIII   Principal Uses of Land Not in Farms in ICAD Study Countries (thousands of hectares).

Country	Total land areas	Land in farms	Total	Forest land [a]	Wasteland, brushland, and natural grassland [b]
			Land not in farms		
Argentina	274,821	173,850	100,971	48,367	52,604
Brazil	846,989	232,211	614,778	505,657	109,121
Chile	73,377	27,712	45,665	11,771	33,894
Colombia	108,400	27,372	81,028	63,001	18,027
Ecuador	43,930	6,000	37,930	13,709	24,221
Guatemala	10,510	3,721	6,789	4,017	2,772
Peru	124,457	18,605	105,852	67,715	38,137

Notes:

[a] Figures obtained as a difference between total forest-land (FAO estimates) and brushland and forests in farms taken from the agricultural census of each country.

[b] Difference between the totals of land not covered by the census and the forest-land area.

Sources:

Argentina: Consejo Federal de Inversiones, Consejo Nacional de Desarrollo, *Tenencia de la Tierra*, Buenos Aires, 1963.

Brazil: Conselho Nacional de Estadística, *VI Recenseamento Geral do Brasil, 1950. Censo Agrícola*, Rio de Janeiro, 1956.

Chile: Dirección de Estadística y Censos, *III Censo Nacional Agrícola Ganadero*, Santiago.

Colombia: Departamento Administrativo Nacional de Estadística, *Censo Agropecuario 1960.* Bogotá, 1962.

Ecuador: Dirección de Estadística y Censos. *Primer Censo Agropecuario Nacional, 1954.* Quito, 1956. Junta Nacional de Planificación y Coordinación Económica, *Plan General de Desarrollo Económico y social del Ecuador*, Quito, 1963.

Guatemala: Dirección General de Estadística, *Censo Agropecuario 1950*, Guatemala, C.A. 1955.

Peru: Dirección General de Estadística y Censos, *Primer Censo Nacional Agropecuario 1961*, Lima, 1963.

FAO, *Yearbook of Forest Products Statistics 1962*, Rome, 1962.

FAO, *Production Yearbook 1962*, Rome, 1963.

TABLE IX Relationhips Between the Value of Agricultural Production, Agricultural Land, Cultivated Land, and the Agricultural Work Force by Farm-Size Class in Selected ICAD Study Countries.[a]

Country and size-groups	Per cent of country total in each size-group			Relative Value of Production as Per Cent of Sub-family Farms		
	Agricultural land	Agricultural work force	Value of production	Per hectare of agricultural land	Per hectare of cultivated land	Per agricultural worker
Argentina (1960)						
Sub-family	3	30	12	100	100	100
Family	46	49	47	30	51	251
Multi-family (medium)	15	15	26	51	62	471
Multi-family (large)	36	6	15	12	49	622
Total	100	100	100	30	57	261
Brazil (1950)						
Sub-family	°	11	3	100	100	100
Family	6	26	18	59	80	291
Multi-family (medium)	34	42	43	24	53	422
Multi-family (large)	60	21	36	11	42	688
Total	100	100	100	19	52	408
Colombia (1960)						
Sub-family	5	58	21	100	100	100
Family	25	31	45	47	90	418
Multi-family (medium)	25	7	19	19	84	753
Multi-family (large)	45	4	15	7	80	995
Total	100	100	100	23	90	281

Chile (1955)						
Sub-family	c	13	4	100	100	100
Family	8	28	16	4	47	165
Multi-family (medium)	13	21	23	12	39	309
Multi-family (large)	79	38	57	5	30	437
Total	100	100	100	7	35	292
Ecuador (1954)						
Sub-family	20	b	26	100	100	b
Family	19	—	33	130	179	—
Multi-family (medium)	19	—	22	87	153	—
Multi-family (large)	42	—	19	35	126	—
Total	100	—	100	77	135	—
Guatemala (1950)						
Sub-family	15	68	30	100	100	100
Family	13	13	13	56	80	220
Multi-family (medium)	32	12	36	54	122	670
Multi-family (large)	40	7	21	25	83	706
Total	100	100	100	48	99	224

Notes:

[a] Gross value of agricultural production in all countries except Argentina, where the estimates are of added value. Comparable data are not available for Peru.

[b] No information available.

[c] Less than one per cent.

137

smallholdings as on the large estates. There is a strong presumption that the same relationships hold for marginal returns.

In summary, more land per farm family could be made available in most rural regions almost immediately by bringing suitable lands now in extensive uses into more intensive uses. One barrier to doing this is institutional—the land-tenure structure. Large church-owned estates in Chile recently turned over to peasant cultivators now have 50 per cent more land under cultivation than four years ago. The change in land tenure, however, was accompanied by credit, marketing aid, and technical assistance, making it impossible to say what part the increase in available land alone played in the changed production patterns.

Land is not the only resource in short supply for the small producers. Agricultural capital amounts to only an equivalent of $100 or $200 per family in many minifundia areas. It usually consists of rudimentary shelter, a few animals, hand tools, and an occasional plow and cart.

It is pointless, however, to think of raising incomes through greater investment in existing kinds of capital unless more land is made available per family and technology is improved at the same time. More livestock, hand tools, or farm buildings would bring scant returns. Erosion of overcultivated hillsides is prevalent, and overgrazing is already a widespread seasonal problem. What is required by the smallholders is not more capital of the types now used, but new kinds of capital and more land.

The one resource most small peasant producers have in abundance is labor. Underemployment is prevalent. The ICAD studies estimated that on the average from one-fifth to one-third of the available labor supply is underemployed in the sense that the same output could be obtained with existing techniques and capital but less labor if work organization were improved. Contrary conclusions of some economists who have looked at the employment problem are not at all persuasive. Busy-work expands to occupy available time. Peasants are seldom found sitting idle, but this does not mean that through reorganization of farm activities, the same work could not be accomplished with fewer people—even after taking account of seasonal peak demands for labor. Examples are cited of production falling when peasants leave their parcels to work on a road or construction project, but these prove nothing about the degree of underemployment. Outside jobs increase family incomes far above anything experienced in the past, making it unnecessary to continue cultivation with the same intensity as before. Also, the area sown to subsistence crops tends to be geared to family consumption needs; if the number of consumers decreases, the immediate response is likely to be less production irrespective of the available supply of inexpensive labor.[47]

2) *The backwardness of agricultural technology* in Latin America also keeps incomes low. In Peru nearly one-third of the farm units are cultivated entirely by hand, without even the help of draft animals. In 1961 only 2.6 per cent of Peruvian farms had any kind of mechanical power and most of these were on the coast; in the Sierra there were only 953 tractors for over a million farm families. One animal-drawn plow is available per thousand farm units in upland Guatemala. Many crop varieties and livestock breeds have not changed since colonial—or even precolonial times. Non-organic fertilizers are unknown to most peasants.

Of course, it is practically impossible to improve technology without also increasing the amount of resources per family. Better seeds, fertilizers, or implements raise operating costs and capital investment. Increasing economic returns to scale are not significant with hand methods; but they quickly become apparent when investment is made in a tractor, a stud bull, or a silo. In any event, capital of these kinds can hardly be supported from an acre of potatoes and wheat, ten sheep, a cow or a yoke of oxen even if the peasants should resort to custom service or a cooperative. Cash income is too small and the advantage of replacing overabundant labor is too slight.

Optimists will point out that even though most peasant farms are small there are innovations that are labor intensive such as fertilizer and improved seeds, resulting in more product from the same area, or higher quality sheep that yield more wool and mutton per head. Japan is often pointed to as a successful example of a country following this path in farm progress; the implication is that it could be repeated in heavily populated areas in Latin America.

It is true that much could be done along these lines, but there are many immediate obstacles. In the first place, the necessary experimental work has not been done in most places with the result that higher yielding varieties often prove less hardy than present stock or unsatisfactory in other counts.[48] An example of inadequate research to adapt technology to local conditions was seen in Chile. There in many areas the volcanic soils are high in phosphate-fixing alumina, making phosphates unavailable as a plant nutrient until after heavy and expensive initial applications.

Politicians and some economists, when comparing United States agriculture with that of underdeveloped countries, like to point out that one farm worker in the United States now supplies 31 other people (including his family) with farm products.[49] The inference is that modern agricultural technology would result in similar productivity increases in Latin America. The corollary of this proposition, however, is often forgotten—that it takes more than ten non-farm workers to supply each farm worker and his family with non-farm produced inputs and producers' goods. In other words, the U.S. farm worker is simply a part of a highly productive and complex society. A U.S. farm worker set down alone in the Andean highlands with only his hands would be in a very different situation than in Iowa, and it is doubtful that even the advantage of his far superior education would help him in such a situation.

Modern agricultural technology cannot be incorporated overnight in any case. The average investment in reproducible farm capital (machinery, livestock, etc.) per farm worker in the United States (not per farm, which is twice as great) amounted to about $18,000 in 1964. The average non-land capital farm investment per farm worker in much of rural Latin America is less than $500. Let us assume that a long-term average growth rate of reproducible farm capital a little better than 3 per cent annually could be attained.[50] The stock of non-land farm capital could then double about every twenty years. At this rate, even if the Latin American rural population does not increase, invest-

140

ment per farm worker could equal that of the present-day U.S. farm worker only after more than 100 years of constant rapid accumulation.

Our concept of agricultural change and how it happens is an outgrowth of U.S. experience. As a consequence it tends to be rather parochial. Agricultural progress is seen as taking place when enough individual farmers abandon their traditional practices for more productive modern ones to affect aggregate production and costs. To accomplish this, farmers must employ new techniques and inputs, such as improved seeds or fertilizer and feeding practices; they must also make adjustments throughout their farm enterprises in order for the innovations to be as profitable as possible. Agricultural progress doesn't take place all at once over a wide area. On the contrary, a few "leaders" among the farmers are seen to pioneer with better methods and as these prove feasible and profitable they spread to other farmers and other areas. Change is promoted by an efficient extension service, specialized agricultural credit agencies, suppliers of farm inputs and the purchasers and distributors of farm products.

In much of Latin America, however, this process of agricultural change and progress is not operative. As was seen earlier, the agrarian structure results in the absence of practically all of the conditions necessary for promoting rapid agricultural change along the lines of this idealized U.S. model.

3) *The services farmers require* for commercial development are woefully inadequate in Latin America. Transportation is normally difficult, expensive, and erratic. For example, the cost of shipping fertilizer from Recife to Santos in Brazil is four times greater than the shipping cost from Tampa, Florida, to Santos.[51]

As was seen in the first part of this paper access to an agricultural extension service, experiment stations, or other types of technical assistance is denied most peasants and the majority cannot even send their children to elementary schools. Credit is available mostly at highly usurious terms from merchants, moneylenders, or large landowners. There are few sales outlets for small quantities of fertilizers, improved seeds, or similar inputs, although these can be imported in bulk by large operators.

In one community studied in the Ecuadorian Sierra the peasants had obtained seeds and a little consumption credit from small-town storekeepers who demanded and received in return a half-interest in the forthcoming crop. Out of thousands of peasant producers interviewed in the ICAD studies, only one or two per cent ever had contact with an extension agent or other agricultural technician, although the majority of the large farmers had received some kind of technical advice or credit.

As in the case of land, limited development gains might be achieved through a better distribution and utilization of existing services. A more equal distribution of services, however, would have only a relatively small impact on the total agricultural problem. In Ecuador, for example, there is only one extension worker available per 4,000 families; although these extension agents now work mostly with large owners, there is no way that they could attend more than a fraction of the small producers.

Greater public investment in services—roads, education, extension agents, experiment stations, credit, and the like—is required. But again, the short-run possibilities are not great. Financing these services could be accomplished only through increased taxes and fiscal reforms or by shifting public expenditures from other items (for example, the military). Both alternatives have limited chances for adoption in the near future unless there are profound political and social changes.

It has been estimated that the income of the large landowners is great enough to permit them to invest much more than they do at present in agricultural services and production. With respect to Chile, Nicholas Kaldor affirms that, "If the ratio of consumption to gross income from property were reduced to levels found in Great Britain, 30 per cent, the personal consumption expenditures of this group would fall from 21.1 to 10.3 per cent of the national income. The freed resources would be more than sufficient to double investments in fixed capital and inventories. This means that, according to official estimates, net investment would increase from 2 per cent to 14 per cent of net national income." [52]

Marvin Sternberg sought to test this assertion for the agricultural sector on the basis of a sample of 20 large landholders

142

in central Chile.[53] The propensity to consume of this small sample was shown to be relatively high in comparison with similar income groups in industrialized countries; on the average they spend on consumption goods about 84 per cent of their disposable incomes (after taxes) of some 40,000 escudos (Eo 1 = US$ 1.00 in 1960). Half of this consumption, Sternberg estimates, was consumptuary (See Table X).

TABLE X   Income and Expenditures of 20 Large Farm Operators of the Central Valley of Chile, 1960 (escudos of 1960).[a]

	Total	Average	Percentage
A. Gross Personal Income	897,300	45,865	100.0
From Agriculture	807,400	40,370	(90.2)
From other sources [b]	89,900	4,495	(9.8)
B. Personal Taxes	46,600	2,330	5.1
C. Disposable Income (A–B)	850,700	42,535	94.9
D. Expenditures:			
Consumption	712,200	35,610	83.7
Personal Investment	119,400	5,970	14.0
E. Personal Savings (C–D)	19,100	955	2.3

[a] Escudo = one dollar in 1960.
[b] As reported by the producers themselves.

Source: Marvin Sternberg, "Chilean Land Tenure and Land Reform" Ph.D. Thesis, University of California, Berkeley, 1962, Table 25.

As already noted (Table V), the 10,000 largest producers in Chile received about 37 per cent of the total agricultural income, and enjoyed an average annual net family income equivalent to about US$16,000. This means that the large landowners received about 3.5 per cent of the gross national income of Chile. If an amount equivalent to only 50 per cent of these incomes had been invested in the country over the past decade, the *net* rate of domestic investment could have doubled. In other countries where agriculture is a more important part of the national income and resource ownership is even more greatly concentrated, such as Peru, the potential investments from this source are relatively even more important.

The possibility of increasing investment in agricultural

services by redirecting part of agricultural income obviously exists. But, the political and social structures in Latin America make realization of this practically impossible.

4) *Market and price policies* in the countries studied are not conducive to agricultural development. Agriculture remains stagnant and peasant incomes do not increase in part because marketing facilities are inadequate and markets are poorly organized, oligopolistic, and inelastic. This is true both for the markets in which farmers must buy their inputs (to the extent that they use purchased inputs) and for those in which they sell their products.

The small peasant producer wanting seed, fertilizers, and tools or even salt, flour, and coffee must buy from the local merchant or hacienda commissary, often paying huge mark-ups. The mark-ups are explained partly by the small volumes required in each village. Also costs of transportation and marketing are high enough to keep potential competition to a minimum even where local monopolies are not politically sanctioned. Cash transactions, in fact, are often of minor importance compared with barter and purchases on credit. More important, institutional restrictions on the entry of new buyers and sellers stem from the land-tenure structure and the accompanying social and political organization. Agricultural inputs such as improved seeds or mineral fertilizers are seldom available for sale in small quantities at any price. Large buyers can import these items in bulk; this is not true for suppliers of many local markets. Effective campesino cooperatives are almost non-existent.[54]

Frequently the small producer is forced to sell his products at low prices to the landlord or to the merchant who has given him part-time employment or credit. Otherwise he deals with itinerant buyers who roam the countryside or he takes his produce to the local market. In either situation, geographic isolation of many rural areas permits relatively few buyers to control the market to the disadvantage of the small producers. Larger regional agricultural markets are frequently regulated by Mafia-like groups that effectively exclude independent producers or merchants from competing freely.

Moreover, the short-run price elasticity of demand for individual farm products is relatively small with the result that a good crop often fetches such a low price that total farm income is less than for a poorer yield. While the longer-term trend is one in which demand for foodstuffs will increase even faster than production in the study countries, this does not protect the peasant producer from disastrous price drops for his produce due to temporary local gluts. On the other hand, as was seen earlier, any tendency for either a short-run or a secular rise in the farm prices of many crops because of poor harvests, increasing population, and incomes is often forestalled by price controls, monopolistic purchasing, and expanded imports from abroad. At the same time tariff protection to encourage national industries keeps prices of many things which small farmers buy relatively high.

Strong government regulation of markets to encourage competition and the organization by producers of efficient agricultural cooperatives with real bargaining power could obviate some of these market difficulties. But even if this were possible, and with the present land tenure structure it usually is not, it would be a long time before sufficient investment could be made in storage and processing facilities, transportation, and the like to improve substantially the present situation.

Assuming that a reasonably efficient marketing system could eventually be created, there are still limitations on agricultural expansion related to the demand and prices of farm products. With overall population growing at about three per cent annually in the Latin American countries, and with urban centers expanding two to five times faster than the rural communities (see Table XI) there should be a possibility for farmers to increase their per capita sales to the cities by at least one or two per cent annually, merely because of population increase. In addition, as per capita incomes in the cities are also growing on the average by one or two per cent per year, this will result in a further expansion of urban markets for agricultural products.[55] Total growth (rural and urban) of domestic demand for foodstuffs should be between three and four per cent per year in all study countries except Argentina. An increase in demand for agricultural experts is also likely, although this is more difficult to estimate because many competing regions, such as Africa, are rapidly increasing their production of export crops.

TABLE XI   Estimated Urban and Rural Rates of Population Change 1950–70, ICAD Countries.

Country	Average annual rate of growth		Per cent rural	
	Urban	Rural	1950	1970
Peru	3.8	1.5	61	47
Ecuador	4.4	1.9	72	60
Colombia	4.8	1.0	72	54
Guatemala	3.1	2.0	75	70
Argentina	2.4	.3	34	25
Brazil	4.9	1.5	64	46
Chile	3.6	.4	41	26

Source: ICAD data.

In practice, not all agricultural regions in Latin America will be in a position to benefit equally from these growing markets. The comparative advantages of favorably situated areas close to metropolitan centers will enable them to supply the cities more cheaply. In remoter areas such as the Andean highlands, which through the use of traditional technologies are already being farmed at close to both their extensive and intensive margins, farmers may be hard-pressed to accommodate the local population increase, despite the migration to urban centers. The profits from using new inputs such as machinery and fertilizer, will generally be greatest in regions where transport costs to urban markets are lowest, the climate is most favorable, the soils are most responsive, and the land-man ratio and topography prove conducive to mechanical cultivation.[56]

Alternative Job Opportunities for the Farm Population

Accelerated agricultural development alone cannot be expected to result in substantially improved incomes for most of the peasantry. Modernization of agriculture offers a solution only if many rural residents move to more productive urban jobs. A continuously growing productivity per worker is only foreseeable if new technology is introduced and the ratio of land and other resources per worker is vastly improved. In other words, accelerated migration from many heavily populated agricultural regions is a necessary condition for their continuous development.

What are the prospects of accelerating migration from poor rural communities? It is difficult to be very optimistic about the short-run possibilities. On the one hand, the absorptive capacities of the industrializing metropolitan areas are limited. On the other hand, usually physical, economic, and institutional barriers prevent poor peasants from depressed areas from obtaining good farm lands or finding remunerative agricultural employment in better farming areas.

1) *Migration to other farming areas:* In Peru, Ecuador, Brazil, and Bolivia there have been impressive local migrations to the lower eastern slopes of the Andes and into the edge of the jungles, such as to *La Convención* in Peru, to the Tingo María area in Ecuador, and the region of Santo Domingo de los Colorados in Brazil. But, quantitatively in relation to the nearly one and one-half million families farming the Peruvian and Ecuadorian Sierra, these migrations have been insignificant. In the four Peruvian provinces located in the *selva* east of the Andes (Madre de Dios, Loreto, San Martín and Amazonas) rural population increased by an estimated 77 per cent, or 153,000 persons between 1940 and 1961.[57] But natural growth of the 1940 rural population in these same provinces would have accounted for all but about eight per cent of this increase, indicating a net migration from the highlands to rural areas of these provinces of not more than 15,000 persons during 21 years, or less than one thousand annually. Meanwhile, population growth in the rural Peruvian highlands, before migration, now probably amounts to about 130,000 annually.

Pioneering in the jungle is difficult. Soils are often unsuited for agriculture. The Tambopata pre-colonization study in Peru supported by the United Nations found much of the eastern Andean slopes already settled or too steep for cultivation. Health hazards and climatic changes make adaption by peasants from other areas to jungle life difficult. Even so, there are immense areas of potentially good agricultural land that are unused. The recent rapid colonization of the Beni area in Bolivia and of Northern Parana and Southern Maranhão in Brazil indicates that

147

with proper stimulus many obstacles to settlement can be overcome.

Why then has there been so little movement to the jungle areas? There are two principal obstacles probably outweighing all of the others mentioned. One is the lack of roads. The second is that much of the land is already claimed by large speculators and what is not yet claimed will be as soon as roads and colonists arrive giving it a market value. Without roads it is practically impossible for the colonists to get to the selva or to market any of their products. In addition, there is little incentive to move to the selva as new arrivals find they have no security but must work as laborers, almost without pay, or as tenants delivering much of their product to the landlord claiming title to the area they have cleared.

With a vigorous road-building program and a thorough reform of the land laws and their administration, colonization of frontier areas would undoubtedly proceed much more rapidly. Even so, it would be naive to expect that settlement of the frontier could take place rapidly enough to relieve population pressures in heavily populated areas such as the Sierra.

It has already been shown that there are many possibilities for using more labor in agriculture by the adoption of more intensive farming systems. It is not realistic, however, to think that intensified production will not also be accompanied by labor-saving technology. In the first place, the principal sources of new technology in Latin America are the United States and Europe, where labor-saving techniques are at a high premium. Secondly, tractors, planting machines, harvesters, milking machines, and similar labor-saving devices have great social and political appeal. Most farmers and planners are ready to make considerable economic sacrifice to have them even though there is a redundant work force. They are symbols of progress.

2) *Rural-Urban Migration:* By far the most important opportunities for the rural peasantry to find alternative employment are found in the cities. Comparing 1950 with 1960 census data, it is possible to estimate net rural to urban migration during that decade for the ICAD countries. Except for Guatemala, where this migration amounted to less than one-half of one per cent of the

1950 rural population per year, the average annual rates of out-migration were between one and three per cent, a little over half of the natural increase in the rural areas of the study countries (see Table XII). The average annual rate for all Latin America was one and one-half per cent or just about 50 per cent of the rural increase.

TABLE XII Estimated Rural to Urban Migration in the ICAD Study Countries between 1950 and 1960.

| Country | Net rural to urban emigration (in thousands) | Net rural to urban migration as a per cent of 1950 | |
		Total population	Rural population
Peru	649	8.3	13.6
Ecuador	390	12.2	17.0
Colombia	1,345	11.9	16.6
Guatemala	75	2.7	3.6
Argentina	1,466	8.6	24.9
Brazil	6,301	12.1	19.0
Chile	685	11.9	29.0

Source: ICAD studies.

A recent study by the Economic Commission for Latin America sees no possibility of urban employment increasing rapidly enough to absorb even the natural increase in rural Latin America during the coming two decades.[58] Instead it foresees a continuation of past trends with rural population growing about 1.5 per cent annually and urban at about 5 per cent. This study points out that the "marginal" unemployed urban sectors (in *callampas* and *favelas,* etc.) are already large in every Latin American metropolis. The growth of industrial output has been relatively slow (four to eight per cent annually) since 1950, and industrial employment has not increased proportionally.

In most of the study countries, it seems probable that urban employment will not expand rapidly enough during the next few decades to pull the excess rural populations into the cities. In spite of an exceptionally high rate of industrial investment in Brazil since World War II, the number of industrial workers has increased only at about 2.8 per cent annually.[59] In Chile indus-trial output was growing at nearly 6 per cent annually between 1950 and 1960, while industrial employment grew only at about two per cent per year during the same period. Modern labor-saving technology and capital make for highly disproportionate rates of growth of industrial output and employment (which, after all, is one meaning of economic progress). Increasing automation in the future will widen this gap.[60]

On the other hand, if industrial output increased much more rapidly in the future even without directly employing propor-tionally more workers, urbanization might also accelerate. The political process in one way or another brings about a wider distribution of the product if it really becomes available. This is reflected in the rapid increase of employment in the "service" sector. The basic determinants then of the cities' capacities to absorb more migrants in the near future will be the relative size of the present urban industrial base and the rate of the country's overall economic growth.

The admittedly very inadequate, available data indicate that at present about one-fifth of the labor force in the five less urban-ized of the study countries is employed in industry and construc-tion, and about one-fourth in services. Both are primarily urban occupations (see Table XIII). Chile and Argentina present a much more urbanized employment structure, however.

Economic growth has been proceeding at from 3 to 5 per cent annually in all of the study countries except Argentina during the last 15 years (see Table XIV). This is approaching the Punta del Este goal of 2.5 per cent per capita, and some develop-ment planners hope to raise the sustained rate of growth to 6 or more per cent (a rate actually achieved by Peru since 1960).

The economic historians, however, are not very sanguine about maintaining such high growth rates for long periods, although they would grant the possibility of rapid spurts in growth during a decade or two.[61] Even the exceptional post-war growth of Mexico looks much less impressive when the two preceding decades are included in the average.

It appears reasonable to conclude then as ECLA has, that the urban populations in the Latin American countries will probably continue to expand at about five per cent annually during

TABLE XIII Distribution of Economically Active Population, 1960.

Country	Basic [a] Thousands of people	%	Secondary [b] Thousands of people	%	Tertiary [c] Thousands of people	%	Undetermined Thousands of people	%	Total Thousands of people	%
Peru [h]	1,622.0	51.9	524.3	16.8	852.5	27.3	125.8	4.0	3,124.6	100.0
Ecuador	784.1	49.8	314.1	20.0	360.2	22.9	115.8	7.3	1,574.2	100.0
Colombia [e,f]	2,338.8	51.1	934.0	20.4	1,302.0	28.5	–	–	4,574.0	100.0
Guatemala [g]	781.6	65.6	182.3	15.3	222.8	18.7	4.7	0.4	1,191.4	100.0
Argentina	1,503.7	19.8	2,426.8	31.9	2,900.0	38.2	768.6	10.1	7,599.1	100.0
Brazil [d]	12,730.9	64.9	2,333.4	11.9	4,501.3	23.0	48.5	0.2	19,614.1	100.0
Chile	735.5	31.5	583.6	24.5	903.2	37.8	148.5	6.2	2,388.8	100.0

Notes:

[a] Includes agriculture, forestry, hunting, fishing and mining.
[b] Includes manufactures, electricity, gas, water and construction.
[c] Includes trade, transport, communications and services.
[d] 1950.
[e] 1957–59.
[f] Includes Chocó, Comisarias and Intendencias.
[g] Estimate.
[h] 1961.

Sources:

Argentina: Consejo Federal de Inversiones, Tenencia de la Tierra, page 92, Bs. As. 1963.

Brazil: Instituto Interamericano de Estadística, America en Cifras, 1961, Tomo VII, pag. 56, Washington 1963. ICAD estimates —1964.

Chile: Dirección de Estadísticas y Censos, Población del Pais (Censo 1960), p. 54, Santiago, 1964.

Colombia: Consejo Nacional de Política Económica y Planeación, Plan General de Desarrollo Económico y Social, Primera parte, pag. 67, Bogotá, 1961.

Ecuador: Junta Nacional de Planificación y Coordinación Económica, Desarrollo y Perspectivas de la Economía Ecuatoriana, Tomo I, Quito, 1963.

Guatemala: L. J. Ducoff, Human Resources of Central America, Panama and Mexico 1950–80, UNECLA, 1960 (B/CN.12/548).

Peru: Instituto Nacional de Planificación. Dirección Nacional de Estadística y Censos, Sexto Censo Nacional de Población, p. 230, Lima, 1961.

151

TABLE XIV   Rates of Increase of Gross National Product at Market Prices, ICAD Countries 1950–1963

| Country | Rates of annual increase | | Per Cent |
	1950–55	1955–60	1960–63
Peru [a]	5.1	4.8	6.7
Ecuador	5.3	4.5	4.0
Colombia	5.3	4.0	4.6
Guatemala	2.6[b]	4.8	0.8[c]
Argentina	3.2	2.7	−0.8
Brazil	5.7	5.8	4.9
Chile	3.1	3.4	4.1[d]

Notes:

[a] Cuentas Nacionales 1958–63.
[b] 1952–55.
[c] 1960–62.
[d] ICAD estimate.

Source: ECLA, Estudio Económico de América Latina, Vol. I, Julio 1964.

the next two or three decades, but not by more. This implies a continued migration during the next few years from rural areas to the larger cities which is less than the rate of rural population increase, except possibly in Chile and Argentina.[62]

It must be remembered, however, that this estimate is based on the cities' probable absorptive capacity for employing new migrants. It does not take into account the possibilities of a major calamity such as a widespread crop failure or rural violence of the type that has recently plagued Colombia, pushing population out of the rural regions more speedily. If such a "push" should occur, urbanization would possibly proceed even faster. There might also be considerable pressure toward migration to other countries—as occurred following the Irish potato famine in the last century.

Lauchlin Currie has suggested that a rapid solution to the agricultural development problem could be found in a big push in industrial output and investment accompanied by rapid migration out of the rural areas.[63] While he neglects to work out the figures, he leaves the impression that a technical revolution could be achieved in agriculture and the number of rural families substantially reduced within a decade.

We have seen that even with a continuation of the recent rapid rates of urbanization there is not likely to be any reduction in the number of subsistence farmers in much of Latin America for the next twenty to thirty years. For Currie's solution to be effective, it would be necessary to urbanize two or three times more rapidly than in the past. This would require a very big push indeed.[64]

He proposes to achieve this "mobilization economy" primarily by means of new fiscal policies, drastically redistributing incomes and increasing investment while at the same time operating existing plants and equipment at full capacity. Attainment of the political conditions required for such an all-out effort appears rather remote and would require a thorough-going social revolution. But assuming that this were possible, it is questionable whether either the increased out-migration or investment that would be necessary to revolutionize Latin American agriculture within ten years or so is within the realm of faintest possibility.

The proportion of U.S. population on farms has fallen steadily since 1820, when it was about 72 per cent (the same as Guatemala's today) to about 9 per cent in 1964. The absolute numbers of U.S. farmers did not cease increasing until about 1920, and did not seriously decline until after 1940. Colombia, with nearly 60 per cent of its population still agricultural, has an occupational structure in some ways similar to the United States economy at the end of the Civil War in 1865. Currie proposes to accomplish in less than a generation the same degree of structural change in employment that cost the United States a full century to make. Granting that the important advances in technology are already available, it is difficult to see how the process of rural modernization could be carried out for a large, under-developed, densely populated region in a few years no matter how stringently and vigorously all available resources are mobilized.

Japan and the Soviet Union have shown that the process of structural change can be shortened substantially, but it took Japan, with its relatively slow population growth, over seventy years of accelerated modernization to reach the point where agricultural population began to decline rapidly. Soviet agriculture is still in difficulties after more than forty years of "forced-draft" industrialization.[65]

Talking about development problems of another part of the world thirty-five years ago, R. H. Tawney observed that economic growth "is a social product that owes as much to the jurist as to the inventor." [66] Development is at best a long process. But there are many limited opportunities for increasing agricultural growth and peasant incomes immediately and for speeding up development. To take advantage of these opportunities both agrarian reform and new agricultural policies are required.

AGRARIAN REFORM AND AGRICULTURAL DEVELOPMENT POLICIES

We have sketched the outlines of three analytically separable issues—agricultural policy, agrarian reform and agricultural development. The three problems are interdependent in the sense that any actions toward solution of one of them will have repercussions on the others. In these concluding paragraphs we will advance some hypotheses about how agrarian reform and agricultural development are related in the Latin American countries studied. It is the main thesis of this paper that the strongest connection between reform and development is to be found in the area of agricultural policy.

In the seven ICAD studied countries there had been no serious agrarian reforms. The Guatemalan reform was too short-lived to warrant conclusions concerning results. Hypotheses about interactions of reform and development based on the ICAD studies can be at best speculations. Actually there have been relatively few experiences in agrarian reform in Latin America. Only Mexico, Cuba, and Bolivia have experienced reforms on a relatively large scale. To a lesser degree Venezuela and Puerto Rico have attempted to speed up changes in their agrarian structures. Chile is commencing a reform process that may assume major proportions.[67]

Effects of Agrarian Reform on Agricultural Production

It was shown that the present land-tenure structure is

associated with an inefficient use of land and labor, with low rates of investment in agriculture and with few opportunities or incentives to adopt new technologies. To what extent would redistributing the rights and benefits of land ownership in favor of the small producers and to landless tenants directly change this situation?

The answer seems to be that increases in agricultural production resulting from a mere redistribution of rights in land would be rather limited. Access to additional land is only one of the many factors limiting agricultural development. It can not be assumed that removing this limitation—and doing nothing more —would cause a great upsurge in production.

Good agricultural land resources are relatively scarce in the regions of heaviest rural population, such as the Altiplano. In such regions the physical possibilities of expanding greatly the areas of more intensive production have a calculable upper limit, at least until some of the other obstacles to agricultural growth are removed. In most areas of intensively cultivated small plots and large extensively used properties (the latifundia-minifundia complex) the shortage of available land would probably keep production from increasing by more than a maximum of 50 per cent above present levels even after many years of using only traditional technologies.

In practice, agricultural production might not change very much at all in the short-run as a direct result of redistribution in some rural areas. Where land reform has been rapid and at times anarchic—as was the case in post-revolutionary Mexico and Bolivia—some lines of production temporarily decreased. Livestock numbers declined, for example, when campesinos sold or ate breeding stock. Sales of some industrial crops also dropped because of general economic dislocation. There is little evidence, however, that food crop production was greatly affected even in these revolutionary reform areas.[68] The ICAD study of Guatemala indicates that during that country's brief experience with rapid large-scale reform there were temporary production and marketing problems for export crops but a marked increase in corn production for consumption. The rural population consumes more food staples, eggs, meat and vegetables following a land reform, thereby reducing their commercial marketings to the cities. This happened to an important degree in Bolivia and to some extent more recently in Cuba. Reform programs that include real incentives for farmers to increase both production and marketing can be expected to avoid most of this difficulty.

Over a longer period, tenure reform can be expected to show much greater effects on production. These effects, however, are not so much from making more land available to the peasants as from changing incentives, services, and marketing facilities. In this respect, the effects of reform could conceivably even be negative if the limited entrepreneurial and organizing functions of the previous landlords were not adequately replaced by the state or by new local institutions.

In considering the productivity problem in relation to reform little has been said concerning possible economies or diseconomies of scale. The omission was deliberate. In the first place, as was pointed out earlier, the very concept of the farm operating-unit has only very limited applicability in the traditional agricultural structure. The large properties are often not operating-units at all but a complex of producing and consuming units under a central administration that may be more political than economic.

Secondly, the real economies of scale in agriculture are associated with particular functions such as plowing, planting, harvesting, marketing, transport, and processing. These functions are all separable one from another. They are not necessarily strictly associated with property rights or even with the farm unit itself; cooperatives, custom work, and numerous other institutional arrangements can be used to obtain economies of scale in different production, processing or marketing functions. The redistribution of tenure rights does not necessarily mean the division of large properties into individual family farms. The *ejidos* in Mexico, the proportional profit farms in Puerto Rico, the state farms in Cuba and the *asentamientos* in Chile are all examples of other alternatives in a land reform process.[69]

Finally, there simply is no convincing evidence concerning economies or diseconomies of scale in relation to size of farm in Latin American agriculture.[70] One reason for this is that operating units and property units do not coincide, nor do census-defined operating units and the multitude of smaller sharecropper and laborers' units that are included in the larger estates.

156

Another is the difficulty of agreeing on what efficiency criteria to use in evaluation. Should labor be counted as a cost valued at current wage rates when there are no alternative job opportunities? If not, what "shadow prices" should be used? What is the cost of land when market values include prestige, political power, social status, credit security, capitalized subsidy payments and its value as a hedge against inflation? Finally, many advantages of scale are offset by disadvantages such as absentee management and problems of labor organization. The net result is that existing studies of economies of scale in the study countries show highly confusing and contradictory conclusions.

Reform and Income Distribution

A second relationship between agrarian reform and agricultural development is to be found in income distribution. There is no question that a real reform can redistribute income to the benefit of the campesinos by absolving them of the tributes and rents by which landlords now expropriate most of the peasants' surplus above subsistence. In Bolivia, for example, peasant incomes and consumption rose after the reform even where production was uneffected.[71] Of course, peasant incomes will not increase if the payments to the landlord are simply made to the state or tradesmen following reform, but this is unlikely. It was seen that in Chile a redistribution of the income now going to the large farmers could theoretically double peasant incomes. In the *asentamientos* [land settlements] organized under the present reform program, peasant incomes have actually increased by about this amount. Without greater agricultural production and accelerated out-migration, however, incomes resulting from reform would be dissipated by population increase within a generation or so.

While there is no question that reform usually can increase peasant incomes, the direct effects on development are more difficult to assess. The demand for industrial goods will undoubtedly be stimulated. But whether this greater domestic market in turn stimulates industrial growth or merely increases imports and inflation depends on the nation's economic and social structure. The beneficial results often claimed for a wider

157

income distribution presuppose changes in national economic policy.

Whether the more widely distributed post-reform incomes help spark development by changing propensities to invest depends on such a host of variables that generalizations are also impossible about this point. If the incomes of the large landlords previously spent on consumption or relatively non-productive capital were redirected into high priority investments either by the state or other groups, this would obviously stimulate economic growth. But there is no a priori assurance that a simple redistribution of land and income would have this result. The land reform would have to be accompanied by tax and fiscal reforms. Otherwise peasant increased consumption might more than offset indirectly increased investments.[72]

Nonetheless, the conclusion seems reasonable that the seigneurial distribution of income is as antagonistic to economic development in Latin America as it has been in other regions in which large plantations and near-feudal conditions prevailed.[73]

Agrarian Reform and Social Structure

Agrarian reform by definition alters the relationships between groups in the use of land—land-tenure institutions are changed. To the extent that reform is effective, rural social structure will be modified, the combination of institutions in rural areas will be different. The traditional "patronal" system is eliminated with much that it implies for social organization if the reform is a real one and not only a slogan. As a consequence the local political structure will change. So too will the social incentives to produce, to invest, to innovate and to migrate.

We know very little, however, about just what these changes will be in Latin America or by what social mechanisms they take place. Clarence Senior attempted to evaluate this for La Laguna region in Mexico.[74] There have been several partial studies of individual communities affected by reforms.[75] There have also been various studies of the effects of reform on rural social structures in other parts of the world.[76] Obviously the degree of social change will depend in part on the nature of the reform, whether it is part of a more thoroughgoing social revolution or is

158

merely limited to local land tenure institutions. It will also depend on the initial situation, on the local social systems prevailing when the reform takes place.

In Bolivia, many observers have reported greatly increased interest in education on the part of the peasants since reform, following the elimination of the old patrons. The author believes he can see a marked difference in the attitudes toward education and political participation in the Bolivian Aymara communities where the hacendados were eliminated and those across lake Titicaca in Puno. Maddox reports an increased propensity to invest and become entrepreneurs on the part of former large landowners in Mexico after the revolution.[77] Many of us visiting the new Chilean asentamientos think we see a dramatic change in the peasants' desires to produce, to build up farm capital, to improve their farming methods, and to educate their children.

While there is wide agreement among students of agrarian reform that the changes in social structure and incentives are possibly the most important of any in their long-term consequences for future development, there has been surprisingly little systematic testing of this hypothesis. The current ICAD evaluations of the reforms in Mexico, Bolivia, and Venezuela should permit a firmer understanding of what the changes in local social systems have been and how they occurred.

Agrarian Reform and Agricultural Policy

The connections between agrarian reform and agricultural policy are more direct and obvious. A profound land reform eliminates the large landowners as the principal policy clientele. If the reform is a real one and not a token program, their hold on local political power is broken. At the national level they cease to be an important interest group either in advocating policies for their own benefit or influencing the policies of other groups. Connections with the large landowning families are no longer an important prerequisite for political recruitment. New channels of political communication are opened between national centers of power and rural groups. Both political structure and political inputs are altered.

Following reform, agricultural policy as a consequence can

be expected to change both in content and in terms of the benefited clientele. The "strategy" of development will no longer call for the large landowners to be the principal modernizers and the capital accumulators. In all probability, however, the new agricultural development "strategy" will not rely only on the campesinos either. The State may take practically all of the initiative in both technical change and capital formation. Or it may leave these functions to new groups of commercial farmers and investors. Or the State may share these responsibilities with campesino and new commercial groups. Which of these alternatives is adopted may depend somewhat on the ideology of the reform movement. It will undoubtedly depend much more on how much representation the campesinos have managed to attain in the new political structure and how well they are organized to press their interests.

Following reform in Mexico, for example, agricultural policy, especially after 1940, became much more development-oriented than before the revolution. The new clientele of agricultural policy, however, does not seem to have been so much the campesinos as the commercial farmers. The larger investors, and the medium- and small-sized commercial operators (the "kulaks") became the new principal beneficiaries of agricultural policies.

In Bolivia and Puerto Rico much the same tendencies as in Mexico are apparent—large commercial operators and medium and small commercially oriented farmers are the new clientele of agricultural policy. In Cuba on the other hand, it seems that the former landless agricultural workers have been among the chief beneficiaries of reform, as have some of the small producers.

In all of these countries, however, the State has assumed a primary role in agricultural development. National technical assistance programs and credit agencies are the chosen vehicles for agricultural modernization. In Chile, for example, present agrarian reform plans call annually for training about 1,000 new agricultural agents of one kind or another to work directly with the campesinos and to take the leadership in agricultural development (the various state agencies combined employed a total of less than 1,000 agents working directly with farmers in 1964). If one reviews the experiences of Egypt, Italy, Japan, Puerto Rico,

Venezuela, Yugoslavia, Rumania, or Poland following reform, the same tendencies are evident.

What were the changes in political structure in these countries? To what extent were these a result of agrarian reform and to what extent were they a cause of it? Do the changes in political structure "explain" the new agricultural policy orientations?

We can only pose these questions here. Our hypothesis is that if the reform really redistributes control of the good land among the peasants, they will become a more important political force. Peasant organizations become feasible. Peasants will be a major interest group. National political parties become concerned with peasant problems. Communications between peasant groups and the State improve. Recruitment from peasant ranks increases. As a result, agricultural policy is altered to take this new clientele into account.

Even if the peasants are not fully incorporated into the political system immediately, and their lack of education and traditional social inferiority makes this difficult, national agricultural policy is still likely to become more conducive for development. The small- and medium-sized farmers, urban investors, middle class tradesmen and government officials replace the former landlord elite. History shows many examples of successful development strategies benefiting primarily these new clienteles, even though the campesinos still get a relatively poor deal from official policies. I know of no examples, however, where development strategy was able to rely principally on aiding the traditional large landowners.

Paradoxically, where orderly land reform is possible through normal political processes, it is less necessary for accelerated development than where it is not. Thus land reforms are commonly the consequence of riots, demonstrations, and revolutions (anomic interest groups), or of outside pressures such as defeat in a war, that have led to a breakdown of the established political and social systems.

If our reasoning is correct, in most situations large-scale land reform is revolutionary in that it changes political structures.[78] Unless there have already been sufficient modifications of political structure to permit the groups pressing for agrarian reform to make their interests effective, reform can not be expected to take place through the established political system. But if the political system has evolved sufficiently to make reform a possible policy "output" so should it be possible to redirect other agricultural policies, even without land reform.

Historical perspective shows agrarian reform to be more a result than a cause of development.[79] As economic development and urbanization progress, and pressures mount to change the traditional rural society there are increasing social and political stresses and tensions. Agricultural policies are increasingly inconsistent with development requirements. At this point, the traditional agrarian structure becomes an obstacle to continued rapid development and agrarian reform can be said to be "necessary."

Land-tenure institutions may be reformed abruptly early in the development process, as they were in Mexico and Bolivia, or the changes may be delayed until development is well under way as they were in Cuba and Chile. Tenure reforms may be revolutionary and violent, they may be rapid but relatively orderly, or they may take place only slowly as rural manpower is absorbed into other activities, accompanied by increasing agricultural productivity and growing competition for workers among landowners. What is certain is that the traditional agrarian structure with its peculiar land tenure institutions will be modified sooner or later as development takes place.

One cannot say that land reform per se is either a sufficient or always a necessary condition for accelerated economic growth, even where traditional agrarian structures prevail. After all, there is ample historical evidence of expanding material wealth being created by slaves and serfs as well as free farmers. More than anything else, rapid development requires firm and capable leadership in modernizing the economy and in providing the appropriate economic organizations and incentives to produce and invest.

Taken by itself, land-tenure reform may neither stimulate nor retard economic growth, at least in the short-run. It may be a prerequisite, however, for new groups to displace the traditional elites—to enable the "modernizers" to mobilize the resources and the efforts required for a big push. In any case, the direct effects of land-tenure reform on agricultural development will be most evident through the reorientation of agricultural policies, policies that before land reform served the interests of the larger land-owners almost exclusively.

Some of my fellow "reform-mongers" have been rather put out with me for concluding that while redistributing rights in land to benefit the campesinos in Latin America lies well within the area of social and political choice, more rapid agricultural development will not automatically follow—that this depends largely on subsequent policies. Also they do not like to admit that orderly land reforms are not likely to be possible in most countries unless there have first been profound modifications in political structures.

Supporters of the agrarian status quo are even less ready to admit that economic disaster will not be the immediate consequence of reform; many have equated this claim of an expanded area of free-will with attempts to subvert society or an attack on Christendom. They fail to recognize that it is idle to expect agricultural policies which would stimulate more rapid agricultural development until there have been real reforms in the traditional agrarian structure.

The argument that one's fellow men should be given more opportunity because it is good for business has always sounded rather hollow. The contrary position—that the selfishness and privileges embodied in the status quo in rural Latin America and institutionalized by the traditional land tenure structure must be preserved to maintain rapid economic growth—is even more hypocritical. One suspects that we economists, like the medicine men before us, have been much more prone to lend (or sell) our support to the second fallacy than to the first one.

NOTES

[1] FAO, *The State of Food and Agriculture*, 1966: Table II-2 and Annex Tables 1-B, 8-B, 12-A and 12-B.

[2] *"El Campesino"* (Revista de la Sociedad Nacional de Agricultura de Chile), Santiago, junio 1966, pp. 34–36.

[3] The Inter-American Committee for Agricultural Development (ICAD) was formed under the "Alliance for Progress" to coordinate the agricultural programs of five international agencies: FAO, ECLA, IDB, OAS and IAIAS.

ICAD, *Relaciones Entre la Tenencia de la Tierra y el Desarrollo Socio-Económico del Sector Agrícola en: Argentina, Brasil, Chile, Colombia, Ecuador, Guatemala y Peru,* Washington, 1966.

[4] Policy combines the political functions of rule-making, rule application, and rule adjudication. It may be regarded as a product of the system's inputs. These inputs include the functions of political socialization and recruitment, interest articulation, interest aggregation and political communications. See Gabriel Almond and James Coleman, *The Politics of the Developing Areas,* Princeton University Press, Princeton, 1960. See especially pp. 3–64.

[5] These are "non-associative interest groups" in Almond's terminology. Almond and Coleman, op. cit.

[6] Almond and Coleman, op. cit. See "Latin America" by George Blanksten, pp. 455–531.

[7] Celso Furtado, *Organización y Administración del Planeamiento,* Instituto Latinoamericano de Planificación Económica y Social, Santiago, mayo 1965 (preliminar, mimeo).

[8] The structure of the Ministry in Brazil, for example, was strongly influenced by a French Technical Assistance Mission in 1906 that based its recommendations on the French colonial agricultural administrative systems in Africa.

[9] The present Chilean Government is finding this administration by "Consejos" one of the biggest obstacles to implementing new agricultural policies: see Plinio Sampaio, *Algunos Problemas Administrativos de la Reforma Agraria en Chile* (Informe Preliminar), ICIRA document, Santiago, 1965.

[10] CORA (Corporación de la Reforma Agraria); INDAP (Instituto de Desarrollo Agropecuario); ONRA (Oficina Nacional de Reforma Agraria); SUPRA (Superintendencia de Reforma Agraria); IERAC (Instituto Ecuatoriano de Reforma Agraria y Colonización); INCORA (Instituto Nacional de Colonización y Reforma Agraria).

[11] A survey among employees of one Latin American agrarian reform agency found that over three-fourths of the professional and technical personnel had been recruited from larger landowners' families.

[12] ICAD, Chile, pp. 175–79.

[13] Charles T. Nisbet, *Interest Rates and Imperfect Competition in the Informal Credit Markets of Rural Chile,* University of Wisconsin Land Tenure Center (unpublished document).

[14] Nathaniel Wollman, *Water Resources of Chile: An Economic Model,* Latin American Institute for Economic and Social Planning, November 1965 (mimeo, preliminary draft).

[15] "In the traditional ascriptive society, with its clear distinctions between social strata, and the continuing estate-like association of each class with the performance of particular economic and social functions, there is an appropriate kind of education for each class and no categorical need for their articulation in a single system, with the possibilities of movement from one system to another." Andrew Pearse, *The Instrumentality of Education Systems,* paper presented to the Cornell Conference on the Development of Highland Communities, Ithaca, March 1966 (mimeo).

[16] ICAD is now carrying out studies of agricultural education facilities and requirements. Studies under the direction of Alvaro Chaparro have

now been made in Ecuador and Chile. See ICAD, *Ecuador, The Future of Research, Extension and Education in Agriculture*, Washington, D.C., Pan-American Union, 1965.

[17] ICIRA, *Informe del Estudio de la Comunidad de Pupuya, Navidad*, Department of Rural Sociology, Vol. I and II, 1966 (draft, mimeo).

[18] See Sergio Bagú, *Economía de la Sociedad Colonial*, Buenos Aires, El Ateneo, 1949. Also Celso Furtado, *The Economic Growth of Brazil*, University of California Press, 1965.

[19] The Economic Commission for Latin America, FAO and the Inter-American Bank are now making an exhaustive study of use and requirements for agricultural inputs and the policies affecting them in Latin America. See: CEPAL/FAO/BID, *Fertilizantes* (Chile, Brazil, Colombia, Argentina), Santiago, 1966 (mimeo, preliminary drafts).

[20] Adams, et al., *Public Law 480 and Colombia's Economic Development*, Michigan State University, 1964.

[21] The material included in this section was developed more fully in: Solon Barraclough and Arthur Domike, "La Estructura Agraria en Siete Países de América Latina," *El Trimestre Económico*, Vol. XXXIII, No. 130, Mexico, abril/junio 1966; and Solon Barraclough, "The Latin American Problem," in *Latin America and the Caribbean*, ed. Claudio Véliz, London, Anthony Blond, Ltd. 1968.

[22] ". . . social structure, as the term is commonly used, refers to. . . . the combination of institutions classified according to the functions each performs. As such it is the most inclusive working unit with which social scientists deal. . . . In choosing the national social structure as our generic working unit, (one adopts) a suitable level of generality: one that enables us to avoid abandoning our problems and yet to include the structural forces obviously involved in many details and troubles of human conduct today." C. Wright Mills, *The Sociological Imagination*, New York, Oxford University Press, 1959, pp. 134–35.

[23] For example, see Dwight B. Heath, "Land Tenure and Social Organization," *International Economic Affairs*, Vol. 13, No. 4 (1960), pp. 46–66; and Andrew Pearse, "Agrarian Change Trends in Latin America," *Latin American Research Review*, Vol. I, No. 3 (1966).

[24] The political basis of land tenure has been emphasized by numerous students of the question. See, for example, Doreen Warriner, *Economics of Peasant Farming*, London, 1939; Kenneth Parsons, "Agrarian Reform Policy as a Field of Research," *Agrarian Reform and Economic Growth in Developing Countries*, Farm Economics Division, U.S. Dept. of Agriculture, Washington, D.C., March 1962; and Erich H. Jacoby, *Agrarian Unrest in Southeast Asia*, Oxford, 1949.

[25] Andrew Pearse, "Agrarian Change Trends in Latin America," op. cit.

[26] The hired labor on many commercial family-sized farms is of a different social class and often from a different ethnic group than the operators. The farm owners' names in parts of southern Chile are almost 100 per cent German, the laborers' Spanish-Indian. Many small commercial farmers are similar to the "kulaks" of Eastern Europe in that they form a distinct economic and social group in a countryside dominated by large landowners and in which workers and small peasants are far more numerous.

165

[28] For an excellent account of these tenure arrangements see Rafael Baraona, "Una Tipología de Haciendas en la Sierra Ecuatoriana," *Reformas Agrarias en la América Latina,* ed. Oscar Delgado, México, Fondo de Cultura Económica, 1965.

[29] Andrew Pearse, *Tenza: Un Estudio de Minifundio,* Bogotá, Universidad Nacional de Colombia, Facultad de Sociología (mecanografiado). Andrés Pascal, *La Localidad Rural como Unidad de Desarrollo: estudio de un caso en Valle de Hurtado, Coquimbo,* ICIRA, 1966 (mecanografiado).

[30] ICIRA, *Informe del Estudio de la Comunidad de Pupuya, Navidad,* op.cit.

[31] Eric Wolf, *Peasants,* Modern Anthropology Series, Englewood Cliffs, N.J., Prentice Hall, 1966, p. 55.

[32] In Chile the ICAD study estimates that sharecroppers and *inquilinos* with plots on the large estates account for about one-fourth of the total value of crop and livestock production of the entire country.

[33] "Production beyond the level of the caloric minimum and the replacement level obeys social incentives and dictates." Eric Wolf, *Peasants,* op. cit. p. 6.

[34] The ICAD investigators in Guatemala visited Panajachel, which had previously been studied by Sol Tax in *Penny Capitalism.* Panajachel was one of the most commercially oriented smallholders' communities encountered in upland Guatemala, confirming Tax's observation that it was atypical in the region with respect to its highly intensive land use. The smallholders were eager to accept new farming methods where they were profitable and were found to be using imported seeds from Holland in some instances. Nonetheless, there were serious institutional obstacles to improving incomes even in this exceptionally progressive community. The principal one was the scarcity of cultivable land available. Tax observed in his study that "The difference between Indian and Ladino is the over-ruling factor in the use of land . . ." (p. 41). Not only did the Ladinos (mestizos) use their land differently than the Indians, but on the average each Ladino family owned eight-and-one-half times more land than each Indian family—obviously a problem associated with land-tenure institutions.

Professor T. W. Schultz in *Transforming Traditional Agriculture,* New Haven, Yale University Press, 1964, has argued that the problem of agricultural development in traditional smallholders' communities can usefully be reduced to purely economic terms without resorting to institutional or cultural explanations. He concludes that the principal problem in transforming traditional peasant societies is one of introducing "unconventional inputs," chiefly education. He uses Tax's data from Panajachel to support his thesis. Tax's study can be interpreted just as well to show that the problems associated with agrarian structure are strategic in developing these communities.

[35] ICIRA, *Estudio de la Comunidad de Pupuya, Navidad,* op. cit.

[36] Economists customarily look at the problem of land redistribution as though compensation could be calculated readily in terms of goods and services. Their remedy for resolving land tenure conflicts is to divide a "bigger pie," leaving every one better off than before. In societies where a high value is put on the possession of power, the problem is not so simple. Power has to do with relationships between persons and groups;

if one has more, others have less. It is a "zero sum game," par excellence. There may be some positive marginal rates of substitution between power, status and material goods, but this would have to be investigated for each society individually as value patterns in one culture may be expected to be substantially different than those in another.

[37] See ICAD, "Peasant Organizations, Community Development and Agrarian Reform," *Tenencia de la Tierra y Desarrollo Socio-Económico del Sector Agrícola: Informe Regional* (Apéndices), UP-G5/058-A, Washington, abril 1966, p. 14.

[38] Several recent studies in Chile have examined the processes by which new values penetrate traditional rural communities. ICIRA, *Informe del Estudio de la Comunidad de Pupuya, Navidad,* op. cit.

[39] Peasants' immediate aspirations, however, may not reveal the full extent of their deep discontent with the traditional structure. "In peasantry, the limitation of expectations becomes socially an act of loyalty to the group, an act of grace and tact. For the individual this limitation is a self-protective measure." Mehmet Begiraj, *Peasantry in Revolution,* Cornell Research Papers in International Studies—V, Ithaca, 1966, p. 10.

[40] Oscar Domínguez, *Aspiraciones de los Inquilinos de la Provincia de Santiago,* ICIRA document, 1966 (informe preliminar).

[41] Arnold J. Toynbee, *America and the World Revolution,* London, Oxford University Press, 1962, p. 185.

[42] The material in this section was developed more fully by Solon Barraclough, *Economic Implications of Rural-Urban Migration Trends from the Highland Communities,* paper presented at the Conference on the Development of Highland Communities in Latin America, Cornell University, Ithaca, March 1966.

[43] The 1964 Census in Chile adopted the FAO definition of a farm unit, counting small tenant parcels as separate farms. While the coverage of these tenant units (*subtenencias*) on the large estates was only partial, the preliminary data indicate that the number of minifundia will be shown to be about double what they were under the 1955 definition.

[44] Oscar Domínguez, *Aspiraciones de los Inquilinos en la Provincia de Santiago,* op. cit.

[45] It is a circular argument to say that investment in more land by the small producers is not justified because returns on the add'ional investment are low. The price of land in smallholder communities is relatively high because it is scarce and greatly in demand. If the *minifundistas* had the possibility of purchasing good land on equal terms with the large owners one could imagine the "land market" allocating this resource more efficiently. Not only must the smallholders pay far higher prices for their land than the estate owners, but they are excluded from the market by their social and legal inferiority, their lack of credit and their lack of knowledge. To draw broader generalizations about returns to land in economic development from the operations of the limited land markets in smallholder communities is a dubious exercise at best. For evidence from Chile of an overvaluation of small parcels in relation to large properties, that may vary from one to twenty times greater in value per hectare, see Oscar Domínguez, *Tributación Agrícola y Reforma Agraria,* Centro de Estudios e Informaciones Sociales, Santiago de Chile, 1965.

[46] The marginal productivity of the various factors of production has

been estimated for the central zone of Chile by Carlos O'Brien Fonck. See *An Estimate of Agricultural Resource Productivities by Using Aggregate Production Functions, Chile, 1954–55*, M.S. Thesis, Cornell University, 1966.

[47] The notion that there is widespread peasant underemployment is criticized by T. W. Schultz in *Transforming Traditional Agriculture*, op. cit. Schultz defines the "labor of zero value" to exclude any possibility of changing work organization. This makes disguised unemployment practically a definitional impossibility. In practice, many producers organize their production as though labor had little real cost. For them, there are no alternative employment alternatives. In addition, wide distribution of the available work is an accepted means of dividing the product among those who must consume it to live. The author has watched many harvesting operations of this kind where the work could have been accomplished easily with only a fraction of the people employed but where dividing the work among many workers was the social mechanism for assuring a distribution of the harvest. This can be visualized theoretically either as operating with a less "efficient" production function than the best one at the command of the enterprise with existing techniques, or as simply operating at a point well below the surface of the production function with existing techniques and knowledge.

[48] For a discussion of the importance of adopting technical progress to be suitable for local conditions in the underdeveloped countries, see F. F. Hill, *Some Viewpoints Concerning Agricultural Development*, Farm Economics Association, New York, December 1965. Dr. Hill's analysis, however, considers only one of the many interdependent factors limiting income possibilities.

[49] *Changes in Farm Production and Efficiency*, Statistical Bulletin No. 233, USDA, July 1964.

[50] This is a reasonable estimate assuming a long-term growth rate of gross national product of only 5 per cent. Of course, investment in roads, schools, and other infrastructure not included in the U.S. investment per worker and figure would have to grow proportionally. See Alvin S. Tostlebe, *Capital in Agriculture*, Princeton, Princeton University Press, 1962.

[51] CEPAL/FAO/BID, Brazil, *Fertilizantes*, Santiago, 1966 (Primer borrador, mimeo).

[52] "Problemas Económicos de Chile," *El Trimestre Económico* (Mexico) XXVI (2) No. 102 (April–June 1959), p. 196.

[53] *Chilean Land Tenure and Land Reform*, Disertation submitted in partial satisfaction of the requirements for the degree of Ph.D. (Economics), University of California at Berkeley, September 1962.

[54] See Antonio García, Enrique Astorga, Pedro Hidalgo, Enrique Contreras, *Cooperativas y Financiamiento Agrícola en un área lechera y forestal de Llanquihue*, ICIRA, Santiago, 1966 (mimeo., preliminary draft).

[55] This income effect, however, is relatively small because the distribution of increased incomes is very unequal with most of it going to families with fairly high living levels already; hence income elasticities of demand for food averaged only about .4 to .5. It is estimated that income redistribution would increase these elasticities considerably. See United Nations Economic and Social Council, ECLA, *Agriculture in Latin America: Problems and Prospects*, Mar del Plata, Argentina, May 1963 (E/CN.12/686).

[56] Nothing is said here about the prospective "Latin American Common Market." While it could result in broader and more competitive agriculture it might also cause some of the poorer regions with competitive disadvantages to be even more hard-pressed.

[57] Maurice Brucker, *Land Settlement in the Peruvian Selva,* Cornell University, 1966 (unpublished research).

[58] United Nations Economic and Social Council, Economic Commission for Latin America, *Geographic Distribution of the Population of Latin America and Regional Development Priorities,* Mar del Plata, Argentina, May 1963, E/CN.12/643.

[59] Celso Furtado in *Political Obstacles to Growth in Brazil,* Chatham House, Oxford University Press, April 1965, p. 252 ss.

[60] "Creation of Employment Opportunities in Relation to Available Manpower," in *Urbanization in Latin America* (UNESCO) Paris, 1962. And also see Gunnar Myrdal, "The United Nations, Agriculture and the World Economic Revolution," *Journal of Farm Economics,* November 1965.

[61] Reviewing the growth rates of today's principal industrial countries (U.S.A., Great Britain, Russia, France, Germany, Sweden) Kuznets finds no three decade periods since the middle of the last century in which gross product grew by more than 4.5 per cent annually or per capita product by more than 3 per cent. Simon Kuznets, *Economic Growth and Structure,* New York, W. W. Norton, 1965, p. 307.

[62] With a 3 per cent population growth, only after *urban* population has increased to over 60 per cent of total population could a five per cent rate of urban expansion absorb all of the rural increase. As the relative size of rural population falls below 40 per cent, migration would begin to cut into the absolute numbers of the agricultural population. This can only be expected to happen after twenty to thirty more years of continued rapid urbanization for Latin America as a whole where the rural population is about 50 per cent of the total.

[63] Currie talks primarily about Columbia but implies more general conclusions. Lauchlin Currie, *Accelerating Development,* New York, McGraw-Hill, 1966.

[64] Alexander Gershenkron, "A Big Push Requires a Big Effort: Either the State or Some Financial Institutions or Both Must Be Willing to Make It," *Economic Backwardness in Historical Perspective,* Cambridge, Harvard University Press, 1962, p. 29.

[65] The papers presented by Polish and Yugoslavian participants at the recent World Land Reform Conference in Rome brought out the difficulties of rapid agricultural modernization given the necessarily gradual change in the urban-rural employment structures. See WM/45444, *Agrarian Reform and Economic Development in Yugoslavia* and WM/45847, I. *Structural Change and Development of Peasant Farms in Poland;* II. *Agricultural Circles and the Process of Structural Change in Private Farms;* III. *Experiences of State Farms in Poland,* FAO, World Land Reform Conference, Rome, June–July 1966.

[66] R. H. Tawney, *Land and Labor in China,* London, George Allen and Unwin Ltd., 1932, p. 130.

[67] There are now ICAD studies going on in Mexico, Argentina, Venezuela, and Bolivia. These analyses provide information that will permit much firmer generalizations about the intimate connection of traditional

land tenure systems and mass exploitation of the peasantry. These studies were begun in 1965 under the direction of Dr. Thomas Carroll of the Interamerican Development Bank.

[68] See W. E. Carter, *Aymara Communities and the Bolivian Agrarian Reform*, University of Florida Monographs, Social Sciences, No. 24 (Fall 1964), and Casto Ferragut, *Reforma Agraria en Bolivia*, FAO, La Paz, November 1964 (preliminary report). The Carter study shows how limited the effects of land reform may be at the local level beyond some immediate income redistribution, if it is not complemented by other measures based on a thorough understanding of the local social structure.

[69] For a discussion of another alternative see: Mario C. Vasquez and Henry F. Dobyns, *The Transformation of Manors into Producers' Cooperatives*, Comparative Study of Cultural Change, Department of Anthropology, Ithaca, Cornell University, January 1964. The conflicting evidence in relation to scale in the Mexican *ejidos* is discussed in Solomon Eckstein's excellent study *El Ejido Colectivo en Mexico*, Fondo de Cultura Económica, Mexico D.F., 1966.

[70] See Solon Barraclough, "Comments on Economics of Farm Size and Agricultural Development" in the forthcoming book *Agriculture and Economic Development* being published under the auspices of the Committee on Agricultural Economics of the Social Science Research Council.

[71] See Carter, *Aymara Communities and the Bolivian Agrarian Reform*, op. cit.

[72] Peasant consumption more than doubled on the church lands in Chile divided among former workers and peasants. See William Thiesenhusen, *The Possibility of a Gradualistic Turnover of Land in Agrarian Reform Programs in Chile*, Land Tenure Center, University of Wisconsin, 1966 (mimeo).

[73] Alfred H. Conrad and John R. Meyer analyzed the economics of slavery in the U.S. South. While slavery as an institution appears to have been economically profitable, they concluded that it produced an income distribution so skewed that it was difficult to support the mass market necessary for the development of local consumer-goods production. "Seigneurial consumption was not likely to be a substitute for the broad market that could have made it profitable in the South to manufacture consumer goods more sophisticated than the most elemental of subsistence wares. Also, seigneurial display that rested upon consumer debt, whether that debt was held within the South or by northern financiers, was inconsistent with economic growth. This inequality need not have restricted income growth in the presence of strong demand pressures in the world cotton markets. However, it is not simply the size but the distribution of income that is crucial for structural change, and it is in respect to the degree of inequality that slavery could have injured the South's early chances for industrialization." Alfred H. Conrad and John R. Meyer, *The Economics of Slavery, and other Studies in Econometric History*, Chicago, Aldine Publishing Co., 1964, pp. 228–229. The analogy with the present development problem in much of Latin America is obvious. Logically inequality of income distribution would not necessarily deter development if a large portion of total income were invested in productive enterprises necessary for economic growth even though returns were low because of limited markets. But this is not a real possibility given seigneurial tastes and ex-

penditure patterns. See also Thomas Carroll, "Reflexiones sobre la distribución del Ingreso y la Inversión Agrícola," *Temas del BID*, Año I, No. 2 (Agosto 1964), Washington.

[74] Clarence Senior, *Land Reform and Democracy*, Gainesville, University of Florida Press, 1958.

[75] For example, see Carter, *Aymara Communities and the Bolivian Agrarian Reform*, op. cit.

[76] For example, R. P. Dore, *Land Reform in Japan*, London, Oxford University Press, 1959.

[77] James G. Maddox, "La Revolución y la Reforma Agraria" in *Reformas Agrarias en América Latina*, ed. Oscar Delgado, Fondo de Cultura Económica, México, 1965.

[78] Neil Smelser, *Theory of Collective Behavior*, Glencoe, Ill., 1962, presents a theoretical framework for "norm-oriented" and "value-oriented" social movements that appears highly applicable for analyzing land reforms. Economists, on the other hand, generally try to fit land reform into an ends-means framework. For example, Professor Thorebecke advances the proposition that land reform may be an appropriate policy measure during the early stages of development and suggests that it be analyzed within the framework of a Tinbergen-type decision model. This approach seems highly unrealistic. Thorebecke himself admits that land reform is a revolutionary measure, but fails to explain how a government policy advisor or bureaucrat can get away with making revolutions. Erik Thorebecke, "Agrarian Reforms as a Conditioning Influence in Economic Growth," *Agrarian Reform and Economic Growth in Developing Countries* (Sponsored by the North Central Land Tenure Research Committee, The Farm Foundation, and the Farm Economics Div., Ec. Research Serv.) Farm Economics Div., U.S. Department of Agriculture, Washington, D.C., March 1962.

[79] Ismail Ajami, *Land Reform, A Sociological Interpretation* (a thesis presented to the Faculty of the Graduate School of Cornell University for the Degree of Doctor of Philosophy), Ithaca, Sept. 1964.

II

Masses
and
Urbanization

5

DANIEL GOLDRICH, RAYMOND B. PRATT,
AND C. R. SCHULLER

The Political Integration
of Lower-Class Urban
Settlements in Chile and Peru

INTRODUCTION

This research report concerns some aspects of the process of
national political integration relating to residents of four lower-
class settlements on the urban periphery of Santiago, Chile, and
Lima, Peru. All these settlements have recently been established,
are permanent, and have obtained or are in the process of obtaining legal title to the land. Three of these settlements have their
origins in squatter invasions.[1] The fourth is a government housing project, composed partly of invaders and partly of applicants
who successfully qualified through the "normal" administrative
process of the National Housing Corporation. The areas are commonly stereotyped by more prestigious elements within the
nations as slums, but they are actually being improved and consolidated, and, as such, should be sharply distinguished from
deteriorating areas, or true slums. The residents have exhibited
a behavior and orientation crucial to the process of national
development. In this respect they represent an increasing, highly
significant human resource, as yet unrecognized by most Latin
American government officials and social scientists generally.

The two components of national political integration of concern here are (1) politicalization, the process of becoming aware of, involved in, and disposed to make use of the political process; and (2) the extent of support for, acquiescence to, and opposition to the political system and its subsystems. It is assumed that the more politicalized and supportive these sectors of the metropolitan lower class are, the more likely they are to develop basic national citizenship orientations regarding rights and responsibilities.

Four problems regarding change in political integration are dealt with: the role of the local association in the settlements, the impact of severe sanctions on the level of politicalization, the assessment of politicalization as a continuous or discontinuous process, and patterns of political legitimacy orientations.

The data are derived largely from interviews, substantially open-ended in character, conducted with samples of male adult residents of the four communities during the period of May through July, 1965.

METHODS

This is a study of lower-class male adults. In Chile and Peru, the work force is divided mainly into workers and employees, the distinction based on manual versus other labor. Our respondents are all such workers or lower-level employees of the janitor, porter, and petty service variety. Also included are such occupations as street vendor, small (home) storekeeper, etc. Within each of the four settlements, the initial sampling unit was the household, with one male adult (18 years or over) interviewed in each selected household. In the two Santiago areas, a very recent census was available, and households were randomly selected from it. The interviewers selected respondents randomly from the household. In the two Lima *barriadas*, block and dwelling maps were used to assign areas to interviewers, who selected households and respondents by availability, although care was taken to disperse the selection throughout the area. The interview schedule had been pretested in Santiago. The same form, with only language changes (suggested by people with experience in the barriadas) to promote comparability, was used in Lima. The interviewers in both cities were social workers and social science students who had had training and experience in interviewing lower-class people.

Since so little survey research has been done on the political orientations of squatters or the Latin American urban lower class in general, it seemed desirable to use mainly open-ended interviewing techniques so as not to constrict the range of responses. However, the cost of this approach is a time-consuming process of code-making once the data are in, and thus only one analysis deck of IBM cards has been available for present purposes. It is clear from our reading of the interviews and our coding experience that the response is a problem, particularly with regard to the (relatively few) items of the Likert-scale, and less so for other forced-choice items. Analysis and control of this phenomenon will be needed. On the other hand, response set seems most apparent in some of the settlements that were studied but are not included in this report, such as a very poor, provisional *callampa*.* Furthermore, it is equally apparent that some interviewers were more committed and effective than others, and this, too, will require control in subsequent analysis. This is all by way of stating that this *is* a provisional report.

URBANIZATION AND SQUATTER SETTLEMENTS

Squatter settlements are a ubiquitous part of the metropolitan landscape in poorer countries—on hillsides, river banks, tidal swamps, and even garbage dumps within and around the city. These are the homes of hundreds of thousands of Latin Americans; many exist in Lima and Santiago. An estimated one-fourth of the metropolitan Lima population of approximately two million resides in such areas, as does perhaps one-tenth of Santiago's roughly equivalent population. The lower figure in Santiago is a reflection of a major program of squatter settlement eradication and building large-scale, low-cost government dwellings to accommodate those housed in shanties and deteriorating *conventillos* (traditional one-story multiple-family dwellings with minimal facilities). Through this program, another tenth of the

* shantytown set up by squatters—literally: "mushrooming"

metropolitan lower-class population has been more or less permanently settled. (The cost of the program has, however, severely strained the national treasury at a time in 1965 when the new reformist government of Eduardo Frei has come into power committed to peaceful but far-reaching reconstruction of the society. Thus, it is questionable whether in Santiago the phenomenon of squatting can be maintained at a level which is lower than elsewhere generally in Latin America.)

Squatter invasions are the consequence of urbanization and population growth without public or private provision for dwellings for the massive metropolitan lower classes. Reinforcing the effect of immigration and population factors are such "normal" urbanization phenomena as clearance of traditional lower-class dwellings in order to build streets, high-rise commercial establishments, and luxury apartments, and the continuous process of dilapidation of the remaining traditional lower-class quarters. As crowding and rent-squeezing of the poor increase, the only outlet for hundreds of thousands is seizure of unused lands or rental of tiny, makeshift quarters in clandestine settlements run as commercial enterprises.

The prevailing image of these settlements (and also of government housing projects) among middle- and upper-class people and local and foreign social scientists is that of the slum. It is an image of apathy, misery, filth, crime, delinquency, prostitution, and family disintegration. It is also commonplace to view these areas as breeding-grounds for political instability and extremism. Their inhabitants are considered to be in the lowest social stratum, mainly emigrants from rural and provincial areas.[2] The settlements are treated as virtually invariant, and are indiscriminately labeled as barriadas, favelas, callampas, etc., which are the local equivalents of slums.

Actually, squatter settlements represent a wide range of conditions. The pioneering work of such people as John Turner,[3] principally in Lima, and Guillermo Rosenblüth [4] in Santiago introduces some typologies of settlement which differentiate vastly variant syndromes of human conditions. For example, Turner has distinguished two types of squatter settlements, the bridgehead and the consolidation. The bridgehead houses, in which live the poorest of the city's lower class, are located near the urban center sources of employment. Here, crowding is extremely high and conditions generally very poor. These areas are declining in living standards and can be considered real slums. The consolidation, on the other hand, represents an attempt by the more organized and effective (but not, generally, the wealthier) segments of the lower class to attain economic and psychological independence. They seek better dwelling conditions—primarily proprietorship and space, within their economic limits—and these motivations find outlet only in the organized invasion of peripheral, unoccupied land. These settlements thus represent considerable investment and continuously improving living standards. The residents consider them to be permanent, incipient communities, or "towns in formation." (Another type discussed by Turner is the mixed settlement, comprising combinations of the above sets of characteristics, but these will not be considered here.) Three of the four research communities are of the latter, permanent type. The fourth is also permanent, but is one of the new Chilean government settlements. Despite its obvious differences from the others in its relations with government—the receipt of dwellings and substantial urban services from the government, and not just post-hoc title to seized lands—as a public housing project composed partly of invaders, it shares the depreciated status of the other settlements and the condition of being a community in formation. Politically these areas are a virtually unknown quantity.

These towns in formation have some experiences and characteristics important to the whole complex of development. While it is useful to keep in mind the questionable romanticism of "community development" mythology, this should not preclude recognition of what these towns in formation demonstrate. If the preindustrial mode of lower-class orientation is resignation before an immutable world, the invaders represent a significant departure, having successfully manipulated an important part of their environment. They have shown initiative and future orientation (the capacity to waive immediate gratification in pursuit of long-range goals). Many have persevered in the face of a hostile state, and even armed attack on the provisional encampments. One of the more elusive capacities in the underdeveloped world is the capacity for organization, but many of these communities were carefully planned, and their successful establishment reflects a rather high level of organization of land allotment, provision for basic services, representation before the public and the state, etc. The capacity for organization seems not to derive from any mystical ancestral communalism,[5] but to be a creative response of a highly selected, self-recruited set of people to an environment otherwise foreclosing opportunity. Theirs has been a major achievement, for independence in dwelling and land is the major way to economic and psychic security for the lower class [6] when industrialization lags far behind urbanization and population growth, and ways out of national poverty remain unknown even to highly educated planners and intellectuals. In the face of their reputation for social disorganization, these settlers reveal remarkably little of it; crime, promiscuity, broken homes occur infrequently, particularly in comparison with the bridgehead settlements and traditional city slums. Though born as illegal invasions, these communities display a prevailing orientation toward law and order.[7]

The Four Research Communities (Table I)

The two barriadas on Lima's outskirts had their origin in organized invasions of undeveloped state-owned land in the arid, rocky slopes and valleys of the Andean foothills. Pampa Seca was thus begun in 1958; its invasion was met by relatively passive hostility on the part of the government. Today, it is a settlement of about 30,000 people, with well-defined, relatively broad, unpaved streets, lined with houses mostly of brick and adobe. The original shacks of reed matting have been largely replaced by permanent structures in various stages of improvement and elaboration. The government has agreed to install water facilities, but despite some substantial installation of pipes, water is not yet universally available, and must still be individually purchased from private trucks that regularly pass by selling water by the barrel.

El Espíritu was invaded in 1962, an act met by the government with both police harassment and army attack on the squatters' huts. After protracted confrontations of this sort, with some

TABLE I   Background Data on the Four Settlements.

	Lima			Santiago		
	Pampa Seca	El Espíritu	Santo Domingo	S.D. Applicants	S.D. Invaders	3 de Mayo
Age of settlement (years)	7	3	4		7	4
Size of settlement (thousands)	30	10	12			1
	%	%	%	%	%	%
Born in capital metropolitan area *	9	12	41	35	51	24
Length of residence in capital:						
less than 3 years	6	6	1	1	0	4
less than 5 years	11	18	3	1	0	12
12 years or more	61	56	80	81	86	64
Education:						
illiteracy	1	2	7	8	7	10
completed 5 or 6 primary years	48	41	35	35	29	30
some secondary or more	19	17	17	10	20	9
Family size:						
3 people or less	8	18	6	5	7	14
6 people or more	65	47	65	77	52	53
Age: 39 years or older	43	28	28	43	15	39
"How far do you think your children can really go in school?":						
primary	17	22	40			46
secondary-tech./commercial	17	21	12			8
secondary-liberal arts	39	34	41			38
university	26	15	5			6
"How much opportunity has a child of this area to attain the position he deserves in society?":						
good opportunity	28	21	34			24
not very good	61	47	50			60
none	10	29	14			15

* Hereinafter, the data reported are from the survey. For each group, N is as follows: Pampa Seca, 127; El Espíritu, 119; Santo Domingo, 191; Santo Domingo Applicants, 79; Santo Domingo Invaders, 59; 3 de Mayo, 98.

deaths and destruction, the invaders were allowed to stay. A second invasion resulted in over-crowding and diminutive lot assignments. This time, the government interceded to reduce the serious internal conflict and to rationalize the settlement, promising services and the acquisition of adjacent private lands to permit more decent individual plots, in return for the settlers' commitment to abide by government plans and to agree to a payment schedule resulting in final individual titles to the land. El Espíritu had about 10,000 residents at the time of the study. Great changes had taken place since the invasion, most apparent in home construction and improvements, although water and electricity were still lacking. At the time of the study, the government had just made available the expropriated adjacent lands, and many of the residents were moving into their new homesites. The level of construction activity on weekends was furious, and work continued into the night.

3 de Mayo is a callampa established apparently with little public notice about 1960 in the Santiago periphery, the location and layout of which have been deemed appropriate by the Housing Corporation for "radication." This means that the settlement has won a presumption of legal permanence from the government. The government began to negotiate with the private owners of the hitherto unused invasion site a few years ago for purchase. This is supposed to be followed by large-scale government assistance in home construction and the installation of urban facilities. In the meantime, water is obtained from standpipes located intermittently along the muddy streets, and electricity is available. 3 de Mayo has a population of about 1,000.

Santo Domingo is one of the new Chilean government housing projects located along the periphery of the capital's working-class districts. At an early stage of site development in 1961, a massive squatter invasion occurred. The police surrounded the area and political tensions rose. The Chilean Left supported the invaders, and the Right was shocked by the seizure of public land designed to meet the housing needs of those who had registered at the Housing Corporation and patiently proceeded to qualify for housing under construction. A compromise was reached such that those invaders who could qualify by "normal" criteria for project housing would receive it, but the

182

remainder would be moved to vacant government lands, where minimal assistance in settlement would be provided. There are two major recruitment patterns in Santo Domingo. About 40 per cent of the residents were successful applicants, having approached the government or been approached as residents of callampas by government social workers and become enrolled, qualifying through a point system based on number of children, prospects for meeting the (relatively low) monthly quota payments consistently, etc. About 30 per cent were either direct invaders of the project site or invaders of other government projects who won recognition of their desperate housing situation and were transferred into Santo Domingo. The remaining residents included (1) those who had qualified through negotiations between the Housing Corporation and labor union or company committees and (2) relatives of the otherwise qualified. Our analysis of Santo Domingo will treat the community sample as a whole, and the "normal" applicants and invaders separately. (The otherwise recruited as described above will not be considered separately because of their small number in the sample, and because we want to focus on the extreme cases represented by normal application and invasion.) Santo Domingo today has about 12,000 residents. They are housed predominantly in single-story dwellings on individual plots. The original housing was minimal. It is currently being replaced by more substantial brick structures. Water, electricity, and sanitary facilities are provided for each dwelling. The size of the lots, though small, allows for gardens and such activities as chicken-raising. As in the case of the two barriadas and as projected for 3 de Mayo, the residents are proprietors, who are to receive legal title upon completion of monthly quota payments amounting to a long-term mortgage.

There is a great deal of variation among the four communities in demographic background and socio-economic indicators, but much that confirms the generalizations made above about permanent squatter settlements. On the basis of our survey data, for example, the majority of the male adult residents are migrants from provincial and rural backgrounds, the proportion ranging from about 90 per cent in the two barriados to 76 per cent in 3 de Mayo and 59 per cent in Santo Domingo. These are not extremely recent, awestruck arrivals in the metropolis. Only

6 per cent or less have resided in the capital less than three years, and less than 20 per cent fewer than five years, while a majority ranging up to 80 per cent have lived there twelve years or more.[8] In countries where even in the capital cities large proportions of the lower class fail to pass beyond the first few years of primary education, these people seem to range from somewhere above the bottom to a relatively high education. For example, a recent field study of Santiago's callampas found that 29 per cent of the sample was illiterate.[9] Illiteracy occurred in 10 per cent of the cases in 3 de Mayo and but 7 per cent in Santo Domingo, while 39 per cent had completed five years of primary schooling or more in 3 de Mayo and 52 per cent had done so in Santo Domingo. Educational attainment was even higher in the two Lima barriadas (though Chilean educational levels in general substantially exceed Peru's), where 67 and 58 per cent of the samples had completed five primary grades or beyond. The residents can thus be distinguished primarily as migrants, but experienced in urban life and as relatively educated (in fact, highly so in the Lima cases) in their lower-class metropolitan context.

Prevailing family sizes are large: from about half to two-thirds of the samples indicate households of six people or more, while small families (three persons or less) are uncommon. Since the great majority of the respondents are less than 39 years of age, this means young children and probably more to come, so that the importance of opportunities for the next generation is apparent. These are high-achieving people, with large families, and relatively high expectations for their children (if we accept educational expectations as a good measure of parental ambition in general). Asked how much education they believed their children could attain, from 53 to 82 per cent indicated some secondary schooling or more, referring usually to a liberal arts education, traditionally a middle-class curriculum, and not merely technical or commercial training.[10] Meeting this expectation will require a very large-scale expansion and improvement of the two nations' secondary and university educational facilities. Along with these ambitions, however, there exists an overwhelmingly widespread sense of deprivation in opportunity for the young. Asked what opportunity a child in this area has to achieve his deserved place in society, the preponderant response was negative, though relatively few aside from the El Espíritu sample replied, "no opportunity."

Local Associations (Table II)

Latin American politics has been characterized by extreme underdevelopment of an infrastructure, or organizations that function to integrate rulers and ruled, to articulate the interests of sectors of the citizenry, and to convey to them the interests of the political elite. This organizational underdevelopment is associated with low levels of national integration. Despite the existence for many decades of labor unions in the Latin American metropolitan areas, this condition has largely persisted, with the qualified exception of the few situations bordering on the totalitarian (Perón's Argentina, Castro's Cuba), where the elite organized the society to an unusually high degree.

In this relative void, one of the potentially significant characteristics of the new settlements is the organization of local associations [11] which invade, represent their interests before outsiders, and promote the internal development of the communities.

The local associations of the new settlements help the settlers meet their needs through mobilizing their own efforts and those of government agencies. Potentially, other functions might also be performed, such as educating the government elite in the capabilities of the settlers and providing it with a means to explain its plans, priorities, and problems to the settlers, mobilizing them for the efforts necessary to implement such plans, etc.

Our data indicate, however, that participation in the local association tends to atrophy as the settlement becomes established, a tendency which Mangin has suggested generally to be the case with barriadas.[12] Of the four, 3 de Mayo and El Espíritu have a distinctly lower level of completion of homes and installation of urban services, while the level of membership in the local association is markedly higher than in the more developed counterparts. Furthermore, within the Santiago pair and the Lima pair, personal interest in the activities of the association is also higher in the less developed settlements; and personal evaluation of the association's helpfulness varies in the same way between

TABLE II Local Association, Local Government, and Associated Programs.

	Lima						Santiago			
	Pampa Seca %	P.S. Orig. Invaders* %	P.S. Late-comers %	El Espíritu %	El Esp. Orig. Invad.* %	El Esp. Late-comers %	Santo Domingo %	S.D. Applicants %	S.D. Invaders %	3 de Mayo %
Membership in local association	10	13	3	22	21	8	6	1	10	21
"How interested are you in what the local association does?":										
very much	8	13	3	8	8	12	28	23	40	36
substantially	13	13	12	21	21	19	15	13	14	26
a little/not at all ("there is no association")	76	70	85	68	68	62	54	64	46	39
Evaluation of extent of help given by local association:										
much	9	23	6	21	22	15	32	26	44	30
some	21	17	12	33	35	35	27	28	24	23
none/do not know	67	53	70	45	37	46	41	46	29	47
"How interested are you in what the municipality does?":										
very much	11									
substantially	17									
a little/not at all	71									
Evaluation of extent of help given by municipality:										
much	6									
some	28									
none/do not know	65									
Evaluation of extent of help given by Cooperación Popular (Lima)/Promoción Popular (Sgo.):										
much	20			10			35	34	36	18
some	18			17			28	32	24	24
none/do not know	62			73			37	34	40	58

* We have distinguished here between original invaders and a set of the most recent invaders in the two barriadas, omitting from analysis those of intermediate residence. The N for Pampa Seca original is 88, of

186

the two barriadas. The only deviation is the slightly more positive evaluation of the association's helpfulness in (developed) Santo Domingo compared to (underdeveloped) 3 de Mayo.

The fact that higher interest and positive evaluations occur more frequently in both Santiago settlements than in both Lima settlements qualifies the relationship. It suggests that the local association may be becoming institutionalized in the two Santiago cases, not in regard to active participation, but as an intermediary political agency, perhaps mediating between the community leadership and the government hierarchy. There is evidence of this in the slightly more prevalent positive evaluation of but lower participation in the association in Santo Domingo compared to 3 de Mayo. This apparently reflects recent government policy of allocating some services to the new projects through the association. The policy could reverse the tendency for total atrophy of intermediary agencies with the increasing consolidation of the community and provide a new integrative mechanism between government and settlers. This mediation role would certainly be an important function, given past lack of communication between them, but the character of the relationship would appear to be paternalistic (participation *is* much lower in Santo Domingo than in 3 de Mayo), and, as such, it would probably not involve some of the other highly significant political functions previously mentioned that would require a more active, contributory role on the part of the settlers.

Within the settlements, those who have taken the most risk are also those who most sustain the local association. Data are available on three of the four cases (excepting 3 de Mayo) that distinguish between original invaders and latecomers in the barriadas and between invaders and "normal" applicants in Santo Domingo. It is clear that the most disparaged of the settlers, the original invaders in the barriadas and the invaders in Santo Domingo, provide most of the active participants in the associations. In two of three cases, they are also more interested in the activities of the association (virtually equal to the latecomers in the third case, El Espíritu), and in all three cases, they more frequently evaluate the association as helpful. At this point, we do not know what the substance of their activity, interest, and appreciation is. Conceivably, it is merely personal interest, reflecting little of value for the communities as a whole. Equally conceivably, these are people especially oriented to and capable of autonomous organizational behavior for community problem-solving, or, as Weiner has put it, integrative behavior.[13] The late-comers to the barriadas and those who gained entry into Santo Domingo by conformity to the bureaucratic rules of the game are not less decent citizens, but they appear to be more passive with regard to the affairs of their community as it struggles for improvement, perhaps more oriented toward the traditional mode of dependence on paternal authorities.

"MUNICIPALIZING" THE BARRIADAS IN PERU

One way in which the local problem-solving function has been structured for greater permanence is the creation of municipal districts of established settlements. This has been done recently in the Lima area; Pampa Seca is one example. The data show that its residents are indeed more interested in municipal activities than in those of the local association and evaluate the municipality as more helpful than the association, but the difference is small in both cases. Furthermore, the municipality's helpfulness in the view of Pampa Seca residents is markedly less than that of the association as evaluated by those of El Espíritu, so that as the barriadas become more established, the formalization of the local settlement's government structure may not be sufficient to reverse the normal decline in relevance of local organizations. (On the other hand, the municipalization of barriadas is such a new policy in Peru that these remarks cannot be considered more than provisional. It is surely possible that the municipal government will become more politically vital with time.)

PROMOCIÓN POPULAR AND COOPERACIÓN POPULAR

Perhaps the major organization to perform national integrative functions in societies seeking to shake off poverty is the mass political party. Such organizations have occurred infrequently in Latin America, and there are very few cases of parties that have focused directly in program or ideology on problems of urbanization and the condition of the settler. (Though little has been done about agrarian reform, it is much more common for "reform" parties to symbolize the *peasant* as the forgotten.) Our data show that, despite the very substantial differences between the Chilean and Peruvian party systems, political parties are evaluated as less personally helpful than the president, government officials, the municipality, and the local association in every case among the four settlements (see Tables II and V). Thus, in neither country does it appear that mass parties have yet developed with reference to the new urban settlements.

However, in Chile and Peru the incumbent national administrations have developed plans for an agency that would incorporate those mass sectors of the population which were previously politically and socially alienated. These agencies, Promoción Popular and Cooperación Popular, respectively, *could* serve as important steps toward the transformation of the governing parties—Christian Democracy in Chile and Acción Popular in Peru—into mass parties of national integration.

In both cases the agencies are seen as contributing technical assistance and initial leadership for community development. Both have important university branches through which students are recruited to participate in community development. This provides one of the few cases in either country where the highly privileged work directly with the highly underprivileged in the field, and the program could of course serve as a major agency of political socialization, broadening the scope of identification of both rich and poor in such a way as to nationalize both.

In Peru, Cooperación Popular has had an auspicious beginning in rural areas with indigenous populations, the integration of which President Belaúnde sees as vital to national development. It is inactive in corresponding urban areas, however, because Belaúnde is not sympathetic to the invasion-established communities, which he apparently considers a blight. Publicity attendant on Cooperación Popular has been plentiful, and despite the presidential exclusion of the barriadas, our data reveal a substantial minority in each barriada who evaluate the program as offering them at least some help. If the program were to acquire an urban direction, it might have additional support-carrying capacity. This potential is underscored in importance by the relatively low level of legitimacy accorded the political system by the settlers in our two barriadas. (We refer to this matter again below in assessing the legitimacy factor.) That this may remain only a potential is suggested by the recently reported cutting of the program's budget by the opposition majority congressional coalition (composed of APRA, Peru's erstwhile radical reform party, and the personalist party of former dictator General Odría), while Belaúnde maintained silence.[14]

In Chile, Promoción Popular has been more elaborately planned by the brain trust of President Frei, and a major dimension is the incorporation of the callampa and new housing project populations. The link between Promoción Popular and those people is the local association, thus building further community development into the structures created by the settlers themselves. Though the program has barely been initiated in 3 de Mayo, the respondents there were relatively evenly divided in evaluation as to whether or not it afforded any help. By contrast, in Santo Domingo, where there has been more activity, the evaluation was considerably more positive. Despite the relatively high support for the Marxist opposition coalition Frente de acción Popular (FRAP) among the Santo Domingo invaders, they are equally as enthusiastic about the program as the more Christian Democracy-oriented applicants. This augurs especially well for the program because of the invaders' high participation and involvement in the local association. In turn, Promoción Popular may contribute to the maintenance of the local association as a basic mechanism for problem-solving in the settlement as well as communication between the government and this sector of citizens. In addition, the substantially lower level of support accorded the political system by the invaders than by the applicants may be counteracted by the program. But if, as Promoción Popular becomes institutionalized, it is used to dominate the local association and to distribute patronage (offices and services) solely to Christian Democrat residents, it may alienate the Frapists * among the invaders, thereby sapping the local association of some of its most active and autonomous participants.

* member of FRAP

Costs of Political Demand-Making:
Sanctions and Depoliticalization (Table III)

Perhaps the most surprising aspect of recent Latin American politics to academic observers is the relatively continuous apoliticalization or low politicalization of the urban lower class in view of its poverty and general deprivation. Elsewhere we have tried to account for this phenomenon, citing the complex structure of the subculture of poverty, the restricted conception of time and space, the perceived immutability of the environment, the nature of lower-class occupations, the nonpolitical supports available, the effects of extreme deprivation, and vulnerability to sanctions.[15]

One might expect a higher level of politicalization among the permanent squatter settlements and housing projects because (1) the residents have had to anticipate dealing with the government before entry; (2) the invasion preparations involve sophisticated planning with regard to mobilizing political support and immobilizing agencies of governmental repression; (3) invasion itself is an illegal—and therefore governmentally relevant —act; and (4) the residents have thus been faced with the problem of acquiring urban services.[16]

An opposing factor, however, is the lower class's particularly high vulnerability to sanctions in preindustrial and transitional contexts. Actual repression or the threat of it may under such conditions be sufficient to discourage any behavior that might antagonize the establishment. The tangible gain through land seizure, in the face of the desperate need to find permanent, independent, economical housing, may represent the extreme case where potentially costly political action is resorted to by lower-class people. If this were so, the level of politicalization might be low, even in the permanent settlements, and the political orientations and behavior associated with the invasion planning and occurrence (or even the application to the Housing Agency) might have been exceptional.

How might such people be considered highly vulnerable to sanctions? First, their level of occupational skill is low, the labor market is glutted, and they have little countervailing power because of restrictions on or under-development of unions. Second, the distance between social classes, particularly between middle and lower classes, is so great that general social support for lower-class people in trouble with the government tends to be low. Awareness of this may also serve to deter political risk-taking on the part of those at the bottom. Third, the bureaucracy tends to be staffed with middle-class people, frequently unconcerned with service to the public, and skilled in the dispensation of subtle humiliations to "inferiors" seeking administrative adjustments. One such form of discouragement is to relegate them to endless waiting. Finally, a different kind of sanction is police harassment of "troublemakers" from the lower class. Although such activity is not directed only at lower-class representatives, they are probably the most assaulted in this respect in all societies.

American political scientists have tended to focus theoretically and empirically on factors that dispose people to enter the political process to the relative exclusion of factors (other than information costs) that discourage their entry, such as sanctions.[17] Theoretically, such sanctions as those mentioned above, or the fear of them, may operate at any point in the political process, discouraging demand-making or the organization of support behind demands or even the communication of wants to preclude their being transformed into the substance of demands. Furthermore, this can involve not only truncated politicalization, but also reversals. For example, if we take such a recent useful formulation as *The Civic Culture's* [18] classification of political cultures according to the prevalence of parochial, subject, and participant orientations of the citizens and apply it to the development of politicalization of individuals,[19] we can project the possibility not only of shifts from parochial to more complex syndromes of political orientation, but of sanction-induced parochialism on the part of formerly more highly politicalized actors.

Frank Pinner cites classic research holding that responses learned under reward conditions are less deeply internalized than those learned under conditions of punishment (positive responses tend toward extinction without frequent reinforcement, while negative responses persist with much less of it).[20] He also suggests that the substance of politics is much more frequently anxiety-producing than rewarding, thereby inducing a variety of avoidance behaviors. Given the greater vulnerability of lower-class people to sanctions, particularly in the condition of societies in transition from preindustrialism, and in view of the limited rewards allocated to the lower class in Chilean and Peruvian governmental processes, we suggest that where severe sanctions have occurred in relation to political activity, the sanctioned will avoid politics. The severely sanctioned will be severely depoliticalized.

Among our four settlements, one, El Espíritu, sharply contrasts with the others in this regard. Though illegal invasions are the origin of all the settlements, and this illegality is a source of anxiety in all, the response by authorities has varied. . . . We have some survey evidence bearing on this matter for the two barriadas. The respondents were asked what problems they encountered in establishing themselves. Only 5 per cent of the Pampa Seca sample referred to traumatic experiences with police or soldiers, but 41 per cent of the El Espíritu sample mentioned the fighting, the encirclement, the necessity for posting night guard, etc. In the context of this kind of background and survey data on the four settlements, we conclude that El Espíritu suffered a distinctively severe sanction.

Following the invasions and settlement, major governmental relations toward the four communities varied in the following manner. Santo Domingo began to receive a relatively full complement of urban services. 3 de Mayo began negotiations with the government for public housing assistance. Pampa Seca gradually began to acquire urban services and was formally made a municipality. El Espíritu has received the least services at this point, but the Housing Agency has acquired additional land to relieve its overcrowding and has participated in the resolution of conflicts over lot boundaries. We conclude that the two Santiago settlements have had more experience with government, while the two Lima barriadas have had less. In terms of meaningful political advantages from the government, our assessment is that Pampa Seca has had more political benefits than El Espíritu, but in both cases received less than their Santiago counterparts. It should be remembered that El Espíritu has an educational level close to Pampa Seca's and substantially higher than that of the

Santiago settlements. Thus, the effect of the severe sanction it experienced must overcome the politicalization resources nurtured by its population's relatively high education.

The data on politicalization reveal a pattern of high consistency, particularly those from El Espíritu, which are clearly in accord with the hypothesized relationship between sanctions and politicalization. El Espíritu respondents report the *least* interest in activities of the national government and the municipality, and the differences between them and the Santiago settlements in particular are extremely large. While only a minority in any of the four report that they have actually tried to get the government to do something or stop doing something, El Espíritu shows almost no such activity. A similar but even more pronounced pattern appears in the proportions of the samples who can imagine what they could do to instigate government assistance. There is not much difference among the settlements in rate of political discussion with primary groups or in attendance at political meetings, though again, El Espíritu tends to have the lowest rate. El Espíritu respondents also report the least dealing with a government agency regarding housing, despite the actual presence of government housing agency personnel engaged in activities previously described. (It is conceivable, in view of their positive evaluation of the housing agency and their negative evaluation of the government generally that they dissociate the two.) Fewer of them than of the Pampa Seca residents indicate they have heard of the Law of the Barriada or that they can evaluate it, although it has received substantial publicity and directly regulates much of the government's dealings with them. A much higher proportion of the Santiago respondents report knowledge and evaluation of Plan Habitacional, the government housing program analogous to that organized under the Law of the Barriada. El Espíritu respondents rank far below those of the other settlements in their capacity to state some conception of the most important problems facing the nation. Although voting participation is on a par with that in two of the other communities, the proportion who either see no personal significance in elections and campaigns or do not answer the item at all is a great deal higher among El Espíritu respondents than among any of their counterparts.

Furthermore, if we distinguish the original invaders from those who came afterwards in El Espíritu, we find that among these people—whom we know to have been sophisticated enough to accomplish the invasion against severe obstacles and who continue to be the main participants in the local association—there are indications of lower politicalization than among the others in the barriada sample. For example, fewer of them (13 per cent) than of the latecomers (19 per cent) can imagine a way in which they could influence the government to act favorably, whereas there is a strong reverse relationship in the Pampa Seca sample (43 per cent of the original invaders have such a conception compared to 18 per cent of the latecomers).

This seems strong evidence in support of our hypothesis. Despite their relatively high education, their politically sophisticated preparations for the invasion, and their close dealings with the housing agency after the invasion, the El Espíritu residents appear to have been powerfully depoliticalized by their traumatic experience associated with the invasion.

Since El Espíritu's original invaders were those directly sanctioned, and since (as we have indicated) they tended to monopolize membership in the local association, it seems reasonable to assume that the depoliticalized community leadership may be an important factor in the low level of politicalization throughout.

In certain obvious ways, this means that El Espíritu residents are not likely to add to the stress on the political system, since their potential for demand-making seems for the present to have been sharply curtailed. But it also means that these people, who have maintained a relatively strong nonpolitical organization in their community and who are working extremely hard to promote its consolidation, will not be participating as full citizens in the national polity, and this represents a waste of human resources. When it is recalled how few of these otherwise very effective people could formulate a national problem, how few recognized or could give an opinion on a national law objectively important to their lives, and how few believed in the significance of the electoral process, the limitations of the civic responsibilities that can realistically be expected of them at this point become clear.

TABLE III Politicalization Indicators.

	Lima		Santo Domingo	Santiago		
	Pampa Seca	El Espíritu		S.D. Applicants	S.D. Invaders	3 de Mayo
	%	%	%	%	%	%
"How interested are you in what the government is doing?":						
very	16	9	39	37	42	32
substantially	20	14	31	34	24	24
a little	44	37	25	24	27	38
not at all	20	35	5	5	7	5
"How interested are you in what the municipality is doing?":						
very	11	6	27	25	29	30
substantially	17	7	32	33	32	24
a little	37	25	31	34	32	36
not at all	34	50	9	6	7	9
Ever tried to get government to do (or stop doing) something: detailed affirmative response	14	2	11	11	15	20
Conception of how he can get government to do (or stop doing) something: detailed affirmative response	32	14	36	32	41	40

Discussion of politics with:							
family:	frequently	15	9	12	13	17	10
	occasionally	23	35	33	25	36	33
	never	57	56	55	62	48	57
friends and neighbors:	frequently	17	9	15	14	24	18
	occasionally	35	47	30	30	30	36
	never	47	44	54	56	46	46
coworkers:	frequently	13	10	18	16	22	22
	occasionally	30	37	32	33	32	39
	never	57	53	50	51	46	39
Meeting attendance or active part in a demonstration: indicates has done something		28	25	32	28	34	39
Has taken some step to get government agency to help solve his housing problem		29	18	56	68	46	64
Has heard of and can evaluate Law of Barriada/Housing Plan		54	40	69	71	71	66
Makes some mention of what is "most important national problem"		87	69	88	89	93	88
Voted in both last presidential and congressional or municipal elections		82	78	81	81	80	66
[ind]icates elections and campaigns have [per]sonal significance		60	34	58	62	56	58

A particularly poignant segment of John Turner's film on the El Espíritu experience, "A Roof of My Own," * expresses this lost opportunity for promoting national citizenship. A spokesman from among the original invaders describes the culminating moment of the invasion, when the first shacks of reed matting were thrown up, signifying the establishment of the barriada. Peruvian flags were run up on bamboo poles, and the spokesman, overcome by emotion, says, "For the first time we felt we were citizens of Peru." Then the troops attacked. While the barriada persisted, the promise of full, participatory citizenship was lost.

Politicalization: A Continuous or Discontinuous Process? (Table IV)

The diffuse "revolution of rising expectations" concept and our tendency to assume progress in human affairs can lead to a logically constructed but empirically unsatisfactory model of the politicalization process. The rising expectations idea has an obvious connotation of automatic improvement in living conditions. In its political aspect, it projects the image of expanding government scope under increasing stress. The very expansion of government functions is seen as contributing to an increasing view of situations as problems requiring government action, which in turn is thought to generate demands. Thus, because previous situations are converted into wants and wants into demands more rapidly than political resources become available, this model suggests that the system undergoes increasing stress and, in the poorer countries, frequent collapse. At the individual level, the implicit assumption is that once one learns to make demands (or engage in other behaviors representing a relatively high level of politicalization), the capacity and disposition to make them is established. Demand-making may not become a constant activity, but a latent orientation to engage in this kind of behavior exists and is easily triggered into operation.

We have been operating with a similar concept of the politicalization process. Although it has been obvious that the intermediate stages may actually occur in a variety of sequences, the

* This film, made by the British architect John F. C. Turner, is part of the "International Zone Series" of United Nations films.

general direction of development has seemed to be: (1) non-awareness of government; (2) awareness; (3) a perception of its utility; (4) a realization of its manipulability; (5) the development of a political preference; (6) an appraisal of one's probable effectiveness; (7) a calculation of gains and costs of action; (8) the making of demands.

We have already suggested the manner in which sanctions can short circuit or reverse the politicalization process. Here we want to assess the experience of our respondents in order to isolate other factors that may produce reversals or constraints.

At what point do we encounter these people? Possibly at that point in their lives where their politicalization is highest. They have all been dealing with the problem of housing. In a bad or extreme situation, they had a tangible alternative: seizure and settlement of unoccupied land or application for government housing. They could see the land, and they knew their own skills in home construction. The invasion itself represents an at least implicit demand that the government not enforce the letter of the law regarding illegal squatting, and for many of the people, there was explicit recognition and planning in terms of this demand. In any event, after the invasion (or application and receipt of public housing), there followed a period of protracted demand-making associated with negotiations for urban services (and, in the case of 3 de Mayo, for housing). A high level of politicalization was reached. The question is whether it became stabilized; in other words, whether the psychological underpinning of demand capability was established.

It has been repeatedly found in American studies that those who feel personally effective in politics tend to participate more. Almond and Verba conclude that personal political efficacy provides a psychological reserve for maintaining the civic culture.[21] They suggest that efficacy needs periodic exercise and testing in order to continue performing this function, but that demand-making need not and cannot be continuous.

Before assessing the psychological condition of the settlers, we need to make our limitations clear. We have data from only one survey at one point in time, and are therefore limited largely to analyses of associations. Comparative data using these same measures are not available. There are no well-defined criteria for distinguishing the person whose sense of political efficacy is stably internalized from the one whose sense of efficacy is unstable. Nor do we know how many stably effective people there must be in a collectivity in order to attain a threshold beyond which that demand-making is likely to be the response to a feeling of need.

Do past demand-making or high levels of politicalization instill a high sense of efficacy? Asked whether "people like you can only wait and accept government programs, or can have influence and make the government help you," a range from 32 to 46 per cent of our sets of respondents opted for the more assertive, effective-seeming alternative. When asked their degree of agreement or disagreement with the proposition, "Only if things change very much will I be able to affect what the government does," a lower range of from 14 to 31 per cent expressed disagreement. Furthermore, not only in the internalization of a sense of efficacy but the very perception of the personal relevance of the government seems in doubt. Confronted with the proposition, "What any government does won't affect my life very much," the response was overwhelmingly affirmative in most cases, with rejection ranging from 23 to 56 per cent. And only a fairly uniform minority of about one-third rejected the proposition that "One gains nothing with political activity." [22] Perhaps one would not expect a higher level of awareness and efficacy among a general cross-section of people, but it would seem more likely among a group that has been involved in demand-making concerning matters of great import. In this situation, it is questionable whether past political demand-making and effectiveness have been converted into a sense of political efficacy. On the basis of these data, therefore, we cannot conclude that an important element of demand capacity has been created.

The tangible alternatives available regarding the housing problem and the tangible gains represented by the acquisition of urban services may not readily be repeated for other problem situations in which these people find themselves, with the result that previous high levels of politicalization will not so readily be reached again. For example, a very high proportion of the respondents in all communities mentioned economic problems as the most important ones facing the country. The responses to this open-ended item clustered around such matters as unemployment, the high cost of living (food staples especially), poverty, misery, etc. Another question asked (a) what one could do to get the government to do (or stop doing) something, and (b) what sorts of problems could be taken to the government. Although the proportion mentioning economic problems as "most important" ranged from 55 to 78 per cent, the proportion mentioning economic problems as the kind of matter they could take before the government was only one-tenth or less in most cases, ranging from 3 to 20 per cent. If alternative solutions to these economic problems are not apparent, the formulation of related demands *would* probably be low. It should be noted here that while there is rather broad agreement in these societies that economic problems, including those mentioned, are the most important, there have been few alternatives posed for their resolution. Moreover, the general lines of attack have been so couched in intellectual, abstract terminology that they have probably not elicited the settlers' interest.

The level of politicalization of this sector of the urban lower class may show considerable fluctuation. Depoliticalization may occur as a function of (a) failure to develop a generalized sense of political efficacy or even a generalized sense of the personal relevance of government; and of (b) failure to conceive or rely on political alternatives to outstanding problems.

It should not be simplistically argued that meeting the demands of people—even where it is vitally important to them—will only result in the generation of more demands from them, and in a situation of extreme scarcity and more stress on the system.

THE CASE OF THE SANTO DOMINGO INVADERS

Once again, the Santo Domingo invaders stand out as a highly politicalized group. Many more of them than any other of our sets can conceive of how to translate economic problems (those considered by all sets as "most important") into personal demands on government. While their levels of efficacy and awareness are not the highest among the various sets, they are relatively high. A series of factors can be proposed at this point that together may suggest the reasons for their demand capability. One factor is a relatively high level of education, in comparison with the other Santiago sets. Another is the relatively high degree of competition within the group between affiliates of Christian Democracy and those of FRAP, which may have defined economic problems in terms meaningful for the poor. Finally, the high demands these invaders made on the government (they invaded valuable public land designed for public housing, demanding not only their right to remain but to housing itself) *and* the successful outcome may have been a particularly potent political experience, establishing a high level of politicalization.

Patterns of Legitimacy and Projected Consequences (Table V)

There has been a tendency to define problems of political legitimacy in societies emerging from preindustrialism in terms of possible political instability. We will now briefly assess the potential for instability in the patterns of legitimacy orientation found in the four settlements, and also treat other possible (and perhaps more common) consequences of lack of legitimacy. One of these is simply the absence of positive support. In other words, low legitimacy may involve the elite's inability to mobilize the citizens or to make policy that assumes their positive support. Another consequence of the failure to find personal significance in the political system may be social disorganization. In this situation, the society and polity must bear the costs of directly anti-social acts, widespread personal aimlessness, and personally destructive behavior.

The actual patterns of legitimacy orientation are quite distinct. Though there is considerable variation in support for the system between the two Santiago settlements, and within Santo Domingo between applicants and invaders, the greatest differences are between the Chilean respondents and the Lima residents. The Santiago set respond much more positively than their Lima counterparts to the system as a whole. They evaluate the President, the municipality, government officials, and a political party as being much more helpful than do the Peruvians. Many more of them report affiliation with a major political party (indi-

TABLE IV Political Efficacy, Awareness, Utility.

	Lima		Santo Domingo	Santiago		
	Pampa Seca	El Espiritu		S.D. Applicants	S.D. Invaders	3 de Mayo
	%	%	%	%	%	%
Can only wait and accept government programs	50	54	63	67	56	59
Can have influence and make government help	46	41	35	32	39	39
"Only if things change very much will I be able to affect what the government does":						
agree strongly	42	37	55	62	44	62
disagree slightly/strongly	31	23	20	16	25	14
"What any government does will not affect my life very much":						
agree strongly	21	30	42	48	34	46
disagree slightly/strongly	56	37	33	23	41	23
"One gains nothing with political activity":						
agree strongly	35	44	42	46	42	50
disagree slightly/strongly	36	32	36	32	39	37
Cite economic problems as most important national problems	74	55	73	68	78	62
Cite economic problems as matters they can take before the government	9	3	17	10	20	10

cating at least provisional acceptance of the parliamentary system). Many more of them than of barriada residents evaluate the government's method of selecting people for public housing as fair. A much higher proportion of them endorse the proposition that people must make sacrifices to help the country develop (potentially a highly significant indicator of the elite's capacity for mobilizing the citizens to implement development policy). Finally, the Peruvians are considerably more disposed to condone violence as a means of settling political questions and to accept social disorder as a consequence of desired social change, which seem probable indicators of dissatisfaction with present political arrangements. Clearly, the Santiago respondents give much more support to and feel they derive much more support from the political system than do the Lima respondents. The Chilean political system has a considerable cushion of legitimacy vis-à-vis the settlers. The government's housing program is a major element in the situation.

Local government (the municipality) substantially contributes to system legitimacy. It exercises some functions regarding urban services that are currently of particular importance to the settlers. Furthermore, in a situation of two-party competition where one party dominates the presidency and congress, election of local councilmen permits another forum for the expression of opposition. However, we lack information in any depth on the local government as a political subsystem. In contrast to the widespread judgment that the municipality plays a small role in Chile, the data indicate it would be useful to study its place in the polity. It is apparent that the political party and administrative bureaucracy are relatively weak integrative elements of the political system, so that despite the many elements of strong support for the Chilean system, the general Latin American political problem of an ineffective or underdeveloped organizational infrastructure remains.

The Santo Domingo invaders show considerably less support for the system than the applicants in the same housing project. In some instances they accord more and sometimes less support than do the 3 de Mayo settlers. It is hard to derive meaningful interpretation from a single cross-section survey. For example, it may indicate a continuing ambivalent disposition toward the

TABLE V Patterns of Legitimacy.

	Lima		Santo Domingo	Santiago		
	Pampa Seca	El Espíritu		S.D. Applicants	S.D. Invaders	3 de Mayo
	%	%	%	%	%	%
"In general our system of government and politics is good for the country":						
agree strongly	22	18	65	76	51	53
agree slightly	38	35	21	16	24	28
disagree slightly/strongly	38	42	11	6	19	15
Evaluation of extent of help given by President:						
much	10	14	50	60	36	33
some	18	24	20	15	24	22
none	50	50	17	10	27	33
do not know	20	11	13	14	10	12
Evaluation of extent of help given by municipality:						
much	6	8	35	38	32	41
some	28	14	24	19	27	24
none	55	66	28	30	32	28
do not know	10	11	12	11	7	7
Evaluation of extent of help given by government officials:						
much	5	7	27	38	14	21
some	17	24	26	20	37	24
none	57	51	31	24	37	42
do not know	17	11	16	16	7	12
Evaluation of extent of help given by a party:						
much	3	2	20	25	15	17
some	12	18	22	23	24	17
none	63	62	44	40	46	51
do not know	20	17	14	11	12	13

TABLE V (continued) Patterns of Legitimacy.

| | Lima | | Santo Domingo | Santiago | | 3 de Mayo |
	Pampa Seca %	El Espiritu %	%	S.D. Applicants %	S.D. Invaders %	%
Affiliation to a party:						
none/independent	54	53	35	35	34	32
government *	21	18	43	49	37	44
opposition †	21	26	18	10	25	24
Evaluation of public housing selection process:						
fair	28	15	54	58	48	48
not very fair	32	49	31	32	34	34
very unfair	34	33	12	8	15	13
In agreement that people should sacrifice for national development	44	45	79	82	71	68
"Violence should never be the way to resolve political problems":						
agree strongly	46	44	75	84	61	69
agree slightly	20	15	12	2	22	14
disagree slightly/strongly	34	38	12	13	17	15
"Social change is acceptable only if it does not provoke disorder":						
agree strongly	49	40	80	85	75	76
agree slightly	26	26	15	13	17	16
disagree slightly/strongly	20	28	5	2	8	6
Change in ideas about politics:						
gov't. more helpful now/better	7	3	22	22	22	4
gov't. less helpful now/worse	11	14	2	1	3	2
Unable to mention anyone to count on for help	30	38	19			20

Finding someone to count on in case of need:						
harder now	37	38	34	35	22	24
same as ever now	34	37	19	18	25	35
easier now	26	23	46	44	52	39
"Do you think people around here are":						
united strongly/slightly	35	50	48	48	46	56
disunited slightly/strongly	64	49	48	48	52	41
Evaluation of extent of help given by rich:						
much	0	1	10	10		7
some	6	5	19	19		21
none	82	82	58	58		67
do not know	10	11	10	10		3
Evaluation of extent of help given by university students:						
much	20	13	46	46		34
some	30	39	15	15		15
none	27	27	10	10		19
do not know	21	21	28	28		30
Evaluation of extent of help given by priests:						
much	35	11	32	32		22
some	32	34	29	29		33
none	26	44	27	27		36
do not know	6	9	10	10		8
Evaluation of extent of help given by JNV (Housing Agency):						
much	40	28				
some	31	35				
none	18	29				
do not know	9	7				

* *Note:* The government party is Acción Popular in Peru and Christian Democracy in Chile.
† The opposition coalition is APRA and *Odriísta* in Peru and Socialist and Communist (FRAP) in Chile.

system and its components; but in view of the recent threatening experiences these invaders have had with the government and the army (during the invasion experience itself), it may also actually represent a trend of growing support. An additional datum here provides some evidence favoring the latter interpretation. We asked the respondents whether their political ideas had changed over the years and, if so, in what manner. The majority of responses dealt with acquiring more information or more experience or more understanding with maturation. But, in Santiago, a much larger proportion of Santo Domingo residents, both invaders and applicants, than 3 de Mayo residents mentioned that the government was more helpful now than in the past. Virtually no one in either Santiago settlement said that the government had become less helpful or more harmful, in substantial contrast to the barriada responses.

It should be investigated over time whether the more cautious or limited support of the system by the Santo Domingo invaders (plus their high politicalization relative to the applicants) (1) stimulates more solicitous government action than if they were considered "safer" constituents, and (2) tends to maintain the invaders as autonomous, as opposed to patron-oriented, dependent actors in the political system.

The Peruvian respondents show more opposition to the system and its components. Neither the President, nor officials generally, nor the municipality, nor the parties stand out as positive elements. Furthermore, these people also perceive less social support than do the Chileans. For example, a higher proportion of the barriada residents say they can count on no one for help when they need it, a distribution found again in response to a question asking whether help is harder or easier to find now than in the past. Moreover, the barriadas report virtually no help from the rich, whereas a minority of about 30 per cent in the Chilean settlements say the rich give at least some help. This indicates a climate of somewhat less inter-class hostility in Santiago than in Lima. Thus, conditions seem present in the Peruvian case that would oppose the continued development of the barriadas toward strong communities, with a respected place in polity and society. In fact, the four settlements' self-image regarding the degree of unity reveals that the more established settlements within each city (Santo Domingo in Santiago and Pampa Seca in Lima) perceive less unity. In the Santiago case, there are many countervailing forces promoting the integration of the residents into the nation. In the Lima case, however, where the least unity is perceived, there is much less in the external environment to deter the tendency over time toward alienation.

PROJECTED CONSEQUENCES

As has been clear throughout, the residents of the four settlements have experienced a great deal of change over a short period of time. The consolidation of these areas may represent a brief historical moment, for generations are short. Quite conceivably, what the settlers have achieved individually and collectively within the past few years may be dissipated tomorrow. Much depends on whether they find some support in the society, and on their integration into the national society. If they do not find support, if neither their achievements nor they themselves win recognition and respect somewhere in the larger society, then the following consequences seem likely in the near future. Children, raised with much parental ambition and sacrifice, may fail to find the means to get ahead or become embarrassed about living in such settlements. In either event, high intrafamilial tensions and a high level of frustration and self-hate among the youth may result. Thus, the next generation could greatly raise the costs to the nation of malintegration of the settlements, by venting their frustrations in either political opposition, across-the-board delinquency, or extreme privatization. Opposition would seem to be promoted to the extent that they are socialized in a home and community environment where the political system is regarded as bad. A second consequence might be that the frustrations and embarrassment of the children could impel many of the original settlers (and presumably community leaders) to relinquish their high hopes for a community and leave for less troubled areas.

Lack of support and its consequences would seem to promote the residents' loss of faith in the achievements of the past. Individual family dwellings once proudly erected through the family's effort could well be vacated for subdivision and renting at high rates to the even more enormous and desperate wave of lower-class urbanites of the future. This sort of shift in orientations toward exploitation would produce neighborhood decline and soon slums.

But if the recent achievements can be consolidated through a commensurate gain in social—or political—status, then it may be possible for the settlements to continue to develop into communities, and the "Watts stage of mass rioting and looting" might be skipped. Even where social status is not forthcoming, political systems *can* deal with resistant societies by providing people with channels to national integration and by giving them political dignity. A partial example is the Puerto Rican experience under Muñoz Marín and the Popular Democratic Party, where the peasant was made the political hero. Tumin and Feldman suggest in their massive study of the Island society that the high morale and sense of national integration of the lower class, in the face of a growing disparity between its material condition and that of the middle class, was a function of this political structure and support.[23] If the political system fails to provide this, and the society continues to be closed to the settlers and their children, then these human achievements and resources seem likely to be wasted. Not only would this involve a failure to integrate a substantial sector of potentially effective citizens, but it could also mean a considerable drain on the scarce development resources needed to maintain a minimum level of social control in the resultant slums and to contain the politically alienated.

Nonetheless, even in the more extreme case of Lima, there are potential bases for integration. A substantial proportion of the barriada samples perceive support from university students, priests (no doubt those operating constructive activities within the barriadas), and the Cooperación Popular program, though little has been done by any of these agents so far. All of them, however, have something to do with plans for community development and the integration of the barriadas into the society. (We have discussed this as a possible nexus of cross-class ties and ties between rulers and ruled in our analysis of the role of the local associations.) A further potential element in this situation is the Junta Nacional de la Vivienda, the Peruvian government housing agency, which has been very helpful and creative with regard to the barriadas, particularly with regard to other government agencies. This support and favorable experience are widely reflected in the evaluation by the settlers of the JNV, which stands in strong contrast to their other political evaluations. The JNV has been engaged in a home improvement loan and title program allowing a great deal of individual decision, responsibility, and labor. The program is helping large numbers of settlers (that is, *lower-class people*) with little administrative overhead and very few cases of default on their part.[24] The JNV has thus depended on the strength of the settlers' experience and skills, as might the Cooperación Popular idea if permitted to operate in the barriadas. Though underdeveloped in this situation, this is clearly an extremely important potential and opportunity. A community development program capitalizing on these elements builds on demonstrated human organizational skills and orientations which are scarce and easily dissipated; it uses relatively little capital, which in this kind of development situation is extremely scarce; and it tends to promote political and social integration under political conditions generally extremely unfavorable toward such a process.

SUMMARY

Thus we have seen that the highly significant local association tends to atrophy with time as the settlement consolidates. This threatens the loss of a potential channel of political elite-citizen integration in societies characterized by political organizational underdevelopment. A Chilean government program may contribute to the transformation of the association into a mediator between government and settlers, but the latter may become less autonomous in problem-solving and more dependent. A similar program of considerable potential in Peru was directed away from these urban settlements, and has now been seriously weakened by political opposition.

Sanctions were suggested as important factors retarding lower-class politicization in transitional societies. The hypothesis presented is that extreme depoliticalization will result from severe sanctions being levied against lower-class people relatively inexperienced in politics. Our data conform closely to the pattern predicted by the hypothesis. The effect can "help" a government by reducing demands and therefore stress, but there is also a loss in the capacity to mobilize support.

Politicalization may be a discontinuous process, contrary to prevailing theory. A high level of politicalization may not be established despite an important demand-making experience. One such experience may not establish the psychological basis for continuing demand-making. Furthermore, the general case regarding the Latin American urban lower class is one where alternative solutions to serious problems are not defined, and this retards politicalization. Consequently, meeting an important demand concerning housing and urban services, for example, does not necessarily trigger a chain of additional demands which would overwhelm governmental capacity in transitional societies.

Considerable variation in patterns of political legitimacy orientations exists between the Chilean and Peruvian settlements. The Santiago residents responded much more affirmatively than those in Lima to their political system and its components. Since the settlers in Santiago also perceive much more social support than those in Lima, they appear to be much more integrated, although such major integrating agencies as the political parties and public bureaucracy appear to be weak links Where political and social support is lacking, as in Lima, internal stress in the barriadas seems likely to promote long-run decline and slum formation, involving social disorganization, personal ineffectiveness, and political alienation. The political costs of maintaining control under such circumstances, and the waste of potential citizenship are considerable for any society trying to move toward development.

NOTES

[1] This term has been defined as forcible preemption of land by landless and homeless people. Cf. Charles Abrams, *Man's Struggle for Shelter in an Urbanizing World*, Cambridge, M.I.T. Press, 1964, chapter 2, "Squatting and Squatters," 12.

[2] See, for example, José Matos Mar, "The *Barriadas* of Lima: An Example of Integration into Urban Life," in *Urbanization in Latin America*,

ed. P. Hauser, N.Y., International Documents Service, 1961, p. 171; James L. Payne, *Labor and Politics in Peru*, New Haven, Yale University Press, 1965, 15; and Tad Szulc, *The Winds of Revolution*, New York, Praeger, 1965, 49–54.

³ John Turner's work is so far available in "Three Lectures on Housing in Peru," presented at the Athens Centre of Ekistics, November 1964 (mimeo); and in the special number edited by Turner, "Dwelling Resources in South America," *Architectural Design* (London), Vol. 8 (August 1963), throughout.

⁴ Rosenblüth's work is available in *Problemas socio-económicos de la marginalidad y la integración urbana; el caso de "las poblaciones callampas" en el Gran Santiago*, Santiago, Universidad de Chile, Escuela de Economía, 1963.

⁵ Matos Mar cites traditional communalism as operative in the barriadas, op. cit. 176. Richard N. Adams presents a contrasting analysis in "The Community in Latin America: A Changing Myth," *The Centennial Review*, VI (summer 1962), 409–34; as does Richard W. Patch, "How Communal are the Communities?" American Universities Field Staff Report, Lima, June 1959.

⁶ See Turner, op. cit.; and Richard Morse, "Recent Research on Latin American Urbanization," *Latin American Research Review*, I (Fall 1965), 35–74. In a study of Lima industrial workers, it was found that ownership of a house was *the* major objective. See Guillermo Briones and José Mejía Valera, *El obrero industrial*, Lima, Universidad de San Marcos, Instituto de Investigaciones Sociológicas, 1964, 71.

⁷ Abrams fears that squatting will promote disrespect for law and government; op. cit. 23. This does not appear to be a major problem in the Lima or Santiago cases, however.

⁸ These data conform closely to the general pattern observed in Lima by anthropologist William Mangin. See his "Mental Health and Migration to Cities: A Peruvian Case," reprinted in *Contemporary Cultures and Societies of Latin America*, eds. D. B. Heath and R. N. Adams, New York, Random House, 1965, 549.

⁹ Comisión Económica para América Latina, "La urbanización en América Latina . . . ," E/CN.12/662/Rev. 1, March 1963, 19.

¹⁰ See Mangin, op. cit. 548, for an appraisal of parental ambitions in the barriadas.

¹¹ What we have termed the "local association" carries such varied titles as *junta de vecinos, comité de vecinos, asociación de la barriada*, etc.

¹² Mangin, op. cit. 549–50.

¹³ Myron Weiner, "Political Integration and Political Development," *The Annals of the American Academy of Political and Social Science*, 358 (March 1965), 52–64.

¹⁴ Selden Rodman, "Peruvian Politics Stalls Belaúnde's Reforms," *The Reporter*, 35 (July 14, 1966), 37–40.

¹⁵ D. Goldrich, "Toward the Comparative Study of Politicalization in Latin America," in Heath and Adams (eds.), op. cit. 361–78; and *Sons of the Establishment: Elite Youth in Panama and Costa Rica*, Chicago, Rand McNally, 1966, Chapter I.

¹⁶ See the Mangin and Turner articles in *Architectural Design*, op. cit.

¹⁷ For a very useful theoretical discussion of this, see Jerry F. Medler,

213

"Negative Sanctions: Their Perception and Effect in the Political System," Ph.D. dissertation, University of Oregon, 1966. See also the treatment of sanctions in R. E. Agger, D. Goldrich, and B. E. Swanson, *The Rulers and the Ruled,* New York, John Wiley, 1964.

[18] G. Almond and S. Verba, *The Civic Culture,* Princeton, Princeton University Press, 1963.

[19] Medler, op. cit. 111–33.

[20] Frank A. Pinner, "Notes on Method in Social and Political Research," in *The Research Function of University Bureaus and Institutes for Government-Related Research,* ed. D. Waldo, Berkeley: Bureau of Public Administration, University of California, 1960, 183–218. See also Henry Teune, "The Learning of Integrative Habits," in *The Integration of Political Communities,* eds. P. Jacob and J. Toscano, Philadelphia, Lippincott, 1964, 247–82.

[21] Almond and Verba, op. cit. "The Civic Culture and Democratic Stability."

[22] Response set may be a problem regarding these items. On the other hand, it is quite possible that the acquiescent (those who tend to agree to such items, regardless of substance) are also those least oriented to political and environmental manipulation.

[23] M. Tumin and A. Feldman, *Social Class and Social Change in Puerto Rico,* Princeton, Princeton University Press, 1961.

[24] John Turner discusses this JNV program in his third Lecture, "Popular Housing Policies and Projects in Peru." op. cit.

6

ANDREW G. FRANK

Urban Poverty
in Latin America *

Latin America already has a great and growing urban population which in several of its countries exceeds 50 per cent.[1] Nonetheless, the city has hardly been studied as an economic system;
and as an economic unit or as part of the economy the city is
only very inadequately understood.[2] Possibly this lacuna in our
knowledge may be traced to economists' emphasis on the sectoral
breakdown of the economy and on the distinctions among primary, secondary, and tertiary sectors. This last sector has become
little more than a residual category for classifying the less stable
structural and less well understood phases of economic activity.[3]
Yet it is precisely this little understood sector which has been
growing at such an alarming rate in Latin America and other
underdeveloped countries.[4] Possibly the same gap in our knowledge of the socioeconomic structure of the city may also be traced
to the sociologists' focus on the urban residential pattern and its
socio-cultural manifestations which, possibly of necessity, relegate economic factors to relatively less well researched dependent
variables.

The so-called floating population of urban areas presents a
particular challenge. Like the indigenous population in rural
areas, the floating population in urban areas is often thought to
be marginal because of the way it is integrated into the society as

215

a whole. Probably the most important study of this population has been of inhabitants of self-built and/or "irregular" [5] residential structures. It has often been thought that these settlements were of a temporary nature and that their inhabitants were merely recent rural migrants in transition to stable urban employment and residence. Recently it has become ever clearer that these settlements are for the foreseeable future not transitional and temporary but rather permanent and growing. Often many of their inhabitants are not migrants from rural areas at all but rather from other, usually smaller cities and notably even from within the same city.[6] ECLA has characterized these self-built settlements as representing "the rejection by the city of native or other people who lived in it, who differ from the rest of the urban population more in the degree of their poverty than in their origins." [7] One student of the problem suggests, moreover, that they "must be considered as a permanent phenomenon which has its roots in the process of economic and social development." [8]

Nonetheless, it is possible to exaggerate the economic and socio-cultural importance of the urban-rural distinction. It may be useful, instead, to consider the distinction between what might be called the "stable," or well structured, and the "unstable" sectors of the economy; and the corresponding distinction between the permanent and the floating populations that are economically active or inactive in them. The stable sectors exist in both rural and urban environments and have been more exhaustively studied in their agricultural and industrial forms. The unstable sector and floating population also exist in both the rural and the urban environments. One may venture to suggest that the rural and urban varieties of this unstable sector probably share a fairly similar economic structure and cause. Possibly more alike still are the rural and urban incumbents in these relatively unstructured and unstable roles. Certainly, they come from substantially the same socio-cultural group, especially if the society is a multi-racial or multi-ethnic one; and often they are the same individuals displaced from one environment to the other (and sometimes back again). Moreover, they often occupy a large variety of these roles simultaneously or in quick succession, shifting rapidly and easily among the unstructured roles, but not between these and the more structured ones.

Insofar as these people and their roles have been studied at all, primary emphasis has been placed on the social and cultural aspects of the problem. Nonetheless, the evidence from these studies does throw some light on and permit some limited insight into the allied economic undertones of the unstable sector. According to studies of internal migration, the economic sources of this problem lie in the failure to expand of the stable primary goods production sector and in the instability of its associated, often speculative, agricultural merchandizing sector and their consequent inability to provide employment and sustenance to the rural population. There is also the corresponding stability of the industrial sector and its associated unstable urban economy, which in turn cannot absorb the population thus expelled from the farms and small towns. Much of this migration is rural to rural, rural to small town, small town to metropolitan, and not only rural to urban in the narrower sense of the word. In the small towns the unstable sector is possibly still larger than in the metropolitan centers in which it has more forcefully pressed itself on the attention of the various students of the problem.[9]

Since the primary and secondary sectors are not expanding fast enough, much of the population in this unstable sector is attracted into, or rather forced into, the tertiary sector. There, it does not of course go into the professions and others of the more traditionally stable and larger service institutions, but rather into small service establishments, and it becomes individual self-employed "entrepreneurs," such as in street vending, odd jobs, and of course in domestic service.[10] Many of these people thus are literally capitalists, but without financial, human, or educational capital. They might be called "Penny Capitalists" in an urban guise; but they lack even the small amount of capital and thus independence that their land affords the peasants in Panajachel, Guatemala.[11] But the overlap between the unstable and the tertiary sector should not blind us to the great extent to which the secondary sector is similarly unstable. Thus, ECLA found in Santiago, Chile, that out of the 42 per cent of the labor force in industry in the self-built *callampa* and out of the corresponding 32 per cent industrial workers in the city as a whole, 19 per cent and 6 per cent respectively (or nearly half in the callampa and one fifth in the city) were in the notoriously occasional and unstable construction industry and not in the stable manufacturing part of the secondary sector.[12] But even in the manufacturing sector, old capital, poor and technologically inefficient small shops, with probably uncertain lifespan and certainly unstable employment, are coming into being at a faster rate than modern, technologically advanced factories. The former unstable ones absorb a larger number of workers than the latter stable ones; [13] but not unlike the relation between agricultural subsistence plots and haciendas or plantations, the small, inefficient, industrial producers have a satellite-metropolis relation with and live in the shadow of the larger efficient ones, often supplying the latter with part of their inputs, and always absorbing the brunt of much of the fluctuations in demand, supply, and price of the modern, stable manufacturing sector.

The existence and expansion of this large unstable—both urban and rural—sector in the structure of the national and international economy produces a correspondingly large unstable "floating" population with low educational and technological qualifications, highly unstable employment, and great insecurity. Thus, ECLA notes that "the worker of the callampa rarely has the security of a stable job; he faces the probability of a succession of badly paid jobs of uncertain duration." A survey of Puerto Alegre, in Brazil, showed 40 per cent of family heads to have work with irregularity and another 55 per cent to be entirely unemployed.[14] Many people shift frequently between irregular unskilled employment and often only partial self-employment,[15] and they must always look forward to having any particular source of income only for a short time. Perhaps paradoxically, multiple employment is closely associated with frequent and high unemployment. Thus a study of the callampa population in Santiago reports 41 per cent of its employable people to have been unemployed between four and twelve months out of the year.[16] These conditions generate such low levels of income that, according to ECLA estimates, the adequate family "model diet" as established by the Department of Food and Nutrition of the National Health Service of Chile would absorb 132 per cent and 121 per cent respectively, of the incomes of Santiago's callampa-dweller and worker. And the instability of employment and insecurity of income is matched only by the 61 per cent of respondents who, though living in Chile, which among Latin American countries is noted for having the best developed social insurance system, said that they are not covered by any social security system.[17]

As in the rural environment, the instability of the labor market, is, if not matched, at least approached by the instability of the product market. Possibly, the urban dweller is less adversely affected than his rural counterpart by market monopoly, fluctuation, and speculation in the goods he buys (and partly sells), because geographical considerations in the larger cities probably reduce the possibility of monopolizing the local market. Nonetheless, the national and urban markets for many goods, including food and often housing, are notoriously monopolistic. Artificially created city-wide shortages, to permit price speculation in this or that consumer necessity, are an all too common occurrence in many parts of Latin America.[18] These inevitably absorb a share of the consumer's income which, though perhaps unknown, is very likely not insubstantial. It has been estimated, for instance, that 40 per cent of the urban food price in Chile represents merchandising costs; and that these costs alone absorb 26 per cent of the urban worker's entire family income.[19]

The degree and impact of this sort of monopolization, restriction of supply, and price speculation in consumer goods is probably greater in the unstable than the stable sector, especially insofar as it is physically and economically located in the self-built and low income suburban residential areas. These latter are far less well provided with urban services, including retail trade outlets, than the city as a whole.[20] Accordingly, retail monopoly and raised prices are that much more possible and likely in these urban areas.[21] The greater instability of family incomes in these areas, moreover, renders its population more exposed to usurious short-term credit practices than in other parts of the city. Since these people's incomes are low, they no doubt receive less credit than other urban dwellers, but they probably pay more for it and spend a higher share of their low incomes on high interest costs.

This economic structure of the city and the disadvantaged position in which it places many of its inhabitants of course has manifold social and cultural manifestations. In multi-racial and multi-ethnic countries this structure manifests itself in very unequal racial and ethnic residential distributions in the city.[22] Most notable, and most widely studied, is the resulting urban residential pattern. Large and usually growing parts of the urban population crowd into self-built, antiquated, sub-standard, and low-income suburban residential structures and areas.[23] Of these, the self-built residential settlements are probably those which have attracted the greatest attention of scientists and policy-makers alike. Though there are undoubtedly differences in occupational structure, income levels, and various social-cultural indices between the self-built and the other two types of low-income urban settlements, ECLA has recently called the extent of such difference into serious question. In Chile, which with Venezuela has had the most ambitious public housing program in Latin America, official estimates place 6 per cent of the population of Santiago in callampas, 20 per cent in *conventillos*, and more in the sub-divisions and developments whose replacement of callampas has been able to reduce their growth in Santiago. In some other cities of Latin America, in which the public building program is very much less extensive than in Santiago, the callampa population reaches much higher percentages, which sometimes exceed 50 per cent. The conventillo population accounts for one third of the families of urban workers and employees.[24] In Mexico City 30 per cent of the population lives in self-built housing, 11 per cent in antiquated sub-standard housing, 14 per cent in proletarian housing, 26 per cent in antiquated housing, and only 19 per cent live in housing that may be classified as good. Commenting on the situation in Lima, UNICEF notes: "The majority of the 'barriadas' are formed because the people want to have their own lot. They organize an 'invasion' which then keeps growing into a continuous flow of people who leave the capital to settle in a place of their own and for which they usually do not have to pay. To this end they may look for vacant lots that are state and even privately owned. A look at the average income of these people shows that almost none of them could live in any other way or pay the rents which the urban areas demand.[25]

The self-built settlements are almost by definition un-planned. As such, they usually are almost devoid of any urban services. They generally lack running water, forcing their usually female and/or minor inhabitants to fetch water in cans from nearby or even from outside communal sources. Sometimes the water is trucked in and sold at a considerable price. Electricity is either unavailable or clandestinely tapped from nearby wires. Sewage systems and often even cesspools are unknown. Garbage collection is nonexistent—on the other hand, the settlement is often built on the garbage dump itself. Paving is nonexistent; and, since these settlements perforce are often on hillsides or in riverbeds, recurrent flooding is all too common. Hospitals are distant, as are telephones with which to call for emergency medical assistance. Schools are far away and crowded or simply inaccessible. Many self-built settlements are far from the center of town, from employment opportunities, and transportation is inadequate and costly in time and money. Police and fire protection are rare. Retail trade, as was noted above, is scarce and costly. But, apart from the insecurity of employment, from the point of view of the inhabitant of self-built residential structures on land owned by others, far and away the worst of its features is the insecurity of his tenancy: "Because here we have no security, on a moment's notice they can kick us out," and "because here we live on charity and may have to move at any time by order of the City." [26]

The inhabitants of conventillo-type antiquated sub-standard housing do not suffer from these shortages of physical facilities to nearly so great an extent precisely because they are urbanized, in the more traditional sense of the word. Their inhabitants also tend to be the members of the working and lower-middle classes whose economic situation and length of residence more nearly afford them this more adequate housing. The low-income suburban settlements, including those planned by public housing authorities, unfortunately appear all too often to suffer from many of the same deficiencies that are so characteristic of the self-built "irregular" settlements. Due to various economic and administrative impediments, many of these housing projects lack many of the same urban, educational, health, and retail facilities.

And, of course, being often even more outlying than the self-built settlements, their inhabitants are seriously disadvantaged with respect to the employment opportunities which were not, and are not, located in these newer residential areas.[27]

Though the population of these settlements is very young—51 per cent of Santiago's callampa population was found to be under fifteen years of age—educational facilities and attainments are extremely deficient. The same study of callampas found 73 per cent of the inhabitants above fifteen years of age to have 0–4 years of schooling. More significant still, it appeared that earning capacity within this group was not influenced by educational attainment, suggesting that only *more than four years of* education —attained by only 27 per cent of the people—equipped them with greater earning capacity than no education at all. Failure to attend school was found in 38 per cent and 45 per cent of school age children.[28] As a consequence of the low-income and sanitary conditions already referred to, health standards are also deplorably low. The Preamble of the Constitution of the World Health Organization defines "a state of complete physical, mental and social well-being, and not just the absence of illness or invalidity." If we were to use this criterion to judge the health of the callampa population, we would have to conclude that the callampa population is a sick population. The rate of days bedridden because of illness is considerably higher than the average despite the fact that the low incomes of these inhabitants probably militate against their sacrificing workdays. The rate of infant mortality is very high and sometimes exceeds that of rural areas. And only 2 per cent received medical attention covered by social security.[29]

The unstable sector of the economy on which the preceding pages have been focused results in widespread mobility and insecurity which call for special emphasis. It was noted above that the contemporary structure of the urban economy in Latin America brings with it a high degree of mobility, both in employment and residence, which tends to be particularly concentrated in the three types of "irregular" residential areas. The same may be said for insecurity, though with respect to this it is important to distinguish between self-built settlements on the one hand and publicly built or sponsored suburban housing projects on the other. Economic insecurity is of course more in evidence in the former because the most economically insecure people perforce tend to settle there. Residential insecurity, on the other hand, is augmented by the very nature of the self-built settlements themselves and particularly by the fact that they are located on land belonging to others. If privately owned, this land is frequently held for speculative purposes and may be claimed by the owner for other uses at a moment's notice. But for various reasons of public policy, including "urban renewal" programs, even publicly owned urban land is often converted from this type of residential use to some other one. In Rio de Janeiro in 1964 a self-built favela was burned to the ground by the city government to make room for a new luxury tourist hotel. One of the principal preoccupations of the self-built housing population is to get and keep even the most modest of roofs over their heads. For this reason among others, this population tends to concentrate its concern and attention on their own immediate day-to-day problems, to the virtual exclusion of any communal, let alone national or international, matters. Their principal social contact tends to be with their own primary group and/or extended family. Neighborhood and other voluntary associations, including political parties, though they may exist in these settlements, enjoy scant participation. This situation appears to be mitigated only in countries with Indian populations, such as Guatemala and Peru, in which neighborhood or city-wide "sons of the . . . (region)" clubs provide recent rural migrants with ties among each other and between them and "back home." Beyond that, the only significant spontaneous communal cooperation is stimulated by the sometimes cooperative efforts to "invade" a new area in order to build there and then to defend it against would-be interlopers or other sources of potential usurpation of their homes. Again, in more strongly ethnically and communally organized countries with large indigenous populations, such settlement and defense of new areas is sometimes organized on the basis of regional affiliation. But in countries like Venezuela and Chile and even in Brazil, such a pattern is hardly to be found. In no case, however, is there any noticeable familiarity with, or interest and participation in, anything that might be called "national affairs" or even in popular programs of national political parties.[30] An observer of the Santiago callampa scene suggests that "the plans that are made at the national level could not take account of the needs of the callampas given that its population is highly unstable and is constantly on the move from one place to another, which practically leaves them out of any activity of national scope." [31]

The same author observes, on the other hand, that "these populations which we have called suburban or 'semi-segregated' urban centers, as their name implies, really are semi-segregated for lack of urban services. But they are on a different and higher level than the callampa settlements in that the fact of having been granted ownership of land offers their inhabitants a degree of security and confidence which they did not have before and permits them to engage in a series of efforts to improve the development of the settlement as far as possible. This new situation creates a new set of responsibilities for them, and to face these they unite into groups which have a clear idea of the goals that they pursue. This also reflects itself in an interest in participating in political activities in contrast to the apathy and disorganization found in the inhabitants of the callampa settlements." [32]

But taking the foreign circumstances into account, it cannot come as any surprise to find ECLA concluding that "in these sectors the problems of urban life acquire an importance beyond those of work itself. Therefore, the collective organizations that are formed do not tend toward the defense of job interests, but toward the improvement of living conditions and, in general, toward obtaining the circumstances that are necessary to permit their members to survive in an urban environment which to them often appears hostile." [33]

The floating urban population is particularly sensitive to and immediately affected by the most common changes in government programs and monetary and fiscal policies. As was suggested above, the instability of the economic sector which forms the base of this population also transforms it into the urban shock absorber of the economic ups and downs of the stable sector and the economy as a whole. To the extent, therefore, that government activity either dampens or amplifies these economic fluctuations, it impinges particularly heavily on the floating population.

This population is the last to be hired and the first to be fired during fluctuations of the urban construction, manufacturing, and service industries. Government monetary and fiscal policy therefore determines their economic situations very immediately via its effects on the private sector. Their employment opportunities are also particularly sensitive to other government programs. In the past in Latin America, the floating population has often seen its sources of employment sharply increased by a surge of public construction, associated usually with particular political circumstances, only to have them reduced again by similarly determined cutbacks in public construction activity. Insofar as the prior increase in jobs attracted still more people into the cities or even into the country itself, its temporary nature contributes to the floating urban population and its insecurity. Such recurrent unemployment may force some people to abandon their homes in the older conventillo slums and seek to establish them in newer self-built ones. Insofar as benefits from social and employment security programs are tied, as they largely are, to the economic institutions in which the population occupies relatively stable places, the floating population which most needs such benefits is left largely uncovered. In all respects, they suffer from the greatest degree of insecurity, and of course, of poverty. Public policy therefore cannot significantly alter, much less eliminate, the deplorable circumstances of this floating urban population in the absence of basic changes in the structure of the society and economy which gives rise to them.

There is, however, one major area in which, it is suggested, public policy can immediately intervene to improve the circumstances of the urban floating population and to lay the basis for other development efforts. This is the area of residential housing and the problems associated with self-built residential structures in particular.

The examination of the urban scene above suggested that there is a significant difference in the kind of social organization and the sense of, and participation in, civic and political responsibility between the inhabitants of self-built residential structures and areas on the one hand and the remainder of the more or less floating urban population in older centrally located run-down and newer surburban project dwellings. Over and beyond economic and other circumstances that distinguish them, this difference between the inhabitants of self-built and those of other residential structures can be traced directly to the difference in security of residential tenure between the two groups. It is the insecurity in their claim to their house and home, coupled of course with job and other sources of insecurity, which appears to be one of the principal obstacles to cooperative and organized civic or political action in their neighborhood or elsewhere by this part of the floating urban populations. The insecurity of residential tenure, in turn, is due in large part to the lack of ownership or other legal claim to the land on which they live and to the relatively much greater power of the private and public owners or claimants who seek repeatedly to expel them from that land.

These considerations create an important task and opportunity for public policy and communal action in the amelioration of the economic and social circumstances of the urban population living in self-built residential structures and areas. It is vain to expect such communal action in these areas in the absence of any external, almost necessarily public, intervention. But with some appropriate, and not necessarily expensive, public intervention, communal action in this part of the population can significantly increase to contribute to the future economic, social, and political development of the society as a whole. Beyond the obvious, but at this time possibly economically prohibitive, measure of building public housing for these populations, there may be other economically immediately feasible measures to stimulate and organize community organization and development among self-built residential areas and their inhabitants.[34]

It would be desirable for central urban municipalities to incorporate or amalgamate with adjoining and even rural townships to form a larger urban or metropolitan area more susceptible to comprehensive urban planning. With a view to the housing problems of the floating urban population, it would then be desirable for the city to pursue a policy of land acquisition by the public authority well in excess of present construction needs.

Two major public policies are suggested with respect to such municipally-owned land and the problem of self-built residential structures. Firstly, existing self-built urban settlements on public land should receive public guarantees against eviction without very long term notice and public provision for better alternative housing in other areas whose location and transportation facilities are not seriously prejudicial to the interests of the potential evictees. In fact, it would seem reasonable to abandon policies and programs of urban renewal which imply the destruction of homes and the eviction of their owners until the still-unforeseeable time when economic conditions permit this policy to be pursued without placing the cost on those members of the society who can least afford it. This applies not only to tourist hotels but also to other urban "improvements." Secondly, the municipality can subdivide publicly-owned urban land and allot it to those in the floating population who have already built on it in settled areas and to those who wish to build on it in new self-built housing developments. These allotments should carry guarantees against evictions and could in return demand some minimal form of responsibility from the occupant. This possibility of transfer of allotments or lots should be provided for, but this must be coupled with measures to prevent acquisition and monopolization of multiple lots by private speculators.

It would be desirable to provide the maximum possible public protection to residents in self-built housing on privately-owned tracts of land. The best protection against private expulsion from and speculation with such privately-owned land is its acquisition under eminent domain and its subdivision by the municipality as described above. The purpose of public land acquisition in excess of residential construction needs is of course to forestall the development of such problems of private urban land speculation (which is also desirable for reasons other than those connected with self-built housing) and of floating populations living on such land.[35] However, it would be desirable to protect present inhabitants of self-built settlements on private lands against arbitrary expulsion as well by, in the public interest, limiting the terms under which such expulsion is legally possible.

More adequate, or less inadequate, self-built housing can be promoted by recourse to several measures of public policy and community action. To the extent that the foregoing measures to increase the security of residential tenure are adopted, it would be possible increasingly to include self-built residential structures and areas in the urban planning and zoning already applied to other parts of the city. Accordingly, it becomes administratively possible to provide a minimum of urban services such as water, sewage, and electricity to the floating population of self-built areas as well. Additionally, it would be possible to provide for their acquisition of building materials that can be at the same time of higher quality and of lower cost than those that are currently accessible to them through exclusively private channels, which are sometimes also monopolized.

Combining all or even some of these public measures to increase the security of tenure and decrease the cost of construction and maintenance for the urban population that must live in self-built housing would provide a substantially greater basis for communal participation of this population in matters of their own immediate interest as well as in those of wider social and political concern. At relatively low cost, these measures would permit the substantial duplication of the social, if not the physical, circumstances of such successful housing developments as "23 de Enero" in Caracas and "José María Caro" in Santiago, which latter incidentally includes a substantial proportion of self-built housing on municipally subdivided and allotted land. These measures, moreover, would permit the organization of residential building and maintenance cooperatives resting on communal participation in the process of planning, construction, and managing substantial settlements of self-built housing.

A further but more ambitious stimulus to such communal participation and organization would be for a public agency to organize the construction of self-built or semi-self-built housing. The public agency would provide the financial resources it now devotes to public housing projects, but instead of channeling them through private contractors who hire construction labor in the usual fashion and retain part of the project funds for themselves, or instead, even, of having the public agency supplant the private contractors and assume the contracting and employment functions itself, the public agency would assume the responsibility of planning the project, supplying the materials, architectural and contracting services, and then employ members of the float ing population in the construction of the project, recompensing them, instead of in wages, in rights to one of the completed dwellings after a certain number of hours of work has been contributed to its construction.

These self-built housing projects should not be confused, however, with such so-called self-built and aided mutual aid housing projects as are reviewed in South and especially in Central America by the Pan American Union in its *Self-Help Housing Guide* [36] and as are often financed by funds from the International Development Bank in Washington. For a look at the cost breakdowns reported in this *Guide* itself shows that these projects are self-built only in name and not in fact. Thus, the attributed labor cost of the participant workers who are to be the subsequent owners is about 11 per cent to 12 per cent in most of the projects reviewed, and 4 per cent in a Guatemalan one. That renders the term "self-built" a cruel joke. Cruel, because it turns out in the same cost breakdown that while contributed labor contributes little more than 10 per cent of the cost of the house, the land the subsequent owners must purchase and have developed, and the management and administration expenses they must pay for, contribute 50 per cent of the cost of the house; and another 40 per cent goes for building materials and professional labor. Having already taken note of high land costs on an earlier page, we may observe that administration and management costs accounted for 25 per cent of the total in Guatemala and 50 per cent and more of the total in Panama. If to these observations we add the one that the total cost of these houses per unit is, more often than not, over \$2,000.00 and sometimes passes \$3,000.00, there can remain little doubt but that this *Guide* to so-called self-help mutual aid housing is little more than a grand scheme for the mutual aid of land speculators, land development contractors, building contractors, and bureaucrats.

To avoid repetition of this sort of thing and to provide for real self-built mutual aid housing projects, the following recommendations are made: build much cheaper houses for much lower income receivers. Reduce the building time from the one and a half years common in the projects reviewed above to a maximum of one half year and preferably less. To achieve these and other ends, build for and rely on the labor of people more largely in the tertiary and self-employed or unemployed sector who have more flexibility in the disposition of their time and residence than workers and employees. Insofar as possible, provide for the participants residing on the building site either in temporary shacks or by designing the houses so that they may be built and occupied in stages, room by room. To that end, in turn, introduce a maximum of standardization of building parts compatible with self rather than professionally built housing. Combine the building facets of these projects with the distribution of food, such as from the Food for Peace Program, and with some of the other urban community-development programs such as community centers where the circumstances demand. It goes without saying, of course, that these recommendations and the publicly aided self-built projects themselves can come to no good whatever if it is not politically possible to eliminate the control of the projects by speculators, politicians, and other interests interested in the perpetuation and extension of the situation reviewed and even recommended as a *Guide* by the Organization of American States and its Pan American Union. Probably not surprisingly in view of the political differences between that country and some others in Latin America, Chile seems to be the country which has achieved the greatest measure of success in this direction; as the Pan American Union's own cost breakdowns show, it is in Chile that the proportionate costs of land and administration, though still high, are quite noticeably the lowest among the countries it reviews with so-called self-built aided mutual help housing projects.

Experience in Caracas suggests that any of these public approaches to the housing problem of the floating population can stimulate substantial social and political awareness and conscientious community action in otherwise very shiftless populations. Moreover, and significantly, it can do so without creating a paternalistic and/or dependency relationship between the government or public agency and the participating population. On the contrary, the Caracas, and to some extent the Santiago, experience suggests that permitting these populations access to minimum security in residential tenure can lead to the development among them of a healthy sense of social responsibility and political independence which manifests itself in very much heightened communal participation in a variety of independent voluntary organizations for the cooperative management and pursuit of housing, neighborhood and other civic interests, and a healthy if sometimes distant mutual respect between them and the government and its public housing agency. Most symptomatic of this sense of civic responsibility and political independence is the extent of self-policing in Caracas' "23 de Enero" Housing Project and the city police force's reluctance to interfere with that urban community's internal affairs. More important perhaps than its immediate implications for the problem of the housing and neighborhood problems of the floating population are the stimulation by these measures of conscious and organized community and political action which can become the basis of this population's more effective participation in other matters of concern to national development and welfare.

NOTES

* This article forms part of a report and recommendations on rural and urban community development which the author prepared under contract to the United Nations Economic Commission for Latin America for their seminar on this topic in 1964. Nonetheless, this organization is not to be held responsible for anything said herein.

[1] For references see especially, Phillip M. Hauser, *La Urbanización en América Latina*, Paris, UNESCO, SS.61/V.9/S,1962; United Nations Economic Commission for Latin America (ECLA), *The Social Development of Latin America in the Post-War Period*, E/CN.12/660, May 11, 1963; United Nations ECLA, *Urbanization in Latin America*, E/CN.12/662 March 13, 1963; Guillermo Rosenbluth L., *Problemas socioeconómicos d · la marginalidad e integración urbana (El caso de "Las Poblaciones Callampas" en el Gran Santiago*, Santiago, Universidad de Chile, 1963; Asociación Venezolana de Sociología, *VI Congreso Latino-americano de Sociología*, Caracas, Imprenta Nacional, 1961, vol. II.

[2] Thus the recent ECLA study, *The Economic Development of Latin America in the Post-War Period*, E/CN.12/659, April 7, 1963, makes no reference to the urban economy; and its companion document, ECLA *The Social Development of Latin America in the Post-War Period*, op. cit., though concerned with the city as a socio-economic unit, is unable to describe and analyze the situation as well as it would have been if economists had prepared the necessary studies of the contemporary urban economic structure.

[3] For a criticism of this classification which indicates the varieties of the tertiary sector, see, Peter T. Bauer and Basil Yamey, "Further Notes on Economic Progress and Occupational Distribution," *Economic Journal*,

March 1954. Also see Solomon Rottenberg, "Reflexiones sobre la industrialización y el desarrollo económico," Santiago, Universidad Católica, 1957.

[4] ECLA, *The Economic Development of Latin America* . . . , op. cit. and *The Social Development of Latin America* . . . , op. cit.

[5] This term is used in G. Rosenbluth L., op. cit. For further discussion, see below.

[6] For migration by stages see, for instance, Bertram Hutchinson, "The Migrant Population of Urban Brazil," *América Latina*, Año 6, No. 2 (abril–junio de 1963), especially pp. 45–50. ECLA, *Urbanization in Latin America*, op. cit. pp. 15, 16 and 33.

[7] *Ibid.* p. 15.

[8] Guillermo Rosenbluth L., op. cit. p. 99.

[9] Cf. ECLA, *The Economic Development of Latin America in the Post-War Period*, op. cit. Chapter VII and ECLA, *The Social Development of Latin America in the Post-War Period*, op. cit. Chapters II and III. Bertram Hutchinson, op. cit. p. 69 notes that 20%–40% of this population in the metropolis comes from other cities.

[10] ECLA, *The Social Development* . . . . op. cit. pp. 63–65, and ECLA, *Urbanization in Latin America*, op. cit. p. 28. Sixty-three per cent of employment in Greater Santiago and 45% in a callampa were found to be in the tertiary sector, and 17% and 33% respectively in the "self-employed" category.

[11] See Sol Tax, *Penny Capitalism*, Chicago, 1953.

[12] *Urbanization in Latin America*, op. cit. p. 28.

[13] ECLA, *The Social Development of Latin America* . . . , op. cit. pp. 59–61.

[14] Reported in G. Rosenbluth L., op. cit. p. 32 (Table 14).

[15] ECLA, *Urbanization in Latin America*, op. cit. p. 28.

[16] G. Rosenbluth L., op. cit. p. 79.

[17] *Ibid.* pp. 64–66.

[18] A document issued by the Presidency of the Republic of Brazil, Conselho do Desenvolvimento, *Questão Agraria Brasileira*, (by Ignacio Rangel), Brasilia, 1961, p. iii, speaks of monopoly which "methodically organizes scarcity" and thus "imposes extortionist prices on the consumer." *Correo da Manha* (Rio de Janeiro), june 6 de 1963, reports price mark-ups of 1,500% on food grown near Rio and sold in that city.

[19] OCEPLAN, *Las Bases Técnicas del Plan de Acción del Gobierno Popular*, Santiago, Chile, 1964, p. 17.

[20] ECLA, *Urbanization in Latin America*, op. cit. p. 10.

[21] J. Chonchol, *La Reforma Agraria en América Latina*, Santiago, Editorial del Pacífico, 1964, p. 63, for instance, argues that the poorest areas and inhabitants of the city pay the highest per unit prices for their food.

[22] See, for instance, "Aspectos Humanos da Favela Carioca," O Estado de São Paulo, April 15, 1960, for Rio de Janeiro; and José Matos Mar, "Migración y Urbanización—Las Barriadas Limeñas: Un Caso de Integración a la vida urbana," in P. M. Hauser, *La Urbanización en América Latina*, op. cit. for Peru.

[23] For distinctions in architectural, economic, social, and cultural terms among these three types of low-income urban dwellings, see, for instance, G. Rosenbluth L. op. cit. chapter III. The self-built settlements

are usually either on the outskirts of the city or on undesirable centrally located hillsides and river embankments. They carry various names: *jacales* (Mexico), *ranchos* (Caracas), *barrios clandestinos* (Colombia), *barriadas* (Lima), *callampas* (Santiago), *villas miserias* (Buenos Aires), *villas malocas* (Puerto Alegre), *favelas* (Rio de Janeiro), *Mocambos* (Recife), etc. Substandard structures and residential zones, like many slums in Europe and North America, are generally centrally located because they consist of old urban housing which is now in an advanced state of disrepair and which supports a very high concentration of occupancy. In Argentina and Chile they are called *conventillos* and in Mexico *tugurios*. Several countries and cities, notably Caracas and Santiago, have undertaken extensive urban renewal programs which "eradicate" self-built and in some cases old housing and which resettle some of the displaced families in state financed housing projects or publicly supervised subdivisions which provide assistance in self-construction of houses. These developments are, of course, usually on the outskirts of town and frequently quite distant from the center of town and/or centers of employment and retail trade.

[24] ECLA, *Urbanization in Latin America*, op. cit. pp. 7, 11, 33.

[25] UNICEF, *Boletín Trimestral del UNICEF*, No. 29, 1962, n.p.

[26] Quoted in ECLA, *Urbanización en América Latina*, op. cit. p. 23.

[27] ECLA, *Urbanization in Latin America*, pp. 9–10; Banco Obrero, *Proyecto de Evaluación de los Superbloques*, Caracas, 1961.

[28] ECLA, *Urbanization in Latin America*, pp.18–21. G. Rosenbluth L., op. cit. p. 90.

[29] G. Rosenbluth L., op. cit. pp. 58–70.

[30] ECLA, *Urbanization in Latin America*, op. cit. pp. 31–32. See also ECLA, *The Social Development* . . ., op. cit. pp. 30–32, 65–67.

[31] G. Rosenbluth L., op. cit. p. 92.

[32] Ibid., p. 96. Similar observations have been made in the other Latin American city with large-scale public housing projects; that is, in Caracas. See, for instance, *Report of a Community Development Evaluation Mission to Venezuela*, prepared for the Government of Venezuela by Caroline F. Ware, Rubén Darío Utria and Antoni Wojcicki, United Nations, Commissioner for Technical Assistance, Department of Economic and Social Affairs, TAO/VEN/15, December 1, 1963, particularly Annex I, E. and Annex E (unpublished). In Santiago "José María Caro" housing project and in Caracas those of "23 de enero" and "Simon Rodríguez" are outstanding in this respect. Each of these has upwards of 100,000 inhabitants. For a somewhat dimmer view, possibly because they compare the project reality with an ideal rather than with the reality of self-built communities, see also, Banco Obrero, *Proyecto de Evaluación de Superbloques*, op. cit.

[33] ECLA, *The Social Development of Latin America in the Post-War Period*, op. cit. p. 136.

[34] In this connection also see Phillip M. Hauser (ed.), *La urbanización en América Latina*, op. cit. Chapter II, "Conclusiones del Seminario," and Chapter XIII, "Algunas Consecuencias Políticas de la Urbanización."

[35] Thus, the *Self Help Housing Guide* of the Inter-American Housing and Planning Center of the Pan American Union in Washington reports land costs that reach such amounts as 57 per cent, 40 per cent and 35 per cent of the total cost of even so-called self-built and aided mutual help

project housing in Colombia, Nicaragua and Costa Rica, including 33% for totally undeveloped land in Nicaragua (pp. 5, 29). Marshall Wolfe attributes such costs largely to speculation in his *Las clases medias en Centroamérica: características que presentan en la actualidad y requisitos para su desarrollo,* United Nations, E/CN.12/CCE/176/Rev.2/1960, p. 1.

[36] Op. cit. The following data are all from this *Guide* and were culled out and combined by the author into a single table covering the dozen or so projects reviewed there. This procedure, which the *Guide*'s authors did not choose to adopt, permits the above general picture which does not emerge very clearly from the presentation, as in the *Guide*, of only the costs for each project taken singly and in isolation.

7

RODOLFO STAVENHAGEN

Classes, Colonialism, and Acculturation

A System of Inter-Ethnic Relations in Mesoamerica

This article will analyze the ethnic relations which characterize the intercultural regions of *Altos de Chiapas* in Mexico and Guatemala. It is not my intention to add new data presently unknown to experts in the area. My purpose is both more modest and more ambitious. I will reorganize known data into a scheme of interpretation differing from those which are currently used in anthropology. I believe that a conceptual scheme based on the role of internal colonialism in inter-ethnic relations will help in clarifying some historical and structural problems in the formation of national societies of Mexico and Guatemala.

The conceptual frame of reference of the analysis of social classes is more adequate to understanding relationships between economy and society than the frames of reference generally employed by researchers. I shall use some concepts that are sometimes ambiguous. In each case I will try to specify their meanings, but this will not always be possible. In such cases these concepts will have to be understood in their more common-sense use. The sources cited are merely illustrative, not exhaustive. Many of the facts analyzed are sufficiently well known so as to require no further documentation. The choice of the region, which includes areas of Mexico and Guatemala, is justified because of cultural and historical similarities of the Indian region on both sides of the border. Political and economic differences between the countries, especially in the course of the last few years, do not seem to have substantially modified the quality of inter-ethnic relationships; particularly is this the case on the analytical level at which this essay is written.

The Maya region of Altos de Chiapas and Guatemala is peculiar in that each local community constitutes a cultural and social unit which is distinguished from other similar communities, and its limits, furthermore, coincide with those of modern political-administrative units called municipalities or municipal agencies. Thus, the Indian population of every municipality (or municipal agency) can be distinguished from others through its clothing, dialect, membership, and participation in a religious and political structure of its own. This usually also involves economic specialization and a developed feeling of identity with other members of the community, reinforced by a somewhat generalized endogamous system. Aside from being an administrative unit integrated in Mexican and Guatemalan national political structures, the municipality in this region represents the sphere of the Indian population's social unit, which has been called "tribe" by some ethnologists, and which others have even termed the germ of the "nation." [1] This coincidence of modern municipal institutions with traditional Indian structures, resulting from the particular historical evolution of the region, has allowed the survival of the traditional structures within the framework of the modern national state.

INDIANS AND LADINOS

In the entire region and in almost all the local communities there co-exist two kinds of populations, two different societies: Indians and Ladinos. The problem of the relationships between these two ethnic groups has been studied in different ways by anthropologists.[2] Only a few of them, nonetheless, have attempted an interpretative analysis of the total society.[3] In these pages I intend to offer some elements for such an analysis.

It is well known that biological factors do not account for the differences between the two populations; we are not dealing with two races in the genetic sense of the term. It is true, of course, that in a general way the so-called Indian population has biologic traits corresponding to the Amerinds and equally, that the so-called Ladino population has the biologic traits of the Caucasoids. But even though Ladinos tend to identify with whites, in fact they are generally mestizo. It is the social and cultural factors that distinguish one population from the other.

For a long time it was common to draw up a list of identifiable cultural elements in order to distinguish both groups: language, clothing, agricultural technology, food, religious beliefs, etc. The advantages of such a list are that it allows an easy quantification of Indian and Ladino populations, and that census returns which include some of these elements—principally the language—can be profitably used. Thus, using these indices, Whetten was able to speak of the "indo-colonial" population of Mexico.[4] Confronted with the obvious insufficiency of this procedure in terms of a deeper analysis, it came to be recognized that these cultural elements were integrated within cultural complexes. Alfonso Caso used as his point of departure the fact that Indian populations live in communities that can be easily distinguished from one another, and he thus offered the following definition: "an Indian is he who feels he belongs to an Indian community, and an Indian community is that in which there exists a predominance of non-European somatic elements, where language is preferentially Indian, possessing within its material and spiritual culture a strong proportion of Indian elements and finally, having a social feeling of being an isolated community within surrounding ones, distinguishing it from white and mestizo villages."[5] This definition no longer considers the Indian as an isolated individual, but as a member of a well-defined social group. The author limits the qualification of Indian to a subjective feeling, and introduces racial considerations when distinguishing the Indian community from white and mestizo ones. We do not find in this definition the elements needed for an analysis of the existing relationships between Indians and Ladinos; quite the opposite, Caso's definition stresses the idea that we are dealing with two autonomous cultural worlds whose co-existence is almost a matter of chance.

The importance attributed by ethnologists to cultural elements of Indian populations has long concealed the nature of socio-economic structures into which these populations are integrated. Sol Tax, for instance, while studying Indian economy in Guatemala, chooses a community in which one third of the population is Ladino. Yet Tax describes only the Indian aspect and leaves aside the mestizo population as though the community's economy were not a complex and integrated whole. When he is forced to describe the inevitable interaction taking place between Indians and Ladinos, he does so as though he were dealing with external relations of Indian society.[6] Siverts, when speaking about monetary exchanges between Indians and Ladinos, even uses the term "external commerce." [7]

Certain recent ethnographic studies, and primarily the efforts of Indianist scholars in Mexico, have shown the weaknesses of an approach based exclusively upon analysis of cultural factors, not taking into account historical evolution. Eric Wolf has recently declared that "the condition of the Indian does not consist in a discrete list of social traits; it lies in the quality of social relationships found among communities of a certain kind and in the self-image of the individuals who identify with those communities. The Indian condition is also a distinctive historical process, since these communities originate at a given moment, grow stronger, decline again, and maintain or lose stability in the face of attacks or pressures coming from the larger society." [8] Thus, it is no longer the cultural *patterns* but the community *structure*, the relationships between its different parts, which are significant. The Indian condition is to be found in those closed "corporate" communities, whose members are bound by certain rights and duties, having their own forms of social control, particular political and religious hierarchies, etc. According to Wolf, these corporate units are the result of Spanish colonial policy, having suffered successive transformations under the impact of external influences. Wolf admits that these units, which are neither totally isolated nor completely self-sufficient, take part in wider economic and political power structures. The Indian communities are related to national institutions and include groups oriented towards both the community and the nation. These groups perform roles as political "power brokers" between traditional and national structures.[9]

Wolf's analysis of the Indian supplies historical depth and structural orientation which are not found among specialists in cultural anthropology. However, while Wolf clearly recognizes the existence of the corporate community's external relations, this community seems to respond mechanically to impulses originated in national and regional sources of power. Wolf does not speak about the relationships between Indians and Ladinos. Tax and Redfield also admit the existence of external relations, with the difference that for them, the controls imposed upon the population from outside the local community "have their origin in natural law"! [10]

Indianist action in Mexico has forced ethnologists to restate the problem in different terms. There has been a shift from the sphere of the Indian community to that of the intercultural region where Indians and mestizos co-exist. This region possesses the characteristic of having an urban complex mainly inhabited by a Ladino population and surrounded by Indian communities which are its economic and political satellites.[11] This new focus allows a better analysis of socio-economic structures and of relationships between human groups. We no longer speak of acculturation alone, but of the Indian's integration to the nation, which is precisely the stated purpose of Indianist policy. The ecological relationships between the metropolis and its satellites are only a part of the complex system of social relationships characteristic of this region. The theoretical framework used until now in the study of these relationships have proved insufficient for their full interpretation.

THE LAND AND SOCIAL RELATIONS

Class relationships in any society appear only through the analysis of the whole socio-economic structure. In the Indian region of Chiapas and Guatemala these relationships are not visible through the study of cultural differences between the two ethnic groups, nor do they show in all of the social situations in which there are inter-group relations. Class relationships emerge clearly through distribution of land as a means of the labor, trade and property relations which link one part of the population to another.[12]

Production Relations

Subsistence Agriculture

The basis of regional production is agriculture, and the basis of agriculture is maize, principally for domestic consumption. Even when other crops are cultivated, maize is the primary agricultural product without which the rural family, the productive unit, would not survive. The soil is poor, agricultural techniques are primitive, and yields are therefore small. Rainfall allows two harvests a year in some regions. The farmer devotes a great part of his time to subsistence farming with participation of family labor. Produce is consumed by the family. Sometimes, when the farmer needs money, he sells part of the harvest, but later, when his reserves are exhausted, he must buy his corn back again. In his position as a maize producer, the farmer remains isolated and does not enter into relations with other sectors of society.

There are exceptions to this situation. Some communities in the area have become specialized in maize production to the exclusion of any other important agricultural activity. Santiago Chimaltenango, in Guatemala, regularly produces a surplus of maize which is sold at the local markets.[13] In this case, the subsistence farmer becomes, in part, a peasant producing for the market. I say in part because the bulk of his production is consumed at home, so he remains within a subsistence economy. It is important to stress the fact that maize is grown almost exclusively by the Indians. Even though the majority of the communities have also a Ladino population, these rarely grow maize. When they devote themselves to agriculture, it is usually to produce cash crops.

We find a primary element for differentiation of the population into social classes: one part of the population predominantly devotes itself to subsistence maize farming—even while it sells

240

some surplus—and another sector does not participate in subsistence agriculture.

Commercial Agriculture

Almost all of the rural communities also participate in agricultural activities whose purpose is not domestic use but commerce. The subsistence farmer is also a producer for the market. Even while he may not devote the greater part of his time to this activity, it allows him to obtain the money he needs. At altitudes lower than 5,000 feet, maize economy is complemented with that of coffee, a cash crop par excellence. There are also cacao, onion, and vegetables of all kinds. At higher altitudes there are fruits. All of these food products are destined for sale, and the different communities specialize in production of one or the other. Maize and coffee (within their geographic limits) are found everywhere. Coffee is destined to national and international markets, while the majority of the other products appear only in local markets. The coffee-growing communities are usually richer than those which, located on higher and poorer lands, do not grow it. The subsistence farmer who grows coffee and other products for the market does not neglect growing his maize. Every community, in fact, possesses lands which are used only for maize, and other, usually better, lands which are used for cash crops. The subsistence farmer secures his maize crop first; only if he has time and additional land at his disposal does he devote himself to commercial farming, even if the latter be more productive than the former. In Panajachel, Guatemala, for instance, growing coffee and onions pays better than growing maize. Yet the Indians do not devote themselves to these activities until they have prepared their maize plots.[14] It is obvious that agricultural factors are involved in this situation; in the poorer and more inaccessible soils only maize can be grown, while the flat and fertile soils, which are nearer to the village, are taken up by commercial agriculture. But there are also reasons of an economic variety: the subsistence farmer has to secure his maize first, because he cannot buy it elsewhere. Panajachel produces only little economic surplus, and should the farmer devote himself exclusively to cash crops, without having the possibility of

241

importing maize from outside, the basis of his economy would crumble. We are therefore not dealing with the individual producer's choice alone, but with a problem of economic development.

Besides corn, in this community Indians are able to grow vegetables and coffee. Yet they grow more vegetables, notwithstanding the fact that these pay less than coffee. Coffee is a perennial plant, and the establishment of plantations requires time and capital. Since the Indians lack the means, they prefer to grow vegetables, with which they are able to obtain quicker, if smaller, benefits. Sol Tax describes the Panajachel Indians' economy as being a "penny capitalism," because they produce commercial agriculture for the market, because they are oriented towards a profit economy, and because they like to make "a good deal." Nonetheless, Tax himself shows that their economy is dominated in the first place by the needs of maize farming, and that they prefer to grow vegetables rather than coffee. The reason for this apparent contradiction lies in the fact that the Indians lack capital and credit institutions. As Wolf has pointed out, it is precisely these two factors—non-existent in Panajachel—which define a capitalist system.[15] The Panajachel Indian *is* integrated to the capitalist system, through the sale of his coffee and acquisition of industrial products. But the subsistence farmer, the Indian, is not the "capitalist" in this case. On the contrary, he is placed at the opposite pole. His agricultural labor is not essentially a commodity, and the money he earns through the sale of his vegetables is not reinvested but spent in current consumption. There is no accumulation of capital.

Differing from the Indians, Ladinos do not grow maize but only cash crops. They settled in the region in the course of the past century, with the expansion of coffee. In the rural communities the Ladino farmers are few in number, and farming is never their only occupation. In Panajachel, they grow the greater part of the coffee, and their farming is exclusively commercial. The coffee producer always employs salaried labor; he therefore must operate within the terms set by the monied economy. He is, in fact, a capitalist farmer, and he is able to afford it because, unlike the Indian, he does not devote his time to subsistence farming. The growing of coffee, as well as those who grow it, were introduced from outside. The Indians have accepted this new kind of farming only as a complementary economic activity.

Here we have a second element for the differentiation of social classes. We distinguish on the one hand, the farmer devoted to commercial agriculture as a complementary activity, and who obtains from it only minimal profits which are wholly destined for consumption; and on the other, the farmer (especially the coffee-grower) who accumulates capital, employs labor, and who usually also performs other non-agricultural activities. Again, the former are Indians and the latter Ladinos.

The Agricultural Workers

Until now we have spoken only about independent farmers, but a large part of the farming population is composed of laborers. In Jilotepeque (Guatemala), laborers constitute 90% of the active population, of which only 9% are Ladinos. All of the laborers work for Ladinos; there is not one Indian in this community who employs labor.[16] In the highlands of Chiapas, the peasants regularly work as laborers in the big coffee plantations, where they spend many months a year. Till only recently, this was forced or semi-forced labor, and the contract and employment conditions were notoriously bad. At present there exist labor unions of Indian workers, and the Mexican government has taken measures for the protection of migrant workers. Nonetheless, recruitment of laborers is still done with pressures and coercion which sometimes exceed the legal limits of what is called a free contract. From an Indian population totalling 125,-000 persons in this area of Chiapas, 15,000 laborers are employed on a seasonal basis.[17] In Guatemala's coffee plantations compulsory labor for Indians existed until recently; up to a maximum of 150 days per year, depending upon the amount of land which they possessed. The pretext for this recruitment was the fight against idleness; yet no Ladino, even those possessing no lands, was forced to perform this kind of work.

It is obvious that the laborer is placed in a class situation. This is perhaps more so for those who emigrate temporarily from their communities in order to work in the plantations than it is for those who remain at home and work as laborers in plantations closer to their communities. These laborers are not separated

243

from the social structure to which they belong; they remain subsistence farmers. They go in search of salaried work only when their corn field is secure. Writing about the *chamulas*, Pozas says that they do not want to work in coffee plantations, and that they do so only when compelled by economic needs.[18] In Guatemala, temporary migrations in search of work annually affect 200,000 Indians,[19] and more than one half of the big plantations' laborers are migratory. "This recruitment," one author says, "has been the means by which the plantations have extended their influence over almost all Indian communities in Guatemala." [20]

Insofar as the monetary needs of these rural communities are concerned, salaried labor has in some the same economic function as commercial agriculture has in others. From the point of view of the global economic structure, the self-subsisting community functions as a labor force reserve.[21] The degree of economic exploitation inflicted upon this labor force is shown by the following datum: in Jilotepeque, a Ladino laborer earns 50% more than an Indian laborer, yet the cost of supporting a mule is even higher than a Ladino's salary! [22]

It can thus be seen that salaried work and commerce notwithstanding, the structure of self-subsisting communities has not been wholly broken down. In Cantel, a Guatemalan community, only when the farmer does not possess enough land to feed his family does he seek work in a textile factory located there. The industrial worker remains integrated in the structure and values of his community. The new class relationships produced by local industrialization have only partially modified traditional structure. Here industrial work has the same function as migratory work and commercial agriculture in other communities.[23]

Salaried work represents a third element of class differentiation in the area. The monetary income obtained by farmers in the manner described above complements a subsistence economy. We find here new production relations, in which the Indian is always the employee and the Ladino the employer. When there are Ladinos employed by other Ladinos, they occupy higher positions and receive higher salaries than the Indians.

We now attempt a first generalization. At the level of agricultural production, the relationships between Ladinos and Indians are class relationships. The former produce exclusively for the market, while the latter produce primarily for their own consumption; Ladinos accumulate capital, Indians sell their farming products only in order to buy goods for consumption; Ladinos are employers and Indians are laborers. These relationships will be seen even clearer when we consider land tenure.

Land Tenure

Communal Property

The system of land ownership in colonial times worked against Indian lands. Through grants and patronage, Indian communities were deprived of their lands. The tutelary legislation of *Indias*, which protected communal property, was difficult to apply in practice. During the national period the collective lands survived only in the more isolated regions of New Spain, such as the one we are now discussing. The liberal reforms of the past century were equally directed against communal property. Part of the population, nonetheless, still possesses communal lands to the present day. There are various forms of collective land tenure, and their legal aspects are not always clear. Sometimes these are lands which in effect belong to a community, in accordance with a land title of the Colonial period, having been revalidated once in a while by some later national government. Another variant is that in which the deed of land ownership is held by an elder of the community who in fact is no more than a trustee. There is no precise data on the subject, yet it seems that traditional kinds of communal lands are not very common in the area. A survey of 80 different villages of West Guatemala showed the existence of communal lands in only one community.[24] In Mexico, the agrarian reform has modified the nature of collective lands in a great number of communities.

The still existing collective property is generally composed of land with poor soils, hardly useful for farming, and of minimal productive and commercial value. These lands are generally used for pasture, for gathering wood and wild fruit. All members of the community have a right to use these lands. Sometimes communal lands are also used to grow corn. In communities where this is done, the extent of communal lands is never sufficient to satisfy all of the farmers' needs. Thus, it can only absorb a part of the farming labor. Only very rarely are communal lands used for commercial farming purposes, and when such is the case, the monetary economy exerts a pressure upon maintenance of collective property. Tax cites the case of some fruit trees planted on communal lands of a Guatemalan village, which are the object of commercial transactions even while the land is still indivisible.[25] In a Chiapas community, the Indians collectively bought an estate which has now been integrated to the communal possessions of the lineage; [26] but usually communal lands are very ancient.

A community still possessing communal lands is also a traditional community, relatively well integrated from a social point of view and more or less homogeneous from an ethnic point of view. For if land cannot be sold, it is unlikely that Ladinos will be allowed to use it. It is also a poor community, with an economy for subsistence, since fertile soils and the possibilities of commercial agriculture attract the Ladinos and tend to transform collective property into private property. In other words, traditional collective lands are infrequent and do not perform an important role in the economy and social organization of Indian communities of this region.

The *Ejido* (Public Land)

Agrarian reform in Mexico reached the Indian region of Chiapas during the regime of President Cárdenas. In some communities traditional collective lands were transformed into ejidos; in others, some of the latifundia were expropriated in behalf of the peasants. In general, the distribution of ejidos respected ethnic differences, so that each ejido includes in effect members of an homogeneous and socially integrated ethnic group, which accentuates its character of being communal property. The proportion of ejido lands varies with respect to total property in the different municipalities. In ten municipalities, in which the density of Indian population is very high, ejido property is distributed in the following way: in three municipalities it embraces almost 100% of the total number of properties. Here we are obviously dealing with traditional communal lands which have resisted the process of disorganization characteristic of other communities, and which are now protected by agrarian legislation through legally sanctioned land tenure. In two municipalities ejido property represents more than 65%; in yet two others, more than 35%; and in the remaining three, less than 25%. Thus in the region there is no general tendency with respect to the proportion of ejidal lands.[27]

In Guatemala the existence of ejido lands may be considered as a tenacious defense of traditional Indian collectivities against the economic system represented by private property and by the Ladino group. In Mexico, on the contrary, the ejido is the result of an active struggle for the land by the Indians against the great latifundists. This struggle, which has had a history of violence, is already an old one, and was recently stimulated by the national movements of agrarian reform. Here, as in other parts of Indian America, the agrarian struggle has often taken the shape of an inter-ethnic conflict. Yet at the same time it is an agent of acculturation, despite the apparently contradicting fact that its manifest objective is the reconstitution of the traditional Indian communities' territorial base.

Despite the fact of being collective property, ejidal lands are tilled individually, or rather by the family group. In Chamula, where all of the land is ejidal, the families control their plots as though they were private property, yet without being able to subdivide them. These plots can be inherited by sons and daughters alike, and this has produced a progressive atomization of family "property," the result of which has been the emigration of a large number of Chamulas in search of lands in the neighboring municipalities. In other communities, the farmer is entitled to the use of ejido lands only as long as he regularly works them. This condition is characteristic of traditional communal organization and follows the Mexican national agrarian reform legislation.

Private Ownership of Land

This is the more usual form of land tenure. It was introduced by the Spaniards and spread greatly after the nineteenth century's liberal reforms. Under the new liberal legislation Indian communities were forced to transform their communal lands into individual property, which contributed to the fact that many communities completely lost their lands.

Private property of land means that land has an economic value and that it has been transformed into a commodity. It also extension of the lands they possess, and new social relationships, means the emergence of inequalities among men, according to the the basis of which is private property of land: sharecropping, tenant farming, wage labor, sale, mortgage, etc. In Panajachel, writes Tax, the land is fully integrated in the commercial cycles which characterize "penny capitalism." But the process is not yet finished. Tax admits that in this community the lands are not considered as an investment (that is, as capital) but only as consumption goods. In Chamula, as we have seen, the land is collectively owned (ejido), yet the concept of private property (even without its juridical manifestations) is developing. The land can be inherited and divided, but not sold. It does not produce rent, but it can be mortgaged under certain special conditions.

In the Indian area, the private property of land has stimulated Ladino penetration. First attracted by the new coffee crop, during the past century, they later took to other kinds of commercial agriculture. Freeing the land in fact accelerated the expansion of the national commercial-capitalist system. In Jilotepeque, Eastern Guatemala, the Indians have progressively lost their lands to such a degree that now only 5% of the Indians possess enough land to satisfy their needs, while 95% of them must rent theirs from the Ladinos. 70% of the land belongs to the Ladinos, who represent only 30% of the population; and this land is primarily tilled by sharecropper or salaried Indians. The Ladinos possess, on the average, 57.3 acres of land, and the Indians 13.2 acres. The results of a survey showed that among the Indians 16% of them were landowners, while among the Ladinos, 55% were.[28] In Panajachel, West Guatemala, the Ladinos represent one third of the population, but they possess 80% of the lands. The average Ladino possesses more than 8 times more land than the average Indian. Besides, the Ladino often possesses lands in other municipalities.[29] How did it come about that the Ladinos have been able to take possession of such a large amount of land? Charles Wagley tells us: "The inevitable result of the series of laws extolling private property in compliance with modern conceptions was that many Indians who were unable to seize the meaning of the new private documents failed to register their lands, and these were often sold to the big plantations as non-validated lands." [30] Pozas quotes the case of a Governor of the State of Chiapas who, as a result of the Reform laws "denounced" the existence of communal land in an Indian municipality, and thus obtained legal title to it. In many instances the Indians' property titles soon passed into the hands of the latifundists, and even when no legal changes in land tenure occurred, the Indians were progressively dispossessed of their land. The lack of land forced the Indians into becoming peons on the big plantations. Many independent farmers were thus depressed to the condition of semi-serfs; and others were recruited for temporary forced labor.[31] This situation was consolidated at the end of the 19th century with the political victory of the conservative forces in Mexico and Guatemala.

These examples show that the private property of land benefits the Ladinos and harms the Indians. The process of appropriation of the land by the Ladino element is a unilateral one; it does not work in the opposite direction.[32] In Mexico, nonetheless, it has been possible to check it somewhat, due to the agrarian reform and the ejido system.

Ultimately there exists a great difference between the Ladinos and the Indians in terms of land property, particularly with respect to their use of it and the feelings and attitudes assumed with respect to it. The Indian is a man who is integrated in his traditional community, which is bound to the land. The Indian tills the soil; culturally and psychologically he ceases to be an Indian when he becomes separated from the land. The tilling of the soil is intimately related to the group's social organization (lineage or tribe), and to religious organization and belief. The Indian needs the land because without it he loses his social and ethnic identity. It does not matter whether this land is communal, ejido, or private. In any case, it will be property and not merchandise. It is a means of production, but it is not capital. It is a source of income, but not of rent. Traditionally, the land is not an exchange value for the Indian. The soil must be tilled, and only by doing so does the Indian come to realize himself (even when it be on someone else's property, as day laborer, sharecropper or tenant). The tilling of the land is primarily performed by the family, yet should the need arise, a few day laborers may be temporarily employed to help in the farming tasks. The Indians do not like to sell their lands, particularly to the Ladinos; yet throughout the years they have done so when they had to. On the other hand, when land is scarce, as in Chamula, those who are the most dynamic or the most needy go in search of land in other places; either to buy it or to work on communal lands of other municipalities. But they do not break their social ties with their group of origin.

The private property of land is only one aspect of the deep transformations which have affected the Indian communities since the 19th century, and which have accelerated during the last decades. Pozas points to the growing contradiction in Chamula between the new principle of private property and the traditional principle of communal and clan equality.[33] This contradiction is not equally profound in other municipalities. In Panajachel, on the contrary, the land is subject to active commerce among the Indians. Yet he who sells his land loses prestige, while he who buys it, increases it.[34] Also in Chimaltenango, it is disapproved of when the Indians sell their lands, and yet "the lands change ownership with a certain frequency" and there are some Indians who have rather large properties.[35]

From the above we can see that among the Indians private ownership of land is still in a period of transition. For the majority of the Indians, who participate in a communal subsistence economy, land as a means of production has not yet acquired the characteristics which it has in a more highly developed economy. The land is still too much linked to the Indian's socio-religious and family complexes to have become a commodity, an object of a distinctly commercial value which it has become among the Ladinos. Finally, as a juridical instrument, the private ownership of this Indian land has not only failed to provide the Indians with the equality and the security which it was meant to provide, according to the liberal ideology, but quite to the contrary, it has exposed the (relative) independence of these populations to the acquisitive spirit of those representing the new economic structure, the Ladinos.

For Ladinos, the private ownership of land has a different meaning than it has for the Indians. It is associated with commercial farming (especially coffee), with a monetary economy, with wage labor, including a type of servitude of the Indians and, finally, with prestige and personal power. For the Ladinos land is a commercial value, independent of the group's social organization. The Ladinos' primary goal is to accumulate land and to exploit it through the use of wage labor. The Ladino still has, in part, the aspirations of a feudal lord (New World variant), but there are very few of them who achieve the privileged position of a big landowner, a position reserved to the descendants of the original owners during the Colonial and post-Colonial period. The Ladino is contemptuous of manual labor; his property serves the purpose of obtaining an income which allows him to devote himself to commerce and politics. Ladinos have not yet acquired a capitalist spirit in the Weberian sense of the word. The development of a regional economy compels him to be an entrepreneur. We have already seen that the majority of the lands belonging at present to the Ladinos were obtained by them at the time of the coffee boom, during the past century. Ladinos use their accumulation of lands to obtain and control cheap labor. The *Instituto Nacional Indigenista* in Mexico has declared that: "In Altos de Chiapas diverse *tzeltal* and *tzotzil* communities have seen their lands invaded by neighboring ranchers. Since it is an overpopulated region, the land has gradually been impoverished by the backward agricultural practices which erode it, and by over-pasturing. With the occupation of their best lands, the Indians find themselves driven each season to the coffee plantations of Soconusco, or working on the margins of the Grijalva under the sharecropping system, subject to the cruel conditions imposed by the owner." [36] Pozas describes the case of a coffee plantation owner who bought a property in an Indian municipality, and who allowed the Indians to grow their corn there under the condition that they would regularly work on his coffee plantation which lay in another region.

This brief analysis has shown that the private ownership of the land has different economic and social functions among the Indians and the Ladinos. It is a social institution linked to the capitalist development of the region. But it primarily benefits the

Ladino group, and it is used by them as an instrument of exploitation of the Indians. The private ownership of land, introduced by the liberal regimes who, ironically, wanted the greatest good for the greatest number, has only served to dispossess the Indians of their lands, thus forcing them to go in search of wage work. The private ownership of land thus constitutes one more element for the differentiation of the social classes of the region.

There are also important differences inside the owners' group, of course, but we do not have the data which would enable us to study them in relation to ethnic differences. The Ladino owners generally possess more lands than the Indian owners. Yet in each of these ethnic groups the extension of properties varies a great deal. Minifundists are many in number, and latifundists, though small in number, concentrate the greatest part of private lands in their own hands. The great latifundists are always Ladinos, of course, and the Indians concentrate at the base of the pyramid. But there are also Ladinos who own only very small parcels of land, while, on the other hand, there are Indians who possess, as in Chimaltenango, 50 times more land than others. The greater part of Indian owners do not possess enough land in order to meet their basic needs, and there are those who sell their minute properties and become day laborers in order to earn a little more.[37]

Commercial Relationships

The Indian economic world is by no means closed. Indian communities are isolated only in appearance. They participate in regional systems and the national economy. Markets and commercial relationships represent the primary link between the Indian community and the Ladino world, between subsistence economy and national economy. It is true that the major part of the Indians' agricultural produce is consumed by them. It is also true that the income generated by the Indians only represents a minimal part of the GNP (even in Guatemala, where the Indian population represents more than one half of the total). The importance of these relationships does not lie in the amount of commercialized products or in the value of the products being bought; it lies in the quality of commercial relationships. These are relationships which have transformed the Indians into a "minority" [38] and which have placed them in the condition of dependence in which they now find themselves.

Markets and commerce in the region have their background in the pre-Hispanic and colonial period. Their importance in some places is such that Redfield even speaks of a "primitive merchant society." [39] Tax calls the system capitalist because it rests on a "monetary economy organized around single households which are units of production and consumption, with a strongly developed market which tends to be perfectly competitive." [40] Such does not seem to be the case in other areas of the region, where the Indian market shows strongly marked monopolistic elements.[41]

Indian markets and the "constellation of regional markets" have been described in many contexts (especially in Mexico). Thus, it should be unnecessary to offer a detailed analysis of their structure. The role of the Ladino city as a metropolis or urban complex of an intercultural region, and its position of economic, political, social, and religious dominance with respect to satellite Indian communities is very well known. Between the city and the communities there develops a network of close and complex commercial relationships. In the city there is a weekly market of regional importance, and regular and permanent commerce in the stores and in the daily market. At the weekly market place there is an influx of thousands of regional Indians who go to the market to sell their handicraft and farm products, and to buy industrial and handicraft goods at the commercial establishments of the city. Some Indians are full-time traders who participate in the cycle of regional markets; Redfield has called them "primitive merchants." [42] But the majority of Indian producers carry their products to the market themselves, usually accompanied by their families. Commerce at the regional urban complex is so organized that the Indian always leaves behind his small monetary income. He sells cheaply and must buy dearly. The Ladino trader perceives a double benefit, through buying the Indian's products and selling him not only the articles which the Indian family needs to satisfy its daily wants, but also those which are related to political and religious life.

Despite Tax's findings in Panajachel, there seems to be a

general tendency towards a monopsonic structure in the Indian markets, in which t ie Indian producer-seller is in no way able to influence the price level. Trading of food products (the basis of Indian production) is controlled by a few Ladino monopolists from the city. As Marroquín has pointed out, the well known bargaining of Indian markets is an instrument used by Ladinos in order to depress price levels of Indian products. In San Cristóbal de las Casas, for instance, the same effect is achieved through the performance of the *atajadoras*, the Ladino women who place themselves at the city's entrance on market days and almost violently force the submissive, incoming Indians to sell them their wares at prices that they impose and which are lower than those which prevail at the market. These varied forms of exploitation which victimize the Indian trader, both as seller and buyer, are due to economic and political dominance of the urban Ladinos. This power is reinforced by their cultural superiority as expressed by their knowledge of price-building mechanisms, of the laws of the country; above all, of the Spanish language, which, being unknown to the Indians, represents one more factor of inferiority and social oppression. It is obvious that under these conditions the Indian has no access to national legal institutions which protect his individual rights.

Not only in the city but also in the "satellite communities" is commerce usually in Ladino hands. The latter are also moneylenders, which is an important function in societies where there is no accumulation of capital and where political and religious life demands considerable expenses. In order to pay their debts, Indians often mortgage their harvest (but seldom their property) and go to work on the coffee plantations.

Among the different kinds of relationships which take place between Indians and Ladinos, commercial relationships are the most important. The Indian participates in these relationships as producer and consumer; the Ladino is always the trader, the middleman, the creditor. The majority of the Indians enter into economic and social relationships with Ladinos at the level of commercial activity, and not at the level of wage labor. It is precisely the commercial relationships which link the Indian world to the socio-economic region in which it is integrated, and to national society as well as to the world economy.

254

Often commercial relationships go together with social relationships of another kind. Pozas writes that these are sometimes familial. He says that "interdependence between Indian and Ladino individuals and families constitutes the real basis of relationships between the Ladino urban complex and the Indian rural villages." [43] These relationships between families can take the form of *compadrazgo* (Godfather complex). Although at first sight compadrazgo may appear to be an institution in which Indians and Ladinos face each other on a level of equality, in fact it contributes to accentuate the Indians' condition of inferiority and dependence. Compadrazgo is one among many institutions in a complex system which keeps the Indian subordinated to the Ladino in all aspects of social and economic life.

The conjunction of all these commercial relationships allows us to carry our analysis further. It is obvious that Indian communities are not economically closed. On the contrary, they are linked to regional structures by means of which they participate in the national and world economy. They are the weakest link of a national economy. On the other hand, these commercial relationships are only a part of the Indian community's economic system. It is precisely this one aspect of all the economic activities of Indian communities which places them in a specific and special situation with respect to the Ladino population: a class situation. Commercial relationships between Indians and Ladinos are not relations between equals. The Indian, as a small producer, small seller, small buyer, and finally small consumer, can influence neither prices nor market tendencies. The Ladino, on the contrary, holds a privileged situation in the region. The Ladinos, small in number, are for the greatest part traders and middlemen. The city, populated by Ladinos, is monopolistic. Regional production is concentrated in it. There finished goods are distributed. True, these activities are a function of regional cities throughout the world. But here the economic inequalities between the city and the community are accentuated by the low level of agricultural production, the high cost of goods brought from other regions, and by all the other means of political, religious, and social power which the city exerts over the neighboring rural environment.

There may be those who see in this situation only an ecologic relation, an "urban-rural" conflict. Others who will see only a situation of contact between two cultures, between two ethnic groups with different economic resources, which would explain or even justify the pre-eminence of one ethnic group over the other. Yet this would be a mistaken view. The city's privileged position has its origin in the colonial period. It was founded by the conqueror to fulfill the very same function it still fulfills; to incorporate the Indian into the economy which the conqueror had brought and his descendants developed. The regional city was an instrument of conquest and is still an instrument of domination. It is not only a matter of "contact" between two populations: *the Indian and the Ladino are both integrated with a unique economic system, in a unique society.*[44] It is for this reason that inter-ethnic relations, insofar as commercial activities are concerned, bear the characteristics of class relationships. The ecologic aspect of interaction between city and countryside, or between urban metropolis and community, in fact conceals specific social relationships between certain kinds of persons who hold differential positions with respect to the means of production and the distribution of wealth.

Social Stratification

There are essentially two ways in which to consider the relationships between Indians and Ladinos: that which only considers two ethnic groups, two cultures brought to a more or less close contact, which might be called the culturalistic perspective; and that which takes as its point of departure the existence of the whole society, of a single socio-economic structure in which these two ethnic groups perform differentiated roles, and which might be called the structuralist perspective. The analysis made thus far is from the latter perspective. Yet this does not mean to deny the value of the culturalist approach. On the contrary, the perspective of cultural anthropology is valid when the analysis of social classes is set aside in order to consider other aspects of the relationships between the two ethnic groups.

In every society there may exist various systems of social stratification. Here it is possible to distinguish three systems of social stratification, that is, three social universes with respect to which social stratification may be studied: the Indian group, the Ladino group, and the total society in which Indians and Ladinos participate (that is, the inter-ethnic system). We may speak of two kinds of stratification: intra-ethnic and inter-ethnic.

Intra-Ethnic Stratification

Indians and Ladinos represent two different cultural communities. Each has a set of cultural values which may be called a value system. To the extent to which the value systems of these two communities are different, so too their systems of stratification shall likewise be different. It is thus easy to distinguish social stratification in each of them.

The Indians' Social Hierarchy

The Indian community is not stratified. All of its effective members equally participate in the same value system, and they are all equal with respect to each other. To participate in an effective manner in the Indian community means that Indians fulfill their duties in the community's political and religious structure.

The corporate community controls its members through control of its resources and through regular distribution of wealth. This is brought about through the cycle of religious festivities and through local government. Community government has traditionally been in the hands of *principales*, family and lineage chiefs who enjoy special prestige due to services rendered to the community, and sometimes due to special supernatural powers which are attributed to them by other members of the group.[45] The council of principales is a group of elders who enjoy an individual pre-eminence; it is not a social stratum. This form of government is linked to the original kinship organization, which is now disappearing. Its real power is decaying, and effective government is in the hands of the so-called Regional Council. This is the pinnacle of the double political-religious hierarchy (also called *centripetal* organization),[46] in which individuals climb to higher status by alternately holding civil and religious positions in the course of their lives. The individual named by

257

his peers to hold a public position within this system is forced to accept it under the threat of strong social ostracism. Public functions imply a series of very heavy duties and monetary expenses. The selected individual (who always tries to escape from his functions before having been elected, but must rigorously submit to his duties once he has forcibly been sworn in) not only must abandon his farming, leaving it to the care of his family or even hired laborers, but must also spend large sums for festivities and ceremonies in the organization of which he must participate. Passing through the hierarchy means years of indebtedness for many. When the public position is well performed it is a source of prestige and moral authority, but it does not bring major benefits. Personal power is strictly limited by the collectivity; authority is exercised for the benefit of the whole community and not for any restricted particular group.

It has been said that the expenses involved in festivities and ceremonies represent a prestige economy, that distribution of wealth (similar to Canadian *potlatch* and African *bilaba*) is the source of prestige.[47] Another author offers an opposite interpretation, which seems closer to reality: it is not wealth as such, but services rendered to the community which create prestige, yet a certain amount of wealth is necessary to carry out these services adequately. Thus, there is not, strictly speaking, a prestige economy, since economic pre-eminence is not automatically translated into prestige. On the contrary, if a poor man performs his public functions well, he may achieve a status of great prestige in the community; that is if he finds the means to finance the festivities and ceremonies which are his charge, even when this may mean running into debts.[48] Apparently economic pre-eminence of individuals is not favored by the community. We have seen that the means available to the Indian for accumulating capital are strictly limited. Also limited are the possibilities of investment. Basically, it is the corporate community itself which limits the economic possibilities of its members. In Chamula, members of the Council sometimes purposefully choose for the presidency individuals whose relative wealth is well known. This is obviously justified by the fact that wealthy persons can more easily perform their duties. But the social consequence of this act is the redistribution of wealth and maintenance of the "principle of equality" in the group's social organization.[49]

Under these conditions it is impossible for a social stratum that stands out among the rest of the population to emerge in the traditional corporate community.[50] Individual economic pre-eminence is not transformed into prestige. It arises, individually, through positions held in the political-religious structure. The political organization of the community is a means to redistribute wealth and channel people's energy into service to the community.

It is important to qualify the phrase "redistribution of wealth." In effect, a fictitious redistribution occurs. It is nothing but elimination of likely economic pre-eminence of those individuals who for some reason have been able to accumulate a greater amount of goods than their peers. This wealth is not reabsorbed by the community. It is consumed in liquor, ceremonial clothing, firecrackers and fireworks, and in hundreds of articles employed in what an observer has named "institutionalized waste." [51] These expenses required by the ceremonial economy associated with the functioning of the political and religious organization are transformed into income for those who provide these articles for the community. These purveyors are urbanized Ladinos, many of whom are craftsmen specialized in the kinds of articles consumed by Indians. Aguirre Beltrán even states that the trading of these ceremonial articles is, in Chiapas, "the real source of life of a city of 18 thousand inhabitants." [52] We may thus conclude that the structure which maintains equality within the Indian community, preventing the emergence of social classes, also contributes to the whole Indian community's dependence on the city, that is, to the differentiation of social classes between Indians and Ladinos.

There exists in the region yet another form of government: the Constitutional Council, which is a part of the national political regime and the only "legal" government, from the point of view of the national constitution. This is the link which unites the community to other political institutions such as political parties, regional and national legislatures and national executive power. It is the means employed by national governments to extend their administrative and political control over Indian populations.

The constitutional council is generally controlled by Ladinos, even though the municipal president may be an Indian. Local Indian government will surely disappear in time, to be replaced by the Constitutional Council. To the extent to which the Indians participate more and more in national politics and in official governmental organisms, the Constitutional Council is likely to become a means of social differentiation within the Indian community, perhaps creating a higher stratum of "court clerks" and functionaries.[53]

Social Strata among Ladinos

Ladino society, like every "Western" society, is stratified. This stratification is influenced by such factors as land ownership, income, occupation, education, and family lineage. The Ladino city is highly differentiated in terms of these diverse criteria, even having its own local aristocracy descending (in fact or in fiction) from important colonial families. Status indices are correlated with one another. The family line, large land ownership, big business, and participation in local politics go together. But on the other hand, a high level of education (especially university) is more typical of the "new rich," the professionals (physicians, lawyers, engineers), who are new to the region but are developing other more traditional interests, and thus frequently associate with older families through marriage.

It would be arbitrary to determine the number of strata existing in the Ladino society. In Guatemala, Adams indicates six "primary economic types": large landowner, plantation owner, medium-sized landowner, small landowner, tenant-farmer and worker. The last three levels often overlap and may be treated as a single stratum. Workers are in turn divided into tenant farmers and day laborers. But on the other hand the same author also speaks of only four strata: the upper cosmopolitan, upper, middle and lower "classes." [54] In Jilotepeque, Tumin differentiates three strata, according to wealth, family prestige, and other characteristics. Combining indices of various scales, which he then divides into three groups: an upper "class," with 45.5% of the Ladinos in his sample; a middle "class," with 40.9%, and a lower "class," with 13.6%. Applying the same indices to a sample of Indian population, the result is no upper class at all, and the concentration of two thirds of the sample in the "lower class." Nonetheless, on Tumin's scale a certain number of Indians and Ladinos hold identical positions.[55]

In terms of our stratification analysis, this exercise in status classification is of only limited value. We have already seen that the Indian community is socially unstratified and Tumin confirms it in his analysis. Tumin's statistical exercise is useful only to establish "standards of living" which may have no major social implications (such is the case, in effect, among the Indians). And with respect to Ladinos, Tumin admits the weakness of his own analysis by showing that in Jilotepeque, Ladinos are in fact divided into only two strata perceived by everyone: the elite, called *society*, composed of 20 families (less than 20% of the Ladino population), and the *populace*. At the lowest level of the Ladino ethnic group, it is difficult to distinguish clearly a Ladino from an Indian. In Panajachel, Tax also speaks of two Ladino classes: the "upper urban bourgeoisie" and the "lower rural." [56] In other communities there also exist specifically defined strata.

Ladinos place high value on wealth and property, which are one of their raisons d'être. These values constitute the foundation of all of their economic activity. Ladino society is mobile, and opportunities for upward mobility exist, in principle, for everyone. As opposed to the Indian, the Ladino conceives his own society as a stratified system. Certain activities, especially manual occupations, belong to an inferior order and must be avoided; there are others, especially commerce, to which they aspire. Finally, the condition of landowner is the most envied. The "good family" plays an important part in these provincial societies, and the fact of being related, through kinship, marriage or compradazgo, to important families is obviously a way of acquiring a high social status. Ladino culture, as opposed to the Indian, is highly competitive and authoritarian.[57]

Inter-Ethnic Stratification

Stratification means that certain characteristics or variables are unequally distributed among individuals. The combination of some of these characteristics and the value attributed to them by members of society account for the existence of a scale or continuum, in which individuals occupy higher or lower positions with respect to one another. If a set of individuals have in common a set of these characteristics, which distinguish them from other groupings, and if this is recognized as such by society, we may then speak of a stratum or social class. When a stratified system has quantifiable status characteristics, and is homogeneous from a cultural and racial point of view, some authors commonly refer to it as a "social class system." But if other factors are involved, and if the status indices are associated with qualitative factors such as "race" or culture, then some specialists speak of a "caste system."

Ladinos and Indians hold different positions in the stratification scale, according to such well known variables as income, property, degree of education, standard of living, etc. Given the fact that Ladinos concentrate along the scale's upper ranks and Indians along the lower ones, the two ethnic groups may be considered as strata within one stratified system. They are in effect the only strata in this system, because in the value systems of both groups ethnic characteristics (cultural and sometimes even biological) play a more important part in stratification than do other criteria. Ladinos hold a higher position not only in the objective scale of socio-economic characteristics, but they also consider themselves, qua Ladinos, superior to the Indians. They are contemptuous of the Indian as such. The latter, on the other hand, are conscious of their social and economic inferiority. They know that those traits which identify them as Indians place them in a position of inferiority with respect to Ladinos.

Even while stratification is objectively presented as a scale or continuum, it in fact functions socially as a system with only two strata which are characterized in cultural and biological terms. Ladinos make use of physical stereotypes to affirm their "whiteness" in contrast to the darker Indians. As Tumin has pointed out, it is a matter of ideal types, since the Ladino population is in effect a mestizo one. This fact notwithstanding, one of the most valued criteria among the higher Ladino strata is that of their supposed "Spanish blood." Other observers have noted that, in San Cristóbal de las Casas, there appears to be a coincidence between the socio-economic scale and the biological continuum.[58] Racial criteria, nonetheless, do not play an important role, precisely because it is impossible to classify the population in either ethnic group on an exclusively physical basis. Cultural factors are essential to stratification: in the first place comes language and dress, but there is also self-identification and personal identification by others. Thus, mastery of Spanish and changes in dress do not ipso facto turn the Indian into a Ladino. Essentially the Indian condition lies in integration with the Indian (corporate) community, and participating in the traditional social structure (kinship groups, civic-religious hierachy). It is the "cultural" and not the "biological" Indian who constitutes the lowest stratum. The Indian is conscious of this situation. Learning Spanish not only represents for him a means of upward mobility, but also an instrument of defense in his daily relationships with Ladinos. The adoption of Ladino dress styles also reduces the stigma of his inferior condition in his relationship with Ladinos. (Let us disregard here a discussion of psychological counter-acculturation, represented by a sharp rejection of everything which is Ladino, a phenomenon which often appears among the more conservative elements of the Indian community.)

The definition of the two ethnic groups depends upon strictly cultural factors which, due to their historical importance in the region, subsume and impose themselves upon all other factors of stratification. While it dichotomizes social relationships, ethnic stratification diminishes the importance of the socio-economic scale or continuum based on quantitative indices. This is true to such a degree that many Indians and Ladinos share the same socio-economic level without the disappearance of ethnic stratification. Robert Redfield noted that in a Guatemalan village, "the greater the Ladinos' upward mobility, the more they tended to be contemptuous of the Indians and to identify lower-class Ladinos with Indians." [59] And, naturally, those "lower-class" Ladinos considered themselves superior to Indians.

These cultural values are reflected in inter-ethnic relations. Ladinos always behave in an authoritarian or paternalistic manner towards Indians. These are treated with familiarity, yet it is expected of them to show signs of respect and submission.

Unskilled manual labor is considered an attribute of the Indian. Notwithstanding legal equality proclaimed in the Constitution, Indians are subject to discrimination, particularly in the cities, where they are exposed to all kinds of arbitrary and humiliating behavior by the Ladino population.

Effective social contacts between Indians and Ladinos are, with the exception of the already mentioned economic relations, very limited. There exists no real social interaction between the two ethnic groups. Traditional religious and political activities are performed separately; common participation at parties and sports is almost non-existent. The only non-economic relationship in which Indians and Ladinos formally participate is compadrazgo, yet as has already been pointed out, here too the Indian's inferiority is obvious, and here too there are economic implications.

SOCIAL MOBILITY

There is upward mobility from the Indian stratum to the Ladino; but its nature and characteristics are by no means simple and they vary from region to region. A public opinion poll carried out by Tumin in Jilotepeque showed that there are relatively more Indians than Ladinos who believe that movement from one group to the other is possible. Indians tend to believe they can achieve this through the accumulation of wealth, while Ladinos believe that the modification of strictly cultural characteristics is needed. Given the Ladinos' superiority, they have an interest in checking the Indians' mobility. Adams has pointed out that in a community where cultural differences between Indians and Ladinos are small, the latter resort to a whole series of ruses in order to maintain their superiority—even the invocation of "racial" factors where no biological differences exist.

Upward mobility among Indians represents a process of acculturation.[60] But learning Spanish and adopting Ladino dress styles is insufficient. The Indian must also become socially (generally meaning physically) separated from his community. In order to become a Ladino, the mobile Indian must cut his ties with the social structure of his corporate community. He must not only modify his cultural characteristics, but also his "social" condition as an Indian. It is very unlikely and one might say impossible, for an Indian to become a Ladino in the midst of his own community. The "ladinized" Indian is a marginal man. Well known are cases of Indians in the process of acculturation, who wear Ladino clothes when going to the city, and change again into their Indian costume upon returning to their community. The difficulties encountered by the cultural promoters of the Instituto Nacional Indigenista in Mexico are also well known. It should be noted that these promoters, in their positions as teachers, nurses, and practical farmers at the service of the State, come to achieve a higher socio-economic status than the local Ladinos. This suggests that mobility increases when the community's traditional structure begins to disintegrate. Researchers have pointed to the existence of diverse stages in the Indian's acculturation process. We thus speak of the traditional Indian, the modified Indian, the ladinized Indian, the armed Indian, etc. These are descriptive categories rather than analytical ones, and since they possess such diverse connotations, they should be handled with great care. On the other hand, there are also "indianized" Ladinos and, to be sure, Ladino culture as such contains innumerable cultural elements of Indian origin.

The Indian's upward mobility means both a process of acculturation and an elevation in the socio-economic scale. It is neither the poorer Indians nor the subsistence farmers who become Ladinos. To become a Ladino in a cultural sense also means being a trader or regularly producing for the market and, in general, acquiring a higher standard of living. This does not mean that all of those who become traders or sell their produce in the market or who achieve a better standard of living necessarily become Ladinos. Nor does it mean that Ladinos who descend the socio-economic scale become Indians. In effect, a Ladino will always be a Ladino, low as he may fall in the socio-economic scale. But an Indian, provided that he ascend the socio-economic scale, may become a Ladino; what is more, he will never be a Ladino unless he ascends on the socio-economic scale (that is, unless he obtains higher indices on the objective hierarchies of social status). Hypothetically the Indians may ascend the socio-economic scale without becoming Ladinos. This occurs in the case of a general rise in the community's prosperity, provided that it maintain its Indian cultural characteristics. This situation could be the result of community development programs, but only if the directors at the same time applied a deliberate policy of conserving and stimulating the Indian culture. This is not the case at present.

According to the perspective which is adopted, inter-ethnic stratification may be considered as a scale (composed of various levels), as a continuum (a series of quantitatively different positions), or as a dichotomy. In social life these perspectives cut across each other. For the Indian moving upward within the stratification system, inter-ethnic mobility represents both a gradual or quantitative evolution (his income increases, he improves his house, he buys a pair of shoes, he learns how to read and write in Spanish, etc.) and a radical metamorphosis, a qualitative "leap" (he abandons his community, earns a salary in the city, marries a Ladino woman, denies his origins). At which point of the individual's cultural evolution does this metamorphosis take place? It varies according to circumstances. It is obvious that when the mobile Indian's point of departure lies high in the socio-economic scale, ethnic transformation will occur with a certain smoothness. The individual departing from a lower level, on the other hand, may accelerate the process by breaking off with his community and migrating to another region. But in this case he is placed outside of the given stratification system, and thus his transformation is not, strictly speaking, upward mobility within a given system of social stratification. Frequency and speed of mobility also depend on other factors: rigidity of the community's traditional structure, rigidity of the ethnic barrier maintained by Ladinos, the region's economic situation, and finally, the effectiveness of Indianist policy.

THE DYNAMICS OF INTER-ETHNIC RELATIONS: CLASSES, COLONIALISM, AND ACCULTURATION

Let us attempt a general formulation of the system of relationships between Indians and Ladinos. Our historical point of departure will be the Spanish Conquest, although we do not deny the importance of pre-Hispanic social processes in the subsequent character of the Mayan region. The Spanish Conquest was a military enterprise and part of the political and economic expansion in post-feudal and mercantilistic Europe. The Conquest was fundamentally influenced by commercial factors (the lust for gold and spice). As a military enterprise the Spanish Conquest was a violent confrontation of two societies, two different cultures. The weaker one—the Indian—succumbed. The Indians received from the conqueror the treatment accorded since ancient times to the vanquished: looting, dispossession, slavery, even extermination. Yet the Conquest of the New World was not like preceding ones. In Spain, deep transformations were taking place due to the *Reconquista*. The American continent would perform an essential role in Europe's economic development, and to the native populations were ascribed specific functions in this development. For different political and economic reasons, destruction and enslavement of native populations had to come to a stop. The military conquest was transformed into a colonial system. Just as other colonial systems which the world has known since then, this one was managed over three centuries on behalf of the interests of certain powerful social classes of the metropolis, and that of their representatives in New Spain. The Crown's policy reflected these changing and often conflicting interests.

At first Indian chiefs and the Indian aristocracy were kept in their positions, which suited the colonial administration's *Realpolitik*. But toward the end of the 16th century Indian communities had become socially and economically homogeneous. Their internal social differentiation was no longer in the interests of the colonizer. Residential segregation of Indians (through settlements of converted Indians and other mechanisms) and the *encomiendas* (lands which the Crown granted as trusteeship to the conquistadores) were the first instruments used by the conquistador to levy taxes and services. Part of the Indian society's wealth was simply transferred to the conquering society. Indian communities were transformed into labor reserves of the colonial economy. Systems of serfdom and forced labor in plantations, mines, and workshop constituted the basis of the economic system.

Colonial society was the product of mercantilist expansion:

of the dawning of the bourgeois revolution in Europe. Its structure still retained much of the feudal era, especially in the character of human relationships. Some researchers even affirm that feudalism grew stronger in America after it had begun to decline in Spain, and that America "feudalized" Spain once again.[61] Exploitation of the Indian population was one of the main goals of colonial economic policy. In order to maintain this labor reserve, it was framed by a complex of laws, norms, restrictions, and prohibitions which kept accumulating during three centuries of colonialism, and which resulted in the corporate "folk" communities. All things were determined for the settler's benefit: the land tenure of the Indian community, its local government, technology, economic production, commerce, residential pattern, marriage norms, education, dress styles, and even its idiom and use of language. In Spain, nobles, landowners, commercial bourgeoisie and petty bourgeoisie were at times fighting, at times co-operating in the struggle for their respective interests. But in Spanish America a rigid social hierarchy based upon centralization of political and economic power and validated in the *Legislation of Indias* kept the natives in their position of inferiority with respect to all of the other social levels.

The colonial system worked on two levels. The restrictions and economic prohibitions which Spain imposed upon her colonies (and which were to forment the independence movements) were repeated, often aggravated, in the relations between the colonial society and the Indian communities. The same commercial monopolies, the same restrictions on production, the same political controls which Spain exerted upon the Colony, the colonists imposed upon Indian communities. As Spain was to the Colony, so the Colony was to Indian communities: a colonial metropolis. Since then mercantilism penetrated even the most isolated villages of Spanish America.

The social groups in Spanish America which took part in the processes of economic production and distribution which sustained the Spanish empire also participated in the class structure of the colonial system. In the same way the Indian population participated in the class structure of the Colony. Colonial relationships and class relationships underlay ethnic relationships. In terms of *colonial relationships*, the Indian society as a whole confronted colonial society. Primary characteristics of the *colonial situation* were ethnic discrimination, political dependence, social inferiority, residential segregation, economic subjection, and juridical incapacity. In the same way, class structure was defined in terms of labor and property relations. These relations were not defined in ethnic, political, social, or residential terms. Only juridical coercion (supported by military power) as well as other economic and extra-economic pressures intervened in the establishment of labor relations. Labor relations were not between two societies, but only between two specific sectors within them. Colonial and class relationships appear intermixed throughout this period. While the former primarily answered to mercantilist interests, the latter met the capitalist ones. Both kinds of relationships were also opposed to each other: the development of class relationships came into conflict with the maintenance of colonial relationships. Indian communities were constantly losing members to the developing national society. Despite tutelary legislation, the biologic and cultural mixing was a constant process which kept producing new problems for colonial society. Those Indians who for various reasons were absorbed by the larger society, therefore, quit the colonial relationships to become integrated simply in a class structure. In consequence, they were no longer Indians.

These two kinds of socio-economic relationships in which the Indian ethnic groups were involved received moral sanction with the rigid social stratification in which the Indian (biologically, culturally, and juridically defined) was always at the bottom (with the exception of the slave). From these conditions there emerged the corporate community and the formation of indocolonial cultural characteristics, which we today call Indian culture. Ethnic relationships of the period thus presented three main aspects: two kinds of relationships of dependence and one kind of relationship of order.[62]

The dynamics of these systems of relationships were varied. Tho colonial relationships between Indian communities and the larger society tended to strengthen the Indian communities and foment their ethnic identity. The subordinate group usually reacts to a dominant-subordinate relationship of the colonial kind with a struggle for liberation (at the most diverse levels). Colonialism produces nationalism and struggles for independence. The colonial period was not devoid of native rebellions. Conversely, class relations contributed to the disintegration of the Indian community and its integration to the larger society. Both kinds of relations complemented each other in terms of the Indian's oppression. But the opposed tendencies which they engendered explain why certain Indian communities survived, while others were transformed into peons' or squatters' enclaves, in the *haciendas* which displaced the encomiendas of the 16th and 17th centuries. Colonial relationships usually dominated class relationships. Although colonial relations were only one aspect of a worldwide system of mercantilist class relations, the more narrowly defined class relationships between Indians and Spaniards (including criollos, Spaniards born in the Colony) usually appeared in the form of the colonial relations described above. This was essentially due to the nature of colonial economy.

Finally, social stratification, which has sometimes, because of its rigidity, been called a caste system, reflected more the colonial character than the class character of the Indian's subjugation. The stratification system, in turn, exerted its own influence upon the development of class relationships.

Political independence in Spanish America did not basically change the relationships between Indians and the larger society. Despite the legal equality of all citizens (including Indians), various factors joined to maintain the "colonial" character of these relations. First, internal struggles which lasted many decades and second, the economic depression during the first half of the 19th century. Both kinds of factors helped to keep Indian communities marginal, isolated from the outside world, and increasingly corporate. Another reason should also be taken into account. At the beginning of the colonial period tutelary laws were established because it was considered that Indians were inferior beings. But by the end of three centuries of colonialism, these laws had served to maintain and fix that inferiority. In consequence, when legal equality was declared, the Indian was effectively in a condition of inferiority to the rest of the population, in every area of economic and social life.

The first effective changes occurred during the second half of the 19th century: first with the Reform laws and later with the introduction of new cash crops (principally coffee) into the Indian region. Both phenomena, of course, are closely related. Legal equality and disamortization of communal land had two immediate consequences: the Indian could now freely dispose of himself in the labor market, and the land he held could become private property. In fact, this did not take place in the abstract, but in the specific situations that have already been mentioned: extension of commercial farming; penetration by Ladinos into communities inhabited by Indian ethnic groups; appropriation of land by Ladinos; formation of great latifundia and the Indians' wage labor on these properties and haciendas. Coffee plantations became working centers for a considerable mass of Indians, legally or illegally recruited from their communities. At the same time the first products of industrialization penetrated into the more distant villages of the Indian region in the form of goods carried by Ladino traders. In this way new economic relationships were established between the Indians and the rest of the population.

Expansion of the capitalist economy during the second half of the 19th century, together with the ideology of economic liberalism, once again transformed the quality of ethnic relationships between Indians and Ladinos. We consider this stage as a second form of colonialism, which we might call internal colonialism. Indians of traditonal communities found themselves once again in the role of a colonized people: they lost their lands, were forced to work for the "strangers," were integrated against their will to a new monetary economy, and fell under new forms of political domination. This time, colonial society was national society itself, which progressively extended its control over its own territory.[63] Now there were not only isolated Indians who, abandoning their communities, joined the national society; but Indian communities themselves, as a group, were progressively incorporated to expanding regional economic systems. To the extent to which national society extended its control, and capitalist economy dominated the area, relations between colonizer and colonized, between Ladino and Indian, were transformed into class relationships.

The corporate community has been characteristic of colonial society in Indian America. Corporative social structure has an ecologic and economic basis. When colonial society is transformed into "underdeveloped" society, when the economic structure of the corporate community is modified (loss of lands, wage labor, commercialization of agricultural produce, etc.), then it is rather unlikely that the corporate quality of the community's internal social relationships should survive for long. As we have seen, some of the Indian's cultural characteristics are bound to the highly structured corporate community. If this structure should progressively disappear, these cultural characteristics would become weaker.

Ethnic stratification in the region is the result of this historical evolution. It reflects the colonial situation which has been maintained till present times. Behind inter-ethnic relationships, which show themselves as a stratification system, there is a social class structure. When an Indian works for a Ladino, the main point is not the inter-ethnic relationship but the labor relation. During the decade of the thirties, the Indians of Chiapas organized to defend their working conditions in the coffee plantations; not as Indians, but as workers. During the years 1944–1954 there were also labor unions of Indian agricultural workers in Guatemala. They have become organized in their struggle for land, under the agrarian reform programs but as landless peasants. These relationships sometimes assume cultural shapes. The struggle for land, for instance, is carried on in the name of restitution of communal and clan lands. At times there have also emerged messianic movements against Ladinos. Yet it was always a matter of structural changes within the traditional community.

Inter-ethnic stratification no longer completely corresponds to new class relationships which have developed along with a monetary economy. "Colonized" Indians are not a social class. We are not saying that Indians and Ladinos are simply two social classes. This would be over-simplifying a deeply complex historical situation. During the course of economic development (or more precisely, of the development of economic underdevelopment, as a result of colonial economy), various new social classes emerge. They are not yet totally formed, because "colonial" relationships still determine the social structure at different levels. The Indian participates in various kinds of socio-economic relationships. He holds various occupational roles at the same time. He may be a small farmer in the communal lands, an ambulant trader, a salaried worker during different periods of the year, or during the course of his life. This situation may last as long as the regional economic structure allows it. But this structure is suffering rapid changes: monetary economy is expanding, capitalist labor and trade relations are becoming generalized, regional communications are developing, and local industrialization is getting started. These different kinds of class relationships contribute to separate the individual from his corporate community. The community's corporate structure is breaking up. Should it disappear, inter-ethnic stratification will have lost its objective basis.

Nonetheless, the inter-ethnic stratification system which, like every stratification system, is deeply rooted in the values held by the members of the society, is an essentially conservative force within the social structure. While it reflects a situation of the past (the clear dichotomy between Indians and Ladinos in every area of social, economic, and political life, characteristic of the colonial situation), it curbs the development of new class relationships. We should not forget that the landless peasant and the salaried worker are *also* Indians. Even though relations of production will be determinant of future transformations in the region, ethnic consciousness may weigh heavier than class consciousness. Thus, exploited or poor as a Ladino may be, he feels privileged as compared to the Indians, even those who may have a standard of living higher than his own. Indians, on the other hand, tend to attribute all of their misfortunes to the Ladinos as such (a position which, by the way, is shared by certain indigenous romantic intellectuals), an attitude which contributes to the concealment of objective relationships between classes. This range of problems has been little studied in the region and it represents, in my opinion, an interesting field of research.

To the extent to which class relationships become more clearly defined, there emerges a new stratification, based on socio-economic indices. This stratification already exists among Ladinos, and is progressively expanding to the Indians. The status symbols of the Ladinos are beginning to be valued by the Indians too. It is no longer sufficient—or even desirable—that the Indian should become "ladinized." The situation will have radically changed when social stratification includes Ladinos and Indians independent of their ethnic characteristics. Ideally this would mean the maintenance of Indian cultural identity independent of stratification. To what degree this situation is workable depends on many special factors. It has been noted that in Quetzaltenango (Guatemala) something of the sort is taking place, and this also seems to be the case in Mexico among the Maya of Yucatán, the Zapotec of Oaxaca, and the Tarascans of Michoacán.

This also depends on the attitudes and reactions of Ladinos, whose position is not stable within the class society. Ladinos have always accepted (at least from one generation to the other) the admission of acculturated Indians into their group. It is difficult to foresee reactions of the Ladino community faced with two hypothetical alternatives of the inter-ethnic stratification system's evolution: on the one hand, the complete assimilation of Indians (which is rather unlikely); and on the other, a general economic rise of the Indian ethnic group as such (which would be a challenge to Ladino superiority). Development of a class society leads toward either of these hypothetic situations. The final result will depend on how class conflicts are solved. Indian-Ladino acculturation is a process operating on several levels. Adams foresees the ladinization of Guatemala, while in Mexico there is some talk about the integration of Indians into the Ladino culture. Yet it is necessary to study which aspects of Indian culture will be transformed in this process. Here it is convenient to distinguish structural from cultural. Those cultural elements intimately associated with the corporate structure of the community and with inter-ethnic stratification will surely disappear with the transformation of the colonial situation into a class situation. In this sense, the Indian will stop being an Indian (or will only be so in a cultural sense, and no longer in a social or structural sense). Tax has pointed out that in Guatemala social relations are civilized, while the world view remains primitive.[64]

There may also exist a class culture, and many "Indian" cultural elements will accompany the development of class society as elements integrated to a new structure. One author has recently suggested that the "Indian" culture of Chiapas is nothing but a "rural" culture, similar to rural cultures in other parts of the world.[65]

The system of inter-ethnic stratification can only be understood as part of the corporate structure of the Indian community and its cultural characteristics. This structure, in turn, can only be explained in terms of its colonial past. The colonial situation has become progressively transformed. The Indian thus finds himself in the midst of diverse and contradicting situations: at times he is "colonized," and at times he is a member of a class (in the sense that he is in a typical *class situation*).[66] In other words, not only does the Indian perform various roles (as everybody else), but he also participates in *dichotomized role systems,* which are historically and structurally conflicting.[67] Nor does the Ladino escape ambiguity: at times he is the "colonizer," at times bearer of national culture and member of national society, and at the same time he finds himself in most diverse class situations, in confrontation with Indians and other Ladinos.

Until now our analysis has mainly focused on corporate community as prototype of one of the poles of inter-ethnic relationships. This position is obviously inadequate. It overlooks, at the cultural level of inter-ethnic relationships, those cultural Indians who are not incorporated into a corporate community; that is, those modified, ladinized, acculturated categories referred to by the anthropologists. Nonetheless, this approach finds its justifications from the fact that the analysis was not carried out on the cultural but rather on the structural level. On the other hand, it has been stressed that two main structural units are involved in the structure of inter-ethnic relations: the corporate community and society as a whole (in its diverse manifestations). The task now remains to approach the problem from the point of view of the total society.

Contemporary inter-ethnic relations partly result from colonial policy. They also represent the disintegration of that policy and are a function of present economic and class structures. As has been shown by various economists, underdeveloped economies tend to polarize into areas of growth and structurally related areas of stagnation. The Maya region of Chiapas and Guatemala constitutes such an area, as do other Indian areas of Mexico. The marginal populations inhabiting these areas are growing in absolute numbers, despite national economic development.[68] If this happens in Mexico, despite accelerated economic growth in recent years, then in Guatemala, where there has been no such development, it must surely happen with greater intensity. During the colonial period, *colonial relations* in the Indian regions served the interests of a well defined dominant class which in turn subdued the colonial society as a whole to its own interests, insofar as relations with Spain would permit. In the situation of *internal colonialism* (which might be called the *endo-colonial situation*) class relationships within the whole society are more complex. The regional dominant class, represented by Ladinos, is not necessarily the dominant one in the national society. In Guatemala, since the defeat of the nationalist bourgeoisie in 1954, these two groups became identified. There is no contradiction between landowners, commercial bourgeoisie (particularly coffee-growers) and foreign capital.[69] In Mexico the situation is different. National power is held by a bureaucratic, "developmentist" bourgeoisie, a product of the 1910 Revolution. This bourgeoisie has displaced latifundists on a national level, but in more backward regions, such as Chiapas, it tolerates them while seeking the support of a new rural bourgeoisie composed of traders, neo-latifundists and public employees.[70] In both Mexico and Guatemala the regional dominant class is composed of "power brokers"—to use Wolf's term [71]—of mestizo origin who have come to fill the power vacuum left by the old feudal landowning aristocracy. In Guatemala the endo-colonial situation is stronger than in Mexico, where latent contradictions between the "developmentist" bourgeoisie in power

276

and its weak shadow in the Indian hinterland contribute to a rapid development of class relationships to the detriment of colonial relationships, and have allowed the development of a structural development-underdevelopment dichotomy. Thus, inter-ethnic relations at the level of total sociey may be considered as a function of the development-underdevelopment structural dichotomy (in its social aspect of internal colonialism), and of the dynamics of national class structure.

For purposes of analysis, four elements may be isolated in the inter-ethnic situation: colonial relationships, class relationships, social stratification, and the acculturation process. These four elements constitute interdependent variables and with them we may attempt to build a hypothetic model of inter-ethnic relations.

Colonial Relationships

These relationships are a function of the structural development-underdevelopment dichotomy, and they tend to be in force for as long as the dichotomy persists. As long as there are areas performing as internal colonies in underdeveloped countries, the relationships characterizing their inhabitants tend to take the form of colonial relationships. These are strengthened where there exist, as in the Maya region, marked cultural differences between two sectors of the population, leading to a rigid stratification defined in cultural and biologic terms (which is sometimes called *caste*). Colonial relations tend to limit and impede acculturation, cultural ladinization, and to maintain a rigid stratification. There exists an obvious interest on the part of the dominant ethnic group (Ladinos) in maintaining colonial relations, especially when their predominance depends on the existence of cheap and abundant labor. This is the case when possibilities of expansion of the economy are few, when agriculture has a low level of productivity and when the labor-capital relation in agriculture is high, when local or regional industrialization is weak or non-existent; and when the region's internal market is poorly developed. Therefore the maintenance of colonial relations is rather a function of the degree of development of national economy than of local or regional decisions.

In contrast to Ladinos, the Indians—the subordinate ethnic

group—derive no benefit from the colonial situation and may try various forms of reaction to it. The first is withdrawal into the corporate community, both physically and socially. As Wolf pointed out, this has happened on various occasions in the history of the region, and it represents on the part of the Indian ethnic group a latent tendency which becomes manifest when the economic and political situation allows it. In association with this withdrawal, the Indians also react to the colonial situation in terms of nationalism. This form of reaction may have as its objective the strengthening of the Indian government (regional council), and possibly the struggle for the Indians' national political representation. It also becomes manifest through measures adopted to encourage education in the Indian language and development of Indian culture. It particularly becomes manifest through an extreme anti-Ladinism and resistance to ladinization. Here there also intervene other counter-acculturative factors such as messianism and, on certain occasions, armed upheavals and other violent manifestations. Finally, there is a third form of reaction to the colonial situation, and this is assimilation. It is an individual process which, as has been seen, represents a separation from the corporate structure of the community. From a cultural point of view it represents ladinization. From a structural point of view it means that the individual becomes integrated to the class structure, no longer as an Indian (that is, a colonized person), but simply due to his relationship to the means of production. Ladinization, as we have seen, may be the result of upward mobility in the scale of socio-economic indices. But generally it only means the proletarianization of the Indian.

Of the three main forms of reaction to the colonial situation, the first, simple withdrawal, does not seem to have many adherents at present. Among those who are still clinging to it we find a few traditionalistic elders. But other members of the community know that there are better ways to combat the harmful effects which colonial relations have upon Indians. The reaction which we have called "nationalism" (for lack of a better term) assumes diverse shapes. Some of them are spontaneous and circumstantial (such as armed upheavals and messianic movements); others have been induced by external agents (such as education in the Indian language); and still others may be the consequence of a political consciousness of Indian communities (such as the election of a person participating in corporate civic-religious political structure, to a position in the constitutional municipal government). At present, the main forms of national-istic reaction are promoted—at least in Mexico—by the national government's specialized agencies. Measures such as literacy in the Indian language and adequate political representation of the Indians show that those responsible for Indianist policy are con-scious of the colonial character of inter-ethnic relations, despite the fact that the problem has never been formulated in those terms by the ideologists of *indigenismo*. Yet paradoxically, these measures are only taken as a means to an end which represents its absolute negation, that is, the incorporation of the Indian to Mexican nationality, in other words, the disappearance of the Indian as such. The paradox, nonetheless, has a practical justifi-cation: national integration can only be achieved if contradic-tions inherent in colonial relations are overcome. This can be done either by suppressing one of the terms of the contradiction, or by a qualitative change of content in that relation. By en-couraging measures of a nationalistic kind, Indianist policy is committed to the second of these alternatives. Yet if the contradic-tion inherent to the colonial relation between Indians and La-dinos is solved, there would be a greater contradiction resolved at the same time: that which exists between those colonial rela-tions and national integration (since the existence of the former represents an obstacle to the latter). In other words, national integration may be achieved, not by eliminating the Indian, but only by eliminating him as a colonized being.[72] Mexican Indian-ism has admitted this timidly and not without some ambiguities. But in this respect it is much more advanced than the rest of the national society. Indianism certainly does not escape the contradictions of national society when, for instance, it is stated that literacy in the Indian language in Chiapas only serves to facilitate the teaching of Spanish, and a series of "assimilationist" measures (particularly the action of "acculturation agents" or "promoters of cultural change") are simultaneously put into practice.

279

Class Relationships

We cannot over-emphasize that the class character and colonial character of inter-ethnic relations are two intimately related aspects of the same phenomenon. They are separated here only for the purpose of our analysis. Class relationships have developed parallel to and simultaneous with colonial relations and tend to displace them more and more. But the colonial character of inter-ethnic relations impresses particular characteristics upon class relations, tending to stop their development. In this context, class relations mean mutual interactions between persons holding opposed economic positions, independent of ethnic considerations. These relations develop together with the region's economic development. As agricultural production increases, as the market for industrial products expands, as monetary economy develops, and as the labor market expands, colonial relations lose their importance and give way to the predominance of class relations. The latter's development also depends, to a great degree, upon structural factors of national economy and is not the result of decision-making at the regional or local level. At any rate, this development tends to impress upon the class relations between Indians and Ladinos a characteristic mark while the feudal or semi-feudal aspects, so frequently indicated in the literature, tend to disappear.

Consequently, measures for local or community development such as improvement of agricultural techniques, establishment of production co-operatives, etc., may change colonial relations into class relations, but not necessarily so. This transformation can only take place if such developments are accompanied by parallel development of the regional economy as a whole, and particularly of its Ladino metropolis. If such is not the case, the likelihood is that the fruits of local development will enter the traditional socio-economic circuits without modifying the regional structure.

It has already been seen that on certain occasions Ladinos are interested in maintaining colonial relations. There also exist circumstances in which they are interested in strengthening class relationships to the detriment of colonial relationships. This happens particularly with the development of the productive forces: when Ladinos are presented with new opportunities of investment, when they need seasonal labor which can only be obtained through monetary incentives, or when they require non-agricultural labor (for certain manufacturing industries or for construction work in the cities or on the roads); finally, when they need to develop new regional markets and the strengthening of the Indians' demand for manufactured products. The Ladinos' interest in the development of class relations also arises when the agrarian reform manages to really break the land monopoly and when the possession of his own land can turn the Indian back to subsistence farming. In this case, class relations develop particularly through the marketing of crops and the agricultural credit structure.

Under certain circumstances Ladinos may have an interest toward curbing the development of class relations: for instance, when their interests are affected by the establishment of plantations by foreign companies, which modify the status quo by attracting a certain amount of labor and paying higher wages than those which are usual in the region, etc. This has happened in Guatemala. Or, for example, when economic development of the region contributes to the liberation of labor, thus increasing its emigration or at the least its capacity to demand higher salaries, in which case the Ladino latifundists are forced to invest a greater amount of capital in agriculture, and this capital they do not possess.

Indians are also interested in the development of class relationships because these imply the existence of better economic opportunities and of wider alternatives for action. On the other hand, they may be interested in curbing the development of class relations because they tend to destroy the subsistence economy, because they contribute to economic and psychological insecurity and encourage proletarianization and disintegration of Indian culture.

The development of class relations involves new forms of sociability and social organization; there emerge new social categories and new groupings and social institutions. The development of these relations tends to destroy the rigidity of social stratification, to modify its bases (from ethnic characteristics to socio-economic indices) and to encourage ladinization of the Indian.

Social Stratification

Insofar as the regional system of social stratification has only two strata based essentially on ethnic characteristics it tends to maintain the appearance of a colonial situation. At the same time, it tends to change into a clearly defined socio-economic stratification. The already existing stratification among Ladino ethnic groups tends to become extensive to both ethnic groups. Perhaps the day will come when both ethnic groups—independent of their cultural characteristics—will be included into a single stratification system, based exclusively on socio-economic criteria. The old stratification system, based on ethnic characteristics (sometimes called *castes*) tends to conflict with the development of class relations and the socio-economic stratification based on them. Thus, for instance, an Indian trader or landowner receives discriminatory treatment from Ladinos who are in a socio-economic situation inferior to his own, while Indian day laborers tend to receive smaller wages than the Ladinos who are in the same position. Among the Ladinos there exists an obvious concern over maintaining the bases of ethnic stratification; especially among the lower strata of the Ladino population, who in this way avoid competing with mobile Indians. This is the same phenomenon as that of the poor whites in the south of the United States and other such cases in other parts of the world.

Social stratification, as we have seen, comprises two aspects: inter-ethnic stratification reflects its colonial past, while Ladino socio-economic stratification, in which Indians are increasingly participating, reflects the development of new class relations, devoid of their ethnic content. The Indians' upward vertical mobility in the socio-economic scale is accompanied by a certain degree of ladinization, but, as has already been pointed out, not all of the aspects of Indian culture change at the same rate. Development of class relations tends to facilitate the Indian's upward mobility, since an ascent in the socio-economic scale renders the conservation of a low status based upon exclusively ethnic criteria more precarious. Upward mobility, as much in the socio-economic scale, as in the shift from the Indian to the Ladino ethnic group, is a function of the transformation of the colonial situation into a class situation.

Ladinization

This process of acculturation of the Indian is hard to place in a structural analysis, since it is used in the literature to refer to processes which are highly varied in content. In a general sense it means the adoption of Ladino cultural elements by individuals or groups (communities) of the Indian ethnic group. Thus, the change in dress, the substitution of folk medicine by scientific medicine, and the change of occupation, to take only three examples, are all part of the process of ladinization. Yet the structural significance of these three examples, taking each by itself, is very different. Without considering for the moment the motivational determinants leading to a change in dress, this by itself has no consequences for the social structure; except if, carried out collectively by the Indians, it should lead to certain changes in the value systems of both ethnic groups, which in turn might influence the systems of mutual action and interaction, thus affecting social structures. But this kind of chain argument does not lead to a better understanding of the phenomena being studied. Of the preceding examples, the second—the shift from traditional medicine to modern medicine—does not by itself represent a structural change in either. But it may lead to demographic consequences which will have important structural results. Change of occupation, on the contrary, can only be understood within the frame of a structural analysis. The above shows that the concept of ladinization may mean anything from a simple change in the daily use of an object (using a spoon instead of a tortilla to eat soup), up to a complete change of the Indians' life and world view. Within the limits of this essay, concern over the process of ladinization is only meaningful insofar as it has immediate structural implications.

NOTES

The author expresses his thanks to Guillermo Bonfil, Andrew G. Frank, Carlos Alberto de Medina, and Roberto Cardoso de Oliveira for the comments, criticisms, and suggestions which they have contributed.

[1] Sol Tax, "The Municipios of the Midwestern Highlands of Guatemala," *American Anthropologist*, Vol. 39 (1937); Henning, Siverts, "Social and Cultural Changes in a Tzeltal (Mayan) Municipio, Chiapas, Mexico," Proceedings of the 32nd International Congress of Americanists, Copenhagen, 1956.

[2] By *ethnic group* we understand a social group whose members participate in the same culture, who may sometimes be characterized in biological or racial terms, who are conscious of belonging to such a group and who participate in a system of relations with other similar groups. An *ethnia* may be, depending upon circumstances, tribe, race, nationality, minority, caste, cultural component, etc., according to the meaning given to these terms by different authors.

[3] The global society is the widest operational social unit within which the studied relations take place and which is not a part of the immediate experience of the actors in the social system. It includes the community, the municipality, the region, the ethnic group, etc., and their diverse systems of interrelation. It is sociologically structured. The global society has been termed a macroscopic group embracing the functional groupings, social classes and conflicting hierarchies. Generally, in this essay, it is identical to the nation (or to the Colony), but it sometimes also refers to the wider economic system, in which the nation participates. See Georges Gurvitch, *La Vocation Actuelle de la Sociologie*, Paris, 1950, p. 301, *passim*.

[4] Nathan Whetten, *Rural Mexico*, Chicago, 1948.

[5] Alfonso Caso, "Definición del Indio y lo Indio," *América Indígena*, Vol. VIII, No. 5 (1948).

[6] Sol Tax, *Penny Capitalism, A Guatemala Indian Economy*, Washington, 1953.

[7] Loc. cit. p. 183.

[8] Eric Wolf, "The Indian in Mexican Society," *Alpha Kappa Delta*, Vol. XXX, No. 1 (1960).

[9] Eric Wolf, "Aspects of Group Relations in a Complex Society: Mexico," *American Anthropologist*, Vol. 58 (1956).

[10] Robert Redfield and Sol Tax, "General Characteristics of Present Day Mesoamerican Indian Society," in *Heritage of Conquest*, Glencoe, The Free Press, 1952.

[11] Alfonso Caso, "Los Fines de la Acción Indigenista en México," *Revista Internacional del Trabajo*, December, 1955, and Aguirre Beltrán, G., *El Proceso de Aculturación*, Mexico, UNAM, 1957, which still constitutes the most complete theoretical exposition on Mexican nativism.

[12] I use here the terms "class," "class relations," and "class situation" as analytical concepts and I completely distinguish them, as shall be seen later, from the concept of social stratification generally associated with them. For theoretical justification of this methodological procedure see my article on "Estratificación y Estructura de Clases," in *Ciencias Políticas y Sociales* (Mexico), No. 27 (1962), and my paper on "Las Relaciones entre la Estratificación Social y la Dinámica de Clases," presented at the Seminario sobre Estratificación y Movilidad Social, Rio de Janeiro, 1962 (to be published by the Pan American Union).

[13] Charles Wagley, *Santiago Chimaltenango*, Guatemala, 1957.

[14] Sol Tax, *Penny Capitalism*, op. cit.

[15] Eric Wolf, "The Indian in Mexican Society," loc. cit.

[16] Melvin Tumin, *Caste in a Peasant Society*, Princeton, 1952.

[17] A. D. Marroquín, "Consideraciones sobre el Problema Económico de la Región Tzeltal-tzotzil," *América Indígena*, Vol. XVI, No. 3 (1956).

[18] R. Pozas, *Chamula, un pueblo indio de los Altos de Chiapas*, Mexico. 1959.

[19] M. Monteforte Toledo, *Guatemala*, monografía sociológica, Mexico, 1959.

[20] A. Y. Dessaint, "Effects of the Hacienda and Plantation Systems on Guatemala's Indians," *América Indígena*, Vol. XXII, No. 4 (1962).

[21] Dessaint, loc. cit., writes: to "obtain an adequate supply of labor has always been of basic importance ever since the Spanish Conquest" (p. 326). And Oliver La Farge has said: "Two methods have been used to tap the great source of labor of the highlands: violence and the destruction of the economic bases which allowed the Indians to refuse voluntary work in the lowlands." Cf. "Etnología Maya: Secuencia de Culturas," in *Cultura Indígena de Guatemala*, Guatemala, (1959).

[22] Melvin Tumin, op. cit.

[23] Cf. Manning Nash, *Machine Age Maya: The Industrialization of a Guatemalan Community*, Glencoe, 1958.

[24] Cf. Goubaud's remarks in the discussion of the report by Sol Tax, "Economy and Technology," in *Heritage of Conquest*, ed. S. Tax, op. cit. p. 74.

[25] *Penny Capitalism*, op. cit.

[26] Calixta Guiteras Holmes, *Perils of the Soul*, Glencoe, 1961.

[27] Ricardo Pozas, *Chamula, un Pueblo Indio de los Altos de Chiapas*, Mexico, 1959.

[28] Melvin Tumin, *Caste in a Peasant Society*, op. cit.; John Gillin, *San Luis Jilotepeque*, Guatemala, 1958.

[29] Sol Tax, *Penny Capitalism*, op. cit.

[30] Charles Wagley, *Santiago Chimaltenango*, op. cit., p. 67.

[31] Cf. Calixta Guiteras Holmes, *Perils of the Soul*, Glencoe, 1961. "In the course of the years more than half the lands of the Pedrano Indians were bought by rich and influential foreigners. . . . The man who bought the land acquired the right to exploit its occupants" (p. 14). "In 1910 the Indians had not only lost their own lands but had also become peons" (p. 16).

[32] One rare exception to this historical trend is the Guatemalan village of Chitatul, quoted by Richard Adams in his *Encuesta sobre la Cultura de los Ladinos en Guatemala*, Guatemala, EMEP, 1956.

[33] Op. cit., p. 63.

[34] Sol Tax, *Penny Capitalism*, op. cit.

[35] Charles Wagley, op. cit., p. 73, *passim*.

[36] "La Situación Agraria de las Communidades Indígenas," *Acción Indigenista*, No. 105 (March, 1962).

[37] When general considerations are made on the Mayan area in Chiapas and Guatemala, certain local aspects and particular situations of great interest are necessarily neglected, the inclusion of which would perhaps modify the general scheme. It is a risk of which the author is wholly conscious, yet which he had to assume, considering the limits of space. Such

is the case, for instance, of the Agrarian Reform in Guatemala, initiated with the revolution of 1944, but checked and diverted by the governments subsequent to the 1954 counter-revolution. Thus, the redistribution of the lands, the law of compulsory renting and the constitution of rural workers' labor unions during the decade of 1944–54 surely affected, in diverse ways, the class relations here analyzed. Yet as these processes are no longer in force, I have chosen to ignore them, at the risk of neglecting some facts which might be important to this analysis.

[38] In the sense given to this sociological term by Charles Wagley and Marvin Harris in their *Minorities in the New World*, New York, 1958.

[39] Robert Redfield, "Primitive Merchants of Guatemala," *The Quarterly Journal of Inter-American Relations*, Vol. I, No. 4 (1939).

[40] Sol Tax, *Penny Capitalism*, op. cit., p. 13.

[41] A. Marroquín, "Introducción al Mercado Indígena Mexicano," *Ciencias Políticas y Sociales*, No. 8 (1957).

[42] Robert Redfield, op. cit.

[43] Ricardo Pozas, *Chamula*, op. cit., p. 111.

[44] The word "integration" is understood here in its more general sense, that of being a functional part of a whole.

[45] G. Aguirre Beltrán, *Formas de Gobierno Indígena*, Mexico, 1954.

[46] F. Cámara Barbachano, "Religious and Political Organization," in *Heritage of Conquest*, ed. S. Tax, Glencoe, 1952.

[47] G. Aguirre Beltrán, *Formas de Gobierno Indígena*, op. cit.

[48] Ricardo Pozas, *Chamula, un Pueblo Indio de los Altos de Chiapas*, op. cit. In an interesting work recently published, F. Cancian proves that in Zinacantan (Mexico), the prestige of a position depends on various factors which are difficult to measure, among them the cost of the position, the authority it conveys, and "idiosyncratic" factors. Cf. F. Cancian, "Informant Error and Native Prestige Ranking in Zinacantan," *American Anthropologist*, Vol. 65, No. 5 (1963).

[49] Ibid. Pozas attributes the principle of equality to vestiges of clan organization.

[50] Cancian (loc. cit.) suggests that in Zinacantan there does exist a rudimentary "economic stratification."

[51] G. Aguirre Beltrán, *Formas de Gobierno Indígena*, p. 103.

[52] Ibid.

[53] In Chiapas, the Instituto Nacional Indigenista de México is training young Indians as municipal secretaries for the positions held by the Ladinos. In Guatemala, the penetration of the national political parties into the Indian communities during the democratic regimes of the 1944–54 decade modified the traditional structure. These problems have been treated in a collective work on *Political Changes in Guatemalan Indian Communities*, New Orleans, 1957.

[54] Richard N. Adams, *Encuesta sobre la Cultura de los Ladinos en Guatemala*, Guatemala, EMEP, 1956.

[55] Melvin Tumin, *Caste in a Peasant Society*, op. cit.

[56] Sol Tax, *Penny Capitalism*, op. cit.

[57] B. Colby and Van den Berghe, "Ethnic Relations in Southeastern Mexico," *American Anthropologist*, Vol. 53, No. 4 (1961).

[58] B. Colby and Van den Berghe, loc. cit.

Classes, Colonialism, and Acculturation

[59] Robert Redfield, "The Relations Between Indians and Ladinos in Agua Escondida, Guatemala," *América Indígena*, Vol. XVI, No. 4 (1956).

[60] We use the terms "transculturation" and "acculturation" interchangeably, in the sense in which the latter is used by G. Aguirre Beltrán in *El Proceso de Aculturación*, Mexico, 1957.

[61] Angel Palerm, "Notas sobre la Clase Media en México," *Ciencias Sociales* (Washington), No. 14–15 and 16–17 (1952). (Reproduced in *Las Clases Sociales en México*, Mexico, s.f., 1960.)

[62] On the concepts of relation of dependence and relation of order and their application to the study of class structures, see S. Ossowski, *Class Structure in the Social Consciousness*, London, 1963.

[63] Pablo González Casanova, in a different and independent analysis, also brings forth the existence of internal colonialism in Mexico. The present essay bears a particular case, which may be considered within González Casanova's general approach. See his study, "Internal Colonialism and National Development," *Studies in Comparative International Development*, Vol. I. No. 4 (1965).

[64] Sol Tax, "La Visión del Mundo y las Relaciones Sociales en Guatemala," *Cultura Indígena de Guatemala*, Guatemala, EMEP, 1956.

[65] V. Goldkind, "Ethnic Relations in Southeastern Mexico: A Methodological Note," *American Anthropologist*, Vol. 65, No. 2 (1963).

[66] We use the term "class situation" not in the sense given by Max Weber (*Cf.* H. H. Gerth and C. W. Mills, eds., *From Max Weber: Essays in Sociology*, New York, Oxford University Press, 1946, p. 181), but in the sense that the individual who finds himself in such a situation participates with others in a kind of relation having the character of class relations.

[67] See S. F. Nadel, *The Theory of Social Structure*, London, 1957, especially chapter IV. It would be interesting to do a formal analysis of the roles of inter-ethnic situation here described. Nadel's model, nonetheless, does not seem to include a situation as that which is brought about between Indians and Ladinos when they face each other as colonizer and colonized and as belonging to opposite classes *simultaneously*. In other words, the same process of interaction between individuals and groups may be understood at different levels of an analysis of roles and in varying conceptual terms. Nadel's concept of "summation" comes closest to this situation.

[68] *Cf.* Pablo González Casanova, "Sociedad Plural y Desarrollo: el Caso de México," *América Latina*, Year 5, No. 4 (1962).

[69] Jaime Díaz Rozzotto, *El Carácter de la Revolución Guatemalteca*, Mexico, 1958. Also see Richard N. Adams, "Social Change in Guatemala and U.S. Policy," in *Social Change in Latin America Today*, New York, (1960).

[70] *Cf.* Rodolfo Stavenhagen, "*La Réforme Agraire et les Classes Sociales Rurales au Mexique*," Cahiers Internationaux de Sociologie, 34, 1963.

[71] *Cf.* Eric Wolf, *Sons of the Shaking Earth*, Chicago, 1959.

[72] The term "national integration" is very ambiguous. The way it is used by Myrdal, for example, referring to its economic aspects, it simply means equality of opportunities (*Cf.* G. Myrdal, *Solidaridad o Desintegración*, Mexico, 1956). When Aguirre Beltrán, in *El Proceso de Aculturación*, speaks of "intercultural integration" at the regional level, he rather refers

to the homogenization of the cultural differences between Indians and Ladinos, that is, to the predominance of the mestizo culture, which is Mexico's national culture. In the preceding paragraph the term has been used in the sense given by Myrdal, which is why we affirm, differing from Aguirre Beltrán, that national integration may be achieved without the disappearance of the "cultural" Indian.

RMANI

migration
lernization in Argentina

Contemporary Argentina cannot be understood without a thorough analysis of the role of immigration in its development. In the first place, immigration was a powerful factor in the total process of modernization. In the second place, the intensity and volume of immigration caused a substantial realignment of the population: economically, socially, and politically. In no other country did the proportion of adult foreigners reach the level that it did in Argentina, where for more than 60 years foreigners represented around 70 per cent of the adult population in the capital city (which contained one-fifth to one-third of the total population of the country), and almost 50 per cent in the provinces which were heavily populated and economically important.

Immigration resulted from a conscious effort by the elites to replace the old social structure inherited from colonial society with a structure inspired by the most advanced Western countries. This plan was based on three assumptions: (1) massive immigration; (2) universal and compulsory education; (3) import of capital, development of modern forms of agriculture and a livestock-breeding industry, and heavy investment in social overhead capital, especially railways.

The principal aims were not only to populate an immense

territory that had a low population density, but also to modify the *composition* of the population. Underlying this are other aspects of the plan: education, and the expansion and modernization of the economy. To understand these aims it is necessary to remember the point of departure for the elites which conceived and carried out national organization. Only then can we understand the essential role that immigration played in the transformation of the country, although there were consequences which were unforeseen and undesired.

The revolution that initiated the successful movement for national independence was led by an elite inspired by eighteenth century enlightenment. It was composed of creoles belonging to the upper urban class, especially from Buenos Aires. It was numerically very small, and its Western and modern (1800 style) outlook contrasted sharply with the traditional nature of the vast majority of the population, urban and rural (but mostly rural). The failure of the elite which came into being after national independence to establish a modern state was basically the result of this contrast. The years of anarchy and autocracy did not fail to teach the modernizing elite a lesson. They saw that a modern national state could only be established on the basis of a transformed social structure and a change in its human composition. This attitude was reinforced by ideas about the role of racial factors and the national character. The intention of many was to modify the "national character" of the Argentine people in a way that would suit the political ideal of national organization to which these elites aspired. It was necessary to "Europeanize" the Argentine population, to produce a "regeneration of the races," to use Sarmiento's expression. Insurmountable limits in the psycho-social characteristics of the existing population made it all the more necessary to physically bring Europe to America.

A CENTURY OF FOREIGN IMMIGRATION

One of the first changes introduced by the new regime which replaced colonial rule in 1810 was to open the country to foreigners, thus eliminating the strict isolation enforced by the

Spaniards in their colony. The governments of the following two decades stressed the need to attract immigrants. This was especially true of Bernardino Rivadavia, who took concrete steps to create a stream of European immigration into the country. But these attempts were doomed to failure for the same basic reasons which destroyed the dream of establishing a modern national state soon after formal independence had been reached. Only a limited number of immigrants arrived in Argentina during the first two decades of independence, and in the next thirty years the Rosas dictatorship practically re-established the old colonial barrier against foreigners. In the second half of the century, after the downfall of the autocracy, immigration increased. The promotion of immigration became a formal function of the State, according to the 1853 Constitution. For nearly seventy years thereafter, European immigrants arrived in Argentina in a continuous stream, broken only occasionally by domestic events like the economic crisis of 1890 or by international upheavals like the First World War.

Of the nearly sixty million Europeans who emigrated overseas, Argentina received some 11 per cent, a proportion much smaller than that of the United States, but still considerably larger than that of any other immigration country.[1] But what really makes Argentina a special case is that the six and a half million foreigners who arrived * between 1856 and 1930 found a very small local population, estimated at 1,200,000 in 1856. This meant that for many decades the proportion of the foreign born was higher than that of the natives within many important sectors of the population.

During the first decade after 1853 immigration did not exceed a few thousand per year. But as soon as some of the more pressing internal problems were solved, the inflow of foreigners increased to an annual average of nearly 180,000 in the decade preceding the First World War. After the war, large-scale immigration resumed, deterred only by the great depression of 1930. From 1947 to 1952 there was another large inflow of European immigration, after which it practically disappeared.

Thus, three major periods can be distinguished in overseas immigration. The first stage ended in 1930, the second stage

* This figure refers to arrivals. For net immigration see Table I.

extends through the thirties and most of the forties, and the last stage corresponds to the period of post World War II. It must be noted that after the end of the first stage another stream of foreign immigration was added: immigration from the neighboring countries, especially Bolivia, Paraguay, and Chile. This process became more important as the demand for industrial labor increased. But in many ways this stream resembles the mass internal migrations, which also occurred in response to industrial development.[2]

In Argentina, as in other immigration countries, not all the immigrants remained. A certain number of them returned to their native lands or emigrated to other countries. Unfortunately, available immigration statistics do not distinguish between permanent and transitory arrivals or departures. The figures for net overseas immigration included in Table I result from the difference between total departures and total arrivals for European passengers travelling second and third class.

TABLE I   Net Overseas Immigration in Argentina. 1857–1965.

Years	Net immigration (in thousands)
1857–1860	11
1861–1870	77
1871–1880	85
1881–1890	638
1891–1900	320
1901–1910	1,120
1911–1920	269
1921–1930	878
1931–1940	73
1941–1950	386
1951–1960	316
1961–1965	206

Sources: Alessandro Bunge, "Ochenta y cinco," *Revista de Economía Argentina,* 1944; and information provided by the Dirección Nacional de Estadísticas y Censos.

It must be noted that the idea of permanent immigration is difficult to define. It is well known that most of the overseas emigrants to South America, especially in the period under discussion, did not intend to become permanent citizens of the new country. Their chief motivation was to save enough money to return to their native villages and buy land.[3] This motive, which affected the assimilation of the immigrants, made difficult the interpretation of migration statistics. In any case, it must be noted that the "return" movement included, in addition to seasonal immigrants and temporary visitors to native lands, a number of permanent returns. These last were probably of two kinds: those returning because of their inability to adjust to social, economic, and personal conditions; and those returning because they had earned the money they desired.

TABLE II   Number of Foreign Passengers Departed for Every 100 Admitted (Second and Third Class).

Years	Departed passengers
1857–1913	40
1914–1920	151
1921–1930	38
1931–1940	67
1941–1946	79
1947–1950	14
1951–1958	56

Sources: Alessandro Bunge, "Ochenta y cinco," *Revista de Economía Argentina*, 1944; and information provided by the Dirección Nacional de Estadísticas y Censos.

After the First World War seasonal immigration disappeared, and the high rate of departures since 1951 corresponds to the last cycle of overseas immigrants, whose assimilation became increasingly difficult.

Almost half of the incoming immigrants were Italian, and a third were Spanish. A fifth of the total were Polish, followed numerically by Russians, French, and Germans. Italian immigration maintained its predominance throughout almost the whole period. In the decade following the First World War, there was a notable Polish immigration, which continued during the period of low immigration, becoming then the largest national group up to 1940. Russian immigration was high between the end of the nineteenth century and the beginning of the twentieth, and again in the decade following the First World War. In this same period there are major immigrations from Germany and other Eastern European countries. This inflow included a large proportion of Jews.

TABLE III   Net Immigration by Principal Nationalities. 1857–1958.

Years	Italian	Spanish	Polish	Others	Total
1857–1860	17	21	—	62	100
1861–1870	65	21	—	14	100
1871–1880	44	29	—	27	100
1881–1890	57	21	—	22	100
1891–1900	62	18	—	20	100
1901–1910	45	45	—	10	100
1911–1920	12	68	—	20	100
1921–1930	42	26	13	19	100
1931–1940	33	—	58	9	100
1941–1950	66	29	4	1	100
1951–1958	58	34	—	8	100

Sources: Alessandro Bunge, "Ochenta y cinco," *Revista de Economía Argentina*, 1944; and information provided by the Dirección Nacional de Estadísticas y Censos.

THE DEMOGRAPHIC IMPACT OF IMMIGRATION

In 1869 Argentina had a population of a little more than 1,700,000; in 1960 it had become more than 20,000,000, thus having increased almost twelve times in ninety years. Immigration decisively contributed to this extraordinary expansion. The proportion of foreigners to the total population does not accurately indicate the immigrants' contribution to national growth. For example, the proportion of immigrants in the labor force was especially large.

A number of demographers and other social scientists have in the past challenged the common-sense notion that immigration always involves an increase in the receiving population.[4] Malthus maintained that immigration would produce no lasting effect, since the available or potential resources would put an absolute limit on population increase. By different routes other authors have reached the same conclusions as Malthus, and in the United States a "substitution theory" was widely discussed.[5] It is recognized now that the effects of immigration are quite complex. Most of these hypotheses cannot survive the test of facts, even though they continued to circulate as ideological arguments against immigration. In any case, nobody has contested the essential role of immigration in a sparsely-populated country like Argentina.

An estimate formulated by Mortara suggests the contribution of immigrants and their children to the Argentine population. Table IV indicates that the joint contribution of immigrants and their descendants to the national population exceeds the natural

TABLE IV Components of Population Growth in Four American Countries. 1841–1940.

Countries	Native natural increase		Immigration		Immigrants natural increase	
		%		%		%
All America	163.0	70.9	36.0	15.6	31.0	13.5
Brazil	28.6	81.0	3.3	9.4	3.4	9.6
Argentina	5.2	41.9	3.6	29.0	3.6	29.0
Canada	8.0	78.4	1.0	9.8	1.2	11.8
United States	67.7	59.1	25.0	21.8	21.8	19.0

Summarized from Giorgio Mortara, "Pesquisas Sobre Populaçoes Americanas," *Estudos Brasileiros de Demografia*, Monografia No. 3, July 1947.

increase of native population. In this sense Argentina represents an extreme case, even in comparison with the United States. With regard to the other Latin American states, it is clear that immigration made a crucial contribution to population growth. During the period 1869–1959, Argentine population grew more than ten times, while the population of another immigrant country like Brazil increased six times, and Chile, where immigration was practically nonexistent, needed 110 years for its population to grow less than four times. Mortara has estimated that without immigration the population of Argentina in 1940 would have been 6,100,000 instead of over 13,000,000.[6]

The demographic impact of immigration was increased by the geographic concentration of the foreigners. About 90 per cent of them settled in the Buenos Aires metropolitan area and

GINO GERMANI

in the central provinces of the country, a region which includes
no more than one-third of the national territory. This concentration was further intensified because most immigrants went to the
cities. The urban counties contained a large majority of the foreign population. After 1914 this tendency was reinforced, and in
the last census 68 per cent of the immigrants lived in the big
cities.

TABLE V   Geographic Distribution of the Foreign-born. 1869–1960.

Years	Buenos Aires Metropolitan area * %	Provinces of Córdoba, Buenos Aires, Entre Ríos, Mendoza, Santa Fé, La Pampa %	Rest of country %	Total %
1869	52	38	10	100
1895	39	52	9	100
1914	42	48	10	100
1947	51	35	14	100
1960	57	27	16	100

Source: Argentine National Census.
* Includes population in the rural sector of the area.

Finally, the proportion of foreigners in certain key sectors
of the population was increased by the age and sex composition
of European immigration. Over 71 per cent of the immigrants
were male, and about 65 per cent were adults between twenty
and sixty years of age. This proportion did not change significantly throughout the period of mass immigration.[7] This
demographic concentration greatly affected the age and sex composition of the Argentine population. The most important economic and social consequences were the great expansion of the
labor force and an extremely high proportion of foreigners among
adult males. The demographic effects of immigration on sex and
age composition began to wear off after 1930, but in the last
census (1960) they were still visible. In 1960 most of the immigrants were concentrated in the older age groups. Two-thirds

TABLE VI Distribution of the Foreign-born Population by Urban and Rural Counties.**

Counties including cities of population specified in 1947 Census	1869 %	1895 %	1914 %	1947 %	1960 %
Buenos Aires metropolitan area	52	39	42	51	57
100,000 and more	5	10	12	12	11
50,000–99,000	3	3	3	3	2
2,000–9,999	34	42	39	30	25
Less than 2,000	6	6	4	4	5
Total	100	100	100	100	100

Source: Argentine National Census.

** The counties were classified on the basis of the size of the major cities they included according to the 1947 Census. Each category of counties also includes a proportion of "rural" population (living in centers of less than 2,000 inhabitants). Such proportion was very small (in 1947) in the first two categories, but it was increasingly larger in the other categories.

of the foreigners were more than forty years old, and nearly one-third was over sixty.

TABLE VII Sex Ratio and Age Composition in Argentina. 1869–1960.

	Sex ratio			% 14–64 years old		
Census	Total population	Native-born	Foreign-born	Total population	Native population	Foreign population
1869	106	94	251	56.5	—	—
1895	112	90	173	57.9	48.6	85.0
1914	116	98	171	61.4	50.3	87.4
1947	105	100	138	65.2	61.9	83.7
1960	101	99	110	63.0*	61.3*	75.0*

Source: Argentine National Census.

* Estimates on the basis of a sample of the 1960 Census.

IMPACT ON THE ECONOMIC AND SOCIAL STRUCTURE

The role of immigration in the rapid economic growth of Argentina can hardly be over-emphasized. However, it is very difficult to separate this role from its general context. Immigration provided the labor needed to occupy the unexploited land and to develop the agricultural production which transformed Argentina from an importing country in 1870 to one of the principal world exporters. At the same time immigration supplied the manpower to build a railroad system, public works, and housing, and to expand the commercial activities and the service sectors. Finally, it was the immigrant population which provided most of the labor and entrepreneurship in the beginnings of industrial development. But relative political stability and heavy capital investment were needed in order for this role to be carried out.

No less important was the contribution of foreign immigration to modification of the social structure. The system of stratification and many traditional social values were sharply affected by the overwhelming mass of foreign population. The old creole stock was replaced by a new type which has not yet been clearly defined.

Immigrant participation in economic areas varied a great deal. Such participation was not only a function of their original skills but also of the kind of socio-economic structure they found in the country and the conditions under which economic expansion occurred. Most immigrants came from the poorer strata of their native lands. About 41 per cent were peasants, 23 per cent were unskilled workers, and about 36 per cent had various manual and non-manual skills. Up to 1890, more than 70 per cent of the immigrants were peasants, but this percentage decreased sharply in following years. It is known that even those who were originally peasants did not remain in the rural areas. A considerable proportion went to the cities and worked in secondary or tertiary activities.

The populating of the countryside through rural immigration was limited by the traditional distribution of land ownership and by the methods of the successive governments in subdividing and allocating the remaining public lands. Two facts must be recorded: throughout the history of the country, property tended to be concentrated among a relatively small number of families, with the consequent predominance of latifundium. These procedures caused serious difficulties in the realization of one of the declared aims of massive immigration: the settlement of European population in the deserted or semi-deserted rural areas of the country. This settlement was successful to a certain extent,

TABLE VIII Farm and Non-Farm Occupations of the Immigrants. 1857–1954.

Years	Farm %	Non-Farm %	Total %
1857–1870	76	24	100
1871–1890	73	27	100
1891–1910	48	52	100
1911–1924	30	70	100
1925–1939	39	61	100
1940–1945	20	80	100
1946–1954	41	59	100

Sources: Alessandro Bunge, "Ochenta y cinco," *Revista de Economíca Argentina*, 1944; and information provided by the Dirección Nacional de Estadísticas y Censos.

but it was undoubtedly much smaller than what might have occurred if there had not been a predominance of latifundium.

In the second place, the traditional system of land distribution did not ensure peasant ownership of the land. For the whole massive immigration period, the so-called "colonization" was carried out through the intervention of commercial companies or individuals who took over the subdivision of the land and the organization of the colonies, making these operations lucrative through what amounted to selfish speculation.

In many cases, the owners of vastly extensive properties in the more favored areas preferred to exploit their lands by means of renting or similar devices, rather than transferring their property.[8] We should also bear in mind that land exploitation often favored the permanence of large units; this applies not only to cattle breeding but also to extensive farming. Finally, insofar as

TABLE IX Foreign-born per Every 100 Persons in Primary, Secondary and Tertiary Activities. 1895–1947.

Activities	1895	1914	1947
Primary	30	37	18
Secondary	46	53	26
Tertiary	42	30	22
Total occupied population	38	47	22

Source: Argentine National Census.

agricultural and cattle-breeding activities developed, the land became increasingly valuable, thus making it less accessible to immigrants, who continued to arrive in great numbers. Very few immigrants acquired property after 1900. This meant that only a minority of the European peasants could settle in the country on the stable basis of land ownership. A considerable number were able to secure land only by renting, and the majority finally settled in the cities, returned to their own lands, or emigrated to other countries. Moreover, the limitations and conditions under which the immigrant appropriation of land occurred caused a great deal of instability for the peasant and his family. This was particularly true of the renters, for whom this situation meant almost always the last stage of their social ascent, since they never became owners of the land they worked on, and moreover were frequently displaced from one area to another in search of better conditions.[9]

In summary, we can say that, while the tremendous increase in agricultural production was mainly the result of European immigration, such participation rarely developed into ownership. Frequently it was subjected to the conditions established by the titleholders of the land, who either rented it to immigrants or hired them as laborers or managers. In the cattle-breeding sector the immigrants' participation was even lower. The development of this sector began earlier. Because of its nature and traditions, its expansion and modernization was undertaken by the big Argentine landowners. Also, labor was provided by the native-born population, traditionally related to this kind of occupation. The rural creole workers, who did not adapt to agricultural work, either migrated to the cities or gathered in the *estancias* (cattle ranches), devoted to stock breeding.

These circumstances explain the varying participation of foreigners in the different economic activities. The figures given in Table X, although fragmentary, give a clear illustration of the foreigners' participation in the different levels of ownership and control of the primary sectors. Only 10 per cent of the landowners, and no more than 22 per cent of the owners of stock-breeding operations, were immigrants. The proportion of the foreign-born approximates the national average in the labor force only in the census category, which lumps together administrators,

TABLE X Proportion of Foreigners in Some Occupational Categories in the Primary Sector. 1914.

Occupational categories	Foreigners per every 100 persons in each category
Landed property owners in general *	10
Owners of cattle-breeding operations	22
Renters of cattle-breeding operations	34
Administrators, directors, managers of cattle-breeding operations (including owners and renters)	44
Administrators, directors, managers of agricultural operations (including owners and rentiers)	57

Source: Third Argentine National Census.
* Excluding the city of Buenos Aires.

managers, and rentiers. In the agricultural enterprises foreigners reach higher proportions than in the national average (but still below the proportion among the owners of commerce or industry).

TABLE XI Proportion of Foreigners in Some Occupational Categories in the Secondary and Tertiary Sectors. 1895–1914.

Occupational and economic category	1895	1914
Owners of industry *	81	66
Owners of commerce **	74	74
Personnel in commerce (workers and white collars) *	57	53
Personnel in industry (workers and white collars) *	60	50
Liberal professions	53	45
Public administration **	30	18
Persons in artisan and domestic activities **	18	27
Business administration **	63	51
Domestic service workers **	25	38

Sources:
* Second and Third Argentine National Census: special census.
** Second and Third Argentine National Census: population census.

The result of the agrarian policy which conditioned foreign immigration was not so much to populate the extensive semi-deserted rural areas as to create an abundant urban labor force and on a lesser scale a rural one, since a minority of the landless immigrants remained in the countryside as salaried peons. The growth of the cities, the emergence of industry, and the resulting transformation of the social structure were consequences of this process, and in turn originated new social conditions affecting the ruling elites. All these circumstances contributed to shaping the geographic and economic distribution of foreigners.

Immigrant participation in certain sectors was preponderant. As we have seen, in the secondary and tertiary sectors foreign participation in the cities was always higher than within the total labor force. The rates included in Table XI indicate the varying proportions of immigrants in some activities. According to the 1895 Census, the conduct of about 80 per cent of industry and trade was in the hands of foreigners. Among salaried personnel the proportion was lower but always higher than in the national average. The native born predominated in artisan activities, other domestic industries, the public bureaucracy, and domestic services.

The data presented in Table XI are too incomplete to offer a basis for systematic observation. Nevertheless, the figures are useful at least to illustrate the orientation of immigration and its distribution in the different strata of the occupational structure. Apparently, in the process of Argentine society's transformation, foreigners were preferentially placed in the emerging strata. Entrepreneurs, workers, and managers in strategic areas of industry and commerce were at the root of modernization. They predominated especially in the middle class and the new urban industrial proletariat, both categories belonging to the new economic structure which was replacing traditional society. It was precisely in the older economic activities that the native born continued to predominate, as well as in activities directly related to government operations.

From the economic point of view the recent industrial activities were of only secondary importance. A larger proportion of industry was directly linked with agriculture and stock breeding. This sector, some 40 per cent of the total industrial production, included the industries devoted to perishable goods and the meatpacking plants, which must be considered the only large scale industries of that time. The remaining industry was devoted mostly to the production of inexpensive and low-quality consumer goods for the lower strata, while the market for the elite and the upper middle class was mostly supplied by imports. Many of the industrial enterprises were small,[10] and did not represent a key sector in the national economy of the time, even if they supplied two-thirds of the total consumption of the internal market.[11] Nonetheless, the growing number of local industrial enterprises eventually played an essential role in the transformation of Argentine society. The rapid growth of the population and the general economic expansion stimulated the internal market. This resulted in a great increase in the number of industrial and business enterprises and a growth of public services. This expansion not only absorbed immigrant labor but stimulated a crucial change in the social structure: urbanization and the rise of a large middle class. By 1895 the urban population had increased to 37 per cent, and by 1914 the majority of the inhabitants lived in urban centers. As noted earlier, this increase was mostly due to the immigrants, whose proportion was about 50 per cent of the population of all ages in the Buenos Aries metropolitan area and more than one-third in the other large cities.

At the same time, the structure of stratification had been drastically modified. The two-strata system of the mid-nineteenth century was replaced by a much more complex structure, in which the middle layers increased from less than 11 per cent of the population in 1869, to 25 per cent in 1895, and to more than 30 per cent in 1914. Within this emerging middle class the pro-

TABLE XII Percentage of Foreign-born in Different Occupational Strata. 1895–1914.

Occupational strata	(a) 1895	(a) 1914	(b) 1960
Middle strata in secondary and tertiary sectors	59	51	16
Middle strata in primary sector	43	45	16
Lower strata in secondary and tertiary sectors	39	48	15
Lower strata in primary sector	25	35	15

(a) Computed from an unpublished re-classification of the 1895 and 1914 Argentine Census prepared for the Institute of Sociology of the University of Buenos Aires by Ruth Sautú and Susana Torrado.
(b) Estimates on the basis of a sample of the 1960 Census.

portion of foreign-born was larger than in the total labor force. This was especially true of industry, commerce, and services.

While these estimates are imprecise, they illustrate the importance of foreign immigration in the modernization of the stratification system.

This process, on the other hand, did not only involve the rise of a substantial middle class. It also stimulated the transformation of the lower class by causing the emergence of a modern urban proletariat, predominantly foreign. This process did not affect the occupational structure alone. When we speak of *middle classes* and *urban proletariat,* we are also referring to attitudes, ideologies, aspirations, and self-identifications. The reality of this transition is clearly expressed in the political events of the period corresponding to the appearance of middle-class political parties, and the typical protest movements of the rising urban proletariat. But, as we will indicate later on, the overwhelmingly foreign origin of both the modern middle class and the modern urban workers was itself a basic factor in the political development of the country.

Between 1870 and 1910 a great part of the transition from a predominantly traditional structure to a more advanced pattern was completed, at least in the Buenos Aires metropolitan area and in the provinces of the Littoral region (which included two-thirds of the national population). However, those geographical areas and social groups less affected by foreign immigration tended to maintain archaic traits. The persistence of these internal contradictions had a lasting effect on the subsequent economic and social development of the country. It is true that the landowning elite was not an entirely closed class, even at that time; its origins were fairly recent, and a number of new families were able to reach the upper social level. However, regardless of the degree of fluidity within this group, the important fact is that the elite became increasingly concerned with maintaining the economic and social structure favorable to its interests. This meant strictly limiting the process of modernization which the elite itself had initiated. While its attempt to completely control the process was doomed to failure, it managed to maintain a key economic position and continued to orient the economy to the exporting of primary products. For another thing, the existence of a large proportion of the population within the less developed regions and still mostly traditional, involved the problem of its future mobilization and integration into the modern pattern. Both problems were to acquire a dramatic expression after 1930.

The rapid rate of the transition after 1930, especially the expansion of the middle class, made social mobility an important factor in shaping the historical process. A large majority of immigrants belonged to the lower strata of their societies. Table XIII does not give a precise measure of the social composition of the immigrants, but at least it suggests the kind of people who were arriving by the thousands in those years. Only very few immigrants had middle-class backgrounds. As a result, the new Argentine middle class, so heavily recruited from among the immigrants, was mostly of lower-class origin. Between 1895 and 1914 no less than two-thirds of the middle classes were of popular class origin; that is, they were formed by individuals who either had begun their occupational careers as manual workers, or were sons of manual-worker fathers.[12] Social mobility

TABLE XIII   Socio-Occupational Strata of Immigrants, According to Their Occupation Declared at the Moment of Admittance to the Country. 1857–1925.

Socio-occupational categories	1857–1870	1871–1899	1900–1920	1921–1924	Total: 1857–1925
Employees in business, industry, services, agriculture; free professionals, technicians; white collar and kindred occupations	4.4	5.4	8.6	13.4	7.2
Skilled and unskilled workers, day laborers and kindred occupations	95.6	94.6	91.4	86.6	92.1

Source: *Resumen Estadístico del Movimiento Migratorio*, Ministerio de Agricultura. Buenos Aires, Argentina, 1925.

became a normal pattern in Argentine society (or at least in the central areas), and this trait was accompanied by corresponding attitude changes and ideological expressions. Social mobility must be considered an important factor not only in explaining the process of absorption of the foreign immigrants, but also in explaining essential aspects of the Argentine political and social history in the twentieth century.

THE ASSIMILATION OF THE FOREIGN POPULATION AND ITS IMPACT ON THE CULTURE

The problem that Argentina had to confront between 1870 and 1930 is probably without precedent in other immigration countries. Even the United States, which received the largest share of the great international migrations, was never in a similar situation; the proportion of foreigners in its total population and in the annual migratory stream, although much higher in absolute terms, was relatively much lower than in Argentina. Moreover, the size of the native-born population was large enough to ensure the possibility of real assimilation; also, the stability of the existing social structure was much stronger, which made it better-equipped to resist the migratory impact. In the United States the maximum proportion of foreign-born population was 14.7 per cent in 1910, and after 1920 it decreased steadily to the present 5.4 per cent. In Argentina immigrants were more than one-fourth of the total population in the last decade of the nineteenth century. This proportion grew to nearly 30 per cent just before the First World War, and it stayed as high as 23 per cent until 1930. In 1960 it was still nearly 13 per cent; that is, a proportion quite similar to the highest ever reached in the United States. But even these figures fail to suggest the immigrants' impact on Argentine society. As we have seen, the demographic concentration for certain ages and for the male sex, coupled with the regional and urban concentration, increased the proportion of foreigners in the more strategic areas of the country and in most of the important sectors of the population. Immigrants comprised from two-thirds to three-quarters of the total adult population in Buenos Aires City for more than sixty years since 1869. In the remaining provinces of the central area, this proportion remained close to 50 per cent. If we consider only the adult males, we see that for many decades there were in Buenos Aires more than four foreigners for every native-born Argentine, and in the central area

TABLE XIV   Total Population and Percentage of Foreign-born in Argentina and the United States. 1810–1960.

Years	Total population (millions)		Per cent foreign-born in total population	
	United States	Argentina	United States	Argentina
1810	7.2	.4	11.1	*
1850	23.2	1.3	9.5	*
1870	39.8	1.7**	14.1	12.1**
1890	62.9	*	14.6	*
1895	—	4.0	—	*
1900	76.0	*	13.6	*
1910	92.0	*	14.7	*
1914	—	7.9	—	29.9
1920	105.7	8.8	13.2	24.0
1930	122.8	11.7	11.6	23.5
1950	150.7	17.0	6.8	15.8
1960	150.7	20.0	5.4	12.8

Sources: Brinley Thomas (ed.), *Economics of International Migration.* London: Macmillan, 1958, p. 136; Francisco De Aparico y Horacio Difrieri (eds.), *La Argentina, Suma de Geografía.* Buenos Aires: Peuser, 1961, p. 94; and *Boletines de la Dirección Nacional de Estadísticas y Censos* (various years).

* No date available.
** 1869 Census.

the immigrants were considerably more numerous than the natives. We do not have specific rates for the inter-census years, but we can guess that this proportion must have continued during

TABLE XV   Foreign-born Over Twenty Years Old (Both Sexes) for Every 100 Persons of the Same Age and Sex. 1869–1947.

Years	Buenos Aires City	Central area. Provinces of Buenos Aires, Córdoba, Entre Ríos, Mendoza, La Pampa	Peripheral area. All other states and territories
1869	67	*	*
1895	74	44	11
1914	72	51	20
1947	37	23	16

Source: Argentine National Census.
* No data.

TABLE XVI Argentine and Foreign Males Aged Twenty Years and Over. 1869–1947 (thousands).

| Years | Buenos Aires City | | Central provinces of Buenos Aires, Córdoba, Entre Ríos, Mendoza, La Pampa | |
	Argentine males	Foreign males	Argentine males	Foreign males
1869	12	48	*	*
1895	42	174	287	309
1914	119	404	557	752
1947	614	433	2,115	747

Source: Argentine National Census.
* No data.

the early thirties, especially before the mass internal migrations from the peripheral regions began to accelerate the Argentinization of the population.

We insist on the sheer size of the proportion because it introduces a factor rarely cosidered in studies on the assimilation of foreign immigrants. Usually one speaks of assimilation as a concept presupposing a native population with the capacity to assimilate the incoming groups. But how well will the host society be able to maintain its identity if the incoming population is larger than the existing one, and if the absolute size of the latter is very small in the first place? We suggest that, other things being equal, these two quantitative aspects definitely limit the absorption capacity of the receiving society. There are other, equally important conditions which affect the process: the power structure of the receiving society; the immigrants' position within the structure; their location in the stratification systems of both the native and receiving societies, the differences between immigrant and native cultures, and their relative prestige; the degree of segregation of the immigrant population in relation to the receiving society and to its different sectors and strata; the degree of cultural homogeneity of the immigrants; their solidarity; their attitudes; their level of education; the strength of their original national identifications; the degree of acceptance they find in the new country; and especially the degree of social mobility they experience in the receiving country. Only in the case of a heterogeneous and subordinated immigrant population, characterized by a much lower cultural level than that of the host society and placed under conditions of severe segregation, could a smaller native population limit the impact of immigration on the existing culture and social structure. An illustration of this extreme case would be a large slave population of immigrant origin placed in a society composed of a smaller number of free individuals. But even in this example the receiving society would eventually change in response to the immigrants' impact. In Argentina conditions were not this extreme. The immigrants were neither nationally nor culturally homogeneous, but there was at least one extremely large national group. The degree of their identification with their country of origin varied, but it was probably fairly low because many immigrants came from backward and traditional cultures. However, they did not regard the receiving country as a superior culture to be imitated. Although many were illiterate, they introduced new skills and new attitudes toward economic activities. Also, the fact of having emigrated involved a rupture with their traditional past. They had been released from that past and were now mobilized, even if their basic motivation was not to settle permanently in the new country but to get rich, return to the native village, and buy land. In fact, their attempts to fulfill their purposes set them on the path which led them to abandon their traditional mores. And this change was irreversible: unconsciously and unwillingly, the immigrants were the bearers of modernization.[13] On the other hand, they soon gained a better social and economic position than the native born of the lower strata. At the same time, however, they remained practically excluded from positions of economic power, which as we have seen remained firmly in the hands of the elite.

After the deluge of immigration there was still an Argentina; the country did not lose its identity. But the old and new elements had been fused and transformed. A new country emerged, and is still emerging, since the historical process set in motion by the mass nineteenth century immigration cannot be considered complete. In Argentina the immigration process implied the virtual disappearance (in the areas of immigrant settlement) of the existing native social types and the partial destruction of the social structure which corresponded to them. In their place emerged a new type, still not well-defined, and a new structure.

Among the rural population, which made up its large majority, the typical native had adapted to the occupations and social conditions of the countryside during the colonial epoch. Many of his psychological features were those that characterize the Spaniards. The image of the *gaucho*, who later became a national myth, may illustrate the prevailing values of rural society prior to the impact of immigration. The gaucho was a kind of *peón* on horseback. He worked at intervals, never having a permanent occupation or home. His personal life was characterized by freedom. He could move freely in the immense open spaces of the Pampas, which at that time had no limits fixed by wire fences. His work depended only on his ability, on his talent as a horseman and on his courage. These were the values which identified him to himself and to others. There were no habits of regularity, frugality, foresight, or rational calculation in his behavior. On the contrary, these were considered negative characteristics, opposed to the manly ideal. He had no aspiration for social ascent, no special desire to acquire land. Because the gaucho sometimes worked as a peón in the estancia, he has quite often been confused with the ordinary peasant, which he was not. However, there is little doubt that most of his traits were shared by the rural inhabitants who formed a majority of the population. Their relation to the masters of the estancias was wholly particularistic, and did not correspond at all to the relationship between a salaried worker and his employer. Insofar as the master displayed some of the traits valued by the gaucho, especially personal courage, physical strength, and ability, the latter felt a personal adherence to him, based on sentiments of fidelity, loyalty, and admiration.

The material aspects of the culture were a function of the necessities of a life based on livestock, technically and socially at a primitive level. Agriculture and sedentary work in general were considered inferior; work itself was despised. In the rural areas, and probably in the lower strata in the towns and urban centers as well, the population lacked national identification; their loyalty was mainly local, and it was usually personified in the *cau-*

dillo. This, of course, was the social basis of the dissolution of the "unitarian state" which occurred soon after Independence.[14]

Thus Argentina in the middle of the nineteenth century, before the beginning of mass overseas immigration, was permeated by traditional values and behavior patterns. Its more modern sectors were found in the urban elites; that is, in a small proportion of its inhabitants sharply contrasting with the rural masses and also with the lower urban strata. The overseas immigrants were the bearers of different attitudes toward agriculture, saving, economic life, and mobility aspirations. Partly because of a different cultural heritage and partly as an effect of displacement, they became a powerful impulse toward modernization. Certainly, even if the majority of the foreigners had little or no education, a considerable number of professionals, technicians, and skilled workers did arrive, and they were able to provide most of the specialized personnel for the many new activities required by modernization in all fields. But even the uneducated peasants became innovators. In the Argentine pampas, for example, they showed a much greater flexibility and creativity than did the local population.[15]

Under the impact of immigration the old cultural patterns practically dissolved. Objects of previously great material value and symbolic meaning, like the horse, lost all importance. Similarly, many aspects of the traditional culture, such as clothes, tools, vehicles, food, housing, furniture, forms of leisure, were totally replaced or profoundly transformed. These changes were mainly due to material necessity, not merely to a wish to emulate. Each immigrant group imprinted its characteristics on the different aspects of the material and non-material culture, and in this way innovation, implicit or explicit, was stamped with the cultural forms imported from Europe.

According to Gori, the immigrant did not easily shed his European culture. On the contrary, "he tried to reaffirm it, especially the Swiss and German, through family training and the schooling of his children. He had staked his sights more on the consulate of his country as an agent of legality than in the formal representatives of Argentine authority, whom he mistrusted, even while being forced to accept."

According to this author and others, the immigrant generally spoke his mother tongue, read newspapers in his native tongue, and maintained organizations to encourage ties with the fatherland. Whenever he could, he chose a wife of his own nationality. Sometimes, in the beginning, the immigrant agricultural colonies chose their own authorities, and quite often geographic isolation made such colonies akin to foreign fortresses in the middle of the nation.[16]

In the cities the isolation and segregation which prevailed in the rural colonies was absent, although there was, particularly in Buenos Aires, some ecological segregation by nationality. The term *colony* was applied to a native group residing in an urban center; this term also referred to settlements of immigrants of any origin throughout the country. They developed separate communities with advanced organizational structure which included newspapers, schools, hospitals, and all kinds of voluntary associations connected with their country of origin.

In some cases the actions of foreign governments through these associations went farther than the attitudes of the emigrants would have justified. In the case of the Italians and the Spanish the degree of national identification with their country of origin was quite low. Patriotism among the Italians often came *after* emigration, perhaps as an effect of nostalgia, as Sarmiento noted.[17] Moreover, the strongest expressions of national identification with the country of origin came not from the inarticulate masses but from the elites of each national sector. If, as we suggest, the national identification of the largest immigrant sectors was weak, this must be counted as an important factor in the survival of an Argentine national identity.

The prevalence of these voluntary associations is remarkable if we consider the low cultural and economic level of the majority. At first the organizations provided many services which Argentina was unable to offer. Later on, however, education, sanitary facilities, mass communication media, and other services were provided by public and private Argentine institutions, and the need for the foreign national asociations was less obvious. Some contemporaries have observed that their underlying purpose was to keep alive the language and traditions of the fatherland.

The asociations had other latent functions. For instance, they provided the traditional immigrants with a means of integra-

312

tion into the Argentine society. These functions may account for the fact that the enthusiasm for associations was much higher among the immigrants than among the native born. This fact cannot be explained simply as a consequence of the emigration and of their special situation in a foreign land. Under similar conditions half a century later, the degree of formal and informal participation of Argentine internal migrants was extremely low; in fact, one obstacle to their assimilation was precisely their disorganization upon their arrival in the city.[18]

The remarkable propensity to cooperate and to create voluntary associations among the foreign immigrants was also due to other factors. In the first place, the associations expressed values and attitudes widely different from the anarchic and at the same time "submissive-authoritarian" character predominant among the natives, especially in the rural areas. In the second place, foreign immigration included an important working-class elite, which often had not left their native lands for economic reasons alone. This elite provided leadership both to the voluntary associations and to the protest movements arising within the new industrial proletariat.

TABLE XVII Voluntary Associations by Nationality of the Majority of Their Membership: Number of Affiliates for Every 1,000 Native-born and for Every 1,000 Foreign-born. 1914.

	No. of members for every 1,000 Argentines and for every 1,000 foreign-born living in the area		No. of associations	
Types of associations	Buenos Aires City	Rest of the country	Buenos Aires City	Rest of the country
Argentine Associations	104	21	19	153
Foreign Associations:				
one nationality	145	151	97	752
multi-national (includes workers' centers)	197	14	98	83

Source: Third Argentine National Census.

The tremendous challenge to Argentina created by the

avalanche of foreigners is reflected in the writings of the decades around the end of the nineteenth and the beginning of the twentieth century. Sarmiento described Argentina as a "republic of foreigners," served by a small number of nationals performing unprofitable and burdensome tasks, such as keeping order, defending the territory, administering justice, and preserving the rights and the special privileges of the immigrants themselves.[19] Even the Italians, who later revealed themselves as the most amenable to assimilation, appeared as a powerful threat to national independence and identity. This was a consequence of their high proportion and concentration, their powerful organizations, and the attitudes of the Italian government, which regarded the Italian immigrants and their descendants as Italian citizens, in keeping with the principle of *Jus Sanguinis*. The problem of foreign schools, the deliberate attempt to create alien national communities, the absence of an Argentine tradition among the immigrants, and their complete political alienation continued to be serious concerns of the Argentine elite for a long time.

The problem was aggravated by certain basic contradictions in the policy followed by the elite in fostering immigration. These contradictions resulted from the difference between the declared and manifest aims of constructing a modern nation, and the limits within which many members of the dominant group wished to restrict the process of modernization. These problems were especially apparent in the political participation of the immigrants.

One of the proclaimed aims of immigration was to provide a stable basis for the functioning of democracy. But it soon became evident that those who were expected to become the new citizens remained totally outside the political life of the country. Indeed, despite the legal facilities for obtaining naturalization (which only required two years' residence and a relatively simple procedure), almost none of the immigrants sought it. There were several reasons for this. The Constitution accorded foreigners the same rights as those of the native-born, except the right to vote and to run for election. Under certain conditions, the foreigner, even without naturalization, could participate in local elections for city administration. In any case, not only economic activities but also all jobs in the civil service of the federal and provincial governments or other public bodies were open to the foreign-born without any requirements of citizenship. Consequently, there was no economic incentive for naturalization. Also, many immigrants were reluctant to lose their foreign national identification, for it gave them additional rights since they were protected also by their respective native governments. In most cases, the immigrant looked down on the native-born as an inferior. Often he simply expected to return to his fatherland as soon as possible after getting rich, This situation caused many heated discussions between Argentines and foreigners, whose point of view was expressed by the booming foreign press. Some foreign sectors requested that naturalization be automatic but not compulsory. That is, foreigners would receive full citizenship rights, without renouncing their previous nationality and without being compelled to accept Argentine citizenship.[20] For certain nationalities and for the more highly educated, the failure to naturalize was certainly an expression of loyalty to the country of origin. But the reasons for the majority of the immigrants, especially Italian and Spanish, were probably different. Their lack of interest in political participation was an expression of the low political culture of the lower-class foreigners who came from countries whose voting was quite restricted and where politics was an activity monopolized by the middle and higher classes.

TABLE XVIII   Naturalized Foreigners for Every 100 Foreigners Residing in Buenos Aires and in the Rest of the Country. 1895–1947.

Regions	1895	1914	1947
Buenos Aires City	0.2	2.3	9.5
Rest of the Country	0.1	0.9	7.2

Source: Second, Third and Fourth Argentine National Census.

The political elite wanted a genuine functioning of the democracy anticipated in the Constitution, and immigration was stimulated with this in mind. But they found themselves faced with the paradox of a country in which 60 to 80 per cent of the adult male population in the most important areas had no right to vote and was governed by the remaining minority, con-

315

stituting 20 to 40 per cent. But even these were not the true proportions. Only a minority of the native-born effectively participated in politics, and elections took place amid the general indifference of Argentines and foreigners alike, at least among the popular classes. And the governing elite, whatever its explicit purposes may have been, for a long time resisted the relinquishing of power through elections based on effective universal suffrage. They yielded only when the urban middle and popular classes became endowed with sufficient size and solidity to impose their influence.

When the foreigners created movements that suggested active political participation, the elite became indignant and fearful. It is true that these organizations could not be considered real channels of integration into the national life, since they were found in the context of the so-called Political Centers for Foreigners [21] and not in national political parties. But other attempts by the immigrants at political participation which were not linked to their nationalities were also opposed. This happened in the case of the workers' movements, which were especially vigorous in Buenos Aires since the end of the nineteenth century, and which lacked specific national identification. On the contrary, although the majority of the members were foreigners, they did not possess any unified national character; they were international and cosmopolitan in ideology and composition. These "cosmopolitan" societies and "workers' circles" had a real function in the assimilation of immigrants; they channeled the immigrants' activities into the political life of the country. This participation was not determined by national origin but by location in a given sector or stratum of Argentine society. However, the immigrants' ideologies still could not be readily accepted by the liberal elite. In this sense it was historically impossible for the elites to recognize the latent integrating function of workers' organizations. In fact the ruling group not only did not welcome the immigrants but repressed them through severe laws and systematic police persecution. The elite wanted to populate the desert, but they were not ready to introduce the necessary reforms in the agrarian structure. They wanted to integrate the immigrants into the body politic but did not want to share power with them.

In fact, political participation by the immigrants is only one aspect of this more general problem. We have given some indications of the many problems and internal tensions caused by immigration. What remains to be understood is how, after some sixty years, a relatively integrated and unified nation finally emerged. Systematic research on this subject is not available. Suggestions can be made, but we must recognize that they are speculative.

Perhaps it will be convenient to clarify first the meaning of *assimilation* as the term is used here. We will base our analysis on a preliminary distinction between *individual adjustment, participation, acculturation* and *identification.*[22]

(a) The notion of *adjustment* refers to the manner in which the immigrant performs his roles in the various spheres of activity in which he participates. What is important here is his ability to perform the roles without excessive or unbearable psychological stress.

(b) The concept of *participation* treats assimilation from the standpoint of the receiving society. Here we distinguish between three different dimensions. (1) *Extent* of participation: what roles is the immigrant performing within the social institutions and sectors of the host society; how much is he still connected with his fatherland; what roles is he playing in the social institutions and sectors of the host society, but socially segregated from it. (2) Another important aspect of participation is the *efficiency* with which the roles are performed. In this case we define efficiency from the point of view of the receiving institutions and groups. (3) Finally, we must take into account the *reception* given by the country to the immigrants. It is important to emphasize that participation may be granted in certain spheres of activities but not in others; indeed, this is usually the case.

(c) By *acculturation* we mean the immigrants' absorption of the cultural patterns of the host society. Such absorption may consist of relatively superficial learning or it may penetrate deeply into the personality. Acculturation is never a one-way process. It affects not only the immigrants but the receiving culture as well.

(d) Finally, an important aspect of assimilation is the degree of *identification* of the foreign-born and their descendants with the new country. To what extent do they lose their previous identification, and acquire a new one; how deep is the new identification, and how does it affect their attitudes and behavior.

These four aspects of assimilation are not necessarily all present in the same group or in the same individual. It is true that in certain spheres of activity adjustment, participation and acculturation will usually be associated, but this does not necessarily include national identification. Given the heterogeneity of the immigrants and the different conditions under which they settled, there should be a variety of situations, according to the different national origins and the educational and socio-economic status of the individuals involved.

In terms of *individual adjustment* there are reasons to believe that massive immigration involved a high cost. The high proportion of "returnees" indicates this. Among the causes were the relative inaccessibility of land ownership and the hardships of life in the rural areas. But in the cities too the adjustment must have been relatively painful. The documents of the period under consideration abound in descriptions of the sufferings, restrictions, and poverty of the immigrants. On the other hand, many acquired a degree of economic and social well-being beyond what they could have expected at home. We know very little about the degree of family organization. It is estimated by some that family organization among the native rural population was not high. If this is true, then immigration helped to establish a pattern of more regular and organized family life among the lower strata.[23]

The *participation* of immigrants varied according to the various spheres of activity. In the economic sphere it was always high. Since immigrant participation in the nation's economic life involved upward social mobility, this must have been a powerful means of integration. Thirty years after the end of mass immigration, in the Buenos Aires area, second generation immigrants were mostly in the middle and higher strata, and together with the foreign-born constituted more than three-fourths of the individuals located at these levels.[24] Among the entrepreneurial elite this proportion was even higher: almost 90 per cent at about the same date.[25] Intermarriage was another essential means of participation and integration into the life of the country. During the period from 1890 to 1910, about 40 per cent of the immigrants married outside their national group, many marrying Argentine women.[26]

The participation of foreigners in the intellectual life of the country was another means of integration. Although of course it was not a means of mass participation, it gave the immigrants an important role among the intellectual elite, and it contributed very much to the national patterns of intellectual and artistic expression. The consequences of this fact are still controversial. Nationalists of the Right as well as the neo-nationalists of the Left feel that the typical cosmopolitism of the Argentine intelligentsia is one of the major obstacles to the rise of an "authentic" national consciousness. Often the blame has been placed on the "oligarchy" and its intellectual establishment.[27] But whatever the evolution of the process, its existence cannot be denied.

TABLE XIX   Argentine and Foreign-born Heads of Family by Socio-Economic Status. Buenos Aires Metropolitan Area, 1961.

	Native-born Argentine family heads				
Socio-economic status	Both parents Argentine-born	One parent foreign-born	Both parents foreign-born	Foreign-born family heads	Total population heads of family
Lower (unskilled and skilled manual)	45.6	30.0	33.3	48.2	41.5
Middle (lower middle and upper middle)	49.0	65.6	60.8	49.8	55.4
Upper (lower upper and upper upper)	5.4	4.4	5.9	2.0	4.1
Total %	100.0	100.0	100.0	100.0	100.0
Number of men interviewed	519	262	534	736	2,051

Source: "Stratification and Mobility in Buenos Aires" (Buenos Aires Institute of Sociology, unpublished data). Survey based on a random area sample. Socio-economic status is computed on the average of four indicators: occupation, income, education, and standard of living.

As we have seen, the direct political participation of the foreigner was low and frequently inconsistent because of the ambivalent attitudes of the ruling elite. But this was true only of those actually born abroad, not of their children. After 1916 the proportion of second-generation immigrants began to rise among the active politicians. In 1889 their proportion among legislators (deputies and senators) was only 38 per cent, but it had risen to 55 per cent by 1916.[28] The degree of participation of second-generation immigrants reflected the political history of the country. Participation rose with the access to power of the middle class and decreased again when the "oligarchy" returned to power through the military revolution of 1930. After 1945 participation increased again.[29] It is worth noting that the last two constitutional presidents were second-generation Italian immigrants. If we consider the other two sectors of the leading elite— the military and the Church—we will see that the paricipation of immigrants' descendants is very high. In the last twenty-five years 77 per cent of the generals and admirals in the Army, Navy, and Air Force and 77 per cent of the bishops were of immigrant origin, mostly sons of foreigners.[30]

One aspect which alarmed the native elite was the immigrants' tendency to segregate themselves in colonies and communities often supported by their respective national governments. At least up to the First World War, Argentina appeared to many observers to be composed of juxtaposed segments, each of which claimed the loyalty of its members. Even in the economic sphere, which was a major field of interaction, the tendency to segregate by nationality appeared to a certain extent. But as time elapsed it became apparent that, below the seemingly chaotic surface of heterogeneous fragments, a sort of unity was being formed. In the first place, for the majority of immigrants ethnic segregation was really limited to certain special sectors of their life. More pervasive segregation occurred only among the higher strata. Moreover, segregation in one area did not affect the adequate fulfillment of universalistic roles within the society as a whole.[31] In fact these segregated structures functioned as intermediaries between the national society and the immigrants. Thus, even while preserving the cultural traditions of their members' homelands, they nonetheless facilitated social integration. In any case a certain degree of survival of native cultural traditions was perfectly compatible with a high degree of integrated participation in other spheres, especially in a society comparatively free from antagonistic ethnic tensions.[32]

Another integrative force was the fact that the immigrants' descendants frequently entered the same voluntary associations as their parents. In this way, such organizations gradually lost their specifically ethnic character. For example, the use of the language of origin in many foreign associations decreased steadily until it almost disappeared, to be replaced by Spanish. It is obvious that the end of immigration in 1930 was a factor in this process.

The participation of immigrants in these organizations varied according to nationality and socio-economic level. The participation of Italian and Spanish immigrants of the popular classes was less frequent and briefer. Although the large voluntary associations were primarily composed of persons from the lower strata, the proportion of members was probably smaller than for the higher strata. Separate social stratification systems were probably maintained only at the higher class levels. But this segregation was certainly much more limited among the lower strata, and continued to decrease in time.

In addition to the progressive Argentinization of the foreign voluntary associations and the lower formal participation among the working class, there were other factors which favored integration into the national society. In the lower strata the ecological segregation of ethnic groups steadily diminished. In the Buenos Aires area, for example, there was a gradual reduction of the "ghetto" areas occupied by given nationalities. It is important to add that these zones did not have some of the characteristics common to cities in the United States. In some cases in the big cities, for example, certain types of slum, like the *conventillo* (a one or two-floor building with a central courtyard around which the rooms are located; usually a family lives in each room), had a real integrative function for the different nationalities. Obviously the disappearance or drastic reduction of ecological segregation was in many cases due to the replacement of the immigrants by their children.

The process of assimilation should be considered as part of the emergence of new cultural forms and a new human type. This synthesis is the outcome of the interaction of the native and foreign cultures.

This observation brings us to the problem of acculturation.

Even though we lack scientific studies concerning this process, there is an abundant literature, mostly impressionistic essays, attempting to characterize the society born of massive immigration.[33] The result of mass immigration was not the assimilation of the immigrants into the existing Argentine culture. The outcome was a synthesis that created a new cultural type, which is still not well-defined. In this emerging culture it is possible to recognize the contributions of the different national groups, particularly the Italian and the Spanish. But all of them are substantially modified and submerged in a context which gives them a new meaning. Particularly visible in most of the largest cities is the Italian influence in language, gestures, food, and many customs. The Spanish influence, no less strong, is perhaps less visible because it is more easily confused with creole elements. Some popular products of this fusion, like the *tango*, have great emotional and symbolic importance as expressions of the new Argentine society.

The bearers of this new cultural type are the children of the immigrants and their descendants. They are almost completely acculturated. Italian, Yiddish, Polish, and other Eastern European languages are seldom spoken by second-generation immigrants. Also, they would never refer to themselves as belonging to a particular national stock. For example, an Italian immigrant's son would mention, when asked, that his father was Italian, but nobody would differentiate people on the basis of their ancestry. Instead, Italian language and customs have been adapted to new cultural patterns. The Italians' sons do not speak Italian, but everybody regardless of their national origin understands Italian and would be able to learn to speak it quite easily. This is not only because of its similarity with Spanish but because Italian is so familiar in many ways. Words, idioms, the typical pronunciation of Spanish in Buenos Aires and the central area, as well as manners, inflections, facial expressions, and gestures, all bear the mark of many generations of Italians.

The immigrants' upward social mobility facilitated the acculturation of their children. Often the second generation was assimilated into a different social class, values, style of living and expectations that greatly diverged from those of the previous generation. This is of course a well-known phenomenon in a country of heavy immigration, but the huge proportion of immigrants in Argentina accentuated its consequences.

THE ARGENTINIZATION OF ARGENTINA AND THE SURVIVING FOREIGN POPULATION

Let us now examine to what extent the process of assimilation was facilitated by the interruption of mass overseas immigration thirty-five years ago. We may also consider the role of the mass internal migrations in this process.

The Census of 1947 is the only one to give some information on the national origin of the parents. By that time more than one-half of the population was born of native Argentine parents. The rest were sons of immigrants or immigrants themselves. The proportion of the foreign element was higher in Buenos Aires. By 1961 only one-quarter of the heads of family were third-generation Argentines on both parents' sides, this proportion increasing to one-third among the adults. One-half of the families living in Buenos Aires included at least one member born abroad.

TABLE XX National or Foreign Origin of the Population. 1947–1960.

National origin	Whole country— 1947 * (all ages) %	Buenos Aires City—1947 * (all ages) %	Buenos Aires metropolitan area—1961 **	
			Heads of family %	Population aged 18 and over %
Argentine-born from Argentine parents	53.3	30.9	25.2	33.1
Argentine-born from foreign parents (one or both)	31.1	41.1	39.3	39.3
Foreign-born	15.6	28.0	35.5	27.6
	100.0	100.0	100.0	100.0

Sources: * 1947 Census and ** "Stratification and Mobility in Buenos Aires," op. cit.

Thus, the composition of the population is still rather heterogeneuos, even taking into account no more than the birth place of the present population and of their parents, and disregarding the origin of grandparents. Only a process of rapid synthesis and a large cultural distance between the first and second generation immigrants can explain the degree of homogeneity apparently achieved. The impact of time on the foreign population was another factor in facilitating the homogenization. Not only the immigrant group is becoming older, but it is composed of a higher proportion of persons with longer residence in the country.

TABLE XXI   Foreign-born Population by Age Groups. 1947.

Age Groups	Buenos Aires metropolitan area	Rest of country
Up to 39 years old	26.2	25.3
40 to 59 years old	51.8	50.1
Over 60 years old	21.2	24.5
Age unknown	0.8	0.1
	100.0	100.0

Source: Fourth Argentine Census.

Some information on the degree of assimilation and identification of the surviving immigrant population may be found in recent surveys. In Table XXIII only the two major immigrant groups were included.

TABLE XXII   Percentage of Foreign-born Population by Number of Years of Residence in the Country. 1947–1961.

Years of Residence	Entire country	Buenos Aires City. 1947 *	Buenos Aires metropolitan area 1961 **
Up to 9 years	7.9	6.9	13.9
10–19 years	16.5	20.7	17.5
20–29 years	25.5	26.7	12.1
Over 30 years	45.2	41.5	56.5
Unknown	4.9	4.2	—

Source: * Fourth Argentine National Census (unpublished data).
** "Stratification and Mobility in Buenos Aires," op. cit.

Some differences may be noted between Italians and the Spanish, especially between lower and higher socio-economic

TABLE XXIII   Some Indicators of Acculturation, Participation, and Identification in Italian and Spanish Population Aged 18 Years and Over. Buenos Aires Metropolitan Area, 1961.

| Indicators | Socio-economic status: ** | | |
	high	medium	low
Feel closer to Argentina than to home country:			
Italian Immigrants	48.6	48.7	46.8
Spanish Immigrants	28.9	46.4	51.3
Not affiliated to any foreign association:			
Italian Immigrants	88.9	95.7	95.3
Spanish Immigrants	75.0	86.3	89.5
Do not wish to return permanently to native land:			
Italian Immigrants	94.4	91.7	93.2
Spanish Immigrants	83.5	92.7	94.5
Closest friends are Argentinians, or Argentinians and foreigners in same proportion:			
Italian Immigrants	100.0	89.5	86.1
Spanish Immigrants	78.6	91.7	88.2
No communications with persons in home country:			
Italian Immigrants	34.3	46.1	47.6
Spanish Immigrants	13.8	40.1	51.0
Never experienced discrimination:			
Italian Immigrants	94.3	92.2	94.9
Spanish Immigrants	96.6	96.0	93.9
Never or seldom read in native language:			
Italian Immigrants	80.0	71.9	88.9
No preference for films, theatre, etc. in own language:			
Italian Immigrants	21.4	54.1	49.7
Speak only Spanish or Spanish and own language in the same proportion when at home:			
Italian Immigrants	92.9	67.6	39.2
Number of respondents:			
Italian Immigrants	20	274	335
Spanish Immigrants	33	228	257

Source: data summarized from Francis Korn, "Algunos aspectos de la asimilación de immigrantes en Buenos Aires." Instituto de Sociología, Universidad de Buenos Aires. Unpublished paper based on the "Stratification and Mobility in Buenos Aires" survey, op. cit.

** Composite index of occupation, education, income and consumption level.

strata, the former being more easily assimilated than the latter. On the whole, however, these two immigrant groups seem largely assimilated.

Even if they have not lost all emotional ties with their fatherlands, they show an increasing identification with their new country. Practically nobody in these two groups wishes to return to his ancestral land. With the exception of the upper class, one-half of them feel closer to Argentina than to their fatherlands. Only a minority of the Spanish and Italians participate in foreign associations or have predominantly foreign friends. Among the Italians, the use of their native language seems confined to their homes.

Argentina has been rather successful in achieving a high degree of cultural homogeneity and national identification, as well as in capturing the loyalty of immigrants. However, many Argentine writers have challenged this suggestion. Such doubts have been expressed not only when the country was submerged in the flood of foreign immigration, but also in recent years. One prominent Argentine historian has described the present society as a "hybrid mass, formed by creole and foreign elements co-existing without predominance by either." [34] In other Argentinians we find a nostalgia for the homogeneous creole society. This attitude is typical not only of Right wing nationals but also of liberal intellectuals like Erro, Borges, or Mallea.

The political instability since 1930, the economic stagnation of the last fifteen years, and especially the fragmentation of many groups and institutions have been imputed to the lack of real community feeling. However, Argentina was stable and economically prosperous when the degree of cultural homogeneity was much lower and the threat to national identity far more serious. The present troubles have other causes, even if they are in part an expression of the painful process of national integration. In fact, one of the consequences of the great internal migrations was precisely to halt the segregation of the old creole population and to facilitate its fusion with the descendants of immigrant stock.

Perhaps doubts and fears could simply be dispelled or confirmed by empirical evidence alone, even if such evidence were actually available. The contrasting interpretations may be caused by divergent expectations of the degree and kind of cultural homogeneity and national consciousness that can be achieved in Argentina. If one takes into account the risks involved in the incorporation of such a mass of foreigners in so short a time, then the present situation can be viewed with optimism. But if this same situation is measured by the yardstick of a country with a longer historical tradition of homogeneous culture, then of course there is less cause for optimism. The problem is primarily one of time, and this is a limit which even the most efficient assimilation cannot possibly overcome.

NOTES

[1] The other countries which received the largest share of inter-continental immigration were Canada (8.7 per cent), Brazil (7.4 per cent), Australia (5 per cent), New Zealand (1.0 per cent), and South Africa (1.3 per cent). The United States, Argentina, and the above-mentioned countries account for some 90 per cent of the total immigration of the period. See Julius Isaac, *Economics of Migration,* New York, Oxford University Press, 1947, p. 62.

[2] Gino Germani, "Inquiry into the Social Effects of Urbanization in a Working-class Sector of Greater Buenos Aires." In Philip Hauser (ed.), *Urbanization in Latin America,* Paris, UNESCO, 1961.

[3] José Luis Romero, *Las Ideas Políticas en Argentina,* Mexico, Fondo de Cultura Económica, 1956, p. 176; and Domingo F. Sarmiento, *Condición del Extranjero en América,* Buenos Aires, A. B. Sarmiento, 1900, *Obras Completas,* Volume V, pp. xxxvi and 73 and passim.

[4] Julius Isaac, op. cit., chapter VI.

[5] Joseph J. Spengler, "Effects Produced in Receiving Countries by Pre-1939 Immigration." In *Economics of International Migration,* ed. Brinley Thomas, London, Macmillan, 1958, pp. 22 ff.

[6] Giorgio Mortara, "Pesquisas Sobre Populaçoes Americanas." *Estudos Brasileiros de Demografia,* Monografia, No. 3, Rio de Janeiro, Fundação Getulio Vargas, 1947.

[7] Walter F. Wilcox (ed.), *International Migrations,* New York, National Bureau of Economic Research, 1929, Volume 1, p. 540.

[8] The diffusion of the system had many causes, but the interests of the big landowners, coupled with the nearly complete lack of official support for a real colonization, are the basic factors. Other complementary causes have also been mentioned. At the beginning the rent was generally low and some immigrants, even if they had the required capital, were therefore more inclined to rent. Given the high market demand, the immigrant was induced to produce as much as possible and preferred to rent large areas of land rather than buy smaller ones. This must be related to the immigrants' basic aim to get rich and return to the homeland. At the same time, the landowner found it much more convenient to rent than to sell, since the price of the land was rapidly increasing. Also, many landowners pre-

ferred cattle breeding to agriculture, and the renting system allowed them to convert from one to the other while at the same time improving the condition of the land and benefiting from its increasing value. One of the most negative aspects of the renting system was the duration of the contracts, mostly less than three years. This caused a kind of "nomad agriculture," and a very high instability of the peasant, with all its economic and social consequences. On this problem see Manuel Bejarano, "La Política Colonizadora en la Provincia de Buenos Aires," Instituto de Sociología y Centro de Historia Social, Universidad de Buenos Aires, 1962, especially paragraph two. Also see Mark Jefferson, *The Peopling of Argentine Pampas*, New York, American Geographic Society, 1926, pp. 114–15 and 141 ff. The classic book on the high concentration of land ownership is Jacinto Oddone's *La Burguesía Terrateniente Argentina*, Buenos Aires (no publisher indicated), 1930.

[9] Gastón Gori, *El Pan Nuestro*, Buenos Aires, Raigal, 1958, p. 84.

[10] In 1913 only one-half of the industrial enterprises could be considered "factory industries"; these enterprises concentrated some 60 per cent of the capital, 80 per cent of the production, and approximately 65 per cent of the workers. The average number of workers per plant was 8.4; in 1947 it had risen to 14.7. See Adolfo Dorfman, *Evolución Industrial Argentina*, Buenos Aires, Losada, 1942, pp. 16–17. See also Gino Germani, *Estructura Social de la Argentina*, Buenos Aires, Raigal, 1955, p. 130.

[11] Adolfo Dorfman, op. cit., pp. 21–22.

[12] Gino Germani, "La Movilidad Social en la Argentina," Appendix to Spanish translation of Reinhard Bendix and Seymour M. Lipset, *La Movilidad Social en la Sociedad Industrial*, Buenos Aires, Eudeba, 1964.

[13] Domingo F. Sarmiento, op. cit. pp. 229–30, 64 ff., and passim.

[14] The literature on the *gaucho* is very extensive; for evaluation and synthesis, see Ezequiel Martínez Estrada, *Muerte y Transfiguración de Martín Fierro*, Mexico, Fondo de Cultura Económica, 1948, v. I, pp. 237–92; see also, for contrasts with the immigrants, Gastón Gori, op. cit., and Gastón Gori, *La Pampa sin Gaucho*, Buenos Aires, Raigal, 1952.

[15] Domingo F. Sarmiento, op. cit. pp. 64 ff.

[16] Gastón Gori, *La Pampa Sin Gaucho*, op. cit.

[17] Domingo F. Sarmiento, op. cit. p. 76. Sarmiento calls this attitude "retrospective patriotism."

[18] Gino Germani, "Inquiry into the Social Effects of Urbanization," op. cit.

[19] Domingo F. Sarmiento, op. cit. p. 101.

[20] Domingo F. Sarmiento, op. cit. pp. 301 ff., 328 ff., and *passim*.

[21] Gastón Gori, *La Pampa Sin Gaucho*, op. cit.

[22] Some parts of the following typology have been summarized from Gino Germani, "The Assimilation of Immigrants in Urban Settings." In *Handbook of Urban Studies*, ed. Philip Hauser, Paris, UNESCO, forthcoming. The typology follows the theoretical suggestions of S. N. Eisenstadt in his *Absorption of Immigrants*, London, Routledge and Kegan Paul, 1954, chapter 1.

[23] In 1942 this difference was still observed. Cf. the remarks by Carl C. Taylor, *Rural Life in Argentina*, Baton Rouge, Louisiana State University Press, 1948, chapter 13.

[24] The average socio-economic status of the native Argentines whose

parents were both natives was lower than that of second-generation immigrants. The average relative position of the foreigner was lower than that of the native, but slightly higher than that of the native internal migrants. Here the emigration to the city was another important factor in determining the socio-economic status. Cf. Gino Germani, Blanca Ferrari, and Malvina Segre, "Características Sociales de la Población de Buenos Aires," Instituto de Sociología, Universidad de Buenos Aires, 1965 (unpublished manuscript).

[25] José Luis de Imaz, *Los que Mandan*, Buenos Aires, Eudeba, 1964, pp. 136–38 (Tables 72 and 73).

[26] Franco Savorgnan, "Homogamia en los Immigrantes en Buenos Aires," *Boletín del Instituto Etnico Nacional*, 1957.

[27] Especially by the ideologues of the "national Left." Cf. Juan José Hernández Arregui, *Imperialismo y Cultura*. Buenos Aires, Amerindia, 1957 and *La Formación de la Conciencia Nacional*, Buenos Aires, 1960.

[28] Darío Cantón and Mabel Arruñada, "Orígenes Sociales de los Legisladores," Instituto de Sociología, Universidad de Buenos Aires, 1960, unpublished paper.

[29] José L. de Imaz, op. cit. p. 9.

[30] José L. de Imaz, op. cit. p. 60 and p. 175. In the Armed Forces the high officers of Italian origin accounted for one-fourth of the total, 35 per cent were of Spanish origin, while the remaining 16 per cent were of French or Anglo-Saxon (including German) descent. Among the bishops, the Italian influence was higher: one-half of them were sons of Italian peasants.

[31] Cf. S. N. Eisenstadt, op. cit. chapter 1.

[32] In Argentina there is some anti-semitism. However, its degree and diffusion are not higher than in other Western countries, like the United States or France. Some episodes which have received international attention are an expression of the complex political situation, but not of a widespread or intense racial prejudice. In a survey it was found that about 22 per cent of the family heads in a random sample of the Buenos Aires metropolitan area gave anti-Jewish answers (when asked specifically about Jews). For similar questions, the verbal attitudes reported in studies in West Germany, France, and the United States indicated a similar or smaller proportion of prejudiced answers. Cf. Gino Germani, "Antisemitismo Ideológico y Antisemitismo Tradicional," *Comentarios*, 1962, no. 34. In any case, it is well-known that the prejudice against Italians or the Spanish is much lower. In the same survey the anti-Italian answers were 4.4 per cent and the anti-Spanish 3.5 per cent. These reactions were obtained from respondents of all national origins and all social classes. The attitudes of native Argentinians classified by socio-economic status (see Table A) showed the usual correlation between low education (and socio-economic level) and prejudice.

The hostility against Italians and Spanish was the lowest and very small at all socio-economic levels. The anti-North American and anti-English attitudes indicated more of an ideological orientation than an ethnic prejudice. There was strong evidence that negative reactions regarding the Jews and other lower-class eastern Europeans were more frequently an expression of "traditionalism" than of ideological anti-semitism. Francis Korn, "Algunos Aspectos de la Asimilación de Immigrantes en Buenos

TABLE A   Attitudes toward Immigrants by Native-born Family Heads. Percentage of Respondents who would "Exclude" the Different National or Ethnic Groups. Buenos Aires metropolitan area, 1961.

National and ethnic groups "excluded"	Low socio-economic status	Middle socio-economic status	High socio-economic status
Italians	12	3	1
Spanish	9	2	0
Jews	34	22	14
North Americans	24	13	5
English	18	10	3
Polish	17	10	7
Rumanians	15	8	7

Aires," Instituto de Sociología, Universidad de Buenos Aires (unpublished paper based on the same survey).

[33] Among Argentine social commentators, the most important are Ezequiel Martínez Estrada, Jorge Luis Borges, José Luis Romero, Carlos Alberto Erro, Eduardo Mallea, and Raúl Scalabrini Ortíz.

[34] José Luis Romero, *Argentina: Imágenes y Perspectivas*, Buenos Aires, Raigal, 1956, p. 62.

9

EDMUNDO FLORES

Financing Land Reform:
A Mexican Casebook

Abajo la deuda agraria
No pagar ni un solo cobre,
Dar la tierra necesaria
Para el campesino pobre.*
Mexican folksong popular c. 1920

In an international conference on land-tenure problems held in
Madison, Wisconsin, in 1951, a group of experts headed by
John Kenneth Galbraith and Walter Morton discussed the prob-
lem of financing land reform. The following is from their report:

> In financing land distribution, the government acquires
> credit for the above purposes from various segments of society.
> In turn, it extends credit to the new farm owners for the acqui-
> sition of land and capital, and it acquires from them obligations
> to repay such advances, usually in the form of mortgages. The
> government usually pays the large landowners in bonds when
> land is purchased from them for distribution purposes. This in
> effect forces the landowners to lend to the government in the
> amount equal to the price they receive for the land.[1]

* Down with the agrarian debt
  Not a single copper cent
  To give the necessary lands
  To the poor peasant

331

As far as Latin America is concerned, this approach to the problem is misleading. Instead, the financing of agrarian reform must be formulated by establishing from the outset a clear distinction between two different conflicting isues: how to acquire the land, and how to finance agricultural development.

Judging by the Mexican experience, it can be said that any attempt to pay compensation—except symbolically—leads to an insoluble situation. This happens because an agrarian reform is primarily a redistributive measure, and compensation defeats the end pursued by redistribution. In order to succeed, an agrarian reform needs to be followed immediately by a vigorous effort to increase the rates of capital formation. It would be self-defeating to take resources from investment and give them to the old oligarchy, particularly if we consider that giving buying power to the old oligarchy means putting in their hands more elements with which to finance counterrevolution. The acquisition of land should not be conceived as a real estate transaction, since it is neither possible nor convenient to buy off the old landowners.

From the viewpoint of economics, agrarian reform is a redistributive measure which transfers the ownership of land and, therefore, its income, from one group to another—from the landlord minority which monopolized it, to the peasants who worked it but received only a minimal fraction of its produce. Its ultimate purpose is the same as that of all other redistributive measures such as fiscal policies, subsidies, tariff protection, rationing, nationalization, and the like—*to reduce the income and consumption of the group that is taxed and to shift elsewhere the resources released.* However, the fact that the vehicle for redistribution is land introduces an intense emotional charge of pseudoagronomic, physiocratic, and juridical prejudices which distort and obscure the essence of the process behind what, paraphrasing Marx, I call a "terrestrial veil."

To have a clear idea of how a redistributive measure works, take progressive income taxation, the legality and equity of which nobody seriously questions nowadays. This tax is imposed according to capacity to pay; high income groups are taxed heavily, while low income groups are largely exempt. Modern states utilize

332

the goods and services which are thus released to defray their costs and to supply a fast-growing group of basic services, such as education, public health measures, unemployment insurance, public works, and so on. There is no close correlation between the taxes paid by any individual and the public services he consumes. Whoever pays the higher taxes receives, so far as public goods are concerned, the same services as any other member of the community. The State does not indemnify him. It does not give him bonds, nor does it exempt him from the payment of future taxes. To compensate him would be absurd because the purpose of the tax lies precisely in curtailing his buying power and in keeping part of his income for redistribution in accordance with the general objectives pursued by the community. From the viewpoint of orthodox liberalism, this tax may be considered confiscatory; but after Marx and Keynes, two world wars, the Great Depression, the New Deal, and the Mexican, Russian, and Chinese revolutions, such a view is sadly irrelevant, at least in the underdeveloped world.

Income taxation is a sophisticated measure which requires a mature equalitarian tradition, a political organization in which all the important interests and groups of the community are effectively represented, and an efficient public administration which cannot be operational without a sizable middle class. These basic conditions are found only in the advanced countries. Richard Goode lists six prerequisites to a successful income tax: (1) a monetary economy (2) widespread literacy (3) minimum accounting records (4) acceptance of the idea of voluntary compliance with tax laws (5) political acceptance of an income tax, and (6) an efficient public administration. Few countries in Latin America satisfy such conditions.[2] The absence of the above conditions escapes many well-intentioned scholars from the international agencies who propose policies which take for granted the basic conditions present only in the advanced industrial societies.

In countries ruled by tradition-directed, ignorant landlords, policed by trigger-happy military hucksters,[3] and administered by corrupt politicians, it is impossible to apply sophisticated redistributive policies. Income redistribution can be achieved only by radical methods such as agrarian expropriation and nationalization. To expect that when a revolutionary government undertakes agrarian reform it should compensate the landowning oligarchy is equivalent (reductio ad absurdum) to proposing that an industrial country should indemnify income-tax payers.

This thesis emerges from the experience of Mexico, a country which tried to follow a conventional pay-as-you-go course, only to be forced in the end to expropriate virtually without compensation.

Eyler N. Simpson says in *The Ejido: Mexico's Way Out,*

> If the government had continued along the lines upon which it actually did proceed during the first fine flush of revolutionary fervor, the problem of financing land grants to villages would have been solved with neatness and dispatch. As in the case of many another social revolution, the tyrants and the oppressors would simply have been thrown out and their property confiscated; for revolutions of the sort which Mexico went through from 1910 to 1921 have never been distinguished by their regard for legal delicacy. But partly because of the Don Quixote strain in the Mexican character, and partly because of the strong pressure brought to bear by foreign powers, Mexico was forced into the position of trying to accomplish by the slow and painful processes of law and order the work which might have been done by the revolution itself . . .
>
> Having once accepted the principle that lands given to villages must be paid for, the question then became: how? That is, how could a country which had just been through ten years and more of revolutionary strife, a country without money or credit, nevertheless acquire properties of great value owned by private individuals, with the intention and for the purpose of turning these properties over to indigent villages? [4]

Mendieta y Núñez, an influential Mexican scholar, dealt with the same theme and concluded:

> In our view, the agrarian debt must be paid, because it represents a revolutionary pledge of honor expressly made in the Law of January 6, 1915, and afterwards in Article 27 of the Constitution.[5]

From a strict juridical viewpoint, the position of Mendieta y Núñez may be right. From a wider perspective, however, it could be proved that the decadent landed class and its heirs have been generously compensated by the revolution. Thanks to it, many of them came to form part of a new and vigorous elite made up of owners of urban real estate (which was exempt from expropriation), stockholders in financial companies, and captains of industry. Thus the revolution not only gave them the opportunity to atone for sins which date back to the Conquest, but contributed handsomely to their fortunes.

Faced with the alternative of paying either for the lands or for public works and services, the Mexican government chose the latter and, as Simpson predicted in 1934, "left the problem of compensation to sink deeper and deeper in the morass of bureaucratic inaction until finally it disappears altogether." [6]

EVADING AN ONEROUS PLEDGE

Were it not for its value to future land reforms in other Latin American countries, it would be better not to disinter the awkward history of the agrarian debt. Its record is confused and contradictory precisely because the intention underlying the whole process was to create confusion and thereby postpone the payment of compensation. Such an end was achieved by contriving a legal conundrum with all kinds of dilatory subterfuges, changes in the denomination of obligations, mergers of bonds, and the enactment of contradictory laws and decrees which were never regulated and could not be enforced.

Mexico's original problem consisted in redistributing lands owned as follows: 3.1 per cent of the total population, or around 470,000 persons, were landowners; the remaining 96.1 per cent, or more than 14 million people, were landless. Considered in another way, the nation owned 19.4 per cent of the total land (including the territory of Quintana Roo); 64.4 per cent belonged to Mexican citizens; and the remaining 12.2 per cent belonged to foreigners.[7]

Public lands could not be given to anybody simply because they were submarginal. No Indian community had settled on these lands. They had incited the greed of neither the Spanish conquerors nor the Catholic Church. Even at the turn of the century, to settle there would have required a public works policy which the government of Porfirio Díaz could not finance—much less imagine. Only because the governments of the revolution were forced to resort to every conceivable innovation in their quest to build an economic structure that would assure the survival and eventual welfare of the mass of the Mexican people was it possible, years later, to start reclaiming these lands and adding them to the productive stock of the nation.

To start the land reform, there was no course other than to take the lands in excess of one hundred hectares, belonging to nationals and foreigners alike, and give these lands to the peasants. Initially there was the well-meaning, optimistic intention of expropriating with prompt and adequate payment. But since this proved impossible, because after seven years of armed struggle the government was bankrupt, the law of January 6, 1915, gave the affected owners the right to claim compensation only within the first year after their lands had been taken. Afterwards, Article 27 of the Constitution allowed for expropriation, for reasons of public use, without immediate compensation; that is, compensation could take place before, during, or after expropriation.

However, these laws specified neither the way in which compensation would be paid nor whether the government was assuming final responsibility for payment or was only acting as an intermediary between the landlords and the peasants who received lands. Judging from other sources, it seems clear that the original intention of the government was only to assume the function of financial intermediary.

According to Simpson, the principal evidence in support of this view is to be found in Circular 34 of the National Agrarian Commission (issued on January 31, 1919) requiring the inhabitants of villages petitioning for lands to agree in writing "to pay the Nation the value of lands which they were going to receive by donation, in accordance with the indemnity which the

336

Nation must pay to the proprietors of the land expropriated; and second, in the original enabling act of January 10, 1920, that authorized the Public Agrarian Debt." [8] The government was thus authorized to issue 20-year, 5 per cent bearer bonds. Amortization was by annual drawings when the market quotation of bonds was equal or greater than par. If the market value was less than par, bonds were retired by purchase in the open market. In 1921, Obregón rescinded Circular 34.

An approximate idea of the magnitude of the agrarian debt assuming compensation had been paid is given by the estimated value that the 1950 census attributed to all *ejido* lands: 1,914 million pesos. [9] GNP (gross national product) in 1950 amounted to 43,299 million pesos, so the value of *ejido* lands was 4.4 per cent of the GNP.

The paragraph of Section VII of Article 27 referring to compensation read:

> The amount fixed as compensation for the expropriated property shall be based on the sum at which the said property shall be valued for fiscal purposes in the cadastral or revenue offices, whether this value be that manifested by the owner or merely impliedly accepted by reason of the payment of his taxes on such a basis. This value shall be increased by ten per cent. [10]

Indemnification was not to be paid to *ejidos* in the case of lands usurped or illegally appropriated.

On January 10, 1920, the Agrarian Debt Law regulated this point as follows:

> *Article I.* The Executive of the Union, in accordance with Article 27 of the Constitution and with the Law of January 6, 1915, shall indemnify those owners of the land which has been granted or will be granted hereafter to villages, hamlets, groups, communities, etc., and shall equally indemnify owners of lands restored or being restored to villages, etc., such indemnification to be in accordance with the Law of January 6, 1915, and Article 27 of the Federal Constitution.
>
> *Article 2.* In order to cover the indemnification referred to in the preceding article a Federal debt shall be created to be known as

337

the "Agrarian Public Debt," to be in charge of the Nation, which shall be guaranteed and paid in the manner and on the terms established by the present law.

Article 3. The Federal Executive shall be empowered to issue Agrarian Public Debt bonds, up to the amount of 50 million gold pesos. These bonds shall be issued by series as necessary and shall be required to be and must be paid by the Nation, by means of annual drawings within a period of 20 years, counted from the date of issuance, crediting the holders during the said period with an interest of 5 per cent per annum of silver or gold in current national currency.

Article 4. Bonds shall be given to the holder and shall have annexed 20 coupons for the annual collection of interest. The interest coupons payable shall be accepted, from the same month, at par, by any federal tax office in payment of taxes.

Article 5. The above-mentioned bonds shall be issued at par at any time by the Federal Government in payment of claims which must be made by adjudication or leasing of idle or national lands, for the payment of interest or the total or partial price of lands granted to villages divided among their neighbors and as guarantee or deposit, in all cases in which under the circumstances of contract or concession it is possible to substitute a cash deposit by Public Debt bonds.

Article 6. The payment of bonds and interest coupons of the Agrarian Debt will affect income of the Nation, of lands granted or restored, divided among the neighbors of the villages, hamlets, groups, and others indicated by the Constitution. The Federal Government shall not otherwise invest the funds constituting this guarantee.

Article 7. The Federal Executive of the Nation is empowered to issue regulations covering this law.

Twenty-Year Agrarian Public Debt Bonds [11]

Regulations under the law of January 10, 1920, were issued on January 28, 1922 (*Diario Oficial*), and later on December 31, 1925. The substantive articles state that claims must be presented within one year, in accordance with article I of the Law of January 6. The articles which follow concern the administrative requirements for making claims:

Chapter II. The Ministry of Agriculture shall be the authority fixing compensation and its amount.

The Treasury Department may request the Secretary of Agriculture to reconsider indemnifications.

Chapter III. Bond Issue. These will be issued in five series of 10 million each, on dates fixed by the Treasury Department. New series will not be issued unless the previously issued bonds have been retired.

Chapter IV. Amortization of the bonds and their coupons. This will be done by annual drawings, one for each series of bonds issued. The coupons will be paid by years due. The bonds not drawn will be paid, at the latest, 20 years after the date of issue.

Only the first two series of 10 million pesos each (January 1926 and January 1928) and $4,426,800 for the third (January 1930) were issued. The agency charged with placing them was the Treasury Department. Amortization services for both capital and interest were provided by the Bank of Mexico.

In January 1930, the Executive solicited and obtained the right to amortize the bonds of the Agrarian Public Debt by means of direct open market purchases; the bonds were quoted at 16 centavos per peso of nominal value. Service on this debt was suspended in 1931 and was reestablished in 1933.

Forty-Year Domestic Public Debt Bonds

On December 31, 1932, a decree was promulgated which authorized the Federal Executive to issue Domestic Public Debt 40-year bonds for 60 million pesos. Article 15 of this decree says: "The Agrarian Public Debt will continue to be governed (for the effects of their title and amortization) by their own regulations." Acceptance of agrarian debt bonds in payment of tax debts was authorized by a decree published in the *Diario Oficial* on July 23, 1934. The same provision was repeated in another decree published on January 1, 1935. In April 1935, the Treasury Department published a circular from the Income Tax

Bureau in which it accepted public debt bonds in payment of 70 per cent of the extraordinary tax on income.

In 1938 the Federal Government authorized *National Financiera* to change agrarian public debt bonds which had attached to them interest coupons from 1932 for 40-year domestic public debt bonds. In December 1940, during the presidency of Manuel Ávilla Camacho, the Agrarian Code was amended. Article 75 states:

> Owners affected by resolutions granting or restoring lands or waters to *ejidos* which have been made in favor of villages, or which may be made in the future, shall not have any right or ordinary legal recourse, nor shall they be able to call upon the right of protection.
>
> Those affected by grants shall have only the right to appeal to the Federal Government for payment of corresponding indemnity. The interested parties must exercise this right within a period of one year, counted from the date that the resolution is published in the *Diario Oficial* of the Federation. No claim shall be admitted beyond this date.
>
> *Article* I. The indemnification to which Article 75 refers shall be in accordance with dispositions to be issued.

Such dispositions were never issued.

On December 31, 1951, during the presidency of Miguel Alemán, the decree of December 31, 1932, authorizing the issue of 40-year domestic public debt bonds was amended, indicating in paragraph VII of Article 6 that the credits "arising out of claims made by small landholders who had nontransferable certificates but from whom land had been taken anyway, and who had been granted favorable decisions from the Federal Executive, must be obligatorily changed for 40-year domestic public debt bonds."

Present Situation of the Agrarian and Domestic Public Debts [12]

The state of the agrarian public debt on December 31, 1959, was as follows:

340

Total issue of bonds authorized by the Law of January 10, 1920	50,000,000 pesos
Total bonds approved by the Ministry of Agriculture for issue to claimants	27,322,060 pesos
Total claimants authorized to receive bonds	170
Total claims approved by the Ministry of Agriculture (in many cases, one person has presented several claims)	387
Total bonds actually delivered to claimants by the Ministry of the Treasury	24,426,800 pesos
Total claims covered by bonds delivered to claimants	381
Total area of expropriated land for which bonds have been delivered to claimants	222,797 hectares
Authorized	50,000,000.00 pesos
Issued	24,426,800.00 pesos
Redeemed	23,155,300.00 pesos
In circulation	1,271,500.00 pesos
Interest:	
By amortization period	8,459,086.38 pesos
Paid	5,941,384.26 pesos
Not due by exchange	329,760.00 pesos
Due	1,978,942.12 pesos
Balance of capital and interest	3,250,442.12 pesos

Domestic Public Debt Series D and E

Authorization for issue: Decree of December 31, 1941, and presidential edict of September 18, 1944, and September 8, 1945.

Object of the issue: to pay obligations pending in kind and to continue the exchange of the agrarian public debt bonds. Issue of $10,000,000.00 was authorized, but only $8,989,600.00 was issued. The state of the debt at December 31, 1959, of the series D and E was $6,267,720.00.

Domestic Public Debt Series G, H, I

Authorization for issue: Decree of December 30, 1951, and presidential edict of January 23, 1952.

Object of issue: To pay credits arising from claims in respect of small agricultural properties. An issue of titles to the value of $50,000,000.00 was authorized, of which only $48,169,700.00 was issued.

State of the debt on December 31, 1959:

Authorized	$5,000,000.00
Issued	48,169,700.00
Redeemed	7,225,455.00
In circulation	40,944.245.00

Domestic Public Debt Series I

Authorization for issue: Law of December 29, 1932, and presidential edict of February 10, 1953.

Object of issue: To pay compensation for land taken from small landowners.

Date of issue: January 1, 1953.

Situation of the debt on December 31, 1959:

Authorized	$30,000,000.00
Issued	—
Redeemed	—
In circulation	—

CONCLUSION

Only 170 national claimants, who presented 381 claims for the expropriation of a total area of 222,797 hectares, were indemnified. This amounts to less than 0.5 per cent of the total of .55 million hectares distributed until 1960. Compensation amounted to 24,426,800 pesos—2.8 million dollars—and was paid in agrarian debt bonds.

These bonds were redeemed by purchases in the open market, at prices which fluctuated between 5 and 16 per cent of their nominal value; or by rendering them, also with a penalty, in payment of certain taxes; or by changing them, in certain cases, for 40-year domestic public debt bonds.

In addition, an unspecified number of influential landowners were indemnified with domestic public debt bonds or compensated with rural or urban lands, cash, or both. Neither the area of the lands paid for in this way nor the amounts disbursed are known, but it may be conjectured that, as in the case of the agrarian debt bonds, the lands and sums involved represent an insignificant fraction of the total distributed. The rest of the lands granted to 2.5 million *ejidatarios* who were heads of families were expropriated without compensation. The peasants who benefited from the agrarian reform received free land grants.

In the case of expropriation of small holdings or of *ejido* lands for reasons of public use, compensation was paid in domestic public debt bonds.

NOTES

[1] See Parsons, Penn, and Raup (eds.), *Land Tenure: Proceedings of the International Conference on Land Tenure and Related Problems in World Agriculture,* Wisconsin, 1956, pp. 492–500.

[2] See Richard Goode's classic paper, "Reconstruction of Foreign Tax Systems," *Proceedings of the Forty-Fourth Annual Conference of the National Tax Association,* 1951, pp. 212–22.

[3] See Edwin Lieuwen, *Arms and Politics in Latin America,* New York, Council on Foreign Relations, Frederick A. Praeger, 1960.

[4] Chapel Hill: The University of North Carolina Press, 1937. I am heavily indebted to Simpson for his pioneering work on this subject. See his chapter XIII, "Financing Land Grants to Villages," pp. 217–29.

[5] Lucio Mendieta y Núñez, *El Problema Agrario de México,* México, Editorial Porrúa, S.A., 1959, p. 449. For a wider legal statement of the problem, see also Kenneth L. Karst, "Latin American Land Reform: The Uses of Confiscation," *Michigan Law Review,* December 1964, Vol. 63, No. 2.

[6] Simpson, op. cit., p. 225.

[7] Frank Tannenbaum, *The Mexican Agrarian Revolution,* New York, Macmillan Co., 1929.

[8] Simpson, op. cit., pp. 218–19.

[9] In 1950 the exchange rate was 8.65 pesos for one dollar. 1,914 million pesos equal 221 million dollars.

[10] *Constitución Política de los Estados Unidos Mexicanos*, Mexico, Herrero Hermanos Sucesores, 1923.

[11] See *Legislación sobre deuda pública*, Vols. I, II, III. Mexico, Secretaría de Hacienda y Crédito Público, Dirección de Crédito, 1958.

[12] Data taken from Simpson, op. cit. p. 221 and brought up to date with data from *Anuario Financiero de México*, Vol. XX, 1960.

10

BRYAN ROBERTS

The Social Organization
of Low-Income Families

This chapter explores the social activity of low-income families in Guatemala City.[1] It aims to contribute to an understanding of what are often described in the literature as the "urban masses." These sectors of the population have often been regarded as having no part in the organizations and networks of social relations that influence the direction of social change in Latin America.[2] Low-income families have thus been characterized as "marginal populations." In presenting the data from Guatemala City, I wish to examine certain of the implications of this concept of "marginality." I am concerned with the relations that exist between low-income families and other sectors of the urban population. In particular, I examine the reciprocal influence between low-income families and urban political and economic organizations. I regard low-income urban dwellers as having an active influence on social change in Guatemala and not as being passive recipients of change.

I also take up the more general question of the extent to which low-income urban families are "integrated" in the national society. Integration has been variously defined.[3] I shall be interested in three aspects of integration. These are (1) the extent and nature of low-income families' participation in political and social life, (2) the extent to which low-income families are prepared to cooperate with others of like or different social positions to effect changes in Guatemala's social and economic structure, (3) the extent to which low-income families differentiate themselves from more prosperous and more powerful groups in Guatemala and do not identify their interests with those of other groups.

My analysis focuses on two sets of factors that influence the relations of low-income families with other sectors of the urban population. These are (1) the physical and social organization of Guatemala City and, in particular, the structure of urban occupations, organizations, and residential areas, and (2) the career experiences of low-income families, such as rural-urban and intra-urban migration, employment experiences, and the recent economic and political history of Guatemala. My analysis is thus concerned both with the effects of an urban milieu on social behavior and with the effects on low-income families of the social and political experience of urbanization.

Mitchell has recently warned us of the necessity of explaining urban behavior primarily in terms of the pressures of an urban social system.[4] The behavior of rural migrants is thus to be understood in terms of their position within an urban social organization and not in terms of their previous rural experiences. In the following analysis, I attempt to show that the behavior of low-income families in Guatamela City is closely related to the constraints exercised by particular forms of urban social organization. Families are not bound by previous or traditional cultural patterns to an inflexible mode of adjustment to urban life. Their social and economic behavior changes with different urban situations and with changes in their social and economic position. I shall, however, stress the importance of the particular life experiences of individual families. These are important in influencing families to choose one of several behavior patterns appropriate to an urban situation. For example, in their political and economic behavior, low-income families must often balance long- and short-term advantages. This is a dilemma faced by all irrespective of their educational level or income level.

In many studies, socio-economic variables, such as income and occupation, differentiate urban families and influence an individual's participation in urban activities.[5] It is argued that membership in voluntary associations, recreation, and social visiting depend on an individual having the financial resources and social skills to undertake such activities. In this study, the sample is confined to low-income families, and thus the range of income, occupation, and education is not great. We can expect, however, that social and economic position will be an important influence on the social and economic activity of this sample of Guatemalan families. The higher an individual's income and education and the more his occupation brings him into contact with others, the greater will be his participation in a range of urban activities. Another set of variables which we must consider are ecological variables. The location of a neighborhood and its social characteristics can have relatively independent effects on the behavior of an individual family by affecting communication between neighbors and affecting contacts with other sectors of the urban population.

Attention must also be given to other variables which have an especial relevance to the social organization of low-income families in rapidly growing cities. Consider the degree of discontinuity produced by urbanization in the life-careers of low-income families. By discontinuity I refer to a relatively rapid change from one set of social experiences to another. Migration from small towns and villages to a city can be an example of discontinuity. Discontinuity due to migration may arise from cultural differences between city and provinces, or it may arise from changes in work situations and social relationships. This type of discontinuity is affected by the degree to which a migrant encapsulates himself in relations with people from his town or village.[6] Likewise, movements within a city contribute to discontinuity insofar as change in physical location entails change in social relations. Historical events such as radical changes in government or social structure also add to discontinuity in an individual's life career. We can expect discontinuity to be a stimulus to an individual's participation in urban social and economic life. When an individual's horizons have not been rigidly confined by one set of social experiences, he is more likely to be aware of, and seek out, the possibilities of changing his social and economic position. Discontinuity is not productive of felt integration with other sectors of the urban population. The discontinuity of life experiences stimulates low-income families to be aware of inequalities of wealth. It also weakens traditional values and social relations that provided support for the existing structure of wealth and power.

Finally, the significance of the relative degree of formality in urban organization is considered. By formality, I mean the operation of urban economic and administrative organizations according to impersonal and standard rules of procedure. Urban organizations can be characterized as informal when they operate in terms of individual considerations and do not apply standardized rules in their contacts with the population. Informality of urban organization stimulates social and economic activity and contributes to the differentiation of low-income families.

One consequence of informality of urban organization is that the social and economic situations in which an individual is placed in urban life are not integrated with each other.[7] By situation, I refer to the people and expectations that an individual meets in carrying out a part of his urban life such, for example, as his job, religion, recreation, or political activities. When there are few stable jobs and urban organizations operating informally, neighborhood-based relations cannot cater to all aspects of an individual family's life. Families are likely to seek out individual means of obtaining needed services and employment. These means are likely to involve them with different sets of people. Where an individual is placed in a variety of situations in which he must deal with different sets of people and different expectations of behavior, his social behavior is not likely to be consistent from one situation to another. Low-income families will be flexible in their interpretation of the possibilities offered by urban life and unstable in their commitments to any one urban situation. Furthermore, an individual's activity will not be confined by any one set of experiences or one mode of coping with urban life. This contributes to the differentiation of low-income families. They will be less likely to recognize their common interests and positions.

Informality of urban organization also entails that there be no formal structure of educational or organizational requirements to define when an individual has failed or succeeded. The possibilities of trying to change one's social and economic position are thus not foreclosed. In this way, a city whose organization is informal contrasts with a developed city where the life chances of individuals will often be decided for them by the time they have left school.

Low-income families in Guatemala have had discontinuous life careers, are faced by a highly informal urban organization, and are placed in a variety of unrelated urban situations. These factors contribute to the social and economic activity of low-income families. The presence of these factors is likely to differentiate the social and economic activity of our Guatemalan sample from that of families living in other types of cities under different conditions of urbanization.

Two Neighborhoods in Guatemala City

The present population of Guatemala City is approximately 600,000.[8] This population has doubled in the last fourteen years, and much of this increase has been produced by migration from small towns and villages to the city. The migration has come mainly from the eastern part of the country, and migrants are predominantly *ladino*.[9] Before coming to the city, many had migrated seasonally to coastal areas to work on plantations. Others had traveled within and without Guatemala in search of work. Migrants often have had considerable mobility before arrival. Furthermore, the small size of the country and the prevalence of small trading or construction employment among the urban poor has meant that many city-born have also traveled to work in the countryside. During the land reform programs of the last twenty years, city dwellers as well as rural families have benefited from grants of farming land.

Geographical mobility between city and countryside is matched by geographical mobility within the city. The rapid expansion of the population has radically altered the urban residential distribution. Expansion has far outrun the available supply of urban housing. This has meant increasing densities in older neighborhoods, the spread of the city into outlying rural areas, and the proliferation of shanty towns. Accommodation near the center of the city is expensive. Cheap accommodation is not conveniently located for the centers of work. Low-income families change residence frequently in the course of their life cycle, searching for the accommodation whose price, size, and location best suit their needs of the moment. The expansion of the city thus means geographical discontinuity in which neighborhood-based social relations are frequently being disrupted. This discontinuity is high even for the city-born, many of whom were reared at a time when work and friendship relations were still based on relatively stable and cohesive urban neighborhoods. Several informants described the city before 1944 as composed of a number of clearly defined *barrios*, each with its own name and distinctive character. Inhabitants of one *barrio* felt a common identity in opposition to inhabitants of another. Relations within and between the sexes were confined to the *barrio*. The traditional organization of the city was thus composed of a series of communities as "closed" as the rural communities from which migrants had come. Thus, like rural migrants, those born in the city have had to cope with new forms of social organization.

Expansion in industrial activity in the city has not kept pace with the expansion of the population. Large-scale industrial enterprises are still relatively scarce and employ a minority of the working population. The majority of low-income workers find their sustenance in a variety of small industrial and commercial establishments, in urban services, or in self-employment. Self-employment, whether in craft or trading activities, has not decreased over time. Instead, it has provided one of the major means of absorbing migrants into the urban economy. This economic structure entails a wide variety of work situations requiring distinctive sets of work relations and orientations. Urban workers move quite frequently from one job to another and have few opportunities to build up extensive and lasting social relations based on their work. Residential mobility means that workers and neighbors are usually distinct sets of people.

Few secondary associations have developed to cater to low-income urban families. Labor unions include less than five per cent of the working population. Geographical mobility and low incomes are not conducive to the formation of mutual benefit associations or sporting clubs. There is little opportunity for workers or neighbors to cooperate together in different social

350

situations. An individual's leisure activities and means of coping with emergencies are not often based on work-place or neighborhood.

People living in Guatemala City retain close links with towns and villages outside the capital. Distances are not great, and bus service is frequent and cheap. There is considerable visiting back and forth between country and city. City dwellers will usually return at least once a year to visit relatives or friends in the places they have lived before coming to the city. Many city dwellers retain business or land interests outside the city. This is seen most dramatically in the cases of the many urban traders who extend their activities into the provinces. People outside the capital come to the city on business and will stay with relatives or friends who live in the city. This interpenetration of city and provinces contributes to diminishing the cultural discontinuity experienced by migrants. It also enables urban low-income families to compare their conditions of life with those of people living outside the city. The outlook of these families is thus not confined to the urban milieu. This is another reason why the activity and attitudes of low-income families are not circumscribed by any one urban social and economic situation.

There are few occasions when low-income families are exposed to formal organizational requirements. Education is compulsory for children between seven and fourteen, but absenteeism is rarely punished. Few jobs open to low-income families require formal qualifications, and at best, educational attainment is an insecure means to better one's work position. The various governmental bureaucracies have few contacts with low-income families. A tax of a dollar a year is collected of all heads of family, but many of the urban working population do not fulfil this minimal requirement. Funds are short in the city, and consequently, the provision of urban services does not extend throughout the city. Also, welfare provision is scarce and, in the face of numerous applicants, tends to be administered by informal procedures. An abundance of legal requirements exists to regulate residence and work behavior. The relative scarcity of police and the rapid expansion of the urban population have meant that these regulations have also been administered informally. This lack of formal organizational constraints on the lives of low-income families means that their means of coping with urban life are individual and flexible. Merely to survive in Guatemala City, low-income families must learn to manipulate the urban social structure. Even though the possibilities of low-income families substantially improving their position are minimal, informality of urban organization is thus conducive to the urban poor actively participating in urban life.

In the last 30 years, many Guatemalans have directly experienced radical changes in the political and social life of the country. The Revolution of 1944 and the reforms of the years immediately following produced changes in the rate of urban migration, the system of landholding, the participation of low-income families in elections, and the protection given to the worker. The city has been the location since 1944 of two successful coup d'etats and a host of unsuccessful ones. Under successive regimes, whether of right or left wing persuasion, political demonstrations and processions have been frequent and have included substantial numbers of low-income workers. Low-income families have become increasingly exposed to events with the spread of mass communications. Approximately 70 per cent of the urban male population is literate. Attendance at films and ownership of radios is widespread. Despite attempts at political censorship, low-income families are likely to be aware of political events and to have directly experienced the impact of these events.

In the context of a city like this, I focused my study on two low-income neighborhoods. One, which I will call San Lorenzo, is a shanty town located near the center of the city. It was illegally invaded in the late 1950's and is composed of wooden shacks with tin roofs. It contains only the rudiments of urban services. The second neighborhood, which I call Planificada, is located at some distance from the city center. It was laid out in equally spaced lots in the early 1950's and has gradually become filled by a variety of construction ranging from spacious concrete dwellings to shacks of the type found in San Lorenzo. The inhabitants of Planificada either own or rent their homes. Planificada had been provided with some urban services, contains a public dispensary, police station, and schools, and is connected to the city center by frequent bus service.

Ecological factors make these two neighborhoods distinct

from each other and not wholly representative of the low-income urban population. San Lorenzo has a high density; interaction among neighbors fomented by the proximity of shacks and the use of communal services. It attracts the attention of urban politicians because of its central location and ambigouus legal status. San Lorenzo thus has very high levels of political awareness. It also attracts people whose work and low pay make it essential for them to live near the center of the city, but whose families are too large for the rented rooms of the center.

The distance of Planificada from the center of the city makes active use of sports and entertainment facilities difficult. It is not densely settled and provides few occasions for interaction among neighbors. It has a higher average income and a greater range of property types, attracting more prosperous as well as low-income families. However, occupational patterns, family status, and length of urban residence are broadly similar in both neighborhoods (see Table I). In the remainder of the paper, I use the combined sample and differentiate the neighborhoods only where appropriate.[10] Unless otherwise indicated, the statistics refer to interviewed heads of households.

Social and recreational life involves low-income families in city-wide activities. Guatemala City offers numerous sporting events, cinemas, and parks. Forty-two per cent of male heads of households attend a sporting event once a month or more, most going to a football match every week or fortnight. Thirty-eight per cent attend a cinema once a month or more, and 62 per cent of this sample go either to a sporting event or a film during the month. When asked their favorite diversions, 14 per cent cited doing things in the home, such as playing with the children or listening to the radio. The majority cited recreations that took them elsewhere in the city or countryside. Many neighbors are also active in Catholic affairs; 61 per cent attended Church at least once a fortnight. These religious activities are not neighborhood-based, but take these families to chapels and churches in various parts of the city.

Families in both neighborhoods also interact quite frequently with friends and relatives. In the majority of cases, these interactions are not based on neighborhood. Sixty-six per cent reported that they visited or went out at least once a week with

TABLE I Social Characteristics of San Lorenzo and Planificada.

Variable	San Lorenzo	Planificada
Length of urban residence:		
Born in City	25%	18%
Resident more than 20 years	33	38
Resident 10 to 20 years	23	18
Resident less than 10 years	19	26
	100%	100%
Number of respondents	108	121
Average monthly income of head of family	55 dollars	65 dollars
Family status:		
Nuclear family (husband, wife, child)	77%	76%
Woman and children	17	17
Single man or single woman	6	7
	100%	100%
Number of respondents	109	127
Average number of children per family	3.5	3.5
Occupation of male head of household:		
Self-employed [d]	33%	40%
Employed in small enterprises [a]	24	15
Employed in large-scale enterprises [b]	32	31
White-collar worker [c]	4	9
Unemployed	7	5
	100%	100%
Number of respondents	88	102

[a] Employees in small-scale enterprises include watchmen, odd-job men, operatives in small workshops and businesses. The criterion is the number of persons employed by the enterprise which, in these cases, does not exceed ten.

[b] Employees in large-scale enterprises include factory operatives, construction laborers (modal occupation), bus drivers, and inspectors. None of these jobs requires high levels of skill or obtains high levels of pay.

[c] White-collar workers in this sample are low-level office worker and male nurses.

[d] Self-employment covers artisans working in their own houses (i.e., shoemakers), small traders, and job laborers.

friends made through their work or previous residence. Only 10 per cent reported that their best friends lived in the same neighborhood.

354

Sixteen per cent reported that they had no known relatives in the city, and a further 19 per cent said that they saw their relatives less than once a month. Of the remainder, more than half had relatives living the neighborhood, and all visited relatives at least once a month; most made a practice of visiting parents, siblings, or more distant relatives on Sunday or Saturday afternoon. Respondents were more likely to have relatives living in their neighborhood than to have their best friends living there.

Low-income families make extensive use of radio and newspapers. Sixty-six per cent own and listen regularly to a radio, 50 per cent listened to foreign stations as well as national, and 54 per cent read a newspaper at least two or three times a week (17 per cent do not read a newspaper at all).

The families generally take advantage of the scarce economic opportunities and public services available in the city. Forty-five per cent have used the free public medical services four or more times in the past year (25 per cent had not used them at all); of those with children of school age, 37 per cent had been four or more times to visit the school and talk to the teachers about their child's progress, while 34 per cent had not visited the school at all.

Families in both neighborhoods show enterprise in finding additional sources of revenue or improving on existing ones. In San Lorenzo there are approximately 40 small shops in a neighborhood of approximately 400 families. Most wives supplement their husband's wages by keeping shops or through petty trading activities outside their neighborhood. Self-employed workers in both neighborhoods are constantly seeking new ways to improve their businesses. Several small craftsmen have utilized contacts made through religion or politics to develop retailing networks for their products. In San Lorenzo, several small traders have used the money they have saved on rent to invest in expanding their businesses. One has fully equipped a barber's shop, and another has purchased a truck for wholesale deliveries. Employed workers in both neighborhoods are also quick to exploit opportunities to better their position. Visits with friends and relatives are often used to learn of new and better job opportunities. Of the employed workers, 73 per cent got their present jobs through contacts in the city. Only two of the 120 male heads of house-

355

hold who were interviewed twice remained unemployed and dependent on their families in the five months of the interview period. Even in times of temporary economic depression, the unemployed neighbors rapidly found new jobs of permanent or temporary nature.

Both these low-income neighborhoods have demonstrated quite high degrees of community organization. Betterment committees, set up mainly through local initiative, have organized neighbors to improve their neighborhoods with their own labor and to act as pressure groups on the city administration.

The general survey given above indicates that these low-income families are active participants in an urban social life that is not confined to their neighborhood. At a certain point, notably through community organization and political activity, they exercise a definite influence on urban organization. They are exposed to a variety of urban situations—in recreation, in social interaction, in their occupations, and in their neighborhood, each of which entails different patterns of social relationship and norms of conduct. We should expect, therefore, that families be affected by the problems and opportunities of the larger society.

DETERMINANTS AND CONSEQUENCES OF SOCIAL ACTIVITY

We will now consider the variables that I suggested would influence the social activity of low-income families. To recapitulate, these are (a) individual social and economic variables, (b) ecological variables, (c) life experiences, and (d) informality of urban organization and the degree of integration between an individual's urban situations.

Social and Economic Variables

Income, occupation, and length of residence in the city are the three social and economic variables whose effects I examine here.[11] These variables differentiate low-income families in both neighborhoods, but there is little evidence for sharp differences in behavior between different groups of low-income families.

In general, the higher level of income, the more likely a family is to participate in an activity. Newspaper reading, listening to a radio, and visiting school are directly related to level of income. Attendance at sport and films and visiting with friends, however, are not so directly related to income (Table II). In fact,

TABLE II Income and Social Activity.

| Activity | Monthly income of head of family | | | |
	30 dollars or less	31 to 49 dollars	50 to 89 dollars	90 to 120 dollars
Read newspaper at least once a month	30%	49%	64%	74%
	(11)	(19)	(32)	(23)
Listen to radio every day	38%	66%	73%	90%
	(13)	(26)	(33)	(28)
Have visited school where have children three or more times in past year	5%	33%	45%	52%
	(1)	(5)	(14)	(13)
Do not attend sporting events [a]	80%	40%	18%	53%
	(12)	(10)	(4)	(7)
Attend films at least once a month	27%	38%	44%	37%
	(7)	(10)	(14)	(6)
Interact with friends at least every week	51%	61%	78%	74% [b]
	(23)	(27)	(48)	(28)

[a] Only those under 40 were included, since age affects attendance at sport.
[b] The percentage for the highest income category (110 to 120) is 59 per cent.

Note: The number in parentheses is the number of people to which the percentage refers. Both are derived not from the total persons in each category but from the number in a particular category who answered a particular question.

in all three of these activities, it is the lowest and highest income levels that participte least. Many of the wealthier heads of household in both neighborhoods claimed that they had little time to engage in such time-consuming activities.

On most of these activities, the very poorest families—those with an income of less than 30 dollars a month—have markedly lower levels of activity than do other families. Families at this income level were the only families in the sample who were not in the majority favorable to urban life. Other families who answered a question asking them to compare urban and rural life saw city life as being more pleasant and having more opportunities. Only at the lowest income level were people more favorable to rural life. In understanding why families in both neighborhoods continue to be active participants in urban life despite difficult political and economic conditions, it is important to remember that for most of them urban life represents a definite improvement upon rural life.

Occupation influences reading of newspapers, radio listening, attendance at sport and films, and interaction with friends (Table III). The size of the sample makes it difficult to take into account the influence of income and urban experience, but in the case of occupation, as in the case of income and urban experience, I analyzed the data within the categories of the other relevant variables and found that the direction of the relationship was not affected. Self-employed workers are less likely than employees in either small or large-scale enterprises to participate in an activity. Employees in large-scale enterprises are most likely to participate. Part of the explanation of these findings lies in the type of work associated with different types of occupation. Self-employed workers in both neighborhoods have irregular hours of work which often take them outside their homes for considerable periods, day and night. They often do not have leisure time that is conducive to participation in either organized or home-based recreation. Employed workers have more regular hours of work, usually arriving home at a fixed time and ready to relax after a tiring day's work. Occupation has also a more indirect effect. Part of the reason why workers in large-scale enterprises were more active participants in these forms of recreation is that they engage in them as groups of workmates. Newspapers are shared between workers. They often attend sports and films together. Discussions between workers about films, sports, and news topics also encourage participation.

Concerning the persons to whom respondents turned for loans and getting jobs, differences also emerge between occupational categories (Table IV). Self-employed workers, as might be expected, were most likely to say that they had started their present job through their own efforts. They are also more likely than employed workers to say that they have no one to go to for a loan.

TABLE III   Occupation and Social Activity.

Activity	Self-employed [b]	Employed in small-scale enterprises	Employed in large-scale enterprises
Do not attend sporting events [a]	62%	41%	25%
	(16)	(9)	(7)
Attend films at least once a month	27%	37%	39%
	(17)	(13)	(23)
Read newspapers at least once a week	50%	51%	72%
	(32)	(19)	(37)
Listen to a radio every day	59%	62%	82%
	(37)	(23)	(40)
Interact with friends at least every week	63%	77%	74%
	(41)	(31)	(40)

[a] Only those under 40 were included, since age affects attendance at sport.
[b] The occupational categories used are the same as those used in Table I.

Employed workers, on the other hand, are more likely to say they can obtain loans from their work-friends or their bosses and are able to cite a greater range of possible sources of loans.

Yet, despite the apparent isolation of the self-employed, I have already indicated that they are as resourceful manipulators of urban organization as are other categories of workers. On certain variables self-employed workers participate as much, if not more, than other categories of workers. This is true of political activity in the neighborhoods (see below). Self-employed workers are also as likely as other workers to visit schools to talk about their children's progress and to use urban medical facilities. When asked what recourse they would have if they wanted to obtain something that was beyond their financial capabilities, self-employed workers cited as many possible recourses as employees in large-scale enterprises (Table V). They cited more recourses than employees in small-scale enterprises. Self-employed workers were also more likely than other groups of workers to cite contacts with social and economic superiors as possible

TABLE IV Occupations and Obtaining Loans and Jobs.

People to whom workers would turn for help to obtain loans or jobs

Occupation	Family		Neighbor		Work Friend		Other Friend		Employer, Patrons		Fellow Villager		No Source		Total Respondents	
	Loan	Job	Loan	Job	Loan	Job	Loan	Job	Loan	Job	Loan	Job	Loan	Job	Loan	Job
Self-employed [a]	29%	7%	12%		19%		32%	38%	7%	19%	5%	5%	(26%	43%)	65	42
Employed in small-scale enterprises	24%	14%	12%		38%	39%	9%	27%	35%	31%		4%	(19%	17%)	37	29
Employed in large-scale enterprises	21%	19%	13%		55%	29%	4%	30%	35%	21%	2%	4%	(9%	25%)	52	47

[a] Total percentages do not sum to 100; respondents could cite more than one possible recourse for loans and jobs.

TABLE V Occupation and Obtaining Help in Emergency.

Where a worker would obtain help in emergency or great necessity

Occupation	Welfare Institution	Relative	Work Friend	Other Friend	Employer, Patrons	Fellow Villager	Neighbor	No Source	Total Respondents
Self-employed [a]	58%	14%	1%	20%	42%	8%	3%	(22%)	65
Employed in small-scale enterprises	52%	22%		14%	31%	6%	3%	(24%)	37
Employed in large-scale enterprises	61%	20%	2%	23%	32%	2%	8%	(10%)	51

[a] Total percentages do not sum to 100; respondents could cite more than one possible recourse.

sources of aid in times of need. While the constraints of the job may make self-employed workers less able to interact with or frequently exchange services with other people, they do maintain a range of relationships, many of which remain latent until they are needed. The participation of self-employed workers does not reflect a general withdrawal from urban social activity, but rather, a selection of activities appropriate to their occupational situations.

Length of residence in the city has always been regarded as a crucial variable in understanding the participation of low-income families in urban activities. It has been argued that with increasing length of residence, migrants participate more in urban social activities.[12] The evidence from this Guatemalan sample is inconclusive on this point. Length of residence has little effect that cannot be accounted for by age or occupation on the behavior of migrants.[13] There are, however, certain differences between those born in the city and migrants. Those born in the city interact with friends more frequently, visit their children's schools more frequently, and attend sports and films more frequently (Table VI). Those born in the city and migrants are similar in their participation in newspaper reading and use of medical facilities. The city-born are less likely than migrants to listen frequently to the radio (45 per cent of the city-born listen rarely or not at all in comparison with 31 per cent of migrants). There is thus some suggestion that those born in the city are more active in those aspects of urban life involving interacting with other people. Yet, on other indicators reflecting the manner of an individual's participation in urban life, differences between migrants and non-migrants are the reverse of what has been found in other studies. With respect to type of marital union, the city-born are more likely to be united by consensual union than are migrants (87 per cent against 66 per cent). Migrants are more likely to have been married by either church or state authorities. We shall see that in San Lorenzo the politically active are migrants and that length of urban residence is not associated with voting in city elections. I would suggest that these latter findings reflect both rural social conditions in Guatemala and the different means of coping with urban life open to low-income migrants and low-income city-born.

Table VI Length of Residence and Social Activity.

Length of Residence	Interact with friends every week at least	Visited school at least 3–4 times	Have not attended sports	Read newspapers at least once a week	Attend film once a month at least [a]	Use medical facility 3 or more times in past year
Less than ten years	72%	25%	47%	48%	37%	43%
Number	(34)	(5)	(15)	(16)	(12)	(15)
Ten to twenty years	71%	33%	47%	65%	31%	52%
Number	(32)	(7)	(18)	(26)	(12)	(21)
More than twenty years	61%	32%	67%	43%	35%	39%
Number	(44)	(12)	(40)	(30)	(18)	(24)
Born in City	85%	61%	30%	57%	44%	45%
Number	(35)	(11)	(10)	(19)	(14)	(15)

[a] The percentages for attendance at films are based on the sample of 40 and under.

Categorizing heads of household in the two neighborhoods by their length of residence provides us with further evidence of change in an individual's social behavior with change in urban situation. Living near relatives and interaction with friends varies directly with length of urban residence (Table VII). Recent mi-

TABLE VII   Length of Residence and Interaction with Friends and Family.

Interaction	Less than ten years	Ten to twenty years	More than twenty years	Born in the city
Relatives in neighborhood (weekly)	53%	37%	27%	23%
Relatives in other parts of city (weekly)	15%	26%	36%	46%
See relatives infrequently or not at all	32%	37%	37%	31%
Percentage	100%	100%	100%	100%
Number	(47)	(46)	(78)	(47)
With friends in neighborhood (weekly)	40%	38%	21%	22%
With friends in other parts of city (weekly)	32%	33%	40%	63%
Interact infrequently with friends	28%	29%	39%	15%
Percentage	100%	100%	100%	100%
Number	(47)	(45)	(73)	(41)

grants to the city are the most likely to have relatives living in their neighborhood. In both neighborhoods it is usual for recent arrivals in the city to come and stay with their relatives and to find accommodation near those relatives. With longer residence in the city, migrants are less likely to have relatives living near them. Frequent residential moves throughout the city disperse relatives. Those born in the city are least likely to have relatives living in their neighborhood. (Both neighborhoods are recently developed neighborhoods.) A similar pattern emerges with respect to interaction with friends. Recent migrants have fewest friends in other neighborhoods and are most likely to have friends in their own neighborhood. With increasing urban residence, friends become spread throughout the city until, for those born in the city, the overwhelmingly proportion of their friends are in other neighborhoods of the city. Recent migrants were most likely to cite relatives as having got them their present job. Those with longer urban residence were more likely to cite friends or work-mates.

Ecological Factors

The two neighborhoods present very different living conditions for their inhabitants. These living conditions are important influences on the social behavior of our sample of low-income families. The contrast between San Lorenzo and Planificada is between a relatively urbanized and planned neighborhood and one that was unplanned and arose spontaneously to meet the housing needs of low-income families. The conditions that differentiate San Lorenzo and Planificada are (a) density, (b) centrality of location, (c) degree of urbanization, and (d) the legal status of the two neighborhoods.

Because of greater living density, people in San Lorenzo can be mobilized more rapidly for communal projects or meetings than can those in Planificada. Gossip and information travel fast in San Lorenzo. At any time of day or night the narrow streets of San Lorenzo are filled with children, young and old men, and women. In contrast, families in Planificada keep to their houses to a much greater extent. Lack of urban services has been a further stimulus to the cooperation of San Lorenzo families. They have worked together to install the urban services they lack and to put pressures on the municipal authorities to have them installed. Furthermore, the possibility that they might be evicted has encouraged San Lorenzo families to form neighborhood committees and has exposed them to the play of urban politics. Political groups in the city have seen the insecurity of such areas as San Lorenzo as providing a useful lever for the establishment and propagation of local branches of their parties. These stimuli to community organization and interaction are lacking in Planificada. Also because of the distance of the neighborhood from the center of the city. Planificada families have less time to spend on such activities or even on recreation. In contrast, San Lorenzo's central location means that its inhabitants spend only a short time in journeys to work and are in easy reach of most urban services and amusements. We can summarize the effect of these differences between San Lorenzo and Planificada by saying that San Lorenzo has both higher interaction among neighbors and higher exposures to outside urban social organization.

San Lorenzo inhabitants do participate more in urban life. People from San Lorenzo can be seen leaving the neighborhood to attend a sporting event or a cinema more frequently than seems to be the case in Planificada. The sample of San Lorenzo heads of family claimed that they attended sports or cinema more often than was claimed by the sample in Planificada. In comparison with those in Planificada, the San Lorenzo sample also claimed to interact more frequently with friends and to see their relatives more frequently (Table VIII). We should note that these findings occur despite the fact that incomes in Planificada are higher. As we have seen, higher income is positively associated with attendance at sports or film.

TABLE VIII   Ecology and Social Activity.

Neighborhood	Interact with friends every week at least	Interact with relatives every week at least	Have not attended sports in last year	Attend film at least once a month
San Lorenzo [a]	78%	70%	47%	41%
	(108)	(108)	(47)	(41)
Planificada	65%	60%	57%	25%
	(98)	(116)	(36)	(15)

[a] The change in size of sample occurs because data was available on the full sample about friends and relatives, but was available for the reduced sample on the other two questions.

The centrality of San Lorenzo's location is not the only factor affecting its inhabitants' use of recreational facilities and ability to maintain relationships outside the neighborhood. It is common in San Lorenzo for people to persuade others in the neighborhood to accompany them in their leisure activities. A small group of men will make their way up the mud street of San Lorenzo and call on those they meet to join them to see a football match or a wrestling exhibition. The spaciousness of Planificada makes such contacts less likely. Since the journey to work is longer in Planificada heads of families arrive home later and do not wish to leave again. However, in the case of institutions located in or near the two neighborhoods such as the public health clinic and the schools, the sample of families in both neighborhoods showed no difference in the frequency of their use of such facilities.

Community organization has been more successful in San Lorenzo than in Planificada. In San Lorenzo, families have laid their own sewage system, built chapels and a community church, and erected a community center. Pressure exercised by betterment committees and other groups has persuaded the municipality to help San Lorenzo, though it is not a legally recognized neighborhood. Water faucets have been installed, building materials provided, and a medical dispensary constructed. In comparison, the various betterment committees organized in Planificada have had less success. Planificada still lacks an adequate sewage system, and though a legally settled neighborhood, it has been unable to secure the paving of all its streets or the provision of an adequate water supply.

Part of the reason for San Lorenzo's relative success in community organization has been the higher levels of political awareness and organization in San Lorenzo. In San Lorenzo, a neighborhood of 400 families, there existed at least five political committees at the time of the last elections. Each of these had at least six active office holders and many more active helpers. Similar committees existed in Planificada; but they were proportionately less numerous. Levels of political awareness are high in both neighborhoods. Most neighbors found no difficulty in discussing present and past political events. In San Lorenzo, over 80 per cent of heads of families were able to give a definite preference about past presidents of Guatemala. Seventy-five per cent of Planificada heads of family gave definite preferences. Seventy-seven per cent of San Lorenzo male heads of family and 65 per cent of Planificada heads of family voted in the elections.

Life Careers

Each low-income family has an individual experience of spatial and job mobility. Families also differ in the exposure they have had to social and political changes in Guatemala. Age, for example, is one determinant of exposure; occupation and residence are others. The cumulative life experience of an individual provides him with an orientation with which he interprets contemporary events and the various urban situations in which he is placed. Though each experience is unique, general distinctions can be made between these life experiences and can be related to the contemporary social activity of low-income families. In this section, however, I limit myself to providing examples of the relevance of life careers to an analysis of urban social organization.

The influence of their life experiences appears in the political attitudes of heads of family. All those heads of family over 35 have experienced the regimes of presidents Arévalo and Arbenz. These regimes attempted to introduce a measure of agrarian and industrial reform to benefit low-income workers. Both regimes were examples of times when political parties improved the position of low-income families, if only temporarily. These improvements would have been felt most by those working in large-scale enterprises. The overwhelming majority of heads of households who were over 35 and had always been employed in large-scale enterprises replied positively to a question asking them if they thought a political party could improve the situation in Guatemala. These same heads of household were also overwhelmingly in favor of Arévalo as the best past president of Guatemala. These were the people who in the interviews would list the achievements of the Arévalo regime in discussing the past presidents of Guatemala. Their past experience gave them more confidence in the political process than any other group. Younger heads of family working in large-scale enterprises did not think that a political party could improve the situation. This latter opinion was true of self-employed workers and employees in small-scale enterprises, whether these were over or under 35. As I have describe elsewhere, working in large-scale enterprises predisposes heads of family to be favorable to cooperating politically with fellow workers and neighbors.[14] It is only experience of successful reformist regimes that converts these attitudes arising from the work situation into confidence in the political process.

The relevance of life experience comes out most sharply in examining political activity within San Lorenzo. All those who were politically active in one of the national political parties were with one exception migrants. The one exception had spent a major part of his working life in the rural areas of Guatemala. Apart from their experience of rural areas, these political activists were similar in the range and type of job experience they had had. They had worked in various areas of the countryside, often in connection with large-scale enterprises such as plantations, construction or government enterprises. The life careers of these political activists had been highly discontinuous. They had experienced different types of social situations and different sets of social relations. They had also experienced political activity before coming to the city. In the neighborhood they were vigorous proponents of national as well as neighborhood political issues. Like other neighbors, they were interested in short-term gains for the neighborhood and in their own personal self-advancement. Many of them got jobs through their political activity. They were in the main self-employed which gave them the flexibility they needed to spend time in political activity. They contrast with another group of neighbors who were almost solely concerned with neighborhood issues. This group was composed of men who were mostly migrants but who had been in the city a considerable number of years. They had obtained fairly steady and well-paid jobs and had remained in these jobs for many years. This second group had more of their children continuing into secondary education than was usual for the neighborhood. This locally orientated group had experienced events under Arévalo and Arbenz and were politically aware and sympathetic to reform governments. Their experiences had been less discontinuous than that of the nationally orientated group. Their life had been a slow attempt to improve their own position and that of their children. They were committed to urban life, had many friends throughout the city, and felt that improvement, even on a neighborhood basis, was a worthwhile objective.

In the complex political events of San Lorenzo, both groups, locals and nationals, responded in very similar ways to the inducements held out by the national political parties interested in the neighborhood. Both groups were influenced by the prospect of jobs, short-term benefits, and the power of competing parties. Yet, their activity was still heavily influenced by the basic orientation that they took to politics. The neighborhood-orientated group always tried to limit political activity to neighborhood improvements. They gave little support to programs designed to convey the extra-local significance of what was being done. The nationally orientated group attempted to extend the significance of local activities, fostering literacy programs, cooperative schemes, and meetings designed to explain to neighbors the general significance of neighborhood improvements.

Families in both neighborhoods differ in the extent and nature of their residential and occupational mobility. I expect such differences to affect not only their political behavior, but also their attitudes to their present job and neighborhood. These differences will also affect commitments to urban life as measured by such indicators as the educational level of the children. My analysis of these variables must await the collection of more detailed information concerning the life histories of these families. My aim here has been to emphasize that individual life experiences contribute to our understanding of the behavior of families placed in different social positions. Furthermore, characterizing families by the prevalent type of life experience is a necessary complement to an analysis of organization at the group level.

Informality of Urban Organization and Articulation of Social Situations

The social activity of families in the two neighborhoods is spread throughout the city. Activity is not based either on the home or on ties formed with neighbors. In our description of the city we noted that this is a necesary consequence of the social and economic structure of a city in which urban organizations operate informally. Family heads in the two neighborhoods work independently or in small enterprises scattered throughout the city. Few families work in the same enterprise as their neighbors. Work contacts are thus different from neighborhood contacts. Recreation, as we have seen, is usually taken outside the neighborhood and often in the company of friends and relatives living elsewhere in the city. Religious activity is not primarily based on neighborhood. Catholics attend several churches with little opportunity to establish enduring relations with other worshippers. Protestantism involves close-knit but small communities whose relations extend to fellow believers in other parts of the city rather than to neighbors.[15] In the recent history of Guatemala, political parties have not received consistent support from low-income families. Both neighborhoods are fragmented politically. The enduring political relationships made by a politically interested family head will not be with fellow neighbors or workmates. They will often be with middle-class political organizers who themselves may shift from political party to political party.

Neighbors are thus involved in diverse sets of relations that differ not only between individuals, but also as individuals move from one urban situation to another. Heads of households operate within one set of relations at work, within another in their religious activity, within another when cooperating for community organization, and within yet another when active in a national political party. Few relations are common to these different situations. There is thus little social pressure for people to be consistent in their behavior from one situation to another. One man in San Lorenzo was active in a left-wing national political group. He was also a member of the local Catholic brotherhood, most of whose members were conservative politically. He helped in community organization and was ritually related to another community organizer of opposed political persuasion. His political group was suspicious of the value of local drinking or sports with workmates. He came from the same rural village as several other families in the neighborhood and was distantly related to them. They all maintained contacts with their home village and would exchange gossip about events there. These ties with fellow villagers were used as one base for political recruitment. However, another relative and fellow villager was one of his chief political opponents in the neighborhood.

This fragmentation should not be over-emphasized. Certainly common birthplace, kinship, and religion are bases for interactions that are common to many spheres of activity. In general, however, families in both neighborhoods move between urban situations in which they deal with distinct sets of people and expectations.

The social activity of low-income families is often socially heterogeneous. Most low-income families in both neighborhoods could cite social and economic superiors on whose help they counted in time of emergency. These relations were formed on a variety of bases. Often they were with former or present employers. In the case of employed workers, employers are almost as frequent sources of small loans as are workmates. Women establish loan relations with the women at whose houses they work. These relations are often latent. Low-income workers do not make a frequent practice of visiting possible patrons, but they maintain the relation by visiting when the opportunity arises or the occasions demand. One man makes a practice of visiting the house of an army colonel with whom he had served. He goes about twice a year and does a small service for the colonel without expecting anything in return. He admits, however, that the colonel would be one source of aid to him should the need arise.

Coming from the same rural village, kinship, membership in a religious group, or in a political organization are also bases on which families in these neighborhoods establish relations with people in different social and economic positions. These relations become a significant frame of reference for neighbors. They estimate their possibilities of improving their position in terms of the kind and range of contacts they have.

These social contacts are factors differentiating one low-income family from another. Families in the two neighborhoods do not interact frequently with each other. Their relations are often with people of different social and economic positions. The social life of these low-income families thus does not encourage them to recognize their common social and economic interests.

The social relations of low-income families in both neighborhoods lead them to be flexible participants in urban life. I discuss the implications of this in terms of residence, employment and politics. In both neighborhoods some 15 per cent of the families leave every year for other parts of the city. Both San

Lorenzo and Planificada are stopping places in the search for good urban accommodation. This residential mobility does reflect the heterogeneity of neighbors' relations. Families do not have intensive contacts with neighbors that bind them to any one urban locale. Having contacts in various parts of the city provides a family with opportunities to obtain other urban housing that suits changes in a family's size or income. Sometimes it will be rented accommodation. Sometimes a family will buy a plot of land after a period of saving in their present neighborhood or when their financial situation improves.

San Lorenzo inhabitants and those renting in Planificada are eager to receive information about new housing developments. They will travel considerable distances to inspect a new development and discover the costs entailed. When the local priests of San Lorenzo launched a scheme to locate shanty-town inhabitants on cheap land on the far outskirts of the city, a large proportion of San Lorenzo inhabitants went singly or in groups to inspect the property. They examined the bus routes and talked with people already living in this development. They concluded that the development was too rudimentary and too distant from their places of work. Almost everyone I interviewed was able to recite these facts about the development project.

It is thus not attachment to their neighborhoods or lack of knowledge of alternative possibilities that keep these low-income families in what is often low-standard housing. In fact, their mobility constitutes a major problem for the urban planning of Guatemala. The city has expanded to suit the pressures of its mobile low-income population. Low-income families have given little credence to government promises or threats. They have not been prepared to rent overcrowded and expensive accommodation. In considerable numbers they have moved to illegally settled shanty towns scattered throughout the city. Now urban administrative problems have thus arisen, and the framework of urban administration has been changed. Municipal administration has tacitly recognized the existence of shanty towns and has sponsored betterment committees in low-income areas. These committees have become an informal but important part of the administrative structure of the city.

These low-income families are also flexible in their attitudes toward employment. In these two neighborhoods, the relations a man forms at work and those he forms in his leisure are different. This means that there are few social pressures to keep a worker in an employment when better opportunities become available. No family head that I interviewed said that he was unprepared to change his type of work. During my stay, some men returned to the countryside to agricultural employment and others went to development projects in distant parts of the nation. Information about new job possibilities circulates quickly in these neighborhoods. As soon as a new construction project is started, for example, laborers without employment will be there seeking employment. Apart from the best paid and securest jobs, job turnover is quite high among low-income heads of household in the sample. This introduces a flexibility into urban employment that is both an economic advantage and an economic disadvantage. Labor is available and flexible, but it is not stable.

The flexible behavior of low-income families is perhaps most apparent in the field of politics. Families in both neighborhoods do not cooperate politically in support of any one political group. Instead, they are available to the variety of political interests that seek the support of low-income voters.

Throughout its short history, San Lorenzo has been divided between competing political committees.[16] These committees gain the temporary allegiance of groups of neighbors. They are usually sponsored by national or municipal political parties. These political parties vary in their ideology from left to right of the political spectrum. They are all controlled by middle-class Guatemalans.

Political parties establish themselves by using kinship, religion, common rural origin, or work relations to approach San Lorenzo family heads. If the relation is a strong one or if sufficient favors are offered, a neighborhood political committee will be established in support of the national or municipal political party. This neighborhood committee will make use of their neighborhood relations to recruit other members to the committee.

At any one time, there are likely to be at least three or four competing political committees existing within San Lorenzo. Families shift from one committee to another or join new committees as political circumstances change. The political histories of members of both neighborhoods usually include temporary membership in three or four distinct political committees in the last five years. Members of the neighborhood betterment committee, for example, had informally sponsored candidates in the last two municipal elections. These candidates lost the elections, and the committee switched their political allegiance to the victorious candidate.

The bases of a neighborhood political committee are loose alliances of different interest groups. Each interest group is based on one of the differentiating experiences to which these low-income families are exposed. Religion, occupation, life experiences, kinship, rural origin are the most common of these. The interest groups are temporarily united in a political alliance through the personal contacts that members of one interest group have with members of another interest group. They are also united in opposition to other political committees existing in the neighborhood.

An analysis of one of the political committees formed before the last municipal elections illustrates these features of the composition of a committee. This committee was formed when the area organizer of a national political party used the local priest to make contact with some members of San Lorenzo's religious brotherhood. These members agreed to help and in turn suggested that he contact another neighbor with extensive kin contacts in the neighborhood who was known to be discontented with the activities of the neighborhood betterment committee. Members of a national political party were also included in the committee. Their support was gained partly through kinship ties with committee members, but it was mainly obtained because other committees were thought to be supporting a rival national political party. The committee also gained the support of Protestants angered at the supposed hostility of other neighborhood committees and their candidates to Protestant interests in the city. This political committee was united by the municipal election campaign. Its members shared few life situations that gave them a common and enduring political position. After the election, the area organizer attempted to maintain the committee and use it to promote neighborhood political organization. The committee, however, split into its component parts, and some of these formed new alliances to begin new political groups around fresh political interests.

The type of political flexibility described above influences political organization in the city. It means that most political parties can find some support among low-income groups. This encourages the proliferation of political parties and means that the style of urban politics includes the use of public agitation and demonstration. The political flexibility of low-income families also contributes to the lack of organization among existing political parties. Since a political party can easily gain grassroots support by sponsoring neighborhood committees, political parties have established only the skeleton of an organization. There are few full-time party workers dedicated to continuously fomenting support in local neighborhoods. When not in power, political parties do not have well organized local support that makes them a continuing and important influence in national decision-making. Furthermore, since political parties depend on sponsoring local political committees, they are under considerable pressure to reward their supporters by obtaining favors or jobs for them. As we have seen, local political committees are not united by an organized and common political position, but by a variety of temporary considerations. Under these conditions, urban political organization is fluid and orientated to short-term issues. Ideologically sophisticated political parties compromise their long-term political goals to the exigencies of the urban political organization under which they work. In these ways, lowincome families are an active influence in urban political life. Whereas decision-making remains in the hands of middle-class Guatemalans, national and municipal political parties are highly exposed to, and sensitive to, the short-term demands of lowincome families.

POLARIZATION OF LOW-INCOME FAMILIES

I have so far emphasized the interconnection and reciprocal influence of low-income families and other sectors of Guatemalan society. These interconnections modify, but do not invalidate, a conceptualization of Guatemalan society as composed of two discrete social sectors differentiated by life styles and access to power.[17] Indeed, we have already noted that low-income families do not frequently participate in formal, urban organizations and that many of their relations with social and economic superiors are of a patron-client nature. In this section my argument is directly relevant to the dual sectors model of stratification in Latin America. I now examine the extent to which low-income families in Guatemala see themselves as a distinct sector of society with interests and life styles opposed to those of more powerful members of their society.

In Guatemala City there are few bases on which an individual obtains prestige in the eyes of his fellows. Wealth and occupation are the most visible bases of social prestige in the city, and low-income families are low on both. Almost everyone in the city is classed as a *ladino,* and ethnic status is thus not an effective, comparative ground for social prestige. Many low-income families in the two neighborhoods are independent in their work. Yet, they, like the employed, are dependent on others for effectively coping with urban life. Furthermore, mobility within the city and the relative absence of organizations in which low-income families participate mean that it is difficult for an individual to build up prestige through the course of long acquaintance or service in an organization. Sectarian religious organizations are almost the only organizations through which low-income families in these neighborhoods obtain prestige through service. There is thus a sharp contrast with the situation that holds in the rural areas, as described by Méndez.[18] In the village he discusses, there were several bases on which prestige is allocated and the village stratified. Individuals can be ranked high in prestige on one dimension and low on another. Wealth is only one dimension of prestige, and others include ethnic status, ownership of land, experience, and community service. There are few individuals in the village who cannot claim some measure of prestige on one of these dimensions. Conflict did exist between the various social groups in the village. Most individuals, however, felt that they had a place within the village structure and were committed to its preservation or change.

Families in San Lorenzo and Planificada attempt to maintain some basis of social discrimination. In conversation and

interaction, a notion of respectability often occurs. The respectable are regarded as those with regular jobs, who wear decent
clothes and keep their houses or huts in some semblance of
order. Those who are not respectable are regarded as those who
drink too much, do not attempt to improve their accommodation,
and pay little attention to their personal appearance or that of
their children. Even in the shanty town, San Lorenzo, neighbors
will talk of holding a party only for respectable people. They
classify many neighbors as not respectable enough for community office. In their personal dealings, most heads of family
emphasize that it is desirable to maintain reciprocity in social
relations. Most stated that they preferred to borrow money either
from those to whom they also lent or under some system of
interest payment where the debt relation is a commercial one.
Some neighbors commented that they were no longer able to
visit certain relatives, since these relatives were rich and they
could not hope to return any favors received. In these conversa-
tions, the norm that was emphasized was that of the independence of the individual family. In their dealings with me, the
"respectable" made a point of not asking for any favors.

Yet, the conditions of urban life in Guatemala make it impossible for any low-income family not to enter into some relations of dependence. The norm of independence is constantly
being violated in practice. Also, the differentiations in prestige
that these low-income neighbors make are insignificant when
compared with the prestige that accrues to wealth and power in
the city. The improvements any low-income family can make on
their house, their clothes, and their financial status are marginal
when compared with the life-styles of the wealthy in Guatemala
City. Consequently, almost without exception, families in both
neighborhoods made their major classification of urban social
groups that of rich and poor. Even the relatively highly paid
among these low-income families classified themselves as among
the poor. People of widely opposing political preferences referred
to the gulf between rich and poor as the central problem facing
Guatemala. Thus, one elderly inhabitant of San Lorenzo chose
Ubico, the old dictator, as his preferred past president of Guatemala. This same man then stated that the root of Guatemala's
contemporary ills lay in the fact that the rich did not help the

poor. A Protestant who claimed to be apolitical stated that he sympathized with the *guerrilleros* since the rich merchants and landowners had done nothing but exploit the poor. Neighbors of left-wing sympathies were equally vociferous in making polar distinctions between rich and poor. Polarization of urban groups into rich and poor is encouraged by an individual's life experience. Those most ready to make this distinction, in the two neighborhoods, were the older heads of family and those whose life had been devoted to trying to improve their own position or that of their fellows. One political activist, in a tape recording of his life history, described the sequence of events by which he tried to improve his economic situation. At each stage, his ambitions had been thwarted by the political and economic climate of Guatemala. He told of his increasing conviction that the rich did not wish to help the poor and of his increasing pessimism that peaceful action would improve the conditions of poorer Guatemalans.

Low-income families are thus highly conscious that the major bases on which prestige is allocated in the urban social structure are irrevocably denied to them. Yet, apart from the categorical distinction between rich and poor, there is, as we have seen, no situational basis for group solidarity among low-income families. Each family has its own set of social relations that differentiates it from other low-income families. Each family attempts to improve its position individually. The consequence of polarization and differentiation among low-income families in Guatemala City is low involvement with the formal processes of urban life. Low-income families are active manipulators of urban social organization. They, however, see themselves as apart from the formal mechanisms by which this social organization is maintained or changed. The majority of heads of family in both neighborhoods had no confidence that any political party, no matter what its political complexion, could improve the economic and political situation in Guatemala. Most family heads regarded the activities of both political reformers and political reactionaries as outside their concern. Their awareness of the significance of the distinction between rich and poor thus contributed to their sense of apartness from the formal political structure.

Few low-income families identify with the national concerns of Guatemala. The actions of the United States or of any other foreign power, with respect to Guatemala, are evaluated in terms of how they individually affect these low-income families. Individual experiences of employment in U.S.-owned enterprises were the most important determinants of attitudes towards the United States. Protestants in both neighborhoods identified more closely with their religious brothers in the United States than they did with their fellow citizens. It is this which gives a peculiar character to urban social organization in Guatemala City. Low-income families are active members of the city, but they feel no commitment either to maintaining or to changing the urban social structure. It is this which makes it difficult to effect planned change in Guatemala City. Low-income families are neither passive recipients of change nor consistent supporters of change.

In looking at the social activity of low-income families in two neighborhoods of Guatemala City, the articulation of these families with the rest of the urban social structure has been emphasized. There is sufficient differentiation among them to render difficult their common organization. Each family is linked by an individual set of relations and activities to other sectors of the urban population. These families have a varied and extensive experience in both rural and urban social organization. The social activity of an individual family is determined by the orientations derived from their life careers and by the various urban situations in which they find themselves. Their experiences have led most of them to an active attempt to improve their individual positions within the city. Their activity is an important condition upon the operation of urban organizations and the behavior of other segments of the urban population. The lack of continuity in life careers and the lack of integration between different urban situations are important factors stimulating both unity and differentiation among these low-income families. In terms of prestige, their urban experience has led them to distinguish themselves as an underprivileged group that is distinct from richer sectors of the city's population. This apartness, together with their internal differentiation means that low-income families direct their activity to the informal manipulation of urban life. They do not attempt to change the formal structure of power and wealth.

NOTES

[1] The research on which this chapter is based was carried out while the author was on leave of absence from the University of Manchester and in receipt of research grants from the Wenner-Gren Foundation, the Institute of Latin American Studies, University of Texas, and the Ford Foundation. The research reported in this paper is still under way (May, 1968) and was begun in April through December 1966. The statistics used in the paper refer to the preliminary stage of the investigation and must be regarded as provisional. The conclusions reached in the paper may be modified by later research, but they do reflect my position after the first period of research and writing. It should also be noted that this study will appear in a volume to be edited by Richard N. Adams entitled *Cruxifixion by Power* and to be published by the University of Texas Press, Austin, Texas.

[2] This viewpoint has often appeared in the writings of Gino Germani and Torcuato di Tella: Gino Germani, *Política y Sociedad en la Epoca de las Masas,* Buenos Aires, Paidós, 1962; Torcuato di Tella, "Populism and Reform in Latin America," in *Obstacles to Change in Latin America,* ed. Claudio Véliz, London, Royal Institute of International Affairs, 1966. Oscar Lewis, in his writings on the culture of poverty, has also tended to concentrate on the isolation of low-income families from other sectors of the urban population: Oscar Lewis, *The Children of Sánchez,* New York, Random House, 1961.

[3] Myron Weiner, "Definitions of Integration," in *Politics and Society in Developing Nations,* New York, Wiley, 1967.

[4] J. C. Mitchell, "Urban Structure, Situations, and Networks," *The Anthropology of Complex Societies,* ed. Michael Banton, A.S.A. (Monograph no. 4), New York, Praeger, 1965.

[5] The literature is extensive. For Latin American cities, there are among other studies the analysis of Caplow *et al.* in San José, Puerto Rico, and of Mexico. Theodore Caplow *et al., The Urban Ambience,* Bedminster Press, 1964.

[6] An example of such encapsulation is provided in Mayer's study of migrants to a South African city. Philip Mayer, *Townsmen or Tribesmen: Conservatism and the Process of Urbanization in a South African City,* Cape Town, Oxford University Press, 1961.

[7] I use the concept of the integration of different social situations in the sense that Mitchell uses it. It refers to the extent that the people an individual interacts with in one situation will interact with him in other situations. J .C. Mitchell, "Introduction," *Networks and Social Situations,* ed. J. C. Mitchell (forthcoming).

[8] As of 1966.

[9] Alvan Zarate, "Migraciones Internas de Guatemala," *Estudios Cen-*

troamericanos, No. 1, Seminario de Integración Social Guatemalteca, Guatemala, 1967. As has been noted in earlier chapters, many of these migrants will have been ladinized.

[10] The statistics presented here and in later tables are drawn from interviews with a 33 per cent sample of San Lorenzo and with all family heads of a representative sector of Planificada. The San Lorenzo sample was drawn randomly, and 85 per cent *of those selected* were interviewed. Two interviews of approximately an hour each were conducted with each family. There was an interval of approximately three months between the two set of interviews. The interviews were conducted after a period of two months when families in both neighborhoods had become used to my presence. In Planificada, the sector selected represented approximately 5 per cent of the neighborhood. A first interview was conducted with all families in the sector (approximately 127), and a second interview with every second family. This procedure was adopted for lack of time. The remainder of the eight and a half months field work was spent in participant observation—mainly in San Lorenzo. The qualitative data is drawn from this observation.

[11] Education is one important variable that has not been examined. Most heads of family have low levels of education. Whether a person is literate (approximately 70 per cent of the male heads of household) does affect his activity—notably newspaper reading and attendance at films. The illiterate are disproportionately concentrated in the lowest income group. The effects of education are a variable that is being considered in the present stage of the research. Age, another important variable in social activity, was considered in terms of its influence on income, occupation, and length of residence. Analyzing within age categories left the direction of the results reported unchanged. The general effect of age is to diminish activity.

[12] Gino Germani, "Inquiry into the Social Effects of Urbanization in a Working-Class Sector of Greater Buenos Aires," *Urbanization in Latin America,* ed. Philip Hauser, UNESCO, Paris, 1961.

[13] Migrants with more urban experience are older and are more likely to be concentrated in self-employment. This accounts for some of the difference among migrants. When younger migrants who work in small- or large-scale enterprises, are compared with non-migrants of similar age and occupational range, the differences shown in Table VI persist.

[14] Bryan Roberts, "The Politics of an Urban Neighborhood of Guatemala City," *Sociology,* May, 1968.

[15] Bryan Roberts, "Protestantism and Coping with Urban Life in Guatemala City," *American Journal of Sociology,* 1968.

[16] I use the term "committee" to cover the semi-formal political groups that exist in the neighborhood. During the year preceding an election and for a short period afterward, these political groups are constituted as committees with office-holders and the task of inscribing supporters for their political parties.

[17] Richard Adams, "Political Power and Social Structures," *The Politics of Conformity in Latin America,* ed. Claudio Véliz, London, Royal Institute of International Affairs, 1967.

[18] Alfredo Méndez, *Zaragoza,* Seminario de Integración Social Guatemalteca, Guatemala, 1967.

III

Masses
and
Politicalization

11

FRANCISCO C. WEFFORT

State and Mass in Brazil

The profound upheaval in the Brazilian export economy as a consequence of a 1929 crisis and the depression of the thirties created the political and social conditions needed for the democratization of the State. Indeed, the Revolution of 1930 was the beginning of a new stage in the history of Brazil. A complex historical-political development with two main characteristics began. One is a trend toward the elimination of the oligarchic State based upon large agricultural properties whose production was oriented toward export. The other is the formation of a democratic State based upon the popular urban masses and the social sectors linked to industrialization. This period initiated the transition from a "limited participation" democracy to a "broad participation" democracy.[1]

The period between 1945 (the end of the Vargas dictatorship and the beginning of re-democratization) and the overthrow of the Goulart regime in 1964 reflects the trends and political forces which make up that process. Because it is a period in which there was wide freedom of expression, the analyst is better able to appreciate the structure of power and its internal tensions. It is furthermore a period during which various forces matured, reaching the limits of their growth in the succession of crises ending in April 1964. Thus, our analysis of this post-1945 period will constitute the historical and empirical basis for our interpretation.

Nonetheless, it is necessary to present this study within the framework of the wider historical pattern which begins with the 1930 Revolution. To grasp the process of State democratization historically, it is essential for us to comprehend its nature and limits. The sociological analysis of this process, oriented to the "Western model" of economic development, often considers necessary what is merely possible, thus overextending the limits which the Brazilian historical situation allows for in the way of planned social change.

As Celso Furtado notes, the decadence of the export economy as a simple reflection of the decrease of external stimulus does *not* lead to an open conflict between the potentially industrial urban sectors and the traditional sectors. The breakdown of the coffee economy during the thirties, due to the crisis of the world markets and to internal overproduction, made possible the strengthening of the ruling class, based upon excluding coffee interests, and their replacement by new elements less linked to export sectors. This marked the beginning of serious political planning for the economy (in contrast with the traditional policy of increasing revenue by simply manipulating the price of coffee); it created conditions for the establishment of industrial capitalism by transferring the losses of the coffee economy to the population as a whole, thereby maintaining the employment level at a time when the import capacity was decreasing. These factors created favorable conditions for investments linked to the internal market. The Brazilian economy thus ceased to depend exclusively on external stimuli.[2]

From the above analysis there clearly emerges a fact of profound importance for understanding the Brazilian historical process, at the economic level no less than at the social and political levels: namely, that the industrialization process is marginal to and dependent upon the traditional agrarian structure.[3]

The dependence of the Brazilian economy on marginal forms of production is so important that the economic factors appear both as a condition and a consequence of backwardness. Indeed, the economic condition, characterized by a decrease in the influence of external stimuli, operates upon the industrialization process through a power structure which supports the coffee economy by maintaining the employment level. This *historical* perspective of the Brazilian economy (historical in the sense that the analysis operates at the economic, social, and political levels in order to determine the basic nature of a concrete structure) is the point of departure for the study of the structure of the State in Brazil. The question suggested by Furtado's analysis brings us directly to our subject. We know that the crisis in the coffee economy did not lead to an open conflict between the industrial interests and the traditional sectors (as the Western model presupposes). The marginality of the industrialization process suggests, on the contrary, the existence of tensions checked by a compromise. The question becomes: *What kind of political power structure could have favored, since the 1930 Revolution, the industrialization which took place in Brazil during the following decades?*

The urban middle classes were the most important pressure groups for overthrowing the oligarchy. From these strata, composed mainly of public officials, military men, service branch employees, and liberal professionals, came the more radical leaders (among the military generally the lieutenants) of the movements of the twenties. They also represented the dominant sector of public opinion, which they channelled toward the realization of liberal-democratic aims (particularly the secret ballot). Settled mostly in the big cities and therefore outside of the direct sphere of influence of *coronelismo*—the ideology of officer corps political leadership—which dominated the rural areas and the small municipalities, these sectors constituted the basis for nonconformist movements against a power structure based upon agricultural interests, particularly those of coffee.

The 1930 Revolution was the climax of the political pressure exerted by these urban groups. Yet this event took place under such difficult conditions that the middle classes were unable to establish, after the crisis of the oligarchic regime, a democratic regime in accordance with their liberal aspirations.

The traditional Brazilian middle classes, as seems to be the case in most Latin American countries, did not have the social and economic characteristics which would allow them political autonomy from the interests of the large agricultural estates. As opposed to the old American middle class, they did not have their social and economic base in small independent properties but in subsidiary activities (State and services) of the social structure of the large estates. Compelled by their dependence on the estates as the prevailing social and economic pattern, these sectors never achieved a fully radical political position. They were never able to formulate a program that was adequate for Brazilian society as a whole. They adopted the ideological principles of liberal democracy, which in broad terms constituted the ideological framework of the agrarian sectors. These traditional middle classes were never able effectively to overcome the institutional limits set by the dominant groups; their most radical acts, generally undertaken by young military men—the *tenentes* —lose all effectiveness in a romantic negation of established society to which they are driven by social desperation.

Greater effectiveness can only be achieved by suppressing radicalism, since effectiveness is sustained only within the institutional framework on which these sectors are ultimately dependent and with which they achieve solidarity in times of realistic action.

Thus, while these middle sectors had the dominant force for opinion and action which led to the serious crisis of the oligarchic regime of 1930, they lacked the social and economic means of effectively rejecting the institutional framework, merely being able to redefine the relationship.[4]

Indeed, the 1930 Revolution brings to light various aspects of this compromise between the urban sectors and the dominant agrarian groups. The nature of this revolution is clearly shown in the famous saying of one of its leaders, Antonio Carlos, head of the government in the state of Minas Gerais and representative of one of the strongest agrarian sectors: "Let us make the revolution before the people make it." It might be said, indeed, that in 1930 the agricultural sectors anticipated the urban sectors, thus defining the limits for the latter.

The oligarchic regime's equilibrium was based upon the axis established between the state of São Paulo (still suffering from the effects of the coffee crisis) and that of Minas Gerais, with the latter's support of the Rio Grande do Sul administration

(Getulio Vargas), which was also linked to the traditional groups. Once this equilibrium had been broken, there arose the need for a new configuration of power. The old structure based upon the coffee interests could no longer survive.

Given the circumstances of the Revolution, which resulted from a tacit agreement between the middle classes lacking in political autonomy and the traditional sectors less linked to exportation, the bases of the new power structure could not be firmly established. Indeed, none of these forces possessed the elements necessary to constitute a new State structure. These groups were able to upset the political representation of the coffee interests, but it cannot be denied that coffee remained the decisive basis of the economy.

This is, therefore, a situation in which those who hold political power do not directly represent the groups which control the basic economic sectors. This means that the new State structure differs from the old in one fundamental aspect: it no longer constitutes an immediate expression of the hierarchy of economic power.

This resulted in a *décalage* between the State and the economy. The oligarchy and the State assign different degrees of importance to the particular interests of a given group (stronger in the former than in the latter) and to the expression of general social interests (stronger in the latter than in the former), and so we enter the phase of State formation and liquidation of oligarchic interests.

We have a situation in which none of the groups (middle classes, coffee sector, agricultural sectors less linked to export) holds exclusive political power. This situation creates the possibility of a State as a political organ which tends to separate itself from immediate interests and to exercise its sovereignty over the society as a whole.

But such a compromise does not confer *legitimacy* upon the State, and without legitimacy the State cannot survive. Indeed, even within the oligarchy we find a compromise solution, based upon the coffee interests, with the participation of the same groups. But in this case the legitimacy of the oligarchy is limited by the political horizons opened by these interests.

After 1930 a new type of compromise was established, in which none of the power groups was able to offer a basis for legitimacy: the middle classes lacked political autonomy vis-à-vis the traditional interests in general; the coffee interests were disconnected from political power as a consequence of the economic crisis; and those sectors less linked to export were connected to the basic sectors of the economy.

In none of these cases could the particular social and economic interests serve as a basis for the political expression of the general interests. It was under these circumstances that a new element appeared on the scene of Brazilian history: the urban popular masses, which constituted the only possible source of legitimacy for the new Brazilian State.

The mechanism by which the masses were able to assume that historical role is clearly shown after the country's return to democracy, and shall be analyzed later in greater detail. The political conditions which allow for this process were already visible during the institutional crisis which began in 1930.

The means of acquiring and maintaining power becomes of decisive importance when none of the dominant economic groups is able to offer a solid base for the State, and when the middle classes lack the economic and social conditions for the establishment of a pluralist democratic regime. The 1930 Revolution had done away with the system of access to power through the traditional families and economic groups, which would have enabled the oligarchy to renew itself within its own group.

Even if the oligarchy had access to power, none of the social and economic groups was in a position to legitimize it. Under those circumstances, the power acquired by the revolutionists through a compromise could only be maintained as long as the individuals who exercised power were relatively free of the dominant groups and were able to widen their sphere of compromise solutions by introducing a new force subject to their manipulation alone.

There thus appears in Brazilian political history the popular phantom, which was to be manipulated by Getulio Vargas for fifteen years. Through him the State created a labor union organization which it controlled during the following decades. It "granted" labor legislation for the cities (thus responding to the

390

pressure of the urban masses, which it manipulated without interfering with the interests of the latifundists). It established, through the official organs of propaganda, the image of Vargas as the "father of the poor." In other words, it legalized the "social question"; that is, it formally recognized that the masses have a right to express their aspirations.

Basing his personal prestige upon the urban masses, Getulio Vargas established State power as an institution. The State thus became a decisive factor within Brazilian society. Through manipulative methods it asserted itself as an institution, even in relation to the economic potentates. Nonetheless, the State still represents a compromise solution, performing the role of mediator between the interests of the dominant groups. Yet, since it can be legitimized only through the masses, the State finds in this transaction a new source of prestige: it becomes the arbiter who decides in the name of national interest. As a result, it often formulates economic and social policy which is contradictory and discontinuous because it is subject to the conflicting pressures of the dominant groups' immediate interests. This can be seen in the policy of protecting coffee. Yet this new role of the State has an historical significance which supersedes particular circumstances.

The social substratum of this historical significance lies in the mechanisms of acquiring and maintaining power, which ultimately constitute the elements upon which the legitimacy of the State is based. Since the individuals who exercise power need the support of the urban masses, they are forced to choose alternatives which would elicit the least popular resistance or the most popular support. Under these circumstances, it is sometimes difficult to know whether a particular decision made by the State originally corresponds to a deliberate policy or whether it is merely a means to widen the base of power.

Thus, the State is able to respond to all kinds of pressures, without becoming exclusively subordinated to the immediate interests of any of them. In other words, there is no longer an oligarchy, nor is the State conceived in the Western tradition. It is a kind of mass State, resulting from the prolonged agrarian crisis, the independence of the urban middle sectors, and popular pressures.

DEMOCRACY AND AUTHORITARIANISM

During the dictatorship, State sovereignty over the different social sectors is obvious. In a dictatorship the State is able to manipulate the masses and through them acquire legitimacy. It can also make donations to the masses or economic groups, serve as arbiter between them, and thereby manipulate them. Furthermore, in its arbitrating, manipulative, or donating roles, the holder of power will try to maintain or increase its control by means of a realistic policy of equilibrium between the different groups' pressures and its own need for popular support.

Would not the fall of Vargas's dictatorship in 1945, and the country's return to democracy, fundamentally have altered political conditions, thus making the existence of a pluralistic regime possible? Would this not have minimized the State's sovereignty—which was confused during the dictatorship with Vargas's personal power?

These questions, to which historical experience replies in the negative, are nonetheless pertinent, since together with Vargas's downfall a new party system emerged in Brazil. Furthermore, the collapse of dictatorship, which coincided with the end of the war against fascism and with which it was confused, apparently ended fascism in Brazil, thereby uniting large urban sectors. It seemed to indicate the beginning of true democracy, a dream which had been the ambition of the urban middle classes since the twenties.[5]

But the return to democracy resulted in complete frustration for the traditional middle sectors. The new Brazilian democracy had the masses as its foundation and populists as its leaders. As Touraine observed, it was a process of "democratization through authoritarian channels."[6]

During the period following the thirties there was an increase in the process of industrialization and urbanization. After 1945, the political participation of the urban masses acquired far greater importance than might have been foreseen during the dictatorship. Popular leadership emerged decisively in all national elections. In 1946, Gaspar Dutra won the presidency by covering himself with the popular mass prestige of Getulio Vargas and the two parties linked with him—the Social Democratic Party (PSD) and the Brazilian Labor Party (PTB). Using populist slogans the deposed dictator was elected in 1950 by a remarkable majority. Juscelino Kubitschek then took office in 1955 supported by the PSD-PTB formula. Jânio Quadros defeated this formula in 1960. Finally, João Goulart, Getulio Vargas's favorite disciple, was elected Vice-President in 1954, and in 1961 became President after Jânio Quadros's resignation.

Brazilian democracy thus radically differs from the Western traditional model. The most outstanding difference is that in this mass democracy the State has immediate contact with all its citizens. Indeed, all the important organizations functioning as mediators between the State and the individual are really entries connected with the State itself rather than effectively autonomous organizations. The labor unions maintain to this date their links with the State apparatus established during the dictatorship. These links, which are not only administrative but also political, are among the elements which explain why the labor unions seldom organized wide and successful strikes without the protection or at least the partisan abstention of the federal government.[7]

The party system is based upon the two groups (Social Democratic Party and Brazilian Labor Party) created by Getulio Vargas, which originally depended largely upon his personal prestige. These parties emerged at the end of the dictatorship as a new form of the compromise upon which the State was based. The Social Democratic Party gave political expression to the conservative sectors linked to agrarian activities; and indeed, it maintained for many years, on the basis of a "clientele policy," the control of rural areas. The Brazilian Labor Party gave political expression to the urban working masses.

Born from power and always linked to it (with the exception of the six months of Jânio Quadros's Presidency), these two parties became agents of patronage, especially the Social Democratic Party.

In the sphere of popular leadership, a similar phenomenon occurred in the relationship between the leader and his mass of followers. Adhemar de Barros created a new party (the Social

Progressive Party—PSP) upon which he exerted full control from 1947 to the collapse of the mass party system following the seizure of power by Castelo Branco in 1964. His popular prestige depends upon the positions which he holds in the institutional system. Like Vargas, this populist leader considers the party apparatus almost exclusively an instrument for the exercise of personal power.

Jânio Quadros, for his part, was unable to establish permanent ties with any party structure. This leader, who made a spectacular appearance on the Brazilian political scene, offers an extreme example of the nature of the democratic process initiated in 1945. Supported almost exclusively for his charismatic style, he was elected in 1953 to the Prefecture of São Paulo against the whole system, including the followers of Getulio Vargas and Adhemar de Barros. In his electoral participation he used the parties (which electorally are of secondary importance) merely as labels (in his postulation for the Prefecture and government of São Paulo) or as occasional allies (in his postulation for the Presidency, at which time he joined forces with the National Democratic Union—UDN).

Within this framework in which the State, through the populist leaders, comes into direct contact with the masses, ideologies do not occupy a place of importance. The decisive aspects of political struggle, the ways to acquire and hold power, are related to a struggle between personalities. Under these conditions nationalism became politically significant when the federal government (especially during the Kubitschek administration) adopted it as the ideological justification for the "development policy." It thus appeared as a form of consecration of the State, as a theoretical transfiguration of populism.[8]

In this democracy, in which power is in effect in the hands of the masses, we are a far cry from the model described by Tocqueville on the basis of his observations on nineteenth century United States. We are equally far from the model presented by Lipset. What are then these differences, and how can they be explained? Or better still, what is the nature of Brazilian democracy and how can it be explained?

If we consider *massification* as a process of atomization of the social classes which, especially in Europe, were once characterized by strong internal solidarity and by social consciousness with respect to society as a whole, we would have to admit that in Brazil, as in other underdeveloped countries, we are witnessing a process of *premature massification.*

Massification in Brazil does not mean the fragmentation of those classes which are the bearers of a political and ideological tradition, but rather the incorporation into urban life and the political process of the popular strata from the interior and the countryside. Massification therefore does not mean the dissolution of the collective loyalty of those sectors already integrated into the industrial process, through the widening of their consumption capacity and of techniques of manipulation. Rather, it contributes to the dissolution of loyalties toward the traditional employers in the rural areas.

The particular situation of the masses in Brazil is better understood when we take into account the marked disproportion between the processes of urbanization and industrialization. The growth of the cities bears no relation to industrial development. Excluding greater São Paulo, where the bulk of Brazilian industrial capacity is concentrated, the old incentives for urbanization are still there: growth of the State apparatus (civilian and military activities), commercial activities, and services linked to exports. In addition to these factors we must keep in mind that the pressures created by the poor conditions of rural life act as an important impulse toward urban growth.

In this situation only some of the immigrants can integrate into the industrial activities as workers, who hold a privileged position with respect to the overall urban popular masses of the country. The standard of living of the urban masses, while higher than that of the rural masses, is in effect unsatisfactory. It is difficult to establish a meaningful similarity between these masses and the "satisfied" masses of the advanced countries. The basic perspective from which to understand the former's political behavior is not their affluence but their poverty.

These unsatisfactory social conditions, which tend to move the masses to some form of political expression, are related in their consequences to another important aspect of the process of massification. The transition from the countryside to the city and from the interior of the country to the big coastal cities represents the first step toward individual political identity and the dissolution of the traditional patterns of submission to the rural potentates. The large Brazilian cities function as a sounding board of the whole national political process. From them emerge the popular leaders and the politically decisive currents of opinion. This means that the process of urbanization places large sectors of the population in a situation of political mobilization.

While in advanced societies there is growing political apathy among the popular masses, in the present case the reverse is true. In advanced societies the traditional forms of popular politics based upon class situations gradually lose importance with the increase of the possibilities of consumption by the popular strata. In Brazil the process is different, as we shall see through an analysis of the political composition of Jânio Quadros's followers, mainly workers and salaried middle class from São Paulo.

Jânio Quadros himself is the clearest indication of the popular pressure upon the State structure in Brazil. In little more than ten years he covered the entire range of political positions: alderman of the city of São Paulo, state deputy and later governor of São Paulo, and finally President of the Republic. In all these positions and in his successful political campaigns, he maintained an arrogant and distant attitude toward the parties and an authoritarian-charismatic position toward the masses. He is probably the only Brazilian politician after 1945 who was able to carry the populist style to its ultimate consequences.

He suffered his first electoral defeat, which perhaps put an end to his political career, in 1962, when he ran together with Adhemar de Barros, populist leader of a paternalistic variety, for the government of the state of São Paulo. This political campaign [9] had certain characteristics which make it particularly useful in an analysis of the populist leader-mass relationship. It coincided with a period of decrease of Jânio Quadros's political importance, since the campaign took place one year after his resignation as President. Jânio Quadros ran for election without any ally of importance who might be able to attract the remaining groups. This condition of isolation and relative ostracism in which the candidate found himself made possible the isolation of the São Paulo electorate which had voted for him as President a little more than one year earlier. Further, it allowed for a purge of the social and political elements that had made possible Quadros's rise to power in the first place.

If we examine the distribution of the general electoral results, there immediately appear several significant factors: (1) Quadros tended to obtain more votes in the peripheral districts (composed predominantly of workers) of São Paulo than in the central districts; (2) He obtained more votes in the capital of the state than in the interior; (3) He tended to obtain more votes in the larger cities and in those where there is a more significant mass of workers. Any comparison between the style of Jânio Quadros's leadership and that of the other populist leaders would clearly point out the radicalism of Quadros's style. While the others exercised a patriarchal type of domination demanding compromise solutions with some form of party structure, Jânio Quadros approximated charismatic leadership, which denies in principle all established forms of power. This charismatic leadership is radical, since it is a call to obedience and dedication toward the leader's *person*, thus denying by definition all established norms. This irrational characteristic of the Quadros leadership, while it does not completely describe its quality, is one of the most important aspects to be considered in an analysis of it.

The combination of these two clear-cut aspects—the predominantly urban and working-class trend in electoral penetration and the charismatic domination—diverts interpretation from the usual course of considering the permanence of traditional patterns as a basic element of populist leadership, which would otherwise expect from the workers organized political expression in the form of parties. Both elements—the presence of traditional patterns and the rationality of parties—are immediately rejected by the charistmatic leadership of Jânio Quadros. In this case there is a distance between the authoritarian leader and the subdued mass which cannot be bridged by any form of communication which would grant the mass the right to approach the leader and have a direct influence over him (as occurs in a democratically structured party or in traditionally structured organizations).

Our analysis eliminates any similarity between these urbanized masses from an underdeveloped country and the satisfied masses from the advanced countries, since such a wide diffusion of charismatic leadership is an unequivocal sign of social dissatisfaction. This dissatisfaction is expressed in another basic trait of Quadros's approach: moralism. By demanding devotion toward his person, Jânio Quadros presented himself as an honest, incorruptible, energetic, and altogether moral man. This clarifies the meaning of charismatic leadership: the denial, through the consecration of the leader's person, of established political norms means the denial of established political structures associated with corruption; and for the masses, the struggle against corruption means fighting against privileges.

This political expression of popular dissatisfaction is the form chosen by the more satisfied sectors within the urban masses. Let us compare the supporters of Jânio Quadros with those of Adhemar de Barros. The former are more optimistic with respect to the present standard of living; they tend to perceive an improvement in the post-war period. Further, within the working class the followers of the Quadros style were generally better qualified and more permanently fixed in their jobs. In this sense they were better integrated into the process of industrial production and economic development as a whole.

This opposition between satisfaction and dissatisfaction is of a dialectical nature. The dissatisfaction of the Quadros masses had deep-rooted origins. Their members were placed at the lower limits of the urban and industrial social ladder, whether because they declined as a middle class whose hopes for personal welfare had been frustrated, or because they went upward in their shift from rural occupations to the urban working classes. They were therefore more stable in the sense that they had nothing to lose with industrial development. They did not feel so much like members of a decadent small bourgeoisie, but rather like operators with a stable position moving toward the better. They were optimists because, by their very integration to the industrial process, they improved their standards of living.

In this situation, they no longer turned toward power with the hope of obtaining personal protection, but justice, since what now counted was not favors but the capacity for work. These were sectors for which the links with the past had little importance in the present. They no longer felt the weight of tradition, nor even the simple petty-bourgeois memory of a recent past of relative prosperity. Integrated into urban life, there was no possibility of their adapting traditional habits to the new patterns. They could not expect personal help from anyone.

The source of the ambiguity of these masses, "satisfied" and "unsatisfied" at the same time, was in their relations with society as a whole in its historical development. They were still rancorous at the disintegration of traditional patterns and with them their hopes for personal well-being. Yet this frustration also constituted a satisfaction, since it incorporated them into capitalist development. This relative adjustment of the masses to the capitalist system suggests the present political importance of their past frustration.

Since they could no longer hope for the favors and privileges associated with the traditional forms of power, they turned against them and came to expect justice and the unconditional enforcement of law from the State. They thus acquired the image of an abstract State considered as res publica. Yet owing to their traditional heritage, they did not have the background to express this aspiration rationally. They were radical, but in the clearly individualistic sense of confusedly and irately perceiving that there no longer was any possible individual solution. They thus expressed their ultimate disappointment, their ultimate frustration as masses of small-bourgeois or rural origin, in the recognition of a charismatic leader through whom they manifested a social hatred whose *class* origins were unknown and obscured by the leadership of Jânio Quadros.

The radicalism of the Quadros mass following was only a traditional varnish covering class reformism. Yet this reformism cannot be confused with what Lenin described as working-class economism. It was tinged with bitter resentment, as if it had to break the traditional spell of established norms in order to express itself clearly in ideologically rational forms.

Now we are getting at the heart of the Quadros drama, in terms of both his leadership qualities, and in terms of the characteristics of his mass support. The masses, insofar as they adjusted as a *class* to the capitalist system and denied the traditional patterns, aspired to a rational State. But as a *mass* they found a means of expression only through charisma, the most irrational of political manifestations. They placed all their aspirations for political and social change in one person whom they believed endowed with unlimited power. Thus the leader had possibilities of manipulation, as, for example, associating the radical moralism of the "poor against the millionaire" with the conservative moralism of the "celebrities." Yet he did not forget the popular hopes for change, since he would thus have run the risk of destroying his image.

The full domination exercised by the leader upon the mass translates itself into an immense responsibility, since he had to put into practice an objectively sober, realistic, and progressive policy by means of violent and arbitrary measures which would demonstrate his unlimited personal power. Miracles are expected from charisma, and Jânio Quadros's resignation represented a confession of impotence which spread doubt among the masses.

This analysis of an extreme manifestation of mass politics in Brazil offers a few suggestions for the political interpretation of the process of massification. (1) Popular pressure upon the State is caused by dissatisfaction, even in the case of sectors which are relatively integrated into the process of economic development. (2) This dissatisfaction is manipulated by the populist leaders, and, through them, by the State. (3) The mass situation tends to dissolve the links with traditional patterns and to obscure class consciousness. Nonetheless, the mass situation and its political forms are in no way independent of specific class positions. Despite the fact that political mass expressions deny these class positions, in the cases of both Jânio Quadros and Adhemar de Barros they constitute possible political expressions in the concrete context of specific class positions. (4) Thus, the mass manipulation by the populist leaders or by the State is limited by those class positions; insofar as the leader or the State is unable to offer any satisfaction of the concrete social aspirations (not necessarily conscious) derived from these positions, their popular image begins to dissolve, even though it may not appear to be related to those aspirations.

400

THE STATE: MYTH AND COMPROMISE

The continuity of mass democracy from 1945 until the fall of Goulart is due to the persistence of the structural conditions which began to take shape as early as 1930. According to Celso Furtado's analysis, even though the process of industrialization became intensified during the fifties, it could not become independent of the influence exercised by the external market.[10] In addition, as Fernando Henrique Cardoso has suggested, industrial development itself increasingly depends on foreign capital, impeding the formation of an entrepreneurial stratum capable of formulating a policy independent of foreign interests.[11] This constituted a frustration of the only possibility of moving beyond a compromise solution, which characterized the power structure since 1930. The new entrepreneurs were simply incapable of providing the State with a basis for legitimacy.

The existence of a compromise solution to the conflict between the dominant groups, as well as the pressure of the masses upon the institutional structure, became increasingly evident. There then arises a peculiar situation. All contending groups, including the popular masses, directly or indirectly participate in power. Yet since none has hegemony, they all see the State as a higher entity from which they expect a solution to all problems.[12] This reliance on the State by the different groups is a fact ever since the crisis which put an end to oligarchy. Yet now that the process of industrialization is reaching the limit of its coexistence with the archaic sectors of society, expectations of the State's possible actions are growing in all sectors. But this situation of potential conflict does not politically express itself in a direct manner, through an open struggle between the industrial and the traditional agrarian sectors. The tension cannot become overt because industrial development proceeds hand-in-hand with a growth of the most anachronistic sectors of the traditional economy, such as agriculture, which supplies the internal market, which in turn politically identifies its interests with the general interests of agriculture.[13]

Under these conditions, in which none of the dominant

groups is able to offer a basis for reform, the popular masses appear once more as the only force capable of providing such a basis. Yet the new situation poses more difficult problems. In the previous decades the action of those who exercised power did not go beyond the choosing, through the interplay of particular interests, of the path of least popular resistance. At present, the State finds the need to *place itself above this interplay of interests and plan, in the name of the national interest, a structural reform*. In the previous period the political process created, through populism combined with the political incapacity of the dominant groups, the image of a sovereign State, but presently the State is faced with the necessity of proving its sovereignty.

If we consider the nature of the political participation of the popular masses, we shall perceive the serious limitations of this attempt to affirm the sovereignty of the State and the politics of reform. Indeed, although the popular masses constitute the basis for legitimacy, they are by the same token unable to exercise an autonomous political action. They constitute the actual source of power, but they are no more than a mass which can be easily manipulated. They confer legitimacy upon a populist leader (and through him, upon the State) only insofar as they serve as an instrument for acquiring and holding power, an instrument which is particularly useful when none of the dominant groups has hegemony over the rest.

The masses are in a position to serve as a basis for State legitimacy only when a compromise between the dominant groups is still possible. Thus, the gravity of the situation since Quadros's resignation in 1961 is because the structure of the compromise is unstable. There no longer exists between the dominant groups that relative satisfaction of interests which allowed those in power to be sensitive to popular dissatisfaction. Insofar as the scope of the compromise is reduced (that is, when the State is forced to prove its sovereignty), there is a reduction of the conditions which enable it to manipulate the masses, and thereby hold and increase its power.

Under these circumstances, popular Left-wing organizations begin to demand of the government political action guided by explicitly ideological criteria. Nationalism acquires political importance. Its point of departure is the idea that the people is a

402

community (thus minimizing class distinctions) oriented toward the State as the only solution to national problems. This ideological transfiguration of populism alters the usual manipulation of the masses by the State. In the case of populism, a spontaneous expression of the political emergence of the masses, the individual in power has the initiative concerning the political manifestation of popular aspirations, therefore following a *Realpolitik* whose limits are defined by the equilibrium between the dominant groups. In a government inspired by nationalism, which deals with popular pressures at the ideological level, the State is increasingly forced to actions leading to the elimination of the political expression of certain conservative agrarian sectors. In other words, the policy ceases to be realistic and purports to represent national interest.

We are not suggesting that the reform policy of Goulart's administration was disinterested. The changes in the government's orientation clearly indicated that reform was both an ideology and a technique for the preservation and extension of power. Further, the government could not clearly establish these differences in concrete situations, since reformism was conceived within an ideological framework of consecration of the State as the only solution to social and economic problems. For another thing, it was clear that some kind of reform in the structure of power was necessary in order to produce a program of change.

The whole complexity of the Brazilian political situation from the resignation of Jânio Quadros to the fall of Goulart is contained in the following conjunction of factors. Structural problems became aggravated; since none of the dominant groups had hegemony, they all turned to the State conceived as an independent entity, awaiting its initiatives. But the State became practically paralyzed as possibilities of compromise between the different groups decreased, thereby increasing the pressure. As a result, the possibility that populism, through manipulation, could keep functioning as an agent conferring dynamism upon the political structure was correspondingly reduced. In this situation, popular pressure became increasingly ideological, resulting in the alteration of the traditional model of mass manipulation. When the individuals in power were no longer able to bring dynamism to the political process by means of concrete action, ideology

acquired an important function. Nationalism, aside from conceal-
ing the State's inefficiency in practice, established as a reality
the myth of a democratic State of the whole people, independent
of class distinctions.

Thus the actions of both the State and the popular political
organizations become increasingly guided by the belief in a
sovereign State able to control any possible reaction on the part
of the conservative groups. These groups (not only the agrarian
sectors but the industrial entrepreneurs as well) look upon the
State as revolutionary, and therefore radically oppose it.

It would be premature to define the road followed by the
Brazilian political process after Goulart's fall. Nonetheless, we
might tentatively suggest that, with the military's rise to power,
the democratization of the State through populism has reached
an end. This does not mean that in the future popular pressures
might not in some way be felt. It does mean that conditions no
longer exist for popular pressures to maintain their former spontaneous effectiveness. The new power established by the military
seems to have ended the myth of a democratic State of the whole
people. The military regime thus marks a turning-point in Brazilian political history.

NOTES

* This paper is only a first attempt to analyze the power structure in
Brazil. It was written for later use in research on the political conditions
of development and planning in Latin America. My aim here is to propose
a preliminary outline for the study of this problem. The research needed
to arrive at a more concrete treatment of this subject is still being prepared
in Brazil. (I am referring in particular to the studies by Paula Beiguelman
and Octavio Ianni on the Old Republic (1889–1930) and on the nature of
State interventions upon the economy, respectively). Indeed, only recently
have Brazilian sociologists taken an interest in the structure of national
power as a specific subject of analysis. For this reason, available studies
on the Brazilian State as a whole are frequently characterized by an accentuated and limiting normative prescription (I am referring in particular to the work of Hélio Jaguaribe and Guerreiro Ramos). As a result, it is
not surprising that the more fruitful suggestions for the sociological interpretation of the State are not found in specialized studies, but rather,
even though in a relatively marginal form, in analyses on economic development, industrialization, and urbanization, problems which have been
the subject of special concern by Brazilian scholars. I wish to make special
reference to two recent books upon which the present paper is widely
based: Celso Furtado, *Dialéctica do Desenvolvimento,* Rio de Janeiro, Edi-

tora Fundo de Cultura, 1964; and Fernando Henrique Cardoso, *Empresario Industrial e Desenvolvimento Econômico*, São Paulo, Difusão Européia do livro, 1964. In addition to these works, the studies on class consciousness and the working-class movement effected in Brazil by Alain Touraine and Daniel Pecaut are of critical importance ("Working Class Consciousness and Economic Development in Latin America," *Studies in Comparative International Development*, Vol. 3, No. 4, 1967–68).

[1] Gino Germani, *Política y Sociedad en una Época de Transición: De la Sociedad Tradicional a la Sociedad de Masas*, Buenos Aires, Editorial Paidós, 1962.

[2] Celso Furtado, op. cit., Second Part, Chapter 2, Section I.

[3] From an economic point of view, the industrialization process is limited by the traditional structures, in terms of the possibility of creating an internal market and in terms of import capacity.

[4] It is possible that a detailed historical analysis of the period ending in 1930 might prove the adequacy, in the Brazilian case, of one of the most important aspects of the "limited participation" democracy model worked out by Germani and which according to him can be applied to all situations in which underdevelopment obtains. Indeed, perhaps these middle sectors, which ultimately brought oligarchy to a crisis, can be characterized as one of the decisive social factors accounting for the stability exhibited by the oligarchic regime during three decades. This hypothesis matches some aspects of the condition of political ambiguity of the traditional middle sectors.

[5] During the stage of the struggle against dictatorship, the National Democratic Union (UDN), which is presently a Right-wing party, had the appearance of being, not a party, but a wide democratic front.

[6] Alain Touraine, op. cit., p. 87.

[7] "Labor unions are then not so much an instrument in the hands of the working class but rather the expression of an indirect and involuntary participation in power . . ." (Alain Touraine, op. cit., p. 88).

[8] Populism as compared to nationalism might be characterized as a circumstantial and spontaneous expression of the process of incorporation of the masses to the political regime, while nationalism appears as the total and ideological expression of this same process.

[9] For a study on this political campaign, see Francisco C. Weffort, "Raizes Sociais do Populismo en São Paulo," 1963 (mimeograph).

[10] "The process of formation of an industrial capitalism in Brazil encountered obstacles of a structural nature, which cannot be overcome within the present institutional framework and through the means usually utilized by the ruling classes. With respect to both the external sector and the agricultural and fiscal sectors, there are obvious contradictions between the way in which the economy operates under present conditions and the requisites necessary to maintain a high rate of investment. Only with the emergence of unforeseeable factors, such as a sudden improvement in the relationship of exchange, could the present trends be modified for some time." (Celso Furtado, op. cit., p. 128; also Second Part, Chapter 2, Sections III, IV and V).

[11] Fernando Henrique Cardoso considers two phases as sociologically important in the process of industrialization. In the first, the aspiration for progress and national independence "accounted for the definition of

goals which allowed the long-term achievement of structural changes." In the second phase, there occurred the penetration of the existing industrial sector owing to the models and practices spread by the "pressures in favor of development." Nonetheless, it is important to note that "the total support by the bourgeoisie of the State-oriented values which guided the movements toward national emancipation" did not take place. Cf. Fernando Henrique Cardoso, op. cit., pp. 84–85.

[12] The industrial entrepreneur, for example, does not identify with the government, but subjectively considers himself as part of the People, and as such demands protection and government support. Thus, "the entrepreneur derives the maximum advantage from belonging to a class which is economically dominant without quite being so politically." Cf. Fernando Henrique Cardoso, op. cit., p. 168.

[13] "Since the ideological position of the agricultural sector is oriented toward the defense of the institutional status quo on the basis of the secure positions which it holds within the legislative power, the more reactionary latifundist group has always achieved to move within a wide front in which its interests are confused with those of agriculture as a whole and also of those who have the ownership of the means of production. For this reason it is difficult for the industrial capitalist class to grasp the contradictions between the interests of industrialization and those of the groups which control the land used for the production of food." (Celso Furtado, op. cit., p. 123.)

12

JULIO COTLER

The Mechanics
of Internal Domination
and Social Change in Peru

Peru exhibits two very different and coexisting patterns of social relations. It is a society characterized by a structural dualism.[1] This often-cited image is based on socio-cultural contrasts between the coast and the sierra, the two most important regions of the country.

Those sectors of economic activity with the highest productivity, such as fishing, agriculture for export, manufacturing, and financial services, are concentrated on the coast. This concentration is reflected in the income and occupational mobility of the population. In 1961, 47 per cent of the total population of the country lived on the coast and contributed 67 per cent of the national income, while the proportions in the sierra amounted to 46 per cent and 34 per cent respectively. As a result, the average per capita income on the coast was 23 per cent above the national average, while in the sierra it was 29 per cent below it.[2] In the same year, 69 per cent of the coastal population resided in urban areas, in contrast to only 29 per cent in the sierra. 79 per cent of the coastal population over fifteen was literate, versus 47 per cent of that in the sierra within the same age group.[3] This contributed in part to the fact that in 1966, 69 per cent of the electorate was

407

from coastal departments, and only 26 per cent was from the sierra.

Most of the newspapers, journals, and books (domestic and imported) are published and sold on the coast. Most radio and television stations are located on the coast. In 1966, only a scant 0.4 per cent of the television sets existing in the country were to be found in two cities of the sierra.[4] All these factors lead to an intense intra- and inter-regional communication on the coast.

The Spanish conquerors carried out an early eradication of native culture on the coast. At the turn of the century, the coast became integrated into the international capitalist market, thus growing further apart from Indian cultural patterns. The result was a variation on Western colonial culture, known as "creole culture." [5]

These characteristics have given rise to a conception of the coast as a region of "Western modernizing development," while the sierra continues to be branded as a "traditional, underdeveloped region."

With the exception of mining centers, the predominant activities in the sierra are agriculture and cattle-breeding, characterized by a low rate of productivity. This means that a great part of the population participates but scantily in the internal market and lives in widely disseminated areas.

The limited access to the sierra region and its preindustrial forms of production account for extremely restricted internal communication and limited acculturation. There are vast pockets which allow for the survival of the *Quechua* and *Aymará* languages and the traditional social forms of organization with which those languages are associated. This situation is largely due to the fact that in the sierra public investment is six times smaller than on the coast.[6]

On the coast there is relative diversification and occupational mobility, in conjunction with the development of industrial patterns of production and property. In the sierra preindustrial patterns predominate, with the exception of mining centers, which are enterprises organized and directed from abroad.

Contrary to the situation on the coast, the landholding system in the sierra exhibits two preindustrial patterns of organi-

408

zation: Indian communities and latifundia. The former constitute corporate organizations based on kinship which, through common utilization of land and water, maintain political-religious functions and ties of internal solidarity. Latifundia are characterized by the feudal character of social relations. These establishments, which emphasize ascriptive criteria, further the continuance of obsolete social and cultural patterns.

The disparity noted between coast and sierra is true to the extent that it does not discriminate internally originated differences in each one of these regions, and endeavors to emphasize the relationship between a geographical region and socio-cultural patterns of existence.

This stereotyped image gives rise to a perception of the country as presenting strikingly opposed social situations. Moreover, Peru is often viewed as a non-integrated nation, the sierra being considered marginal and the coastal region representing the country. This concept of a lack of national integration has led some authors to view the country as a social archipelago, or as an inarticulate, plural or heterogeneous society.[7]

These concepts are useful to illustrate internal differences through various indicators, such as those mentioned above. Nevertheless, it is important to point out that this perspective overlooks the relations between the regions and their social strata, insofar as they are affected—though in different degrees—by one historical process.

Although it would be inaccurate to state that the population of the sierra is not incorporated into the life of the nation, this must be qualified by pointing out the context of social relations of dependence. The existing terms of interaction between the two regions and their respective social sectors are unfavorable to the sierra, insofar as its population does not have access to the opportunities and resources in the global society. This does not mean that as a whole the sierra is marginal with respect to the country, but rather that it is *made* marginal by a sector of the latter. In Frank's words:

> . . . this "marginal" or "floating" population is in the process of becoming, or in some instances, is fully integrated into the society in a way which prejudices its welfare and opportunities

409

to develop, and which defines the urban or rural economic sector, social position, and economic region or locality as "underdeveloped."

These considerations suggest that Latin America is not a "dual" society, but rather an integrated one, and that many of its members are not so much marginal as they are integrated in a way that prejudices their most vital interests. . . .[8]

Some writers have suggested that just as relations between developed and underdeveloped countries are set in metropolitan-colonial terms, the same obtains between the developed and underdeveloped regions of a country.[9] In addition to this regional stratification, in each one of the regions stratification relationships of the same nature are produced and successively repeated in a branching pattern. Thus, developed social sectors may include metropolitan and colonial social sectors, which may in turn have, as a whole, their own area of influence, thus performing a metropolitan role with respect to other social sectors.

The structure of relations between the developing metropolis and the underdeveloped periphery of the international market appears, in the course of the historical development of Latin America, to have been duplicated within the continent, within each of its countries, and indeed within many of the latter's internal regions. Within each of these there developed a metropolitan center and a corresponding underdeveloped periphery. At the same time these national metropolises, as is the case with the world metropolises, maintain structured economic relations with their respective provincial peripheries, which is an extension of the relationship between the world metropolises and themselves. A similar relationship can be observed in turn at the regional level, whose commercial centers are in an economically disadvantageous position, being in the periphery with respect to national and international metropolises—yet performing a metropolitan role in terms of their respective peripheral rural hinterlands. The metropolis-periphery relationship at the national, regional, and in certain cases sectoral levels, no less than at the international level, exhibits a transfer of capital from the periphery to the metropolis, as well as the determination of the fortunes of the periphery by the metropolis.[10]

Stavenhagen, in his description of dualist societies in Latin America, points out that the underdeveloped regions of these countries remain in this state because of the human exploitation in underdeveloped areas: "The underdeveloped regions of Latin American countries perform the role of internal colonies. Instead of stating the problem of Latin America in terms of dualism, it would be better to speak of internal colonialism." [11] In the same sense, an expert in Mayor Lindsay's administration in New York City declared that "Harlem has many of the features of underdeveloped countries. . . . The basic similarity between Harlem and an underdeveloped nation is that the local population does not control the area's economy, and therefore most of the internally generated income is rapidly drained out. That money is not returned or applied to any local community improvement." [12]

Various writers have described the deprivation of Indian sectors in Latin America—in the Mezo-American region as well as in the central Andean region—on the basis of the dependence and domination imposed upon the Indians by the immediate "superior" element, the ladino or mestizo. [13] Bourricaud refers to the status of the Indian in terms of his dependence upon the mestizo. Stavenhagen and González Casanova define the status of the Indians as that of a colonized class or a *Lumpenproletariat* with respect to the ladinos.

Wolf points out that the marginality of the Central American communities stems from the Indians' unwillingness to establish relations with the ladinos, inasmuch as it might entail patterns of domination. [14] Bourricaud, on the other hand, defines the Indian community as essentially alien with respect to the mestizo. [15] The Regional Plan for the Development of Southern Peru states that the Indians "in many cases appear to have conducted a war of exhaustion, consisting of a passive resistance, or of retiring into areas where there is a minimum of contact with the higher classes." [16]

These authors have endeavored to explain the relations between metropolitan and peripheral social strata—without explaining how this situation is linked with the metropolitan region and its different social sectors. In other words, if, as stated by

411

Bourricaud and the Plan del Sur among others, the Puno mestizo is the dominant element in that circumscription, the question could be raised as to what extent his status is sustained by and at the same time dependent upon the metropolitan area and social strata established in the coastal region. And if such relations exist, which are the mechanisms that furnish the mestizos with such regional standing? And what consequences does that situation entail for the social system as a whole, and for the coastal peripheral elements in particular?

The purpose of this analysis is to provide some tentative answers to these questions, within the Peruvian context, on the basis of bibliographical sources and in some cases of primary sources.

INDIANS AND MESTIZOS

Bourricaud characterizes Indians and mestizos as socio-cultural groups having their own particular attributes and constituting a sort of caste. These attributes refer to traits such as language, place of residence, consumption, occupation, as well as the prestige of same. Thus, the Indian speaks only Quechua or Aymará, is always bound to rural areas, has a distinctive style of consumption (generally characterized by lesser ties with the market), and is always a shepherd or farmer. In other words, he fills positions of minor social prestige. Conversely, the mestizo always speaks Spanish and masters some other aboriginal tongue, resides in or is attached to urban areas, his consumption is linked to the market, and he is never a shepherd or peon. Nobody would classify a lawyer or a physician in the Indian group, nor an army or police officer. Bourricaud points out:

> Occupations which do not require previous instruction are regarded as the exclusive property of the Indians. Inversely, we could say that the fact of being white or a *'misti'* is incompatible with certain activities. The peon of the hacienda is always an Indian. Also the *'misti,'* even of the lowest status, will have a position which confers upon him a minimum of authority; he will be at least a warden, or a gatherer. Should he descend in the social scale to the status of peon, he would suddenly find him-

412

self in the same status as the Indian. We would even go as far as to assert that an Indian is never the holder of a position that entails high prestige. . . ." [17]

Likewise, in the Plan del Sur it is stated that "in Puno there is a pronounced dichotomy between the mass (85 per cent) of the population who live in rural areas, speak an indigenous language, perform manual tasks and are regarded as a separate class (almost a caste), and the dominant urban society of three intermediate classes which participate to different degrees in the Peruvian economy and culture." [18]

But, as these writers point out, within the Indian group there are internal differences, if one considers the institutional framework within which the Indian status is located. Though the Indian is always a shepherd or farmer, these activities can be performed within the hacienda or in the Indian community, which involve different patterns of social control in the mestizo-Indian relationship.

Among the mestizos there are different social gradings based on class criteria, such as education, occupational prestige, income, place of residence, etc., but they always have one common trait: the domination of the Indian peasant. The distinctions between Indians and mestizos are therefore discontinuous in nature, since the latter, despite their internal differences, are characterized by their control over the Indian.

In 1961, the region commonly referred to as "Mancha India," which included the departments of Ancash, Apurímac, Ayacucho, Cuzco, Huancavelica, and Puno, comprised 29 per cent of the country's total population. Of this group 87 per cent of those over five years of age communicated with each other in an Indian language. Of the economically active population, 69 per cent was engaged in agriculture and cattle-breeding, whereas the average for such occupations in the rest of the country was only 42 per cent.

These occupational conditions entail a reduced diversification and are reflected in the average income of the population of the area, which is 39 per cent lower than the national average.

The agricultural and cattle-breeding activities were carried on within a system of property characterized by latifundism and

TABLE I Distribution of Landholdings in "Mancha India" and in the Remainder of the Country.

Hectares	Mancha India		Rest of Country	
	Productive Units %	Hectares %	Productive Units %	Hectares %
0– 4	87.5	7.8	79.3	5.8
5– 9	6.6	2.7	11.4	3.3
10– 19	2.5	2.0	4.6	2.9
20– 99	1.9	4.6	3.5	6.2
100–499	0.5	8.5	0.7	7.2
500– +	0.4	60.7	0.2	65.4
Within incorporated communities	0.03	13.1	0.03	8.8
	99.43	99.4	99.73	99.6

Source: Primer Censo Nacional Agropecuario, Lima, 1961.

a high fragmentation of productive units—a situation which does not differ much from that existing in the rest of the country.

The Haciendas

The haciendas of this region are mainly used for sheep-grazing and, in a complementary form, to agriculture. While wool is destined primarily for the international market, mutton is shipped to the large cities in the country. It would appear that agricultural production is aimed chiefly at local consumption or limited commercial circles. In certain cases, however, it has an essential function, especially in the case of haciendas in subtropical valleys, where the cultivation of *coca* and of sugar cane (the latter for the production of vodka) is intended for consumption by the Indians, while coffee and tea are destined for the international market.

The abundance of manpower in the area—due to a landless or minifundist population—contributes to make it cheap, and thereby intensively used with a correspondingly low capitalization. Such an abundance of cheap manpower explains why re-investment is chiefly aimed at increasing production and not labor productivity.

As a result of this structure of property and production, the population is scattered—especially in hacienda zones—with only a few important population centers in the area. In 1961 there were only six cities with over 20,000 inhabitants, housing but 61 per cent of the total population—while 87 per cent resided in centers with less than 2,000 inhabitants, contrasting with an average in the rest of the country of 31 per cent and 60 per cent respectively.[19]

The conditions of the structure of property and production, together with the high dispersion of the population and the lack of occupational diversification, favor the existing relations between mestizos and Indians, and do not allow for alternatives to the hacienda system.[20]

The manpower of landless Indians is employed in the hacienda of the region through a peculiar form of "hooking" generally referred to as *colonato*, in which the mestizo owner offers the Indian worker the use of a plot of land for cultivation or grazing, conditioned upon the latter's paying him back through the fulfillment of certain obligations. The obligations that the Indian is committed to are varied: unremunerated work in the land of the hacienda during a certain number of days per week, grazing of the cattle of the hacienda, domestic service at the farmhouse or in the urban residence of the boss; selling to the owner the produce of his small plot at a price established by the owner, as well as any surpluses that the Indian may have been able to achieve, etc. This last duty is fundamental in the case of haciendas in the subtropical valleys. This enables the landowner not only to recruit workers almost free, but also to monopolize the marketing of high-priced goods such as coffee and tea.

This relationship established between landlord and worker determines that the latter be in a permanent state of insecurity, unable to anticipate with any degree of certainty the character of his duties, and with no time to accomplish any task of his own: "At plowing and potato-digging time they work for the hacienda a whole month, and therefore have no time left to tend their plots." [21] The workers' possibilities to migrate temporarily from the hacienda are severely limited, as this would imply a nonfulfillment of their duties—with the consequent loss of their rights over the plot of land they use.

The situation of uncertainty which characterizes the tenant-farmer has led some authors to consider that his state of mind probably verges on the pathological. His constant fear that the boss might expel him from the plot or take possession of his live-stock, his fear that, through illness, he will be unable to fulfill his duties or tend his plot, surrounds the Indian with a complex of fears and repressions.[22]

> The Vicos manor serf suffered from a number of forms of fear—so many, and often so serious, that we entertain some doubts as to whether the local subculture really worked out effective escapes from danger that permitted the serfs to enjoy a state of relaxation at any time. In the most general terms of personal interaction, the serf regarded all human relationships as hostile, since they were basically power-oriented.[23]

In this situation the boss is perceived as the all-powerful source, whose good graces the Indian must woo in order to maintain his unstable position. Because the Indian has no other possi-bilities of livelihood within his reach he must accept the asym-metrical ties of reciprocity proposed by the landlord. Toward this end, he seeks to establish paternalistic ties with the boss and also with the figures of authority in general, so as to commit them to a situation which might place him in a preferential status with respect to the other tenants. If he gets the boss to be godfather to one of his children, he may have fewer duties to perform, and there may be a chance that he obtain a certain degree of indul-gence in case of nonfulfillment of his duties or, at best, he might even be taken as the boss's man.[24] The landlord, for his own part, uses this paternalistic relationship to strengthen the ten-ant's ties of personal loyalty—highlighting the latter's excep-tional status and thereby constituting himself as the single source of identification of his tenant-farmers—thus avoiding the forma-tion of class identifications.[25]

> There is a common ideology between landlords and peasants (*japas*). The former regard themselves as protectors of the Indians, whom they call their "little ones"; they offer them eco-nomic security in times of famine, and social security when they are summoned to appear before the local authorities on charges of misdeeds or misdemeanors. The Indians call the land-lord *patrón,* and sometimes look upon him as a father and

protector. They do not feel scorned . . . when regarded as servants; on the contrary, on certain occasions they identify with their landlords.[26]

With these conditions of control and social identification, cultural forms proscribe patterns of aggressivity toward the boss and prescribe instead that these be directed toward the other tenant-farmers competing for the boss's favors. As a result the Indian views his well-being in terms of the deprivation of other workers.[27] This provokes a situation of distrust and envy, characteristic of the "familial amorality" described by Banfield, which contributes to social fragmentation.[28] The Indians' lack of social articulation—encouraged by the authority figure on the basis of services and personal rewards which tend to divide the tenant population—determines the establishment of dyadic [29] and asymmetric relationships between landlord and tenant,[30] suggesting the existence of multiple disconnected radii which converge on one single vertix.

This situation of structural and normative dependence of the Indian upon the mistis, gives rise to considerable social and cultural distance between both sectors of the population. For if the mestizo considers the Indians an animal which most resembles man, the Indian, on his part, internalizes his subordinate condition. Thus, of 499 Indians interviewed in six communities and one hacienda of the department of Cuzco, 52 per cent agreed that "Indians are born to serve and obey the misti.[31]

The Indian Communities

Together with the hacienda, the Indian community is the other type of rural social organization characteristic of the area. Indian communities, in contrast to what happens in the hacienda, exhibit a high population density and incipient occupational differentiation.

Indian communities are characterized by the internal solidarity ties that exist between their members, which encourage them to regard themselves as particular collectivities. The identifications developed in these centers have a local familial character, as indicated by the fact that an individual belonging to a certain community may be recognized by certain distinctive aspects of his clothing.

Despite the existence of such internal solidarity, the situation of the communities continues to be precarious. Indian communities are generally located in the most barren lands, on hillsides with a large degree of erosion. As a consequence of the distribution of communal plots, there is a high degree of fragmentation and dispersion of the land, which is the chief, if not the only source of capitalization. This forces the free peasants to seek land in neighboring areas, and there are cases of status combinations, such as when middle-sized peasants rent land from the haciendas, which they in turn sublet to other tenant-farmers who are thus committed to render service both to the hacienda and to the commoner-renter.[32] Yet another arrangement is that of a community collectively integrated into the hacienda system, which has been called a "dependent or captive community." [33] Another alternative for free peasants facing the problem of land shortage is to emigrate. This does not affect their rights or affiliation in the community, in contrast to the situation of tenant-farmers.[34]

Thus the communities in Mancha India constitute a reservoir of manpower for the haciendas whenever the latter want to extend their areas of work or replace any number of tenant-farmers.

The intense fragmentation and dispersion of the commoners' farmland may incline them to a permanent state of anxiety, expressed by manifold internal conflicts. These circumstances account for the existing discord between communities, to which must be added their ethnocentric identifications, all of which favors the development of endless lawsuits.[35] Moreover, with no new occupational opportunities, these circumstances are aggravated by population growth.

Under these conditions a new form of Indian dependence is generated: this time with respect to the mestizo. In order to resolve lawsuits, the Indian woos the favors of a mestizo to obtain (through the latter's good offices) a favorable judicial ruling —since the Indian does not speak Spanish, is illiterate, and there is a generalized belief that juridical proceedings are not subjected to universal criteria. Thus, of 499 interviewed in Cuzco, 56 per cent considered that judges base their rulings on personal influence and on the amount of money paid by plaintiffs.[36]

> The Indian seeks the (mestizo) middle-class member as a protector and, above all, as an influential factor to tilt justice on his side in his all-too-frequent lawsuits with other Indians or with people of higher strata.[37]

The mestizo's role as middleman and "protector" of the Indian extends not only to judiciary cases, but to all the relationships that the Indian must establish with official institutions. Under such conditions, commoners are in effect clients of the mestizos, whom they must reward in some way. They are tacitly committed to sell them their products, thus becoming dependent upon *atajadores* ("intercepters"). They are recruited to perform tasks of a private nature gratis, and "public" labor in district capitals under the pretense of retribution for favors that it is in the hands of the mestizos to grant. Such recruitment is carried out through the indigenous authorities of the haciendas or communities. Thus, in contrast to what some "indigenists" assume, community autonomy is spurious in that Indian authorities channelize the landlord's or the district authorities' orders and the requests for favors—in addition to the fact that the commoners are also clients of the town mestizos.

> In the communities or in the haciendas, the Indians have their own traditional authorities designated annually by the commoners, whose duty it is to maintain relationships within the system in force. They receive orders from the *mistis* and see that they are carried out, and seek to obtain the mestizo's favors.[38]

As a result of the structural and normative conditions of dependence in which tenant-farmers and commoners find themselves with regard to the mestizos, the predominant personality trait is one of fatalism. They also exhibit political lethargy and an inability to modify such a situation, since designs of the mestizos appear to them as uncontrollable, a perception which is manifested through servile behavior usual among subordinate groups.

THE MESTIZOS AND THE NATIONAL SYSTEM

Even though property is a sufficient condition to establish a relation to domination over the Indians, this condition is not necessary since, as already seen, those commoners who are in no direct relation with the hacienda system are nonetheless equally involved in ties of dependence. The necessary and sufficient requirements of the system of domination described are a function of the mestizo's access to the system of authority through his knowledge of Spanish, and through literacy which allows him to elect or be elected to and to designate or be designated to fill positions within the system of national authority or within the public administration—thus securing State resources to legitimize his lineage and his domination of the Indian mass.

As stated above, the mestizo is not only the owner or administrator of the hacienda: he is also lawyer, middleman, judge, governor, policeman, trader. As expressed by Bourricaud: ". . . the *misti,* even of the lowest strata, occupies a position which bestows upon him at least a minimum of authority. . . ."

Monolinguism and Illiteracy

In 1961 there were in Peru 1.8 million inhabitants over five years of age who spoke Quechua or Aymará, 87 per cent of whom were concentrated in Mancha India, constituting 19 per cent of the total population of the country within this age group.[39] These departments, especially Huancavelica, Apurímac and Ayacucho, head all departments in their degree of illiteracy, with a correlation of .84 between literacy and ability to speak Spanish.[40]

Despite the relative weight of Indian languages among the population of the country, those who speak them are discriminated against in all spheres of the institutional life of Peru. The educational system ignores the Quechua and Aymará languages and imposes Spanish. Teachers sent to Mancha India usually do not speak Indian tongues, and if the teachers do, being of mixed racial origin, they only use them in personal relations in which they invoke their privileged status. The help rendered by govern-

Internal Domination and Social Change in Peru

ment and university institutions for the study of Indian languages is insignificant, and the little research in this field is subsidized by foreign foundations.

TABLE II   Distribution of Population in Terms of Total and Rural Illiteracy and by Degree of Functional Literacy.

Departments	Percentage of illiterate adults, 15 years or older in the total population	Percentage of illiterate adults, 15 years or older in rural areas	Percentage of functional literacy
Ancash	51	82	19
Apurímac	76	86	10
Ayacucho	72	81	10
Cuzco	72	80	16
Huancavelica	66	88	9
Puno	64	66	10
Average	65	81	12
National average	39	78	31

Source: Censo Nacional de Población, volume II, 1961.

Indians themselves appear to recognize that their lack of knowledge of the Spanish languages and illiteracy are associated with their status. Of 495 interviewed in Cuzco, 76 per cent felt that if Indians had the same level of education as mestizos they would be on equal terms to perform any occupation; and 91 per cent agreed that "through education a man can achieve what he wants." [11] Mario Vázquez likewise testifies:

Vicosinos recognise the importance of the Spanish language as an instrument of communication and knowledge, for at present Spanish is the chief barrier between the Indian and the mestizo, and is perhaps one of the causes of Vicos' isolation and cultural backwardness. The following confirm our statement: "I am afraid of going to other towns because I do not speak Spanish. . . . I am ashamed of being unable to answer when spoken to in Spanish. . . . Many people scoff at us when we cannot answer their questions. . . . they keep saying, why do you come here if you cannot speak Spanish? If I could only speak Spanish I would not be afraid because I would feel equal to the others.

. . . Mestizos have better opportunities to make money because they work more with their eyes, while we are tied up in the fields. . . . If I knew Spanish perhaps I would be more courageous and the educated would not humiliate me." [42]

Public administration lacks the necessary mechanisms to communicate with this population. The Ministry of Labor and Communities has only one official Quechua or Aymará translator at the Indigenist Institute of Peru. Regarding the administration of justice, the situation is truly pathetic, as the Indian defendants have no possibility of understanding their cases as they are carried out in a language unknown to them. It goes without saying that the Indians lack the means to learn of their rights, and as a consequence are at the mercy of the mestizos, their obligated middlemen.

The Electoral System

Due to Peru's electoral regulations, which stipulate that only literate individuals have the right to elect or be elected, the Indian population has no access to the polls or to true representation. Nonetheless, in accordance with those regulations, they are considered in the computation of the number of representatives that each area sends to Congress—for which the total population of each department is taken into account. Thus, Mancha India, which holds 20 percent of the total population of the country, has 14 per cent of the electoral population—since only one out of every five of its inhabitants over twenty years of age is entitled to vote. This fraction of the population, however, elects fifty of the 185 representatives who constitute Congress. Likewise, these departments require an average of five times less electors to elect a representative than those required for the department of Lima, which has the highest proportion of electoral population in the country—86 per cent of its population over 20 years of age are electors.

This electoral mechanism, besides contributing to discrimination against the population of Mancha India, discriminates against the peasant population of the country as whole, be it in sierra or coastal departments: 78 per cent of the rural population over fifteen years of age is illiterate. Thus, there is a positive rank correlation of .83 between the economically active population dedicated to agricultural activities and the illiterate population—and a negative correlation of .87 between the population dedicated to agricultural labor and the electoral population, at the national level. In 1965 the electoral population was of about two million. At the same time there were six million people of voting age.

Ignorance of the Spanish language, the strong incidence of rural illiteracy, the dispersion which characterizes the population of Mancha India, the situation of structural and normative dependence that the Indian suffers in relation to the mestizo, are all factors which suggest that both the electors and the elected are mestizos. In this way the mestizo authority is institutionalized and the Indian population placed outside of the institutional resources.

Gamonalismo

Through knowledge of the Spanish language, education, and through restriction of these resources for the Indian population, mestizos are able to control economic, political, juridical, repressive, and cultural resources: they are the representatives and senators, hacienda owners or administrators, departmental prefects, sub-prefects, and governors; they are likewise the judges and teachers, dominating all authority spheres, a fact which defines the gamonal, or landlord, system.

Mestizo domination over the Indian separates the two along caste-like lines. Both the mestizo and the Indian sectors have a group of reference or of affiliation, and belonging to each involves well-defined values, activities, and relations. From this it may be concluded that mestizo activities in Congress, the bureaucracy, tribunals, etc., are aimed at strengthening the position of the group.

Thus, mestizos make decisions at local and regional levels —and through these at the national level—without having to take into consideration a dominated mass incapable of autonomous initiatives or decisions.

This privatization of power exists at different levels. The

423

mestizo group is free to act in accordance with its own initiatives, even re-interpreting dispositions which could reduce the range of its attributions.

> In the Chawaytiri hacienda (Cuzco), as a result of a movement which brought about tenant-farmer syndicalization, district authorities appointed a literate tenant-farmer as lieutenant-governor. . . . Upon his visiting the hacienda owner in order to inform him of his appointment, he was told by the owner: "Who do you think you are, to have yourself appointed lieutenant-governor. . . . I do not know you. . . . You should know that in this hacienda there can be no lieutenant-governor or any other authority for that matter, so go and paper the walls of your house with your appointment. In the hacienda the only authorities are those appointed by me.[43]

Moreover, the owner or his administrator, even without holding any political office, through the control they exercise over the tenant-farmers and their affinity and closeness with those in authority, in fact perform such functions:

> Until three years ago, the landlord was the maximum political, social, and juridical authority. When quarrels broke out, theft, or even crime was perpetrated, the administrator or his representative were the first to intervene. If the case warranted it, it was then transmitted to the competent authority. Traditional local authorities were appointed by and took oath before the administrator; there was no need to travel to the Pisac governorship in order to receive a ruling on the case.[44]

This privatization of power has geographic connotations. Landázuri states that at La Convención the district capital is but a village within the hacienda, which is the real seat of authority.[45]

Due to lack of social diversification in Mancha India, and also to a lack of peasant mass articulation, whole regions are under gamonal domination, thus the popular saying: "Abancay is the only hacienda with a Prefecture." (Abancay is a city of 9,000 inhabitants.) A district, province, or even a department may be dominated by a single family or group of families.[46]

There are ample possibilities for the mestizo group to expand its economic resources, either through illegal coercive means, or through legal means. Of particular importance is the renting of land owned by the government, religious congregations, public charities, universities, schools, etc. In fact, extensive holdings belonging to these institutions are rented in public auctions at rates which have not changed for several decades. Thus, in mid-1966 the Ministry of Public Education discovered that it owned nearly a million hectares which were rented at ridiculously low rates. In order to participate in the auctions it is necessary, among other things, to be literate, to be the holder of a voting card, and to possess a commercial guarantee—requisites which only mestizos of certain status are able to achieve.

The Bureaucratic Clientele

One of the manifestations of the rigidity of the social system existing in Mancha India is evidenced by the well preserved consistency of the criteria of classification of the population. Wealth (land and/or cattle), education, place of residence, type and prestige of occupation, and scope of influence remain constantly associated. Indians do not possess land or are but very small landowners, are always agricultural laborers, are monolingual and illiterate, reside in rural areas, and their scope of personal influence is limited to their fellows or relatives. In contrast, as the mestizo moves upward along the social scale, the wealthier he is, the higher his level of education, the less time he dedicates to activities related to agriculture; he resides in increasingly important urban areas, filling positions of political influence of increasing scope.

> The political participation of the social classes is circumscribed by the geographical categories where their personal influence exists. The lowest class (Indians) is circumscribed by the community and the neighborhood; the low class (called *chola* class) plays a dynamic role in village politics, while the middle class acts in provincial politics, with a good degree of participation in departmental politics.[47]

The big landowners reside in cities, departmental capitals such as Arequipa, Cuzco, Puno, Huaraz, or in Lima, holding important positions in the public administration, magistrate, or Congress, dedicating themselves to a lesser degree to trading. Different authors point out the existence in provincial cities of Mancha India, of a white group, with lineage, wealth, education, and positions of prestige, closely tied to Lima.[48]

The Pisac district, for example, in the department of Cuzco, has 10,000 inhabitants, of which 84 per cent are Indians.[49] The people of the district recognize the existence of four social strata: landowners, mestizos, the Cholada, and the Indians. In the district there are ten haciendas, one of them the property of a religious congregation, and fifteen communities spread over the hillsides, which, administratively, constitute extensions of the district capital. The landowners rent or own the haciendas. They do not reside in the district capital but in the departmental capital, occupying positions as judges, high functionaries of the public administration, or as university professors—their holdings being rented and managed by mestizos. The latter constitute the high class of the town, jointly with the small and medium-sized landowners, traders, and public officials. They maintain close contact with the high class at provincial or departmental levels—for they must remain "in their good graces" if they wish to continue their climb up the social ladder.[50] Through the electoral mechanism and the particularistic pattern in which juridical and political authorities are designated, the Pisac mestizos become political figures, owing to the support of high class mestizos.

> Taraco is a district . . . and as such, authority within its jurisdiction is exercised by a governor who is appointed by the departmental prefect, having been proposed by the subprefect of the province. The latter suggests three "neighbors," one of which is chosen to fill the post in question. Ostensibly, the chief requisite in order to qualify for the post of governor is to be a "prominent neighbor" in the district, *i.e.*, a prominent mestizo residing in the district capital, who enjoys certain prestige amongst the group constituted by mestizos; but in fact the man who gets elected is he who has the best relationship with sub-prefect or prefect.[51]

High-placed officials secure appointments for teachers, post office employees, judges, prefects and sub-prefects, irrigation administrators, etc., namely, the key positions at local and regional levels, and thus take care of individuals who wish to promote their status through politics. It is understood that the appointees perform their jobs in such a way as to avoid severing such ties, for this would leave them in a helpless situation.

This system of recruitment and promotion in the public administration is not limited to the level of local or regional decisions, since the big landowners place ("recommend" is the currently employed euphemism) their allies in positions connected with decision-making at the national level. It could be surmised that in the public administration of Peru there exists the phenomenon of "clientelism," similar to the *panhelinas* of Brazil,[52] since the livelihood of a bureaucrat depends on the personal protection he is able to secure from an influential person—who must be rewarded in an equally personal way. Influential figures take it upon themselves to distribute favors among their kin or close friends with understanding that they, once placed in key positions, will be of service not only to reinforce their position, but that they will also help their protectors in contacting new entities, thus expanding their economic and political opportunities.

If the recruitment of the bureaucracy and of individuals in positions of authority is carried out among the clients of powerful figures, it may be concluded that the bureaucracy is characterized not only by its origins, but also by its class orientation—and that identification with their patrons and the distance that separates them from the dominated sectors, favors their association with the situation and with the culture of domination. In other words, the value orientations of public employees are characterized by their discrimination against the Indians and of all underprivileged sectors generally.

Although favoritism in the public administration is generalized all over the country and at all social levels, it undoubtedly loses its aspect of clientelism as the social environment presents a greater diversification and the social mobility of the population increases. In fact, under these conditions it is possible to alternate between different sources of influence, and the population is able to develop institutional resources which limit the power of patronal figures.

NEUTRALIZATION OF "PARTICIPANTS"

The participant sectors, or sectors integrated within the national society, namely, manufacturing, mining, and agricultural workers; governmental and private-sector employees; professionals, who live in urban sectors with access to education and to the polls, who are incorporated to the internal market and participate in unions or political organizations; in sum, those who have means of representation, have achieved considerable gains with regard to the unorganized peasant mass, the Indian mass, and the unemployed population of the cities.

The socio-cultural distance between the participant and marginal sectors explains why the gains that the former are trying to secure are exclusively for themselves. They ignore any type of massive redistribution which could immediately affect their consumption. Their aspirations follow the life style of the higher classes.

Segmentarian Incorporation

The privileges of the system of domination are expanded by incorporating segments of the population to that system, extending the number of social sectors which directly or indirectly benefit from the peasant marginality. Thus it can be argued that though the basic problem underdeveloped societies confront is that of creating ways and means for new population sectors to gain access to social and political resources—it might be added that to the extent that such incorporation is partial or in progressive steps it favors the maintenance of the system of domination as it expands, neutralizing the activities of those promoted by alienating them from the marginal sectors.[53]

In seeking to improve the income of their members, unions gain many advantages at the expense of non-organized sectors. The pressure they originate in enterprises often brings about a greater technicalization and a stabilization in the number of employees.

The reduction or at least the strict limitation of individuals employed is very probably the counterpart of the advantage gained by the higher-paid and better organized agricultural workers. Their privileged status is very high in comparison with that of their non-unionized fellows—even more so if it be considered that those who might have found employment in the exploitation of sugar and have been unable to do so due to technification, have had to remain in their miserable plots.[54]

Although unionized workers have achieved a certain degree of autonomy from patronal constraints, as evidenced by benefits gained such as social security, improved working conditions and higher salaries than the non-unionized,[55] paradoxically, they have fallen into new patterns of dependence as their demands for improvement and benefits are directed exclusively toward the unionized—without taking into consideration the national context. For example, the agricultural unions on the northern coast and the central sierra mining unions, after tough and protracted struggles, have achieved relatively high wages and improved standards of living through legal dispositions that bind enterprises to provide lodging, medical assistance, education, etc., which transform such enterprises into company towns." Consequently, leaving the enterprise would entail loss of the right to use those public services, which are in fact private, inasmuch as they are a "property" of the enterprise.[56] In fact there are still places in which it is necessary to produce a special permit to gain access to them.

To the extent that such organized sectors do not promote an opening of the system, but only particularized benefits, they determine the inflexibility of their own possibilities in terms of market consumption, production, and employment, thus creating a low rate of occupational mobility, all the more evident because there is a growing demand for employment. Thus, recruitment in enterprises is based on favoritism and family connections, which encourages a familial-regional climate, as well as an arrangement in which employer-employee relations are in fact a new version of the old style.[57]

Narrow and segmentarily-oriented worker groups push for State investment in urban development projects, chiefly in the coastal region, thus creating not only a greater socio-cultural alienation between the coast and sierra, but also a more acute stagnation of agricultural production, as the greater urban demand is opposed by a rigidity in the supply of food. Thus the growing demands of the participant sectors to improve their standards of living—without implying redistributive measures at the national level, especially in the rural sector—leads to an inflationary pressure which works against their own aspirations.

The rural sectors' marginality and the narrow and specific orientation of the participant sectors leave the road clear for individuals with access to large property, to the control of production and marketing of exports, and of credit—items in which foreign capital plays an important role. They are the ones who establish economic restrictions within the political sphere, thus varying the economic policy of the State to suit their own ends.[58]

One reason why the Peruvian economy is based on the export of raw materials is the lack of an effective mass movement advocating national economic development, along with a redistribution of income and wealth, and a nationalization of the government, placing the latter in a position to control industrial development.

The Political Parties

The tendency toward segmentation and State privatization is favored by the political parties. These organizations are characterized by a recruitment of their members and orientation of their activities in terms of the participant sectors, with an exclusive insistence upon measures conducive toward increasing the latters' income. At present, for example, no party has made universal suffrage an issue in its political platform. We once asked an Apra leader why his party had not sought to organize the Indian masses, and he replied that ". . . there was no interest in it, in view of the fact that Indians do not count politically, as they do not vote. . . ." We obtained a similar reply from another leader, this time of Acción Popular: ". . . there is very little interest in this matter as it would arouse too much opposition. . . . Internally, many in the party would oppose such a measure. . . . The vindication of such a measure would be unpopular, we would be very much criticized and moreover we would have major opposition from the Army."

During almost 35 years, Apra sought to combine the different strata of the population: agricultural and urban workers—whom it helped unionize—clerks, students, and professionals, in order to break down the control that the "oligarchy" exercised over the government. This situation met with a stubborn opposition from *fuerzas vivas* and the armed forces, as the achievement of the objectives that Apra pursued would lead to the emergence of the former social sectors to State power, with the subsequent subordination of the armed forces to civil authority.

In view of the strong opposition of the fuerzas vivas, and armed forces, Apra retained a segmentarian orientation in order to obtain their support. Its alliance with these sectors was with the understanding of an adherence to the rules of segmentarian incorporation and a rejection of any attempt at a massification of society. The new parties formed during the last decade have adjusted to the same rules, resulting in what is referred to in journalistic jargon as "superaccommodation."

With the incorporation of political parties into the political system, which grants representation to the participant sectors thus offering a new legitimacy to the State, the mechanism of segmentation has become institutionalized, as shown, for example, by "parliamentarian initiatives" and "surname laws." Parliamentarian initiatives consist of the power endowed upon each representative to personally mobilize a given budget assignation for any purposes that he should determine. Surname laws refer to laws which exclusively affect—benefit or hurt—a particular individual, or sector of the population. The national budget is compounded through such legal mechanisms. It seems to benefit a determined political clientele, without taking into consideration the national requirements. It can truly be said that there are two budgets: one compounded by representatives in order to neutralize and win over a specific social sector, and another based on international loans devoted to furthering new possibilities in order that new sectors be segmentarily incorporated to national life.

431

DYNAMICS OF SOCIAL CHANGE

Despite the dependence of the peasant mass, especially the Indians, the segmentary orientation of the participant sectors, and the privatization of power by the oligarchy, chief axis of the social system, new social forces are emerging within a context of social and political mobilization,[59] exhibiting an organized confrontation and an awareness of the limitations of the prevailing social order.

Urban Ruralization and Rural Urbanization

During the last 25 years the country has undergone great urban growth and experienced increased physical mobility of the population. While in 1940 the urban population (those living in localities of over 2,000 inhabitants) comprised 25 per cent of the population, the proportion has swollen to 42 per cent, with an annual average growth rate three times above that of the rural population, at the expense of the migratory movement from rural areas.[60]

Migration originates chiefly from rural sierra zones and moves toward urban coastal zones, especially in the central area, Lima being the main focus.[61] In 1961, about 15 per cent of the total population of the country resided in departments other than those of their birth; the strongest movement was to the Lima-Callao complex. During the last 25 years Lima has tripled its population, of which over half is made up of first generation immigrants. Likewise, the country has witnessed the sprouting of two cities, Chimbote and Huancayo, chiefly composed of immigrants and cities competing in importance with those (except Lima) that were founded by the Spaniards.

Urban growth due to internal migration has produced "city ruralization," a phenomenon consisting of an accommodation to the new habitat—without eradication of the social and political rural behavioral patterns. The industrial labor characterizing the urban and modern world [62] absorbs but a small number of these immigrants—insofar as industrial recruitment tends to select literate individuals from urbanized areas.

> Very few textile workers come from densely populated rural areas, from mines or plantations. Most come directly from urban areas . . . or from other mechanized labor. The growing number of rural migrants in Lima and in Arequipa is chiefly employed, as might be expected, in non-industrial "entry" occupations, such as construction work, domestic service and the Armed Forces.[63]

Immigrants perform chiefly service activities or crafts of a family variety, and are often underemployed. Due to the political pressure originated by their presence, the State has been forced to develop housing construction, destined especially for the high-income sectors, and to grant facilities for industrial development, in order to create stable and gainful employment. Thus, a part of this migrant population has joined unions and political life, with the arousal of class-consciousness and ideological interest. But even this new occupational pattern and the political participation it encourages does not sever the ties that this sector maintains with rural areas, either because they have dependents in those areas, or because such ties are reinforced through the arrival of other immigrants that they attract.

The rural areas, however, especially the communities, continue to be sources of social identification for the immigrants. The city slums witness patterns of traditional reciprocity, cooperative labor, and festivities, reflected in a reinforcement of the original regional and communal solidarity ties. This identification is also seen in the high rate of participation in regional and local provincial association which exist in Lima.[64] Likewise, the occupational instability of these sectors, the holdings that they preserve in their communities of origin and the family and communal links of solidarity they maintain, act to provide a very fluid and temporary residential mobility. Many city slums group people from one part of the country in a pattern of extended families. They often are all engaged in one single occupational specialization. On the other hand, due to the marginal status of the slums and to the social and political mobilization of their dwellers, the latter tend to become increasingly interested in local problems, as manifested by the association of dwellers.

This new type of urban proletariat has the opportunity of becoming politically socialized at quite different levels. There is

433

both class consciousness and a party contest, and both urban and rural contexts. Multiple loyalties and identifications are developed, and thus their social and political mobilization is devoid of any segmentarian character. The organization which groups the construction workers, for example, stands out as one of the most aggressive at two quite different levels: personal benefits and the advocating of political change at the national level.

As a result of this urban ruralization, there is a growing "sierranization" of the coast. Because of the large population originating from the region and residing in the coast, a great number of radio and television stations give a large part of their programs to news and music from Mancha India, to advertising in Quechua, and to creating a stereotype of urbanized Indians. The production of sierra music records has achieved considerable volume, sierra folk programs have gained interest and are now combined, for the first time, with creole groups.

This new urban proletariat leads in great measure to the inverse process of urban ruralization: rural urbanization. The close links which immigrants maintain with their places of origin encourage the diffusion of new social, cultural, and political customs in the rural areas, as well as diverse social innovations, propagating new technologies and styles of consumption, diffusing new mass communication media, and recreating identifications with the rural society by means of a new cultural style. It is important to notice that this group with its traditional values is determined to achieve a position of civic equality within the national context.

Further, a new and autonomous group is being formed which incorporates modern values, without destroying all of the traditional patterns, encouraging a climate of civic equality which is creative in its form, and not just a copy of that part of the culture from which it has been borrowed.

These immigrants spread new organizational and ideological patterns which emphasize the relationship between people and nation, family and peasant status in general. This movement has been fostered by the State, the Church, and other international organizations, which have sent representatives to channelize this social mobilization. Cooperación Popular, United States and

Canadian missionaries, and the Peace Corps, by making an appearance in rural areas, have also influenced the process of peasant urbanization, leading to the development of social diversification and of new patterns of social stratification.

On the other hand, due to the occupational demands of the urban population and of rural urbanization, the State has been forced to develop a policy of public works, opening new regions to communication facilities and connecting a greater number of rural sectors. Finally, the growth of the urban population itself has had repercussions in rural areas. The expansion of urban centers has increased the demand for agricultural goods, and because these could not be met under the prevailing structure of property and production,[65] technical innovations have been introduced and further occupational diversification has occurred, especially in those areas close to the population centers and free of the encroachment of the traditional haciendas.

The Marginal Urban Population and the State

The social and political mobilization which characterizes the marginal urban population also has a special force in the character of its relations with the authorities and with the State. Due to the massive and far-reaching scope of its claims, and also because of the existence of numerous spheres which compete to satisfy the requirements of the population of marginal slums (with the purpose of expanding their clientele), this group has avoided situations of dependence, since their members alternate between different power figures. Though the associations of dwellers seek to use influential middlemen in order to achieve their claims, the terms of reciprocity achieved through such links do not result in personal identifications or loyalties.

Moreover, this population reinterprets and adapts to its own interest the ties originated through the rendering of services, in order to avoid relations which could result in a condition of dependence or in the restriction of its activities. Thus, government functionaries, political parties, and prominent figures have felt defrauded by the reaction of this population once it had been granted certain services.

435

Due to the type and magnitude of the demands of this population, only State entities are in a position to offer a convincing answer, which leaves no place for the middleman.

Cholification

As a result of the confluence of urban ruralization and of rural urbanization, there has been a change in the patterns of social stratification of Mancha India, with an emphasis upon the elimination of caste lines. These new patterns of social stratification have come about through the phenomenon of "cholification." [66]

This form of social mobilization which affects urban and rural populations has resulted in an increasing number of Indians who, through contract with urban areas, learn Spanish, become literate, and are thus able to perform new occupations, but this time independently of mestizo patronage. Thus, in 1959, the Plan for the South estimated that Cholos constituted 70 per cent of the urban population and 13 per cent of the population in the department of Puno. [67]

The Cholo is characterized by an incompatible status: due to his social origins and to the low prestige of his occupation, he resembles the Indian; yet in terms of his income and the occupational independence he enjoys with regard to the mestizo, he does not fit into these ethnic-social groups. His reference group is ambiguous for he maintains Indian cultural traits while adopting some of the mestizo's, impregnating them with a new, elusive element. While the Cholo often settles in his own local area and engages in agricultural labor, he also undertakes new occupations which involve residential mobility, and which provide him with the means of obtaining a larger income and discovering new opportunities. He appears to be indifferent to the sacred character of agriculture and to the relations of communal solidarity—all of which occasions a loosening of ties with the extended family, typical of the Indian kinship structure.

As the mestizo social system blocks Indians from possibilities of achieving prestige, wealth, and power through the traditional roads of access to authority and property, the Indian moves upward socially to the Cholo status—without severing his original roots—through engaging in new occupations unhindered by mestizo patronage, such as laborer in public works, truckdriver, door to door salesman, trader of meat and wool, etc. These occupations afford the Cholo the means and status which make him important in the eyes of his family, friends, and country-men who remain in the Indian status, and also in the eyes of the town mestizos. The Cholo adopts an aggressive and mobile behavior which differentiates him from the polite mestizo, and from the servile and apathetic Indian.

This new social type is most frequently encountered in places unhindered by the domination of the hacienda—the Mantaro valley, for example. There, the Cholo carries on an in-tensive commercial activity and contributes to the formation of new population centers. A good example of the latter, outside Mancha India, is the city of Huancayo.

> It is significant in this sense to note that in Sicuani, where the process of *Cholification* is more evident, there are but few haciendas; there is a certain alienation from the control of Cuzco and a very important commercial movement. Such a process resembles greatly what happend at the end of the middle ages, when opportunities for commerce and for craftsmanship arose and the serf became a free citizen.[68]

But due to the political-economic limitations in Mancha India, social opportunities for the Cholo are somewhat limited, although this is not the case in the Mantaro valley. The mestizo blockade against the Cholos of Mancha India forces them to orient their aggressiveness toward trade union and political ac-tivities, in an effort to develop a national orientation. The proximity of the Cholo group to that of Indians—fundamentally due to their social origin and family connections—and their estrangement from the mestizos, has led to a form of political activity geared toward the mobilization of the rural, communal, and tenant-farmer masses. The growing political importance that the Cholo sector has achieved by "grabbing political initiative as a representative of the peasant indigenous mass with the purpose of dominating the upper classes" [69] has conferred prestige upon this sector in the eyes of certain sectors of the lower mestizo class, which would favor the development of "a pressure tending toward the amalgamation of the middle class downwards and of the Cholo class upwards." [70]

This situation suggests that the Cholo group in fact organized and heads the peasant movement existing in Mancha India,[71] which determined a series of hacienda invasions by the communities, and of tenant-farmer strikes, which had to face mestizo repression.[72]

The political importance of the Puno Cholos is shown by the success achieved by the Frente de Trabajadores y Campesinos (Workers' and Peasants' Front)—a regional organization which is made up chiefly of Cholos—in the municipal elections of December 1966, in which it won in all the provinces, with the exception of the chief mestizo bastion, the city of Puno.

As this new agrarian union movement originating in the Indian region takes on a political character, and as it pushes for distribution of property and of regional power—in contrast with the guild benefits character of the coastal unions—it conditions the articulation [73] of the Indian peasant, who thus appears about to sever the patterns of domination previously described.

On the other hand, the appearance of the Cholo sector into economic and political activities, creating new occupations and symbols of prestige, has brought with it signs of competition with the village and town mestizos, since the latter are not always able to compete adequately with the Cholo either in terms of consumption or politically. This is at least one reason why the small and medium-sized landowners in the area, who face an uncertain and threatening situation, have emigrated to urban zones—mainly coastal—where they fill subordinate positions in the State bureaucracy or in small business concerns, with the help of family connections and friends. This is done after selling, parceling off, or abandoning their holdings in order to avoid the lowering of their social status. As an alternative, they enter the ranks of the official political parties, thus facing the prospect of retaining political control only by soliciting and gaining peasant support.

This weakening of mestizo prestige in Mancha India implies that the support they recived from the higher mestizo classes, who in turn were sustained by the Lima oligarchy, is being eliminated. In fact, spokesmen of the National Agrarian Society have even publicly declared the need for parceling off large haciendas in the southern sierra.

To the extent that the weakening of the mestizos in rural areas is becoming visible and their power image is fading in the eyes of the peasants, the status of the Cholo gains stature among the Indians and becomes a new model of social behavior. It should also be noted that some urban Left-wing groups have found in this emergence, apparently initiated and led by the Cholo sector of Mancha India, a reinforcement of their ideology, and they have offered to support the various activities.

The Cuban Revolution and the Sino-Soviet conflict have contributed—among other factors with which we shall not deal here—to the rebuff by some Left-wing intellectual sectors of the reformist political parties, especially of the Communist Party.

The affiliation of these new groups has been reinforced by land invasions, strikes, and peasant uprisings which have kept recurring in the region in the past few years. It is felt that the revolutionary violence of this peasantry is the only road to social change. On the other hand, small and medium-sized land-owners, workers, employees, and professionals seem to be "bourgeoisified" or neutralized. Thus the revolutionary Marxist leader, Hugo Blanco, declared while in prison: "The peasants of La Convención are petit bourgeois; any future uprising of Indians will take place in the highlands, not in La Convención." [74]

Though the frustrated guerrilla activities in the southern sierra have not achieved their final purpose, they have indeed contributed to the political mobilization of tenant-farmers and commoners and to the continuous deterioration of the structural and normative dependence which they suffer at the hands of the mestizos. It would appear that one of the guerrilla groups has been less dedicated to guerrilla activities than to dispelling the image of omnipotence that the boss embodies before his serfs, by scoffing at the former and scattering to the four winds the signs of his authority—vindicating at the same time the local authorities.

Although the guerrillas have been subdued, this activity as well as the peasant organizations have prompted various political, intellectual, economic, and even military circles into discovering the existence of this "alien" country, with the limitations and dangers that its existence signifies to the social structure. They have pressed for State intervention in the region, not only with repressive measures, but also through the elimination of the dependence of the Indian at the hands of the mestizo. Agrarian reform and communication media in the region would allow the incorporation of this population within the national market and into the mainstream of the neutralized sectors.

But such measures are continually being postponed, even in their most timid manifestations, since, as we have tried to point out, certain previous measures of internal reorganization of the State apparatus would be required, thus necessitating a revamping of the social system as a whole.

The new urban proletariat and its Cholo counterpart in Mancha India are—each in its own way as well as in a combined form—breaking in upon the structural and normative dependence of the Indian mass by mobilizing it socially and politically. Such mobilization entails a change from the local-family Indian pattern to another with class connotations. The confrontation with the mestizo system takes place especially in the political sphere as such, since this type of resource is at the very root of the mestizo class status. Therefore, the "access crisis" of the peasantry presupposes the questioning of the legitimacy of the caste system and thereby of the economic, social, political, and cultural cleavages which it entails.

If rural marginality allows for the neutralization of the participating sectors and the privatization of State power, the political sphere demands, with pressing urgency, a new line of social integration based upon the full participation of the different sectors of the population in the distribution of social resources; a form of pluralistic participation. In other words, this crisis pursues the nationalization of Peruvian society.

The crisis of mass participation evident in the country is a consequence of the rejection of a consensus based on domination criteria and of an attempt to establish in its place one based on the participation of citizens of the different sectors of society.

NOTES

[1] *Informe sobre la Situación Económica y Social del Perú,* Instituto Nacional de Planificación, 1963–1964.

[2] *Cuentas Nacionales del Perú,* 1950–1965, Lima, Banco Central de Reserva, 1966.

[3] National Census, 1961.

[4] Walter Thompson, *Perfil del Mercado Peruano,* May, 1966.

[5] Ozzie Simmons, "The Criollo Outlook in the Mestizo Culture of Coastal Peru," *American Anthropologist,* Vol. 57 (1955), pp. 107–117; and Richard Morse, "The Heritage of Latin America," in *Founding of New Societies,* ed. Louis Hartz, New York, Harcourt, Brace & World, 1964, pp. 123–177.

[6] *The New York Times,* March 27, 1966.

[7] José Matos Mar, *Idea y Diagnóstico del Perú: La Pluralidad de Situaciones Sociales y Culturales,* Instituto de Estudios Peruanos, Serie Mesas Redondas y Conferencias No. 5, Lima, September, 1966; and Augusto Salazar Bondy, *La Cultura de la Dependencia,* Instituto de Estudios Peruanos, Serie Mesas Redondas y Conferencias No. 8, Lima, October 1966.

[8] Andrew G. Frank, "La Participación Popular en lo Relativo a Algunos Objetivos Económicos Rurales," p. 9 (ditto).

[9] François Perroux, "Consideraciones en Torno a la Noción del Polo de Crecimiento," *Cuadernos de la Sociedad Venezolana de Planificación,* Vol. II, No. 3–4 (1963), pp. 1–10; and John Friedmann, "Core Region Strategy as an Instrument of Development Policy," September 1966 (mimeo).

[10] Andrew G. Frank, op. cit., pp. 7–8.

[11] Rodolfo Stavenhagen, "Sept Thèses Erronées sur l'Amérique Latine," *Partisans,* No. 26–27, p. 4.

[12] *The New York Times,* December 11, 1966.

[13] François Bourricaud, *Changements à Puno: Étude de Sociologie Andine,* Institut des Hautes Etudes de l'Amérique Latine; Pablo González Casanova, "Sociedad Plural, Colonialismo Interno y Desarrollo," *América Latina,* year 6, No. 3 (1963), pp. 15–32; and Rodolfo Stavenhagen, "Classes, Colonialism and Acculturation in Mezoamerica," *Studies in Comparative International Development,* Vol. I, No. 6 (1965).

[14] E. Wolf, "Corporate Peasant Communities in Mezoamerica and Java," *Southwestern Journal of Anthropology,* Vol. 13 (Spring, 1957).

[15] François Bourricaud, op. cit.

[16] *Plan Regional para el Desarrollo del Sur del Perú,* Vol. V PS/B/9, (1959), p. 20. (Further references below will use the title, *Plan del Sur.*)

[17] François Bourricaud, op. cit., p. 17.

[18] *Plan del Sur,* PS/B/9, p. 13.

[19] Censo Nacional de Población, Vol. I (1961).

[20] Some descriptions of the hacienda system can be found in François Bourricaud, *Changements à Puno,* op. cit.: Carlos Ferdinand Cuadros y Villena, "El Arriendo y la Reforma Agraria en la Provincia de la Convención," *Forum sobre Desarrollo Económico,* Sociedad de Ingenieros del Perú, 1966, pp. 61–99; Gustavo Palacios P., "Relaciones de Trabajo entre el Patrón y los Colonos en los Fundos de la Provincia de Paucartambo," *Revista Universitaria del Cuzco,* year 46, No. 112 (1957), pp. 174–222; Mario Vázquez, "La Antropología Cultural y Nuestro Problema del Indio," *Perú Indígena,* Vol. 2, No. 5–6 (June 1952); and *Hacienda, Peonaje y Servidumbre en los Andes Peruanos.* Lima: Editorial Estudios Andinos, 1961.

[21] T. C. Cevallos Valencia, *Informe sobre Chawaytiri.* Instituto de Estudios Peruanos, Estudio de Cambios Rurales del Perú, 1965 (ms).

[22] Allan Holmberg, "Relationships Between Psychological Deprivations and Culture Change in the Andes." Paper presented at Cornell Latin American Year, Conference of the Development of Highland Communities in Latin America, March 21–25, 1966; and Jacob Fried, "Social Organization and Personal Security in a Peruvian Hacienda Indian Community: Vicos," *American Anthropologist*, Vol. 64, No. 4 (August, 1962), pp. 771–780.

[23] Ralph Klein, "The Self-image of Adult Males in an Andean Culture: A Clinical Exploration of a Dynamic Personality Construct." University Microfilms, 1963, p. 113. In A. Holmberg, op. cit., p. 2.

[24] G. Foster, "The Dyadic Contract in Tzintzuntzan: Patron-Client Relationship," *American Anthropologist*, Vol. 65, No. 11 (1962), pp. 1280–94.

[25] W. Mangin, "Estratificación Social en el Callejón de Huaylas," in *Estudios sobre la Cultura Actual del Perú*, Lima, Universidad de San Marcos, 1964, pp. 298–305.

[26] César Fonseca and Juan Murrugara, "Huaychao," in *Sociedad, Cultura y Economía en 10 Áreas Andino-Peruanas*, Lima, Ministerio de Trabajo y Comunidades, Instituto Indigenista Peruano, October 1966, pp. 36–37.

[27] G. Foster, "Peasant Society and the Image of Limited Good," *American Anthropologist*, Vol. 67, No. 2 (1965), pp. 293–315.

[28] E. Banfield, *The Moral Basis of the Backward Societies*, Free Press, 1958.

[29] Foster, *The Dyadic Contract* . . . op. cit.

[30] Stanislaw Ossowski, *Class Structure in the Social Consciousness*, The Free Press, 1963, p. 149.

[31] Instituto de Estudios Peruanos, Estudio de Cambios Rurales en el Perú, Marginales.

[32] Cevallos, op. cit.; and Virgilio Landázuri, "Informe sobre el Problema de los Arrendires del Valle de La Convención," 1960 (mimeograph).

[33] Rodolfo Vizcardo Arce, *Pacaicasa, una Comunidad de Hacienda*, Universidad Nacional de San Cristóbal de Huamanga, Ayacucho, 1965 (thesis).

[34] Apparently this possibility is conditioned by the relative importance of the hacienda system in a given area. The hypotheses may be suggested that the larger the holdings under hacienda domination, the smaller the amount of immigration. It should also be noted that there is seemingly no relation between the amount of emigration and the number of communities or commoners in a given department. Thus, for example, 21 per cent of those born in Ancash, Apurimac, Ayacucho and Huancavelica have emigrated from these departments—while only 11 per cent of those born in Cuzco and Puno have chosen this alternative. Similarly, in the first four departments mentioned 50 per cent of the land is concentrated in holdings of over 500 hectares (communities not included), while in Cuzco and Puno this percentage rises to 80 per cent.

[35] Uldrich P. Ritter, *Comunidades Indígenas y Cooperativismo en el Perú*, Estudios sobre la economía iberoamericana. Bilbao: Ed. Deusto, 1965.

[36] Instituto de Estudios Peruanos, op. cit.

[37] *Plan del Sur*, PS/B/11, p. 28.

[38] Cevallos, op. cit. See also Mario Vázquez, "Autoridades en una Hacienda Andino-Peruana," *Perú Indígena*, Vol. X, Nos. 24–25 (1963), pp. 24–36.

[39] Censo Nacional de Población, 1961, Vol. III.

[40] Censo Nacional, 1961, Vol. III, p. viii.

[41] Instituto de Estudios Peruanos, op. cit.

[42] M. Vázquez, Cambios en la Estratificación Social en una Hacienda Andina, *Perú Indígena*, Vol. VI, Nos. 14–15 (July, 1957), p. 85.

[43] Cevallos, op. cit., p. 17.

[44] Cevallos, op. cit., p. 19.

[45] V. Landázuri, op. cit.

[46] M. Vázquez, *Hacienda, Servidumbre y Peonaje*, op. cit., p. 18.

[47] *Plan del Sur*, PS/B/11, p. 28.

[48] W. Mangin, "Classification of Highland Communities in Latin America," Cornell Latin American Year, Conference on the Development of Highland Communities in Latin America, March 21–25, 1966.

[49] F. Garmendia, "Informe sobre Pisac," Instituto de Estudios Peruanos, 1965 (ms).

[50] One might well ask if these haciendas with low productivity are not maintained more as a political power bone than as an economic entity. They may be used to obtain political positions which in turn are a source of wealth and social prestige.

[51] H. Martínez, "La Subárea Quechua de Taraco," Instituto Indigenista Peruano, Programa Puno-Tambopata, March 1958, p. 98 (ms).

[52] Anthony Leeds, "Brazilian Careers and Social Structure: A Case History and Model," in *Contemporary Cultures and Societies of Latin America*, eds. D. Heath and R. N. Adams, New York, Random House, 1965, pp. 379–404.

[53] Gino Germani, *Política y Sociedad en una Época de Transición: De la Sociedad Tradicional a la Sociedad de Masas*. Buenos Aires: Editorial Paidós, esp. Chapter 3.

[54] François Bourricaud, "Syndicalisme et Politique: le Cas Péruvien," *Sociologie du Travail*, No. 4 (1961), pp. 48–49.

[55] David Chaplin, "A Discussion of Major Issues Arising in the Recruitment of Industrial Labor in Peru," (ms.); and James Payne, *Labor and Politics in Peru*, Yale University Press, 1965.

[56] Luis Soberón, "Cerro de Pasco, Ciudad-Empresa," *Revista del Instituto de Planeamiento de Lima*, Universidad Nacional de Ingeniería, No. 1, 1966, pp. 27–35.

[57] David Chaplin, op. cit.

[58] François Bourricaud, "Structure and Function of the Peruvian Oligarchy," *Studies in Comparative International Development*, Vol. II (1966), No. 2.

[59] Karl W. Deutsch, "Social Mobilization and Political Development," *American Political Science Review*, September 1961.

[60] "Diagnóstico y Programación de los Recursos Humanos Población del Peru," *Servicio del Empleo y Recursos Humanos*, March 1965.

[61] Ibid. "Diagnóstico de la Situación de Los Recursos Humanos," Instituto Nacional de Planificación, January 1966.

[62] Alex Inkeles, "Industrial Man: The Relation of Status to Experience, Perception and Value," *The Bobbs-Merrill Reprint Series in the Social Sciences*, S-131.

[63] David Chaplin, op. cit. See also Stillman Bradfield, "Some Occupational Aspects of Migration," *Economic Development and Cultural Change*,

Vol. XIV, No. 1 (October 1965), p. 10; and G. Briones y J. Mejía V., *El Obrero Industrial, Aspectos Sociales del Desarrollo Económico del Perú*, Instituto de Investigaciones Sociológicas, Lima, Universidad de San Marcos, 1964, pp. 29–30.

[64] W. Mangin, "Clubes de Provincianos en Lima," in *Estudios sobre la Cultura Actual del Perú*, Lima, Universidad de San Marcos, 1964, pp. 289–305.

[65] CIDA: *Perú, Tenencia de la Tierra y Desarrollo Socio-Económico del Sector Agricola*, Unión Panamericana, Washington, D.C., 1966.

[66] José María Arguedas, "Puquio, una Cultura en Proceso de Cambio," *Revista del Museo Nacional*, Vol. XXV, pp. 184–232; Ibid., "Evolución de las Comunidades Indígenas. El Valle del Montaro y la Ciudad de Huancayo: un Caso de Fusión de Culturas no Comprometidas por la Acción de las Instituciones de Orden Colonial," Ibid., Vol. XXVI, pp. 140–194; F. Bourricaud, "Aparition du Cholo" and "Cholification" in *Changements à Puno*, op. cit., pp. 25–27, 215–228; *Plan del Sur*, op. cit.; Aníbal Quijano, "La Emergencia del Grupo Cholo y Sus Implicaciones en la Sociedad Peruana," (thesis), Facultad de Letras, Universidad de San Marcos, Lima, 1965; and Mangin, "Classification of Highland Communities in Latin America," op. cit.

[67] *Plan del Sur*, PS/B/9, p. 16.

[68] *Plan del Sur*, PS/B/9, p. 18.

[69] Ibid., PS/B/9, p. 18.

[70] Ibid.

[71] A. Quijano, "El Movimiento Campesino Peruano y sus Líderes," *América Latina*, Year 8, No. 4 (Oct.–Dec., 1965).

[72] Hugo Neira, *Cuzco, Tierra y Muerte*, Lima: Editorial Populibros Peruanos, 1964; and Wesley W. Craig, Jr., "The Peasant Movement of La Convención, Perú: Dynamics of Rural Labor Organization" (mimeo).

[73] A. Quijano, "Contemporary Peasant Movements," in *Elites in Latin America*, eds. S. Lipset and A. Solari, Oxford University Press, 1967, pp. 301–342.

[74] Quoted in W. Craig, op. cit., p. 33.

13

GERRIT HUIZER

Peasant Organization
in Agrarian Reform in Mexico[*]

Among the most important gains of the Mexican Revolution are
Article 27 and Article 123 of the Mexican constitution of 1917,
dealing with agrarian reform and labor respectively. It has been
recognized that legislation, especially concerning agrarian reform,
was introduced by the Carranza government (1915–1920) to
appease strongly organized and violent pressure from the peasantry in various regions of Mexico—a prominent example being
the peasant guerrillas led by Emiliano Zapata in the state of
Morelos and the surrounding areas. At various times these groups
became so powerful that they threatened to take or actually took
power in Mexico City. The peasantry could be quieted only after
land reform legislation was accepted, land distribution in Morelos
was well under way, and the main leader of the revolt, Zapata,
had been assassinated in 1919 by an officer of the Government
troops. The existence of an agrarian reform law, and the fact
that the most violently contested areas of land had been given
back to the communities, did not mean that land reform in
Mexico was effective. A constant struggle by the peasants to demand enforcement of the new laws proved necessary. Numerous
obstacles, not infrequently involving violence, had to be overcome
in order to wrest the land from the large landowners as the law
indicated.

445

The effectiveness of the movement organized by Zapata and his followers was mainly due to the fact that the peasants, through armed force, could establish political and social control in large areas, where land could then be distributed. Toward the end of Carranza's presidency, an increasingly sharp division could be noted between the groups which worked for the acceptance and implementation of articles 27 and 123 in the 1917 constitution and those conservative and landed interests headed by Carranza, which opposed directly or indirectly the implementation of those articles. Marjorie Ruth Clark noted that although the effects of the constitution under the Carranza regime were minimal, nothing "could destroy many of the gains which labor had made during the revolutionary years preceding the constitution. . . . Once the peasant and the industrial worker had been given arms and had learned how to use them, most of the worst features of the old order disappeared." [1]

CROM AND LABOR PARTY

For many years efforts to bring unity into the labor movement had been difficult. Carranza saw the jealousies, rivalries, and various social doctrines which divided the movement as an advantage in gaining control over it. One of his trusted partisans, Gustavo Espinosa Mireles, Governor of Coahuila, called together a meeting of representatives of all unions on March 22, 1918, in Saltillo. Here the CROM (Confederación Regional Obrera Mexicana) was founded, and Luis Morones became its leader. Although the government paid all its expenses, the CROM did not fall completely into the government party's hands. Its program, however, was moderate and inconsistent regarding the land tenure problem. [2]

General tactical considerations of its leadership were (1) that its program be no more radical than its organized strength permitted; (2) that its aims be cautiously expressed in order not to provoke American propaganda on behalf of intervention; and (3) that good relations must be maintained with the government in power, if possible. [3]

CROM very closely followed the dictates of a small and select inner circle known as the Grupo Acción. This group was practically dominated by Luis Morones and consisted of around twenty of the initial organizers. Marjorie Ruth Clark noted: "This group, in a country where both the political and the social movements have been one long history of treason and bewildering shifting of fealties, is the more remarkable for the loyalty and the discipline it has shown. Its action is secret, and even its membership is largely a matter of speculation among members of CROM unions. Differences of opinion within the group have been at times very strong, but it has always managed to arrive at a compromise and present a united front to the rank and file of the union members. Morones has been from the first the dominating figure in the Grupo Acción, as he has been in the entire CROM, and whether the loyalty shown by the members of this group has been to him personally, or to the group as a whole, it is one of the noteworthy aspects of the Mexican labor movement.[4]

In 1919 the Grupo Acción formed the Partido Laborista Mexicano to support presidential candidate Alvaro Obregon, after he had signed an agreement favorable to labor with all of the group's members.[5] This gave labor more political power and, at the same time, put the members in line for political jobs.[6]

National Agrarian Party

Although initially the *agraristas*, headed by Díaz Soto y Gama, tried to gain influence within CROM, CROM paid attention to agrarian problems [7] in relatively few areas. At the II Convention of CROM in 1919, Antonio Díaz Soto y Gama, a peasant delegate, tried to strengthen peasant influence and accused the top leaders of dishonesty. His further participation in the CROM was practically made impossible.[8] Then in 1920 Díaz Soto y Gama, together with other former collaborators of Zapata's peasant movement in Morelos and some intellectuals, founded the Partido Nacional Agrarista (National Agrarian party). The National Agrarian party also made a deal with Obregon to support him, in return for a radical land distribution program.[9] By setting

447

this group as a rival against the Labor party, Obregon was able to prevent any group from becoming a threat to him during his presidency (1920–1924).[10]

COMPETITION

In Oscar Lewis's account of the life of a peasant, Pedro Martínez of Tepoztlán, Morelos, we find information about the activities of CROM and its increasing competition with the National Agrarian party.[11] This peasant related how the CROM entered the community in the person of two ex-villagers who lived in Mexico City. One of them was a member of the Typographical Union affiliated with CROM. They came to help the Tepoztecans to defend the community's forests from uncontrolled exploitation and complete ruin. Some of the large landholders who had ruled the village before the Revolution, or their sons, had come back and managed to reconquer the important posts in the municipality. Those men, called *caciques,* tried to make quick profits by production of charcoal from the municipality's forests —thus ruining completely this valuable community resource. In addition they started to claim restitution of cattle they had lost in the turmoil of the revolution. Those who opposed these practices, with support from CROM and some other community members who had gone to Mexico City, were soon called "bolsheviques" or "socialists."

In 1922, at the advice of the CROM member who lived in Mexico City, the villagers requested the removal of the municipal president and the cessation of the exploitation of the forests. But, of two hundred petitioners, 17 were immediately put in jail. After they spent 22 days in jail in Cuernavaca, the violent attitude of the angry peasants and pressure from President Obregon and leaders of CROM convinced the Governor to be helpful in having the municipal council resign within a few days. The petitioners marched back to the center of Tepoztlan in a glorious demonstration. However, notwithstanding this peasant strength, obtained through common action and suffering, not much changed in Tepoztlan.

In 1925 two members of the Comisión Nacional Agraria,

dominated by the National Agrarian party, came to Tepoztlan to redistribute land. The local heads of the CROM Union saw this as a threat and were afraid that the Union would disintegrate. The young men who had come to organize the distribution of hacienda land were killed. The granting of the land then was delayed administratively in Cuernavaca.

One might suspect from this instance that CROM as well as the Agrarian party used improvement measures partly, or perhaps only, to win political support from the peasants. It is possible that because of such competition between CROM and the PNA, in some areas certain benefits were obtained for the peasants, while in other areas such competition became destructive and benefited the common enemy, the large landholders. In 1926, owing to increased activities, CROM could claim 1,500 peasant workers' syndicates as their affiliates.[12]

OBSTACLES

A case which may demonstrate what difficulties the union organizers in the rural areas had to face was described by Gruening: "In Aguascalientes in 1925, the *jefe de operaciones* [local military commander] was General Rodrigo Talamantes. In connivance with the large landholders he used his forces to drive peasants off their *ejidos*. More than one head of a village committee he strung to a convenient pirú tree. The Mexican Federation of Labor [CROM] sent one of its organizers, Miguel Ricardo, to investigate. Finding conditions as reported, he presented himself to General Talamantes and said that if these killings were without the General's knowledge it was time he knew about them, and that in any event he, Ricardo, had come to demand protection for the *ejidatarios*. The General called in his chief of staff, Colonel Estrada. It was agreed that . . . they should go out to the villages and there prove his charges. Ricardo arranged that the *campesinos* in one of the most flagrantly robbed pueblos should assemble to meet them. As Ricardo got off the train, the Colonel lined up a file of soldiers and had him shot. Several of the assembled villagers were also killed; the rest fled. Nothing whatever was done by the War Ministry. General Talamantes is still a jefe de operaciones. Colonel Estrada, however, was waylaid by a group of campesinos a year later when he tried the same tactics in the State of Nayarit and killed." [14]

In addition to repressive actions of *hacendados* and the state authorities Gruening reported the attitude of church authorities as an obstacle to agrarian organizations. Although some exceptions were noted, most of the church hierarchy ignored the existence of an agrarian problem at all, expressing the belief that peasants would not be able to cultivate the land decently anyway. In September 1922 the Union of Campesinos of the State of Durango addressed a memorandum to the Archbishop complaining about the anti-agrarian activities of various priests in the area. This request for support was never answered, although the activity of those priests was at the point of producing serious conflicts.

YUCATÁN

An agrarian movement which was rather independent but had fraternal relations with CROM developed in Yucatán. In that state the revolutionary General Salvador Alvarado began to take agrarian measures in 1916 favoring the Maya Indian peasants. He liberated 60,000 peasants from serfdom. He had already forced the annulment of debts and released many Indians from jail during the previous two years. [15]

In 1916 Felipe Carrillo Puerto, one of the agronomy students who formed part of the Agrarian Commission which helped to distribute lands to the peasants of Morelos in the areas controlled by Zapata's peasant army, returned to Yucatán to offer his help to General Alvarado. There he became the effective organizer of the Resistance Leagues (Ligas de Resistencia), affiliated with the Socialist Party of the Southeast (Partido Socialista del Sureste). [16] The organization started to pressure for a transformation of the serfs of the haciendas into agricultural workers protected by legislation regarding hours of work and decent wages.

The socialist and labor movement in Yucatán was inextricably bound to the henequen industry, which in turn was controlled by the state government of Yucatán through the Henequen Regulating Commission, created by Alvarado. The control of this highly profitable product gave Yucatán a certain independence. In 1922, with support from the Socialist party, Carrillo Puerto became governor. Because of control through the strongly organized peasant and labor movement, various reforms were introduced—for example, distribution of land to ejidos in accordance with the law of January 6, 1915. Carrillo Puerto had translated the constitution of 1917 into Maya and instituted "peasant Thursday," when instruction about rights and obligations was given. In the first eleven months of his governorship he distributed almost 210,000 hectares among 36 communities.[17] Carrillo Puerto tried to extend his political control beyond the state of Yucatán and to impose his followers on the government of the neighbouring state of Campeche. But Carrillo Puerto's governorship lasted less than two years. As soon as the landholding elite of Yucatán got a chance for revenge, during the military coup of Adolfo de la Huerta, Carrillo Puerto was shot, along with three of his brothers and nine other leaders, in January 1924. Actual power was regained by the hacendados.[18]

BROADENING PNA ACTIVITIES

Because the land distribution agency or National Agrarian Commission, was in the hands of the PNA under Obregon's government, the regional branches of this agency could be used to create leagues of agrarian communities (Ligas de Comunidades Agrarias) in many states, which later could be united into a National Peasant League (Liga Nacional Campesina). Such leagues were formed in Veracruz, Puebla, Michoacán, Tamaulipas and various other states. These leagues and other organizations were invited on May 1, 1923, to the I Congreso Nacional Agrarista. President Obregon attended this Congress, which was held under the auspices of the National Agrarian party. One thousand seventy-eight delegates participated in it. Travel expenses of the delegates were paid by the federal government.[19]

Antonio Díaz Soto y Gama played an important role in the Congress, defending the land distribution of Christian socialist doctrines. He also defended the right of the peasants to possess arms. He denounced the state governors who did not comply with the laws, the leniencies of the courts, and the obstructions by the army and clergy of the reform process.

Veracruz

The league of the State of Veracruz was probably the most important one. Carleton Beals indicated that besides Morelos and Yucatán, only in Veracruz was there an agrarian movement which went so far as occupying land: "In Veracruz the hacendados attempted to disarm the peons who had received lands, in some cases to drive them off their newly acquired properties. The agrarian elements thereupon retaliated by occupying various large haciendas." [20] Because of its density of population, relatively high educational level and the presence of various industrial centers, Veracruz had conditions favorable for a peasant movement.[21] In those years, too, Adalberto Tejeda was governor of the state, and he not only tolerated but strongly supported such a movement.[22]

In the city of Veracruz there had existed for some time the Revolutionary Syndicate of Tenants (Sindicato Revolucionario de Inquilinos), which had organized a great part of the population in a strike against high rents. This organization had become so strong that it had its own periodicals and newspapers and could afford to send out agitators to organize the peasants in the state. It was hoped that with help of all sectors of the population a kind of socialist revolution could be brought about.[23]

In March 1923 the I Congress of the League of Agrarian Communities of the State of Veracruz (Liga de Comunidades Agrarias del Estado de Veracruz) was held in Jalapa. The main purpose of the league was to obtain a strict application of the agrarian laws, but it also wanted to obtain political influence, although not through the existing political parties (including the National Agrarian party), which were not considered to be sufficiently radical.[24] The movement, however, encountered severe obstacles. Because General Guadalupe Sánchez, the army commander for the State of Veracruz, was strongly identified with landholding interests, the campaign to organize the agrarian communities into a league was very difficult. Various peasant leaders were assassinated.

452

The large landowners (united in the Sindicato de Agricultores de Veracruz) formed a Revolutionary Junta with help of the military commander and armed their serfs. The peasants of the communities had been disarmed by the Obregon government, and thus were practically defenseless against the cavalry of General Guadalupe Sánchez, and the armed serfs and the cattle herds of the landowners when they destroyed the harvests of the ejidos and burned the houses of the ejidatarios. The daily newspaper of Veracruz undertook a campaign against the organized peasants, calling them agrarian bandits.[25]

The military coup of General de la Huerta against Obregón was launched in December 1923 in Veracruz, Yucatán, and other states with a strong opposition movement.[26] In Veracruz this rebellion had the support of General Guadalupe Sánchez.[27] Although the peasants did not particularly favor Obregón, whose agrarian policy never had been very radical, the league supported him against the generals headed by de la Huerta when his government was threatened.

Michoacán

In Michoacán, another densely populated state, a strong peasant movement was developed in the early twenties by Primo Tapia. Under the regime of Porfirio Díaz the Tarasco Indians around Lake Zacapu had been despoiled of their best lands by the hacienda Cantabria. In 1921 Primo Tapia, a local peasant who had worked as a wetback in the United States, had returned to his village, Naranja—one of those which had been victim of the hacienda usurpations. He succeeded in arousing the peasants from their indolent conformity and into a struggle for the restitution of the village lands promised in the new legislation.

Tapia organized and headed a commission of peasants to the municipal president, but the local government was, as everywhere, controlled by the hacendados. Various efforts were immediately undertaken to assassinate Tapia, or to get him in jail under some legal pretext.[28]

As if there had been no new constitution, in 1921 the land tenure situation in Michoacán was practically the same as before 1910. The peasants either did not know about their new rights,

453

or, under influence of the Catholic clergy, insisted on conforming to the old pattern. Thus, under religious guidance, the indigenous community of Patzcuaro refused to accept ejidal lands when the state government, headed by Francisco Mujica, wanted to start complying with the agrarian law.[29]

As a countermeasure against activities in favor of land reform, the Sindicato Nacional de Agricultores, the association of large landholders which was strong in Michoacán, started to form "white syndicates" in which peasants, foremen, and landowners united under the motto "Justice and Charity." The CROM had not been able to expand in Michoacán beyond Morelia, the capital of the state. The Michoacán Socialist party, which was founded to campaign for General Francisco Mugica, the well known agrarian protagonist, as governor, was permanently in danger. Its main leader, Isaac Arriaga, was liquidated in early 1921, as were a peasant leader named Felipe Tzintzun and a group of his followers.[30]

Tapia continued to have meetings with peasants in their houses although the soldiers or "white guards" [31] sent by the Cantabria hacienda tried several times to capture him. After four villages, Zacapu, Naranja, Tirindaro, and Tarejero, had united for common action and had chosen him as their representative, Tapia began the first transactions with governor Mujica for the formation of an ejido. Notwithstanding strong opposition, Mujica had been able to distribute 23,000 hectares to various ejidos.[32] He was, however, soon thrown out by Enrique Estrada, the military commander of Michoacán and neighboring states, who allied with the landholders and got support from a rebellious movement led by priests and landowners against the government in 1922. The central government of Obregón did not interfere with this situation because the President had to keep General Estrada quiet.[33]

In December 1922 an Agrarian Convention was organized in Morelia, instigated by the local representative of the Comisión Nacional Agraria and with help from the Federación de Sindicatos Obreros y Campesinos de la Región Michoacana, an affiliate of CROM. This Convention intended to found a Liga de Comunidades y Sindicatos Agraristas de Michoacán with delegates from many communities. Primo Tapia was elected secretary-general, and Apolinar Martínez internal secretary. Headquarters were established in Morelia. Initially the main part of the work consisted of sending complaints to the national government about violations against members, such as a case of a peasant who was mutilated into a eunuch without ears. Such violations were frequent: in one community where Apolinar Martínez and another organizer had assisted in the election of an agrarian committee, the house in which they had passed the night was searched by "white guards" who, not finding them, killed some other peasants instead.

In 1923 many peasants from the Liga of Michoacán participated in the I Congreso Nacional Agrarista in Mexico City. Primo Tapia brought with him a proposal for a new agrarian law to replace the one in force. The main point was to give the *peones acasillados* (workers living on haciendas) full rights to petition for land. Another issue was that large units for the cultivation of sisal, cotton, sugar, henequen, or rice would not be left untouched but given as a whole to the peasants. This proposal was considered utopian by opponents and even by many adherents of the Revolution.[34]

One of the major manifestations of the Liga was a demonstration of 8,000 peasants at the railway station of Patzcuaro, when the presidential train passed, to request the return of Francisco Mujica as governor. Once Mujica returned, his life was in constant danger because of the activities of the military commanders of the area and the landholders. For the same reason the Liga had to work mainly in a clandestine way. A painful dilemma arose for the Liga when the zonal commander General Estrada participated in Adolfo de la Huerta's military coup against the government of Obregón in December 1923. Neither Estrada nor Obregón had been favorable to the agrarian movement in Michoacán. Thus the Liga found it difficult to support either of them. In that period Apolinar Martínez left for the United States, while Primo Tapia and other leaders fought against both sides.[35]

At the II Convention of the Liga, in November 1924, it was indicated that the gravest danger for the movement were the persecutions of peasant leaders by the authorities and the assassinations of leaders by the landowners, who generally were not even punished. There were 180 delegates at the Convention, among whom was Ursulo Galván, representing the Liga of Veracruz.[36]

Primo Tapia was again elected secretary-general. He travelled constantly all over Michoacán, to organize and assist the unions. He organized women, too, in order to counteract the influence of the clergy. One of the results of the increasing strength of the organization was that in March 1924 the communities Naranja, Tirindare, and Tarejero received official possession of about 2,200 hectares, mainly from the Cantabria hacienda. Thus the domination of Cantabria was broken, and the peasants could have their own authorities in the municipality. After his home town of Naranja had gotten justice Tapia said that his ambitions were fulfilled, and that he asked nothing more of the world. At that time the Liga was an important force in Michoacán and even some landowners became friendly.[37]

Opposition had not disappeared, however, and a heavy blow to the Liga was given when on April 27, 1926, Primo Tapia was taken captive in Naranja and shot by a unit of the federal army in hacienda El Cortejo. A few days later two other leaders were taken in Opopeo and assassinated in Oyamel. Tapia, whose growing influence was feared by President Calles, was accused of rebellion through intrigues by the landowner of Cantabria. Shortly before, Tapia had signed a manifesto for the Liga, which denounced a number of criminal practices of the owner of Cantabria, and other hacendados, as well as criticized the weakness of government intervention against such practices.[38]

Similar techniques to repress the peasants in the years around 1925 in different areas were summarized by Gruening: "A state governed at that time by a man closely allied with the hacendados and hostile to the land programme; peons working on the haciendas at wages still as low as twenty-five cents a day sought an increase in wages; the governor using his state guard (which as a rule is nothing more than a strong-arm squad to serve his private interests) to kill some peasants audacious enough to ask for higher pay, thereby terrorizing the remainder, and at the same time discrediting the agrarians by blaming them for this violence."[39]

456

UNITING THE LIGAS

On the initiative of the Liga of Veracruz, the leagues of Michoacán, Morelos, and other states came together in Toluca, July 22–25, 1924, to sign a pact of solidarity. In November 1926 this led to the I National Congress of Leagues which was called together in Mexico City by Ursulo Galván [40] with help from Adalberto Tejeda, former Governor of Veracruz, who had become a Minister in the cabinet of President Calles. At this Congress the Liga Nacional Campesina was founded. One hundred and fifty-eight delegates participated in it, representing (it was claimed) 300,000 peasants from 16 of the 27 states of Mexico.[41]

The declaration of principles which was accepted advocated adopting articles 27 and 123 of the Constitution as a guarantee of the rights of the peasants; perfecting the ejido system and complementing it with various forms of co-operative action; accepting as a final aspiration the socialization of land and other means of production; stressing that the peasant problem is international and pointing out the need that organizations of different countries unite for common interest; and emphasizing solidarity with all proletarians and their fight for liberation from the capitalist system.[42]

It was declared that the League should support governments which wanted to free the peasants from clerical influence and economic exploitation. Manuel P. Montes, José Guadalupe Rodríguez and Ursulo Galván were elected to the National Executive Committee. Montes and Rodríguez were later assassinated.[43] Marte R. Gómez formed part of the Advisory Commission.

Tamaulipas and Portes Gil

Another League which was to play an important role in the national political scene was that of the state of Tamaulipas, strongly supported by Emilio Portes Gil. Portes Gil became governor of his home state in 1924 and started to organize the peasants into the Liga de Comunidades Agrarias y Sindicatos Campesinos de Tamaulipas.[44] The fact that Portes Gil had distributed land among the peasants in 1924 gave a solid base to

457

peasant organization. As governor he further promoted rural education and an anti-alcoholism campaign. Various unions of workers were organized as well as the Partido Socialista Fronterizo, a political party in which all the new organizations worked together. The achievements of Portes Gil in his home state gave him the reputation of being a radical agrarian.

Tamaulipas was one of the few states which during the years of the Calles's government (December 1924–December 1928) stayed outside the absolute control of CROM. Luis Morones who continued to be both the Labor party's and CROM's leader, formed in those years part of Calles's cabinet as Minister of Industry, Commerce and Labor. He tried vainly to get control of the labor movement in Tamaulipas by dividing the workers. This led to some bloody struggles at one time.[45] It was said that Morones had ambitions for the presidential elections in 1927. However Alvaro Obregón became the strongest candidate and was elected with support of the National Agrarian party. Shortly afterwards, on July 15, 1928, Obregón was assassinated by a religious fanatic.

Immediately after the assassination (on which, according to rumors, the Labor party headed by Luis Morones as well as President Calles himself may have had a certain influence), the leaders of the Agrarian Party, Soto y Gama and Manrique, initiated pressure for the nomination of Emilio Portes Gil as provisional president. They were distrustful of Calles and saw in Portes Gil the best guarantee for a continuation of the agrarian reform program of the Revolution.[46]

During his term as provisional President (December 1, 1928–February 5, 1930) Portes Gil gave strong backing to the land distribution program. This was not to the liking of ex-President Calles, who was still very powerful. Portes Gil explained to him, however, that land distribution was the only way to guarantee peasant support for the government in case the discontented military should undertake another coup (which indeed happened in mid-1929).[47] Portes Gil claimed that he had reliable indications that in such a case 400,000 peasants were willing to take up arms and defend the government. As one sign of the cordial relationship between Portes Gil and the agrarian movement, he nominated Marte R. Gómez, advisor of the Liga Nacional Campesina, as his Minister of Agriculture.[48]

In January 1929 the Liga Nacional Campesina, together with the Mexican Communist party, the Labor Federation of Tamaulipas and some other groups and federations, created the Workers and Peasant Bloc (Bloque Obrero y Campesino). The Bloc adopted a very radical program including the abolition of the present form of government and the substitution of workers' and peasants' soviets for the Chamber, Senate, and Cabinet; nationalization of industries; confiscation of Church properties; elimination of all latifundios; creation of voluntary, armed, peasant defense groups to prohibit using good agricultural lands for cattle-raising, etc. Besides Ursulo Galván, outstanding members of the Communist Party, such as Diego Rivera and Hernán Laborde, were elected to direct the Bloc. The Bloc's candidate for the 1929 presidential elections, Pedro V. Rodríguez Triana, an old revolutionary and peasant leader of the North, was nominated.[49]

DIVISION OF THE MOVEMENT

After the military coup in March 1929, the peasant movement split up. Most leaders unconditionally supported President Portes Gil and fought on his side. Some leaders, such as José Guadalupe Rodríguez, got involved, however, in a plot to use the opportunity to defeat the military and overthrow the government, and thus to establish a proletarian regime. The Communist party expelled Galván, Rivera and the other leaders who had supported the constitutional government.

In January 1930 the National Revolutionary party (PNR) was created by former President Calles to bring together various competing political factions. All government officials automatically became members of the party, because they had to give seven days of salary per year for its financial support.[50]

The new party immediately wanted control over the National Peasant League. The VI Convention of the League in February 1930 was a scene of confusion and violence. "The first directive board of the convention, of which Galván and Enrique Flores

Magon were members, was replaced by one more favorable to governmental control. Members were forced to disarm before entering the meetings, and police were stationed everywhere throughout the meeting place in a twofold attempt to prevent violence and to make obvious the determination of the government to have a part in the proceedings." [51] The government representatives gained control, and a split in the League resulted. One group followed the Communist party, one group joined the PNR, but the overwhelming majority followed Galván, who continued as President of an independent League, until he died very suddenly—of natural causes—later in 1930. The League then changed its name into Liga Nacional Campesina "Ursulo Galván."

As Marjorie Ruth Clark indicated, "Agrarianism has become a political game second to no other in Mexico," generally to the detriment of the peasants. "Unfortunately, nothing has yet been done to free the peasant from the politician. From this point of view it makes little difference to the peasant which of the many organizations he joins. He must take care to belong to the one which is strongest in his region, if he wishes to escape persecution. Whether it is the National Peasants' League "Ursulo Galván," claiming to take no part in political action, or the National Peasants' League, member of the National Revolutionary party, or a state league of agrarian communities independent of any central organization, or the CROM, the peasant is always, either directly or indirectly, under the control of some political faction." [52]

Eyler N. Simpson quoted from the field report of a zonal representative of the National Agrarian Commission, an agency responsible for land reform: "The greatest difficulties in the ejidos of this zone come from the political parties. . . . Each group tries at all costs to maintain control of the ejido and of the ejidatarios in order to . . . place in office its own members. This has created a great gulf between the peasants and gives rise to constant complaints from all sides." After studying a number of cases Simpson concluded: "There is hardly a state without an assortment of Agrarian Leagues, Peasant's Syndicates, and Ejido Parties, organized and led by astute politicians all too often with their eye on the main chance. In the beginning some of these parties and their leaders were honestly and sincerely devoted to protecting the ejidatarios and improving their economic and social conditions. And this is doubtless still true of a few of these organizations. But most of the rest of them, if they have not been destroyed or absorbed by even more powerful political forces, are dominated by self-seeking individuals whose only interest in the peasant is his votes or his guns." [53]

The peasants were used by politicians mostly for their own benefit—sometimes including benefit to the peasants, sometimes not: when the 1931 electoral campaign for state governor started in Tamaulipas, there were certain pressures from peasants and workers to re-elect Portes Gil in the hope of a continuation of the agrarian program. Calles, who had certain economic interests in Tamaulipas tried to bring in an opposition candidate, because Portes Gil's policy in favor of the peasants and workers was not appreciated by those who had interests to lose in Tamaulipas. Through various maneuvers including military intervention, Calles got his candidate, Villarreal, to the governorship. This led, as Portes Gil has noted, to two years under Villarreal of oppression of those who protested against injustices. Hundreds of peasants were killed and still more expelled from the state, till finally a widely publicized demonstration of 40,000 people of all social classes in the four major towns of the state forced the Governor to resign.[54]

Michoacán and Cárdenas

Although many politicians and military commanders abused their position for their own pecuniary benefit, there were a few exceptions. One of them, Lázaro Cárdenas, had become famous as a loyal and effective military commander in the years of the Revolution and in the crushing of the military uprising of Adolfo de la Huerta.[55] But special attention was drawn to him because he did not take advantage of his power as a military commander to become rich, as most of his colleagues did. In 1927 representatives of the state of Michoacan came to ask him if he could run for the governorship of this state for the years 1928–1932.[56]

461

Since his candidacy had the support of Calles and Obregon, his rivals immediately abandoned the field, realizing that they had no prospect of success.

Michoacán was in a state of chaos. Conservative Catholic rebel groups, called Cristeros, were operating in various parts of the State to defend the interests of the Church, which coincided generally with those of the landlords. The Weyls say: "The Cristero bands were mainly composed of resident hacienda workers, the *acasillados*, who were stirred to rebellion by their priests and maintained in arms by their landlords. Economically dependent on the hacienda system, the priests were not only the intellectual instigators of the revolt, but frequently were its military leaders. They taught that land distribution was contrary to the will of God and that the peon owed his hacendado implicit obedience." [57]

In those days the peones acasillados were not benefiting from the land distribution program, because they did not fall into any of the categories which, according to the constitution, could petition for land. The Calles government at that time was well disposed toward the large estates and did not change the law to the benefit of the resident workers. These workers depended completely on the hacendados and let themselves be used against the government. Yet, "the peasantry of the land-hungry villages and the ejidatarios who had already wrested land from the hacendados supported the government and were prepared to sacrifice their lives for the agrarian programme." [58]

Cárdenas had to leave the governorship for various months to act as military commander in the campaign to pacify the Cristero revolt. In addition to gaining control through military action he tried to create a basis of popular support in Michoacán through the formation of class organizations of peasants and workers. In January 1929 he founded the Confederación Revolucionaria Michoacana de Trabajo, to unify the various existing and the newly created syndicates and communities.[59] One of the activities of this federation was an anti-religious campaign, transforming churches into libraries, schools, or granaries. The main activity however was to struggle for land distribution.

In those years Cárdenas distributed more land in Michoacán than all his predecessors together: 181 villages with 15,373 inhabitants received land "wrested from the haciendas." [60] Even the women were organized to support this effort: "After the distribution of lands in Langostura, the 'white guards' of the hacendados attacked the ejidatarios in the fields. The men and women of the village repelled the invasion. Mauser in hand, the members of the feminine league stood guard over the fields while their hubands worked." [61]

Cárdenas's successor in Michoacán, Benigno Serrato, tried to destroy Cárdenas's work by creating a rival labor organization and at the same time boycotting the existing one.[62] Many leaders had to take refuge in the neighboring states.

In 1966 Landsberger and Hewitt studied a number of ejidos in the municipality of Taretan, Michoacán.[63] The first challenge to the hacienda system in that area came in 1920 when 135 petitioners presented a request for an ejido to the authorities. About one third of the petitioners were local businessmen or craftsmen of the town of Taretan. The other two thirds were mainly laborers on the haciendas. Nothing happened, however, for a long time. The countermove of the hacendado in 1926 was to offer land for sale in parcels of 5 to 7 hectares for such a price that only the better-off petitioners could afford it. This could have been a way to alienate the leadership from the movement. There was for many years no open agitation to support the petition. It was difficult to rally the fearful peasants. The clergy was active in those years to keep people in many areas from insisting on their rights.

But in 1929 a local branch of the Confederación Revolucionaria Michoacana de Trabajo was founded in Taretan and started to demand higher wages. One of the leaders of this movement was killed by the troops of the hacienda. In 1930 another leader, Emilio Ruiz, the son of a local orchard owner, who considered Francisco Mujica as his "ideological father," took the lead in the movement. With his brothers, he sent letters to the capital to support the petition for land, and, with support from Governor Cárdenas, obtained the expropriation of hacienda lands (2,515 hectares, of which 1,015 were irrigated). Former demands for higher wages were abandoned for petitions for land in many surrounding villages where the movement spread.

The main obsbtacle to effective organization continued,

however, to be the fear of violent acts of the "white guards" and the more subtle methods used by clergy and landowners to convince the peasants that their leaders would only use them for their own benefit. After Serrato became governor in 1932 and gave support to the landowners, the movement suffered a severe setback. Only a few peasants had the courage to join the movement, which was again under constant threat of violence. Manipulated by the hacendados most peasant workers refused to sign petitions for land.

CÁRDENAS AND THE AGRARIAN MOVEMENT

Later Cárdenas was called to become president of the PNR, the official political party, which, as Cárdenas recognized, had as a function to "control the popular vote" in an epoch in which counterrevolutionary forces time and again tried to impose themselves.[64] On January 1, 1933, Cárdenas became, at Calles's request, Minister of War in the cabinet of interim-President Abelardo Rodríguez. This fact shows that Calles had great confidence in Cárdenas since the War Ministry was a key post as regards national political emergencies which could occur during the coming presidential elections.

As the elections for the presidential term 1934–1940 approached, various personalities who were in favor of a more radical agrarian policy than the one followed by President Calles and the successors under his powerful tutelage, looked for an appropriate candidate within PNR. The ideal choice had to combine high favor with Calles with more radical inclinations. This candidate was General Lázaro Cárdenas, known for honesty and his serious reform efforts while Governor of Michoacán.

Graciano Sánchez, a leader of the National Peasant Federation who had joined the PNR, Emilio Portes Gil, and some other agrarian leaders organized in 1933 the Confederación Campesina Mexicana partly to promote Cárdenas's candidacy in the name of the agrarian cause. To this effect in May 1933 a convention was held in San Luis Potosí of the Ligas de Comunidades Agrarias of the states of Tamaulipas, Michoacán, San Luis Potosí and Chihuahua. Later the peasant league of Tlaxcala joined the movement. A manifest, drafted by Marte R. Gómez, was published, proposing that the peasants of Mexico support the candidacy of Lázaro Cárdenas. The manifesto was directed especially to the Liga Nacional Campesina "Ursulo Galván," proposing to form a united campaign in favor of Cárdenas. The manifest was signed by the president, secretary, and treasurer of the peasant leagues or federations of San Luis Potosí, Tamaulipas, México, Chihuahua and Tlaxcala.[65]

At the same time, General Gildardo Magaña, the old collaborator with and successor of Zapata, now military commander of the state of Puebla, started to propose General Cárdenas through other channels. Support had to be won from those who were discontented with Calles's policies as well as from his ardent followers. When Calles was approached about the campaign for Cárdenas, he immediately approved, although he had possibly thought of others initially. He trusted Cárdenas as a loyal follower and believed that he would be less radical in practice than he was in words. As the Weyls observed: "Calles also knew that the firebrands of the revolution graduated easily into the ranks of its millionaires, and he may have counted on the corrupting influence of power to curb the idealism of his young protégé."[66]

For his official victory as candidate at the next PNR convention Cárdenas thus counted on support from the agrarian movement but also from the army, labor organizations, and even some pro-Catholic leaders. In addition: "Mexico's long indoctrination with semisocialist theory and the existence of a vital agrarian and labor movement made leftist political candidates almost a political inevitability."[67] Thus the more conservative candidate within the PNR withdrew, and at the Party Convention in Queretaro, December 1933, Cárdenas was nominated presidential candidate for the PNR by acclaim.

At the same convention a Six Year Plan, which would serve as a guide during the new presidential term, was accepted. This plan was proposed by Calles months before and had in the meantime been elaborated, as a compromise between the conservative and the radical elements. At the party convention, however, the leader of the National Peasant League, Graciano Sánchez, took the floor and helped to push through a number of last minute changes which reaffirmed the revolutionary road abandoned during the last years. As regards the agrarian program, the Plan indicated: "the only limit to the distribution of land and waters shall be the complete satisfaction of the agricultural needs of the centres of rural population." It foresaw measures to speed up the land distribution; reorganization of the state agrarian commissions with participation of peasant representatives; the creation of an independent Agrarian Department instead of the National Agrarian Commission; and provisions so that resident hacienda peons could benefit from land distribution. These proposals represented a revolutionary break with the past.[68]

As the Weyls summarized: "Until 1933, the PNR had devoted itself almost exclusively to the important task of keeping opposition voters away from the polls and counting in its own candidates. Elected officials were kept in line with a strict caucus system and the threat of expulsion from the one political machine that possessed effective electoral power. But the young revolutionaries who were sent to the II National Convention of the party took the Calles catchwords of democracy and socialism seriously. They swept the conservative delegates along a torrent of left-wing oratory and committed the PNR to frank support of the democratic principle of government and the workers' and peasants' movement of Mexico. By promulgating the Six Year Plan, the convention frightened Mexico's conservatives into desperate opposition." [69]

Following the party convention, President Abelardo Rodríguez (1932–1934) issued a few decrees which would lay foundations for an agrarian policy in agreement with the plan: the decree of January 15, 1934, creating the Agrarian Department; the promulgation of the first Agrarian Code (Código Agrario) on March 22, 1934.[70]

Notwithstanding the fact that his election as president was assured when he was nominated the candidate of the National Revolutionary party, Cárdenas insisted on traveling to all corners of the country to get acquainted with local problems. He thus became very popular and won the election with an immense majority: about 2,270,000 votes against about 40,000 for the three other candidates together.[71]

Cárdenas indicated that one of the important problems in Mexico was the lack of unity in the country as a whole. While in one state a strong impetus was given to agrarian reforms, in another the policy could be contrary to such reforms. It was one of his objectives to create a united revolutionary front. On various occasions he tried to mediate in the "inter-proletarian" struggles. It was part of his program to unite the workers and the peasants, as he had done when he was governor of Michoacán.[72]

As regard the peasants Cárdenas proposed to give them back arms, in order to overcome the violent actions of vested interests and their "white guards" against the accomplishment of the agrarian laws. "I always maintained that only by giving arms to the agrarian elements which have been, are and will be the firm supporters of the Revolution, one can teach them to continue accomplishing their apostolate rather than become victims of attacks as happens in the whole republic. . . . I will give to the peasants the Mausers with which they made the Revolution, so they can defend it and the ejido and the school." Cárdenas proposed to organize a peasant militia which would be a reserve to the army, and would make it possible to economize in army expenses.[73]

The Weyls noted that in the years before 1934 the peasant organizations of Mexico were divided and weakened in all states except Veracruz, Michoacán and Tamaulipas. As a first requirement for a dynamic land reform program, and to promote a strong peasant organization, Cárdenas issued on July 10, 1935, a decree in which the National Executive Committee of the PNR was put in charge of organizing a league of agrarian communities in every state. Once these leagues were organized a national federation would be created.[74]

The main task of organization fell on Emilio Portes Gil, President of the PNR, but Cárdenas himself participated in the campaign by attending some of the state conventions where a league was founded. In Jalisco, one of the most difficult states, where the Cristero rebellion had violently opposed the agrarian reform, Cárdenas promised at the Convention that the zonal military commander would organize the distribution of arms, after the peasants at the meeting had indicated that this was a first necessity for them.[75]

Cárdenas indicated in a speech at the I Convention of the League of Agrarian Communities of the Federal District, September 7, 1937, that the government and the PNR would pay the costs for the delegations but would not interfere with the elections of leaders, nor with the internal affairs of the leagues or unions.[76]

The fact that communities or other entities which wanted to apply for land were legally obliged to be organized into an agrarian committee, helped the organization process considerably.

President Cárdenas and the Labor Movement

In order to cope with the forces opposing a radical government program, the labor sector badly needed to be strengthened. "By 1934, the Mexican trade-union movement had become a chaos of bickering factions. While the people hungered, politicians promised the New Jerusalem and used the evanescent labor federations they created as the building blocks of power. The Regional Confederation of Mexican Labor (CROM) had originally organized the working class of Mexico. Acquiring unqualified government support during the Calles presidency, the CROM leadership became corrupt and control was vested in the self-appointed 'action group' of Luis Morones's friends. After its fall from official favor, the CROM lost its power, but retained its vices. 'Self-defence against the Red menace' became the battle standard of a narrow and embittered factionalism. The lavish entertainments given by Morones, the leader's diamonds and his far-flung property holdings contributed to working class disillusionment with trade unionism." [77] In 1932 the CROM had split into three groups, while various state governors had created their own federations. The group which would become most important was led by Vicente Lombardo Toledano,[78] who had been in CROM for many years, but had never been allowed to enter the *Grupo Acción*. Lombardo Toledano and other younger members of CROM were weary of the long dictatorship of Morones and his group. Although the dissident group did not get control of most of the unions in the federal district, they enjoyed increasing influence outside it. The new group was called Confederación General Obrera y Campesina de México (CGOCM). Lombardo's group was sceptical of Cárdenas's promises until he proved his sincerity by supporting labor demands and strikes against the vested interests, including those of former members of the government.[79]

Calles's attack on Cárdenas in mid-1935 helped to unite the forces of peasants and labor behind the government. The same day that Calles published a threat against Cárdenas in the newspapers, CGOCM promoted the organization of the National Committee of Proletarian Defense, which branded Calles as a traitor and an enemy of the working class.[80] Paul Nathan [81] indicated that this Comité de Defensa Proletaria represented 70 per cent of the workers who, although disarmed, were trained militarily and ready to defend the government against any insurrection.

The National Committee of Proleterian Defense issued a call for a National Unification Congress, February 26–29, 1936. At this Congress the Confederación de Trabajadores de México (CTM, Confederation of Mexican Workers) was created. The CTM included a total of 3,594 separate organizations: individual factory unions, industrial unions whose jurisdiction spread throughout the country, and organizations of agricultural workers and of peasants who have received land in the form of ejidos.[82]

The new organization managed to rally effective support for Cárdenas, in the critical moments of his struggle with Calles. After a massive popular demonstration in April 1936, Cárdenas had no problem in expelling Calles from the country. Calles had dominated Mexican politics for about ten years.

The CTM was reported to have participated in the efforts of the government to unify the peasants into a National Peasant Confederation: "The Confederation has co-operated in the unification of the peasants of the country by urging its members to join the Leagues of Agrarian Communities, and is awaiting the organization of the National Peasant Confederation in order to sign a pact of solidarity and mutual aid with it, which will constitute a true united front of the two principal sectors of the Mexican people, formed to struggle efficaciously for the betterment of the living conditions of the producing masses and to guarantee the uninterrupted development of the Mexican Revolution.[83]

The CTM could significantly increase its influence because the strikes it organized were generally supported by the government. This happened in urban as well as in rural areas.

National Peasant Confederation (CNC)

It has been observed that the Confederación Nacional Campesina (CNC) was created not only to defend the interests of the peasants but also to form a certain counterweight against the increasing influence of the CTM, under the leadership of Vicente Lombardo Toledano.[84] Its foundation was decreed on July 10, 1935, and was executed in a process of working from below. In all the states and territories of Mexico the ejidos and agrarian committees (groups which petitioned for land) were brought together into regional committees and these were united into a Liga de Comunidades Agrarias y Sindicatos Campesinos for each state. Thirty-seven such organizations, from all over the country sent delegates to participate in the foundation of the Confederación Nacional Campesina, at its constituent congress, August 28, 1938, in Mexico City. Graciano Sánchez was elected Secretary-General. In contrast to the peasant leagues and confederations which existed in earlier years, the CNC was given legal standing.[85]

The CNC's main objectives were to foster the continuation of land distribution, to help the peasants with the solution of problems, to transmit peasant grievances to the competent offices and to ensure that local officials would not obstruct the distribution process.

Francisco Gómez Jara noted that the CTM had difficulties in giving up many affiliates, unions of peasant workers on the sugar, henequen, or cotton plantations who had been organized with great effort. First, recognition from the hacendados or plantation owners had been achieved, then improvements in standards of living, and finally many of these unions were active in preparing petitions for land reform on a large-scale and on a collective basis, such as the union in the Laguna area. Cárdenas had made it very clear, however, that he wanted the peasants to be organized independently in their own organization. CTM decided to give up many of its affiliates, although a good number did not want to leave and kept a double affiliation.[86]

Some observers stressed that the objective of the CNC was to organize the ejidos for political action within the party. Emilio

Portes Gil initially charged with the task of creating the CNC and purging the Calles followers from the official party ranks, replaced them with his own supporters. Thus Miguel Aleman was adjudged governor-elect of Veracruz, although he had about one-third of the number of votes which his opponent received. Also in Tamaulipas certain irregularities took place. Portes Gil resigned in 1936.[87]

Then Cárdenas, influenced by the popular front experiments in Europe, and in consultation with Lombardo Toledano, decided to broaden the National Revolutionary party to include the main forces supporting his revolutionary program, especially peasants and labor.[88] In March 1938 the PNR was transformed into the party of the Mexican Revolution (PRM), in which four autonomous sectors were fused: labor (CTM), peasants (CNC), "the popular sector," and the army. This happened in the days that Mexico was united behind its President because of the expropriation of the oil industry.

The Constituent Congress of the PRM was composed of 393 members, 100 from workers' organizations, 96 from peasant organizations, 96 from the middle class (teachers, petty industrialists, artisans) brought together as the "popular sector," and 101 from the army. The 101 votes of the army were controlled by the government (Ministry of War). This was done to integrate the military into the civil political establishment. Its influence was strong and not proportional to its relatively weak numerical strength; thus it could function as a balance to combinations of either peasants or workers with the "popular sector." Since both the CNC and the CTM practically lived from government subsidies there was almost complete control over the whole system of the Party.[89]

Immediately after the CNC's creation, complaints arose that certain leaders were not radical enough in representing the peasants' demands. They were accused of being too bureacratic and an obstacle to getting land. The question arose if an independent and more combative revolutionary organization should be formed, but among such groups as the Communist party it was considered more useful to stay within the CNC. It was considered essential that, when leaders were not active enough on a certain issue, the radical elements should form an independent committee (Comité de Lucha) to direct the struggle, thus showing the members who were their true leaders.[90]

Armed Peasantry and Politics

The peasant sector became an important pillar of the national power structure through its influence within the official party. It had already obtained some effective power through the distribution of arms, which created the peasant reserve, also known as the peasant militia. This power gave weight to their participation in political life, and on various occasions proved to be an important guarantee for political stability.

That the need for armed peasant groups was not exaggerated can be concluded from the fact that *The New York Times* reported 53 battles between agrarianists and their opponents during the first eighteen months of Cárdenas's government. Not a few landowners hoped to escape distribution of their lands by burning down the villages in which the potential petitioners lived. According to the law lands of estates within a radius of seven kilometers around a village could be expropriated to the benefit of that village. Through making a village disappear or move elsewhere, several estates tried to take away the legal basis for a petition.

Under Cárdenas's regime as well as under those of his predecessors, people who organized peasants to make a petition according to the law ran the risk of being eliminated by men hired by the landowners. Even government officials ran this risk. In the first years of Cárdenas's government 2,000 persons were reported assassinated for such reasons in Veracruz alone. During the three most critical months of 1936, 500 persons were killed in various states.[91]

Moisés T. de la Peña indicated how difficult it was for the peasants to take the benefits of the revolution which they themselves had brought about with great sacrifices. He gives various examples, some as late as 1938 in which only 30 or 40 peasants of 400 who had benefited from the allotment of an ejido, took actual possession of the lands. The rest, fearful and timid under the preachings of the local priests and the threats of the landowner, stayed aloof. Only exceptionally courageous peasants were "agrarianists" (*agraristas*). They were called "robbers" (*agarristas*) by the priests.

Because only few such agrarianists had the courage to work for a petition, they occasionally had to rely on doubtful practices, such as inscribing babies as petitioners, in order to fill the minimum number of petitioners required by the law, for most villagers hesitated to join the action.[92]

The psychological effect on the peasants of the legal possession of arms for the defense of their rights should not be underestimated. This factor was helpful in overcoming the fear of the landowners and their allies and in making the agrarian reform program more vigorous.

According to statistics supplied at the end of the Cárdenas regime, the rural reserve created by decree of January 1, 1936, contained 60,000 men in 1940, all with arms and almost half of them with horses. They were divided into about 70 battalions and 75 cavalry regiments, directed by more than 400 chiefs and officers, altogether under 9 generals. The functions of the rural reserves was to organize and control the armed peasantry defense. The Ministry of Public Education co-operated in literacy work among the members of the reserves.[93]

At times the government seemed to have more confidence in these forces than in the regular army itself. The forces defended not only the rights of the peasant class, but on various occasions they were used to safeguard the national government from severe threats of being overthrown by conservative forces.[94]

All this happened in the days when international fascism gained its initial victories and organized many subversive activities in Latin America. These forces had a strong impact in Mexico. Partly because of this the country was in serious turmoil around 1940 during and shortly after the election of Manuel Avila Camacho, the successor of Cárdenas.

The American journalist Betty Kirk said of Manuel Avila Camacho: "He was a successful army general, able administrator, and vigorous leader who hated communism and was determined to purge it from Mexican life." [95] His candidacy for the presidency was first launched unofficially at a banquet offered by his brother, governor of Puebla, and was supported by the majority of state governors, the conservative bloc of the senate and the conservative army officers. Camacho's candidacy was backed by the Confederación Nacional Campesina within the PRM structure. Some sources indicated that the CNC, the "Graciano machine," already supported Camacho several months before the PRM had issued a call for a nomination congress.[96]

Lombardo Toledano and CTM, who were more inclined to support the radical General Francisco Mujica as the PRM candidate, gave in, so as not to divide the popular front at the time when the danger from extremely conservative and fascist forces, such as the Sinarquist movement, was alarmingly strong.

Before and after the elections, controlled and—according to Nathan—probably falsified by the official party, thousands of peasant militia were brought into the capital to guard against unrest and possible uprisings. Betty Kirk noted, "This peasant horde of thousands of men was to be unleashed if trouble should break." She indicated that on September 1 still more armed peasants came to the Capital to guard, from the roofs of surrounding buildings, the installation of the newly elected Congress. It was reported that the opposition, mainly from Catholic organizations with fascist tendencies, was finally brought down when President-elect Camacho declared that he was a faithful Catholic.[97]

It is difficult to say whether the existence of the peasant reserve was the reason that a certain peace began to rule in the country. The coincidence of progress in pacification and the official support of the peasant reserve was, however, noted as striking. Under Cárdenas's successors, various disarmament campaigns (*despistolización*) have been undertaken, with only partial success, since, as was reported, the peasants have felt this to be an intolerable humiliation.[98]

There is strong evidence that political participation through the National Peasant Confederation and the fact that the peasants were armed were inseparable from a vigorous land distribution program which took place during the years of Cárdenas's presidency. During his regime 10,651 ejidos were formed through the distribution of 18,352,275 hectares to 1,020,594 peasants. Together with the land distributed under former governments, this amounted in 1940 to 13,091 ejidos, with 25,324,558 hectares to 1,442,895 peasants. Outstanding among the land distributions under Cárdenas were those in the Laguna region, Yaqui area, Los Mochis, Yucatán, Lombardo y Nueva Italia, el Mante, Mexicali and Soconusco. These lands were owned by powerful proprietors, many of whom were foreigners. Before the reforms these areas had formed nuclei of serious unrest and oppression, and generally had had increasingly strong peasant movements against this.[99]

Rise at the Middle Sector

During the last part of the Cárdenas regime certain measures were introduced which appeared to be more favorable to the private commercial farmers than to the peasants and ejidatarios. On March 1, 1937, a decree was issued to protect the livestock industry, since many cattle ranchers had stopped investing in their industries for fear of expropriation of their lands. The decree was an addition to the Agrarian Code, declaring non-expropriable so much cattle land as was needed for the breeding of 500 head of big cattle, or its equivalent in small cattle. The law of Livestock Development (Ley de Fomento Ganadero) promulgated by Cárdenas, giving the guarantee of non-expropriability to large extensions of land dedicated to cattle breeding, led to the hidden persistence of many latifundios in the hands of those who simulated cattle-breeding on a large scale, but who in reality did not use a large part of the protected lands or who dedicated them to agriculture.[100] The number of peasants with provisional rights to land (*derecho a salvo*) increased at the same time considerably.

In July 1940 Cárdenas invited the National Congress to a special session to discuss a new agrarian code. This was approved on September 23, 1940, and published in the *Diario Oficial* of October 29, 1940.[101] One of the important changes introduced which was also favorable to private commercial farming was Article 173, declaring non-expropriable not only 100 hectares of irrigated land, but up to 300 hectares of irrigated land on plantations of such cash-crops as bananas, coffee, cacao and fruit trees.

During Avila Camacho's government (December 1940–December 1946) this tendency was strengthened to meet the needs for national unity and an increase in production of raw materials to help the Allied forces in the struggle against fascism. In those years the so-called march to the sea was initiated, consisting of the opening of new lands for agricultural exploitation through irrigation schemes and road building in the coastal areas. One of the main objectives of the agrarian policy of president Avila Camacho was a consolidation of the gains made during the Cardenas regime and a continuation at a more moderate speed of the distribution of ejidos. Thus, while Cárdenas distributed lands to about 770,000 peasants, Avila Camacho did this to only 115,000.[102]

In 1943 the Agrarian Code was again adapted so as to give more guarantee of land ownership to "small proprietors" as well as to ejidatarios. The giving of individual titles to the plots of the ejidatarios was introduced, thus protecting the ejidatarios from possible malversations of the authorities.[103] Special protection was given to "small properties," generally those lands which were left to hacendados after part of their land had been distributed to ejidos. They could be considered middle-sized farmers.

The increasing importance in the early forties of the "middle sector" in Mexico was indicated by the fact that between 1939 and 1945 the manufacturing industry augmented its production 39 per cent. It was noted however that between 1945 and 1946 increase was only 1 per cent which meant that at that time the stimulating influence of the Second World War on the production of manufactured goods in Mexico had come to an end, and that decline was entering, especially because the productive capacity of the United States had tremendously increased in the meantime.[104]

Since many members of the growing middle classes were inclined to be favorable to the conservative party (Partido de Acción Nacional) or the Sinarquistas, the official party (PRM) had to increase its appeal for these classes. For this reason the so-called popular sector in the PRM was strengthened. The army representation in the PRM was dissolved and advised to enter into the popular sector which in September 1942 was organized into the Confederación Nacional de Organizaciones Populares (CNCP).[105]

The transfer of army representation to the CNOP was made easy because Cárdenas was at the head of the Ministry of War during the Second World War years. Many revolutionary generals were occupying important political posts, including for many years the presidency of the official party and a considerable number of governorships. This was another factor which eased the transition.[106] The CNOP has won the majority of the seats in Congress since 1943. Avila Camacho strongly supported and found support in this sector.

The Confederación Nacional de Organizaciones Populares is composed of the following organized nuclei: small agriculturists; small industrialists; small merchants; artisans; members of co-operative enterprises; professional men and intellectuals; youth groups; women's clubs, diverse groupings.[107] CNOP's largest affiliate, the National Confederation of Small Agricultural Proprietors (Confederación Nacional de la Pequeña Propiedad Agrícola) claimed—according to a source in 1957—750,000 members.

While the ejidataries and many kinds of workers more or less obligatorily belonged as members to the official organizations, CNC and CTM, the CNOP membership was voluntary and less formalized. This implied that the leaders of CNOP had to be able to achieve certain benefits in order to make membership advantageous and maintain their following while this was much less needed in the other organizations. As was noted: "Confederation leaders push harder than do most leaders in other organized social segments in order to maintain a continued drive toward consolidation and expansion of the extensive gains that have been achieved." [108]

Regarding the general orientation of the CNOP Padgett remarked: ". . . it is necessary to keep in mind that the CNOP is dominated by professional people who are often also propertied people. Thus the CNOP tends to stand against any raise in property and income taxes. It also promotes the cause of the rural property owner in relation to demands for expropriation on the part of landless peasants, and it stands for increased emphasis upon urban improvements and investments, and investment in the industrialization process as opposed to larger allotments of government money for credit to those on the ejidos." [109]

The fact that the agrarian problems were looked upon in a different way, from the last year of Cardenas's government (1940) onward, is noted in the statements of the CNC at the

477

First National Revolutionary Congress of Agrarian Law, which took place July 4–17, 1945, in Mexico City. It was organized by the Agrarian Department and various related ministries together with the CNC, the Sociedad Agronómica Mexicana and the National University. Leopoldo Flores Zavala, lawyer and chief representative of CNC, indicated that between 1940 and 1943, of 1,112 petitions for land, 691 were negatively decided while in this same period more than 8,000 resolutions of agricultural expropriability were issued, covering almost 550,000 hectares, as well as 203 decrees of livestock inexpropriability, covering almost 2,400,000 hectares. The CNC indicated that although in 1940 about 1.5 million peasants had received land, the need of almost the same number had not yet been satisfied. There existed more than 2,000 villages without ejido-lands, but 5 million hectares which had been distributed by presidential resolution had not yet been handed over to the peasants. More than 8,000 cases were still under consideration.[110] It was also noted that thousands of petitions accumulated at the state level, without being transferred to the Agrarian Department.

One of the points the CNC tried to have accepted in the legislation was the elimination, from the procedure of land petition, of the influence of the state governors and the "Comisiones Agrarias." Because petitions for land had to pass through those channels at the state level, considerable delay was suffered, especially since the governors of some states were in favor of the large landholders, and created obstacles to petitions for land.[111] A more direct treatment by the Agrarian Department through its state delegate was proposed.

Complaints of the peasant Confederation at the Congress of Agrarian Law concerned a great variety of subjects. Some of them were critical of the functioning of the Ejido Bank. It was noted by the CNC representative that this bank bought the products from the ejidatarios at a very low price. For this reason a "moralizing" of the Ejido Bank was recommended.[112]

Among other problems brought forward by spokesmen for the peasants was the availability of water for the distributed lands. One of the representatives of the CTM, Emilio López Zamora, indicated that in the Laguna area the peasants could irrigate only a small part of the irrigable land they had received, because of lack of water, while the "small proprietors" in the area received proportionally much more water. This was noted as one of the reasons why many of the local credit societies in the ejidos could not pay their debts to the Ejido Bank.[113]

Similar things happened in other areas, the ejidatarios receiving less water than they should have been able to claim if distribution of water had been proportional between them and the private farmers. A change in the land reform legislation was proposed, to the effect that the water distribution would be legally fixed the same way as the land distribution.

Another thesis defended by the CTM representatives and unanimously accepted, at the Congress of Agrarian Law, was to reform the irrigation law in such a way that newly irrigated lands, resulting from government investments in irrigation schemes, would be used exclusively for distribution among peasants who petitioned for land, but for whom there was no land available. It would be the responsibility of the Agrarian Department to create the so-called *nuevos centros de población agrícola* (n.c.p.a.) from the lands which benefited from new irrigation schemes. "Small properties" which might be created in such newly irrigated areas should not exceed 20 hectares. This would prevent the frequently occurring practices of land speculation in those areas.[114]

One of the problems brought up, but not discussed at the First Congress of Agrarian Law was that of the sharecroppers and renters who worked on the "small properties" and lived in great misery. The Ligas de Comunidades Agrarias (state branches of the CNC) systematically excluded these peasants from their ranks. It has indicated that they easily fell into the hands of the *sinarquistas* and similar groups which were basically conservative and "against the government." [115]

An increasing number of agricultural workers, peasants who were not in condition to become ejidatarios, sons of ejidatarios who did not inherit the right to their father's parcel (subdivision between sons was prohibited) and other categories of landless peasants had practically no representation in the CNC, nor in the CTM. The CTM generally organized peasants only when they belonged to a specific group, such as the sugarcane and cotton workers, who often were also ejidatarios.

479

The CTM under direction of Fidel Velasquez, the successor of Lombardo Toledano after the latter's term was over in 1941, followed during the years of the Second World War a moderate line, in order not to disturb the production process in those crucial years. Conservative forces had chances to consolidate their position in those years. In order to avoid a turn to the right and an increasing alliance with foreign capital interests, the CTM supported Miguel Aleman for the presidential election of 1946; the candidacy was spearheaded by the CNOP. Ezequiel Padilla, the other candidate, was denounced for his rightist tendencies and for being under the influence of U.S. interests.[116]

At a meeting of the CTM National Committee on June 6, 1945, Lombardo Toledano gave a speech in favor of the candidacy of Miguel Aleman. Aleman himself, at this meeting, stressed that he would continue the work of the Mexican revolution.[117] The review *Futuro*, which was edited by Lombardo Toledano and which strongly supported the Aleman campaign, noted a number of demands in relation to agrarian reform. There were 15,-000 proceeding cases of petitioning peasant committees of ejidos which needed definitive solutions. It was requested that the newly irrigated lands, which would become available the following years when various irrigation schemes were completed, would be dedicated to the solution of the agrarian problem through ejidal settlement (*colonización ejidal*). Another most urgent problem noted was to extend the ejidal credit system, since only 13 per cent of the ejidatarios were attended by the Banco Ejidal. Most peasants continued to receive credits on very unfavorable terms, including usury from private sources.[118]

The CNC supported the candidacy of Miguel Aleman also. At the national congress of the CNC, in July 1945, where his candidacy was proposed, Miguel Aleman said that during his regime 1,440,000 hectares of land would receive irrigation. The need for a redistribution of the rural population, away from the too densely populated areas, was emphasized and an increase of the ejido credits was foreseen.[119]

At the same meeting the secretary-general of the CNC, Gabriel Leyva Velazquez, noted the continuous struggle of the CNC against the "white terror" of landowners and caciques. He indicated that many "white guards" were still operating, causing the death of "thousands and thousands" of peasants in addition to pillage, destruction, and migration in leaving many ejido communities. According to Leyva, this "silent and bloody civil war" was revived particularly by the sinarquistas in the early forties. That the secretary-general of the CNC did not exaggerate can be verified by consulting the press of that epoch, especially the independent and leftist papers, which reported various case histories almost every day.[120]

The serious obstacles which the Mexican revolutionary program was facing have been evaluted in 1944 by Jesús Silva Herzog, Mexican scholar and diplomat. As chief in the Mexican government enterprise which managed the oil industry after its expropriation in 1938, he had considerable experience with the inner aspects of the Mexican political and economic life. Herzog resigned from his post because he found it impossible to introduce an honest and rational administration.

Regarding the agricultural sector, Herzog noted that the credit system had only limited results because of the paternalistic attitude with which credits were distributed and because often political, rather than technical, criteria were followed in the distribution. According to Herzog, something had been done to improve the standard of living of the population, but considerably more could have been done. The main problem in this respect, according to his opinion, was that of honesty.[121]

He criticized the fact that improvements for the workers were not so much gained in hard struggle against employers and police, but to a great extent simply through government support. The result of this was that many labor and peasant leaders became politicians, and politicians became union leaders. This led to a certain lack of syndical education among the organized workers and peasants and to a great liability for rhetoric and demagogy. Since political success in the official party was frequently based more on personal favors and "friendships" than on technical capacity, the higher politicians were not always the most capable people.[122] Being a politician was, according to Silva Herzog, the most easy and most lucrative profession in Mexico, a profession in which shrewdness was more important than knowledge and culture. The labor movement especially suffered from a great number of rather immoral leaders, who worked only for

481

their personal benefit,[123] although there were a number of quite honorable exceptions, as has been noted.

Another evaluation of the Mexican revolution was made in September 1944 by Vicente Lombardo Toledano at an assembly of the revolutionary sector, consisting of CTM, CNC, and CNOP. Lombardo did not stress political corruption but indicated that although the Mexican revolution had made considerable progress, it continued to face some severe problems. These were the poor natural resources, the remnants of the feudal-colonial past and the economic intervention of foreign interests. He stressed that industrialization was one of the basic solutions for Mexico, if it would be directed towards national autonomy and economic independence.[124] For this reason a close collaboration of the various "popular sectors" was needed.

As a follow-up to this assembly, in April 1945 the CTM and the National Chamber of the Manufacturing Industry (Cámara Nacional de la Industria de Transformación) signed the Pacto Obrero-Industrial to build up a basic industry for the country, while each partner would defend its own particular interest.[125]

Consolidation of the Middle Sector

The increasing control of the country's economy by the "middle sector" at the cost of the interests of labor and the peasants became visible, however. One of its symptoms was the change in the official party brought about during Aleman's presidential campaign. Brandenburg noted: "Aleman's grand debut in January 19, 1946, dramatically redesigned the official party in the image of Alemanism: the PRM became the PRI (Partido Revolucionario Institucional), or the party of the Institutionalized Revolution (and how can revolution remain revolution if institutionalized?) and the old party theme 'For a Democracy of Workers' gave way to the PRI theme of 'Democracy and Social Justice.' Aleman exercised his new power by arbitrarily informing party leaders that he had selected Rafael Gamboa, his personal campaign manager, to be first president of the new PRI." [126]

Lombardo Toledano later indicated that this move by Aleman came as a surprise. He also noted that the PRI was less independent than the PRM and was controlled by the government in a way which reminded one of a corporative state.[127]

Symptoms of the increasing influence of the middle and commercial sector in agriculture, at the cost of the ejidatarios and the landless peasants, were additional changes in agrarian legislation, confirming and accelerating the tendency which had started in 1940. Similar to the change in the party slogan, many of the modifications introduced into the official declarations and legislation appeared to be mere changes in terminology, or to be of minor importance. Over the years, however, they proved to have a considerable impact and to represent a significant change in approach and policy.

Article 8 of the Declaration of Principles of the PRI dealt especially with agrarian and agricultural problems. It stressed the needs for land in the villages which had no land or not enough land in the first place; agricultural technical improvement, agricultural credit, and social security for the agricultural workers were other important points: Emphasis was also given to the need that "the agrarian laws determine the responsibilities of the ejido authorities and the corresponding sanctions as means to morally improve the respective administration to give the peasant true securities as regards his work and stimulus to dedicate all his capacities to it." [128] Land distribution, however, followed a considerably slower rhythm than in the Cárdenas period.

One of the modifications in the agrarian legislation to be introduced immediately after Aleman took power in December 1946 was a change in article 27 of the Constitution, giving "small proprietors" the right to request injunction (*derecho de amparo*) against expropriation. During his presidential campaign Miguel Aleman explained that although he agreed that perhaps this right was not an effective means to defend "small property" it would be judicially absurd not to give this right to the "small proprietors." Of course, he noted, it should not be used as a means to protect the still existing latifundios. The right to injunction against expropriation had been left out of article 27 of the Constitution by decree of January 9, 1934, because it had been abused by the large landholders and led at that time to much rural unrest. Already in 1931 the elimination of the landowners right to injunction had been brought about through a modification of the law of January 6, 1915 at the request of the Liga Nacional Campesina "Ursulo Galván." Aleman brought it back into the constitution, however.[129]

At the First National Revolutionary Congress of Agrarian Law, in July 1945, various CNC representatives expressed their objections to bringing the right to injunction against expropriation back into article 27. The change, however, was defended by professor Lucio Mendieta y Núñez.[130] Among the important counter-arguments was the opinion that real small property was constitutionally guaranteed against expropriation, and so-called small properties which resulted from a simulated division of latifundios, should not be given such legal protection. Various speakers denounced this kind of "small proprietor" as different from real small farmers who work their lands and who do not create problems for the ejidatarios. Conflicts in rural areas generally arise because of the simulated "small proprietors," who maintain "white guards," try to divide neighbouring ejidos, and prevent the creation of new ejidos.[131]

One of the CNC representatives observed that it was not the group of *rancheros* and authentic small owners which pressured for changes in article 27 of the constitution, but the large-owners who simulated the division of their states into fractions, without changing the feudal structure. It was said that those representatives of the old landholding families were not infrequently supported by the Supreme Court even against the decisions of the President. It was noted that two hundred villages, contrary to official decisions, were despoiled of their ejido lands, mainly in the states of Jalisco, Michoacan, and Guanajuato. (From these states also came most of the braceros who migrated to the United States, a coincidence which was not accidental.)[132] It was for this reason that the CNC strongly rejected the proposals to give the judicial authorities more influence in the land reform process through such changes as those brought about by Aleman in article 27 of the constitution.

Another change in article 27 of the constitution was related to the definition of "small property." According to the current Agrarian Code 100 hectares of irrigated land were inexpropriable and up to 300 hectares, if cultivated with certain cash crops. In the discussion of this point at the First National Revolutionary Congress of Agrarian Law, it was stressed, especially by Lucio Mendieta y Núñez, that including 300 hectares of cash crops as "small property" within article 27 of the Constitution was superfluous since they were already legally protected. It was emphasized that a change in the constitution could give easy opportunities to the large landholders with simulated "small properties" to escape the agrarian reform. A declaration against a modification of article 27 in this respect was unanimously accepted at the Congress of Agrarian Law.[133]

Only a few days after Miguel Aleman took office in December 1946, however, the debated changes of article 27 of the constitution were brought about, in spite of the apparent disagreement of peasant representatives and prominent agrarianists. There appeared to be little expression of such disagreement in the first years of the Aleman government, however.

With regard to the attitude of the peasantry toward the changes in the law, there is evidence that participation of the peasants in the discussion of changes was avoided. There was no evidence of campaigns to teach the peasantry about the consecutive changes, many of which were disadvantageous to the ejidatarios who were petitioning for land. Changes in the legislation were brought about within the official party and the National Congress. Some deputies or other representatives of the official peasant organization, CNC, noted at times quite openly that it was not convenient to bother the peasants with the details of legislation, even those disadvantageous to peasant interests; they wished to avoid agitation in the countryside, which was considered bad for the economy of the country as a whole. Thus a declaration of CNC's Secretary-General Roberto Barrios (later chief of the Agrarian Department) about changes in the Codigo Agrario promulgated in 1949, said: "we have faith that the revolutionary deputies and that the CNC will struggle so that no step back will be made." The organ of the Frente Zapatista, a group of followers of Zapata, related to the CNC and the PRI, stated: "The political moment is not fit for discussion of the proposed additions, because the simple announcement that the Agrarian Code will be reformed in a sense favorable to the creation of new latifundios has provoked unrest among the peasants, unrest, which, if not soothed, may disturb the huge and patriotic plans of work which the government of President Aleman is realizing." [134] Although a great deal of lip service was still being paid to the agrarian-reform cause, the main slogan related to agriculture became "increase of production." [135]

One of the ways to cope with the postwar economic problems was to achieve self-sufficiency in the production of foodstuffs which formerly had to be imported. One of the products the cultivation of which had to be stimulated at all costs was sugar. During the roundtable meetings organized for the presidential candidate Miguel Aleman, the Union Nacional de Productores de Azúcar, S.A., de C.V., an organization of the sugar industrialists, proposed as a measure to increase sugar production that all sugar cane produced in areas where sugar mills existed be delivered to those mills and that the primitive production of alcohol be prohibited and controlled. It was also proposed that any mill which was not economical be transferred to an area where it could produce more. The representatives of the Sindicato de Trabajadores de la Industria Azucarera at the roundtable meeting mentioned, among other obstacles to sugar production, the fact that the large private sugar mills kept the sugar prices artificially high through the temporary storage of large quantities, thus making immense profits.[136] The representative of the Unión de Productores de Caña de Azúcar (Union of Sugarcane Producers) at the roundtable meeting proposed the establishment of a special tribunal to concilate the many controversies which arose between the producers of sugar cane and the sugar industrialists.[137]

As Wise noted, for the policy of the government to promote industrialization and attract foreign capital, an orientation of the labor movement was needed which stressed conciliation rather than class struggle and which also helped to promote a more favorable attitude toward the United States. A new line of action, in agreement with government policies, was adopted at the IV

National Congress of CTM in 1947. Instead of the former "struggle for the complete abolition of the capitalist system," the declaration of principles accepted at this congress proposed to defend the democratic system and to struggle against any form of fascism, to support the Good Neighbor Policy between Mexico and the United States, and to respect the will of the people. The motto "For a classless society" was changed to "For the emancipation of Mexico." [138]

Aleman was not as favorable to labor as were the former governments. Brandenburg noted an official opinion: "Governmental defense of strikes was nonsense: the courts would settle peacefully and in accord with the promotion of constructive relations with management. Company unions were protected, promoted, and given immunity from mandatory membership in a big central. Rapid industrialization, an Aleman fetish, required low wages and the sacrifices of the labor force to capital accumulation. Aleman insisted that Communists had no place inside the labor movement. His intimate knowledge of Communists, acquired while holding the post of government minister under Avila Camacho, was based on personally compiled biographical records of all labor and peasant leaders. Perhaps nobody in Mexico knew the Communists better than Aleman, and he maintained close surveillance over them." [139]

One consequence of the new government policy was a drastic decrease in strike activity. The number of national strikes showed a decreasing tendency: [140]

Year	Strikes
1943	569
1944	374
1945	107
1946	24
1947	13
1948	11
1949	9
1951	3

As regards the peasantry in those years, indications that the Aleman government was not favorable to the ejidatarios and

487

small peasants became obvious especially in the distribution of the lands which benefited from newly built irrigation systems. Up to 300 hectares of irrigated land planted with cashcrops was inexpropriable according to the Agrarian Code of 1940 and such lands could, after the change in article 27 of the constitution made in December 1946, be considered "small properties." As a consequence much newly irrigated land could easily fall into the hands of businessmen and "friends of the government." [141]

Through legal tricks these "small proprietors" had possibilities to go beyond the limit of 300 hectares, occasionally getting large plantations of thousands of hectares. This kind of neo-latifundio did not show itself easily in the statistics of land tenancy and was difficult to evaluate, because it was in the hands of influential personalities and powerful interests and thus practically above critique. Thus in Matamoros, close to the U.S. border, where 20 per cent of the Mexican cotton was produced, only 20 per cent of the land was in the hands of ejidos while the rest was owned mainly by politicians who could obtain those lands on government credit in 100 hectare plots for 6,000 pesos.[142]

As a result, while in 1940 half of the irrigated land, 994,320 hectares, was in the hands of ejidos and 905,770 hectares in private hands, by 1950 the irrigated land in ejidos had increased to 1,221,000 hectares, but the privately owned to 1,788,000; by 1960, 1,428,000 hectares were in ejidos and 2,087,000 privately owned.[143]

Chevalier indicated that thus only a few tens of thousands of ejidatarios—perhaps 2 or 3 per cent of the total—benefited from the spectacular agricultural development of Mexico, which tripled its production in 25 years. Of the "small proprietors" with more than 10 hectares of irrigable land, many were city-dwellers, ironically called "nylon farmers." Chevalier noted that because many of these were related to the government through friendships [or even more directly] and because their products were important for the national export balance, many irregularities were generally overlooked by the authorities.[144] An additional reason for this was the fact that some of the new commercial crop areas in the hands of these "nylon farmers" were located far from the densely populated areas of subsistence farming and thus did not form a major source of social tension.

There existed a potential for problems however. As González Ramírez noted, too many of the "nylon farmers" used their newly acquired lands for speculation more than for improved agriculture. Another source of difficulty was the fact noted by López Rosado that while profits in commercial agriculture were high, the real value of the agricultural minimum wage was lowered 46 per cent, between 1940 and 1950.[145]

Various critics noted that under the government of Miguel Aleman official corruption increased considerably. It took various forms: public officials and politicians formed companies and then gave government contracts to these companies; because policies as regards new irrigation projects were known long in advance, lands which in the future would benefit from the schemes were bought at cheap prices and held for high profits. A case of this in the area of Matamoros was so outstanding that Lombardo Toledano indicated that the government had made Matamoros a great monument against agrarianism.[146]

A way to keep this system intact against pressure from below was what Padgett called "continuism." [147] Persons in key posts in the official labor or peasant organizations and local politicians, who were accomplices of the "establishment," were kept in power. Thus many corrupt *comisariados ejidales* were maintained through pressure from above, notwithstanding that the Agrarian Code obliged a change every three years. Various means existed to get the same person "re-elected" such as bribery, threats to cut off credits, and threats to evict unwilling ejidatarios from their plots. To indefinitely postpone general assemblies of ejidatarios was another way of preventing democratic processes from functioning. These practices strengthened what has been called *caciquismo,* government by one leader.[148]

Reaction in the Lower Classes

It could be seen as a reaction to these tendencies that ideas developed for the formation of a popular party consisting of workers, peasants, intellectuals, national industrialists, and other sectors of the middle class, under the direction of the proletariat. This idea was defended by Lombardo Toledano in a meeting of various groups, organized in January 1947. The PRI was described as no longer able to fulfill the ideals of the Mexican revolution.[149] These ideas found positive response within the CTM's National Council and National Congress. It was noted that this was a reason why Lombardo supported the election of Fernando Amilpa as the successor of Fidel Velazquez, as secretary-general of the CTM, thus opposing Luis Gomez, the candidate of various radical federations. When those radical groups saw that they had no chance to win, they separated from the CTM.[150]

Because various radically oriented unions and federations split off from the CTM, this organization came more and more into the control of the moderate leaders. Lombardo Toledano supported this tendency while the National Committee of CTM was favorable to his activities to form a new popular party (Partido Popular). Members of this party stayed initially within the CTM, but under pressure of the government the CTM's National Committee expelled Lombardo and other Popular Party activists from its ranks in January 1948.[151]

Later the CTM leaders proposed that they change the statutes of the CTM, break connections with the CTAL (Conferación de Trabajadores de América Latina) and the WFTU (World Federation of Trade Unions) and seek contact with the AFL (American Federation of Labor), headed by George Meany. This happened when the Cold War started to make its impact.[152]

Shortly after being expelled from the CTM, Lombardo organized in January 1948 the Alianza de Obreros y Campesinos de México, affiliated with the CTAL and the WFTU. Various organizations of rural workers joined this Alianza in addition to oil workers, metal workers and railroad workers.

After long preparations on June 20, 1948, the Popular party (PP, Partido Popular) was officially founded, with Lombardo Toledano as secretary-general. Its undersecretary-general was Vidal Díaz Múñoz, one of the top leaders in the Alianza de Obreros y Campesinos. In order to escape the obligatory link with the

PRI and to let members be free to support the political party of their liking, more and more unions left the CTM and proposed to join the Alianza. As a massive national congress in June 1949, this organization was then transformed into the Unión General de Campesinos y Obreros de México (UGOCM). Lombardo indicated that it had 77 regional federations, six state federations with about 300,000 members in all, 70 per cent of whom were peasants.[153] One of its strongest affiliates was the Federación Nacional de Cañeros (sugar cane workers), headed by Vidal Díaz Múñoz.

As a counteraction to the dissident unions the government interfered militarily—for the first time—to dissolve the ruling National Committee of the Railroad-workers Union, imposing a leader called "El Charro," who was favorable to the government.[154] Since that time the word "charro" has been used for leaders who were not democratically elected.

Lombardo noted that many of the unions which initially joined the UGOCM soon disappeared from its ranks, because the directing committees of those unions were imposed by the government. Soon the government again had strong control over the labor movement, except the UGOCM. It has also noted that the article on "social dissolution" of the Penal Code which had been accepted in the early forties to cope with subversive activities of Nazi agents was adapted by Aleman in such a way as to include labor agitators and opponents to the policy of direct government interference with the unions. Various radical labor leaders, including Luis Gómez, were imprisoned.[155]

In 1950 the legal registry as a labor union of the UGOCM was refused by the Ministry of Labour.[156] One of the results was that for the industrial workers UGOCM could not function as a bargaining agent. This was one of the reasons why many urban labor unions had to leave the UGOCM. The peasant unions were practically the only ones to remain.

The peasant strength of the UGOCM existed mainly in the more developed states of Mexico, where the CTM rather than the CNC had been influential. These states included Veracruz, where the sugar workers were important, the cotton-producing Laguna area, where the Unión de Sociedades de Crédito Colectivo Ejidal,

491

headed by Arturo Orona, was affiliated with UGOCM, and Sonora, where the state's Federación de Trabajadores del Estado de Sonora, which included most of the ejidatarios and other peasants, had joined UGOCM at its foundation.

Various efforts were undertaken to weaken or divide the UGOCM. Vidal Díaz Múñoz, secretary-general of the Federación Nacional de Cañeros (sugar cane workers), withdrew with his union from the UGOCM in 1956.[157] The Unión de Sociedades de Crédito Colectivo Ejidal in the Laguna area lost its legal status because of changes brought about in the legislation for agricultural credit in 1955.[158]

In Sonora as early as 1951 the CTM started a campaign to reconquer the unions from UGOCM. A leaflet of one of UGOCM's affiliates, the Federación de Trabajadores y Campesinos del Sur de Sonora (Región del Yaqui) of April 1951, warned the members of a congress to be held by the CTM in Ciudad Obregón, the main center of the area. It gave the names of those who were leading the CTM movement, and denounced many of them as merchants and small businessmen. The leaflet accused the movement of waiting for government money to start its campaign, and it noted that some ejidos had already been divided through government support of various forms.[159]

Some sources claimed that in the beginning UGOCM had a membership of about 500,000 in affiliated organizations, which soon diminished considerably because of the strong counter pressure from the government.[160] Other estimates went as low as 20,000.[161]

In Sonora, the state which was a main UGOCM stronghold, there was considerable activity in the rural sector. This took such proportions that various scholars indicated this as an important reason for the acceleration of the agrarian program during the presidency of Adolfo López Mateos (1958–1964).[162]

In this context some of the most spectacular peasant movements in 1957 and 1958 were the invasions, organized by the UGOCM, of the lands of the Cananea Cattle Company in Sonora owned by U.S. citizens. These lands fell within the legal terms for expropriation, not only because of their size, but also because of the fact that according to the Constitution, no foreigners can own land within 100 kilometers of the national border. The local peasants had petitioned for expropriation for many years, but without results, although the government of Adolfo Ruíz Cortines (1952–1958) had made some initial steps to acquire the 400,000 hectare estates. Schmitt reported the following about the happenings in the late fifties: "During 1957 the UGOCM complained that government officials were not following up the presidential order for the nationalization of the property, and for much of the year carried on agitation to this end. In the first week of February 1958 a band of men led by Jacinto López and local Communist party leader Ramón Danzos Palomino, recently returned from Moscow, seized control of the radio station in Cananea and announced their intention to invade lands of the 400,000 hectare Cananea Cattle Company in the area. They added that they had at their disposal twenty-three trucks to transport those campesinos who desired to participate in the land seizure. Federal Troops and the Judicial Police repelled them, but López shifted his attack to the Culicán Valley in Sinaloa, to the south, where some properties were invaded by squatters. Dislodged by federal forces, López then shifted his operations westward to the Mexicali region in the neigbouring state of Baja California, Norte, where he was again repulsed. On February 24 a UGOCM meeting of 2,000 farm workers, led by Lazaro Rubio Felix, threatened to renew the invasion of all lands held by foreigners along the frontier. Farm owners in the three states appealed to President Ruíz Cortines and to the Department of Defense for army protection against future incursions." [163]

In mid-1958, the federal army and the state police seized Jacinto López and other leaders of the movement and jailed them for about half a year. Thousands of peasants were dislodged by the army from the lands on which they were squatting. The agitation attracted wide publicity and considerable sympathy in Mexico, however.[164] The lands of the Cananea Cattle Company were finally expropriated in 1958.

In the post-reform efforts in the area the government gave strong support to the CNC, the official peasant organization belonging to the PRI. Channeling credits and other benefits through this organization it was possible to win over from

493

the UGOCM an important segment of the Cananea peasants.[165]

After coming out of jail Jacinto López said he would continue to be active in urging land reform in areas where it still had to be carried out. As Schmitt noted: "True to his word López returned to Sonora where his agitation was renewed. Early in January 1959 he led 3,000 squatters in the seizure of lands just outside Ciudad Obregón in the southern part of the state. They remained in peaceful possession for about a week, when city and state police intervened. The squatters, organized in groups of 50, wrapped themselves in Mexican flags as the police approached, but evacuated the land without violence. The state government provided trucks to carry the squatters to their homes, and the Chief of the Department of Agrarian Affairs promised a solution of the land problem within the law." [166]

In 1961 and 1962 several hunger caravans were organized by UGOCM or other independent organizations, but the invasions were especially effective; as Schmitt indicated: "In March 1961 the Attorney General reported that his office had about two thousand complaints against squatters under study. The government in most instances has moved swiftly with a combination of force and concessions to head off these demonstrations before serious violence developed. The UGOCM may not be able to take credit for all agrarian agitation, but it has done more than any other organization in Mexico to point up the needs of the Mexican peasant and to do something about them." [167]

The effectiveness to pressure for completion of the land reform of organizations not dependent on government support stood in contrast to a lack of proper functioning of the CNC which increasingly suffered from the phenomena of continuism and caciquism. As Padgett noted: "When López Mateos took office in 1958 it was clear that the CNC was not maintaining a desirable level of support among peasants, agricultural workers, and others within its organizational sphere. Many rural people were not sharing in the prosperity of industrialization. Moreover, the militancy and determination of the CNC as a channel for effectively presenting the demand of the peasants seemed to be more lacking every year. In these circumstances demonstrations in the rural areas and even violence on occasion were followed by efforts on the part of minor figures among agrarian leaders to create new types of organizations which would have the militant spirit necessary to articulate demands of the rural people." [168]

It was partly due to this situation that in January 1963 a number of peasant unions and leagues which had split off either from the CNC or from UGOCM, because they wanted a more radical policy, formed the Central Campesina Independiente (CCI). Padgett noted that this new organization or its affiliates at the state level could be effective in bringing some urgent regional abuses and demands to the attention of the federal government through demonstrations and similar activities although, after the problems were more or less solved and the emergency was over, the movement lost some of its vigor.[169] Leadership rivalries and differences over policy which came up on various occasions within the CCI resulted in a split. One group, headed by Ramón Danzos Palomino and Arturo Orona, insisted on a radical line and complete independence from the official party or the government, while the other group, headed by Alfonso Garzón, tried to gain benefits by making overtures to the PRI and the CNC.

NOTES

* This paper is part of a larger study on the role of peasant organizations in agrarian reform in Latin America, sponsored jointly by the International Labour Office and the Comite Interamericano de Desarrollo Agricola.

[1] Marjorie Ruth Clark, *Organized Labor in Mexico,* Chapel Hill, University of North Carolina Press, 1934, p. 55.

[2] Clark, op. cit., pp. 60–61.

[3] Carleton Beals, *Mexico: An Interpretation,* New York, 1923, p. 137. See also Vicente Lombardo Toledano, *La Libertad Sindical en México,* Mexico, 1926, pp. 124–128.

[4] Marjorie Ruth Clark, op. cit., pp. 62–64.

[5] Clark, op. cit., pp. 70–74; see also Rosendo Salazar y José G. Escobedo, *Las Pugnas de la Gleba 1907–1922,* Mexico, Editorial Avante, 1923, Segunda Parte, pp. 68–70, who indicate that the name of the party was inspired by the English Labor Party example.

[6] Ibid., p. 70.

[7] Ibid., p. 68.

[8] Antonio Díaz Soto y Gama had been Zapata's legal advisor and

mentor at various times; Rosendo Salazar y José G. Escobedo, op. cit., pp. 73–75 give a description of the Convention, dominated by Luis Morones and his political followers.

[9] Julio Cuadras Caldas, *El Comunismo Criollo*, Puebla, Mexico, 1930, p. 53.

[10] Marjorie Ruth Clark, op. cit., p. 77.

[11] Oscar Lewis, *Pedro Martinez: A Mexican Peasant and his Family*, New York, Random House, 1964, pp. 127–151. The village Tepoztlan carries the name Azteca in this book.

[12] Apolinar Martínez Mugica, *Primo Tapia: Semblanza de un Revolucionario Michoacano*, 2nd ed., Mexico, 1946, pp. 93–100.

[13] Vicente Lombardo Toledano, op. cit., p. 111.

[14] Ernest Gruening, op. cit., p. 324.

[15] Moisés T. de la Peña, *El Pueblo y su Tierra: Mito y Realidad de la Reforma Agraria en México*, México, 1964, pp. 131–135 and p. 316; A. Pérez Betancourt, *Revolución y Crisis en la Economía de Yucatán*, Mérida, 1953; and Marjorie Ruth Clark, op. cit., pp. 198–213.

[16] Marte R. Gómez, *Las Comisiones Agrarias del Sur*, México, 1961, p. 140; Manuel González Ramírez, "El Problema Agrario," *La Revolución Social de México*, vol. III, México, Fondo de Cultura Económica, 1966, p. 263; an interesting description of the effect of the Ligas de Resistencia in the struggles against serfdom and afterwards, in civic education (e.g. anti-alcoholism and community development) can be found in the example of village Muxupip, taken from Juan Rico, *Yucatán, la Huelga de Junio*, in Rosendo Salazar y José G. Escobedo, op. cit., pp. 75–79.

[17] Marjorie Ruth Clark, op. cit., pp. 201–204, 206–207; see also General Salvador Alvarado, *Carta al Pueblo de Yucatán*, 1916. Reproduced in *La Cuestión de la Tierra*, Colección de Folletos para la Historia de la Revolución Mexicana, directed by Jesús Silva Herzog, Mexico, Instituto Mexicano de Investigaciones Económicas, 1962, pp. 153–203, esp. pp. 169 ff.

[18] Marjorie Ruth Clark, op. cit., pp. 208, 404–405; also Nathaniel and Sylvia Weyl, *The Reconquest of Mexico: The Years of Lázaro Cárdenas*, Oxford University Press, 1939, p. 136.

[19] Julio Cuadros Caldas, op. cit., p. 55, indicates that he organized the league in Puebla in 1922, at a meeting of 528 delegates; Apolinar Martínez Mugica, op. cit., pp. 93–100, 109.

[20] Carleton Beals, op. cit., pp. 102, 105.

[21] Manuel Maples Arce, *El Movimiento Social en Veracruz*, Conferencia, May 1, 1927, Jalapa, Talleres Gráficos del Gobierno del Estado, pp. 9–10, 29.

[22] Arce, op. cit., p. 29.

[23] Francisco Gómez Jara, *Las Organizaciones Campesinas en México*, 1966, manuscript, p. 15; also Francisco Gómez Jara, *Las Organizaciones Campesinas de México*, Magisterio, Revista Mensual de Orientación del Sindicato Nacional de Trabajadores de la Educación, No. 71. May 1966, p. 26.

[24] Liga de Comunidades Agrarias del Estado de Veracruz, *La Cuestión Agraria y el Problema Campesino*, Jalapa-Enríquez, Veracruz, 1924, pp. 23, 25.

[25] Ibid., p. 30.

[26] Manuel González Ramírez, op. cit., p. 261, indicates that the coup in 1923–1924 was clearly a struggle between militarism and agrarianism, in which militarism was defeated.

[27] Ernest Gruening, op. cit., p. 320.

[28] Apolinar Martínez Mugica, op. cit., pp. 13–20, 24, 93.

[29] Mugica, op. cit., p. 35.

[30] Mugica, op. cit., pp. 36, 38. For a brief description of this organization founded in Mexico City in 1921, see Vicente Lombardo Toledano, op. cit., pp. 99–100. The organization was reported to be a cover for political activities aimed at introducing elements favorable to the owners of land and capital into the government, and at exercising pressure through press campaigns and other means to modify the existing legislation, especially concerning agrarian questions.

[31] "White guards," *guardias blancas*, were groups of armed men hired by the landowners to fight against those peasants who petitioned for land or those who had received it. See Jesus Silva Herzog, op. cit., pp. 287–288.

[32] Apolinar Martínez Mugica, op. cit., p. 53.

[33] Mugica, op. cit., pp. 51–71.

[34] Mugica, op. cit., pp. 93–100, 105–108.

[35] Mugica, op. cit., pp. 121, 123–131.

[36] Mugica, op. cit., pp. 141–143, 153, 157–159; also Liga de Communidades Agrarias del Estado de Veracruz, op. cit., pp. 36–43.

[37] Mugica, op. cit., pp. 194–195, 199, 200.

[38] Mugica, op. cit., pp. 134, 203, 213, 216, 217, 219.

[39] Ernest Gruening, op. cit., pp. 152–153.

[40] Ursulo Galván attended the First International Peasant Conference held in Moscow in 1925. There he became acquainted with new ideas and forms of land tenure practiced in the Soviet Union. See Liga de Comunidades Agrarias del Estado de Veracruz, op. cit., pp. 48–73.

[41] Karl M. Schmitt, *Communism in Mexico: A Study in Political Frustration*, Austin, University of Texas Press, 1965, p. 14; Julio Cuadros Caldas, op. cit., p. 55; see also Marjorie Ruth Clark, op. cit, p. 156.

[42] Caldas, op. cit., pp. 55–58.

[43] Caldas, op. cit., pp. 58–59.

[44] Emilio Portes Gil, *Quince Años de Política Mexicana*, 2nd ed., México, 1941, p. 446.

[45] Gil, op. cit., pp. 105–107.

[46] Gil, op. cit., pp. 30, 64.

[47] Gil, op. cit., pp. 42–43; on the influence of the army in Mexican politics, see p. 243. Also Pedro González Blanco, *Una Experiencia Política* (*Las "Memorias" del Lic. Portes Gil*) Mexico, Ediciones Rex, 1945, p. 126 and p. 130.

[48] Emilio Portes Gil, op. cit., p. 78.

[49] Marjorie Ruth Clark, op. cit., pp. 156–157; Julio Cuadros Caldas, op. cit., pp. 60–72; Karl M. Schmitt, op. cit., pp. 14–15.

[50] Emilio Portes Gil, op. cit., pp. 197 ff.; Carlos Alvear Acevedo, *Lázaro Cárdenas: El Hombre y el Mito*, Mexico, Editorial Jus, 1961, p. 36.

[51] Marjorie Ruth Clark, op. cit., p. 157.

[52] Clark, op. cit., pp. 161–162.

p. 31.

[53] Eyler N. Simpson, *The Ejido, Mexico's Way Out,* Chapel Hill, University of North Carolina Press, 1937, pp. 335–336, 350.

[54] Emilio Portes Gil, op. cit., pp. 448–450.

[55] Nathaniel and Sylvia Weyl, op. cit., pp. 91–94.

[56] Weyl and Weyl, op. cit., p. 74.

[57] Weyl and Weyl, op. cit., pp. 78–79; also Francisco Gómez Jara, manuscript, op. cit., pp. 30–34. Daniel James, *Mexico and the Americans,* New York, Praeger, 1963, pp. 231–232, indicated that the Cristeros received help from Catholic groups in the United States.

[58] Weyl and Weyl, op. cit., p. 79.

[59] Weyl and Weyl, op. cit., p. 79; also Carlos Alvear Acevedo, op. cit.,

[60] Weyl and Weyl, op. cit., p. 80.

[61] Weyl and Weyl, op. cit., p. 79.

[62] Weyl and Weyl, op. cit., p. 106.

[63] Henry A. Landsberger and Cynthia N. Hewitt, *Preliminary Report on a Case Study of Mexican Peasant Organizations,* Ithaca, New York State School of Industrial and Labor Relations, Cornell University, mimeo., 1966, esp. pp. 15-22.

[64] Carlos Alvear Acevedo, op. cit., p. 39.

[65] Emilio Portes Gil, op. cit., pp. 461–468. Also L. Vincent Padgett, op. cit., p. 110; Graciano Sánchez started out as a rural schoolteacher in his native state of San Luis Potosí. During the Revolution he enlisted in the army of General Lucio Blanco, who first distributed land in the north of Mexico. Later he joined Pancho Villa for a time. After the turmoil was over he went into politics and union organization in San Luis Potosí and Tamaulipas, and became one of the main organizers of the National Peasant Confederation.

[66] Eduardo J. Correa, *El Balance del Cardenismo,* Mexico, 1941, pp. 9–17; Weyl and Weyl, op. cit., p. 108.

[67] Weyl and Weyl, op. cit., pp. 109–110.

[68] Weyl and Weyl, op. cit., pp. 115, 118, 119.

[69] Weyl and Weyl, op. cit., p. 344.

[70] Jesús Silva Herzog, op. cit., pp. 365 ff; also Manuel González Ramírez, op. cit., p. 334.

[71] Partido Nacional Revolucionario, *La Gira del General Lázaro Cárdenas: Síntesis Ideológica,* Mexico, 1934, p. 38.

[72] Partido Nacional Revolucionario, op. cit., pp. 23, 49–50; see also Alfredo Cisneros, *El Gobierno Mexicano es Socialista,* Mexico, 1937, pp. 60–61.

[73] Partido Nacional Revolucionario, op. cit., p. 63; Julio Cuadros Caldas, op. cit., p. 74, claimed that over the years more than 3,000 agrarian leaders have been killed by "white guards," rebelling generals and the state governors' police.

[74] Weyl and Weyl, op. cit., p. 189; Manuel González Ramirez, op. cit., pp. 341–342; also Lázaro Cárdenas, *La Unificación Campesina,* Partido Nacional Revolucionario, Biblioteca de Cultura Social y Política, Marzo, 1936.

[75] Lázaro Cárdenas, op. cit., p. 17.

[76] Francisco Gómez Jara, op. cit., p. 41.

[77] Weyl and Weyl, op. cit., p. 235.

[78] For a short biography about Lombardo Toledano see A. Kawage Ramia, *With Lombardo Toledano*, México, 1943. For an extensive description of Lombardo's life and thoughts see Robert Paul Millon, *Vicente Lombardo Toledano*, Biografía Intelectual de un Marxista Mexicano, México, 1964 (translation of Ph.D. Thesis, presented in 1963, Chapel Hill, University of North Carolina.

[79] Víctor Alba, *Historia del Movimiento Obrero en América Latina*, México, Libreros Mexicanos Unidos, 1964, p. 447; Nathaniel and Sylvia Weyl, op. cit., p. 236.

[80] Confederación de Trabajadores de México, *Informe del Comité Nacional 1936–1937*, signed by Vicente Lombardo Toledano as General-Secretary and other members of the Committee, pp. 64–65.

[81] Paul Nathan, op. cit., p. 378; Francisco Gómez Jara, manuscript, op. cit., p. 36, quoted from a newspaper of that time (*El Día*, June 24, 1935) that about a million peasants were represented in the Committee.

[82] Confederación de Trabajadores de México, op. cit., p. 67.

[83] Confederación de Trabajadores de México, op. cit., p. 84.

[84] Francisco Gómez Jara, op. cit., pp. 41–43.

[85] Manuel González Ramírez, op. cit., pp. 341–342. Francisco Gómez Jara, op. cit., p. 43; also William P. Tucker, *The Mexican Government Today*, Minneapolis, University of Minnesota Press, 1957, p. 54.

[86] Francisco Gómez Jara, op. cit., p. 43; also Carlos Alvear Acevedo, op. cit. p. 170.

[87] William P. Tucker, op. cit., p. 53; Eduardo J. Correa, op. cit., pp. 85–86; Paul Nathan, op. cit., p. 451.

[88] Nathaniel and Sylvia Weyl, op. cit., pp. 344–349.

[89] Paul Nathan, op. cit., pp. 456–457.

[90] Dionisio Encina, *Informe al Primer Congreso Extraordinario del Partido Communista de México*, March 19–24, 1940, México, D.F., Editorial Popular, pp. 132–134.

[91] Paul Nathan, op. cit., p. 236.

[92] Moisés T. de la Peña, *El Pueblo y su Tierra: Mito y Realidad de la Reforma Agraria en México*, Mexico, Cuadernos Americanos, 1964, pp. 320–323.

[93] *Seis Años de Gobierno al Servicio de México*, 1934–1940, El Secretario de Gobernación, November 30, 1940, La Nacional Impresora, pp. 95–96.

[94] Paul Nathan, op. cit., p. 240.

[95] Betty Kirk, op. cit., p. 233.

[96] Ibid., p. 234, where the CNC is classified as "middle-of-the-road"; Weyl and Weyl, op. cit., p. 358.

[97] Paul Nathan, op. cit., p. 468; Betty Kirk, op. cit., pp. 245–246, 248.

[98] Paul Nathan, op. cit., pp. 240, 241.

[99] Seis Años de Gobierno al Servicio de México, op. cit., pp. xiv and 331.

[100] Oscar Figueroa Felix, *Reestructuración del Proceso Agrario: Supresión de la Primera Instancia*, U.N.A.M., Facultad de Derecho, Tesis Profesional, México, D.F., 1965, p. 52; Manuel González Ramírez, *La Revolución Social de México*, op. cit., p. 397.

[101] *Diario Oficial,* México, D.F., 29 octubre 1940; also: Oscar Figueroa Felix, op. cit., p. 53.

[102] Jesús Silva Herzog, op. cit., pp. 452, 453.

[103] Manuel González Ramírez, op. cit., pp. 375–377; also *International Labour Review* XXIII, no. 5, Geneva, May 1941.

[104] Manuel German Parra, *Conferencias de Mesa Redonda,* presididas durante su Campaña Electoral por el Lic, Miguel Aleman, 27 de agosto de 1945–17 de junio 1946, México, 1949, p. xvii.

[105] Eduardo J. Correa, *El Balance del Avila Camachismo,* Mexico, D.F., 146, p. 158; also William P. Tucker, *The Mexican Government Today,* op. cit., pp. 44, 56–58.

[106] Frank Brandenburg, *The Making of Modern Mexico,* Englewood, N.J., Prentice-Hall, 1946, p. 94.

[107] CNOP, *Bases Constitutivas,* article 2, pp. 15–16; quoted in L. Vincent Padgett, op. cit., p. 124.

[108] L. Vincent Padgett, op. cit., p. 127.

[109] Padgett, op. cit., p. 127.

[110] Departamento Agrario, *Primer Congreso Nacional Revolucionario de Derecho Agrario,* op. cit., pp. 330–332.

[111] Departamento Agrario, op. cit., p. 329.

[112] Departamento Agrario, op. cit., p. 188.

[113] Departamento Agrario, op. cit., pp. 149–151.

[114] Departamento Agrario, op. cit., pp. 165–167, 222–235.

[115] Departamento Agrario, op. cit., pp. 498–500.

[116] Robert P. Millon, *Vicente Lombardo Toledano (Biografía Intelectual de un Marxista Mexicano),* op. cit., pp. 152–153.

[117] Vicente Lombardo Toledano, *El Proletariado ante la Sucesión Presidencial,* and Miguel Aleman, *Continuaré la Obra de la Revolución Mexicana, Futuro,* July 1945, Mexico.

[118] Jorge Fernández Anaya, *Consumación de la Reforma Agraria, Futuro,* June–July 1945, Mexico.

[119] Miguel Aleman, "La Reforma Agraria y la Producción Agrícola," *Futuro,* June–July 1945, Mexico.

[120] *Futuro,* Agosto 1945.

[121] Jesús Silva Herzog, *La Revolución Mexicana en Crisis,* Mexico, Ediciones Cuadernos Americanos, 1944, pp. 22, 26, 27.

[122] Herzog, ibid., p. 31.

[123] Herzog, ibid. pp. 33–34.

[124] Vicente Lombardo Toledano, *El Nuevo Programa del Sector Revolucionario de México,* Mexico, 1944, pp. 4–14, 16–21.

[125] V. Lombardo Toledano, *La Perspectiva de México: Una Democracia del Pueblo,* April 15, 1955, leaflet, p. 6.

[126] Frank Brandenburg, op. cit., p. 101.

[127] Vicente Lombardo Toledano, op. cit., pp. 39–40, 42.

[128] Jesús Silva Herzog, op. cit., p. 487 (translation by this author).

[129] Manuel German Parra, *Conferencias de Mesa Redonda,* presididas durante su campaña electoral por el licenciado Miguel Aleman, 27 de Agosto de 1945–17 de Junio de 1946, Mexico, 1949, p. 149, par. 37; Departamento Agrario, *Primer Congreso Nacional Revolucionario de Derecho Agrario, Memoria,* op. cit., pp. 333, 426–427.

[130] Departamento Agrario, op. cit., pp. 397, 481.

[131] Departamento Agrario, op. cit., pp. 415–418, 420–423.

[132] Departamento Agrario, op. cit., p. 506.

[133] Departamento Agrario, op. cit., pp. 158–159.

[134] El Campesino, Organo del Frente Zapatista de la República, December 1, 1949. (translation by this author.)

[135] See, for example, a leaflet for peasant education, published by CNC, Futurismo, el Enemigo Común, Asamblea del Mejoramiento de la Vida Rural, November 6–7, 1950.

[136] Manuel Germán Parra, op. cit., pp. xxviii, 43–46; Henry A. Landsberger and Cynthia N. Hewitt, op. cit., p. 26.

[137] Manuel German Parra, op. cit., pp. 47–49.

[138] George S. Wise, El México de Alemán, Editorial Atlante, México, 1952, pp. 249, 250.

[139] Frank Brandenburg, op. cit., p. 102.

[140] Vicente Lombardo Toledano, Teoría y Práctica del Movimiento Sindical Mexicano, México, Editorial del Magisterio, 1961, p. 91; George S. Wise, op. cit., p. 240; for similar data regarding strikes of all types and numbers of strikers, see Pablo González Casanova, La Democracia en México, Editorial Era, México, 1965, pp. 14–15 and Cuadro III, pp. 170–171.

[141] François Chevalier, Ejido y Estabilidad en México, America Indigena, XVII, No. 2, 1967, Mexico, pp. 176–177.

[142] Chevalier, op. cit., p. 179.

[143] Chevalier, op. cit., p. 177; from census data of 1940, 1950 and 1960.

[144] Chevalier, op. cit., p. 181.

[145] Manuel González Ramírez, op. cit., p. 397.

[146] Robert P. Millon, op. cit., p. 81; Vicente Lombardo Toledano, Teoría y Práctica, op. cit., p. 81.

[147] L. Vincent Padgett, op. cit., pp. 114–120, which includes a case study.

[148] Ibid.; also René Dumont, Terres Vivantes, Paris, Ed. Plon, 1961, chapt. VI, p. 104.

[149] Robert P. Millon, op. cit., p. 170.

[150] Millon, op. cit., p. 154.

[151] Millon, op. cit., p. 172.

[152] Vicente Lombardo Toledano, Teoría y Práctica, op. cit., pp. 82–87.

[153] Toledano, op. cit., p. 89.

[154] Toledano, op. cit., p. 86.

[155] Ibid., p. 87; also Robert P. Millon, op. cit., p. 155.

[156] L. Vincent Padgett, op. cit., p. 94; also Karl M. Schmitt, Communism in Mexico, op. cit., p. 179.

[157] Karl M. Schmitt, op. cit., pp. 178–179.

[158] Marco Antonio Duran, "El Estancamiento en la Organización Interna de los Ejidos," El Trimestre Economico, XXXII, 3, No. 127, México (July–September, 1965), p. 465; for a comparison of regulations in the agricultural credit laws of 1943 and of 1955 see next chapter.

[159] Alerta Obreros y Campesinos del Estado de Sonora, Ciudad Obregón, April 1951 (Secr. Gen. Ramón Danzos Palomino), leaflet.

[160] Robert P. Millon, op. cit., p. 155.

[161] Howard F. Cline, Mexico: Revolution to Evolution: 1940–1960,

Oxford University Press, 1962, indicated that the UGOCM had only 20,000 members.

[162] Karl M. Schmitt, op. cit., p. 14; also Howard F. Cline, op. cit., p. 211 and Martin C. Needler, "Mexico: Revolution as a Way of Life," in Political Systems of Latin America, ed. Martin C. Needler, Princeton, N.J., Van Nostrand Political Science Series, 1964, pp. 23–24.

[163] Schmitt, op. cit., p. 180.

[164] Schmitt, op. cit., pp. 113–114, 201.

[165] Schmitt, op. cit., p. 201.

[166] Schmitt, op. cit., p. 181.

[167] Schmitt, op. cit., p. 182.

[168] L. Vincent Padgett, op. cit., p. 120.

[169] Padgett, op. cit., p. 122.

14

CAMILO TORRES RESTREPO

Social Change
and Rural Violence
in Colombia

SCOPE OF ANALYSIS

To determine the magnitude of a change it is necessary to establish three aspects: (1) the situation before the change; (2) the factors that contributed to the change and the way in which they contributed to it; (3) the situation after the effect of these factors. Before undergoing the phenomenon of violence, rural Colombian society was relatively static.[1] To a certain extent this makes it easier to perceive that a change has taken place. Nevertheless, a study of social change must be limited to certain variables because its complexity rules out the possibility of an exhaustive analysis. In the present study we shall consider only those areas that have been affected at some time by violence. Nevertheless, according to the studies carried out, especially by Germán Guzmán, this includes almost all the rural areas of Colombia.[2]

Many of the variables that we will take into account are by no means exclusive to Colombian society. They constitute defining factors in any rural society. We have singled them out here because we believe that they have been particularly affected by the phenomenon of violence.

The present analysis refers almost exclusively to the de-

503

scription made by Germán Guzmán in the first volume of his book, *La Violencia en Colombia,* and to studies on rural Colombian society before it underwent the impact of violence.[3]

We will try to fit the information contained in those studies into a theoretic framework relative to social change brought on by violence. We shall discuss: the selected variables as they appeared before violence; how these variables were affected by violence; the final result. We will classify the variables into three groups: (1) those common to all rural societies; (2) those that pertain to rural societies of underdeveloped countries; and (3) those characteristic of Colombian rural society.

VARIABLES COMMON TO EVERY RURAL SOCIETY

Lack of Division of Labor and Specialization and Scarcity of Social Roles

Farming and cattle raising are almost the only activities of the Colombian farmer. They condition every other aspect of life —the market, religion, the family, etc. The occurrence of violence confronts the farmer with new needs, which in turn impose a division of labor in resulting new activities: in the active groups, in addition to what is required for any act of war as such, there arise those needs specific to guerrilla warfare, e.g., espionage, clandestine communications, supplies, medical and other social services, public relations, etc.[4]

New needs also arise for the passive groups. Both among these and between them and the guerillas co-operation is essential in order to keep watch and be prepared for repressive acts by the government.

It has proved indispensable that one member of the rural community be appointed to regularly take charge of these needs. Hereby a kind of specialization has been achieved; although elementary, it is important in terms of social relations.

In rural society, because of the lack of division of labor and specialization, social relations are more intimate, frequent, and personal than elsewhere. The result is a folk society, which has been described by Redfield:

504

Such a society is small, isolated, nonliterate, and homogeneous, with a strong sense of group solidarity. The ways of living are conventionalized into that coherent system which we call 'a culture.' Behavior is traditional, spontaneous, uncritical, and personal: there is no legislation of habit or experiment and reflection for intellectual ends. Kinship, its relationships and institutions, are the type categories of experience and the familial group is the unit of action. The sacred prevails over the secular. The economy is one of status rather than of the market.[5]

These were exactly the characteristics of Colombian rural society before it underwent violence.

The lack of division of labor also accounted for group solidarity, i.e., mechanistic solidarity.[6] This mechanistic solidarity produces a coherent system of life based on tradition and sentiment.

In Tönnies' terms, Colombian rural society resembles the community (*Gemeinschaft*) more than the society (*Gesellschaft*). Subsistence economy stimulates primary relations much more than it does secondary relations and is one of the causes of the lack of division of labor.

These phenomena produce important effects on attitudes toward social change. The predominance of primary relations over secondary relations tends to disappear as there is a greater division of labor and greater specialization, and therefore as social roles become multiplied and diversified.

In those communities affected by violence, social interaction is increasingly based on the functions of the individual rather than on the individual himself. Group solidarity becomes organic rather than mechanistic, that is to say, based on the complementariness of roles rather than on their homogeneity.

Social relations are increasingly based on reason rather than on tradition and sentiment. Behavior is no longer traditional and spontaneous but becomes critical and impersonal.[7] The "community" changes into a "society." Colombian rural society affected by violence begins to organize itself around patterns of urban behavior. This process of urbanization is carried out exclusively through tertiary activities (personal services, commerce, transportation, war, etc.) and is not connected with the secondary activity of industrialization.

505

The socio-economic effects are obvious: the urban way of life implies a rational, anti-traditional attitude with respect to social change. In the present case, however, this attitude is not accompanied by industrialization, which might allow for a higher standard of living. In sum, violence in Colombian urban society produces urban attitudes without the instruments peculiar to an urban society.

Social Isolation

Among the variables common to all rural societies we find social isolation, an element that Redfield includes within the folk society. This ecological phenomenon is produced by a low demographic density and by the absence of communication media that characterizes rural societies. In underdeveloped countries social isolation is aggravated by the lack of transportation and the absence of all kinds of communication media. In Colombia isolation is particularly severe. Population is concentrated in the mountainous zone and in the valleys separated by mountains. In addition to being isolated from the cities and from the centers of their respective communities, the *veredas*—typical small settlements found, in the manner of a colony or outpost, along the trails—or rural neighborhoods are isolated from each other.

Violence increased rural migrations, not only to the city but also among the various peasant localities. The armed forces, aside from their regular system of communication, functioned as a human system for transmitting news and introducing social values and standards of behavior from the city to the rural areas and among the various rural neighborhoods.

As a result, rural populations have come into contact with each other, becoming aware of common needs and acquiring a group solidarity, as they compared their own socio-economic conditions with other sectors' higher standards of living, both rural and urban.

Local cultural patterns began to spread, producing a phenomenon of assimilation of these factors and thereby beginning the formation of a Colombian rural subculture. In terms of social change, the emergence of a group solidarity or class consciousness among Colombian peasants evolves into the formation of a pressure group from below which, when organized, can become important in the transformation of the country's social, political, and economic structure.

Importance of the Rural Neighborhoods in Social Life

In view of the isolation described above, it is logical that the neighborhood should be of the greatest importance in the social life of the rural community. Human activity in this society is directly related to geographic location. The lack of division of labor almost completely rules out the need to move from one place to another. Thus, the neighborhood and the family constitute the most efficient institutions for social control within present society. The approval or disapproval of the neighborhood has a great influence on the behavior of the peasant.

There is a close relationship between the forces of social control and the standardizing of patterns of behavior. Phenomena of anomie rarely appear in an isolated and strictly controlled society. There are no demands of adaptation to new norms, inasmuch as life in such a society requires only a mechanical compliance with traditional patterns of behavior. Hence the coherence in the system of folk society spoken of by Redfield. Hence, too, the lack of experimentation and of intellectual reflection.

The occurrence of violence breaks down the barriers around the rural neighborhood. Guerrilla groups become the new controlling elements, not just in the veredas but on a regional scale. In many rural areas government pressure is felt for the first time. This ranges from physical violence to economic enticements. The possibility—and, in some instances, the necessity— of migrating frees the rural groups from the social control of the surrounding community. Reference groups for social control become multiplied; besides the family there is the guerrilla group; besides the neighborhood itself, there are more or less belligerent groups of fugitive peasants. The government army and the groups of civilian armies, as well as the urban groups that participate directly or indirectly in the patterns of violence and through it intervene in the rural communities—all these groups with their different norms and standards of behavior relax social control in a way similar to what takes place in the cities. The peasant, accustomed to act without reflection or criticism by merely following the patterns, loses all standards of behavior and adapts as best he can to the different reference groups. In this way anomic behavior spreads through the peasant conglomerate as an effect of the peasants' emergence from the social isolation of the neighborhood. Rural communities that have undergone the phenomenon of violence are exposed to all kinds of cultural contacts.

The peasants' emergence from social isolation has caused the neighborhood to lose importance in their social life and has established, on a regional and national scale, new institutions that characterize the new subculture originated by violence.

As in the case of social isolation in rural areas, local social control has been relaxed by the multiplication of controls independent of geographic locale. This is explained by the diversification of rural activities. Nevertheless, that diversification is not the result of a development of economic productivity; rather, it is linked to activities of destruction, defense, or simply self-sustenance, which hardly fit into a plan of socio-economic development for the country. Thus there are sociological phenomena of urbanization without concomitant processes of industrialization or city-building.

Individualism

In general, isolation makes for closed groups and societies. However, when each person is also isolated in his work, individualism arises as a logical outcome. This happens in rural societies that are made up of *minifundios* or are based on seasonal employment in the harvests. In these instances, each individual is concerned with his own interest and cooperates only to serve his own interests. Institutions like *la minga, la mano vuelta, el convite* [8] are transitory and do not contradict but rather confirm the individualist pattern of behavior, in the sense that this behavior results from the pursuit of objectives that serve predominantly personal interests. Individualism is an attitude defined by motivation. Nevertheless, social behavior is an index and at times the only index that is known or can be known.

508

In view of the predominance of minifundio owners and harvest workers within the Colombian peasant population, we can be certain that the individualist attitude is quite general, especially in more isolated areas. The collectivist habits that some indigenous communities had in the past have almost disappeared.

To a great extent the emergence of violence breaks up the peasants' individualism and forces the introduction of patterns of behavior in which teamwork becomes indispensable. On similar grounds, so-called guerrillas for peace are organized by the government to combat the real guerrillas. Unofficially, guerrillas work as teams both in their combat activities and in providing for themselves. There are even established groups like the one at El Pato, where, through collective effort, a mill was built, an orchard grown, the production of cane sugar organized, and the fields were weeded, tilled, sown, irrigated, and harvested.

The group solidarity peculiar to every marginal community and especially to every outlaw group is fully confirmed within the guerrilla groups. Among the peasants, the emergence of violence creates circumstances which force them to abandon their individualism. Joint migrations, defense of the rural communities, organization of production, etc., encouraged a mentality of co-operation, initiative, and class consciousness. A new situation has transformed Colombian rural communities into social units with internal cohesion, initiative, and their own dynamics.

Conflict with the Out-Group

The members of rural groups described have "a strong sense of solidarity." [9] This is usually directly linked to the degree of conflict with out-group elements. Colombian rural communities are distrustful of institutions and leaders—and of all persons who do not belong to their own social group.

The institutions belonging to the out-group can be classified as official, ecclesiastic, and private. Many of the government, ecclesiastic, and private institutions belonged to the peasant sector as such, in the sense that they were identified with the rural community much more than with the national level of the government, church, or other entity. The use of the first person plural pronoun "our" in relation to the church (as a building), the county courthouse, and some of the haciendas reveals this sentiment of solidarity with those institutions. Nevertheless, the attitude toward official institutions at a level higher than the county level was not one of open conflict but rather of reserve and even of distrust. The same is true with respect to non-local ecclesiastic and private entities.

In rural areas it is essential to distinguish between two very different kinds of community: one belongs to the town and the other belongs to the vereda. Between these two there existed, before the emergence of violence, a relationship of accommodation whereby the vereda communities were subordinate to the town communities. This accommodation sometimes flared into open conflict, especially for political reasons, which were a mere pretext to allow expression of latent conflicts rising out of the vereda's inferior situation with respect to the town that served as a kind of county seat. Among the different veredas there was also a rivalry which was at times settled by conflict—only very rarely violent. Although there was seldom a relationship of accommodation between one vereda and another, the common conflict with the town that served as county seat made tensions between the veredas diminish, creating a relationship of solidarity among the veredas themselves.

The occurrence of violence fundamentally changed human relationships within the rural society. Government ecclesiastic and civil institutions—even the local ones—came to be considered in many instances as out-group institutions that broke up the peasant sector into splinter groups. Moreover, since the peasant group was engaged in open conflict—sometimes violent —with the national or state level of these institutions, a relationship of conflict was established with these institutions at the local level, too.

Accommodation with respect to the government, the church, and the landlords was destroyed. The relationship of accommodation between the vereda and the town also underwent a change. Some elements in the towns joined in alliance with civil, ecclesiastic, and government institutions that were in conflict with the peasant group; others joined the peasants and opposed the established groups. Thus, town-dwellers entered into a relationship of co-operation with either the vereda inhabitants or the outside institutions.

The veredas' relationships with one another have gone through various stages. After violence erupted, frictions that had been minor became more serious, at first taking on an entirely political cast. Divided and rallied around the flags of the two traditional parties—liberal and conservative—the peasantry engaged in violent conflict. The communist groups rose as a third faction, at times as a peasant group made up of those who wanted to fight not other peasants but formal and informal authorities.

Thus, the first effect of violence was to divide the peasants. As violence became a chronic condition, an important phenomenon of social change appeared: whenever violent pressure by the out-group diminished and socio-ec nomic needs increased, a new type of solidarity emerged among the peasants—liberal, conservative, or communist.

This new type of solidarity was organic rather than mechanistic, and rational rather than sentimental, eliminating not only those political divisions that had been sharpened by violence, but also the divisions existing between the peasant groups prior to the emergence of violence. Before the occurrence of violence, bureaucratic leadership was concentrated in the town or county seats, though leaders were also found in the veredas. But they had little influence in official decision-making for the rural community at the county level. All they could reserve for themselves was a small share of unofficial power at the vereda level.

The structure of peasant leadership changed with the onset of violence. The charismatic leaders of the vereda grew in importance with respect to the leaders of the town or county seat. When the traditional leaders and the *gamonal* leaders—large landowners operating within a feudal-style latifundism as local political leaders—of the towns were obedient to the institutions responsible for violence against the peasants, they lost their positions of leadership among them. The same thing happened to the charismatic leaders, who were therefore no longer such in the true sense of the word.

Electoral processes developed a new kind of gamonal leadership, more attuned to the needs of the peasantry, and with which the national executives of the political parties were forced to deal, in their attempt to obtain the co-operation of the peasant masses.

Sentiments of either solidarity with or distrust toward other individuals in the out-group were strictly conditioned by peasant attitudes during the occurrence of violence. Indeed, many out-group elements, even some of upper-class and urban origin, were trusted by the peasant group, provided they showed solidarity toward the peasants' armed struggle, while many genuinely rural elements were rejected if they showed solidarity with the enemy groups. Solidarity with individuals was decided on the basis of common interests rather than common origins, and for rational rather than traditional reasons.

Conflict with the out-group elements and the restructuring of social relations in rural communities fundamentally altered the structure of Colombian peasantry by creating a new and more rational type of solidarity.

Feeling of Inferiority

The peasants' feeling of inferiority to urban inhabitants has usually been described as an individual psychological phenomenon. However, when this represents a collective attitude, its study can be transposed to the psycho-social level, if we make the appropriate conceptual adaptations. The peasants felt fundamentally inferior to urban institutions and individuals. This feeling was translated into different kinds of relationships: at times, of accommodation; at other times, of conflict. The occurrence of violence made the peasants feel safe to oppose elements, institutions, individuals, and patterns of behavior that they associated with the urban community. Actually, peasant guerrilla groups have never directly attacked the big Colombian cities. Even so, in warfare the feeling of inferiority has been replaced by one of superiority. In guerrilla warfare, the peasants know they have overcome the army and defeated an urban institution that constitutes the principal bastion of defense of the cities.

512

Putting to one side the truth of falsity of this new feeling, what must be noted is the psycho-social change that it implies, inasmuch as one element essential to the formation of a pressure group is that the group should feel safe to act with regard to others against whom it considers the exercise of social pressure to be necessary.

VARIABLES PECULIAR TO THE RURAL SOCIETIES OF UNDERDEVELOPED COUNTRIES

Absence of Vertical Upward Mobility

Social mobility has always been considered an element of social change. Nevertheless, it seems necessary to distinguish between a simply material social mobility and a socio-cultural mobility. Material social mobility consists of a simple shift of individuals from one social group to another, from one geographic area to another, from one status or social class to another. Cultural social mobility necessarily implies a change in values, behavior, and, consequently, in social institutions as a consequence of the material mobility. There is a relationship between material social mobility and cultural social mobility, from both a quantitative and a qualitative point of view.

Quantitatively, if the shift of individuals from one group to another or from one area to another is carried out en masse, it is very difficult to prevent socio-cultural changes from occurring in the process of assimilation, as much in the individuals who admit the newcomers as in the newcomers themselves. In contrast, if the shift is made slowly and by a small group it is very probable that the socio-cultural patterns of the society that admits the newcomers will remain almost unchanged, and the new elements will be the only ones changed by the social mobility, inasmuch as in this case conformity will be imposed on the new elements as a requisite for acceptance.

Qualitatively, it is necessary to distinguish the type of individual who becomes mobile. The ascent of a leader is not the same as the ascent of a person with no influence in his social group. Also it is necessary to define the requirements for social mobility. It is possible that in horizontal mobility no demand is made by the host community, whereas for a vertical upward mobility it is necessary to adjust to the patterns of social ascent of the institutions that control this ascent—that is to say, it is necessary to conform.

In the present analysis we consider social mobility not only from the physical point of view but also from the socio-cultural point of view—since in our opinion the latter aspect is the most directly relevant to the study of social change. Social mobility from rural areas to the cities occurs everywhere, but in underdeveloped countries this migration exhibits more sharply defined characteristics.

It is difficult to make a similar statement with regard to horizontal mobility, understood as a non-ascending migratory flow to urban centers. The rapid growth of big cities in underdeveloped countries, due fundamentally to migration from rural areas, is a sign that horizontal rural mobility in those countries is greater than in industrialized countries. Furthermore, despite the shortcomings of the transportation systems, the "push" factors from rural areas and the "pull" factors from the cities are more significant in countries not yet industrialized.

In view of the existence of self-fulfilling prophecies within the socio-economic structure of developing countries, vertical downward mobility is much greater than in the developed countries, especially in rural areas. The increase of production cannot keep pace with the increase in rural population. The continual re-dividing of the land aggravates the problem of minifundio, which worsens with each new generation. Manpower becomes cheaper because the increase of the population is not accompanied by a proportional increase of opportunities for work and productivity.

ECONOMIC CHANNEL

The ownership of manufactured and consumer goods is, in general, a rapid means of upward social mobility. In a social system based on private enterprise, the ability to acquire wealth depends on the average inhabitant's business ability. In other words, the capacity to ascend economically does not necessarily require long-range training, as it does in the cultural, military, or ecclesiastic fields. Ownership and use of goods and services requires only superficial training and, by its very nature, this channel of ascent makes no demands.

To own and to use is something that everybody knows how to do. It is much easier than, say, giving orders. Therefore, the economic channel is, in itself, even more rapid than the bureaucratic and the political. Moreover, in a regime of private enterprise and even in a collectivist regime, as far as consumer goods are concerned, satisfaction of man's vital needs depends on economic ascent. For these two reasons, among others, the blocking of the economic channel of social ascent constitutes one of the most serious social frustrations, especially in the underdeveloped countries, where levels of training are low and the national income is limited.

When this frustration is recognized and possibilities for relieving it are offered, the real "social problem" appears. One of the characteristics of underdeveloped countries is the concentration of goods and services in a few hands. The few propertied people block the channels of economic ascent unless they profit from opening them. Those who begin to emerge from the feudal mentality of owning rather than producing, those who begin to have a capitalist mentality of greater productivity, will open economic channels to those who could become better consumers —and will open them at the rate at which social pressure from below becomes a serious threat to the economic structures that benefit these few propertied people. Nevertheless, these two circumstances (mentality of productivity and social pressures from below) are indices of incipient development. Where they do not exist, there is almost total obstruction of the economic channel of ascent. This obstruction is greater in rural areas. The low productivity of the farming and animal husbandry business and the subsistence economy in rural areas of underdeveloped countries result in a slower increase of consumer demand in relation to the increase of income per capita than is the case in industrial areas. Moreover, rural traditionalism impedes rapid change in the consumer habits of the peasant population. As a result, although some of the propertied people do think in terms of opening channels of economic ascent in order to increase consumer demand, rural inhabitants are the last to be considered prospective customers.

Regarding social pressure, the peasantry was likewise in a position of inferiority. Social isolation, individualism, and traditionalism made it difficult for the peasantry to become a pressure group. Until they had social contacts that could spark changes in these and other variables, the peasants would not pose a threat to the ruling economic structure. The occurrence of violence impelled the peasants to become a pressure group. They became aware of their needs and their human resources to meet them. This drew them out of their traditional passiveness and brought out a feeling of group solidarity as they organized for very specific purposes. Violence developed the conflict with respect to the out-group and institutionalized it.

With regard to social ascent by the economic channel, the new framework of violence had two principal effects: it created the contacts necessary to arouse the peasants concerning their wretched poverty—and made that poverty more deeply felt in all the areas in which violence occurred. Simultaneously, violence made it possible for individuals at all social levels to achieve economic gains. Violence had the political-economic effect of assuring bureaucratic favors to the governing class, for example, through acquisition of large properties devaluated by the phenomenon of violence,[10] confiscation of crops, withholding of payments of debts to public and private persons, traffic of arms, confiscation of animals and small properties, etc. Together with an awareness of his wretchedness, the peasant acquired instruments that Colombian rural society considered anomic, but that turned out to be effective for social ascent. We will show that, whenever there is pressure to ascend, obstruction of the normal routes of ascent results in the use of abnormal channels if these seem to be more effective.[11] Since violence began, the peasant has used any available means to try to ascend economically or at least support himself.

Admittedly, there is a marked rate of criminality among the guerrilla groups. Yet the new generations of peasants will not be able to end the pattern of violence unless normal channels of economic ascent are opened and prove to be effective for the majority of the rural population.

CULTURAL CHANNEL

We understand "culture" to be the combination of values, patterns of behavior and institutions which are transmitted from one generation to another within a society. The term implies no value judgment.

Cultural ascent in society refers to the acquisition of those cultural forms corresponding to a higher class or social status. These forms can be acquired directly or indirectly. Indirectly, when a given status or class has been reached by some channel other than the cultural, and these forms are acquired by integration and assimilation into the new class or status. Directly, when the formal integration and assimilation of the new values or institutions have been achieved through academic education.

Primary Education

Because there is, in the underdeveloped countries, a shortage of teachers and schools for primary education (and a high rate of illiteracy); because teaching is concentrated in the cities; and because there is student absenteeism (principally for economic reasons), the possibilities of acquiring new cultural forms are limited to only a part of the society and the distribution is by no means favorable for the peasant. In Colombia the rural system of shift schools [12] makes this situation even worse. Due to the scarcity of classrooms, the low number of class hours, and the urban priority, there is a definite correlation between economic status and amount of primary schooling received. This correlation becomes greater when we consider that student absenteeism is seriously detrimental to learning. Thus the blocking of the economic channel of ascent has an important influence on the blocking of this primary phase of the cultural channel of ascent.

Secondary Education

The economic factor's effect on the cultural channel becomes decisive at the secondary level of schooling in those countries in which, as in Colombia, most secondary schools are either private or parochial. (82 per cent of all Colombian students attend such schools.) It is logical that without subsidies and adequate controls, secondary schooling is costly and becomes the almost exclusive property of the higher economic classes. Even the few government or low-tuition secondary schools that do exist are kept in operation only by the influence of persons who have economic power. The economic factor is clearly predominant. At this secondary stage of learning, cultural ascent is determined by the possibilities of economic ascent. If economic ascent is obstructed, cultural ascent will likewise be obstructed.

University Education

University education in underdeveloped countries is not costly as far as tuition is concerned. Private institutions lack the prestige to charge high registration or tuition fees. In Colombia approximately 50 per cent of the university students attend private institutions. Among these are a few private universities where high tuitions are paid by a small minority of the students.

The blocking of the cultural channel at this higher level is caused mainly by quantitative limitations. The quota for admissions is usually very small compared to the demand. In Colombia, where secondary schooling is so severely restricted, out of 16,000 students who applied for university admission in 1958, only 9,800 were accepted. Furthermore, it is estimated that among those who do enroll, only 40 per cent complete their courses.[13] This quantitative limitation on the basis of a competitive elimination of candidates has many causes—among them, bureaucratic red tape. Thus, the economic factor determines, to a great extent, the blocking of the cultural channel at this higher level of education. Even so, it is necessary to carry the analysis further. The excessively strict requirements for enrollment and specialization—insisted upon by the universities—serve the intellectual elite as a device to obstruct the cultural channel of social ascent and exclude, as much as possible, the competition that could threaten the positions of the members of that elite. We know that when competition increases in any professional field those who practice that profession lose a certain number of prerogatives and privileges. Therefore, although the structure of developing countries makes it inadvisable, and modern peda-

518

gogic trends are quite the opposite, Colombian universities insist on offering professional courses keyed to industrialized countries, and on selecting a minimum of future professionals according to exceedingly high standards of excellence.

In conclusion, the upper level of the cultural channel of ascent is obstructed by economic and cultural factors. Attention must be called to the fact that in these developing countries anyone who does not have a conformist attitude toward the cultural elite will find it very difficult to achieve social ascent through a professional education. Because this elite controls upward mobility, only very rarely does it tolerate ascent by individuals who want to reduce its control. In the university we clearly see how the level of conformity rises as graduation draws near and as it becomes necessary to be accepted by the professional elite that maintains itself as such owing to the prevailing power structure. These requirements for ascent make social mobility through the cultural channel an economic rather than socio-cultural undertaking, and thereby imply an absence of change in the social structure of the country.

With regard to the rural areas, it would be interesting to conduct a more inclusive study showing the percentage of students of peasant origin who are in the university, and in the secondary schools.[14] In view of the social structure described above, we can state here that this percentage represents a minority. Hence, the peasants find the cultural channel of social ascent even more drastically blocked than is the case for urban underprivileged social sectors.

Despite the guerrilla groups' sporadic requirements that their members undergo educational training, the occurrence of violence has not brought about social ascent by the formal cultural route. On the contrary, the already precarious educational programs of rural areas were further affected by the destruction of schools, the flight of teachers, and the impossibility for children to attend class. Nevertheless, it is important to note that after what they have undergone, the peasants are more aware of the need to be educated. Now that they have constituted a pressure group, the need for education and advancement will be one of the foremost objectives of their action.

Surveys made preliminary to projects of land reform showed

that the first need felt by Colombian peasants in areas affected by violence was for a school to which they could send their children. Thus the occurrence of violence has represented an advance toward formal education by awakening a desire for progress among the peasantry affected.

POLITICAL CHANNEL

We find that like the culture channel of ascent, the political channel is divided into various levels and into official and unofficial aspects. By "political ascent" we understand, in general, a rise in power within an authoritarian regime in which force may be exercised by the state itself or by individual and collective pressures. We will use the restricted concept of "political power" and regard it as "political action as such," that is to say, within the structure of the State as official political action.[15] Since this official political action is exercised by means of State functions, we will limit our examination to the possibility of ascent in government political positions and exclude from this channel the administrative. Political positions are found at national, state, and county levels.

In underdeveloped countries the peasant mass is excluded from positions at the state and national levels. The only exceptions occur in those few underdeveloped countries in which true agrarian parties with wide popular support and electoral power exist.

Selection of government functionaries in underdeveloped countries—especially in Latin America—is made not on the basis of objective standards of professional competence and administrative efficiency but rather according to economic and social criteria and in order to secure votes.

Although gamonalismo is an unofficial institution of politically oriented action [16] rather than an official political institution, by which government positions are filled. The gamonal is either himself a candidate or casts a decisive vote in the election of some other candidate to the office of advisor, mayor, judge, etc., at the county level. The gamonal's influence is based on economic and social power that has an important effect on electoral results.

Even in countries in which (as in Colombia) the selection

of most county functionaries is by appointment rather than by election, influence over voters is a decisive criterion in their selection. Nevertheless, in order to differentiate the bureaucratic channel from the political channel we will consider only those functionaries who have repressive power over the citizenry. Among the official political functionaries there are county advisors, mayors, and judges (in the case of Colombia). Since we do not consider the military as functionaries, we will devote a separate analysis to that social group. Other county functionaries may have political influence, but they are not political functionaries in the sense explained above.

In some underdeveloped countries, such as Colombia, certain municipal political functionaries are named by regional and central authorities. In such cases, appointments are made principally on the basis of candidates' support of government policy—provided this support is combined with social prestige in their communities. The factors decisive for political ascent, then, are those that determine the criteria used by central authorities to make their choices and those that constitute social prestige at the county level.

In order to make well-founded statements about these factors it would be necessary to conduct detailed research. Even so, as a working hypothesis we can state that because those who hold power are a minority, and because their advancement has not been due to qualifications and objective criteria of selection, they will be characterized by a conservative attitude with regard to the prevailing power structure; social insecurity; and aggressiveness toward members of the out-group.

(1) The term "power structure" refers to the channels of social ascent already analyzed—the economic and the cultural. We believe that the political minority is interested in mechanisms to obstruct those two channels because any modification in them would cause their heads to fall—if not as individuals, certainly as a privileged class. Therefore, only conformists are granted social ascent.

If this political elite does not itself own the means of production, it depends heavily on the economic elite by which its public—and therefore also its private—life is subsidized; in turn economic policy, so basic in general politics of the underdeveloped countries, cannot be carried out without the co-operation of this political elite. Even if the political leader belongs to the cultural elite (the merit he must usually have in the eyes of the ruling class to compensate for not belonging to the economic elite), the latter is also directly and indirectly influenced by economic power, as we explained when we spoke of the cultural channel of social ascent.

(2) Social insecurity in a position of leadership is a result of subjective standards of ascent. The individual who ascends is dependent on another person, not on objective and impersonal requirements which might ensure his occupational stability. For the political functionaries whose appointments to office depend on the political elite, and even for members of that minority which exercises central power, the above-mentioned characteristics of the political elite block the political channel of social ascent. Among the factors of obstruction, the economic factor, together with and through the cultural factor, seems to be the most predominant. The fundamental criterion for political ascent must, therefore, be an attitude of conformity with regard to the ruling class. Of course, among those who conform to an equal degree, the most capable will be chosen. Nevertheless, this structure of political ascent makes vertical mobility purely material and prevents any social change in the socio-cultural structure.

The economic factor is found to be just as predominant with regard to social prestige at the county level. This factor is basic in the political influence of the gamonal. Personal appeal and ability must take second place to economic backing—be it the candidate's own or from some other source. Nevertheless, at the county level, the first two qualities are relatively important since primary relationships are important—especially in rural areas.

At the county level social prestige is the basis for selection not only of functionaries appointed through the hierarchy but also of those elected in a democratic way. Therefore, standards of social prestige also rule the political ascent of the elected functionaries.

Even so, the influence of the economic factor does not operate merely through prestige but also directly with respect to the functionaries elected. Elections are carried out with a series of economic pressures on the voter, for example, threat of being dismissed from a job or promise of some reward. In the under-developed countries, even without mentioning electoral fraud, elections are controlled by minorities through the executive com-mittees of the political parties and the gamonal leaders who exert economic, social, and religious pressures that tend to sup-port the power structure, and keep the channels of social ascent firmly blocked—that is to say, pressures that allow only the conformist elements to be elected.

Thus in the underdeveloped countries the political channel of social ascent is obstructed for a majority of the population that does not have economic resources or personal ties with those holding economic power, nor enough formal education combined with economic power and/or the appropriate contacts—the latter closely linked to conformity with respect to the status quo. The occurrence of violence established a new informal system of government in the peasant areas in which it broke out. Although it would be difficult to determine the percentage of old traditional or gamoral leaders within the new guerrilla leadership, it is obvious that within the normal structures of social ascent many of the new leaders would never have achieved the power that they did obtain through violence.[17]

There has been talk of the existence of republics in the central regions of the country. Certain zones are known to be controlled by guerrilla chiefs. The fact is that at the regional level there has arisen an informal and anomic government which at times has more power than the legal government. As we said before, it is not surprising that the executive committees of the political parties try to make alliances with the new leaders. The influence of the traditional gamonalismo is being wrested away by the guerrilla leaders, who are far less conformist. This transfer of power has affected the social structure of Colombian rural communities. The importance acquired by these peripheral groups headed by new leaders in the county veredas has resulted in a loss of power for the middle classes who are established in the county centers and who in the past enjoyed the benefits of power, administration, and economic and social control gen-erally.

To a certain extent informal political power has become more democratic in Colombian rural areas, and a frankly non-conformist attitude—presently exhibiting abnormal and anomic forms—has emerged. Nevertheless, this change provides a basis for the advancement of vereda peasants, who had heretofore been a marginal group not only with regard to the rest of the country but even with regard to the rural community.

If the Community Action Program, Land Reform, and other popular movements organized by the government within the agricultural communities do not succeed in opening normal channels (indirectly of course) for the political advancement of peasant leaders, violence will continue to be the only effective political channel of ascent for the nonconformist Colombian peasant. Even if new channels of normal ascent should open, these will necessarily have a structure different from that of the channels now in existence. The requirement for future ascent can no longer be political conformity. New agreements will have to be made with the peasant leaders on the basis of their influence among the people, and this influence will be measured by criteria of efficiency rather than by subjective standards.

BUREAUCRATIC CHANNEL

The bureaucratic channel of social ascent operates through exclusively administrative positions—that is to say, through positions that have executive functions with pre-established norms in the field of public, as well as private, organization. We must therefore examine bureaucratic ascent both within public and private administration.

Public Bureaucracy

Just as was described for the political channel of ascent, in underdeveloped countries in general and in Latin America in particular,[18] the criteria for social ascent within government bureaucracy follows standards that are more subjective than objective. One of the subjective standards is the influence—political, social and economic—the candidate may have in the eyes of the prospective employer. This is not to say that these influences cannot be objectively controlled—for example, through the number of votes cast in the zone of influence, family prestige, income per capita, etc. Subjective standards include the candidate's personal appeal, his ideological tendencies, and the commitments of family and friends. We are emphasizing that these standards are reflected through the person who makes the appointment.

The concept of subjective standards disregards professional qualifications relevant to the functions to be performed. By no means do we want entirely to exclude objective criteria from the standards of upward mobility. We are merely trying to indicate the priority of subjective criteria for social ascent—among which the most important are those conditioned by political and economic factors.

In underdeveloped countries bureaucracy is the most common source of employment. Here we find the heaviest proportion of investments from the national budget and the least requirements for professional qualifications.[19] For this reason the number of candidates for jobs in government bureaucracy exceeds the number of opportunities. The employer takes advantage of this surplus in the supply of workers: he requires that the candidate possess qualities that can make the employer's own position more secure.

As we explained above, the positions occupied owing to subjective criteria are unstable because they depend on persons rather than on those pre-established universal requirements accepted in developed countries, where administrative careers are relatively strict and efficient. In underdeveloped countries security is provided by the candidate's political influence and economic position.

The political influence of the employee guarantees the employer the respect of the politicians who participate in the government directly as functionaries and indirectly through organs of the party on which the employer's own position depends. Not only does economic influence have indirect effect on politicians, but in the case of retirement from public bureaucracy, economic influence guarantees a possibility of ascent in private enterprise.

In this situation, much of the political struggle is motivated by the prospect of sharing bureaucratic favors and hence, too, the political ideology of government employees follows the twists and turns of election results and politics in general. The effect produced in Colombia by the establishment of administrative parity is interesting from the viewpoint of political sociology. The bureaucratic struggle was carried to the heart of each of the traditional parties, producing wide splits in them with the obvious bureaucratic consequences for the internal factions. Social ascent through the bureaucratic channel is thus conditioned by obstructions in the economic and political channels. Bureaucratic ascent in government ultimately depends on conformity with the minority that holds economic, political, and cultural power.

Private Bureaucracy

In order to establish the criteria for upward mobility within the bureaucratic circles of private enterprise it is necessary to define the kind of private enterprise in which this bureaucracy is employed. When it is an enterprise more feudal than capitalist, standards will be more subjective than objective. When an enterprise is more capitalist than feudal, standards will be more objective than subjective. In this sense subjective standards will have a negative rather than positive orientation. That is to say, they will be used as standards of exclusion more than of promotion. Principal among standards for promotion is the conformity of the candidate. A well-qualified but nonconformist individual would find it quite difficult to ascend the ladder of private bureaucracy. This leads to the conclusion that even on this scale the privileged minority will keep the situation under control by preserving the stability of the power structure and by preventing the ascent of anyone who does not strengthen the position of this elite.

Three of the principal ways by which the pattern of violence affected the public administration are establishment of an informal military administrative system; decentralization of administration; and emergence of new pressures for the control of administrative positions.

(a) *Establishment of an informal military administrative system.* The guerrillas had an informal military administrative system. As *La Violencia en Colombia* tells us, there were several levels in the guerrilla organization—from the guerrilla unit as

526

such through the section, the company, the guerrilla group, and the guerrilla division. The whole military administration had to be developed within this hierarchy and nonmilitary administrative positions were created—for example, political commissary, community leader, Land Distribution Officer, vereda Delegate, and Secretary General.[20] Besides the rules of warfare, the norms imposed on the fighting men included a series of elementary administrative principles. According to these principles established by the National Liberation Democratic Front of Colombia, the attainment of officer rank required—in addition to political knowledge of Marxism—the ability to read and write, elementary notions of spelling, the ability to perform the four basic operations of arithmetic, and good behavior in public and private life.

The administration of justice is beginning to be practiced among the guerrillas and even among those peasant groups which in the past enjoyed impunity. Informal codes of punishment and incentives provided for military and administrative control of the peasant population in general—and combat groups in particular.

Subsequently, the so-called Independent Republics have multiplied in Colombia. Inside these territories, where official government authority has no access, an administration parallel to the government administration has been organized. This new informal administration has constituted an avenue of access to bureaucracy, with different selective standards based on military qualifications, political sectarianism, and elementary administrative ability as charismatic leader.

(b) *Decentralization of administration.* The informal administration is beginning to enjoy great regional autonomy. The revolutionary commands establish themselves with eminently practical standards as regards local conditions and guerrilla activity.

La Violencia en Colombia lists the guerrilla commands that existed during the first stage of this period:

Command of the Revolutionary Forces of the Eastern Plains
Revolutionary Command of Santander
Command of the Revolutionary Forces of La Plama and Yacopí
Command of the Revolutionary Forces of Southern Tolima
Command of East Tolima

Command of Sumapaz
Command of Pavón
Command of the Forces for Self-Defense of Gaitania
Command of the Forces of Self-Defense of Tequendama
Command of Río Chiquito and Símbola-Páez
Command of Nare
Command of Anorí
Guerrilla Command of La Rivera

As Guzmán states, "Except for some parts of the Plains, those commands never succeeded in co-ordinating with each other nor in carrying out joint actions.[21]

Decentralization is autonomous and unco-ordinated. Peripheral and local communities acquire greater importance than the administrative groups of the government.

(c) *Emergence of new pressures to control administrative positions.* As we saw above, advancement in bureaucratic circles of government administration requires—in addition to a certain degree of competence—strict conformity, which guarantees the hierarchical control of the ruling classes down to the lowest ranks of public administration. In the new informal guerrilla administration, positions and promotions are granted according to different standards, many of them considered anti-social but in any case based on qualities more likely to be possessed by the majority of the population. Selection is made more by pressure from below than by decisions of decentralized and distant groups. The guerrilla leader himself is subject to pressure from those with whom he lives and on whom his prestige, his safety, and his life depend. To advance within this informal guerrilla administration, conformity with the power structure became an obstacle, and another kind of conformity was demanded: an unconditional revolutionary position.

The pressures of the newly organized peasant group were exerted not only on their own informal guerrilla administration. The pressure of the fighting groups had a decisive influence on the administration of justice and the replacement of judicial functionaries. Likewise, many other functionaries have to respect the opinions of the fighting groups' main regional leaders.

As a result of violence, many peasants at various levels of the administrative hierarchy have become accustomed to exerting pressures. The peasant masses affected by the phenomenon have also become accustomed to exerting pressures on the administration. They have found within their reach a bureaucratic channel of ascent that they did not have within the government administrative structure.

If the formal public administration does not set sufficiently objective requirements and does not provide instruments that will enable the majority of the population to meet these requirements, the informal guerrilla administration will continue to be the more effective channel for social ascent through bureaucracy.

MILITARY CHANNEL

The military channel of upward social mobility is comprised of all the formal ranks of the army, navy, air force, and police.

The function of the military institutions is to maintain the established order. In underdeveloped countries the elite has the greatest interest in maintaining this order, on which their privileges depend. Furthermore, the economic life of the army depends on the government budget approved by the Parliament. In certain instances, such as in Colombia, the highest ranks are conferred or approved by Parliament. In this way the Armed Forces also depend, significantly, on the dominant group which, in turn, depends on them to maintain order. In general, because they are politically, culturally, economically, and bureaucratically inferior, military institutions have been the instrument of the dominant groups. Inasmuch as those groups are usually unpopular in the developing countries and are responsible for maintaining a social structure that is unfavorable to the majority, there are frequent disturbances of public order. When popularity is lacking, recourse is had to bayonets. Naturally, the military leaders can select the political sub-group that they want to support within the elite. When they exercise government power directly they always do it supported by a sector of the propertied class; the military government will fall when this support disappears without being replaced by another. In this way, control by the ruling minority is exercised through agreements with the military. The political, economic, and cultural elite will be willing to turn even the government of the country over to the Armed

Forces on the condition that they preserve the power structure. The military will make the ruling classes respected, provided they are granted privileges in proportion with the urgency of their intervention. In case of international or civil war, or should the violence in the country grow, these privileges will have to be greater than those granted normally. If the privileges do not increase proportionately, there will be a conflict that can culminate in a military coup. Still, even in this case, the only channel that would be interrupted—at least temporarily—would be the political channel. If political power is used against the interests of the economic elite, the latter will scheme and maneuver to overthrow the government. We have already stressed the importance of economic power over political power.

Thus the military channel is controlled by the economic, political, and cultural elite which also controls bureaucratic power. Nevertheless, it is necessary to note some traces of independence in the military channel, with respect to the economic and cultural channels. For economic and social reasons rather than because of functional qualifications, there is almost an insurmountable barrier between the ranks of noncommissioned and commissioned officers. However, higher military training provides officers with a few opportunities for social ascent.

Military education is quite inexpensive compared to private education in general. Furthermore there is a simultaneous remuneration that helps overcome economic obstacles. These facilities result in social ascent by the lower classes—even by the middle class—with standards relatively independent of the general economic and cultural structures. Nevertheless, although there is notably more possibility for ascent through this channel, the control by the dominant minorities is not to be overlooked. Indeed, at every level there is a requirement that culminates in the "contractual conformity" which we discussed above with reference to the highest ranks of the military hierarchy.

The emergence of violence had several effects on the structure of the regular Colombian army. However, here we are concerned with its effects upon peasant society, which gained, through violence, an informal military channel for social ascent. In this sense the most important effects regarding socio-cultural changes were: creation of an informal army, and new standards of determining promotions within the new army.

(a) *Creation of an informal army.* As with the administrative channel, the guerrilla army had a well established structure, copied from that of the regular army, combined with an informal administrative structure adapted to the needs of guerrilla warfare. In addition to the traditional ranks there were duties that permitted women and children to enlist.[22]

(b) *New standards to determine promotions within the new army.* Although in every military institution conformity to superiors is a basic criterion for advancement, it is necessary to determine whether the military institution as such is a conformist institution with respect to the power structure.

As we showed above, the army in an underdeveloped country has as its primary function the keeping of internal order, which, in political terms, means maintaining the power structure. The guerrilla army has precisely the opposite purpose—to transform these structures. Therefore, the criteria for advancement must be keyed to the revolutionary efficiency of the one receiving the promotion.

Besides these basic criteria there are others such as the desire to serve, loyalty, courage, and nerve.[23] There are also some intellectual and political criteria the guerrillas have taken into account in making promotions. Likewise worth noting is the guerrillas' more democratic relations between officer and subordinate, as well as the introduction of the subordinate's right to criticize and to express his opinions. Within the informal army the peasants found a channel of social ascent that they would never have found in Colombia's regular army.

Guerrilla leaders, to whose social extraction we referred above, could hardly have attained in the regular army the rank that they have today—general, colonel, captain, etc.

In the first edition of *La Violencia en Colombia,* we find pictures such as the one of "Mariachi" in a general's uniform, reviewing his troops. It is highly improbable that "Mariachi" might have attained even the lowest officer's rank within the regular army. If he had, it would have been by adapting to the standards of conformity with the status quo, and by obtaining

531

the necessary economic and poltical support of the ruling classes.

In this way violence opened another channel of social ascent. As was the case in those channels for mobility analyzed earlier, here too, when the need for ascent cannot be satisfied by normal means, anomic or pathological means are created to open a channel.

The possibility of massive upward mobility through the regular military channel would not, however, prevent the formation of these informal armies, insofar as other main channels for upward mobility remain obstructed. The very structure of this informal guerrilla army changed the values, attitude, and behavior, not only of those peasants who joined that army, but of those who have come into contact with it. The guerrillas have enforced discipline as requested by the peasants themselves. They have made authority more democratic and have given confidence and a sense of security to rural communities. As mentioned earlier, the spirit of inferiority disappeared in those rural areas where the phenomenon of violence manifested itself.

All these socio-cultural transformations among the peasantry have enabled them to become a pressure group working toward a general change—as we shall see further on—in the social structure.

ECCLESIASTICAL CHANNEL

In the underdeveloped countries of Latin America the ecclesiastic channel for social ascent is comprised of the different ranks and offices established by the Catholic Church. In view of the importance, both social and institutional, of other channels that depend on a religious institution, we will not consider them at this time. Moreover, official ranks should be distinguished from those that correespond to the social scale as such.

Within the latter we can establish the ranks of seminary student, chaplain, rural parish priest, urban parish priest in a working-class neighborhood, urban parish priest in a residential neighborhood, monsignor or canon, auxiliary bishop, full bishop, archibishop, and cardinal.

Within each of the foregoing categories there can be a con-

Social Change and Rural Violence in Colombia

siderable range of status. Nevertheless, in a tentative classification we propose the following as average for each stratum.

Seminary student	Lower middle class
Chaplain	Middle middle class
Rural parish priest	Middle middle class
Urban parish priest in a working-class neighborhood	Middle middle class
Urban parish priest in a residential neighborhood	Upper middle class
Monsignor or canon	Lower upper class
Auxiliary bishop	Middle upper class
Full bishop	Middle upper class
Archbishop	Middle upper class
Cardinal	Middle or upper upper class

This classification, having the disadvantage of being founded only on participant observation can prove to be somewhat arbitrary. However, all we are trying to show is the openness of the ecclesiastical channel for promoting upward social mobility. This fact is made even more clear if we consider that the majority (in absolute terms) of the clergy is of rural social extraction. Nevertheless, since its rural social origin is middle middle class (merchants, small farmers, teachers, etc.), the beginning of the ecclesiastic career does not constitute an ascent.[24]

The ecclesiastic channel is relatively independent of the economic channel. In fact, it is the most independent channel in terms of the economic elite, because of the low tuition cost of seminaries, upper as well as lower, and because the number of scholarship students is usually greater than the number of tuition-paying students.

In the second factor the economic level has a certain degree of influence in that the preferred candidates for the scholarships are those whose social levels are high. As described earlier, social level is closely linked to the economic and cultural levels.

The first stage of social ascent in the ecclesiastic channel—the seminary—is predominantly academic. This first ascent is usually accomplished from primary school (apostolic school) through the university level (upper seminary). The criteria for ascent at this stage are intellectual capacity and conformist behavior.[25]

In the next stages, the main criterion for ascent in the present structure of the Latin American Catholic Church is conformity. For example, in some countries bishops are not elected without the acceptance of the candidate by all national bishops. This provision implies a uniformity of the candidates, principally on the basis of conformity.

There are two reasons why the ecclesiastic channel is not widely used as a channel of social ascent in Latin American countries: the slowness of ascent in the first stage (from six to seven years of upper seminary); and the high drop-out rate (in Colombia approximately 50 per cent of the enrolled students drop out during the first year of upper seminary).

These limits demand a high degree of conformity and intellectual and emotional maturity in the individual's family or in the individual himself, if he is an adult candidate.

Entering a seminary presupposes a series of goals (desire for change, progress, leadership) to be reached over a long period of time. These goals, as a rule, are not found in the lower class, but rather from the lower middle class upward. The ecclesiastic channel is an effective means for upward mobility, in which the obstacles are cultural rather than economic, political, or bureaucratic.

Nevertheless, it is necessary to estimate how far-reaching is the effect of cultural blocks. The requisites of intellectual ability are objective requisites, although always imposing a limit by the kind of demand made. If the test is made on the basis of a system, that is inadequate for today's needs, a high rating does not represent effectiveness.

In an underdeveloped country the requisite of conformity can bring about economic mobility without socio-cultural mobility. In other words, an individual from the lower middle class, or even lower class, can become archbishop or cardinal. However, he may very well be tolerated in this position only at the price of absolute conformity with the values of the dominant minority. Thus, the ecclesiastic channel of social ascent proves to be mate-

534

rial rather than socio-cultural. This situation becomes even worse in those countries in which political power intervenes—formally or informally—in the appointment of bishops and general clergy of the Church. In the developed countries, too, change of class does not fail to imply a change of values. Nevertheless, here it is not a condition sine qua non for advancement, as it seems to be in the ecclesiastic channel in countries such as Colombia.

The foregoing analysis is clearly over-simplified. The economic factors—family, political, cultural, and bureaucratic—act upon the ecclesiastic channel at various levels and in a variety of combinations. We merely wish to emphasize its main characteristics.

At the present time popular pressure has little influence over ascent by the ecclesiastic channel. It is true that the acceptance or rejection of a priest in a given community has some influence on his ascent. Before the phenomenon of violence took place, the acceptance or rejection taken into account for social ascent or descent was not that of the majority of the community but fundamentally by the traditional or bueaucratic leaders of the community. It is common for a priest who is popular among the majority of his parish to be transferred because of pressure by an influential minority. This occurred in the past especially because the majority of the peasantry did not constitute a pressure group and because their attitude—especially in rural areas —with respect to the priest was passive and uncritical.

Due to the union of interests between the higher Church hierarchy and the ruling class, one of the basic criteria for ecclesiastic ascent is conformity with the status quo—manifested at the local level by conformity with the minority ruling groups of the local community.

During the occurrence of violence we have witnessed the death of several priests as well as blasphemies and other sacrilegious acts, all of which reveal a change in the peasants' attitude toward ecclesiastic institutions.[26]

The peasants' disaffection and negative sentiments toward this institution is probably not solely produced by those elements of the clergy who in some way encouraged the killing of peasants. It would be interesting to conduct a systematic study of the religious attitudes of Colombian peasants in those areas affected by violence. As a working hypothesis, we can say that Colombian peasants rejected the Church in those areas where they did not find priests to show sincere solidarity with them.

There may very well have been a change in the criteria for the priests' popularity in rural communities. It is no longer enough for a priest to be a good administrator or avoid downright antagonistic acts. The peasant must feel that his interests are defended by the priest.

If the majority of the peasantry forms a pressure group, the standards for ascent through the ecclesiastic channel will perhaps change over a long period of time. Nevertheless, for a far-reaching change in the standards for ascent to occur, the criteria of the hierarchy would have to cease being invariably linked to the standards and interests of the ruling classes and thereby to maintain the status quo. If—in addition to becoming the most effective pressure group by expression of their approval or rejection of the priest—the peasantry should come to provoke a divorce between the interests of the ruling class and the interests of the Church, the ecclesiastic channel for social ascent would change fundamentally, imposing criteria based on the peasants' interest instead of criteria based on the interests of the ruling class. In a country such as Colombia, where the religious institution still has great influence, the importance of a change—based on the interests of the majority—in the attitude of the Church leaders cannot be ignored.

CONCLUSIONS

1. In the underdeveloped countries of Latin America, and in Colombia in particular, the majority of the population finds the channels for social ascent blocked.

2. The economic factor is what most definitely conditions the blocking and control of all channels.

3. The elite that controls upward social mobility is interested in keeping the channels of ascent obstructed; therefore conformity is an indispensable condition for achieving social ascent.

4. Upward social mobility is accomplished by small groups

rather than en masse; is material rather than socio-cultural; and therefore has no immediate effect on social change.

5. This immobility is more acute in the rural areas of these countries.

6. The phenomenon of violence simultaneously produced a class consciousness and abnormal instruments for social ascent.

7. The abnormal channels of ascent established by the emergence of violence changed the attitudes of Colombian peasants, transforming them into a majority pressure group.

Latent Aggressiveness

Aggressiveness can be individual or social. Individual aggressiveness results from a destructive urge rooted in frustration. Destruction is sought as a compensatory release and in the hope that the eventual reconstruction will present an opportunity to satisfy the unfulfilled desires that caused the frustration. In the case of social aggressiveness the characteristics of individual aggressiveness are extended to the social group.

Social aggressiveness is usually found in those countries where aspirations are frustrated. If that frustration forms a part of the social consciousness and if violent and effective instruments of fulfillment are found within the social institutions, aggressiveness will become manifest.[27]

In the rural areas of developing countries there is much social immobility, which produces a frustration of aspirations if there is awareness of such immobility. That awareness is acquired through an induced social change. When human communications are extended and increased, social consciousness increases, and when points of comparison are established, frustrations arise. When there is an awareness of frustration without the institutional means for relieving that frustration, aggressiveness will remain latent. If effective institutional instruments do exist within the prevailing social structure, latent aggressiveness will be resolved into institutional action that will not violate the prevailing social order. If, on the other hand, known effective instruments are in conflict with the status quo, latent aggressiveness will become manifest. This manifest aggressiveness will become greater as awareness of frustration increases, and in proportion with the effectiveness of the instruments working against the social structure as compared to the low effectiveness of those instruments working in support of the social structure.

In the rural areas of Latin American countries we find different degrees of frustration and awareness, and different combinations of normal and abnormal instruments (both for and against the prevailing order). Throughout the history of Colombia latent social aggressiveness has intermittently become manifest, from the time of pre-Colombian wars among the Indians through the subsequent struggles of the Conquest, the uprisings of the Colonial era, the War of Independence, subsequent civil wars and the manifestations of violence such as that of 1930—down to today's phemonenon of violence.

The above analysis has shown how the occurrence of violence introduced simultaneously: a sense of frustration; an intensification of that frustration; and effective abnormal instruments to relieve frustration. The armed action of government forces was the element of induced social change by which the three foregoing effects were produced. The phenomenon common to underdeveloped rural areas—described as latent aggressiveness—was present in Colombian peasant communities and has been transformed into manifest aggressiveness through the phenomenon of violence.

CHARACTERISTIC VARIABLES OF COLOMBIAN RURAL SOCIETY

Political Sectarianism

What has usually been called "political sectarianism" is a form of group aggressiveness—specifically of a group that is part of an organization exercising or trying to exercise government power. In addition to the element of aggressiveness, political sectarianism includes the correlative notions of in-group and out-group security.

Every group affiliation is simultaneously the cause and the effect of every individual's need for security. The security function of the group will increase in intensity as insecurity increases outside the group. In the developed countries, further, there exist institutions that guarantee social security independently of group affiliation. Therefore the need to belong to groups is smaller in the developed countries than it is in underdeveloped countries. Since, furthermore, social aggressiveness is greater in underdeveloped countries because frustrations are greater, political sectarianism is a byproduct of the lack of socio-economic development.

In non-industrialized countries the minority that holds power constitutes a closed group with the greatest degree of security inside society. The only way to lose this security would be through a structural change that would occasion the loss of social control by this elite.

Obviously social change can only come from the majority of the population unable to ascend. Thus, the very fact of being a minority constitutes an element of insecurity should the majority show discontent. Therefore, the minority needs some mechanism to satisfy the majority, maintain the status quo, and, if possible, make it dangerous for any of the prevailing structures to be changed.

The political party can fulfill the above functions provided it meets certain requirements: in the first place, it must make a few concessions—enough to ward off discontent. In the second place, it must relate concessions to the maintenance of the prevailing social structure, and in the third place, create systems that would make it dangerous to change this social structure.

The political party in Colombia is an instrument to satisfy certain needs of the majority of Colombians. Inasmuch as bureaucratic favors are important in an underdeveloped country (with mostly unskilled manpower), inasmuch as a high percentage of the national income is allocated to administration (and there are few technical requirements on the part of that administrative system), and given that these favors are distributed by the political party, the latter is an important source of livelihood for many Colombians. In other words, through their hopes of obtaining public jobs, there are more people dependent on public jobs than the number who exercise them. Therefore, many Colombians depend directly or indirectly on the political party. Nevertheless, for their dependence on the party to be a guarantee that the socio-economic structure will be maintained, it is necessary to make them dependent on the ruling class.

For the party to be an adequate instrument for the preservation of this class, it has to be organized to include people of all social needs. If affiliation brings neither technical nor rational advantages, it is necessary to look for sentimental motivations to justify it. Hence the traditional or sentimental basis of the party systems. The majority of the population could—in a more technical and rational way—administer the bureaucratic favors which are distributed by the ruling class.

In order to ensure the permanence of the social structure, its collapse must entail a danger for the classes that do not benefit from the status quo. Political sectarianism is the device by which the ruling class provides the majority with a feeling of in-group security proportional to the out-group insecurity.

To summarize, the political party has functions as much with respect to the ruling class as with respect to the majority under that rule. For the ruling class it constitutes an element of conservation of the structures through party sentimentality and party sectarianism and by refusing to rebuild the parties along rational lines that would transform the social structure by establishing majority rule.

For the classes over which rule is exercised, political sectarianism produces an atmosphere of insecurity, and the party constitutes a refuge—the only group capable of connecting these classes with the ruling elite—that is to say, with the source of security. The indispensable condition of the relationship is conformity with respect to the party. This conformity is displayed and reinforced through manifestations of sectarianism against the opposing party. Political sectarianism is, then, the two-edged sword that prods the majority to conform and thus guarantees the stability of the social order enforced by the ruling class.

Violence was unleashed as a device to serve sectarianism to fulfill the functions outlined above. Therefore, the outbreak of violence occurred not among the ruling classes but rather within the peasant masses sentimentally divided among traditional parties and suffering great social insecurity that bound them even more tightly to these parties.

Even after the ruling classes made a political alliance, the pattern of violence has been prolonged to ensure the continuation of the sectarianism necessary to prevent the parties from being rebuilt along rational lines that would transform the social structure. Under this system it is logical that any individual who risks disagreeing with the leaders of the traditional parties will be pushed aside and regarded almost as an outlaw. It is significant that there emerged McCarthyite societies composed of elements from the ruling classes of both parties. The stated and formal purpose of these societies is to fight communism; the unstated and informal purpose is to isolate every nonconformist individual or movement that appears on the political, social, or economic scene. The pattern of violence, therefore, did not favor one political party over another. At times it can favor a minority party by balancing political forces that would be unequal at the polls. Nevertheless, violence fundamentally benefits the ruling class irrespective of party affiliation.

All this notwithstanding, violence has started a social process that the ruling classes did not foresee. It has awakened the class consciousness of the peasant, given him group solidarity and a feeling of superiority and confidence to act. It has opened possibilities for upward social mobility and has institutionalized aggressiveness, making the Colombian peasants begin to give precedence to their own interests over those of the party. This will have the effect of constituting a social pressure group—economically and even politically capable of changing the social structure in the way least expected and least desired by the ruling class. It is very possible that, due to violence, political sectarianism will be changed into class sectarianism, as has already occurred in many Colombian rural areas.

Lack of Class Consciousness

The present analysis does not purport to investigate the fine points in the definition of social class. For our purposes a generally accepted definition suffices. When we speak of the peasant class we refer to a certain social group which has the lowest economic status within Colombian society, and which engages in an occupation within the primary sector of production, predominantly located in the rural areas of the country. Class consciousness is what exists with respect to a series of social relationships within a group such as that defined above—relations of a kind that excludes the out-group. When this class consciousness is added to initiative in, and organization for, group action, it is capable of influencing government decisions and, therefore, is capable of becoming a pressure group.

In many underdeveloped countries, the peasantry has become organized in various ways. In most Latin American countries agrarian movements have had an importance that contrasts with their lack of importance in Colombia.

The most characteristic features pointed out above—especially individualism and isolation—have kept the Colombian peasants from developing a class consciousness. At the same time the cultural isolation in Colombia, together with backwardness in communication media, have blocked the cultural interaction necessary to bring about social change which in turn could create a class consciousness. The absence of contacts—and hence the lack of visibility of reference groups—has kept the peasants unaware even of their own needs. The lack of upward social mobility has resulted in an institutionalization of fatalism regarding the solution of the few needs which they do recognize. Even where there is awareness of needs and where fatalism may have been replaced by an attitude of initiative and action, this has generally come about on an individual basis. Conflicts with out-group peasants have prevented the creation of rural solidarity, and political sectarianism has aggravated disunity.

Subsequent to the onset of violence, those rural communities that have neither directly nor indirectly undergone its influence exhibit the characteristic lack of class consciousness, defeatist attitude regarding progress, and lack of collective security among the peasants.

As we consider how violence has resulted in the emergence of class consciousness in the Colombian peasant, we can summarize the changes that have taken place in the society as a whole.

The excessive importance of the local neighborhood, isolation, individualism, in-group and out-group conflicts, sense of inferiority, absence of upward social mobility, latent aggressiveness—all of these imply a lack of class consciousness. By altering these features, violence created a class consciousness; it generalized social relationships among the peasantry at a national level, making them aware of the exclusiveness of these relations, and provided solidarity for action by exercising an informal influence in government decision-making and, through political alliance, in the power structure. Overcoming the lack of class consciousness, the peasantry gradually formed a pressure group of definitive importance in the change of Colombian society.

Respect for Private Property

From the various reports in the Chronicles of the Indies, colonial historians and Latin American historians, we can conclude that the most generalized form of property among Indian communities was collective ownership of the land.[28]

The Spanish colonization did not fundamentally affect the native mentality with respect to property. Collective rural organizations continued under new ecclesiastic, military, or civil patterns.

The Emancipation Movement introduced liberal ideas, among them the notion of private property as the basis for Colombian political and social structure. Respect for private property became part of the Colombian heritage of cultural values. Prior to the onset of violence, Colombian peasants had a formal respect for private property, although that respect was occasionally not evident in their behavior. During the occurrence of violence the institution of *jus primi possidentis*—right of the original occupant—was introduced.[29]

With expropriations indemnified below value, invasions, and control over harvests and markets exercised by the guerrilla groups, Colombian peasants lost that cultural value that they had acquired in the previous historic stage.

In the communities where this phenomenon occurred, land invasions have been organized with an ease that cannot be explained solely on the basis of economic pressure, but, also by the practice, during the occurrence of violence, of making use of other people's property for the immediate needs of survival. Although this effect of violence is secondary and apparently intranscendental, it is important with regard to social change. If, as we saw above, the peasants are gradually forming a pressure group, it is important to study the cultural patterns of that group.

If respect for private property has ceased to be a positive value, it is very possible that, in the structural changes that the pressure of this group can achieve, private ownership will be attacked outright.

CONCLUSION

The phenomenon of violence has constituted for Colombia the most important socio-cultural change in the peasant areas since the Spanish Conquest. Through the guerrillas the rural communities have become integrated within a process of urbanization, with the full range of implications: division of labor, specialization, socio-cultural contact with other groups, socialization, a mental orientation toward change, awakening of social expectations, and the use of methods of action to realize social mobility through channels which the power structure had not foreseen. Furthermore, violence has established the systems necessary for the establishment of a rural sub-culture, a peasant social class, and a revolutionary pressure group constituted by this same class. Violence has wrought all these changes through pathological channels and without an orderly process of economic development of the country as a whole.

NOTES

[1] The phenomenon of violence in Colombia can be defined as a social conflict that manifests itself through armed action of groups, especially in peasant neighborhoods—those with rural inhabitants, ranging from the most deprived coca-chewing peon to the more highly developed small farmer—which are geographically widespread in Colombia. This situation became endemic, inasmuch as it has continued for several years without solution. For a more detailed explanation see C. Germán Guzmán, Eduardo Umaña Luna, and Orlando Fals Borda, La Violencia en Colombia, Monografías Sociologicas, No. 12, Bogota Facultad de Sociología, Universidad Nacional de Colombia, 1962, p. 368.

[2] Ibid., Vol. I. [The author often refers to Guzmán throughout the text as the author of La Violencia, but it should be noted that he is but one of three authors of the book listed in the first footnote.—ed.]

[3] Gustavo Pérez, El Campesino Colombiano, Un Problema de Estructura, Bogotá, Centro de Investigaciones Sociales, 1962 (2nd ed.); Orlando Fals Borda, Campesino de los Andes, Bogotá, Editorial Iquelma, 1961, and El Hombre y la Tierra en Boyacá, Bogotá, Editorial Anteres, 1956.

[4] See Guzmán, et al., op. cit., pp. 147, passim.

[5] Robert Redfield, "The Folk Society," *The American Journal of Sociology*, Vol. 52, January 1947, p. 293.

[6] Emile Durkheim, *The Division of Labor in Society*, Glencoe, Ill., The Free Press, 1960, Chapter XXXII.

[7] For theory on the transition from folk society to urban society due to division of labor, see E. C. Hughes, "Personality Types and the Division of Labor," *American Journal of Sociology*, Vol. 33, 1928, pp. 754–768; and Leopold Von Wiese and Howard Becker, *Systematic Sociology*, New York, John Wiley and Sons, 1932, pp. 223–225, passim.

[8] *Minifundios* are small parcels of land under 20 hectares. Often in Latin America, they are much smaller than that, and seldom is the land fertile enough for such a small plot to be productive—or even to suffice for a family to be fed and clothed adequately.

La minga is a pre-Colombian Indian expression for community cooperation in public works. Under the Inca empire—which stretched as far North as Pasto, Colombia—the *minga* was compulsory and provided labor for building roads, bridges, silos, aqueducts, etc.

La mano vuelta is a Colombian expression for reciprocal help at the individual level.

El convite is the modern version of the *minga*. *Convites* are massive and impressive efforts by entire communities. For example, more than 20,000 citizens of Pereira, Colombia, worked for three days in a *convite* to clear the land for a new local airport. Unlike the pre-Columbian *minga*, the *convite* is voluntary and is usually carried out in a festive spirit.

[9] Robert Redfield, op. cit.

[10] C. Germán Guzmán et al., op. cit., pp. 274, passim.

[11] We use the terms "normal" and "abnormal" to refer to the cultural patterns formally accepted by most of Colombian society.

[12] *Escuela alternada:* school with two or three shifts daily—usually girls in the morning, boys in the afternoon, and sometimes adults in the evenings. Necessarily, the school day is shorter than in a one-shift school.

[13] Data taken from *Estadística de la Educación Superior*, 1958, Bogota, Asociación Colombiana de Universidades.

[14] Robert Williamson, *El estudiante Colombiano y Sus Actitudes*, Facultad de Sociología, Monografía No. 13, Bogota, 1962. This publication reports that only 6 per cent of the university students are sons of peasants.

[15] See Max Weber, *Wirtschaft und Gesellschaft*, Tübigen, J.C.B. Mohr, 1922.

[16] Ibid.

[17] C. Germán Guzmán, et al., op. cit., Chapter VI.

[18] See Oscar Handlin, *Clases Sociales en América Latína*, Social Sciences, Pan American Union, Washington, D.C.

[19] In 1961 the budget for bureaucracy *was* approximately 30 per cent of the National Budget. In Bógota it was approximately 60 per cent for the same year.

[20] C. Germán Guzmán, et al., op. cit., Chapter V.

[21] Guzmán, op. cit., p. 163.

[22] Guzmán, op. cit., pp. 163–64.

[23] Guzmán, op. cit., pp. 158–59.

[24] See Gustavo Perez, *El Problema Sacerdotal en Colombia*, Madrid, Editorial Rivadeneira, 1962.

[25] Although formally virtue is spoken of in terms of self-control, in practice it is usually a matter of conformity.

[26] Guzmán, op. cit., p. 171.

[27] Fulfillment in the sense that Talcott Parsons explains of "performance." See Talcott Parsons, Robert F. Bales, and Edward A. Shils, *Working Papers in the Theory of Action*, Glencoe, Ill., The Free Press, 1953, Chapter V, Section 5; and T. Parsons and Neil J. Smelser, *Economy and Society*, New York, Free Press of Glencoe, 1956.

[28] For a study on the evolution of the concept of property in Colombia, see Alfonso López Michelsen, *Introduction to the Study of the Constitution of Colombia*.

[29] C. Germán Guzmán, op. cit.

15

NELSON AMARO VICTORIA

Mass and Class in the Origins of the Cuban Revolution

Before the Castro Revolution of 1959, Cuba exhibited a general malaise of class disequilibrium. Many social strata were simply powerless: including agricultural field hands, the landed proletariat such as sugar growers and cattle breeders, unemployed and underemployed Negroes, and all those workers lacking in any union protection. Class exploitation was also present among small self-employed sectors, whose means of production were limited and who were unable to hire labor. This social sector which dotted the Cuban countryside can be defined operationally by the possession of 66 hectares of land. As the only remaining private sector in the revolutionary regime, this sector has been institutionalized as the National Association of Small Farmers (ANAP). Members still till their own soil. They may be considered as that sector of the lower middle class whose characteristics have changed relatively little since the 1959 transformations.

The exploiting social groups were the landholders and the major farmers and cattle-breeders in the countryside and the industrial capitalists in the cities. The middle classes were the farmers and small owners in the countryside and professionals, traders, small entrepreneurs, and white-collar workers in the cities. White domination of blacks and mestizos was present to a certain extent, and members of these groups were unlikely to attain positions of authority.

Economic domination came from the United States because of its investments in Cuba and the degree to which they determined Cuba's economic structure. But by 1959, these investments were becoming increasingly concentrated outside industrial production, and were declining in political influence.

After the Revolution of 1933, industrial workers had an organization to defend their interests against those of the industrial capitalists. This division of interests was a consequence of a system of free enterprise oriented toward profit, and it led the entrepreneur to want larger profits and the worker to demand higher wages. These urban workers structured the conflict on a legal basis, aiming for a legitimation of such conflict. The movement became oriented toward promotion of working-class interests exclusively. Wide-ranging social legislation benefited unionized workers, and they enjoyed the highest salaries among the exploited classes. The situation of the seasonal agriculture and sugar workers was peculiar because most of them were underemployed. Despite being unionized, they worked under different conditions from workers employed all year or those who worked in the sugar mills.

Aside from these privileged workers and the landholders, farmers, cattle-breeders, and a few others in secondary agriculture, no organizations in the countryside could be said to constitute interest groups. Nonetheless, in the cattle-breeding and agricultural associations there were small groups opposing the dominant interests regarding possession of the means of production.

The immense peasant mass also constituted a quasi-class, though it had not yet taken shape as an interest group. This delay may have been due to several factors: (1) peasants lacked class consciousness; (2) they were isolated from one another; (3) they lacked leadership and a unifying ideology; (4) they lacked the means to maintain an organization. Each of these factors affected agricultural workers in the authority relationships to which they contributed labor power. The same factors affected the unemployed sectors of rural Cuba.

The authority of the dominant classes derived from their ownership of the land and their control of the means of production. This was legitimized by the Cuban Constitution. In the cities, the industrial capitalists were expanding throughout the early years of the century, up until the world-wide depression of 1929. In the countryside a similar process was taking place: cattle-breeding and rice-growing were responses to the crisis of 1922 and 1929, which came about because of the single-crop economy. With the curb on *latifundia* and Cuba's dependence upon external markets, the sugar industry had entered a period of stagnation. In addition, sugar is subject to inelastic demand.

The lines of authority extended from the supreme political authority to the least employee executing orders under the hierarchy. The government derived its power from the interplay of interest groups, whose members were part of political subgroups. Before 1959, these particularistic interest groups were chiefly represented by the army, a quasi-autonomous group, and secondly by the remaining sectors of the armed forces.

Conditions of exploitation were a result of a crisis of authority rather than a consequence of legal authority as in developed countries. The deterioration of confidence in the government throughout Cuba sharpened that crisis, and it reached its climax with Fulgencio Batista's coup d'état in 1952. Its main participants declared that the coup aimed to re-establish authority—a rhetorical device used in all Latin American countries to legitimate army intervention in civic life.

Between 1898 and 1959 Cuba's economic and political spheres were split at the institutional level. Values which condemned politics as the work of thieves and gangsters reinforced this. The dominant classes abstained from active participation in the political sphere in order to retain their prestige, and limited their influence to the manipulation of interest groups. The middle classes, especially professionals, abstained from participation in Cuba's public life. At one time, a record of non-participation in public life—or better still, one of refusing a position —became a mark of prestige. Among the remaining social classes, the split was reflected in general skepticism.

Classes with roots in conditions of economic domination had vested interests in the industrial growth of the island, and espoused capitalist values, such as honesty and dependability in the fulfillment of commercial transactions. Because these values were in sharp contrast to prevailing political style, the support of

Castro's 26th of July Movement by all social classes should not be surprising.

The Gestation Period

HYPOTHESIS: THE HIGHER THE DEGREE OF INDIVIDUAL OR CLASS MARGINALITY, THE GREATER THE SUPPORT OF REVOLUTIONARY MOVEMENTS BY SUCH INDIVIDUALS OR GROUPS.

A common characteristic of developing countries is the low degree of power held by marginal interest groups. This contributes to a conflict of interests. Black and mestizos were in the most critical situation, since aside from their exclusion from positions of authority, they were also denied access to non-economic associations. This limited their institutional access in general.

The urban unemployed were marginal mainly because of the slow growth of industry. From 1954 to 1959, 606,000 rural inhabitants moved: 82.3 per cent migrated to urban areas. According to the 1953 national census, 30 per cent of the population of Havana came from the provinces.[1] These urban unemployed ranked very low within the system of economic exploitation. Finally, they were totally marginal in the institutional sphere.

Agricultural workers were even more marginal than were urban workers, since they lacked the means of participation provided by urban styles of life. This was heightened because the ideas of modern industrialization held by agricultural workers isolated the countryside as an entity distinct from the city.

The most critical conflicts between the entrepreneurial sectors and the working classes resulted from the totally excluding system of authority to which blacks and mestizos, urban and rural unemployed, agricultural workers, urban workers, and small owners were subjected. The first and second categories had the highest level of conflict; the level decreased progressively in the remaining three sectors. Since being black or mestizo and being in the unemployed category are often overlapping conditions, the fusion of racial with class strife is apparent.

Support of revolutionary movements, which signaled the gestation of the Revolution, may be defined as an attitude which consciously or unconsciously favored total changes in society. This definition is supported by data prior to 1959 and by research carried out in Cuba in 1962 by Maurice Zeitlin.

In a survey made by the Catholic University Association [2] in 1957 among peasants, the following question was asked: "Where do you expect the solution of your problems to come from?" Answers were as follows: jobs, 73.46 per cent; schools, 18.36 per cent; roads, 4.96 per cent; hospitals, 2.96 per cent. The institutions capable of resolving those problems was identified as: government, 69 per cent; employers, 16.72 per cent; labor unions, 6.82 per cent; freemasonry, 4.30 per cent; Church, 3 per cent. Here we should note that the exploited peasant class expected its economic problems to be resolved politically. They equated the ultimate economic power with the highest political authority. At the same time an extremely critical situation prevailed in the economic sphere. Because such institutionally marginal groups had no access to associations of exploitation, they began to question the nation's legal order, since the legal structures, with which the exploited groups identified ultimate political power, supported the associations of exploitation. Only 16.72 per cent of the peasants expected solutions to come from employers; this is not surprising.

Zeitlin's study [3] confirms our statement: he found that the greater the degree of marginality of industrial workers to positions of authority, the greater their support of the Revolution. Further, workers employed for longer periods of time were less likely to support the Revolution than were the underemployed and unemployed.

Zeitlin [4] found further evidence of institutional marginality: while 80 per cent of Negroes favored the Revolution, only 67 per cent of the whites had the same attitude. The favorable attitude was 91 per cent among Negroes who had worked nine months or less before the Revolution. Thus, among the most critically marginal—the black and unemployed—was the strongest support for the Revolution.

Economic and social resources were less accessible to the marginal groups than to the exploited classes. This factor alone does not produce support of the Revolution, but it provides evidence for our second hypothesis: THE GREATER THE DEGREE OF

CONFLICT OVER ECONOMIC RESOURCES IN SOCIAL CLASSES, THE
GREATER THEIR SUPPORT OF THE REVOLUTION. AND, THE LOWER
THE DEGREE OF INSTITUTIONALIZATION, THE GREATER THE SUP-
PORT OF REVOLUTIONARY MOVEMENTS.

Conversely, a high degree of marginality makes the process
of institutionalization impossible. The exploiting classes inflict
the effects of underdevelopment upon the politically marginal
classes, thereby preventing them from adopting institutionalized patterns of behavior toward the economic and political
environment.

Following Parsons,[5] we define institutionalization as the
process by which generalized normative patterns are established,
defining prescribed, allowed, and prohibited behavior in social
relationships, for individuals and for mutual interaction in
society and its various subsystems and groups. It may seem surprising that we should use a concept of integration when a conflict model is being discussed. Nonetheless, the sense we have
given to the concept of "institution" is one within the legitimate
order.

A crisis of authority generates a certain ambivalence toward
institutions. Those in existence do not meet the needs of the
time, and those being created prove unsuccessful. Institutions
that do prove successful are usually ones that most clearly allow,
prohibit, or prescribe social behavior. Such institutions require a
certain degree of permanence to allow the individual to internalize patterns of behavior. The system that rewards good behavior
and represses that which deviates from institutionalized patterns
is significant in this process.

At the social level, this process can be traced through different "political generations," in which individuals belonging to
each have shared experiences providing a similar political frame
of reference. Zeitlin's research [6] distinguishes five generations:
that of 1959 onward; that of 1953 (the attack upon Cuartel
Moncada); that of the "republican interregnum," beginning with
the arrival of Grau in 1936; the period following the Revolution
of 1933; and the generation of 1933 itself. The generational
periods began when the workers were between 18 and 25 years
old. The assumption is that to men of those ages the Revolution
is of greatest significance.

We assume that generations which experienced a more severe institutional crisis and were more exposed to a revolutionary climate will also be the most revolutionary members of the exploited classes, irrespective of their ages. Thus we expect that the 1933 generation exhibited maximum support for the Revolution and that there was a decreasing trend for support in generations until 1952, when a new increase was climaxed in the youngest, 1959, generation.

Zeitlin's data [7] on industrial workers show that as age decreases, support of the Revolution tends to decrease. This trend is reversed after 1952, when support of the Revolution begins a new increase, reaching its peak with the generation of 1959. So far, our hypothesis stands confirmed. Yet the generation aged 21–27 in 1962 appears to contradict our assumptions. Its experience is more recent, and its views are doubtless as ambivalent as was the Revolution during those years. Nineteen fifty-nine saw the climax of the general crisis when the emphasis for the country's future was on a humanistic and democratic government. The generation aged 28 to 35 in 1962 experienced the crisis of political authority with greater intensity. Its age span corresponds approximately to that of the chief leaders of the Revolution. More than any other generation, its members were aware of the distrust of political institutions during the democratic period which ended with Batista's coup d'etat.

Two other generations bear out our hypothesis—the generations between 52 and 59, and 44 and 51 years of age in 1962. The members were young men during the revolutionary events of the thirties. It is, of course, possible to argue that, having experienced an abortive revolution rather than a successful one, they ought to be cynical and pessimistic rather than optimistic regarding Castro's Revolution. But although the social revolution was curbed, the political revolution—in a strict sense—was successful, for Machado's regime was overthrown. Furthermore, the revolution brought significant economic gains for the workers in subsequent years by legitimating their right to organize politically and economically. [8]

James Davies has stated that: "Revolutions are most likely to occur when a prolonged period of objective economic and social development is followed by a short period of sharp reverses.

The all-important effect on the minds of people in a particular society is to produce, during the former period, an expectation of continued ability to satisfy needs—which continue to rise—and, during the latter, a mental state of anxiety and frustration when manifest reality breaks away from anticipated reality. The actual state of socio-economic development is less significant than the expectation that past progress, now blocked, can and must continue in the future." [9]

Our analysis will assume that for an institutional process to become consolidated, an expectation of continued ability to satisfy needs is necessary. To the extent that the country's institutions do not provide this, there will be a predisposition toward supporting revolution, especially if retrogression is perceived. The quality of institutions is marked by the associations of exploitation which function within them. These are in turn collectivities constituted in the light of those institutions.

Between 1868 and 1878, Cuba had been struggling against Spain, although it was disadvantaged because Spain could concentrate all its military power on the island, as it could not in the independence struggles of the other Latin American republics. Cuba's main goal in this period, expressed in the speeches of José Martí and in his Manifesto of Montecristi, was to gain its independence in order to create a republic based upon an equilibrium of the various social powers. The two main leaders of the movement, José Martí and Antonio Maceo, died on the battlefield, and the War of Independence (1895–1898) blazed throughout the island, ruining the country's economy.

As a result of the explosion of the *Maine* and the development of North American public opinion because of the denunciations of Cubans exiled from the colonial regime, the United States declared war on Spain in 1898 and achieved an easy victory. A final blow was dealt the Spanish Empire, but in the signing of the Treaty of Paris, the belligerent Cubans were neither recognized nor invited to participate in the negotiations. This occurred despite an alliance between the United States government and the Republic in Arms, based upon the joint resolution which specified: "Cuba is, and must be, free and independent by right." United States intervention was declared and the rebel army was disbanded, thus frustrating the expectations of the Cuban people. For the next four years Cubans exercised pressure upon the United States government until they achieved a partial victory: the election of their own government and the independence of the island. However, the Platt Amendment retained for the United States the right to intervene in Cuban affairs. The Platt Amendment was included in the 1901 Constitution even though opinion among the Cubans was divided on this issue. Some were unwilling to approve the amendment, while others were in favor of doing so, with the ultimate purpose of annulling it. History proved the latter group wisest, in view of the fate of Puerto Rico and the Philippines, which at that time were in the same position as Cuba. In any event, the institutional life of the country was suppressed. Various political forces sought to gain the favor of the United States in order to benefit their own positions. The United States again occupied Cuba from 1906 to 1909, with disastrous effects. The intervener, Magoon, attempted to resolve the political problem by distributing sinecures and privileges in transactions with the Cuban government, setting in motion the administrative corruption which was characteristic of the republic of Cuba.

At the same time, North American investments spread across the island, reaching a peak in 1922, and crashing to a stop shortly after. In 1924 and 1925, economic recovery began, thwarted again in 1929. Economic ruin coincided with the political crisis when President Gerardo Machado attempted to perpetuate his office unconstitutionally, generating the Revolution of 1933. This is in line with Davies's hypothesis, in both the economic and the political spheres.

Cuba next entered a period of political instability having a few presidents in succession, until the situation was stabilized by Colonel Fulgencio Batista, then at the threshold of presidential power. During the interregnum, the United States, at the Conference of the Pan American Union held in Montevideo in 1934, pledged to annul the Platt Amendment when the Cubans announced their desire for total independence. The goals of sovereignty enunciated in 1895 had in fact been fulfilled, but only in a formal sense, since the country was in a condition of economic ruin at the time. What this meant was a set of concessions to the United States in foreign affairs, and to the lower classes in domestic affairs. A new commercial treaty with the United States was agreed to; basic sugar price supports were strengthened; and the relationships between the various factors of sugar production were regulated. A national trade union unity was achieved, and a new constitution worked out. This constitution was a program for action and signified the expectations of those Cubans who advocated social democracy and who had achieved political power during the Revolution of 1933. Unionized workers benefited from extensive social legislation. The only disquieting element was the influence of the army and of Batista, who politically impeded the country's democratization. The process of economic liberalization, especially after 1934, was not without its bloody chapters, such as the repression of the strike of 1935.

The international scene and the general repudiation of military dictatorship after the defeat of the Nazi and the Fascist regimes, together with Roosevelt's Good Neighbor Policy, reinforced legal internal opposition to the Batista dictatorship. Elections were held in 1944, and Grau San Martín, with his almost mystical popular image, was elected to office. Thus, the formal machinery of democratic government still obtained in Batista's Cuba.

When administrative dishonesty and corruption again settled in, Cubans began to fear that political gains might be lost. The coup d'état, supposedly carried out in order to liberate Cuba from these, instead represented a return to old patterns of forceful intervention by the armed forces. This continued until January 1, 1959. Thus Davies's hypothesis is confirmed in the political sphere.

Yet in the economic sphere, expectations were increasingly satisfied. During the period between 1940 and 1959 Cuba tripled its national income. The legitimate government built up an extensive institutional structure, creating such bodies as the National Bank and the Exchequer. Efforts were made to diversify exports in order to eliminate the drawbacks of a single-export economy. Tourism was becoming an extraordinary source of income, and, as means of transportation expanded, seemed to offer incalculable economic potential. Industry was expanding throughout the country, despite the unfavorable direction of investments. However, problems of unemployment and of the countryside remained practically untouched during the period, isolating these sectors from the institutionalization occurring elsewhere in the country. Not until 1958 did a malaise, in the sense named by Davies, begin to be felt. The awareness derived from the extension of the rebel movement in the countryside, which imposed taxation on the bags of sugar within its territory and ordered the burning of cane. Cattle were also confiscated. Fulgencio Batista said of the transactions made around these interest groups that they left the road to power open to the insurgents.[10]

Though to a lesser degree, Davies's hypothesis regarding the economic sphere was also verified by 1959. The movement which came to power then was awaited by Cubans as a political revolution with economic and social manifestations, not a socio-economic revolution with political manifestations.

Institutionalization and Caudillismo

The problem of *caudillismo* has been neglected by present-day sociology. "Modern sociological research," Peter Heintz tells us, "tends to study personal leadership within the framework of small or informal groups, and impersonal domination within the framework of large and formal groups, neglecting the problems of charismatic leadership, as Max Weber would say, or of leadership based upon personal prestige within the framework of large groups. One of the conditions which may favor the emergence of such leadership is an element of 'personalism,' or the extraordinary extension of the personal and emotional sphere, with the consequent rejection of abstract rules."[11]

This suggests that a low degree of institutionalization may be related to subjection to a leader with whom people identify in such a way that he becomes a part of their personal lives—caudillismo. Does this occur in Cuba?

The two chief caudillos of Cuba's republican era emerged from the country's two most severe institutional crises: Fulgencio Batista, after the Revolution of 1933, and Fidel Castro, with the Revolution of 1959. They have differences as well as similarities. After having assumed personalistic power, both undertook institutionalization. During Batista's first term the Constituent Assembly produced the Constitution of 1940, which displaced that of 1901. Likewise, Castro began far-reaching revolutionary legislation. Their differences are equally sharp. Batista based his takeover upon the support of the army, while Castro was supported in the beginning by the whole of the Cuban people.

One may posit a continuum from personal authority incarnate to authority derived from impersonal institutions. The greater the degree of institutionalization, the less important the person of the leader, and vice versa. During the republican interregnum, and within a legal framework, caudillismo had also been manifested; people hoped that Grau would be Cuba's "salvation," or believed that if Eduardo Chibás had not committed suicide in 1951 Batista would have been unable to bring about the coup d'état.

During the first years of the struggle against Batista by radical groups, Cuba's problem was often said to be lack of leadership. At that time Fidel Castro began to perform spectacular acts: with 126 men, he attacked the Moncada garrison, which lodged 1,500 soldiers. As fate would have it, his life was spared, and he was condemned to prison. Batista, in a gesture of pacification, decreed an amnesty in 1955, and Castro was freed.

In November 1956 he embarked upon revolutionary activities with 82 men. Ultimately only a few who had taken refuge in the mountains were left. From then on, Castro's personality gained ascendancy over those of other leaders, and the element of caudillismo was intensified. Longstanding opposition parties, which had leaders with greater maturity in civic strife than had Castro, voluntarily placed themselves under his authority.

Fidel Castro's opinions were regarded more highly than those of men in the Orthodox Party, in which Castro had recently been a rank-and-file militant. In 1957, he personally withdrew his authorization of a unity pact within the Cuban opposition against Batista, over and above the wishes of such groups as the Cuban Revolutionary Party (PRC), the Cuban People's Party (Orthodox), the Authentic Organization, the University Students' Federation, the Revolutionary Directorate, and the Revolutionary Workers' Directorate. The new Cuban generation represented a permanent focus of struggle, and it did not compromise with the past as had other political organizations which had held power.

The leadership of the opposition was increasingly exercised by the 26th of July Movement and its leader, Fidel Castro. This was one of the decisive factors which enabled the rebel army, with hardly any men, to take over power, despite the fact that Fidel Castro's organization was not the only one to have resisted Batista.

The Movement's main problem consisted in undermining the foundations of the constituted order, radicalizing the situation so that groups which opposed the constituted order only moderately should shift to a permanent focus of struggle under the leadership of the 26th of July Movement headed by Castro. This phenomenon took place in the Cuban experience as a natural consequence of the polarization between the constituted order and the movement or caudillo most radically opposed to that order.

Another problem was the high value given to personal courage, which found expression in the Cubans' identification of their republican history with the War of Independence of 1895. Confronted with change in institutions, people traditionally responded with violence.

After the victory of 1959, veneration for the caudillo acquired pronounced characteristics, in which the people associated their leader with their personal lives. The heavy emphasis upon caudillismo in Cuban society gave the Marxist Revolution traits that were very similar to those of Nazi and Fascist regimes, in which one individual was the supreme authority.

THE PERIOD OF GENERAL CRISIS AS A PRELUDE TO REVOLUTIONARY VICTORY

From March 10, 1958, and Fulgencio Batista's coup d'état, to January 1, 1959, when the 26th of July Movement took power, and less pronouncedly, until the present institutionalization, conditions made takeover by a revolutionary group possible. What was the weak link within the institutional framework?

A series of events made the military victory possible. Yet

this was not the most decisive aspect of the Cuban Revolution. The victory was due more to social and psychological conditions, which were such that once strong allies of the exploiting class reversed their loyalties as the revolutionary struggle reached its climax. The middle classes became discouraged, and even deserted Batista. Prohibition of arms transport by the United States and conspiracies within the Cuban Army were political factors. The ideological entente of the 26th of July Movement had a broad base, and it allowed all the oppressed classes of the nation to join the political sphere. It even attracted some in the exploiting classes. Also important were social conditions such as mass media, which contributed to keeping revolutionary fervor alive.

The psychological tone of the strategy and tactics of the resistance now seem curious. Its whole strategy was geared toward producing a psychological impact rather than achieving a military victory, and this in itself reduced the importance of a military victory.

On January 1, 1959 the 26th of July Movement had a number of psychological, political, technical, and social conditions operating in its favor. Among them was a certain caudillismo toward Fidel Castro, which made the Movement more representative and broader than was the Revolutionary Directorate, an organization with roots in the University of Havana. Then, too, the Movement was supported by the new generations which wanted a profound change in Cuba. The remaining organizations were composed of politicians who had either already been in power, or had not been able to organize effectively. For all these reasons, when powerful elements within the government decided to join the revolutionary movement, they contacted Fidel Castro, and this in turn strengthened his position.

When Batista abdicated, Castro, through the resistance communication, called for a general strike against the impending military coup. This call was the counterpart of Lenin's cry in Russia, but instead of being "All the power for the Soviets," it was "All the power for the 26th of July." The strike had two important consequences: it paralyzed attempts to form a junta of military and civilian men to take charge of the government; and the remaining revolutionary organizations became marginal with respect to power.

THE PERIOD OF EXPANSION

During the period of expansion the Movement assumed political power. Due to the clandestine nature of the military struggle, this power was in the hands of only a few individuals. Once military goals had been achieved, the Movement was broadened to include large social sectors which became militant in support of the political, economic, and social goals of the revolutionary group.

The previous period of general crisis complemented the present one of expansion of the Revolution. As the revolutionary movement became further radicalized, successive crises provoked measures which in turn helped it to establish its identity with different interest groups and quasi-groups. At the same time, the movement determined with whom it wished to co-operate and whom it wished to exclude. The most militant groups supporting the 26th of July Movement were the intermediate classes; support from remaining groups occurred on an individual basis and was not determined by class.

The revolution became increasingly radicalized, undergoing total modifications. These changes took forms similar to those of the Nazi transformation of German society, rather than those of Marxist transformations in other countries: "The method consisted," wrote Stefan Zweig of the Nazis, "in administering only small dosages, and, after each one, allowing for a pause. This was their precaution. One pill at a time, and then a moment of rest to verify whether it had not been excessive, and whether the universal conscience was in a condition to assimilate it." [12]

Osvaldo Dorticós confirms this in respect to Cuba: "It was widely due to strategic reasons that an integral revolutionary theory was not formulated here. . . . This would have required great effort and ideological indoctrination, which it was possible to avoid until the Cuban people had been educated by events themselves." [13]

The identification of a large part of the marginal classes with the government excluded the rest of the population. We may distinguish five phases in the Cuban Revolution, in which

561

the principles of totality, identity, and opposition were radically modified.

Democracy

This phase extended from the emergence of the 26th of July Movement—with the attack on the Moncada Barracks—to the first few months of revolutionary victory on January 1, 1959, specifically until the promulgation of the first law of reconstruction of a new order, the "Rent Law." The manner in which the 26th of July Movement dealt with all the characteristics of Cuban society before 1959 may be considered in an examination of this phase.

Practically all the Cuban people identified with the 26th of July Movement, and it in turn tried by every means to disseminate its ideological content as widely as possible. A survey carried out by the magazine *Bohemia* during the first months after the victory showed that 90 per cent of the population supported the revolution.

The intermediate classes, especially intellectuals and students, were the most actively militant. They formed the first revolutionary cabinet during the first month and a half, while the army and Fidel Castro, the former Commander-in-Chief of the Armed Forces, remained apart from government.

The division of power ended after the Cabinet nominated Fidel Castro as Prime Minister on February 16, 1959. This change took place in a climate of collective enthusiasm which extended to all the changes that were taking place, such as the substitution of personnel in the bureaucratic apparatus, the modification of the uniforms of the police force, the demolition of police stations and the construction of parks in their place. These changes were still only superficial, but they symbolized a break with the past and the beginning of a new stage.

The main dilemma in this phase was whether social reforms were to be made before the development of an institutional structure in the economic and political sphere, or whether elections ought to be called before making such reforms. The choice was made in favor of the former.

Humanism

This phase emphasized revolutionary legislation; it extended from the first measure affecting economic and social sectors to the arrest of Commander Hubert Matos, in October 1959.

On April 22, 1959, during an unofficial visit to the United States, Castro announced:

> Our victory was possible because we united all Cubans from all classes and sectors in one single aspiration. Let us unite all the peoples of Latin America in a common aspiration, let us unite, and not divide. . . . This is the doctrine of our Revolution, of majorities. A revolution of public opinion. The first thing our Revolution did was to unite the nation in a great national people, and our Revolution wishes that the peoples of America should likewise reunite in a great American dream. Our Revolution practices the democratic principle for a humanistic democracy. Humanism means that man's dearest desire, his liberty, need not be sacrificed in order to satisfy his material needs. Yet man's most essential freedom does not mean a thing without the satisfaction of his material needs. Neither bread without freedom, nor freedom without bread. No dictatorships of man, nor dictatorships of castes, or class oligarchy. Freedom with bread, without terror. That is humanism.[14]

Immediately humanism was declared the ideology of the revolution, and the mass media began to justify revolutionary measures on that basis. The people continued to be elated. Castro spoke practically every week on television, and was followed in his travels by representatives of all the media. His speeches were often made without warning and lasted for many hours, upsetting the usual schedule of programs. Those in power were constantly in the news, and the country was being rocked by the ongoing changes: the rent laws, the agrarian reform, the tax reform; the military trials of those accused of committing genocide during the Batista regime; the efforts of the various revolutionary organizations, among them the Communist Party, to

563

gain political influence, and also their rivalries; the counter-revolutionary organizations of those of the Batista regime displaced from power; and international opinion regarding the Cuban Revolution. All of these factors figured in a continuing social and political crisis. On April 22, 1959, Castro declared in New York that the holding of free elections in Cuba might mean the return "of oligarchy and tyranny." He gave assurances that elections would be held within the next four years.

In the economic sphere, collective solidarity generated a true mystique of development. Among all the sectors of the people, charities and fairs were held, the proceeds of which went to the Agrarian Reform program. Industrialists participated, and before the agrarian reform law was passed, associations of cattle-breeders, farmers, and landholders agreed to give a part of their lands and cattle, free of charge, to the revolutionary government. Tractors could be seen everywhere, and people contributed their valuables to support the currency. In this year taxes were paid promptly, breaking the record for amount collected.

The government began a close relationship with the "exploited classes," through its revolutionary legislation. Rent laws reduced rent by 50 per cent with practically no forewarning. Even more important, the Law of Agrarian Reform proscribed latifundia and made landowners of those who had tilled the soil. With the Law of Agrarian Reform, the rebel army, a permanent factor in all the stages, shifted its functions to the National Institute of Agrarian Reform (INRA).

Zones of agrarian development were created, headed by a chief named by INRA, almost always a military man. These constituted informal emissaries of a sort, links between the bureaucracy and the peasantry, both uniting and separating them. Within these zones were organized co-operatives which granted credit, opened roads, carried out health and sanitation projects, etc. "People's Shops" were established, which offered merchandise to the peasants at practically cost price. The Prime Minister himself took walks in these zones, and it was rumored that he carried a checkbook and would distribute checks then and there, according to needs in the various zones.

564

Mass and Class in the Cuban Revolution

On July 26, 1959 an enormous demonstration was organized to gather as many peasants as possible in Havana. Once again solidarity functioned at all levels. People with homes in Havana made room to lodge the peasants, the majority of whom had never seen the capital city.

If one date can be said to represent the shift of the quasi-groups to consciousness as interest groups, it was that year of 1959. At the same time, new interest groups emerged. The emergence of a group of men who had no ties to the past, who were determined to bring about Cuba's economic development, and who had, in the beginning, the trust of the Cuban people, brought fresh hope to all social classes that a new era had begun in Cuba. To a greater or lesser extent, those social classes established and defined their objectives within the regime and supported it as long as they were not excluded.

Radio, television, and popular gatherings were the main instruments for creating consciousness. Castro spoke for hours on end, on a popular level, about the significance of "currency," "reserves," "development," "industrialization," etc.

The active incorporation of the marginal social classes into the revolutionary movement conformed to three main patterns: (1) those who had radical ideas, such as the underemployed and unemployed urban workers, but who had not responded to the call of the 26th of July Movement, perhaps due to its emphasis on public freedoms, joined the Revolution when concrete economic measures were passed; (2) those who had no class consciousness, but who acquired it in the process of revolution; here we could place the agricultural workers and landless peasants who, according to research carried out before 1959, had lacked class consciousness; (3) those who responded to the call of the 26th of July and who belonged to the marginal classes, but who had not engaged in political activities before 1959. With the triumph of the Revolution, they established ties between the social movement and the mass of their respective classes through control of the organizations of workers and peasants. This also applies to those professionals and students who actively participated in the overthrow of Batista.

All of these patterns of behavior were present in 1959.

565

Gradually, "humanism" began to decline. A major contradiction was the identity of the revolution with the Popular Socialist Party. This whole period was characterized by the defense of the revolutionary regime against the "infamous campaign" regarding the "Communist" character of the revolutionary movement.

The major groups alienated from the social movement established a pattern of avoiding co-operation in the development of the country. Certain institutions constituted a focus for alienation from the social movement and the classes which supported it. In this phase the main issue was agrarian reform. We have already described the characteristics of the Cuban countryside prior to the revolution. This situation had led to Cuban legislators to proscribe latifundia in the Constitution of 1940, but this had not taken effect until 1959. The Law of Agrarian Reform was signed on May 17, 1959 at Sierra Maestra.

INSTRUMENTS FOR CHANGE

(a) *The Institute of Agrarian Reform* (INRA) practically became a government within a government. Its functions were as follows: (1) organization and management of co-operatives, whose administrative personnel INRA had named, and governing the co-operatives through the "Zones of Agrarian Development"; (2) the total regulation of agricultural production temporarily remaining in private hands; (3) organization and execution of all collateral services necessary to agrarian productive activity: credits, machinery, technical assistance, stabilization of prices, fiscal and tariff studies, etc.; (4) the direction of all rural life, including education, health, and housing; (5) the application of the Law of Agrarian Reform by means of resolutions pending the decree.

(b) *The Zones of Development* were administrative units of the agrarian reform; their heads were responsible for the progress of reform within their zones, and particularly for the development and functioning of the co-operatives.

(c) *Co-operatives* were under the control of INRA, through the heads of agrarian zones, "pending a wider autonomy to be granted by law." (Subsequently there were to be regulations for the constitution and organization of co-operatives.)

Nationalism

The third phase of the revolution, the period of nationalism, emphasized anti-Yankee imperialism, with "Fatherland or Death" as its motto. The first executions among sectors not belonging to the Batista regime took place. This period began with the trial of Matos, on December 2, 1959, and extended to the first Declaration of Havana on September 2, 1960. After that, the revolution was defined by events rather than by its ideology. In 1960 the revolution acquired its definitive direction.

After the trial of Matos in December 1959, the Cabinet was reorganized immediately and the country's politics concentrated on the international front, with a simultaneous intensification of repressive measures against dissident internal elements. The main political battle was fought at the international level, in the beginning, through agreements of all kinds between Cuba and the Soviet satellites. This created an anti-American climate characterized by such direct accusations of sabotage as that made to the American government at the time of the explosion of the ship *Le Coubre*, which carried arms and ammunition for Cuba, or the denunciation of an imminent invasion by U.S. Marines in May 1960.

The trend was climaxed with the arrival of Russian ships carrying raw oil to Cuban ports. The Cuban government requested that the refineries accept the oil; they refused to do so and were confiscated. Immediately, the United States reduced the Cuban sugar quota considerably (by 700,000 tons), while Cuba responded with the Law of Nationalization (No. 851) of July 6, 1960, by which all American enterprises were expropriated.

Those who did not support the government's policies were eliminated from universities, professional associations, trade unions, and from the government itself. Practically all of the country's newspapers and radio stations also fell victim to the campaign. On May 1, 1960, Castro gave a speech in which he attacked democratic procedures of the past, and concluded: "Elections—what for?" On June 27, 1960, Castro defined his relationship with the Popular Socialist Party: "He who is an anti-Communist is a counterrevolutionary."

The Cuban population was polarized: those who supported and those who did not support the revolution. In this case Lenin's words held true: "Have these gentlemen never seen a revolution? A revolution is undoubtedly the most authoritarian thing there is; it is an act by which one part of the population imposes its will upon the other, by means of rifles, bayonets, and cannons, authoritarian means, if any; and the victorious party, if it does not want to have fought in vain, must maintain this dominion through the terror that its arms inspire in the reactionaries." [15]

To the denunciations of "*batistianos*," "latifundists," and "apartment-house owners" was added criticism of "imperialists," "bourgeois," and "sectors damned by reaction." All of them were called "counterrevolutionists," and if they were identified as activists, their possessions were confiscated or they were condemned to prison or execution. The massive exodus abroad began.

Socialism

This period emphasized organization of the people. Internally, the state absorbed the country's whole economy. The period extended from the expropriation of industries belonging to Cubans, under the Law of Nationalization (No. 890) of October 13, 1960, to Fidel Castro's declaration of his Marxist-Leninist militancy on December 1, 1961.

Although the phases into which we have divided the Cuban process are not strict, their climaxes are well defined, as in this case, on May 1, 1961, when Castro proclaimed Cuba a socialist republic.

The socialism of this phase had little to do with a concrete ideology. It was directed to creating organizational ties between the revolutionary movement and the masses, previously scattered. The militia was extensively organized; the Association of Rebel Youths—later to be named Union of Communist Youths—became stronger, as did the Pioneers for Children under Twelve, the Federation of Cuban Women, etc. In the economic sphere, a final guideline of the Central Junta of Planning was issued, and Fidel Castro was named its president. This junta supervised other state bodies. Education was socialized, and all private schools, including Catholic schools, were taken over by the State. The first Brigade of Educators was organized and assigned the goal of making Cuba literate within one year.

Committees for the Defense of the Revolution were created; there was to be one unit on each square block throughout each major city and in rural centers. These committees carried out censuses for the rationing of food, distributed homes, organized voluntary work, fought the black market, and, most important at this stage, carried out supervision designed to prevent the occurrence of "counterrevolutionary" activities.

In the political sphere, the Integrated Revolutionary Organizations (ORI) were constituted: the 26th of July Movement was grouped with the Revolutionary Directorate and the Popular Socialist Party. The abortive invasion of Playa Girón occurred, consolidating the power of the revolutionary movement even further.

In his speech of December 1, 1961, Fidel Castro made a class analysis of the composition of the Integrated Revolutionary Organizations. The Popular Socialist Party, he said, was composed of the more advanced elements within the working class, both in the countryside and in the city. The 26th of July Movement was composed primarily of peasants, but also included large sectors of the urban working classes. He also mentioned the professional sectors, intellectuals, youthful elements, students, and also the more progressive and revolutionary elements from the middle class and the small bourgeoisie. He closed by saying that the Revolutionary Directorate represented "more or less the same sectors, but fundamentally the student sector."

During this period the main source of alienation was any organizational movement competing with the revolutionary movement at the social level. The term "counterrevolutionary" included the Church if it exceeded its authority, the Catholic Action Movement, and even a few Protestant sects. Their lands were expropriated and movements such as "For the Cross and with the Fatherland" emerged. These included individuals of diverse religious tendencies who supported the revolution and constantly attacked the clergy and "non-revolutionary" Catholics. The Freemasons were the targets of similar attacks.

The Marxist-Leninist Phase

Marxist orientation had long been acknowledged in the revolutionary movement, but not until December 1, 1961, did Fidel Castro declare himself and the system affiliated to Marxism-Leninism. In the period which followed, changes were made within the structure of the system itself, as opposed to previous changes which had been oriented toward "phasing out" the previous social system. The Marxist-Leninist phase reached its climax with the constitution of the United Party of the Socialist Revolution (PURS) in March 1962.

Can the class analysis made by Fidel Castro on December 1 be considered valid in the long run? The available data show that the greater an individual's marginality before the revolution, the greater his support of it. Nonetheless, the only existing data are those of Zeitlin's research on workers. In a study conducted at Miami by scholars from Stanford University, it was observed that persons left Cuba in class order; that is, the first to leave were the higher classes, then the middle classes, and finally the lower classes. Irrespective of the exact percentages of support of the revolution or lack of it, it seems certain that the marginal classes exhibited greater support of the revolution, without reference to any special sector. Such support seems natural, since the revolution emphasized marginal individuals. Fidel Castro's personality characterized the revolutionary movement over and above class feeling.

Two variables contributed to producing identity with the revolutionary regime: (1) *The higher the status acquired during the revolution, the greater the support of it.* (2) *The fewer the links with traditional political parties, the greater the possibility of following revolutionary movements.*

As Zeitlin's data (Table I) show, increased status influenced Cubans toward greater support of the revolution. If these occupational data were applied to the remaining categories of social status, such as prestige, income, education, and housing, it would be noted that even though a distinction between manual and intellectual jobs is made, emphasis is placed on the fact that either position does not affect social ascent. The government is

570

TABLE I   Relationship between Race, Change in Job Status, and Attitude toward the Revolution.

	Per Cent Favorable Change in Job Status			
	Same Level		Higher Level	
Negroes	71	(21)	90	(21)
Whites	60	(80)	81	(58)

Source: Maurice Zeitlin, "Economic Insecurity and the Political Attitudes of Cuban Workers," *American Sociological Review*, XXXI, 1 (Feb. 1966).

explicit in emphasizing the values of work over and above the functions of bureaucracy. Regarding incomes, there are no reliable data; some have decreased and others have increased. In general there has been an economic deterioration. Regarding housing, homes which belonged to people who left the country have been distributed, creating a personal link between those who enjoy those goods and the future destiny of the revolution. Education is an area of greatest success for the regime, and has also included the more marginal classes. Furthermore, an overall policy of full employment can be assumed from Zeitlin's research.

Support of the revolution was affected by laws subsequently passed, geared mainly toward those classes dominated in the past, such as the law of compulsory military service, which required citizens to give two years to the state, either in military training or working in production, with a salary of seven pesos per month.

During the Batista regime, the traditional parties consistently lost power. Some of them attempted to mobilize the people for the elections called by Batista, either in 1954 or in 1958, but they never developed the necessary support. Those who chose insurrection were not trusted by the people, because they had already been in power and were largely held responsible for the situation under Batista. As for the (orthodox) Cuban Peoples Party, after the death of Chibas, its leader, no potential leader comparable to him emerged, other than Fidel Castro himself, who practically placed this party under his command by draining it of its youth.

By 1959 there were two movements in Cuba with any organizational base: the 26th of July Movement, with a low degree of organization and a large mass membership, and the Popular Socialist Party, with a great deal of organization and a small mass membership. During this Marxist-Leninist phase and the previous socialist period, both combined their resources admirably.

As the revolution became defined as Marxist, any ideology such as that produced by the previous bourgeois structures was labeled as opposition. Emphasis was placed upon the enemy within, either due to the difficulties brought about by the shift from a capitalist to socialist system, by excessive bureaucratization, or by inefficiency in the area of production. All criticisms had to be made within the revolution and never outside of it; otherwise, criticism was considered a "counterrevolutionary" activity.

In sum, the following aspects should be emphasized: (1) the Cuban revolution underwent an essential change in its nature; the intervening factor was a modification in the thoughts expressed by the principal leaders; (2) the social movement analyzed identified mainly with the marginal classes; (3) the reference to totalitarian principles became increasingly encompassing in each phase; (4) the principle of opposition became increasingly exclusive in each phase.

The 26th of July is probably the most significant date for the regime and is an occasion for gathering the population and announcing important messages; its main attraction is a speech by Fidel Castro. Fidel Castro's three-hour speech in the city of Santa Clara in 1965 was delivered after the regime had achieved a certain measure of consolidation. Frequently the mass responded to the leader's words with applause or interrupted him with statements; this produced a dialogue between the leader and the mass.

What subjects was Fidel Castro dwelling on which produced such mass behavior, and with what frequency did various observations occur throughout the speech?

Some of the above categories need clarification. "Attacks on the enemy" refers to mentions of the dangers suffered by Cuba due to the existence of "Yankee Imperialism" and of the old social classes which had reigned over Cuba. "Praise of the

TABLE II   Theme of Interaction between Caudillo and Mass

Theme	No. of observations	Per cent
Attacks on the enemy	26	22.6
Praise of the revolution	25	21.7
Praise of the people	23	20.0
Opposition to the government	19	16.5
Toward a widening of the National Liberation Movement	9	7.8
Symbols	9	7.8
Other	4	3.5
	115	100.0

revolution" refers to any favorable mention of the regime's performance. "Opposition to the government" refers to an idiosyncratic aspect of Castro's manner of speech, in the sense that he assumed both the role of the defense and of the opposition regarding certain deficiencies within his own government. "Praise of the people" refers to any mention of the unlimited capabilities of the people that he leads. "Toward a widening of the National Liberation Movement" refers to any mention of support of the internal struggles carried out in other countries in order to achieve what the Cuban revolution has already achieved. "Symbols" are words producing reactions by themselves, such as "The United Party of the Socialist Revolution," or the name of some distinguished revolutionist.

Regarding the results obtained, "attacks on the enemy," "praise of the revolution," "praise of the people," and "opposition to the government," exhibited, by a wide margin, the highest frequency in the interactions between the caudillo and the mass. In the latter category, the overt manifestation of the existence of such conflict by the leader himself produces a reaction among the people which releases part of the tension.

The three remaining aspects which had high levels of frequency contribute to integration of the leader, the revolution, and the mass. The statements analyzed in the above table can be summarized as follows: "The enemy lurks and wants to destroy our revolution, the realizations of which have liberated the people from exploitation and egotism. But this people has already demonstrated its capacities to reject those enemies, because they know what the revolution has given them, despite the fact that there remain a few unjust aspects of which I am already taking proper care." This theme unites the mass, the caudillo, and the revolution; they are able to identify with one another. The revolutionary cycle is complete.

Conclusions

The following is a model of explanation of the Cuban revolutionary process, according to the historical periods presented above.

PERIOD OF GESTATION

a. The economically marginal classes tended to support the revolutionary movement, even though it did not become truly effective after the revolution. When Batista was overthrown, the politically marginal classes comprised almost the whole Cuban people. The intermediate classes, mainly professionals and students, performed a decisive role before 1959, constituting the leadership of the Revolution during the period of struggle.

b. People's degree of marginality was in turn an obstacle to the political and economic institutionalization of the country, which led to the promotion of a profound institutional change. Before 1959, that desire to change was considered mainly in the political sphere, even though in underlying form the conflict had been derived from the economic sphere.

c. The lack of faith in the political institutions led to a greater caudillismo, chiefly represented by Fidel Castro and some of his followers, who, interpreting the needs of the moment, presented a wide program together with an intransigent opposition to the constituted political order. This did not extend to the economic order existing prior to 1959, thus reflecting the manifest interests of all social classes.

PERIOD OF GENERAL CRISIS

Fulgencio Batista carried out a coup d'état which generated a general crisis in Cuba, thus breaking down even further the institutional political order. Gradually, Batista lost his base of power. The United States withheld arms, his chief men became corrupted, and his army became increasingly demoralized.

The movement headed by Fidel Castro became the main opposition movement, while at the same time the strongest both militarily and in mass support. At the greatest institutional crisis, after Batista's downfall, Castro demanded total power and got it. The result was a reenactment of the previous process, namely, a time of lower levels of institutionalization and greater caudillismo.

PERIOD OF EXPANSION

1. The revolution defined its historic action in an increasingly total form, going from a democratic phase to a Marxist-Leninist phase in less than two years.[16]

2. The permanent leaders throughout all these phases were in the rebel army and the National Institute of Agrarian Reform, which in 1959 established links with the economically marginal classes. Remaining leaders were gradually replaced by these men, while others gradually accepted the totalitarian aspects of the revolution. Fidel Castro represented the main link between those men who wanted to carry the revolution toward a Marxist system and those who were being gradually displaced.

3. At the appropriate time the revolution was extended to the economic sphere, expropriating the means of production, while it was explicitly stated that "being anti-Communist was equal to being counterrevolutionary."

4. The Popular Socialist Party (Communist) played a preponderant role in the organization of the socialist state and of the people in general.

5. Later the revolution was defined as "Marxist-Leninist."

Throughout the revolutionary process, support of the revolution had as its basis the improvement of the status of the marginal classes, together with the Cuban people's lack of links with institutionalized parties. To this must be added the lack of class consciousness, before 1959, by the dominant classes, and the divorce between the economic and political spheres at the level of institutions and values. The Cuban revolution, by integrating both aspects, made its importance clear, even though awareness of its significance came too late for those who would have wanted a different destiny for the revolution.

NOTES

[1] Aureliano Sánchez Arango, *Reforma Agraria*, Havana, 1960, pp. 59 ff.

[2] R. P. Francisco Dorta Duque, S.J., *Justificando una Reforma Agraria*, Madrid, 1960, M.A. dissertation.

[3] Maurice Zeitlin, "Economic Insecurity and the Political Attitudes of Cuban Workers," *American Sociological Review*, XXXI, 1 (Feb. 1966), pp. 47 ff.

[4] Ibid.

[5] Talcott Parsons, *Structure and Process in Modern Societies*, Glencoe, Free Press, 1963, p. 177.

[6] Maurice Zeitlin, "Political Generations in the Cuban Working Class," *American Journal of Sociology*, LXXI, 5 (March 1966), pp. 493–508.

[7] Ibid.

[8] Ibid., p. 502.

[9] James C. Davies, "Toward a Theory of Revolution," *American Sociological Review*, XXVII, 1 (February 1962), p. 6.

[10] Fulgencio Batista, *Respuesta*, Mexico, 1960, p. 79.

[11] FLACSO, *Sociologia del Poder*, Santiago, Chile, ed. Andrés Bello, 1960, p. 55.

[12] Stefan Zweig, "La Irrupción de los Nazis," in *Nazismo y Marxismo*, *Colección de Política Concentrada*, Buenos Aires, ed. Jorge Alvarez, 1964, p. 43.

[13] Boris Goldenberg, *The Cuban Revolution and Latin America*, New York, Praeger, 1965, p. 244.

[14] R. P. Francisco Dorta Duque, S.J., op. cit., p. 302.

[15] V. I. Lenin, *El Estado y la Revolución*, Obras Escogidas, Moscow, Foreign Language Editions, 1960, p. 352.

[16] Irving L. Horowitz, "The Stalinization of Fidel Castro," *New Politics*, IV, 4 (Fall 1965), pp. 63–64.

16

GINO GERMANI

Mass Society, Social Class, and the Emergence of Fascism

TOWARD A THEORY OF FASCISM:
CHANGING INTERPRETATIONS OF TOTALITARIANISM

A mature sociological interpretation of fascism is only now becoming possible. Our historical experience has broadened as new fascist movements and regimes have appeared in a variety of societies, including the developing nations. The accumulation of theories, hypotheses, and facts also contributes to more refined approaches and comprehensive reformulations.

Interpretations of fascism have changed since its first appearance in Italy. At the time, Italian fascism was considered an unexpected product of World War I—a complete deviation from the mainstream of history. Although the war had shattered the illusion of perpetual progress, most people still considered the permanent or prolonged breakdown of democracy in a European country very unlikely.[1]

When Italian fascism came to power, Russian communism had not reached the totalitarian stage, and German nazism was still in the making. Contemporary interpretations of fascism stressed either accidental and temporary factors (early versions of the "parenthesis" hypothesis) or the peculiar traits of Italian history (the "historical" hypothesis).[2] Even the Marxists, interpreting fascism as an expression of class struggle within capitalistic society, stressed the specific historical conditions of capitalism in Italy.[3] All explanations lacked sociological and psychological approaches: all analyses were formulated in terms of political or economic theories, or in terms of the history of ideas.[4]

In the thirties, especially after the rise of the Third Reich, new analyses appeared. There were now psychological explanations, strongly influenced by Freudian or neo-Freudian psychology, as well as sociological hypotheses emphasizing particular structural traits and historical trends. Theoretical constructs, such as the authoritarian personality, social disintegration, anomie, displacement of large sectors of the society, loss of community, the changing position of the elites, and the rise of the masses, became strategic tools in the analysis of totalitarianism. Psychological theories on the authoritarian syndrome, sociological and psychosocial theories of mass society, and formal definitions and typologies of the totalitarian state were applied to cases ranging from fascism or nazism to communism and the mass regimes in developing nations.[5] The role of class in explaining totalitarianism was secondary in this analytical framework. Totalitarian societies and movements were interpreted as a result of widespread disintegration of processes involving *all* classes.

Historical explanations emphasizing national peculiarities also followed new approaches. Such peculiarities were interpreted, in psychosocial and cultural-anthropological terms, as expressions of a national character or as cultural components.[6] The historical analysis of ideologies viewed the rise of totalitarianism in the light of European social and political thought.[7] Many new approaches emphasized a model of totalitarianism that included both right and left. Though the identification of Soviet Communism as a form of totalitarianism was affected by the changing pattern of international alignments, it became predominant among non-Marxist writers once the Cold War had begun. In the fifties, this interpretation was extended to the new "mass states," with the Latin American states, given certain similarities in cultural traditions, conforming most closely to the model. The interpretation of fascism and totalitarianism then merged with the broader problems of representative democracy and political change. The problem of mass regimes and monolithic versus competitive party systems was now seen within the context of political development.[8]

This paper will explore class and mass society as two explanatory factors in the emergence of fascism and totalitarianism. The theoretical discussion will be complemented by a brief analysis of Perónism in Argentina in comparison with Italian fascism. The main points of comparison are the contrasting social classes giving support to the mass movements in each country; differences in social structure; and differences in degree and rate of economic development and social modernization. The underlying culture, basic values, and attitudes are in both cases Latin, and a substantial part of the Argentine population is composed of first, second, and third generation Italians.

THE STRUCTURAL (MARXIST) VERSION OF THE CLASS HYPOTHESIS

The Marxist approach was the first attempt to explain fascism in terms of a *general* theory. F. Neumann, M. B. Sweezy, R. A. Brady, and others considered fascism (and nazism) "the final stage" in the evolution of capitalism—an outcome determined by the internal dialectics of the system itself.[9] Guerin tried to relate fascism directly to the classic Marxist notions of the fall of capitalist profits.[10] In its ascending stage, capitalism could find democracy "advantageous," but such favorable conditions would change sharply in the more advanced stages of the system. The need to counteract the fall in profit rates and the increasingly severe cyclical crises would require the reduction or withdrawal of all the "concessions" made to the working class. These political, economic, and social concessions which had been possible when the economy was growing, were necessary to stabilize the system under representative democracy. Their withdrawal could not be accomplished under a free regime; hence the need for dictatorship. Though Guerin observed divergencies of interest between different sectors of the bourgeoisie (between heavy industry and light, or consumer goods and industry), he concluded that class interest would prevail. Fascism, however, was a "mass" movement, counting on the active participation of a considerable sector of the society. Where could the bourgeois find his troops? An easy answer, within the framework of Marxian theory, was that the lower middle classes and certain deteriorated or too-traditional sectors of the proletariat could provide the human basis for fascism. The middle classes, according to Marxism, are not real classes. Under the threat of "proletarianization," they were exposed to contrasting pressures, and "false consciousness" could be invoked to explain their alliance with capitalism. As for the proletarians attracted by fascism, such deviance could be explained by the factors that prevented the formation of a class consciousness among them. The Marxian notion of the lumpen-proletariat could be integrated into this analysis.

The Marxist writers did notice a number of additional important traits that could not be directly deduced from their orthodox assumptions. The component sectors of both fascism and nazism could not be reduced to lower middle classes and lumpenproletariat: Veterans, unemployed, young people, and peasants took an active part in these movements. Their common trait was their uprootedness. Thus the human basis of fascism was displacement, caused basically by the deterioration of the capitalist system but accentuated by the war. In Italy, a popular word clearly described this condition. Fascists were called *spostati*—displaced persons.

The Marxists recognized that this uprootedness was not mere accident. The totalitarian solution could not have been generated by the pre-existing capitalist establishment. A body of "outlaws," to use Laski's term, was required for that task.[11] And this leads to two further observations common among Marxist writers: that the fascist rule achieved a degree of independence and autonomy vis à vis the old ruling class, meaning at least the partial removal of the established political elite;[12] and that fascism originated an unprecedented type of state, the totalitarian state. The central role of charisma and other peculiar traits of the new regimes were also clearly recognized.[13] Fascism was nothing more than the last defense of capitalism in its declining phase, but both the *means* (the displaced sectors) and its immediate outcome (the totalitarian state) went beyond the initial purposes of the bourgeoisie and could not be fully explained in Marxist terms. The Marxist interpretations of totalitarianism involved a sharp differentiation of communism from fascism and nazism.

THE PSYCHOLOGICAL VERSION OF THE CLASS HYPOTHESIS

The participation of the lower middle classes in totalitarian movements of the right, which played a complementary role in the Marxist interpretation, became a central factor in the psychosocial version of the "class hypothesis." Resentment, moral indignation, envy, insecurity, and fear were the most common notions used in connection with psychoanalytic models. The whole construct of the authoritarian personality was formulated mostly in relation to lower-class behavior. The psychosocial approach was complemented by sociological analysis. The processes of displacement, uprootedness, and anomie were more precisely analyzed and refined and other sociological factors—status incongruency, status panic, status deprivation—were also emphasized.

The notion of resentment as an important component of attitude and value formation has a long history in European thought. "Slave morality" as described by Nietzsche was further elaborated by Scheler. In his phenomenology of resentment, Scheler suggested a number of typical roles that are likely to generate resentment: those of the woman (especially the spinster and the mother-in-law), the older person, the priest, and the member of a declining traditional intermediate class, such as the artisan. In modern sociological terminology, Scheler saw these social roles and situations as particularly "unbalanced" in terms of present status versus aspirations.[14] In the thirties, these suggestions were elaborated by Svend Ranulf and others. Ranulf built on the classic contributions of Weber, Sombart, and Groethuysen, but he also conducted detailed case studies of different groups to determine the social conditions characterizing resentment. Resentment expresses itself as a "disinterested tendency to inflict punishment" and has always been especially strong in the small bourgeoisie, or the lower middle classes.[15] Again here resentment is related to the stresses, conflicting reference groups, inferiority feelings, and basic insecurity owing to the intermedi-ate position of these social strata. This resentment endemic to lower-middle-class positions may be greatly activated in times of crisis. In Italy and Germany, these classes were threatened both by the rising proletariat and by the increasing concentration in power and wealth of the bourgeoisie. As indicated by Lasswell, such a threat is not identical to the objective proletarianization seen by Marxist writers.[16] It is caused not by actual reduction of income and economic security, but by "psychological impoverish-ment" due to the decreasing distance from the lower strata, and the increasing distance from the upper strata.

Erich Fromm's model of *social character* in interrelation with social structure and change provided the framework to unify structural and psychosocial approaches with some of the contributions of classic sociological theory, such as the transition to new forms of integration (from community to society or from mechanic to organic solidarity), and its consequences in terms of social and individual disorganization.[17] Fromm's model also in-corporated an analysis of displacement, atomization, and other processes emphasized by the "mass society" hypothesis. The growth of rationality and individuation gives rise to the psycho-logical strains inherent in our modern society: feelings of aliena-tion, isolation, insecurity, and fear. The breakdown of the pri-mary links of the traditional pattern originates on a higher level of individuation and freedom, but still deprives the individual of any sense of "belongingness." The emergence of a society domi-nated by huge organizations, and the decreasing importance or disappearance of intermediate structures, intensifies such feel-ings.[18] In response, the individual may develop various defense mechanisms: authoritarianism, destructiveness, and automaton conformity. (The former two correspond to the well-known model of the "authoritarian personality" later used by Adorno and many others.[19]) Which defense mechanism is activated depends on the particular conditions prevailing in the different social classes. Such conditions will pattern their *social character*. In the lower middle classes, the tendency will be toward authori-tarianism and destructiveness; the psychology of resentment is here reinterpreted in psychoanalytic terms. Among the working class, the main defense is automaton conformity, a character structure typical of most normal persons in advanced modern society. Automaton conformity represents alienation and partial loss of identity—a tendency to conform to the expectations of others in a fashion quite similar to the concept of the "other-directed" personality later developed by David Riesman.[20] Fromm reconciles the Marxist interpretation with the psychosocial approach, not only by integrating structural and psychological levels, but also by interpreting nazism as an expression of class struggle in a period of declining capitalism. The process is specific to certain countries because the universal psychosocial propensities are patterned by the specific structural conditions of modern industrial society.

The authoritarian-personality trend became fashionable in the late forties and fifties, especially after the publication of work by Adorno and his group.[21] Abandoning Fromm's more productive approach, their conceptual framework became frankly psychologistic. But despite its highly sophisticated methodology and techniques, it did not escape ideological distortions. Especially noticeable was the one-sided emphasis on rightist authoritarianism. As Shils pointed out, the authoritarian syndrome could also be expressed in extreme leftist ideologies.[22]

MASS SOCIETY AND THE RISE OF TOTALITARIANISM

Theories of mass society have a rather prominent place in contemporary sociology. Their starting point is the transition from traditional to modern, with its familiar negative consequences in terms of growth of rationality and high individuation. To these traits, emphasized also by the "psychosocial hypothesis," the mass society theories add another central theme: the changing relationship between masses and elites. There are two sides to this process: the increasing participation of the masses and the decreasing isolation of the elite. The former corresponds to what Mannheim called "fundamental democratization," a process by which "modern industrial society stirs into action those classes which formerly played a passive part in political life." Fundamental democratization brings into the forefront groups with a lower level of rationality and threatens the "exclusiveness" of elites. Multiplication of elites, new forms of recruitment, changes in their composition, and the destruction of their exclusiveness, undermine the conditions required to maintain their proper function—creativity and a high level of rationality.[23] The "invasion" of the elites by the masses had been noted since the nineteenth century, especially by conservative writers.[24] Mannheim was more concerned with the breakdown of democracy and liberalism as a consequence of "massification" than with the maintenance of aristocratic values. Fundamental democratization, when it reaches the point of massification, would turn into its very opposite—"negative democratization," an inversion of modernization. Its typical form is the totalitarian state.

Mass society is a necessary but not a sufficient condition for the rise of totalitarianism. "Displacement" is also required. Masses and elites must be available for action.[25] Kornhauser suggests that release and high availability are originated by "major discontinuities in social process"—a high rate of change.[26] The later mass society hypotheses, like Kornhauser's, could enlarge their generalizations to include mass movements in developing societies. The notion of "social mobilization," interpreted as release from the traditional pattern and entrance into modern forms of behavior,[27] is closely related to Mannheim's fundamental democratization. It could also be interpreted as a form of displacement and a factor for availability, under conditions of rapid change and lack of proper channels for integration.[28] This concept has evoked another important trend: the analysis of the extension of civic, political, and social rights to the lower classes and finally, to all the population, as described for England by Marshall.[29]

A rapid rate of mobilization is not a *sufficient* cause for displacement and availability; inadequate *channels for integration* are also necessary. Such channels are provided not only by legitimation of rights, but also by the existence of parties or other organizations able to represent the newly mobilized masses within the existing political and social order. These additional considerations provide a suitable framework for interpreting mass movements and regimes in developing countries.[30]

The rejection of the class interpretation is a common feature of mass theory. Mannheim, for instance, recognized the role of the middle classes in the rise of fascism, but emphasized the general trends and conflicts inherent in modern society. Lederer and other writers grant nearly exclusive emphasis to the role of the masses. One class or another may predominate in the first stage of the movement, but the regime itself is a domination over the masses by the masses.[31] Differential class recruitment in the various fascist and totalitarian movements can hardly be denied,[32] but it can be interpreted in two ways. As happens with normal political parties (even in societies with high class cleavages in political life), there are always supporters with deviant social origins. This is clearly true for fascist, nazi, communist, and other mass movements.[33] Or one can recognize the difference in composition but say that "mass society theory is not contradicted by this class difference between fascism and communism . . . since common mass characteristics may subsist along with different class characteristics. On the contrary, just because fascism and communism are not similar in class composition, we cannot use class theory to account for their similarities, especially their totalitarianism." [34]

Lipset has shown that authoritarianism is not necessarily a middle-class phenomenon. Specific environmental conditions (family structure, early socialization, isolation, lack of intellectual stimulation) may explain authoritarian attitudes among proletarians, but Lipset does not conclude from this a deterministic propensity among the lower classes for totalitarian movements. Living in a simplified, rather inarticulate mental environment, the worker is likely to choose the least complex alternative, which *may* (or *may not be*) a totalitarian movement.[35]

Another theoretical approach related to mass society theory has focused on the *formal* characteristics of the totalitarian state. Here class is not considered very relevant. Even if leftist and rightist movements are not alike, "they are sufficiently alike to class them together and contrast them, not only with constitutional systems, but also with former types of autocracy." [36] The problem, however, is not purely one of classification. This approach blurs all differences in economic, social, and political impact. Mass theory does not necessarily rule out a position that recognizes the general relationship between class and authoritarianism. Lipset, for instance, holds that under given conditions all classes may turn authoritarian, but he does not deny class as a meaningful factor. It is impossible, he says, "to understand the role and varying success of extremist movements unless we distinguish them and identify their distinctive social bases and ideologies much as we do for democratic parties and movements." [37]

Another criticism: Mass theory has exaggerated the "loss of community" effect. Primary links still exist in urban or metropolitan society. They are certainly modified, but they still perform the traditional functions—giving individuals emotional support and feelings of belonging. This is true in totalitarian as well as in nontotalitarian states. In the former, most of the impact of displacement was created by specific conditions affecting particular classes and not by general conditions of mass society.

Mass theory's main shortcoming lies not only in its relative neglect of class, but also in its *failure to distinguish between different forms of mobilization and displacement,* especially between those occurring in modernized societies (or some of their component sectors), and those taking place in developing countries. Class and mass theories must be reformulated within a more general framework concerning mobilization, displacement, and availability. Such reformulation has been suggested by the mass and "national-popular" movements in Latin America, both of which have been regarded as fascist or totalitarian.

MOBILIZATION, CLASS, AND MASS MOVEMENT

I have suggested elsewhere a general framework of the mobilization process.[38] To review, a theory of mobilization should distinguish between different phases within the process, and different types of mobilization.[39] These distinctions are usually neglected in current theories. Mobilization's different phases (which may take place simultaneously or successively) are: a state of *integration* (within a specific structural pattern); a process of breakdown or disintegration (affecting some aspect of the existing structure); release of the individual (and social groups); response to the release (withdrawal or availability, i.e., psychological mobilization); objective mobilization; and reintegration (which may occur within a modified structure).

A society is integrated if there exists sufficient correspondence between three levels: the normative level (the institutionalized and legitimate norms, values, statuses, and roles regulating social actions); the psychosocial level (the internalization of the norms, values, etc., in terms of motivations, attitudes, aspirations, and character structure); and the environmental level (the whole external context within which social actions take place). When such correspondence exists, individual behavior will be precisely that predicted by the normative structure. It will be institutionalized and legitimated behavior. Breakdown or disintegration will occur whenever such correspondence is altered by change in one or more of the three levels. The passive response is *withdrawal* (apathy, personal disorganization, and its consequences: mental illness, criminality, etc.). *Availability,* the active response, is a propensity to intervene. The tendency here is to reestablish the correspondence between levels. Availability is only *psychological* mobilization. The passage to actual behavior is *objective* mobilization. Finally, reintegration occurs when this action becomes institutionalized and legitimated within the larger society.

No society ever existed in a state of perfect integration. Change is permanent and universal. Reintegration will always involve structural change, but whether this change will be drastic and assume revolutionary forms will depend on the rate of mobilization and conditions of integration. Integration requires proper channels, such as those formed by changing conditions at the environmental and the normative levels. These changes should permit at least partial satisfaction to the mobilized sectors. (The nature of satisfaction may vary from "substitute" satisfaction—loss of status compensated by alleged national or racial superiority—to "real" satisfaction—upward social mobility or actual participation in decision-making). Legitimate structures for political expression by the newly mobilized sectors also provide a channel for integration. Such structures—parties, unions, or other organizations—may be legitimate in terms of the existing social order, even if their surface ideology is strongly anti-status quo. This was true of the social protest movements in

Western countries: They channeled the protest of the mobilized sectors, but as organizations or groups, they were accepted or at least tolerated. What is important is the degree of resistance such groups encounter, and the level of tolerance for conflict existing in the society. Thus the two main channels for integration are complementary.

When the rates of release (and of objective mobilization) are very high and legitimate channels of integration do not exist, the type of displacement associated with extreme social and political movements may occur. In this case, reintegration will be accomplished through mass movements and drastic changes in the political or social structure. But even with available masses and conditions of high displacement, the actual formation of mass movements (as well as their orientation and nature) will be greatly influenced by two other factors: available elites and available ideologies.

Available elites are created in the same way as available masses, but the elite must be in a state of intense displacement. An established elite cannot assume the direct leadership of an extreme mass movement. A combination of rapidly mobilized masses and established elite may adopt a quite extreme surface ideology, but it will be unable to translate these beliefs into revolutionary action. Such a movement will likely fall into the type of legitimate channel already described. Another condition for the emergence of a political-social movement is the availability of proper ideologies. Any movement must find its proper ideology and this choice is not, as some authors have suggested, arbitrary. The right choice will not only affect the success of the movement, but will help shape its nature.

The main conditions determining the nature of the movements are the type of mobilization—primary or secondary; the predominant class or classes in the mobilized sectors, and the effects of the release in terms of social mobility; the existing pattern of mobilized and nonmobilized groups, their interests and attitudes; the historical climate, at the international level, in which the process is taking place; and the extent and nature of the satisfaction actually given to the mobilized masses.

The distinction between *primary* and *secondary* mobilization refers to the type of pre-existing social structure. Primary mobilization occurs within a traditional, nonindustrial structure. Secondary mobilization denotes disintegration, release, and isolation from a modern, industrial structure. The displaced sector is, by definition, marginal to modern society. Mannheim's "fundamental democratization" and Deutsch's "social mobilization" resemble primary mobilization, while "displacement" and "availability" (as used in the psychosocial version of the class hypothesis and mass society theory) refer to secondary mobilization. The kind of marginality in the two types will be very different. In primary mobilization, the marginality of the mobilizer sector is *previous* to its incorporation into the modern structure. Secondary mobilization affects sectors that are already participants in the modern sector, and which may have been made marginal by inflation, mass unemployment, war, loss of relative status, mass downward mobility, and other similar processes. The difference in marginality may be illustrated by the two types of nonvoter; the traditional who has never voted, and the alienated modern who has become dissatisfied with or uninterested in politics. The lack of distinction or the confusion between primary and secondary mobilization has caused major misunderstandings in the analysis of mass society and totalitarianism.

CONTRASTS BETWEEN ITALIAN AND ARGENTINE FASCISM

The emergence of fascism in Italy was characterized by *primary* mobilization of large sectors of the lower classes, and *secondary* mobilization of large sectors of the middle classes. Both processes were consequences of World War I, but the nature of the impact was very different in the two cases. The first stage of primary mobilization began in Italy in the last decade of the nineteenth century. It assumed the same pattern as in other Western countries with the great protest movements—such as the Socialist Party and the CGL—providing political expression to the mobilized sectors. Though there were serious conflicts, the mobilization found legitimated channels. The second stage of primary mobilization was triggered by World War I. Its nature did not change, but the rate increased enormously. Unionization (in the CGL) jumped from 200 or 300 thousand in the period 1911–1917 to 1,159,000 in 1919 and 2,200,000 in 1920. Another large mass (1,250,000) was concentrated in the Catholic federation.[40] The same sudden expansion occurred with regard to electoral participation. Italy had passed from "limited" to "enlarged" participation in 1913. From some 1,800,000 voters in 1908, it passed to over 5,000,000 in 1913. In the 1919 elections (the first after the war), the Socialists emerged as the largest party, followed by the Popular (Catholic) Party. Both parties represented mass movements, but they were not revolutionary. Both elites were legitimated. The Socialist leadership, despite its verbal ideology, was virtually absorbed into the system. Progressive extension of rights, effective participation at the parliamentary level, and a deliberate policy of political integration [41] checked the revolutionary potential of the Socialist Party. This was the main factor that prevented seizure of power by the organized working class. The displacement caused by the war could not be turned into a revolutionary movement for lack of an available elite.[42] Instead it was quickly dissipated into what was in many cases purposeless social unrest. Mobilization, in terms of increased aspiration to new forms of participation and consumption, had been partially counteracted by the extension of social rights and increased real salaries.[43] The workers' tension began to decline by 1920. The fascist violence that followed this decline interrupted a process of integration that was similar to the Western European experience and that was, in fact, successfully resumed after the Second World War.

Middle-class, secondary mobilization took a very different course. Not being absorbed by any pre-existing mechanisms of integration, it exercised its full impact. There were no channels for political expression: No tradition linked the uprooted sectors to any existing parties or organizations. Re-equilibration could be reached only through the demobilization of the lower strata, or at least strong required such demobilization. Disequilibration had caused loss of status for the urban middle class—decreasing distance from the advancing working class and downward mobility in terms of unemployment, inflation, decreasing income, and decreasing political influence.[44] Loss of relative status was particularly important because of the predominantly elitist or inequalitarian character of the stratification system. The advance of the working class was resented as a usurpation. Further, this displaced elite was available, and the ideology finally adopted by the movement was highly adequate to the deep motivations of the mobilized sector: It satisfied their need for re-equilibration through the emphasis on "order, discipline, hierarchy," and through the demobilization of the lower classes. It displaced their frustrations from an individual or class level to a national level in terms of national vindication, and dreams of imperial power. All these factors account for the formation and growth of a mass movement with a high revolutionary potential and an extreme authoritarian nature. But its actual success, and its transformation into a totalitarian state, was possible because of the predominant interests of the established ruling class. The direct responsibility of the Establishment (the political ruling class, the monarchy, the military, the economic elites) in the support of fascism is generally recognized. The Establishment also needed the partial and perhaps temporary demobilization of the lower classes, but it could not go beyond the limits of its own political tradition. This was also true of the relatively more progressive sector of the ruling class. The movement went far beyond its initial purposes; but the role of the ruling sector in establishing the fascist regime is undeniable.

Argentina presents certain crucial differences that explain the success of Perónism, and its repeated failure to establish a "classic" fascist regime. In the past 38 years, there have been four attempts to establish fascism in Argentina. The first occurred in 1930–32, when a military coup interrupted some 70 years of constitutional government under representative democracy. The second took place in 1943–45; the outcome was Perónism. The third was in September–October 1955, when the Perónist regime was overthrown by a civilian-military coup. In the military takeover of 1966, there was another attempt to establish a corporate state, and the attempt seems to have failed again.

Argentina has experienced very rapid growth and modernization since the second half of the nineteenth century. Economic expansion occurred when it entered the world market as an exporter of food products. Mass European investment (British) and mass European immigration (Italian and Spanish) completely transformed the country in few decades. By 1900, Argentina was highly urbanized. Its middle class had increased from 10 per cent in 1869 to 25 per cent in 1914, and the expansion has continued (45 per cent in 1960). Four-fifths of it is urban—mostly white-collar workers, managers, and salaried professionals. Until the thirties, Argentina ranked sixth among the world's powers in per capita GNP. Argentina's political modernization followed the Western model. Its transition from limited to enlarged participation occurred at nearly the same time as Italy's (1912), through a law that extended suffrage to all adult males. In Argentina, enlarged participation meant a change in the social basis of the government. In 1916, the middle classes came to power through the Radical Party (a populistic party of the liberal-popular variety), replacing the liberal oligarchy. Political modernization seemed to advance smoothly, but after 1930 partial breakdown, discontinuities, and stresses finally led to the rise of Perónism.

As in Italy, we may distinguish two stages of primary mobilization prior to the rise of Perónism, the first following the Western model, and the second one provoked by sudden disintegration. In the case of Argentina, the event triggering the second stage was the great Depression of the thirties and the resulting acceleration of internal migrations and industrialization.

The first stage of primary mobilization affected the central areas of the country (Buenos Aires and the Litoral), which included one-third of the territory and two-thirds of the population. The pattern of regionally imbalanced modernization, with an advanced central region and a backward periphery, corresponded to the north-south cleavage in Italy. In Argentina, the second stage affected the surviving traditional sectors in the periphery and the partially demobilized sectors of the central zone. There were rather sharp differences between the two populations in degree of modernization and cultural background. While the population of the central zone was immigrant, the population of the periphery was composed mainly of the remnants of the old creole population that existed prior to mass overseas immigration.[45] This difference was very important. The protest movements originated by the first stage of mobilization involved foreign immigrants. Though the degree of social unrest was rather high, its *direct* political impact was low because foreigners *did not vote*, nor did they *expect* to vote. Thus these movements were not a real threat to the social order.

The foreign composition of the protest movements was also an important factor impeding the formation of a working-class political tradition (as occurred in Italy), but mas upward mobility was the decisive mechanism. Primary mobilization involved not just the transformation of a traditional lower sector into a more participant modern proletariat, but its partial transformation through upward social mobility into a modern middle class.[46] This rapid change in the class structure prevented the formation of a specific working-class party, since such a party would have required time to form through the long process of socialization and generational replacement. In addition, it substantially modified the ethos of Argentinian society, from the "elitist" traditional pattern (common in Latin America) to a very equalitarian society. Mass mobility created the expectation of rapid social ascent, a climate unfavorable to the formation of proletarian consciousness. And it reduced the cleavage between the lower and the middle classes. The political expression of both was provided by the same Radical Party, whose ideology was "liberal" and whose composition was "popular." A socialist party achieved some importance in the Buenos Aires area, but with social mobility, it changed from a party of working-class foreigners to a party, not very different from the Radicals, of both working and middle class.

The military coup of 1930 was produced by the persistence of the old landed oligarchy, which had never completely abandoned its aspirations to power, and which was activated by the financial crisis of 1929—and by the Latin American tradition of direct military intervention in politics. As in Italy, the oligarchy could not directly and openly assume leadership of a demobilizing movement. There were no available masses, since the middle class did not feel particularly displaced, and there was no deep cleavage between it and the lower class. The only alternative was the surviving tradition of the military coup. A small group of intellectuals and some officers wanted to establish a fascist corporate state, but their attempt failed for lack of popular support and the oligarchy's realistic decision to achieve partial but sufficient political demobilization without changes in the political structure. This was obtained through an electoral fraud that left the opposition (Radicals) with the government of some provincial states and representation in the Congress, and maintained most of the constitutional liberties, but reserved the Federal Executive to the landed interests. Demobilization produced some displacement effects among the lower and the middle classes in the central region. For instance, the activity of the unions could continue, but it was restricted.

The second stage of primary mobilization occurred after the middle thirties, during this conservative rule. It was caused by a sudden wave of industrialization (owing to the breakdown of the Argentinian primary export economy) and by mass internal migration, from rural to urban areas, and from the periphery to the center. The mobilizing new masses were formed by traditionals and marginals, and also by the demobilized lower class of the central areas (especially the younger generation, whose political participation and unionization had been prevented by widespread fraud and other restrictions). The context in which the second stage of primary mobilization occurred was different both from the corresponding Italian case and the first stage of the process in Argentina. No ready channel for political expression existed, since Argentina lacked a working-class party tradition. Cultural cleavages, discontinuities in the process, political restrictions and the unrealistic attitudes of the leadership prevented the established opposition parties (from Radicals to Communists) from exercising any attraction on the mobilized masses. There was displacement and availability of the mass, but no pre-existing channel, and no available leadership *on the left*.

Perón, both a charismatic figure and a realistic politician, provided this leadership. The military coup of 1943 had a mixed fascist-nazi-falangist orientation. It was prepared by a military-lodge sponsorship under strong German influence. All the political parties were dissolved, and a benevolent neutrality maintained vis-à-vis the Axis. Labor, especially Communist-oriented, was strongly repressed. Press censorship and concentration camps completed the picture.

Perón saw that purely military rule could not be maintained for long. The possibility of establishing a classic totalitarian regime of the Spanish, Italian, or German type was impossible, since there were no available masses for that purpose. The only available sector that could be used in a mass movement was the new working class originated in the second stage of primary mobilization. This change in recruitment required a change in surface ideology, which in turn involved a sharp separation (at least in appearance) from the fascist groups that were collaborating with the military. The fascist and nationalist organizations were dissolved, but their leaders collaborated with Perón. The basis of the new political movement was provided by the organization of new unions and Perónist penetration of the older unions. Labor *was* manipulated, but within limits. It never was a unilateral process. The human basis reacted on the leadership and substantially modified the nature of the movement. The surface ideology (social justice, working-class participation, extension of social rights, redistribution of national income) determined to a great extent the policy of the regime. Labor retained much autonomy, especially at the lower level. Perón ruled through an uneasy balance between two opposing factors: the workers and the military. His fall was the result of his inability to maintain this balance under the new economic conditions of the fifties. Confronted with a military coup supported by the middle classes, his only alternative was to appeal to the workers—and this was too much for a fascist leader.

Perón came into power through a legal election, Argentina's first in 16 years. Until the end, he held a genuine majority. Though heavily restricted, representative democracy was not destroyed. The opposition maintained its parties and its representation in congress. Intellectual freedom was curtailed, especially in the universities, but nothing like a truly totalitarian state was established. For the workers, Perónism meant a real advance. Their lot improved not only in terms of salary and social position, but also in terms of concrete freedom and participation in decision-making.

The main difference between the Argentinian and the Italian experiences lies in the different classes out of which the mobilized masses were recruited, and in the different stages of mobilization. Perónism, in contrast with Italian fascism, relied on lower-class recruitment and primary mobilization. It was a national-popular movement, which is perhaps typical of primary mobilization. Perónism had totalitarian traits—but it was not really very different from the popular-liberal movement, the Radical Party, which had given political expression to Argentina's first stage of primary mobilization.

NOTES

[1] It has been common to consider Sorel, along with Pareto, Mosca, and Michels, as one of the ideological sources of Italian fascism. But Sorel's idea contrasts very sharply with the anti-proletarian totalitarian state. For an analysis of this problem, see Irving L. Horowitz, *Radicalism and the Revolt Against Reason*, London, Routledge and Kegan Paul, 1961. p. 176 ff. and passim.

[2] This terminology is used by some Italian writers. See Constanzo Casucci, "Fascismo e Storia," in *Il Fascismo*, ed. C. Casucci, Bologna, Il Mulino, 1961, p. 425. Fascism had been called by Croce a "parenthesis" of 20 years (in C. Casucci, op. cit., p. 174). However, Croce also saw the implications of fascism as a general phenomenon. G. A. Borgese interpreted fascism within the context of the historical development of the Italian spirit since the Middle Ages (in Goliath, *The March of Fascism*, New York, Viking Press, 1937). "Fascism was Italy's autobiography," wrote Bogetti in 1922. Rosselli considered fascism a "gigantic return to the Italian's past." (Cf. P. Gobetti, *La Rivoluzione Liberale*, Milano, Einaudi, 1949, p. 185, and C. Rosselli, *Socialismo Liberale*, Roma, Edizioni U, 1945, pp. 109–112.) A common theme was the weakness of the *Risorgimento* in terms of economic and social modernization.

[3] See, for instance, P. Togliatti, "A proposito del fascismo," reprinted in Casucci. Both Togliatti and the official position of the Communist Party did not follow the thesis of some orthodox Marxists that fascism is the "last stage of capitalism" (as in Guerin and others), but the idea of the "weakest link" in the capitalist world. (See "Theses of the Third Congress of Italian Communist Party in 1926," in *Rinascita*, 1951, pp. 94–98.)

[4] The overwhelming contributions of Italian scholars to the study of fascism have occurred in the field of history. The lack of sociological dimensions was also noted by Renato Treves, "Interpretazioni sociologiche del Fascismo," *Occidente*, 1953, pp. 371–391.

[5] A few proponents of such theories are discussed, pp. 581–583.

[6] A typical illustration of this trend is P. Vierick's *Metapolitics*, New York, Knopf, 1941. This book traces the historical origins of the "two souls" of Germany. Another example is F. Stern's *The Politics of Cultural Despair*, New York, Doubleday, 1965.

[7] E.g., J. L. Talmon, *The Origins of Totalitarian Democracy*, London, Secker and Warburg, 1951.

[8] In the thirties, the problem was posed more in the context of modernization in Western countries, and in terms of the growth of rationality versus irrational and traditional trends. See K. Mannheim, *Man and Society in an Age of Reconstruction*, New York, Harcourt Brace, 1940. The

problem of the required economic and social conditions for the emergence and maintenance of representative democracy, and new formulations on totalitarianism in the context of development, both in earlier industrialized (Western) areas and in presently developing ones, became prominent in the late fifties. Lipset's *Political Man* is one central contribution. The "totalitarian oligarchy" (to use Shils' term), was seen as a possible alternate road to modernization in underdeveloped countries. E. Shils, "Political Development in the New States," in *Comparative Studies in Society and History*, Vol. II, 1959–1960.

[9] In this article on "The Decay of German Democracy," F. Neumann states: "German National Socialism is nothing but the dictatorship of a monopolized industry and of big estate owners, the nakedness of which is covered by the mask of a corporative state." (In *Political Quarterly*, 1953.) But his *Behemoth, The Structure and Practice of National Socialism*, 1933–1944, New York, Oxford University Press, 1944 gives a more elaborate view. See also M. B. Sweezey, *The Structure of the Nazi Economy*, Cambridge, Mass., Harvard University Press, 1941, and R. A. Brady, *The Spirit and Structure of German Fascism*, New York, Viking Press, 1937. For a formulation of the "class hypothesis" in the Mosca-Pareto tradition but also similar to the Marxist approach, see G. Dorso's *Dittatura, Classe Politica e Classe Dirigente*, Milano, Einaudi, 1949.

[10] Daniel Guerin, *Fascisme et Grand Capital*, Paris, Gallimard, 1945, first edition, 1936.

[11] Harold Laski, *Reflections on the Revolution in Our Time*, London, Gollancz, 1942.

[12] Guerin, Chapter VI. However, Guerin sees the process occurring in two stages: the first one in which the "plebeyans" (an equivalent of Laski's "outlaws") conquer and remove the old ruling class, and a second stage characterized by the elimination of the "plebeyans" and the rise of a bureaucratic-military dictatorship. This change in the composition of fascist leadership in Italy and the trend toward a bureaucratic and police dictatorship has been documented by Alberto Aquarone, *L'Organizzazione dello Stato Totalitario*, Milano, Einaudi, 1965, Chapter III.

[13] The role of charisma was particularly emphasized by F. Neumann, *Behemoth*, op. cit. The evolution of Marxist thought on fascism has been described and analyzed by John M. Cammet, "Communist Theories of Fascism, 1920–1935," in *Science and Society*, XXXI (1967), pp. 149–163.

[14] Max Scheler, *El Resentimiento en la Moral*, Buenos Aires, Espasa Calpe, 1938, Spanish translation, especially Part I. For Scheler, situational factors are only *one* condition of resentment; race and heredity are the main determinants. Scheler shares with other representatives of the German irrationalistic orientation many traits of nazi ideology.

[15] Svend Ranulf, *Moral Indignation and Middle Class Psychology*, Copenhagen, Levin and Munksgaard, 1938, Introduction. See also Eugene Raiga, *L'Envie, Son Role Sociale*, Paris, Alcan, 1932.

[16] Harold D. Lasswell, *The Analysis of Political Behavior*, London, Routledge and Kegan Paul, 1947, pp. 235–245 (from an article published in 1933 in *Political Quarterly*).

[17] Erich Fromm, *The Fear of Freedom*, London, Routledge and Kegan Paul, 1942 (published in the United States, in 1941, as *Escape from Freedom*).

[18] The distinction between total fear and diffused anxiety, as opposed to ordinary fear, was noted by K. Riezler, "The Social Psychology of Fear," in the *American Journal of Psychology*, Vol. XL (1944), pp. 489–498.

[19] T. W. Adorno and others, *The Authoritarian Personality*, New York, Harper, 1950.

[20] D. Riesman, *The Lonely Crowd*, New Haven, Yale University Press, 1950. Riesman related this type to the "marketing orientation" described by Fromm in another book, *Man for Himself*.

[21] Both Adorno and Fromm belong to the same scientific tradition. With Horkheimer, they were at the Institute for Social Research in Germany, where Fromm first conducted an inquiry into the German middle and working classes. His whole theory of authority stems from these early studies. The research was later published in France: M. Horkheimer (ed.), *Autorität und Familie*, Paris, Alcan, 1936.

[22] Edward A. Shils, "Authoritarianism: 'Right' and 'Left,'" in R. Christie and M. Jahoda, *Studies in the Scope and Methods of the Authoritarian Personality*, Glencoe, Free Press, 1954. An attempt to operationalize the distinction between right- and left-wing authoritarians was undertaken by H. J. Eisenck, dividing authoritarianism into two dimensions: the "tender mindedness-tough mindedness" dimension and the "radical-conservative" dimension. H. J. Eisench, *The Psychology of Politics*, London, Routledge and Kegan Paul, 1954. See also Milton Rokeach and others, *The Open and the Closed Mind*, New York, Basic Books, 1960.

[23] K. Mannheim, op. cit., especially Part I, section 3, and Part II.

[24] One of the earliest versions was *La Rebelión de las Masas*, first published by José Ortega y Gasset in 1926. This work exercised a deep influence in Latin America. In Italy theories of mass society were not frequently discussed. See G. Perticone, "Osservazioni sul regime di massa," *Rivista Internazionale di Filosofia del Diritto*, Vol. XIX (1939), and *Studi sul Regime de Massa*, Milano, Bocca, 1942.

[25] See R. Aron, *L'Homme contre Les Tyrans*, New York, Maison Française, 1944.

[26] W. Kornhauser, *The Politics of Mass Society*, London, Routledge and Kegan Paul, 1960.

[27] W. K. Deutsch, "Social Mobilization and Political Development," *American Political Science Review*, Vol. LV (1961), pp. 493–514.

[28] This interpretation was applied by the author to the rise of Perónism. G. Germani, "Algunas repercusiones de los cambios económicos y sociales en la Argentina: 1940–1950," in *Cursos y Conferencias*, Vol. XL, 1952, pp. 559–578, and *La Integración de las Masas a la Vida Política y el Totalitarismo*, Buenos Aires, C.L.E.S., 1956.

[29] T. H. Marshall, *Citizenship and Social Class*, Cambridge, England, University Press, 1950.

[30] An interpretation of political development in Latin America based on a model of this type may be found in G. Germani, "Democratie Representative et Classes Populaires en Amérique Latine," in *Sociologie du Travail*, Vol. III (1961), pp. 96–113.

[31] E. Lederer, *The State of the Masses*, New York, Norton, 1940.

[32] See H. Gerth, "The Nazi Party: Its Leadership and Composition," *American Journal of Sociology*, Vol. XLV (1940), pp. 517–541. The only available figures for the Fascist Party are those given in a report to the

Party Congress in November 1921. (See, *e.g.*, R. de Felice, *Mussolini il Fascista*, Milano, Einaudi, 1966.) The works of Kornhauser, op. cit., and Lipset, op. cit., give information concerning different countries. For Perónism, see G. Germani, op. cit., and *Estructura Social de la Argentina*, Buenos Aires, Raigal, 1965, Chapter XVI. Also see H. D. Lasswell and R. Sereno, "The Fascists, the Changing Italian Elite," *American Political Science Review*, XXXI (1937), pp. 914–929; and D. Lerner and others, *The Nazi Elite*, Stanford, Stanford University Press, 1951. Both studies indicate the middle and lower middle class origins of these elites, but middle class intellectuals were also the predominant sector in communist elites. The nazi study showed a high proportion of socially and ecologically "marginal men."

[33] This is the thesis maintained by R. Bendix, "Social Stratification and Political Power," in R. Bendix and S. M. Lipset, *Class, Status and Power*, Glencoe, Free Press, 1953. Bendix points out that most of the support for the Nazi Party could have come from persons who in previous elections were nonvoters (younger persons and "alienated individuals"). The social background of these persons is not known.

[34] Kornhauser, op. cit., pp. 179–180.

[35] Lipset, op. cit., Chapter IV. Also, S. M. Miller and F. Riessman, "Working Class Authoritarianism: A Critique of Lipset," *The British Journal of Sociology*, XII, 1961, pp. 263–276, and Lipset's reply in the same issue.

[36] C. J. Friedrich and K. Brzezinsky, *Totalitarian Dictatorship and Autocracy*, Cambridge, Harvard University Press, 1956.

[37] Lipset, op. cit., pp. 175–176.

[38] An early version has been published in English, Germani, "Social Change and Intergroup Conflicts," in *The New Sociology*, ed. I. L. Horowitz, New York, Oxford University Press, 1964.

[39] Pizzorno has suggested that the notion of "organic crisis" used by Gramsci may be the same as the concept of mobilization and its theoretical framework. See Alessandro Pizzorno, "Sul Metodo di Gramsci (dalla Storiografia alla Scienze Politica)," unpublished ms., 1967.

[40] I. L. Horowitz, *The Italian Labor Movement*, Cambridge, Harvard University Press, 1963, pp. 75 and 124.

[41] This trend is best represented by Giolitti.

[42] "When it appeared that the government forces might not be able to cope with the situation, the Socialist Party sat back and applauded, but offered no leadership or direction, either back to legality or toward insurrection.") Horowitz, op. cit., p. 139.

[43] These rights included the eight-hour day, collective bargaining, representatives in the industrial plants ("internal commissions" in the firms), and certain participation in the control of enterprises. The peasants also achieved important advances. In 1921 and 1922 real salary reached the first higher level of the century, which would be reached again only in 1948–49. A. Fossati, *Lavoro e Produzione in Italia*, Torino, Giappichelli, 1951, p. 634.

[44] The important role of "agrarian fascism" has been noted by several authors. The motivations and attitudes of this sector resembled the reactionary conservative pattern more than the typical fascist (or totalitarian) pattern, but it became absorbed in the latter. See M. Rossi-Doria,

"L'Agricolture Italiana, il Dopoguerra e il Fascismo," Casucci (ed.), op. cit., and De Felice, op. cit., Chapter I.

[45] During several decades, the foreign-born among the adult population was from 50 to 70 per cent.

[46] In 1895 and 1914, two-thirds of the non-manual occupations were held by persons of manual origin (intergenerational and intragenerational mobility); in 1960, one-half of the sons of immigrants of manual origin were located in non-manual categories. Germani, *La Movilidad Social en la Argentina*, Buenos Aires, Instituto de Sociología, No. 60, and "Mass Immigration and Modernization in Argentina," *Studies in Comparative International Development*, II, 11 (1966), pp. 165–182.

Name Index

601

Name Index

Name Index

Obregón, Alvaro, 337, 447–48, 453–55, 458, 462
Odría, Manuel, 87, 190
Onganía, Juan Carlos, 24
Orona, Arturo, 492, 495

Padgett, L. Vincent, 489, 494–95
Padilla, Ezequiel, 480
Palomino, Ramón Danzos, 493, 495
Parsons, Talcott, 552
Patch, R., 74
Peña, Moisés T. de la, 472
Pinner, Frank A., 192
Pozas, R., 224, 249–51, 255
Puerto, Felipe Carrillo, 450–51

Quadros, Jânio, 87, 393–94, 396–400, 402–3
Quiroga, Facundo, 5

Ramírez, Manuel González, 489
Ranulf, Svend, 581
Redfield, Robert, 239, 253, 263, 504, 506–7
Ricardo, Miguel, 449
Riesman, David, 583
Rivadavia, Bernardino, 291
Rivera, Diego, 459
Rodríguez, Abelardo, 464, 466
Rodríguez, José Guadalupe, 457, 459
Roosevelt, Franklin D., 556
Rosas, Juan Manuel de, 291
Rosenblüth, Guillermo, 178
Ruiz, Emilio, 463

Sánchez, Graciano, 464–65, 470, 474
Sánchez, Guadalupe, 452–53
Sarmiento, Domingo F., 290, 312, 314
Scheler, Max, 581
Schmitt, Karl M., 493–94
Scott, Robert E., 14–15
Senior, Clarence, 158
Serrato, Benigno, 463–64
Shils, Edward A., 583
Silva-Michelena, J. A., 84
Simpson, Eyler N., 334–36, 460
Siverts, Henning, 238
Smelser, Neil J., 67–68
Sombart, Werner, 581
Stavenhagen, Rodolfo, 12, 411

Sternberg, Marvin, 142
Sweezy, M. B., 579

Talamantes, Rodrigo, 449
Tapia, Primo, 453–56
Tawney, R. H., 154
Tax, Sol, 238–39, 242, 246, 248, 253, 261, 275
Tejeda, Adalberto, 452, 457
Tocqueville, Alexis de, 394
Toledano, Vicente Lombardo, 468, 470–71, 474, 480, 482–83, 489–91
Tönnies, Ferdinand, 505
Toro, A., 84
Torre, Víctor Raúl Haya de la, 87
Touraine, Alain, 392
Toynbee, Arnold, 128
Trevelyan, George Macaulay, 123
Triana, Pedro V. Rodríguez, 459
Tumin, Melvin, 68, 74, 77, 210, 260–62, 264
Tupac, Amaru, 5
Turner, John F. C., 178–79, 198
Tzintzun, Felipe, 454

Valera, José Mejía, 70
Vargas, Getulio, 21, 389–94
Vázquez, Mario, 421
Velázquez, Fidel, 480
Velázquez, Gabriel Leyva, 480–81
Véliz, Claudio, 10–11
Verba, Sidney, 15, 199
Villa, Pancho, 4

Wagley, Charles, 248
Weber, Max, 557, 581
Weffort, Francisco C., 72
Weiner, Myron, 188
Weyl, Nathaniel, 462, 465–67
Weyl, Sylvia, 462, 465–67
Whetten, Nathan, 237
Wise, George S., 486
Wolf, Eric, 120, 238–39, 242, 276, 278, 411
Wollman, Nathaniel, 102

Zamora, Emilio López, 478
Zapata, Emiliano, 445–46, 450, 465, 485
Zavala, Leopoldo Flores, 478
Zeitlin, Maurice, 551–53, 570–71
Zweig, Stefan, 561

Subject Index

Subject Index

Mexico (see also Altos de Chiapas), 332, 334–43, 445–95

middle class (see also bourgeoisie): traditional, 387–90; urban, 387–90

middleman, 36–37; functions of, 36–37; mestizo as, 419–20

mobility: goals of, 90–91; Indian vs. ladino, 264–66; rural, 513–37; and underdevelopment, 513–37

mobilization (see also participation and politicalization): lower-class, 176, 185, 187, 190; mass, 14–17, 76, 91; theory of, 586–89

model, traditional-modern, 68–69

modern: social system, 67–69; vs. traditional subcultures, 86–87

modernization, and immigration, 289–90

movements: agrarian, 447–95; level of analysis, 91–92

nationalism, 402; and populism, 403; and revolution, 567–68; and the State, 402–4

oligarchy, 387–90

participation (see also mobilization and politicalization), 187; and immigration, 317–21, 325; institutionalization of, 72; and manipulation, 82; mass, 14–17, 71–72, 82–83, 176, 185, 187, 190, 520–24; peasant, 161–62, 428–30, 506–7, 509–13, 516, 520–24, 526–38, 540–44; political, 176, 190; and stratification, 14–17, 191; and violence, 16, 506–7, 509–13, 516, 519–20, 526–38, 540–44

paternalism, 21–22, 187

peasantry (see also Indians, lower class and masses), 33–39, 113, 118–23, 126–27, 547–48; guerrillas, 445, 507, 509–13, 516, 519–20, 526–38, 540–44; incomes of, 128–54; job opportunities, 146–52; marginality of, 428–30, 520–24, 538–43; organization of, 445–46, 448–95, 526–38, 540–44; political participation of, 161–62, 428–30, 520–24, 526–38, 540–44

Peronism, and Italian fascism, 589–96

Peru (see also Lima), 407–40

planning: of development, 99; economic, 107; urban, 226–31

policy: agricultural, 95–112, 154–63; Indianist, 239, 278–79

political integration (see also participation and politicalization), lower-class, 176, 187–90, 428–30

politicalization (see also participation), 198–202; vs. depoliticalization, 191–98; and integration, 176, 187, 190; mass, 15–17, 82, 91, 176, 190–91, 198–202, 506–7, 509–13, 516, 520–24, 526–38, 540–44

political system: archaic, 90; mobilizing, 90; support for vs. opposition to, 176

populism, 403–4; and nationalism, 403

poverty, urban, 217–26

power (see also control): peasant, 445–46, 526–38, 540–44; State, 391–93; working-class, 71–72

production, agricultural, 95–96, 128–29, 154–57

radicalization, of union leaders, 84, 86

reform: agrarian, 95–97, 113, 122–28, 154–63, 331–43, 445–95; and masses, 19–23; vs. revolution, 19–23

revolution: Brazilian of 1930, 385–90; and classes, 547–52; and conflict, 551–57; Cuban of 1933, 548; Cuban of 1959, 547–76; and democracy, 562; gestation period, 550–59, 574; and humanism, 563–66; and institutionalization, 551–57; and Marxism-Leninism, 570–74; and masses, 19–23, 547–52; Mexican of 1910, 445, 455; and nationalism, 567–68; period of expansion, 561–76; period of general crisis, 559–60, 574–75; vs. reform, 19–23; and socialism, 568–69

Rio de Janeiro (see also Brazil), 223

rural: economy, 114–22; illiteracy, 107–9; mobility, 513–37; poverty vs. urban affluence, 82; social change, 506–7, 509–13, 516, 519–20, 526–38, 540–44; social structure, 113–28, 504–44; underdevelopment, 513–44; urbanization, 432–35; violence, 506–7, 509–13, 516, 519–20, 526–38, 540–44

Santiago (see also Chile), 176–212, 224

607

Subject Index

Sao Paulo (*see also* Brazil), working class, 76, 84
socialism, and revolution, 568–69
social organization (*see also* social structure *and* social system), urban, 346, 380–81
social structure (*see also* social organization *and* social system): and agrarian reform, 158–59; dualism in, 407–40; impact of immigration, 298, 302–6; rural, 113–28, 504–44; rural underdeveloped, 513–44; urban, 346, 380–81
social system (*see also* social organization *and* social structure), 68–69; colonial, 266–71; factors of integration vs. questioning, 86, 88–90; modern, 67–69; traditional, 67–69, 113–28
socio-economic status, and participation in urban activities, 346, 356–81
sociology, of change, 65–71
Spanish Conquest, 266–71; economic policy of, 266–71; and Indian culture, 408
squatter settlements, and urbanization, 177–212, 216, 220–26
State: and agricultural development, 160–61; and bureaucracy, 31; and colonialism, 31; democratization of, 385–404; economic intervention of, 71, 90; and the economy, 389; functions of, 32, 291, 391; legitimacy of, 389–92, 401; manipulation by, 392; and the marginal urban population, 435–36; and masses, 385, 390–404, 520–24; and nationalism, 402–4; power, 391–93
strategies: of land reform, 95–97, 154–63; for vs. of the mass, 23–26
stratification(*see also* classes), 256–57, 282–83; castes, 277, 282–83, 412–13; and colonialism, 12–13, 410–40; intra-ethnic and inter-ethnic, 257–66, 272–82, 407–40; international, 13–14; ladino, 260–61; mestizo, 413; and participation, 14–17, 191; socio-economic, 282–83
subcultures, urban, 86–87
subordination, and domination, 235–83, 407–40

substitution, import, 48, 52–54, 57–62

taxation, 332–34; and agricultural policies, 106–7; and land reform, 332–34
technology: agricultural, 139–41; innovations, 59–60
totalitarianism of the Right(*see also* fascism): and fascism, 577–79; interpretations of, 577–89; and mass society, 579, 583–86; and class society, 579–83
traditional: middle class, 387–90; vs. modern subcultures, 86–87; social system, 67–69, 113–28

underdevelopment, and dependence, 73–74, 82; and mobility, 513–37; rural, 513–44
urban: affluence vs. rural poverty, 82; culture, 82–83; experience vs. work experience, 83, 86–90; family, 345–81; immigration, 72–73, 82, 91, 432–35; lower class, 176–212, 345–81; masses, 71–72, 82–92, 345–81, 385, 390–404; middle class, 387–90; permanent vs. floating populations, 216–19, 222–26; planning, 226–31; politics, 91; poverty, 217–26; sector, 30–32; social structure, 346, 380–81; squatter settlements, 176–212, 216, 220–26; subcultures, 86–87; working class, 71–72, 82–92
urbanization, and squatter settlements, 177–212, 216, 220–26

Venezuela (*see* Caracas)
violence (*see also* guerrillas): and change, 504, 506–7, 509–13, 516, 519–20, 526–38, 540–44; and participation, 16, 506–7, 509–13, 516, 519–20, 526–38, 540–44; rural, 506–7, 509–13, 516, 519–20, 526–38, 540–44

work, experience vs. urban experience, 83, 86–90
working class (*see also* lower class *and* masses), 65–92; access to power, 71–72; action, 84, 88–91; ambiguity, 72, 82–84; attitudes, 84–85, 88; migration, 72–73, 82; skilled, 85–86; unskilled, 85–86; urban, 71–72, 82–92

608